Popular Musicians

Popular Musicians

Volume 3

Reba McEntire - Sonic Youth

Editor

Steve Hochman

Project Editor

McCrea Adams

SALEM PRESS
Pasadena, California Hackensack, New Jersey

Managing Editor: Christina J. Moose
Project Editor: McCrea Adams
Acquisitions Editor: Mark Rehn
Research Supervisor: Jeffry Jensen
Production Editor: Yasmine A. Cordoba
Photograph Editor: Karrie Hyatt
Copy Editors: Lauren M. D'Andrea; Douglas Long
Research Assistant: Jun Ohnuki
Design and Layout: James Hutson

∞ The paper used in these volumes conforms to the American National Standard for Permanence of Paper for Printed Library Materials, Z39.48-1992(R1997)

Library of Congress Cataloging-in-Publication Data

Popular Musicians / consulting editor, Steve Hochman ; project editor, McCrea Adams.
p. cm.
Includes discographical references and index.
ISBN 0-89356-986-0 (set : alk. paper). — ISBN 0-89356-987-9 (vol. 1 : alk. paper). — ISBN 0-89356-988-7 (vol. 2 : alk. paper). — ISBN 0-89356-989-5 (vol. 3 : alk. paper). — ISBN 0-89356-990-9 (vol. 4 : alk. paper).
1. Musicians — Biography — Dictionaries. 2. Musical groups — Dictionaries.
I. Hochman, Steve, 1956-

ML105.P66 1999
781.64'092'2—dc21 99-11658
[B] CIP

First Printing

PRINTED IN THE UNITED STATES OF AMERICA

Contents

Popular Musicians

Popular Musicians

Reba McEntire

BORN: Chockie, Oklahoma; March 28, 1954
FIRST ALBUM RELEASE: *Reba McEntire,* 1977
MUSICAL STYLE: Country

With record sales surpassing 35 million copies, Reba McEntire has the best-selling albums of any woman in the history of country music. Through a career that has spanned more than two decades, this fiery redhead has found her voice both on and off the stage. Not only does she coproduce her albums, but she serves as president of her musical empire, Starstruck Entertainment, which has an elaborate presence on Nashville's famed Music Row. She has developed a trademark sound that could be called "vocal aerobics" because it has so many bends, trills, and even hints of yodeling. Through the years, she has drifted from hardcore country songs to a new, more mainstream sound, allowing her to attract more listeners along the way.

The Beginning. Reba McEntire was raised in Chockie, Oklahoma, with her brother Pake, also a country music singer, and sister Susie, a contemporary Christian music singer. Their mother, Jacqueline, was a schoolteacher, and their father, Clark, was a champion steer roper and rancher. The siblings formed a group called the Singing McEntires and began performing at rodeos while in their teens. McEntire even competed as a horseback barrel rider in rodeos on the side. The Singing McEntires recorded "The Ballad of John McEntire," a ballad that paid tribute to their grandfather. Reba earned a degree in education and music at Southeastern Oklahoma State University to use in case her musical career was not successful.

McEntire received her big break in 1974, when country singer Red Steagall heard her sing the national anthem at the National Finals Rodeo. Impressed, Steagall had McEntire record a demo in Nashville, which led to a deal with Mercury Records. (McEntire's brother and sister, who

Reba McEntire (Paul Natkin)

came with her to Nashville along with their mother, also recorded albums in 1975.)

In 1976, McEntire married Charlie Battles, a rodeo rider, just as she was beginning her attempts at launching a national career. Her first single, "I Don't Want to Be a One Night Stand," reached only number 88 on the country charts. She scored her first Top-20 hit in 1978 with "Three Sheets in the Wind." McEntire did not break the Top-10 until 1980 with "(You Lift Me) Up to Heaven." Her first number 1 hit, "Can't Even Get the Blues," came in 1982, followed a year later by the number 1 hit "You're the First Time I've Thought About Leaving." During this time, McEntire, encouraged by her mother, fought with producers to retain her unique sound, which embraced her country roots, rather than move in a more pop-oriented direction. They encouraged her to smooth out the trills and dips in her voice.

McEntire, growing more confident in her music, moved to MCA Records and teamed up with producer Harold Shedd (who had previously worked with the band Alabama) to record the album *My Kind of Country* in 1984. That album spawned the number 1 hit "How Blue" by effectively capturing her pure country sound and helped her clinch the female vocalist awards from the Country Music Association and the Academy of Country Music, which she won for two consecutive years. In 1985, McEntire teamed up with producer Jimmy Bowen for the album *Have I Got a Deal for You,* which produced the number 1 song, "Somebody Should Leave." The year 1985 was an important year in McEntire's life for several reasons. Not only did the album's success advance her career, but she also served as the project's coproducer, which was a rarity in a male-dominated industry. Also that year, she was named a member of the Grand Ole Opry.

The album *Whoever's in New England* followed in 1986, and it has become known as one of McEntire's most significant works. Ironically, this collection was McEntire's first foray into the pop-influenced sounds that she earlier had avoided. (She would continue to explore more contemporary pop sounds in future albums.) McEntire ended the year by capturing the highly coveted Entertainer of the Year Award from the Country Music Association, an award that has traditionally gone to male singers.

The Hits Continue. McEntire became a permanent fixture at the top of the charts in the mid-1980's and would remain there for more than a decade. Chart-toppers included "Little Rock," "What Am I Gonna Do About You," "One Promise Too Late" and "The Last One to Know." Unfortunately, her image, as well as the potential for long-term success, was in the hands of her management, which was pushing her to become flashier and more commercial, failing to realize where she was in her career. A turning point for McEntire came when she was playing in a seventeen-thousand-seat arena and only seventeen hundred fans attended.

In 1987, McEntire divorced husband Charlie Battles after eleven years of marriage, and she assumed control of her career. Two years later, she married Narvel Blackstock, a former steel-guitar player in her band who had become her manager. During this turbulent time in her personal life, her professional life remained steady and successful, with such hits as "I Know How He Feels" and "New Fool at an Old Game," as well as a remake of the Everly Brothers' 1960 hit, "Cathy's Clown."

McEntire, who gave birth to son Shelby Stephen on February 23, 1990, became the voice of work-

For the Record

By the 1990's Reba McEntire had one of the most elaborate live shows on the road, requiring nearly five hundred lights. Fifteen buses and thirteen tractor-trailer trucks were needed to carry all the equipment. McEntire's show included fourteen costume changes, a taxicab driven onto the stage, and a cable car that rose over the audience. In 1994 McEntire was the only country performer among the top-ten grossing touring acts and was one of only two women on the list (the other was Barbra Streisand).

ing women everywhere. Her songs told tales of assertive women getting control over their lives, much different from some of the antifeminist themes sung by Tammy Wynette and others in the 1960's. For instance, McEntire's 1992 number 1 hit "Is There Life out There," which resulted in a television film with the same name, inspired many women to return to college. ("She's done what she should, should she do what she dares?") In the 1992 hit "Take It Back," McEntire urged her lover to take his love back, because she no longer wanted it.

Meanwhile, McEntire became heavily involved in every business aspect of her career, from the elaborate staging and lighting of her concerts to the trucks that carried the equipment from town to town. McEntire established a music publishing company that signed songwriters and pitched their material to other singers, including her. She also established a publicity company and began managing other acts as well.

The 1990's not only brought more hits, including a duet with Vince Gill entitled "The Heart Won't Lie" and "Does He Love You," a duet with Linda Davis that was one of McEntire's biggest records, it also marked the beginning of her acting career. McEntire had a role in the 1990 film *Tremors* and followed that up with several other television films and motion pictures.

Tragedy Strikes. Tragedy struck McEntire in March of 1991, when a plane leaving San Diego crashed, killing her seven band members and her road manager who were onboard. Devastated, McEntire decided to focus intently on her work, performing a few weeks later at the Academy Awards ceremony and a month later at the Country Music Association Awards show.

McEntire's feelings of heartbreak and loss were reflected in her next album, *For My Broken Heart* (1991). The album sold three million copies and *Stereo Review* called it "one of the ten best albums of the year—not just country albums, but across the board." The album reflected both strength and despair, honesty and hope, and it boosted McEntire's career to yet another level. She released her autobiography, *Reba: Starting Over*, in 1994 and she once again rose up the charts, but this time it was *The New York Times* best-sellers list.

McEntire, who has won two Grammy Awards, has released twenty-four albums in thirty years, eighteen of which have gone gold, fourteen of which have sold one million copies or more. Her *Greatest Hits Volume II* (1993) sold an impressive four million copies. She has sold the most albums of any female country star in history; no other woman in Nashville has five triple-platinum albums to her credit. *—Beverly Keel*

SELECT DISCOGRAPHY

■ ALBUMS

My Kind of Country, 1984
Have I Got a Deal for You, 1985
Whoever's in New England, 1986
What Am I Gonna Do About You, 1986
For My Broken Heart, 1991
Read My Mind, 1994

SELECT AWARDS

Country Music Association Female Vocalist of the Year Award, 1984, 1985, 1986, 1987
Grammy Award for Best Country Vocal Performance, Female, for "Whoever's in New England," 1986
Country Music Association Entertainer of the Year Award, 1986
American Music Awards for Favorite Female Country Artist, 1988, 1989, 1990, 1991, 1992, 1993, 1994, 1995, 1996
Grammy Award for Best Country Vocal Collaboration for "Does He Love You," 1993 (with Linda Davis)

SEE ALSO: Brooks, Garth; Parton, Dolly; Wynette, Tammy.

Bobby McFerrin

BORN: New York, New York; March 11, 1950
FIRST ALBUM RELEASE: *Bobby McFerrin*, 1982
MUSICAL STYLES: Jazz, pop, classical crossover, performance art

Composer, symphonic conductor, popular performer, jazz vocalist, artistic collaborator, teacher, and philosopher/thinker are all terms that define

Bobby McFerrin. His motivation for making music is simple and clear: "I consider myself a healer, using music as a potent force to bring people joy. . . . A happy heart is good medicine, and I feel like I'm a channel for fun."

Early Influences. Born into a family of musicians (his father a professional opera singer, his mother a classically trained soprano and voice teacher), McFerrin began formal musical training at the age of six, studying piano and music theory at the Juilliard School of Music preparatory division in New York City. In 1958, his family moved to Los Angeles, where McFerrin continued musical involvement in school and church activities. After high school graduation, McFerrin majored in music at California State University and Cerritos College, taking courses in music theory, composition, arranging, and applied piano study. In the early 1970's, he left school and became a keyboardist with various pop lounge bands and with a traveling band that accompanied the Ice Follies.

By 1977, following several more years on the road and two years as a freelance jazz pianist, McFerrin concluded that he "was feeling pretty burned out and wondering what my direction in life was going to be, when an inner voice told me I should *sing*." Now a self-proclaimed vocalist, McFerrin's performance opportunities changed little. He worked as a singer in a number of piano bars, and in 1979 he settled in San Francisco seeking to make music in a more vital market.

Collaboration. Shortly after arriving in San Francisco, McFerrin met jazz vocalist Jon Hendricks of the popular jazz trio Lambert, Hendricks, and Ross. The group was well known for performing creative arrangements of jazz standards that featured Hendricks's up-tempo, scat-style vocal improvisation. Hendricks invited McFerrin to join the group following an informal vocal jam session that, in effect, served as an audition.

Performing with Hendricks's group created the exposure that boosted McFerrin's career. Building on the foundation of jazz performers of an earlier era, McFerrin integrated the scat-singing dexterity of Ella Fitzgerald with the improvisational genius of saxophonist Charlie Parker to create a unique vocal style that became his trademark. With the assistance of entertainer Bill Cosby, McFerrin was offered engagements in Las Vegas and at the 1980 Playboy Jazz Festival in Los Angeles. In 1981 he appeared at the New York Kool Jazz Festival, where he was met with warm audience response and enthusiastic critical acclaim that referred to his "uncanny ability to simulate the sounds of instruments with boppish overtones." McFerrin continued on the Kool Jazz tour, appearing with jazz legends George Benson, Herbie Hancock, Dizzy Gillespie, and Wynton Marsalis.

For the Record

During the 1988 presidential campaign, Republican candidate George Bush's strategists used "Don't Worry, Be Happy" as a theme song to suggest the prosperity that the nation was enjoying in the 1980's under the Ronald Reagan administration. However, the practice stopped when it was learned that Bobby McFerrin was a supporter of opposing candidate Michael Dukakis.

In 1982, the singer's first full-length album, *Bobby McFerrin*, was released. While much of McFerrin's live concert work was performed with minimal instrumental accompaniment or, as in his later work, completely a cappella, the album was heavily dependent on carefully arranged instrumental accompaniment, giving it a pop character. In McFerrin's own words, "I never wanted to climb up on the pop merry-go-round in the first place. . . . I knew that once I made a solo [a cappella] voice album, people would notice me."

"Wondervoice." Heeding his own misgivings about a pop-music career, McFerrin instead launched a solo concert tour in 1983. A mixture of storytelling, mime, theater, humor, audience participation, and music both new and old, McFerrin's one-man concert was a showcase for his unique vocal instrument. Whether singing a conventional lyric, jazz scatting on an improvised series of nonsense syllables, or using his voice as a surrogate violin, McFerrin's vocal capacity, combined with a fertile sense of musical creativity, becomes difficult to categorize or compare. He stated, "Because what I do is spontaneous, I've been called a jazz singer, but increasingly I've found that label restricting. . . . I see myself as a performance artist." In terms of vocal range, timbre, dynamic control, focused pitch, virtuosic flexibility, sense of phrasing and diction, and creative ability to simulate instrumental sounds with the voice, he earned the accolade *Stimmwunder* (Wondervoice), a term designated by a German audience on hearing McFerrin perform on tour. One such concert was recorded live in Germany in March, 1984, and was released as his second album, *The Voice*.

Recording activities during the 1980's reflect the eclectic nature of McFerrin's musical capacity. *Spontaneous Inventions* (1986) included solo vocal pieces as well as duets with jazz/fusion pianist Herbie Hancock and actor-comedian Robin Williams. McFerrin's voice was beamed into millions of homes each week as viewers heard his recording of the familiar theme music for the long running *The Cosby Show*. *Simple Pleasures* (1988) included the rock classic "Sunshine of Your Love," the Beatles tune "Drive My Car," and five original tunes by McFerrin. The reggae-like "Don't Worry, Be Happy" from the album went on to become a number 1 hit single, spending thirteen weeks on the charts and earning McFerrin 1989 Grammy Awards for Best Male Pop Vocalist, Best Song, and Record of the Year.

Building Bridges. Learning the art of jazz improvisation has traditionally been a process of spending time with experienced musicians in a master-apprentice relationship involving listening, practicing, and, eventually, assimilating musical style and syntax. McFerrin has been asked to share his insights and performance suggestions with young, aspiring jazz musicians, and on one occasion, in 1993, at the University of Northern Colorado School of Music, students had an opportunity to interact with McFerrin in a lecture/demonstration session. The inevitable question "How do you improvise?" was posed. McFerrin responded in characteristically straightforward fashion, suggesting, "Improvisation is the courage to move from one note to the next. It's that simple. Once you conquer that basic fear, when you are able to make that leap from one note to the next without thinking or preparing for it, then you are improvising."

As McFerrin continued to explore new ways of interacting with music, his efforts led him increasingly toward the classical idiom. Substituting his voice for melodic lines scored by Antonio Vivaldi, Felix Mendelssohn, Peter Ilich Tchaikovsky, and others for orchestral and keyboard instruments, McFerrin created an additional way to showcase his voice. The result was a series of albums including *Hush* (1992) with virtuoso classical cellist Yo-Yo Ma, *Paper Music* (1995) with the Saint Paul Chamber Orchestra, and *The Mozart Sessions* (1996) with keyboard legend Chick Corea. Fulfilling a lifelong career goal, McFerrin has established a reputation as an orchestral conductor, making guest appearances with the Israel Philharmonic, Chicago Symphony, and Philadelphia Orchestra, among others. He became affiliated with the Saint Paul Chamber Orchestra in 1994 as Creative Chair, responsible for developing creative and educational initiatives, and in 1996 began conducting subscription concerts with the orchestra. In yet another classical music endeavor, McFerrin has been commissioned to compose an original work for the San Francisco Opera Company. —*William M. Camphouse*

SELECT DISCOGRAPHY

■ ALBUMS

Bobby McFerrin, 1982
Simple Pleasures, 1988
Hush, 1992 (with Yo-Yo Ma)
Play, 1992 (with Chick Corea)
The Mozart Sessions, 1996 (with Chick Corea)

SELECT AWARDS

Down Beat Readers Poll, named Best Male Vocalist, 1984-1989

Grammy Awards for Best Jazz Vocal Performance, Male (with Jon Hendricks), and Best Vocal Arrangement for Two or More Voices (with Cheryl Bentine), for "Another Night in Tunisia," 1985

Grammy Award for Best Jazz Vocal Performance, Male, for "Round Midnight," 1986
Grammy Award for Best Jazz Vocal Performance, Male, for "What Is This Thing Called Love," and Best Recording for Children for *The Elephant's Child* (with Tom Bradshaw, Jack Nicholson, and Mark Sottnick), 1987
Grammy Awards for Record of the Year (with Linda Goldstein), Song of the Year, and Best Pop Vocal Performance, Male, for "Don't Worry, Be Happy," and Best Jazz Vocal Performance, Male, for "Brothers," 1988
Grammy Award for Best Jazz Vocal Performance for "Round Midnight," 1992

SEE ALSO: Fitzgerald, Ella; Hancock, Herbie; Manhattan Transfer.

Loreena McKennitt

BORN: Morden, Manitoba, Canada; February 17, 1957
FIRST ALBUM RELEASE: *Elemental*, 1985
MUSICAL STYLES: Celtic, new age

Canadian singer and harpist Loreena McKennitt, whose Celtic-flavored music touches on mysticism, classic literature, and eras past, has created a successful niche for herself on both the new-age and pop charts.

The Beginnings. McKennitt was born and raised in the Canadian prairie town of Morder, Manitoba, a region filled with Irish, Scottish, and German inhabitants. Classically trained in voice and piano, she briefly studied to be a veterinarian after moving to Winnipeg, Manitoba, as a young woman. It was there that McKennitt was first exposed to the Celtic folk boom. She performed in Canada's Shakespearean Festival in the late 1970's, around the same time she first discovered the Celtic harp.

Setting Literature to Music. Relocating to Stratford, Ontario, in the mid-1980's, McKennitt first visited Ireland in 1982. Enchanted by the poetry of William Butler Yeats and the music of Breton harpist Alain Stivell, she put her newfound Celtic fervor to use when she interpreted Yeats's "The Stolen Child" in a song. It was a tool McKennitt would use repeatedly in her career: taking a piece of classic literature, such as English poet Alfred, Lord Tennyson's "The Lady of Shallot," or English poet Alfred Noyes's poem "The Highwayman," and setting it to music.

After reading Diane Sward Rapaport's book *How to Make and Sell Your Own Recording*, McKennitt established her own record company, Quinlan Road, using ten thousand dollars she borrowed from her parents. She recorded her first album, *Elemental*, there, then literally took her music to the streets.

Self-Promotion Proves Successful. McKennitt built her audience in an unusual way: she would load her car with boxes of her cassettes, bring along her harp, and perform on the streets of Toronto, Ontario, a move that caught the attention of programmers at the Canadian Broadcasting Company.

Her second album, *To Drive the Cold Winter Away* (1987), was a collection of Christmas carols, and her third album, 1989's *Parallel Dreams*, was McKennitt's first move toward a more multicultural sound. Around this time, McKennitt, whose music defied easy categorization, was hired to score music for the National Film Board of Canada's acclaimed film series *Women and Spirituality*.

A growing audience and reputation in Canada led to a licensing deal with Warner Bros. in 1991.

For the Record

McKennitt was concerned that the techno-pop radio-only mix of "The Mummers' Dance" would goad people into buying *The Book of Secrets*, which featured a more ethnic-flavored version of the song. Not wanting to alienate listeners, who might be disappointed with the album version, she convinced Warner Bros. to release a commercial edition of the remix as a single.

Since then, that label has distributed all of McKennitt's work, while she has retained control in every aspect of creation and promotion. As her work progressed, McKennitt began exploring Celtic connections to Eastern and Indian culture and music. Her love of travel eventually led her to explore many exotic locales, and her discoveries often found their ways onto her albums, both musically and thematically.

In 1991, a trip to Venice, Italy, to see a collection of international Celtic artifacts proved pivotal in her career. Seeing Celtic art from countries beyond the United Kingdom, such as Hungary, Ukraine, and Spain, was exhilarating for McKennitt, who later said it made her more open to multicultural music, thus transforming her sound.

A New Direction. The primeval-sounding tamboura beat that opened her next album, 1992's *The Visit*, signaled McKennitt's more global direction, and she displayed new confidence on interpretations of English dramatist William Shakespeare and Tennyson and on an edgy take of the medieval classic "Greensleeves."

Calling her music "eclectic Celtic," a surge of press interest in Irish pop music in the early 1990's drew additional attention to McKennitt, whose mysterious and somewhat mystical persona added to her intrigue and cult status. With virtually no radio airplay, two of her albums, *The Visit* and *The Mask and Mirror* (1994) reached gold status in the United States.

Breaking Through to U.S. Radio. McKennitt's seventh release, 1997's *The Book of Secrets*, complete with Sufi chants and Egyptian percussion instruments, became her most successful commercial effort, reaching platinum status in the United States and adding to her list of more than four million in worldwide sales. A techno-tinged remix of one of the album's songs, "The Mummers' Dance," became a surprise U.S. hit single for McKennitt. —*Nicole Pensiero*

SELECT DISCOGRAPHY

■ ALBUMS

Elemental, 1985

To Drive the Cold Winter Away, 1987

Parallel Dreams, 1989

The Visit, 1992

The Mask and Mirror, 1994

The Book of Secrets, 1997

SEE ALSO: Enya.

Brian McKnight

BORN: Buffalo, New York; June 5, 1969

FIRST ALBUM RELEASE: *Brian McKnight*, 1992

MUSICAL STYLES: Rhythm and blues, pop, soul

Brian McKnight emerged in the late 1990's as one of pop music's premier rhythm-and-blues balladeers. He found a particular niche in preaching love and romance, largely apart from the overt sexuality so prevalent in the soul music of the 1990's.

Background. McKnight came from a musical family. He began singing in a Buffalo, New York, church choir led by his grandfather. His older brother Claude was a member of the gospel group Take 6, which managed to land a record deal with a major label while McKnight was a teenager. With a supportive family, he began composing easy-listening instrumentals while still in his early teens. However, it was his strong vocal style that caught the attention of veteran record executives. After hearing a demo, Mercury Records president Ed Eckstine immediately signed the eighteen-year-old McKnight.

His first single, "The Way Love Goes," hit number 11 on the rhythm-and-blues charts, but his next two releases did not make the rhythm-and-blues Top 40. His first two albums, *Brian McKnight* (1992) and *I Remember You* (1995), both went gold, scoring high on the rhythm-and-blues charts. His biggest hit, however, came from the *Beverly Hills, 90210* sound track. "Love Is" (1993), a duet with Vanessa Williams, went all the way to number 3 on the pop charts, earning him a large crossover audience.

New Ranges. Having earned a reputation as an adult-contemporary songwriter and vocalist, McKnight deliberately expanded the musical range on his third album, *Anytime* (1997), which rose to the top of the rhythm-and-blues charts.

For the Record

Brian McKnight developed a unique songwriting regimen. He would go to the recording studio around 7:00 P.M. at least four days a week, and he would not leave until he had finished writing a new song.

§

At 6 feet, 4 inches tall, McKnight played basketball in high school and college and continued to play with NBA friends in the 1990's. He sang the U.S. national anthem for the 1997 NBA All-Star game.

Introducing elements of funk, rap, and hip-hop into his collection of soulful ballads, McKnight earned a new audience, helping the album go platinum. The Puff Daddy-produced single "You Should Be Mine (Don't Waste Your Time)" was the first single release from *Anytime.*

Other Abilities. McKnight was in heavy demand as a songwriter, vocalist, and producer throughout the 1990's, working with a variety of artists including Vanessa Williams, Boyz II Men, Ce Ce Peniston, Az Yet, George Benson, Quincy Jones, and Take 6. He also helped produce *Rhythm of the Games* from the 1996 Olympics and *The NBA at 50: A Musical Celebration* in 1996. In 1998 McKnight limited his touring in order to pursue an acting career. *—John Powell*

SELECT DISCOGRAPHY

■ ALBUMS

Brian McKnight, 1992
I Remember You, 1995
Anytime, 1997

SEE ALSO: Benson, George; Boyz II Men; Williams, Vanessa.

Sarah McLachlan

BORN: Halifax, Nova Scotia, Canada; January 28, 1968

FIRST ALBUM RELEASE: *Touch,* 1988
MUSICAL STYLES: Folk rock, alternative, folk, pop

Singer-songwriter Sarah McLachlan's life reads like a proverbial fairy tale, from her musical discovery at an early age to rocketing to stardom from her very first album. From the very beginning of her career, at age nineteen, she was compared with other female singer-songwriters such as Tori Amos, Kate Bush, Joni Mitchell, and Sinead O'Connor. Her songs are passionately honest, stark, confessional, and soul baring. Many of her songs have an air of mystery and darkness, revealing her to be a true romantic and realist. She has written about the inevitable pain of relationships that do not work, the struggle for independence from family, and the trials of simply growing up. Songwriting has been a form of therapy for McLachlan, enabling her to learn about herself and to work through her hardships. She has been described as a down-to-earth diva with a haunting voice that soars from the earthy to the ethereal; she is both a humble balladeer and a quiet superstar. She has maintained a devoted, almost cultlike fan base, creating the first-ever mainstream all-female musical festival, Lilith Fair.

The Beginnings. Sarah McLachlan was born on January 28, 1968, in Halifax, Nova Scotia, Canada. She was the last of three children adopted by Jack and Dorice McLachlan. She started singing at age four; her mother taught her "How Dry I Am," the short and simple Prohibition-era song. The first musical instrument she learned to play was the ukulele, because she was too small to play a standard guitar. When she was young, she wanted to grow up to be another Joan Baez. Among the other major musical influences on her career were Simon and Garfunkel and Cat Stevens. McLachlan studied classical guitar and piano and took voice lessons, never becoming popular with schoolmates, preferring to spend time on long winter nights writing songs. In high school, she was voted most likely to become a rock star.

By the age of seventeen, McLachlan was singing in a new-wave band called the October Game. McLachlan's big break came when the group opened for the Vancouver band Moev one night at a Dalhousie University student club. It was her first performance with her first band. Mark Jowett, a Moev band member and an owner of the Vancouver-based Nettwerk Productions, heard her sing and was captivated. He tried to sign her to a contract. Her parents would not let her sign, however, because they wanted her to finish her schooling. Two years later, Nettwerk President Terry McBride offered her a five-record deal that included total creative and image control. She immediately signed the contract and moved to Vancouver. McLachlan wrote her first song, "Out of the Shadows," in early 1987.

McLachlan's first album, *Touch,* was released in 1988 and went gold in Canada. It won wide critical acclaim thanks to underground hits such as "Vox" and "Steaming." She was suddenly rocketing to stardom. Music critics hailed her as the year's most exciting and important new artist. Her early songs were introspective, full of romance and inner turmoil. After completing a sixteen-month tour, she released her second album, *Solace,* in 1991, which was even more successful. Songs such as "Drawn to the Rhythm" and "Into the Fire" took McLachlan's music from the underground music scene to the mainstream. This album succeeded critically and commercially and catapulted her to international prominence. Shortly after the album's release, McLachlan became the victim of a stalker, who sent her threatening letters and followed her from concert to concert. She used his letters as the basis for her song "Possession," which was written from the stalker's viewpoint. Her *Fumbling Towards Ecstasy* album, which was released in 1993, went platinum five times and brought her international acclaim for songs such as "Hold On," "Possession," and "Good Enough." Her *Surfacing* album, which included the hit single "Building a Mystery," turned platinum in less than eight weeks in 1997.

Sarah McLachlan (Ken Settle)

Lilith Fair. In 1996, McLachlan created Lilith Fair, a two-stage road show featuring more than eighty rotating female artists, including Shawn Colvin, Tracy Chapman, Suzanne Vega, the Indigo Girls, and Jewel. Lilith was the mythical first wife of Adam, who was sent from the Garden of Eden for not being subservient. McLachlan had the idea for a show to celebrate women artists when concert promoters grumbled about her choice of a female opening act. The promoters said fans would not pay to see two women on the same stage. McLachlan launched the show to prove them wrong; she wanted to show promoters and fans that women entertainers could do the same as men—earn money by performing together. The show outsold male-dominated events such as Lollapalooza. It also propelled McLachlan into the spotlight with some of the industry's brightest stars, including Sheryl Crow, Fiona Apple, Paula Cole, and Joan Osborne.

McLachlan's performance and role in Lilith Fair put her in the forefront of the rock music scene. She achieved star status without a hit single to drive an album to success. Music retailers and promoters attributed her popularity to her tremendous live performance charisma and her loyal fans. McLachlan established the groundwork for her success through almost constant touring, promoting, and production of new albums. Her reputation grew primarily by word of mouth and through live performances.

Legacy. McLachlan's musical style changed over the years. It evolved from new age to folk rock and then to alternative folk rock. While hard to categorize, she earned a reputation as a gifted musician with a strong voice. Most important, her songs are a simple and sincere account of her own life and her own struggles. Thanks to her efforts, female artists had a chance to grow and to prove they could perform on the same level as men. She proved that fans would pay to see more than one woman in concert, and perhaps most important, she showed promoters and other skeptics that women were a force to be reckoned with in the music industry. —*Fred Buchstein*

SELECT DISCOGRAPHY

■ ALBUMS

Touch, 1988

Solace, 1991

Fumbling Towards Ecstasy, 1993

The Freedom Sessions, 1994

Surfacing, 1997

SELECT AWARDS

Grammy Awards for Best Female Pop Vocal Performance for "Building a Mystery" and Best Pop Instrumental Performance for "Last Dance," 1997

SEE ALSO: Baez, Joan; Chapman, Tracy; Colvin, Shawn; Gabriel, Peter; Indigo Girls, The; Jewel; Mitchell, Joni; Simon and Garfunkel; Stevens, Cat; Vega, Suzanne.

For the Record

Sarah McLachlan sang "O Little Town of Bethlehem" at the Vatican Christmas Concert in 1994.

John McLaughlin

BORN: Yorkshire, England; January 4, 1942

FIRST ALBUM RELEASE: *Extrapolation*, 1969 (first solo release)

MUSICAL STYLES: Jazz, jazz fusion, blues

Guitarist John McLaughlin first made his name in the jazz world playing with Miles Davis and the Tony Williams Lifetime in the late 1960's. Then, in 1971, he founded the critically acclaimed Mahavishnu Orchestra. This commercially successful group was a pioneer of jazz-rock fusion music. Later his recordings with Al DiMeola and Paco DeLucia reached new heights of virtuosity and passion.

The Beginnings. Born in Yorkshire, England, in 1942, McLaughlin became interested in violin and piano at age seven. His mother, a violinist, exposed him to many styles of classical and folk music. He was inspired to take up the guitar after hearing records by American blues artists such as Muddy Waters. At age fourteen he discovered flamenco and jazz music. He was fascinated with the passionate gypsy style of French guitarist Django Reinhardt. The *Jazz at the Philharmonic* series of recordings introduced him to many great jazz guitarists, including Barney Kessel and Tal Farlow. The 1958 Miles Davis album *Milestones* introduced him to post-bop and cool jazz. At age sixteen he quit school to take a job at a musical instrument shop. He began sitting in with local jazz groups and developing his technical skills. On weekends in the late 1950's he would hitchhike two hundred miles to Manchester to hear Spanish guitarists at local clubs. These jaunts led to his first professional job as guitarist with Peter Deuchar and His Professors of Ragtime, who performed in Manchester and London.

In 1960 McLaughlin moved to London and took part in the blues explosion, playing with notable musicians such as Alexis Korner, Georgie Fame, Graham Bond, and Ginger Baker. After becoming interested in abstract forms of music, he recorded with John Surman, Dave Holland, and free-jazz pioneer Gunter Hampel. *Extrapolation*, his first recording as a leader, was recorded

John McLaughlin (Paul Natkin)

in 1969 with Surman and drummer Tony Oxley. McLaughlin's lightning-quick technique and diverse pallet of tonal colors impressed European jazz fans.

In 1968 Dave Holland, who played bass with Miles Davis, persuaded drummer Tony Williams to hire McLaughlin for is band, Lifetime. This job brought McLaughlin to New York City and led to collaborations with bassist Charlie Haden and percussionist Airto Moreira. McLaughlin was becoming well-known in the jazz world, and soon the legendary Miles Davis asked him to play on the sessions for two breakthrough 1969 albums, *In a Silent Way* and *Bitches Brew.* These albums, combining rock beats and jazz improvisation, gave birth to a new style called "fusion." Solid rock grooves, funky electric bass, and complex polyrhythms formed a foundation for jazz-influenced improvisation. The music had the power of rock, the sophistication of jazz, and the instrumental mastery found in classical music.

In the early 1970's McLaughlin became fascinated with Eastern mysticism and theology. This break from traditional European concepts had been a driving force in pop culture and, to some extent, in pop music in the late 1960's. McLaughlin aligned himself with guru Sri Chinmoy. Experiments with Indian ragas and sitar music yielded intricate and fresh textures, and McLaughlin adapted them in his improvisational lines.

With the fusion style gaining in popularity, McLaughlin decided to create his own sound by forming the Mahavishnu Orchestra. The band's first album appeared in 1971, and *The Inner Mounting Flame* astounded the jazz and fusion worlds. McLaughlin had indeed created a sound that no one had heard before. Jazz guitar was traditionally clean-sounding, with little bending of the strings for pitch variation. Mclaughlin played loud and used considerable distortion, and he bent notes frequently, as rock guitarists had long done. The rest of the band was also a loud, powerful unit, with Billy Cobham's ambidextrous drumming style causing nearly as much of a sensation as McLaughlin's guitar work. Also in the band were Jerry Goodman on violin, Czech keyboardist Jan Hammer, and bassist Rick Laird. The compositions involved odd time signatures and were generally played at breakneck tempos; unison melodies were played by guitar and violin, and the band members then took turns playing blazing solos. The music showcased McLaughlin's extraordinary technique and diverse musical background. Rock guitar superstars now had their equal in the jazz world. The band's second album, *Birds of Fire*, like the first, was a critical and—for an instrumental album—commercial success. This version of the Mahavishnu Orchestra then put out a (disappointing) live album and disbanded. McLaughlin applied the Mahavishnu Orchestra name to his new group for his next two albums, then went on to record a number of solo and trio guitar albums. The early 1970's was a prolific period for McLaughlin, as he recorded several albums other than his Mahavishnu work, including *Devotion* (1970), *My Goal's Beyond* (1972), and *Love, Devotion, Surrender* (1973, with Carlos Santana).

Sharing the Flame. In 1981 McLaughlin teamed up with finger-style guitar great Paco DeLucia and guitarist Al DiMeola for the live album *Friday Night in San Francisco*. The trio dazzled the audience with both virtuosity and emotion. At one point during the concert McLaughlin broke into a driving shuffle blues, seemingly paying tribute to his early influences. The second (studio) album by this powerful trio, *Passion, Grace, and Fire* (1982), has become a classic. McLaughlin returned to playing the electric guitar on two solo recordings, *Belo Horizonte* (1981) and *Music Spoken Here* (1982). After this he joined Miles Davis on *You're Under Arrest* in 1984. This recording did not capture the same magic that earlier work with Miles had. In November of the 1985 McLaughlin broke new ground by performing, with the Los Angles Philharmonic Orchestra, a full guitar concerto written for him by Mike Gibbs. That same year McLaughlin also re-formed the Mahavishnu Orchestra with Billy Cobham; the group featured saxophonist Bill Evans instead of a violinist. The new solo voice created a more traditional jazz texture.

McLaughlin began touring with percussionist Trilok Gurtu in 1987. Their sound of classical Indian drums and McLaughlin's acoustic guitar was well received at a concert at London's Royal Philharmonic Hall in 1989. In 1990, McLaughlin was back in the United Kingdom for the premier of his *Mediterranean Concerto* with the Scottish National Orchestra at the Glasgow Jazz Festival. Verve records then convinced McLaughlin to break new ground by recording with jazz greats Joey DeFranceso on Hammond B-3 organ and drummer Elvin Jones. This recording, *After the Rain*, released in 1995, was the first to feature McLaughlin playing classic jazz compositions by tenor saxophone legend John Coltrane. McLaughlin's relentless creativity, along with DeFrancesco's sultry organ, rivaled many classic jazz guitar recordings of Wes Montgomery and Pat Martino. A third recording with DeLucia and DiMeola was released in 1996. This time the trio concentrated on creating rich musical textures instead of blinding technical forays. The result was critically acclaimed and showed the maturity of these three guitar greats.

Legacy. The combination of jazz concepts with rock grooves created the style that became known as fusion, and along with Davis and Weather Report, McLaughlin was a trailblazing figure. The Mahavishnu Orchestra recordings of the 1970's broke ground with the inclusion of Eastern ragas and sitarlike improvisations. The guitar trio of McLaughlin, DiMeola, and DeLucia left audiences in the 1980's and 1990's gasping for breath. Rarely have three such extraordinary solo artists collaborated to redefine an art form.

—Joseph D. Mixon

SELECT DISCOGRAPHY

■ ALBUMS

Extrapolation, 1969

The Inner Mounting Flame, 1972

Birds of Fire, 1973

Apocalypse, 1974

Friday Night in San Francisco, 1981 (with Al DiMeola and Paco DeLucia)

After the Rain, 1995
The Guitar Trio, 1996 (with DiMeola and DeLucia)

SELECT AWARDS
Down Beat Reader's Poll Guitarist of the Year, 1973, 1974, and 1994

SEE ALSO: Davis, Miles; Hancock, Herbie; Morse, Steve; Santana, Carlos; Weather Report.

Madonna

BORN: Bay City, Michigan; August 16, 1958
FIRST ALBUM RELEASE: *Madonna*, 1983
MUSICAL STYLE: Pop

Madonna was perhaps one of the most influential pop icons of the 1980's and 1990's. Her career has been controversial, radical, and always interesting. Her blatant support of sexual freedom and alternative lifestyles, and even her own highly publicized sexual ambiguity, has been a fascination to the media. By 1998, Madonna had recorded nineteen Top-10 singles, eleven of which reached number 1, and seventeen of which were certified gold. Twelve of her thirteen albums were included on music critics' top-ten lists, and each sold from one to four million copies, seven of them going multiplatinum. In the 1980's, Madonna overtook the record set by the Beatles by having six straight Top-5 singles.

Madonna was one of the first artists to take advantage of MTV, the new music video station of the 1980's. Her music videos were revolutionary and an important element to her success, and they also foreshadowed Madonna's successful film career. With more than forty music videos by 1998, Madonna would be one of the most frequently televised artists in MTV's history. Her frequent change of style and persona would continue to frustrate and intrigue even her most ardent critics.

Early Years. Born Madonna Louise Veronica Ciccone on August 16, 1958, in Bay City, Michigan, Madonna was the eldest of six children. Madonna's career direction was greatly influenced by the music of Motown Records, located in nearby Detroit, Michigan, and dance studies, which she began at the age of fourteen. In 1976 she was the recipient of a dance scholarship to the University of Michigan. Uninspired by academia, she left for New York in 1977. While attending an American Dance Festival course at Duke University in North Carolina, Madonna met the modern dance choreographer Pearl Lange. This chance meeting would result in a scholarship with the Alvin Ailey American Dance Theater. Madonna struggled for several years in the dance world while simultaneously trying to promote her music career.

The Early 1980's. Madonna's first important musical success was with the release of her 1983 debut, *Madonna*, on the Sire Records label. The musical style was fresh, upbeat, and included such hits as "Holiday" (her first Top-40 hit), "Lucky Star" (her first Top-5 hit), and her first music video, "Borderline." Although critical reviews were initially mixed, *Madonna* became one of the best-selling albums of all time.

The release of her second album, *Like a Virgin* (1984), defined her "bad-girl" image. Sporting a belt buckle inscribed with the words Boy Toy, dirty blonde hair, and multiple crucifixes around her neck, Madonna would project an image that was particularly appealing to adolescent girls. The notoriety surrounding this album is historical, because it challenged traditional values held by conservative factions. Regardless, *Like a Virgin* would go on to become one of the top-selling albums of the 1980's (seventeen million copies in the United States, another fifteen million worldwide). The title track was Madonna's first number 1 single. It held the position for six consecutive weeks and became a multiplatinum sensation. In 1984, Madonna successfully performed the song on the first MTV Video Music Awards telecast, captivating audiences with her sexy, bold image.

The year 1985 would see Madonna's film debut in *Desperately Seeking Susan*. This romantic comedy received positive critical reviews. While on the set of her "Material Girl" video, Madonna met her future husband, actor Sean Penn. They married on her birthday in 1985. The disastrous reviews of their film collaboration in 1986, *Shanghai Surprise*, with Madonna in the role of a missionary, certainly foreshadowed their turbulent relationship. They eventually divorced in 1989 due to irreconcilable differences.

Madonna (Ken Settle)

The Late 1980's. Madonna projected a new glamorous look in 1986 with the release of *True Blue*. With platinum hair and a stronger voice, *True Blue* sparked political controversy with the release of the single "Papa Don't Preach," which addressed teenage pregnancy. Regardless, *True Blue* became an international success, selling seventeen million albums worldwide. *True Blue* was featured in *The Guinness Book of Records* by becoming a number 1 hit in twenty-eight countries. The film comedy *Who's That Girl* opened to mixed reviews in 1987. Commercially and critically successful in Europe, the film was a box-office failure in the United States. In contrast, the 1987 "Who's That Girl" concert tour was a complete success. With the inclusion of exhausting choreography, multimedia technology, elaborate costumes, previous musical hits, and manic fans, the success of the tour was guaranteed.

Madonna's acting debut on Broadway was in 1988 with David Mamet's *Speed-the-Plow*. With Madonna in the role of Karen, a temporary office assistant, *Speed-the-Plow* was a phenomenal success, receiving several Tony Award nominations. In 1989, Madonna signed with Pepsi-Cola to star in three television commercials. Pepsi also agreed to sponsor Madonna's upcoming "Blonde Ambition" tour. Pepsi's attitude soon changed with the release of her 1989 *Like a Prayer* album. The major controversy was with the title track, Catholic iconography, burning crosses, and an interracial kiss all led to severe criticism from social and racial groups and from the Vatican itself. Pepsi canceled their sponsorship of Madonna and refused to endorse the "Blonde Ambition" tour. Regardless, the album was a tremendous success, selling more than ten million copies worldwide. The single hits "Express Yourself," "Cherish," and "Oh Father" were on top of the record charts for all of 1989. The futuristic "Express Yourself" video became one of Madonna's most popular.

The Early 1990's. The year 1990 was perhaps one of the most successful of Madonna's career. The film *Dick Tracy* was a critical and box office success. Madonna's strong performance of "Sooner or Later" would help win composer Stephen Sondheim the Best Song Academy Award. The success of *Dick Tracy* would also help to launch the critically acclaimed "Blonde Ambition" tour.

The "Blonde Ambition" tour continued to push the conservative envelope. The performances incorporated overt sexual simulation, sexy, futuristic clothing, including Madonna's signature "cone bras," and Catholic icons. Although Pope John Paul II called for a boycott of her performances in Italy, the tour performed in twenty-seven cities worldwide. The final performance was aired on the Home Box Office (HBO) cable network.

The 1990 release of "Justify My Love," which originated on *The Immaculate Collection*, revealed an overt sexual image that Madonna would pursue in the early 1990's. For the first time in its history, MTV refused to air a video, claiming "Justify My Love" was too controversial for the airwaves. It would go on to become one of Madonna's biggest hits, selling 1,000,000 recordings and almost 800,000 videos.

Madonna's popularity soared with the release of two new film projects. The first was *Truth or Dare*, a 1991 documentary of backstage and concert footage of the 1990 "Blonde Ambition" tour. Comparing Madonna's performing life with her everyday life, the film was initially criticized for some insensitive subject matter and depiction of gay sexuality, but *Truth or Dare* was a financial success. Less successful in 1992 was the release of Woody Allen's film *Shadows and Fog*, with Madonna cast as a high-wire artist.

By 1992, critics could no longer deny that Madonna was a musical phenomenon. As an actress, however, critics were still not convinced, though she had more than ten films to her credit. Critics did warm to Madonna's performance in *A League of Their Own*, a film about a 1943 women's baseball team. Both the film and Madonna's performance won critical accolades. It became the top-grossing film of the summer of 1992. The film also produced another hit for Madonna with the popular theme song "This Used to Be My Playground."

Sex. The year 1992 was very controversial for Madonna. This was primarily due to the publication of her 128-page book of erotica, *Sex.* Many critics and fans felt Madonna had acted beyond the limits of good taste. *Sex* included original poetry and song lyrics written by Madonna and hundreds of photographs of her and her friends in various states of erotic activity. The book also included a comic book and a compact disc of an "Erotica" remix, and it was bound in a stainless-steel cover. *Sex* sold 150,000 copies in the United States on its first day, with many bookstores agreeing to sell it under the counter only. Madonna's sixth full-length album, *Erotica*, was released simultaneously with *Sex.* Hailed as one of her best recordings, *Erotica* included the successful singles "Rain" and "Deeper and Deeper" and sold more than three million copies.

Madonna founded her multimedia company, Maverick Entertainment, in 1992. Based in New York and Los Angeles, Maverick Entertainment would represent performing artists such as Alanis Morissette, Candlebox, the Deftones, the Rentals, Me'Shell NdegéOcello, Wank, and Madonna her-

For the Record

According to the *Encyclopedia Madonnica*, "Like a Prayer" is the only video in which Madonna appears with her completely natural brunette hair color.

§

Granada issued the first Madonna postage stamp in 1989.

§

"Like a Virgin" is included on "The 500 Songs That Shaped Rock" in Cleveland's Rock and Roll Hall of Fame.

self. It was the production company behind the 1993 art film *Dangerous Game* (in which Madonna starred) and was instrumental in the publication of *Sex*. In 1998, Maverick Entertainment teamed with the Imagine Entertainment production company.

Madonna's career appeared to be in a slump during the opening of 1993. The reviews of *Dangerous Game* were mixed, and the reviews of her other film *Body of Evidence* were disastrous. Neither film faired well at the box office. In a career low, Madonna became the recipient of the Golden Raspberry and Golden Turkey Awards for Worst Actress. The 1993 "Girlie Show" tour, which only played in three U.S. cities, seemed to revitalize her career. The critical response was mixed, but the fan response was extremely positive. The "Girlie Show" tour included commentary on disco, AIDS, Hollywood, and, of course, sex. HBO televised the show live from Sydney, Australia, and Maverick released it for home video as *The Girlie Show: Live Down Under*. In addition, Madonna's second book, *Madonna: The Girlie Show*, was published in 1994.

The album *Bedtime Stories* was released in 1994. The musical style was in contrast to many of her earlier albums. It showcased a more mature Madonna and was more narrative than danceable. The single "Take a Bow" remained at number 1 on the pop charts for seven consecutive weeks, surpassing her old record of six consecutive weeks with "Like a Virgin" in 1984.

The Late 1990's. Although Madonna had a small role in the 1995 film *Smoke*, her next major project was the 1996 film version of the 1978 Andrew Lloyd Webber and Tim Rice musical *Evita*. Madonna was cast in the title role as the Argentine political heroine Eva Peron. The film was a critical success, although the Argentine populace had some initial dismay at Madonna portraying their beloved national figure. Webber and Rice collaborated to compose a new ballad, "You Must Love Me," specifically for the film. Madonna's commitment to the role and increased vocal training helped to make *Evita* an immediate success.

Madonna gave birth to a daughter, Lourdes Maria Ciccone Leon, fathered by Carlos Leon, in 1996. Motherhood, along with a newfound spirituality through study of a branch of Judaism called Kabbalah, created a new look, sound, and attitude for Madonna. The 1998 release of *Ray of Light* was a phenomenal success. Two months after its release, *Ray of Light* had gone double platinum with sales in excess of more than two million copies. Additional 1998 projects included the VH1 cable special *Madonna Rising* and more film roles.

—Brent Register

SELECT DISCOGRAPHY

■ ALBUMS

Madonna, 1983
Like a Virgin, 1984
True Blue, 1986
Who's That Girl, 1987 (sound track)
You Can Dance, 1987 (compilation)
Like a Prayer, 1989
I'm Breathless: Songs from and Inspired by the Film "Dick Tracy," 1990
The Immaculate Collection, 1990 (compilation)
Erotica, 1992
Bedtime Stories, 1994
Something to Remember, 1995 (compilation)
Evita—The Complete Motion Picture Music Soundtrack, 1996
Ray of Light, 1998

SELECT AWARDS

American Music Award for Favorite Pop/Rock Female Artist, 1985
MTV Video Vanguard Award, 1986
International Music Award for Best Female Singer for "Like a Prayer," 1989
MTV Video Music Award for Artist of the Decade, 1989
Glamour, named Woman of the Year, 1990
Grammy Award for Best Music Video, Long Form, for *Madonna: Blonde Ambition World Tour Live*, 1992 (with others)
American Society of Composers, Authors, and Publishers (ASCAP) Film and Television Music Award for Best Songwriting for "This Used to Be My Playground," 1993

SEE ALSO: Morissette, Alanis.

The Mahavishnu Orchestra. *See* John McLaughlin

See John McLaughlin

The Mamas and the Papas

ORIGINAL MEMBERS: John Phillips (b. 1935), Denny Doherty (b. 1941), Michelle Phillips (b. Holly Michelle Gilliam, 1944), Cass Elliot (b. Ellen Cohen, 1943-1974)

OTHER MEMBERS: Mackenzie Phillips (b. 1959), Elaine "Spanky" McFarlane (b. 1942)

FIRST ALBUM RELEASE: *If You Can Believe Your Eyes and Ears*, 1966

MUSICAL STYLES: Folk rock, rock and roll

Of the many pop groups that rose and fell during the 1960's, one of the most spectacular and most fondly remembered was the California-based the Mamas and the Papas. Although most of this vocal group's members were not from California, their music captured the casual, free-love ethos of California's "flower generation" of the late 1960's and influenced many other performers by helping to bridge the gap between folk and rock music.

Recording and performing mostly their own music, the Mamas and the Papas were unusual in combining male and female vocalists at a time when the vast majority of rock bands were all male. The Mamas and the Papas were noted for innovative vocal arrangements marked by contrapuntal harmonies, with lines sung on top of each other above a solid electric-folk base. While their pleasing harmonies found a wide commercial audience, they managed to remain closely identified with the counterculture. They recorded only four original albums but left a solid body of pop standards. They are also remembered for helping to launch the careers of Janis Joplin, Jimi Hendrix, Jefferson Airplane, and others through the role they played in staging the Monterey International Pop Festival in 1967.

The Rise. The acknowledged leader of the Mamas and the Papas, and the person primarily responsible for both their songs and their innovative arrangements, was John Phillips. The son of a career Marine, he grew up an all-American boy in Virginia. Tall and athletic, he earned all-state honors in track and basketball and received a coveted appointment to the U.S. Naval Academy. After only three months as a cadet, however, he abandoned his military aspirations and turned to a radically different lifestyle in New York's bohemian Greenwich Village in 1957. There he formed a folk group called the Journeymen. In 1962 he married Michelle Gilliam, a native Californian who had come to New York to become a model. She took up music herself and occasionally sang with the Journeymen.

Meanwhile, Denny Doherty, a multitalented Canadian who had joined his first folk group when he was fifteen and helped record two albums while still a teenager, came to Greenwich Village. There he joined Zal Yanovsky, Jim Hendricks, and Hendricks's wife, Cass Elliot, to form a group called Cass Elliot and the Big Three. This group soon went electric; renamed the Mugwumps, it added drummer Art Stokes and John Sebastian on harmonica. After recording one album (not released until 1967), the Mugwumps disbanded. Sebastian and Yanovsky formed the Lovin' Spoonful, Elliot joined a jazz trio, and Doherty joined the Phillipses to form the New Journeymen.

By 1964 popular music tastes were shifting from folk to electric rock. After concluding he should create a less folk-oriented band, one with both men and women, Phillips took Michelle and Doherty to the Virgin Islands to work out a new act. Cass Elliot—whom they were reluctant to admit to the group—followed them there and supported herself as a waitress while occasionally rehearsing with them. After she and her husband relocated to Los Angeles, Doherty and the Phillipses joined her and finally admitted her to the group.

In Los Angeles the New Journeymen renamed themselves the Mamas and the Papas and made Lou Adler their manager. Signing a recording contract with Adler helped to create a new label, Dunhill. Early the following year they scored their first hit with "California Dreamin'," a song Phillips had been inspired to write by Michelle's fond

The Mamas and the Papas: John Phillips, Michelle Phillips, Cass Elliot, Denny Doherty (MCA/Guy Webster)

memories of California during her first winter in New York. That single slowly rose to number 4 on the charts, but its successor, "Monday, Monday," on which Doherty sang lead, quickly rose to number 1 (it later won a Grammy Award). Their first album, *If You Can Believe Your Eyes and Ears*, topped the charts in May, 1966, firmly establishing the Mamas and the Papas as a major recording group. In 1966 and 1967 alone, they had six Top-5 singles.

The Fall. Still riding a succession of hit singles and albums, the group reached their peak in 1967 when they performed at California's Monterey Pop Festival, which Phillips and Adler produced. That festival inspired Phillips to write "San Francisco (Be Sure to Wear Flowers in Your Hair)," which former Journeyman Scott McKenzie turned into a Top-5 hit. The song itself became an anthem of the "flower generation."

By the following year, however, the Mamas and the Papas were unraveling. High living, drug problems, and sexual entanglements among the group's members—which years later the Phillipses detailed in separate autobiographies—turned the group's members against one another. John and Michelle separated, and Michelle left the group briefly—returning after her replacement failed to please concert fans. By the end of 1968, the group's members decided to disband. John and Michelle divorced in 1970. Meanwhile, everyone in the group became embroiled in breach-of-contract and royalty disputes with Dunhill, except Elliot, who was beginning to record with Dunhill as a solo act.

In 1971, the Mamas and the Papas reunited on a new album, *People Like Us*, but it was not successful. As Dunhill issued several reprise albums, the members of the group finally went their separate ways. Doherty made two unsuccessful solo albums, Michelle turned more to acting and achieved some success in films and on television. Among the former Mamas and Papas, Elliot achieved the greatest success as a solo act, but a fatal heart attack brought on by her overweight condition cut her career short while she was touring England in 1974. Meanwhile, John Phillips effectively retired from the music business, content to live on the substantial royalties from the hit songs he had written.

Rebirth. During the early 1980's, renewed public interest in the music of the 1960's prompted John Phillips to organize a new version of the Mamas and the Papas. Rejoined by Doherty, he added his daughter, Mackenzie Phillips, who was by then well known in her own right as a television actress, and Elaine "Spanky" McFarlane, from Spanky and Our Gang, to the group. This new incarnation of the Mamas and the Papas enjoyed modest but steady success on the nostalgia tour circuit. The group recorded no fresh hits, but during this period John Phillips cowrote "Kokomo" for the Beach Boys, who took it to number 1 on the charts in 1988. After he retired from touring in the mid-1990's, a completely new group took over, using the Mamas and the Papas' name, which Phillips still owned. Meanwhile, Doherty continued to perform the Mamas and the Papas music on his own solo tour.

—*R. Kent Rasmussen*

SELECT DISCOGRAPHY

■ SINGLES

"California Dreamin'," 1966
"Monday, Monday," 1966
"Words of Love," 1966
"Dedicated to the One I Love," 1967
"Creeque Alley," 1967
"Dream a Little Dream of Me," 1968

■ ALBUMS

If You Can Believe Your Eyes and Ears, 1966
The Mamas and the Papas, 1966
Farewell to the First Golden Era, 1967
The Papas and the Mamas, 1968
People Like Us, 1971
Creeque Alley: The History of the Mamas and the Papas, 1991 (compilation)

SELECT AWARDS

Grammy Award for Best Contemporary Rock & Roll Group Performance, Vocal or Instrumental, for "Monday Monday," 1966
Rock and Roll Hall of Fame, inducted 1998

SEE ALSO: Beach Boys, The; Hendrix, Jimi; Jefferson Airplane / Jefferson Starship; Joplin, Janis; Lovin' Spoonful, The.

Barbara Mandrell

BORN: Houston, Texas; December 25, 1948
FIRST SINGLE RELEASE: "I've Been Loving You Too Long," 1969
FIRST ALBUM RELEASE: *Treat Him Right*, 1971
MUSICAL STYLES: Country, pop, rhythm and blues, gospel

Barbara demonstrated her musical talents at a very early age and received strong support from her parents. Her father Irby was a singer and guitarist, and her mother Mary was a music teacher and pianist. When Barbara was only five years old, her mother taught her how to play a small accordion. After her parents moved to California, Barbara learned to play the steel guitar and the saxophone, and by the time she was twelve she was playing both instruments on television programs, including *Town Hall Party* and *Five Star Jubilee.*

Rise to the Top. In her teens, Barbara learned how to play two more instruments, the banjo and the guitar, and in 1967, she married Ken Dudney, the drummer in the Mandrell Family Band. After moving to Nashville with her family in 1968 and making a few vocal appearances, Columbia music producer Billy Sherrill signed her to a contract in 1969. Barbara's fifth single release, "Tonight My Baby's Coming Home," finally landed her in the Top 10 on the country charts in 1972 and earned her an invitation to join the Grand Ole Opry. "This Time I Almost Made It," "Standing Room Only," "Married but Not to Each Other," and "Woman to Woman" were all hits that preceded her first number 1 smash hit of 1978, "Sleeping Single in a Double Bed." In 1979, she had another number 1 hit, "I Don't Want to Be Right," and another major hit in "Fooled by a Feeling." Mandrell was named Female Vocalist of the Year in 1978 by the Academy of Country Music (ACM), followed by the ACM's and the Country Music Association's Entertainer of the Year Awards in 1980 and ACM's Female Vocalist of the Year Award again in 1981.

Barbara Mandrell in 1983 (AP/Wide World Photos)

Good Times and Bad. In 1980, Mandrell inaugurated her own television program, *Barbara Mandrell & the Mandrell Sisters,* joined by her younger sisters Louise and Irlene. This national television series brought Mandrell to the attention of millions of new fans all over the world. In 1980, Mandrell had single hits with "Years," "Crackers," and "The Best of Strangers" and three more big hits in 1981, "Love Is Fair," "Wish You Were Here," and the very popular "I Was Country (When Country Wasn't Cool)."

Keeping up with her recording career, concert tours, television series, and motherhood proved too demanding for Mandrell, and, on her doctor's advice, she took some time off. Feeling refreshed, she resumed her concert work in late 1982, received gold certification for her albums *The Best of Barbara Mandrell* (1979) and *Barbara Mandrell Live* (1981), and earned a Grammy Award for her gospel album *He Set My Life to Music* (1982).

In 1984, Mandrell made her television film debut in *Burning Rage*, and when it seemed as though she was on top of the world, she and her two children were involved in a near-fatal car accident on September 11, 1984, when a young driver hit the Mandrell car head-on. Because they had fastened their seat belts just minutes prior to the collision, Mandrell and her children survived.

Coming Back. Having suffered many injuries and much pain from the automobile crash, the energetic Mandrell worked herself back to her normal activities by late 1986, and in 1987, she received the American Music Award for Favorite Female Country Vocalist. Although her recordings would not see much chart success after her accident, Mandrell would continue to draw large crowds in her live stage performances, and she remained a star on the Grand Ole Opry.

—Alvin K. Benson

SELECT DISCOGRAPHY

■ ALBUMS

A Perfect Match, 1972 (with David Houston)
Moods, 1978
He Set My Life to Music, 1982
Greatest Hits, 1985

SELECT AWARDS

Academy of Country Music Female Vocalist of the Year Award, 1978, 1981

Country Music Association Female Vocalist of the Year Award, 1979, 1981

Country Music Association Entertainer of the Year Award, 1980, 1981

Grammy Award for Best Inspirational Performance for *He Set My Life to Music*, 1982

Grammy Award for Best Soul Gospel Performance by a Duo or Group for "I'm So Glad I'm Standing Here Today," 1983 (with Bobby Jones)

SEE ALSO: Atkins, Chet; Cash, Johnny; Jones, George; Parton, Dolly.

Chuck Mangione

BORN: Rochester, New York; November 29, 1940
FIRST ALBUM RELEASE: *The Jazz Brothers*, 1960
MUSICAL STYLES: Jazz, pop

Jazz musician Chuck Mangione went from being an obscure bebop player and second-string trumpeter in the early 1960's to a jazz-pop superstar in the late 1970's. He accomplished this by trading in the trumpet for the soft, warm sound of the fluegelhorn and turning his back on the harmonic complexities of the music begun by Charlie Parker, Miles Davis, and Dizzy Gillespie for Latin-inspired instrumentals that soothed and never challenged. By doing this, Mangione did more than just sell a lot of records: He opened the ears of rock and pop audiences to jazz sounds and did it better than anyone else in his day.

Bop Beginnings. Chuck Mangione's father was a jazz enthusiast who would often take Chuck and his older brother, Gap, to jazz concerts in nearby New York City. Jazz trumpeter Gillespie became a family friend and an inspiration as well; Mangione started to study the trumpet early, while his brother's instrument of choice was the piano.

With his father's encouragement, Mangione auditioned for the prestigious Eastman School of Music and was accepted. There he worked at mastering the subtleties of bebop jazz and learned to copy the style of Clifford Brown, Davis, and Gillespie. (Bebop, or bop, is a style of jazz that originated in the 1940's and features improvisation, fast tempos, unusual chord structures, and complex rhythms.)

With Gap he formed a hard-bop quintet called the Jazz Brothers, who would last for five years and record four albums on several small jazz labels. On these early recordings Mangione mimicked the style of the great bop players of the day, and none of the albums were commercial or critical successes. In 1965, the brothers broke up and went their separate ways.

Success *Feels So Good*. Mangione's reputation as an ace trumpeter made it easy for him to find other work. He performed in the big jazz bands of Woody Herman and Maynard Ferguson in 1965 and in Art Blakey's band in 1966 and 1967. During his time with Blakey's band, he was featured on the successful 1966 *Buttercorn Lady* album.

Chuck Mangione (Lissa Wales)

Needing a change, he returned to the Eastman School of Music in 1967, where he taught for a few years. During this time he experimented with the fluegelhorn, eventually abandoning the trumpet altogether. In the early 1970's, he formed his own small band under his own name. This band began making lighter jazz albums and had some success, especially with 1973's *Land of Make Believe* on the A&M label.

In 1977, *Feels So Good* was released and was an instant hit, selling more than two million copies. The catchy, simple melodies and lack of improvisation made it popular with the general public, and the title track became a huge crossover hit. As with Kenny G in the 1980's and John Tesh in the 1990's, there were accusations that what Mangione was playing was not jazz. Yet it has been argued that these performers make jazz elements palatable to the average listener and often inspire such people to seek out other jazz recordings and artists.

For the Record

The fluegelhorn is a valved brass instrument pitched in B-flat with the same range as the trumpet. The mouthpiece is deeper, and its tone is mellower than a trumpet's. It was first heard in military bands in the ninteenth century. Mangione was one of the first to apply this unusual instrument to jazz.

Mangione followed up the popular *Feels So Good* album with a sound track to the film *Children of Sanchez* in 1978. The title track received significant radio play, as it featured many of the elements heard on *Feels So Good*. Next came the live album *An Evening of Magic: Chuck Mangione Live at the Hollywood Bowl* (1979), which was a greatest-hits collection of his 1970's foray into jazz-pop.

The 1980's. In the 1980's he switched labels and went to Columbia Records, where he made some commercially and critically disappointing recordings. Mangione then made an attempt to return to his bop roots and even recorded with Gillespie, but nothing seemed to revive his career to the level it had attained in the 1970's. By the 1990's, he had all but dropped completely out of music, doing no recording and little live playing. His brother Gap Mangione would be heard more frequently, recording and performing with his own big band. —*Kevin M. Mitchell*

SELECT DISCOGRAPHY

■ ALBUMS

The Jazz Brothers, 1960

Buttercorn Lady, 1966 (with Art Blakey and the Jazz Messengers)

Land of Make Believe, 1973
Feels So Good, 1977
Children of Sanchez, 1978
An Evening of Magic: Chuck Mangione Live at the Hollywood Bowl, 1979
The Best of Chuck Mangione, 1985 (compilation)
Eyes of the Veiled Temptress, 1988

SELECT AWARDS
Grammy Award for Best Instrumental Composition for "Bellavia," 1976
Grammy Award for Best Pop Instrumental Performance for *Children of Sanchez*, 1978

SEE ALSO: Davis, Miles; G, Kenny; Parker, Charlie; Tesh, John.

Manhattan Transfer

ORIGINAL MEMBERS: Tim Hauser (b. 1941), Gene Pistili, Marty Nelson, Pat Rosalia, Erin Dickens
BEST-KNOWN LINEUP: Tim Hauser, Janis Siegel (b. 1952), Alan Paul (b. 1949), Cheryl Bentyne (b. 1954)
OTHER MEMBERS: Laurel Masse (b. 1954)
FIRST ALBUM RELEASE: *Jukin'*, 1971
MUSICAL STYLES: Jazz, swing, Latin, rock, pop, rhythm and blues, country, gospel

Very few vocal groups have performed so many different styles and forms of modern music with the enthusiasm, authenticity, and success of the Manhattan Transfer. Since 1972, the list of the group's hits has been seemingly endless, and the group's impact on the U.S. music scene is equally immeasurable. Manhattan Transfer has been a dynamic live attraction, regularly selling out shows worldwide, while high school, college, and community choirs across the United States sing published versions of the group's music every year.

The Beginnings. There have actually been two versions of the Manhattan Transfer. The group is the brainchild of Tim Hauser and was originally formed in the late 1960's. Hauser, a native of Troy, New York, who cites as his major influences 1950's rhythm and blues, bebop, and soul, would regularly travel to Harlem, New York, to hear his favorite vocal groups. Hauser has sung professionally since high school and recorded with a doo-wop vocal group called the Criterions at the age of seventeen. His primary love was always four-part vocal singing, which led him to form the first version of the Manhattan Transfer, which consisted of Hauser, Gene Pistili, Marty Nelson, Pat Rosalia, and Erin Dickens. This group recorded their first album, *Jukin'* (1971), as well as a few singles, on the Capitol label.

The group dissolved soon after, however, and Hauser turned to cabdriving in New York to earn a living. He never lost his desire to return to the four-part ensemble, however. One night his cab passenger was Laurel Masse, an out-of-work singer who was familiar with the first Manhattan Transfer album and looking to form a group. A few weeks later, another of Hauser's cab passengers took him to a party where he met Janis Siegel, who was then a member of a harmony group called Laurel Canyon. Siegel, Masse, and Hauser began meeting regularly to sing. Soon after, Masse's husband introduced Hauser and Siegel to Alan Paul, who was at that time in the Broadway cast of Jim Jacobs and Warren Casey's *Grease*, and who had appeared on the original Broadway cast recording of Lionel Bart's *Oliver*. Paul was attracted to the trio's cool attitude blended with their strong emotional feeling, and as the four of them began to sing together, they discovered an exceptional musical chemistry. On October 1, 1972, the new Manhattan Transfer was born. With this lineup, the group made four albums: *The Manhattan Transfer* (1975), *Coming Out* (1976), *Pastiche* (1978), and *Live* (1978), the first appearing on the Atlantic label in 1975. A string of Top-10 hits came from these recordings, as did a highly experimental television show. The recordings seemed to fare especially well in Europe. In 1978 Masse was seriously hurt in an automobile accident. During her recovery she felt perhaps she would be unable to match the group's energy from then on, and she elected not to return to the group.

Auditions were held, and among those who auditioned was a singer from Seattle, Washington, a former member of the New Deal Rhythm band who was also doing club work in Los Angeles. The three remaining members immediately felt her impact, and Cheryl Bentyne became the newest member of the group. The group's sound then went through a noticeable change.

New Sound. As Paul explained, with this new sound, "the Transfer's second phase began." This second period ran roughly from 1979 to 1984, and it was during this time that Manhattan Transfer developed "its jazz persona and began associating itself with American jazz music," said Hauser. In addition to the addition of Bentyne, Manhattan Transfer also came under the influences of saxophonist Richie Cole and singer Jon Hendricks of the jazz trio Lambert, Hendricks, and Ross.

Vocalese. Hendricks, considered one of the most gifted lyricists in jazz music, had an amazing facility for vocalese—the writing of lyrics to recorded, improvised, instrumental jazz solos. Hendricks "encouraged us to do more vocalese," said Janis Siegel. "He made us realize what a gift it is to be involved with all this music, and by that I mean not just the jazz or vocalese, but all of it."

Bentyne believed that the Manhattan Transfer's third phase began with the group's 1985 album *Vocalese*, for which Hendricks wrote the lyrics to eleven classic jazz and rhythm-and-blues recordings, and continued with the 1987 release *Brasil*, on which the group focused on contemporary material from that region. "From a musical standpoint, those are our two strongest albums," Bentyne said with justifiable pride.

Manhattan Transfer would break from Atlantic Records after the release of *Brasil* but would return seven years and three albums later. Among those three non-Atlantic albums was a long-awaited Christmas album and a departure recording, *The Manhattan Transfer Meets Tubby the Tuba* (1994), the group's first and only children's album. After returning to Atlantic, the group made three more albums, one of which invited a sizeable number of guest vocalists (Phil Collins, Bette Midler, and James Taylor, among others), a third live album, and *Swing* (1997), with its emphasis on 1930's-era swing music and vocal classics.

Perhaps appropriately so, *Swing* was released in the Manhattan Transfer's silver anniversary year. With this album, the group showed no signs of slowing down, their vocal harmony and four-part jazz vocalese being at their peaks, and their enthusiasm and energy at perhaps their highest levels.

Manhattan Transfer in 1977 (Archive Photos)

Awards. The album *Extensions* (1979) contains the tune that has become the group's signature tune, "Birdland" (written by Joe Zawinul and first recorded by his group, Weather Report). The song earned the group their first Grammy Award for Best Jazz Fusion Performance, Vocal or Instrumental, and another award for Siegel for Best Arrangement for Voices.

In 1981 Manhattan Transfer made music history by becoming the first group to win Grammies in both pop and jazz categories in the same year. "Boy from New York City" broke the Top 10 on the pop charts and garnered them the award for the Best Pop Performance by a Duo or Group with Vocal, and "Until I Met You (Corner Pocket)" also won them the Grammy for Best Jazz Vocal Performance, Duo or Group. Both of these songs appeared on the group's fifth album, *Mecca for Moderns* (1981). Another Grammy for Best Jazz Vocal Performance, Duo or Group, was won in 1982 for the song "Route 66."

The album which the group considers its tour de force is *Vocalese.* Bentyne's pride in calling this one of the group's strongest recordings can be backed by the fact that this recording received no less than twelve Grammy Award nominations (second only to Michael Jackson's *Thriller* as the most nominated album of all time). Manhattan Transfer won in two of the categories in which it was nominated: again for Best Jazz Vocal Performance, Duo or Group, and for Best Arrangement for Voices (this time for Bentyne and Bobby McFerrin). In 1991, Manhattan Transfer released the first of their two albums on Columbia Records, *The Off-Beat of Avenues,* from which the song "Sassy" earned them the Grammy Award for Best Contemporary Jazz Performance.

—*Bart MacMillan*

For the Record

Tim Hauser played Kim Basinger's bandleader and produced the sound track for the 1991 film *The Marrying Man,* in which Alan Paul did some solo work as well. Cheryl Bentyne appears on the 1991 *Mortal Thoughts* sound track, but the album was never released.

SELECT DISCOGRAPHY

■ ALBUMS

Jukin', 1971
The Manhattan Transfer, 1975
Coming Out, 1976
Pastiche, 1978
Extensions, 1979
Mecca for Moderns, 1981
Bodies and Souls, 1983
Bop Doo Wop, 1984
Vocalese, 1985
Brasil, 1987
The Christmas Album, 1992
The Manhattan Transfer Anthology: Down in Birdland, 1992 (compilation)
The Manhattan Transfer Meets Tubby the Tuba, 1994
The Very Best of the Manhattan Transfer, 1994 (compilation)
Tonin', 1995
Swing, 1997

SELECT AWARDS

Grammy Award for Best Jazz Fusion Performance, Vocal or Instrumental, for "Birdland," 1980
Grammy Awards for Best Jazz Vocal Performance, Duo or Group, for "Until I Met You (Corner Pocket)" and Best Pop Performance by a Duo or Group with Vocal for "Boy from New York City," 1981
Grammy Award for Best Jazz Vocal Performance, Duo or Group, for "Route 66," 1982
Grammy Award for Best Jazz Vocal Performance, Duo or Group, for "Why Not!" 1983
Grammy Award for Best Jazz Vocal Performance, Duo or Group, for *Vocalese,* 1985
Grammy Award for Best Pop Performance by a Duo or Group with Vocal for *Brasil,* 1988
Grammy Award for Best Contemporary Jazz Performance for "Sassy," 1991

SEE ALSO: Weather Report.

Barry Manilow

BORN: Brooklyn, New York; June 17, 1946
FIRST ALBUM RELEASE: *Barry Manilow*, 1973
MUSICAL STYLES: Pop, adult contemporary

When Barry Manilow burst upon the popular music scene with the single "Mandy," which was to become his first number 1 hit in late 1974, most of the public had no idea that he had been in the music business for almost a decade. He had begun arranging music for television when he was only eighteen years old, had accompanied innumerable performers for auditions, had performed as a duo with Jeanne Lucas, had been Bette Midler's pianist, conductor, and arranger, had written and/or sung several commercials for national companies, and had one album under his belt before his stardom came with "Mandy."

How It Began. Barry was born on June 17, 1946, to Harold Pincus and Edna Manilow in Brooklyn, New York. By the time Barry was two, his father had deserted his young family, so he was raised by his mother and his Russian-immigrant grandparents in the poverty-ridden Williamsburg section of Brooklyn. His name was soon changed from Pincus to Manilow. When he was seven, his grandmother, Esther, insisted that Manilow take accordion lessons, which he eventually learned to play quite well.

When Manilow was thirteen, his mother married a trucker and jazz buff, Willie Murphy, who introduced Manilow to the cool sounds of jazz and to Broadway show tunes by taking him to Town Hall in Manhattan to hear jazz great Gerry Mulligan. Most of the students his age at Eastern District High School were listening to the rock-and-roll pioneers, but Manilow preferred his stepfather's jazz record collection and Broadway musical albums. At his bar mitzvah, his new stepfather gave him a piano.

After high school, Manilow was tempted to try to become a professional musician, but he decided on a more secure, practical path by enrolling at City College in New York City to study advertising. He soon discovered, however, that advertising did not hold his interest, so he transferred to New York College of Music where he remained until he dropped out due to lack of money. He later attended evening classes at the prestigious Juilliard School.

Working for a Living. To pay his bills, he held down a series of jobs, including one in the CBS mailroom for about one year. He worked his way up to a film-editing job at WCBS-TV, the Manhattan local affiliate of the network. Later he became film editor of *The Late Show*, a nightly feature film spot, for which he arranged a new theme song. When not working, he was busy coaching aspiring singers, accompanying vocalists at Broadway auditions, and playing piano at local night spots.

While he was still in his teens, Manilow wrote new arrangements for several familiar tunes and composed a few new songs for a musical adaptation of the mid-nineteenth-century melodrama *The Drunkard*, which ran for eight years Off-Broadway. Manilow's musical score received praise from critics. It was during this period that he married his high school sweetheart, Susan, but they were divorced within a year.

He then teamed up with singer Jeanne Lucas for a six-month tour of small lounges. At first he played piano and she sang, but some of the clubs wanted a duo, so they rehearsed some duet material. After six months, Manilow headed back to New York City.

When he returned to the city, he found a job as music director at WCBS-TV for a weekly afternoon showcase of young talent called *Callback*. The show gave Manilow the opportunity to write arrangements for a tremendous variety of music. He also began conducting and arranging for Ed Sullivan productions and performing at the famous club Upstairs at the Downstairs.

Jingle King. A good portion of Manilow's income during the early 1970's came from writing, singing, and arranging commercials. Jingles he wrote include those for State Farm Insurance, Stridex, and Band-Aids. He sang for Kentucky Fried Chicken, Pepsi-Cola, Jack in the Box, Dr. Pepper, and McDonald's. (A medley of those familiar commercials found an enthusiastic audience on his later tours and was featured on his 1977 *Barry Manilow Live* album.) In 1972, while filling in as the house pianist at the Continental Baths, a combination Turkish bath and nightclub, Manilow met and accompanied the as-yet-undiscovered Bette Midler. Even though their personalities clashed, he soon became her musical director, arranger, and pianist.

Recording Contract. At about the same time, Manilow recorded a demo of three of his own tunes that caught the attention of Bell Records. They signed him to a recording deal with the stipulation that he would tour to promote the album, *Barry Manilow.* By the time he left on a thirty-city national tour with Midler in the fall of 1971, Bell had arranged for Manilow to open the second act of the show. During the tour, Atlantic Records took Midler into the recording studio to record her first album. Manilow coproduced and arranged the music for the album, *The Divine Miss M* (and later did the same for her second album, *Bette Midler*).

Clive Davis had become the new president of Bell Records (soon to become Arista). One of the few performers that he kept under contract was Manilow. As soon as Manilow returned from the Midler tour, Davis set up recording dates for a second album, *Barry Manilow II.* The first single from the album was "Mandy," a revision of a song originally titled "Brandy." It became Manilow's first chart single and climbed all the way to number 1 in January, 1975. "Mandy" was followed by a succession of Top-10 singles over the next five years, including "Could It Be Magic," "I Write the Songs," which became his second number 1 hit in January, 1976, "Tryin' to Get the Feeling Again," "Weekend in New England," "Looks Like We Made It," which became his last number 1 hit in the summer of 1977, "Can't Smile Without You," "Copacabana (at the Copa)," "Somewhere in the Night," "Ships," and "I Made It Through the Rain."

His biggest hits were written by other composers: Scott English and Richard Kerr wrote "Mandy," Bruce Johnston wrote "I Write the Songs," and Richard Kerr and Will Jennings wrote "Looks Like We Made It." However, Manilow composed more than fifty percent of the songs on his albums. His most frequent collaborators were Marty Panzer, Adrienne Anderson, and Enoch Anderson.

Manilow's last Top-10 single, "I Made It Through the Rain," was in the early 1980's. Seven other songs charted through 1984, when "Read 'Em and Weep" became his last chart single.

Other Projects. After that, he remained active musically with almost yearly albums, several television specials, including *Swing Street* in 1987, and a Broadway revue entitled *Barry Manilow—Live on Broadway* in 1990. He wrote one song for the 1988 sound track of the Disney film *Oliver and Co.*; composed the music, produced the recording,

Barry Manilow, 1984 (AP/Wide World Photos)

and sang the end title duet with Debra Byrd for the animated feature film *Thumbelina* in 1994; composed the original songs for the animated feature film *The Pebble and the Penguin* sound track in 1995; and composed *Harmony*, a 1997 musical which played at the La Jolla Playhouse in California for a pre-Broadway tryout. His *Barry Manilow's Copacabana—The Musical* played in London's West End in 1994-1995 for eighteen months.

Manilow's performing career has included virtually every facet of entertainment, including not only singing and songwriting, but film, television, stage, and publishing work. By the late 1990's, he had released twenty-eight albums. His discography, most of which is included on a 1992 four-compact-disc boxed set, *The Complete Collection and Then Some . . .*, yielded twenty-five consecutive Top-40 hits. He is the undisputed best-selling adult-contemporary artist of all time, evidenced by his record sales which exceed fifty-eight million worldwide. He has toured the world and sold out concerts around the globe. He has received a Grammy, a Tony, and an Emmy Award and was nominated for an Academy Award for "Ready to Take a Chance Again" from *Foul Play*. He is involved with several charities and humanitarian causes. His autobiography, *Sweet Life: Adventures on the Way to Paradise*, was published in 1987. —*Don Tyler*

SELECT DISCOGRAPHY

■ ALBUMS

Barry Manilow II, 1974
Tryin' to Get the Feeling, 1975
This One's for You, 1976
Even Now, 1978
One Voice, 1979
Barry, 1980
Sings Sinatra, 1998

SELECT AWARDS

Emmy Award for Outstanding Special, Comedy-Variety or Music, for *The Barry Manilow Special*, 1977

Grammy Award for Best Pop Vocal Performance, Male, for "Copacabana (at the Copa)," 1978

SEE ALSO: Midler, Bette.

Marilyn Manson

ORIGINAL MEMBERS: Marilyn Manson (b. Brian Warner, 1969), Daisy Berkowitz (b. Scott Mitchell), Olivia Newton-Bundy (b. Brian Tutunick), Zsa Zsa Speck

OTHER MEMBERS: Gidget Gein, Twiggy Ramirez (b. Jeordie White, 1971), Madonna Wayne-Gacy (b. Steve Bier), Sarah Lee Lucas, Ginger Fish, Zim Zum

FIRST ALBUM RELEASE: *Portrait of an American Family*, 1994

MUSICAL STYLE: Rock and roll

Marilyn Manson, also called Mr. Manson and Reverend Manson, created and has served as leader of the band which bears his name. Manson's real name is Brian Warner. Although Warner and the band he formed represented an American parent's nightmare in the latter part of the twentieth century, Warner himself had an untroubled childhood growing up in Canton, Ohio. At the age of eighteen he moved from Ohio to be a journalism student and to work as a music critic in the Tampa Bay, Florida, area.

Soon after his move in 1989, he met Scott Mitchell, a guitarist. Warner and Mitchell found that they had similar ideas about music and American life in general. Warner convinced Mitchell to join him in a band that would display the tawdry tabloid quality of American life. In order to emphasize this aspect of the band, Warner and Mitchell chose names from U.S. tabloids and television sitcoms. They chose first and last names which represented the duality of life, juxtaposing good and evil. Warner named himself Marilyn Manson after film star Marilyn Monroe and mass murderer Charles Manson. Mitchell became Daisy Berkowitz named for Daisy Duke of the television series *The Dukes of Hazzard* and David Berkowitz, 1970's "Son of Sam" serial killer.

Beginnings. Manson originally put together a band in the Fort Lauderdale area of southern Florida. In addition to him and Berkowitz, the original band, Marilyn Manson and the Spooky Kids, had Olivia Newton-Bundy on bass, named for Australian singer Olivia Newton-John and se-

Marilyn Manson in 1997 (AP/Wide World Photos)

of life: chaos opposed to self-control and innocence versus evil. In carrying out their purpose the band often exhibited shocking modes of entertainment, such as self-mutilation, indecent exposure, pyrotechnics, and strange costumes.

In 1992 Manson decided to drop the Spooky Kids from the band's name, making it simply Marilyn Manson. The band's philosophy and mode of performance remained the same. In 1993 the band won several South Florida Slammy Awards. They were voted Best Local Release for a self-marketed cassette, Band of the Year, and Song of the Year for "Dope Hat."

Career Development. In 1994 Marilyn Manson toured with Nine Inch Nails' "Self-Destruct" tour. However, on the tour Marilyn Manson was banned from appearing in Salt Lake City, Utah. After the ban, Manson met with Dr. Anton S. LaVey, founder of the Church of Satan. LaVey named Manson a priest in the church, and, thus, Manson began using the title Reverend Manson.

During the Nine Inch Nails tour, Sara Lee Lucas was fired from the band and replaced by drummer Ginger Fish, named for Ginger Rogers and Albert Fish, executed cannibal killer. Trent Reznor, creator of Nine Inch Nails, was so impressed by the band that he produced their first album, *Portrait of an American Family* (1994) on his Nothing label. The thirteen-track album was a collection of songs which Marilyn Manson had been playing on stage for more than five years. The group was zealous to hold to its original sound, themes, and lyrics. With Reznor as producer, it was able to do this. In general, Middle America was shocked not only by the lyrics of *Portrait of an American Family*, but also by the album cover, which was created by Mr. Manson and showed a family of four, the mother holding a

rial killer Ted Bundy. On the keyboards was Zsa Zsa Speck, whose namesakes were Zsa Zsa Gabor and murderer Richard Speck. Manson himself was responsible for vocals, and Berkowitz was responsible for lead guitar and for programming the band's drum machine, a Yamaha RX8. In 1990 Zsa Zsa was replaced by Gidget Gein, named for 1960's surfer girl Gidget and for Wisconsin cannibal Ed Gein. The next year the drum machine was replaced by Sara Lee Lucas, named for Sara Lee snack cakes and Henry Lee Lucas, accused mass murderer.

From 1989 to 1992 Manson and the Spooky Kids played the South Florida music scene, giving live performances and selling cassettes of their music, which had been influenced by Kiss and Alice Cooper. The group was building a reputation based not only on their music, but also on their antics. Manson claimed that he represented the "part of man which he is ashamed to be." During their performances Manson, as vocalist, acted as ringleader of a group of "freak supremacists" whose purpose was to explore the dualities

cigarette, the father drinking beer and wearing a belt buckle which says, "Nobody ever raped a .38." The family scene was rounded out by an adolescent and a naked baby, and the artwork included needles and guns. In 1996 the band was joined by Zim Zum, a name from an ancient Hebrew mystical text, who replaced guitarist Daisy Berkowitz.

Legacy. Marilyn Manson has been accused by some as being just another hype with a good marketing campaign designed to appeal to those who feel alienated from mainstream society (particularly adolescents). If so, the marketing campaign has been effective. Marilyn Manson's 1995 cover of the Eurythmics classic "Sweet Dreams (Are Made of This)" gave the band much media attention and MTV airtime. The band's 1996 album *Antichrist Superstar* debuted at number 3 on *Billboard*'s charts. The single "The Beautiful People" from *Antichrist Superstar* was widely played by mainstream media. *Mechanical Animals*, released in 1998, received favorable reviews from a number of critics and was another successful seller.

Even though many have charged that Marilyn Manson was designed for its shock value, the band's cultural themes are serious, and critics have commented that in *Antichrist Superstar* the band went beyond carnival antics to produce deep lyrics that took a serious look at those cultural themes. In asking its audience to look at cultural issues, Marilyn Manson has used its artistic efforts to entertain as well as to reflect on society in general. The band has expressed many people's feeling of alienation from a culture that seems fascinated by the very things, such as violence and sexual excesses, that it claims to despise.

—Annita Marie Ward

SELECT DISCOGRAPHY

■ SINGLES

Get Your Gun, 1994 (extended-play single)
Smells Like Children, 1995 (extended-play single)
Lunchbox, 1995 (extended-play single)

■ ALBUMS

Portrait of an American Family, 1994
Antichrist Superstar, 1996
Mechanical Animals, 1998

SEE ALSO: Cooper, Alice; Kiss; Nine Inch Nails.

Bob Marley

BORN: Nine Mile, St. Ann Parish, Jamaica; February 6, 1945
DIED: Miami, Florida; May 11, 1981
FIRST SINGLE RELEASE: "Judge Not," 1962
FIRST ALBUM RELEASE: *The Wailing Wailers*, 1965
MUSICAL STYLES: Ska, reggae, world beat

No artist is so fully responsible for the global popularity of reggae and ska music as Jamaica's Bob Marley. A devout Rastafarian and a musician and writer of unparalleled gift, he made reggae a major influence on rock, rap, and countless other musical styles.

The Duppy. In the last days of World War II, Jamaica was home to a group of unique people, the Maroons. Descendants of slaves who had escaped bondage to forge a stalwart community in the island's mountainous interior, they farmed, traded, and maintained a culture largely West African in origin. In February of 1945, gossip centered around the impending birth of Cedella Malcolm Marley's first child. The nineteen-year-old Maroon woman, daughter of a very strict father, scandalized the locals when she conceived a child with the white British overseer of the plantation where she worked. Captain Norval Sinclair Marley was in his mid-fifties and the son of a prominent family. When Sinclair married Cedella to legitimize their child, his family exiled him to Kingston.

To such ignominy, Robert Nesta Marley was born. Within weeks, he suffered a mysterious illness that his grandfather, Omeriah, attributed to demonic assault. Many inhabitants of the British West Indies believed that evil spirits called "duppies" laid siege to humans at night, and newborns were at particular risk. Although the herbal medications administered by young Marley's kin cured him, Omeriah was certain that an evil presence would shadow this boy throughout his life.

Childhood. Marley spent his childhood in this melange of West African Yoruban culture overlaid with a British veneer. At an early age, he accompanied his mother into the fields, fetching water for the workers. He heard their work songs, call-and-response forms similar to their African predecessors. The tempo of the songs was meant to set a work pace, but the chugging rhythm would one day be reborn in Jamaican popular music.

A shy, well-behaved boy, Marley reveled in the community celebrations replete with feasting, riddle telling, and music. He often passed these festivals in the company of Stepney School classmate Neville "Bunny" Livingston. During the story-telling portions of the celebrations, Marley was transfixed by hero tales about Nestorian Christian king and Ethiopian Emperor Haile Selassie. The importance of Selassie's assumption of the throne had been foretold by Jamaican Marcus Garvey, a leader of the Universal Negro Improvement Association (UNIA) in the United States in the 1920's. Garvey's prediction that the rise of a black king in Africa in 1930 would kindle a new era of pride in diasporic African people was considered dangerous. Garvey was deported back to Jamaica, where his work received serious attention. A result of Garvey's ministrations was the formation of the Rastafarian religion. Marley learned about Rastafarian beliefs around bonfires on those festival nights. As an adult, he would become the world's best-known Rastafarian.

At the age of five, Marley's life took an unexpected turn. Marley's mother and father wanted their son to receive his education in Kingston, whose schools were better regarded than rural ones. When the boy arrived in Kingston, his father met him at the bus station. Inexplicably, Norval did not put Marley in school; instead, he took him to the Trench Town home of a woman named Miss Grey and left him there. It was more than one year before Cedella located Marley, retrieving him to Nine Mile. Ironically, Cedella soon relocated to Kingston, and, after living with a succession of rural relatives, Marley joined her. She had taken up with Bunny Livingston's father, and the four (Cedella, Livingston, Bunny, and Marley) soon became a family.

Marley and Bunny came of age in a poor section of Kingston (later immortalized in the Wailers' "Trenchtown Rock") during a time of growing social unrest. Class conflict and the racial issues in which it was grounded were giving birth to street gangs and labor demonstrations. Marley was spending after-school hours in the streets fighting, courting girls, playing music, and learning about Rastafarians. Cedella was worried.

Early Recordings. In 1960, Marley, certain of his musical talent, ventured into Coxsone's Musik City, a recording studio. Listening to the players who came and went with discs of their music in hand, Marley knew what he wanted to do with his life. Instead of Musik City, though, he would record his first song at Count Boysie's, another such pressing plant. Using studio musicians, Marley recorded "Judge Not" and "Do You Still Love Me?" He was paid just twenty pounds. It was 1962, and Marley was apprenticing as a welder. When he heard the record playing on a bar's jukebox earning money for Count Boysie, not him, he was livid.

Although she knew her son was talented, Cedella feared for his future. Instead of keeping his mind on learning welding, he, Bunny, and another friend, Peter McIntosh, were spending time writing songs. Marley was a street tough known in Jamaica as a "rude boy." His band, the Teenagers, soon added Winston "Pipe" Matthews, Junior Braithwaite, Cherry Smith, and Beverly Kelso. This assemblage became the Wailers.

Not long after Jamaican independence (August, 1962), the Wailers signed a recording contract with Clement Dodd, a producer who owned five labels. Their first sessions showed how amateurish their writing and playing skills were. What the band needed most was a cohesive sound, something best accomplished by choosing a single lead singer. They settled on Marley, and his unique voice was the feature of their next singles.

A forerunner of reggae, ska music's characteristic beat was woven through lyrics that spoke of urban ghetto life. Rude boys and Rastafarians were driving forces in ska, and the poor inhabitants of Trench Town and similar enclaves clamored for the music that told of their lives. The Wailers performed and recorded during much of 1964 as the ska phenomenon spread to Britain and the United States. When it became a focus of tourism marketing, benign acts (those whose lyrics stayed clear of social issues) were promoted. The Wailers were encouraged to write such fare.

Around this time, Marley met a pretty, young nurse named Rita Anderson. She claimed to be a fine singer, but her first job in Marley's employ was as his correspondent, answering letters Cedella was sending to Marley from her new home in Wilmington, Delaware. A romance soon ensued, and the couple married in 1966. Even though Rastafarianism had been around Marley all his life, it would be Rita's conversion that led to his own.

From Ska to Reggae. In 1967, Marley signed with JAD and Cayman Music, fronting a version of the Wailers that included Bunny, McIntosh (Peter Tosh), and Rita. Their earlier ska had transformed into reggae, and they would spend the next two years honing their sound on songs such as "Soul Rebel" and "Duppy Conqueror." Through a deal with England's Trojan Records, the Wailers' first album, *Soul Rebels*, was released in 1969. As subsequent albums spread the gospel of the Wailers' reggae, Leslie Kong, who had produced Marley's first single in 1962, seized the financial opportunity, releasing old tracks as *The Best of the Wailers.* It made him a very rich man.

On the British charts, the Wailers were making steady inroads. Marley had now signed with CBS International, and the company wanted the band to tour. This first road trip was a shoddy affair during which the band mostly played in school gymnasia. Marley had written a song that was recorded by his friend Johnny Nash, and this single, "Stir It Up," was a big hit. It was 1972, and Marley was about to become an international star.

Catch a Fire, released in 1972, sold poorly at first, but Island Records' Chris Blackwell knew worldwide fame for the singer was just around the corner. He courted Marley, finding the Rastafarian not at all the violent, racist, crazy man he had been taught Rastafarians were. The pair were destined to make music history, creating a sensation with Jamaican reggae.

Bob Marley (Archive Photos)

Back in Jamaica, Marley purchased a large house that became a sort of compound for the Wailers and various friends. Bob and Rita Marley's growing family lived there amid an assortment of Rastafarians, their leonine hair falling in the "ropes" called dreadlocks. Smoking the Rastafarian sacrament, "ganga" (marijuana), they communed with the mystic, awaiting the spiritual repatriation to Ethiopia and their deliverance from "Babylon" (anywhere that Africans had been exiled).

By 1973, Blackwell's influence in the band was causing dissent. Tosh would soon leave, fatefully just before the Wailers achieved their dream of global success. Eric Clapton had already recorded the Wailers' classic "I Shot the Sheriff," introducing white rock fans to the infectious reggae beat. Concertgoers clamored for the original version, and Bob Marley and the Wailers (the new name was Blackwell's idea) launched their first major tour in 1975. The following year saw the release of *Rastaman Vibration* and an ominous event: While playing soccer, Marley injured his foot. The injury itself was not serious, but the fact that it never healed properly made it seem like another assault by the duppy.

Problems. On the night of November 22, 1976, armed vigilantes broke into Marley's compound, shooting several of the residents. Rita survived a shot in the head, and Marley received an arm wound. The attack was a result of the growing involvement of Rastafarians in the politics of Jamaica, especially Marley's endorsement of candidate Michael Manley. Manley went on to win the prime ministership, and Marley survived to alert the world to Jamaica's long-time internal strife.

Babylon by Bus, the band's 1979 live release, coincided with another massive tour. The rigors of touring exhausted Marley, and his unhealed soccer injury dogged him. As a practicing Rastafarian, Marley was very strict about his health. He ate a balanced diet and exercised regularly. Aside from his sacramental ganga, he was not a smoker, nor was he a drinker of liquor or beer. If anyone should have had the constitution to recover from the foot injury, it should have been Marley. Unfortunately, even the amputation of the wounded toe did not stop the pain and the dark spot that grew larger every week. Marley had melanoma, a virulent form of skin cancer. His Rastafarian faith did not permit him to have a more extensive amputation, and he did not seek cancer treatment to arrest the lesion. He decided to put his faith in Jah (God) and accept whatever fate awaited him.

In the years after the vigilante attack, Marley had spoken often and to many people about his premonitions. His days were limited, he told them; the duppy that had haunted him all his life was closing in. The predictions notwithstanding, Marley continued making and playing his soulful music, and his exuberant joy on the concert stage was no act. In his reggae element, he truly felt the wonder of the healing effects of music. While it could not stop the growing disease in his body, his spirit was made whole with every performance. This and the knowledge of the equal joy he was bringing to his fans buoyed him through the hectic pace of the 1979-1980 world tour. His records were selling briskly, and his concerts were attended by thousands of chanting, swaying fans.

In September, 1980, Marley realized he was having memory problems. While jogging in New York's Central Park on the morning of the 21st, he had a stroke and collapsed. Not realizing what had happened, Marley returned to his hotel, by-

For the Record

"Money mon-monee! Is plenty things them people don't know, you know. Is plenty wisdom them people don't know. Because is few guys know that figures ain't got no end. You can start all over again. Numbers. They don't go more than nine. But they don't have no end. That means, if numbers is where you get your kicks from—to have plenty—then you're lost. Because it don't have no end. So plenty people don't realize that this thing is something happening here. This s— don't have no end. Ya know. It's just madness. Weirdness. Weird situation." —*Bob Marley*

passing hospitalization. Rita was not told. The following day, a doctor was consulted. After tests, a brain tumor was diagnosed, and Marley was admitted to Memorial Sloan-Kettering Hospital. More tests were done, and it was determined that Marley was suffering from cancer that had spread to his major organs. Radiation treatment was started immediately, but the outlook was bleak. Marley was given one year to live. The foot injury that had not healed had been the warning sign that Marley was facing the beginning of the end.

Desperate for a cure, Marley and his wife traveled to the Bavarian clinic of German doctor Josef Issels, known for treating hopeless cancer cases. Issels was controversial, but whatever the value of his methods, he extended Marley's life an extra half-year. In May, 1981, no longer responding to Issels's treatment, Marley flew to Miami, Florida, checking into Cedars of Lebanon Hospital. On May 11, less than two days after his admission, Robert Nesta Marley died at the age of thirty-six.

Marley's Legacy. The legacy Marley left is immeasurable. He made reggae a worldwide success. His songs have been covered by numerous artists, including his son, David "Ziggy" Marley. Rita continued her singing career and won rights to most of her husband's early songs. Marley's legacy also lives on in the tradition of world beat (or world music) and the revival of ska in the works of such bands as No Doubt and Sugar Hill.

Marley has been honored in many formal ways. A commemorative stamp was issued by Jamaica, and his homeland is also the site of several historical markers celebrating his life. In the London section called Brixton, home to a largely Caribbean population, riots broke out in 1981 over the grinding poverty of the area and the lack of social action being taken by Her Majesty's government. Fueled by reggae and "Oi!" music (the punk rock of Britain's poor, white youth), Brixtonites took to the streets in protest. Years later, with social and economic conditions little changed, the government authorized the renaming of a Brixton street for the late Bob Marley. Adjacent to the street that rained fire from Molotov cocktails sailing over police barricades in the 1981 riots, "Bob Marley Way" stands mute watch over the ghetto. Tellingly, it intersects "Marcus Garvey Way." It was the first street in London named for a contemporary musician.

Although reggae would launch the careers of many stars, including luminaries such as Toots and the Maytals, Jimmy Cliff, Yellowman, and Judy Mowatt, none would reach the heights attained by the Maroon from Nine Mile, Bob Marley. His name has become synonymous with Third World issues and with the need for people to come together, regardless of race, class, faith, or political allegiance. —*Cynthia R. Kasee*

SELECT DISCOGRAPHY

■ SINGLES

"Get Up, Stand Up," 1973

"Roots, Rock, Reggae," 1976

"Jamming," 1977

■ ALBUMS

Burnin', 1973

Live!, 1975

Rastaman Vibration, 1976

Exodus, 1977

SEE ALSO: Clapton, Eric; Clash, The; Cliff, Jimmy; Specials, The; Tosh, Peter.

Dave Mason. *See* Traffic / Steve Winwood / Dave Mason

Johnny Mathis

BORN: San Francisco, California; September 30, 1935

FIRST SINGLE RELEASE: "When Sunny Gets Blue," 1956

FIRST ALBUM RELEASE: *Johnny Mathis*, 1957

MUSICAL STYLES: Pop, rhythm and blues, rock

John Royce Mathis grew up in San Francisco. As a child he studied piano and sang in church, school, and various community events. Aside from his vocal talent, Mathis was an outstanding athlete. As a student at San Francisco State University, Mathis played on the basketball team and also set the high-jump record in track and field. Mathis gave up an opportunity to make the 1956 Olympic Team in order to record his first album. Although the world lost a track-and-field star, it acquired one of its most successful, internationally renowned singers.

Musical Contributions. In 1954, after Mathis was spotted by Columbia Records executive George Avakian, it is said that Avakian cabled his home office with the words, "Have found phenomenal nineteen-year-old boy who could go all the way. Send blank contracts." In 1956, Columbia Records signed the nineteen-year-old Mathis. Since that point, Mathis has compiled a treasury of incomparable music that has soared high and long on national and international record charts. Except for a brief period with Mercury Records (1964-1967), Mathis has recorded for the Columbia label.

With his soothing and stunning vocal range, Johnny Mathis has enjoyed more than forty years of worldwide success on the music charts and in concert performances. Many fans have said that Mathis advances the art of remembering, and his music always starts one moving toward an embrace. An article in *Rolling Stone* magazine stated, "Dancing close was the same as dancing Mathis. He had a voice that could melt steel." The article closed by saying that Mathis is a patron saint of "the romantic candlelight world that doesn't really exist except for people who want it to."

The Legacy of His Career. Mathis's earliest releases for Columbia Records included "Wonderful! Wonderful!" and "It's Not for Me to Say." The latter release stayed on the charts at number 5 for twenty-three weeks and proved to be a harbinger of great things to come. In 1957, one year after signing his contract, Mathis released his first number 1 hit, "Chances Are." Within two years Mathis released "The Twelfth of Never," "Wild Is the Wind," "Come to Me," "No Love (but Your Love)," and his signature song, "Misty." These songs were written and performed with a strikingly beautiful balance between romance, passion, longing, and love.

In 1958, two years after signing his contract, Columbia released *Johnny's Greatest Hits*. In the recording industry, this album was unparalleled for two reasons. First, the term "greatest hits" was created for Mathis as a marketing tool and has since become a recording-industry standard. Second, the album was a national and international success. It held the number 1 spot on the charts for three weeks and then remained for an unprecedented 490 consecutive weeks on *Billboard*'s Top-100 chart. In other words, this album was on the *Billboard* Top-100 chart for nine and one-half years. This amazing demonstration of fan devotion and album sales set a chart record.

Besides *Johnny's Greatest Hits*, two other albums distinguished themselves on *Billboard*'s Top-100 chart. The album *Heavenly* (1959) was on the *Billboard* Top-100 chart for 295 consecutive weeks and the album *Warm* (1957) stayed on the charts for 113 consecutive weeks. During his career, Mathis recorded nearly one hundred albums and has amassed more than sixty gold and platinum albums in his worldwide record sales.

Scope and Longevity. During his extraordinary singing career Johnny Mathis has worked with

Johnny Mathis (Archive Photos)

an outstanding group of producers and arrangers, including Ray Coniff, Ray Ellis, Percy Faith, Don Costa, Mitch Miller, Nelson Riddle, Glenn Osser, and Henry Mancini. Through the blending of his unique touches of phrasing and intonation Mathis has been able to create a sense of remarkable musical intimacy with each producer and arranger. This soft, yet immediate and pervasive intimacy is showcased especially in his romantic ballads. Music critics consistently point to the exceptional Mathis vocal technique that has served to create this marvelous intimacy time after time.

Johnny Mathis is an international concert star. He has performed in South America, Europe, Australia, the Far East, and throughout North America. At home in the United States, Mathis has been a concert favorite since the beginning of his career. In recognition of his vocal talent and concert performances, Mathis was honored in 1972 with a star on Hollywood's Walk of Fame.

In 1978, Mathis recorded "Too Much, Too Little, Too Late" with Deniece Williams. The recording was the very first duet for Mathis. It went on to be a number 1 rhythm-and-blues hit on the *Billboard* charts. Williams and Mathis also recorded "Without Us," the theme song from the hit television series *Family Ties.* Mathis has also performed with a variety of musical stars, including Dionne Warwick, Regina Belle, Gladys Knight, Sergio Mendes, Take 6, Barbra Streisand, and Lena Horne.

Johnny Mathis has enjoyed enormously successful record sales. He is the eighth best-selling album artist and has had eighteen singles in the Top 40 during his career. Evidence of his renowned talent and incredible longevity was again demonstrated by his 1996 album that debuted at number 119 on the *Billboard* 200. This album was released as Mathis gracefully turned sixty years old. In one review, the question was asked, is Mathis "the make-out maestro of MTV?" To millions of fans around the world, the answer was still a definite "yes!" —*Albert Valencia*

For the Record

Johnny Mathis is credited with having the biggest-selling album of all time in the United States: *Johnny's Greatest Hits,* 1958. Mathis's 1957 song "Wonderful! Wonderful!" stayed on *Billboard*'s singles chart for 39 weeks—a record not broken until Paul Davis's "I Go Crazy" made it to 40 weeks on May 27, 1978.

SELECT DISCOGRAPHY

■ SINGLES

"Wonderful! Wonderful!" 1957
"Chances Are," 1957
"The Twelfth of Never," 1957
"A Certain Smile," 1958
"Misty," 1959
"Gina," 1962
"What Will Mary Say," 1963
"Too Much, Too Little, Too Late," 1978 (with Deniece Williams)

■ ALBUMS

Johnny Mathis, 1957
Wonderful, Wonderful, 1957
Warm, 1957
Good Night, Dear Lord, 1958
Johnny's Greatest Hits, 1958
Swing Softly, 1958
Merry Christmas, 1958
Open Fire, Two Guitars, 1959
More Johnny's Greatest Hits, 1959
Heavenly, 1959
Faithfully, 1960
Romantically, 1963
This Is Love, 1964
Love Is Blue, 1968
Love Story, 1971
I'm Coming Home, 1973
I Only Have Eyes for You, 1976
Mathis Magic, 1979
Friends in Love, 1982
Right from the Heart, 1985
In the Still of the Night, 1989
In a Sentimental Mood: Mathis Sings Ellington, 1990
The Music of Johnny Mathis: A Personal Collection, 1993

SELECT AWARDS
Hollywood Walk of Fame, star awarded 1972

SEE ALSO: Knight, Gladys, and the Pips; Mendes, Sergio; Streisand, Barbra; Warwick, Dionne.

Kathy Mattea

BORN: South Charleston, West Virginia; June 21, 1959
FIRST ALBUM RELEASE: *Kathy Mattea*, 1984
MUSICAL STYLES: Country, folk, blues, bluegrass, gospel

Known for her warm voice and down-to-earth accessibility, Kathy Mattea has released a series of albums combining traditional country music with elements of bluegrass, blues, gospel, rock, and pop. Mattea's insistence on maintaining her artistic integrity has led her to select songs whose lyrical depths transcend typical country fare, and her avoidance of emotional excess in their interpretation has won her a loyal fan base while rewarding her with several chart-topping country hits.

Leaving West Virginia. Mattea sang with a bluegrass band while majoring in engineering at West Virginia University; at age nineteen she dropped out of college and headed for Nashville. There she worked as a Country Music Hall of Fame and Museum tour guide before finding work singing on songwriters' and music publishers' demo tapes.

In 1983 she was offered a recording contract and the next year released *Kathy Mattea*, which featured standard country-pop songs. Mattea's voice and style were compared to Canadian icon Anne Murray's, and *Billboard* named her the Best New Country Artist of the Year. Mattea was nonetheless somewhat disappointed with her first record, as her background in bluegrass had been overlooked. Her second release, *From My Heart* (1985) followed suit, and neither album produced any hits.

Even without a hit single, Mattea was able to tour, opening for established country artist George Strait intermittently through 1988. In the meantime she released two more traditional country albums, *Walk the Way the Wind Blows* (1986) and *Untasted Honey* (1987), which produced several hit singles. Mattea's fifth album, *Willow in the Wind* (1989), included the single "Where've You Been," a touching story of enduring love cowritten by Mattea's husband, Jon Vezner. The song won Grammy Awards for both Mattea and Vezner and, with the album, crossed over to the pop charts. Mattea was voted Female Vocalist of the Year by the Country Music Association (CMA) in 1989 and 1990.

For the Record

Kathy Mattea wrote "Leaving West Virginia" (from her 1986 album *Walk the Way the Wind Blows*) just before she left home to become a Nashville songwriter. It is the only song Mattea has recorded that she wrote herself.

Walking Away a Winner. Mattea was taken aback by the awards. Advised to tour strenuously and focus on making money, she chose instead to pursue artistic growth. Influenced by musicians she befriended while traveling in Scotland, Mattea recorded *Time Passes By* (1991), an album of Celtic and folk-influenced songs. Mattea then briefly considered abandoning country music but worked within the country format on her next record, *Lonesome Standard Time* (1992). The critically acclaimed album's sluggish sales were attributed to Mattea's involvement with fundraising for acquired immunodeficiency syndrome (AIDS) research; she spoke about AIDS awareness at the 1992 CMA awards and would be instrumental in recruiting country and folk artists to perform on the AIDS benefit album *Red Hot + Country* (1994).

Mattea tried to produce a breakthrough commercial record with *Walking Away a Winner* (1994). While the album successfully integrated country, folk, bluegrass, and rock, critics felt Mattea's choice of songs and subject matter had been too conservative, and the album's sales failed to surpass Mattea's earlier efforts. Mattea asked her record label for time to find a new creative approach, and she did not release another album until 1997's *Love Travels,* which again incorporated a range of musical styles. While critics noted a new-age sentimentality that marred the album (Mattea was greatly influenced by a workbook designed to help artists link creativity and spirituality), overall it was considered her best work to date.

Although the pinnacle of success as a country queen eluded her, Mattea would remain a respected performer who refused to compromise her artistry to win fame. Her eclectic style and instinct for selecting unusual material are demonstrated on her unconventional Grammy-winning Christmas album, *Good News* (1993), which eschews familiar carols in favor of little-known songs by contemporary songwriters.

—*Maureen J. Puffer-Rothenberg*

SELECT DISCOGRAPHY

■ ALBUMS

Kathy Mattea, 1984
From My Heart, 1985
Walk the Way the Wind Blows, 1986
Untasted Honey, 1987
Willow in the Wind, 1989
A Collection of Hits, 1990 (compilation)77
Time Passes By, 1991
Lonesome Standard Time, 1992
Good News, 1993
Walking Away a Winner, 1994
Love Travels, 1997

SELECT AWARDS

Country Music Association Single of the Year Award for "Eighteen Wheels and a Dozen Roses," 1988
Country Music Association Female Vocalist of the Year Award, 1989, 1990
Grammy Award for Best Country Vocal Performance, Female, for "Where've You Been," 1990
Grammy Award for Best Southern Gospel, Country Gospel, or Bluegrass Gospel Album for *Good News,* 1993
Country Music Association Video of the Year Award for "455 Rocket," 1997

SEE ALSO: Krauss, Alison.

The Dave Matthews Band

ORIGINAL MEMBERS: Dave Matthews (b. 1967), Stefan Lessard, Leroi Moore, Boyd Tinsley, Carter Beauford
OTHER MEMBERS: Peter Griesar
FIRST ALBUM RELEASE: *Remember Two Things,* 1993
MUSICAL STYLES: rock and roll, alternative

Building upon a strong college following and a growing interest in world music, the Dave Matthews Band emerged as one of the top bands of 1996 with the multiplatinum *Crash.* The album rose to number 4 on the pop charts and remained on the charts for more than one hundred weeks.

Beginnings. Dave Matthews, the son of a South African physicist, left his homeland in 1986 rather than face conscription into a military that upheld apartheid. As an expatriate living in Charlottesville, Virginia, he began writing songs in 1990 and early the next year began enlisting the best local musicians he could find to produce a demo recording. Working as a bartender at the area's premier jazz club, he came into contact with all the future band members. After a few rehearsals, they performed for the first time at a rooftop Charlottesville party in May, 1991. From there they moved to malls, restaurants, and clubs. Enthusiastic university students packed the clubs to see them perform.

The Dave Matthews Band benefitted from their policy of allowing fans to tape their concerts by having their live act "arrive" at southeastern venues before the band did. Eventually disc jockeys around the country learned about their hot live act and began asking for recordings. The original demo tape had never been produced, so in August, 1993, they recorded their concert at the Muse Music Club on the island of Nantucket in Massachusetts. The result was released as *Remember Two Things* (1993), a remarkable, independently released first album that sold more than 100,000 copies in less than one year. While they sold albums through their office, they continued a furious touring pace, opening southeastern concerts for groups such as Phish, Blues Traveler, and Colonel Bruce and the Aquarium Rescue Unit.

For the Record

Bassist Stefan Lessard, who joined the Dave Matthews Band when he was sixteen, settled near Charlottesville when his parents became followers of Swami Satchidananda.

Major Label. By 1994, the Dave Matthews Band had become regional headliners, and they signed a major record deal with RCA Records. Their major-label debut, *Under the Table and Dreaming* (1994) sold more than five million copies and earned two Grammy nominations for the single "What Would You Say." Critics had mixed feelings about their unique fusion of jazz, folk, and rock, but fans were fanatic, generating a wave of word-of-mouth publicity. The band continued to perform frequently, including European tours in both 1994 and 1995.

By late 1995 when they went back into the studio, the Dave Matthews Band had developed a formidable worldwide following. Their third album, *Crash* (1996), entered the charts at number 2, sold more than 4 million copies, and was still on the charts two years after its release. In 1997, the band took a break from the gruelling touring schedule they had pursued the previous five years, but that did not slow their phenomenal success. *Live at Red Rocks 8-15-95* (1997) debuted at number 3 and sold more than one million copies in less than six months. The break also enabled the band to produce their most eclectic and ambitious album, *Before These Crowded Streets* (1998), which entered the U.S. charts at number 1. —*John Powell*

SELECT DISCOGRAPHY

■ ALBUMS

Remember Two Things, 1993
Under the Table and Dreaming, 1994
Crash, 1996
Live at Red Rocks 8-15-95, 1997 (live)
Before These Crowded Streets, 1998

SELECT AWARDS

Grammy Award for Best Rock Performance by a Duo or Group with Vocal for "So Much to Say," 1996

SEE ALSO: Blues Traveler; Phish.

The Dave Matthews Band: Carter Beauford, Boyd Tinsley, Dave Matthews, Stefan Lessard, Leroi Moore (RCA/Danny Clinch)

Curtis Mayfield

BORN: Chicago, Illinois; June 3, 1942
FIRST SINGLE RELEASE: "Listen to Me"/"Shorty's Got to Go," 1958 (with the Impressions)
FIRST SOLO ALBUM RELEASE: *Curtis*, 1970
MUSICAL STYLES: Soul, rhythm and blues, funk

Curtis Mayfield was a major artist during the 1960's and 1970's, first as one of the leaders of the singing group the Impressions and later as a solo artist. Mayfield sang, played guitar, wrote songs, produced records, and started his own record label, Curtom. Influenced by gospel music and group vocal harmony singing (doo-wop), Mayfield sang about love and black pride and was one of the most respected artists of his generation.

The Beginnings. Curtis Mayfield grew up in the Cabrini-Green housing project in Chicago. He was first exposed to gospel music as a child by his grandmother, Annabell Mayfield, who was a minister at the Traveling Soul Spiritualist Church in Chicago. Through his family Mayfield heard the music of the black gospel groups, including the Soul Stirrers (which included Sam Cooke), the Five Blind Boys of Alabama, and others.

After singing briefly with a secular group, the Alphatones, Mayfield, still a mere seven years old, joined his first serious group, the Northern Jubilee Gospel Singers, which also included three of his cousins and a friend, Jerry Butler. Mayfield sang in a high tenor and falsetto voice, which he maintained throughout his later career as a professional singer. In addition to introducing him to gospel music, Mayfield's religious upbringing also instilled in him a high moral sense, which would shine through in his lyrics.

By the time he was in high school, Mayfield, now an accomplished and original guitarist, and Butler had sharpened their vocal skills and decided to join an established group, the Roosters, which included Sam Gooden, Fred Cash, Emmanuel Thomas, and brothers Richard and Arthur Brooks. By 1957, Cash and Thomas had left the group, which decided to change its name to the Impressions in hopes of making an impression on audiences.

Good Impressions. The Impressions auditioned for Vee Jay Records, a rising Chicago label, that liked their sound and had them record a song written by Butler and the Brooks brothers, "For Your Precious Love." A perfect marriage of gospel and doo-wop, the record, with Butler singing lead, came out in the spring of 1958 on the subsidiary Abner label and rose to number 3 on *Billboard*'s national rhythm-and-blues charts and number 11 on the pop charts. Unfortunately, their followup, "Come Back My Love," did not fare as well, and Butler decided to leave the group to start a solo career. (He would have a prolific career, putting nearly sixty singles on the rhythm-and-blues charts over the years. In his later life, he successfully ran for political office in Chicago.)

It took until 1961 for the Impressions, now signed to ABC-Paramount Records, with Mayfield singing lead and Fred Cash back in the group, to reestablish themselves, but they came back with "Gypsy Woman," a flamenco-influenced number that rose to number 2 on the rhythm-and-blues chart. That was followed in 1963 by "It's All Right," an uplifting gospel-flavored tune that went all the way to number 1 on the rhythm-and-blues chart and number 4 pop.

By that time, the Brooks brothers had left the group, leaving the Impressions as a trio: Mayfield, Cash, and Gooden. They went on to build an astounding career as an important force in black music. Mayfield began writing songs for the Impressions and other artists, including Major Lance, Jan Bradley, Gene Chandler, and old friend Jerry Butler. He also became a staff pro-

For the Record

"Everybody in this country at one time or another has been a minority, wherever they came from. We just made a good loud noise as far as congregating. From out of that came a lot of my songs."

—*Curtis Mayfield*, in *Goldmine* magazine, 1997

Curtis Mayfield (AP/Wide World Photos)

ducer for the Okeh Records label and produced for artists on other labels.

Success. Meanwhile, the Impressions became regular chart toppers. Whether singing unabashed love ballads such as "I'm So Proud" (number 14, 1964), anthems of self-determination and pride such as "Keep On Pushing" (number 10, 1964), or pure spirituals such as "Amen" (number 7, 1964), the band, with their gospel-soul style, never failed to appeal to music fans of all races, even during times of racial strife in the 1960's. Mayfield's angelic lead vocals and the harmonies of Cash and Gooden combined beautifully, and with Mayfield's poetic words, the Impressions stood apart as a positive, inspirational element in the music scene of the day. Even when black militants began calling for more aggressive solutions to the nation's social problems, Mayfield called for love and peaceful answers.

The Impressions continued to make their mark with strong, positive message songs throughout the remainder of the 1960's. Among their other classic hits were the gospel ballad "People Get Ready" (number 14, 1965) and "We're a Winner" (number 14, 1967), the latter a soulful tribute to the ideals of Martin Luther King, Jr. In 1968, Mayfield (along with a partner, Eddie Thomas) founded a record company, Curtom, which would eventually release Mayfield's own records and those of the Impressions and other artists, such as the Five Stairsteps, Gene Chandler, and the Staple Singers.

The Solo Years. Mayfield left the Impressions in 1970 to start a solo career. The group carried on with a new lead singer, Leroy Hutson, and then others. They continued to have hits on the rhythm-and-blues charts, but did not have as great an impact as they had with Mayfield at the helm.

Mayfield's first solo hit was "(Don't Worry) If There's a Hell Below We're All Going to Go," in 1970, which exhibited a more funk-oriented style than the Impressions had utilized. His crowning achievement as a solo performer was the 1972 sound track for the hit film *Superfly*. From the album, Mayfield scored with two huge singles, "Freddie's Dead" and "Superfly," both funky tunes that were thick with affirmative morals and infectious riffs.

Tragedy. Mayfield continued as a major force in rhythm and blues throughout the 1970's and 1980's (he reunited briefly with the Impressions in 1983 for a tour), recording for such labels as RSO and Boardwalk. Although the hits were no longer as plentiful, he was still considered one of the giants of popular music. Then, on August 13, 1990, Mayfield was struck by a lighting rig during an outdoor concert and became paralyzed from the neck down. Although his spirit never flagged, his musical contributions became fewer as time went on. In the 1990's, he was looked upon, particularly by rap artists, as a major source of inspiration. His 1996 album *New World Order*, on Warner Bros., was as brilliant as any other he recorded during his lengthy career. —*Jeff Tamarkin*

SELECT DISCOGRAPHY

with the Impressions

■ ALBUMS

Keep On Pushing, 1964

The Complete Vee Jay Recordings, 1993

Curtis Mayfield solo

■ ALBUMS

Curtis, 1970

Superfly, 1972

The Anthology 1961-1977, 1992 (compilation)

New World Order, 1996

SELECT AWARDS

Rock and Roll Hall of Fame, inducted 1991 (with The Impressions)

Rhythm & Blues Foundation Pioneer Award, 1991

Rock and Roll Hall of Fame, inducted 1999 (Mayfield solo)

SEE ALSO: Cooke, Sam; Staple Singers, The.

MC Hammer. *See* Hammer

Meat Loaf

(Marvin Lee Aday)

BORN: Dallas, Texas; September 27, 1947

FIRST ALBUM RELEASE: *Stoney and Meat Loaf*, 1971 (with Stoney)

MUSICAL STYLES: Pop, rock and roll

Meat Loaf took the pop world by storm in the late 1970's, seemingly emerging from nowhere and issuing, with his second album, one of the best-selling albums of all time. He largely remained out of the public eye for more than fifteen years, then, with the sequel to his first hit album, yielded another multiplatinum hit in 1993.

Early Days. Marvin Lee Aday was nicknamed Meat Loaf in high school in Dallas, Texas, as a result of his large size. After his mother died and his home life soured, he moved to Los Angeles. There he formed a psychedelic-rock band known as both Popcorn Blizzard and Meat Loaf Soul, who opened for such acts as the Who, Ted Nugent, and Iggy Pop. Meat Loaf won a role in a traveling production of Gerome Ragni, James Rado, and Galt MacDermott's musical *Hair*, during which he met a soul singer known as Stoney. The two recorded an album in 1971 that was unsuccessful.

Meat Loaf then spent time in other musical productions and was featured in the 1975 cult film *The Rocky Horror Picture Show*. He also provided vocals on Ted Nugent's 1976 album *Free for All*. The composer of one musical Meat Loaf appeared in, Jim Steinman, was writing a musical entitled *Never Land*. Much of the music for this show would be recorded by Meat Loaf on his breakthrough album, *Bat out of Hell*.

Major Hit. After recruiting Todd Rundgren as producer, *Bat out of Hell* was released in 1977 to little notice. A heavy touring schedule in support of the album soon brought attention and heavy sales, however. With the hit singles "Paradise by the Dashboard Light," "You Took the Words Right out of My Mouth," and "Two out of Three Ain't Bad," the album went platinum in one year. Though criticized for its bombastic, melodramatic portrayal of teen angst, the album remained on the U.S. charts for eighty-eight weeks and eventually sold more than thirty million copies worldwide, making it the third biggest selling album of all time.

Meat Loaf could not follow up this success, however. Steinman went on to pursue a solo career, and Meat Loaf began drinking heavily. He eventually lost his voice. When the much anticipated *Dead Ringer* was finally released in 1981, it received little acclaim in the United States, although it did reach number 1 in the United Kingdom. The 1980's were not kind to Meat Loaf, as his albums *Midnight at the Lost and Found* (1983) and *Blind Before I Stop* (1986) were failures, he declared bankruptcy, and he underwent rehabilitation to repair his damaged voice.

Back on Top. He made a huge comeback in 1993, however, with *Bat out of Hell II: Back into Hell*, which again teamed him with Steinman. This number 1 album was even bigger than its predecessor, with sales over ten million within its first three months of release. It yielded the number 1 single "I'd Do Anything for Love (but I Won't Do That)," which earned him a Grammy Award for Best Solo Rock Vocal Performance.

Releasing *Welcome to the Neighbourhood* in 1995 without Steinman at the helm was unfruitful, seemingly proving that without Steinman's inspiring anthems, even Meat Loaf's passionate voice could not make an album a hit. His *Live Around the World* album (1996) received positive reviews, however, and Meat Loaf has found success in films, appearing in *Roadie* (1980), *Wayne's World* (1992), and *Leap of Faith* (1992).

—Lauren M. D'Andrea

SELECT DISCOGRAPHY

■ ALBUMS

Stoney and Meat Loaf, 1971 (with Stoney)
Bat out of Hell, 1977
Dead Ringer, 1981
Midnight at the Lost and Found, 1983
Hits out of Hell, 1984 (compilation)
Bat out of Hell II: Back into Hell, 1993
Welcome to the Neighbourhood, 1995
Live Around the World, 1996

SELECT AWARDS

Grammy Award for Best Rock Vocal Peformance, Solo, for "I'd Do Anything for Love (but I Won't Do That)," 1993

SEE ALSO: Nugent, Ted; Rundgren, Todd.

For the Record

Ellen Foley, who sang the female vocals on "Paradise by the Dashboard Light," was featured as lawyer Billie Young on the television program *Night Court* in the 1980's.

§

"Nobody writes like Jim Steinman. All these things—bombastic, over the top, self-indulgent. All these things are positives." *—Meat Loaf*

John Mellencamp

BORN: Seymour, Indiana; October 7, 1951
FIRST ALBUM RELEASE: *Chestnut Street Incident*, 1976 (as Johnny Cougar)
MUSICAL STYLE: Rock and roll

A true small-town boy from Seymour, Indiana, John Mellencamp typified U.S. heartland rock, much like Bob Seger and Bruce Springsteen. Whereas Seger was more urban, and Springsteen was more suburban, Mellencamp grew up with farmers, a fact that would lead to his cofounding of the Farm Aid charity concerts. Feisty and fiercely independent, Mellencamp was Everyman with a rebel attitude.

Roots. Mellencamp grew up in a blue-collar home and married his pregnant high school sweetheart at the age of seventeen. By the time he was twenty-four, he had fled to New York to attempt to be a rock-and-roll star. There he met David Bowie's manager, Tony DeFries of Mainman Management, and was signed to his first recording contract. DeFries thought the handsome singer-songwriter with the rebellious streak would be a good pinup boy. He renamed him Johnny Cougar—without asking Mellencamp's permission—and they released an album for MCA called *Chestnut Street Incident* (1976). Mellencamp had not written a single song on it, and it did not sell well.

Mellencamp, torn between the lure of success and the denial of his true self, almost gave up the music business at that time. He did not stop writing songs, however. Saddled with his new moniker, he recorded an album called *John Cougar* (1979) for a smaller label, Riva. It was not a big hit, but one of his compositions, "I Need a Lover," was picked up by singer Pat Benatar and was a big hit for her.

Mellencamp said of his next album, *Nothin' Matters and What If It Did* (1980), "I phoned in my parts on that one. I was thinking about quitting at that point. I owed the record company a record, but I was honestly thinking at that point I didn't want to make records any more." He had, though, written one song he liked: "Jack and Diane," the tale of "two American kids living in the heartland." He put it on the 1982 album that, as far as he knew, was destined to be his swan song, *American Fool.*

"Jack and Diane" came from Mellencamp's own experience, and most listeners easily identified with it. It hit number 1 on the charts. From that album also came a second Top-10 hit, "Hurts So Good," which also won him a Grammy Award. MTV had by then discovered the handsome and charismatic singer, and John Cougar, as he was still known, was finally successful.

Doing It His Way. The first thing John Cougar did when he topped the charts was change his name back to Mellencamp. His business advisers were upset about the confusion the name change would cause listeners. However, the artist was adamant, and a compromise was reached; from then on, his records were released as John Cougar Mellencamp.

By 1983, Mellencamp was a bona fide rock star. He had divorced his first wife and married his second. He recorded his next album, *Uh-huh* (1983), at a farmhouse near his home in Indiana, with the drums and guitar in the living room and the mixing board in the kitchen. The album was released while *American Fool* was still high on the charts; the singles "Crumblin' Down," "Pink Houses," and "Authority Song" hit the Top 10 one after another.

Scarecrow, in 1985, sold better still, yielding the singles "Small Town," "R.O.C.K. in the U.S.A.," and "Lonely Ol' Night." The man who became known for fighting authority and holding on to his teen years was becoming a successful grown-up, even with his blue jeans, loafers, and white T-shirt. He explained, in regards to "Jack and Diane," "When I said 'hold on to 16,' I didn't mean hold on to your teenage years. I meant hold on to whatever makes your heart beat. Not hold on to being young—hold on to being alive."

Mellencamp always held on to his beliefs and his roots. He continued to live in Indiana, near his old friends and family. He refused alcohol and tobacco sponsorships of his tours and cofounded, with country superstar Willie Nelson and others, the Farm Aid fundraising concerts for U.S. family farmers. He raised his daughters from both his first and second marriages. He also explored indigenous American music in the 1987 album *The Lonesome Jubilee,* an album liked more by critics than by record buyers.

John Mellencamp (Paul Natkin)

Branching Out. The early 1990's saw major changes in Mellencamp's personal and professional life. He married again (fashion model Elaine Irwin) in 1992. He directed and starred in his first film, *Falling from Grace* (1992), a moody, downbeat piece that received limited attention. His albums were also receiving limited attention: *Whenever We Wanted* (1991) and

Human Wheels (1993), both released under the name John Mellencamp, ignoring the Cougar name altogether, spoke mostly to established, older fans.

Mellencamp reached a whole new audience in 1994, however, when he duetted with young funk bassist Me'Shell NdegéOcello on the Van Morrison hit "Wild Night." It went to number 3 on the charts and propelled Mellencamp's *Dance Naked* to gold-record status.

Mellencamp was unable to tour in support of *Dance Naked* because he was felled by a heart attack at the age of forty-three. He spent most of 1995 recuperating and, when he did release a new album in 1996, it reflected his new perspective on life. *Mr. Happy Go Lucky* was an upbeat collection, filled with wonder, love, and joy. "Key West Intermezzo (I Saw You First)" was a hit on album-rock stations.

Throughout the 1990's, Mellencamp would remain an artist who could speak to and for his contemporaries, reassuring his fans that he never changed his values to promote bigger record sales. He remained true to himself, his roots, and his music. —*Ethlie Ann Vare*

SELECT DISCOGRAPHY

■ ALBUMS

Chestnut Street Incident, 1976
John Cougar, 1979
Nothin' Matters and What If It Did, 1980
American Fool, 1982
Uh-Huh, 1983
Scarecrow, 1985
The Lonesome Jubilee, 1987
Big Daddy, 1989
Whenever We Wanted, 1991
Human Wheels, 1993
Dance Naked, 1994
Mr. Happy Go Lucky, 1996
John Mellencamp, 1998

SELECT AWARDS

Grammy Award for Best Rock Vocal Performance, Male, for "Hurts So Good," 1982

SEE ALSO: Benatar, Pat; Seger, Bob; Springsteen, Bruce.

Sergio Mendes

BORN: Niteroi, Brazil; February 11, 1941

FIRST ALBUM RELEASE: *Cannonball's Bossa Nova*, 1963 (with Cannonball Adderley, rereleased as *Quiet Nights*)

MUSICAL STYLES: Pop, Latin, jazz pop

Pianist and bandleader Sergio Mendes has been the driving force behind Brasil '65 (periodically updated to reflect later years), a jazz-pop group which brought his country's bossa-nova style to a string of pop hits. Between 1966 and 1968, Mendes epitomized the South American sound in American popular music, producing four gold albums and three Top-20 hits.

Jazz Stylings. Mendes studied classical piano until the age of fifteen, when he heard his first Dave Brubeck record. That prompted him to start listening to Charlie Parker, Bud Powell, and other great jazz musicians. Around 1960, he began experimenting with a merger of jazz and samba, and he created a band that in 1962 would become widely influential in Brazil, the Sexteto Bossa Rio. With two trombones, tenor sax, bass, and drums, the group had a unique sound and were invited to play at New York's Carnegie Hall as part of a multigroup Brazilian bill designed to capitalize on the growing popularity of the bossa-nova sound.

The growing interest in the bossa nova remained more cultural than commercial, as early Mendes albums sold poorly. Finally moving to the United States in 1965, he showcased his sound in Southern California with little success until he developed a new sound. His two-girl vocals on popular melodies, sung over a Brazilian groove, proved to be a winning combination, and attracted the attention of Herb Alpert, king of the Latin "Ameriachi" sound, who signed him to A&M records. Alpert, who was already famous as a songwriter ("Only Sixteen," "Wonderful World"), producer (Jan and Dean), and performer ("The Lonely Bull," "A Taste of Honey"), had Mendes and Brasil '65 open for his own band, the Tijuana Brass, on a worldwide tour. The understated but hauntingly poignant vocalizations of Lani Hall,

For the Record

In 1964 a telegram to Sergio Mendes in Brazil was interpreted as a subversive communiqué, leading the newly installed military regime to place him under house arrest. Shortly thereafter, Mendes emigrated to the United States.

Janis Harrison, Bonnie Bowden, and Mendes's future wife Gracinha Leporace accentuated the quiet sway of the bossa-nova beat and together provided an anticipatory counterpoint to the brassy sound of Alpert's band.

Pop Hits. The pop potential of Brasil '66 was quickly realized when *Sergio Mendes & Brasil '66* went to number 7 on the pop charts. They hit the peak of their popularity in 1968, however. The single "The Look of Love" from the 1967 film *Casino Royale* rose to number 4 and drove the album *Look Around* (1967) to number 5. *Fool on the Hill* (1968, number 3) featured John Lennon and Paul McCartney's "The Fool on the Hill" (number 6), which spent four weeks at the top of the adult contemporary chart. Finally, "Scarborough Fair" hit the charts in December and peaked at number 16.

With light pop almost disappearing from the charts in the late 1960's, Mendes had little chart success in the 1970's. He made a comeback in 1983 with "Never Gonna Let You Go," (number 4), which featured vocalists Joe Pizzulo and Leza Miller and spent four weeks at number 1 on the adult contemporary chart. In the years out of the spotlight, Mendes recorded regularly and toured worldwide, playing festivals and working with noted international stars, including Antonio Carlos Jobim.

World Music. In 1992 Mendes won a Grammy Award for Best World Music Album with *Brasileiro,* a musical exploration of his native Brazil. Those who preferred his jazz-tinged pop were more satisfied with *Oceano* (1996), which incorporated hints of Portuguese and Swahili influence, as well as a nod to rap. In the late 1990's Mendes toured with Brasil '99, incorporating Bahian hip-hop into his repertoire of hits stretching back to the mid-1960's.

—John Powell

SELECT DISCOGRAPHY

■ ALBUMS

The Swinger from Rio, 1965
In Person at El Matador! 1966
Sergio Mendes & Brasil '66, 1966
Look Around, 1967
Crystal Illusions, 1969
Greatest Hits, 1970 (compilation)
Sergio Mendes & the New Brasil '77, 1977
Alegria, 1980
Sergio Mendes, 1983
Confetti, 1984
Brasileiro, 1992
Oceano, 1996
Grammy Award for Best World Music Album for *Brasileiro,* 1992

SEE ALSO: Alpert, Herb.

Natalie Merchant. *See* 10,000 Maniacs / Natalie Merchant

Metallica

ORIGINAL MEMBERS: Lars Ulrich (b. 1963), James Hetfield (b. 1963), Dave Mustaine (b. 1961), Ron McGovney

BEST-KNOWN LINEUP: James Hetfield, Lars Ulrich, Kirk Hammett (b. 1962), Jason Newsted (b. 1963)

OTHER MEMBERS: Clifford Lee Burton (1962-1986), Jeff Warner

FIRST ALBUM RELEASE: *Kill 'Em All,* 1983

MUSICAL STYLE: Heavy metal

In the early 1980's, dedication to a musical phenomenon known as heavy metal brought together two young men from totally disparate backgrounds who went on to form perhaps the most influential heavy-metal band in the annals of rock.

Death, drugs, and personal discord marked the lineage of Metallica from the very start.

Beginnings. Lars Ulrich, the son of Danish tennis star Torben Ulrich, relocated to Los Angeles in 1980 and placed an advertisement in a music magazine called *Recycler*, looking for fellow musicians with whom to form a heavy-metal band. One of those answering the ad was James Hetfield, the son of a trucking entrepreneur and an opera singer. The two met for a jam session, but nothing came of it. Ulrich then traveled to England to follow the metal band Diamond Head on tour for three months. When he returned to L.A. in the fall of 1981, Ulrich got back together with Hetfield and, adding guitarist Lloyd Grant, recorded a track for a compilation album titled *Metal Massacre* on Metal Blade records. On March 14, 1982, Metallica performed its first live show.

Metallica's James Hetfield (Ken Settle)

Realizing they needed a good demo tape if they were to get meaningful performance dates, the band members bought some studio time and recorded several songs. Originally untitled, this demo later surfaced as a bootleg album with the title *Power Metal* (1982). Most significant, however, was the band's lineup for these recordings: Ulrich and Hetfield, plus Ron McGovney on bass and Dave Mustaine on guitar. This was the first appearance of the original version of Metallica.

On the Way. The rerecording of "Hit the Lights" became the band's entry on the 1982 Metal Blade Records' compilation album *Metal Massacre*, the first release for Brian Slagel's new label. In the middle of that year, the band recorded another demo, titled *No Life 'Til Leather*, which was never officially released but was quickly bootlegged. The band also experimented with a five-piece format by adding Jeff Warner on vocals. According to most fans, the experiment was blessedly short-lived. Warner's crucial contribution to the band was not through his vocals but through his connections; he introduced them to his friend Cliff Burton, who was playing bass for a band called Trauma. Ulrich and Hetfield, who were secretly dissatisfied with McGovney, went to hear the band and were quite impressed by Burton's tight, compact playing style. Burton, however, was dissatisfied with the L.A. music scene and agreed to join Metallica only if they moved to San Francisco.

Anxious to secure his friend's placement in the band, Warner arranged some shows in San Francisco, hoping the band would fall in love with the city. Their best show was with a local band called Exodus, which featured Kirk Hammett on guitar. The show was recorded and released as *Live Metal up Your Ass*. By the end of 1982, McGovney left the band, Burton joined, and they all moved to San Francisco. In early 1983, record store owner Jon Zazula had the band touring the East Coast in search of a contract. When nothing came of it, he started his own label, MegaForce Records, and signed Metallica for the first release. It was during this tour that Mustaine's substance abuse became a major liability to the band, and he was asked to leave. Hammett flew in to join them and finish the tour. Soon after, he became a regular member of the band.

All-New Metallica. In May, 1983, the new version of Metallica recorded *Kill 'Em All.* The working title for the album was *Metal up Your Ass,* but distributors refused to handle it with that name. The final title reflects the band's venomous attitude toward these distributors. Metallica spent the remainder of 1983 writing and recording new material for their next album, *Ride the Lightning,* which was released in mid-1984. In February, 1984, the band toured Europe for the first time. To promote the tour, the British label Music for Nations released the extended-play single *Jump in the Fire.* The band had finally been noticed in Great Britain.

On August 17, 1985, Metallica performed at the legendary "Monsters of Rock" festival in Donnington, England. The band was a last-minute addition, sandwiched between two hard-rock bands, Ratt and Bon Jovi, but they totally amazed the seventy thousand attendees. Then they proceeded to Copenhagen, Denmark, Ulrich's original hometown, to record another album. In March of the following year, *Master of Puppets* was released. That same month, Metallica began its tour with Ozzy Osbourne. This tour was significant for two reasons: It was the ultimate honor to tour in support of the "godfather" of heavy metal, and it was Metallica's last tour as a supporting act.

Bad Luck Stalks the Band. In June, 1986, Hetfield fell off a skateboard and broke his wrist. The band missed a few shows, but they completed the remainder of the tour with Hetfield in a cast and John Marshall filling in on guitar. Marshall was Hammett's guitar technician on the tour and also guitarist for his own band, Metal Church.

Further disaster struck on September 27, 1986, when one of the band's two tour buses skidded out of control on an ice-covered road near Ljungby, Sweden. The vehicle swerved and flipped, coming to a rest in a ditch. A majority of the occupants, including three of the four band members, scrambled to safety with only minor injuries. Unfortunately, the fourth Metallica member, Cliff Burton, was ejected in the accident and the bus came to rest on top of him, killing him instantly. Two days later, the three surviving members returned to the United States. The following month, Flotsam and Jetsam bassist Jason Newsted became the newest member of Metallica. In August, 1992, Hetfield was badly burned when pyrotechnics malfunctioned during a show with Guns n' Roses in Montreal, Canada.

Good Fortune Returns. Just before Christmas of 1987, the band decided to release their first video, *Cliff 'Em All,* in honor of their recently deceased comrade. Since the band had little footage of their own, they solicited bootleg videos from their fans. The project was a tremendous success.

Metallica's first commercially successful album, . . . *And Justice for All,* was released on Elektra in 1988. Their most famous album, *Metallica* (the black album), was released in late 1991, preceded by a video of "Enter Sandman" and a large tour called "Wherever I May Roam." The album *Load* was released in mid-1996, the year Metallica headlined the North American Lollapalooza tour. *Reload* was released in late 1997. —*David A. Clark*

SELECT DISCOGRAPHY

■ ALBUMS

Kill 'Em All, 1983
Ride the Lightning, 1984
Master of Puppets, 1986
. . . *And Justice for All,* 1988
Metallica, 1991
Load, 1996
Reload, 1997
Garage, Inc., 1998 (compilation)

For the Record

After a free outdoor Metallica show in November, 1997, *The Philadelphia Inquirer* reported: "It was part burlesque show, part rugby match and hearing loss, and neighbors who feared the worst from the self-styled Loudest Band in the World complained more about the sound from the news choppers circling overhead."

SELECT AWARDS

Grammy Award for Best Metal Performance for "One," 1989

Grammy Award for Best Metal Performance for "Stone Cold Crazy," 1990

Grammy Award for Best Metal Performance with Vocal for *Metallica*, 1991

SEE ALSO: Black Sabbath / Ozzy Osbourne; Iron Maiden.

George Michael / Wham!

George Michael

(Georgios Kyriacos Panayiotou)

BORN: Finchley, London, England; June 25, 1963

FIRST ALBUM RELEASE: *Faith*, 1987

Wham!

ORIGINAL MEMBERS: George Michael (b. 1963), Andrew Ridgeley (b. 1963)

FIRST ALBUM RELEASE: *Fantastic*, 1983

MUSICAL STYLES: Pop, rock and roll

George Michael has enjoyed a career as one of the best-known singer-songwriters in the world. He began his career while still in his teens as one-half of Wham!, a hugely successful dance-pop duo that helped define popular music the 1980's. He left the group in 1986 to pursue a career as a solo artist. While Michael's first solo album sold extremely well and generated a number of hit singles, later efforts did not generate the same level of enthusiasm.

Early Days. Michael, whose real name is Georgios (or Yorgus) Kyriacos Panayiotou, grew up the son of a Greek restaurateur in the London suburb of Finchley. His English mother worked as a secretary. An ironic fact seems to have shaped Michael's identity as a schoolboy; he was chubby and wore thick glasses (his extra weight has been attributed to American neighbors who introduced him to peanut butter and jelly sandwiches). A striking transformation took place after Michael met close friend Andrew Ridgeley in grammar school. "I never thought about looking good before I met Andrew," he has said. "He was this person who was always incredibly smart looking." Inspired by Ridgeley, Michael soon reduced his bulk and gave up spectacles in favor of contact lenses.

Both Michael and Ridgeley dreamed of becoming pop stars and formed a ska band as teenagers to pursue their shared vision. Called the Executives, the group played for only two dances before disbanding. Michael and Ridgeley, now calling themselves Wham! UK, turned to creating demos of original songs with a portable four-track recorder. Panayiotou also began using the stage name George Michael.

***Fantastic* Success.** Their demos bore fruit when Innervision Records signed Michael and Ridgeley to a recording contract and released their first album, *Fantastic*, in 1983. The infectiously happy sound heard on the album soon yielded three British hit singles for the musical teenagers, "Wham Rap! (Enjoy What You Do)," "Bad Boys," and "Club Tropicana." The album served as a welcome antidote for many to the ear-grating cacophony of punk rock. Listeners, especially young women, also responded to the clean-cut good looks of the pair; posters of the duo started appearing in teenage bedrooms across the United Kingdom. Their dream of becoming pop stars was coming true.

Feeling that they had been cheated out of royalties from *Fantastic*, Michael and Ridgeley engaged Simon Napier Bell as their new manager. He got them out of their contract with Innervision and into one with CBS/Columbia. With international success in mind, Michael and Ridgeley dropped the word UK from their group's name. CBS/Columbia released their second album, *Make It Big*, in 1984. Like *Fantastic*, *Make It Big* generated several hit singles, including "Wake Me up Before You Go-Go" and "Freedom," and success was now worldwide.

As they basked in the glow of fame, Michael and Ridgeley started to grow apart. Michael, the more introverted—and, by far, the more musical—devoted himself to his art. Ridgeley, the more extroverted, pursued an avocation as a race-car driver. In 1986, Michael declared Wham!

would cease to exist after the release of their next album. It appeared in June of 1986 and was entitled *Music from the Edge of Heaven.* It reached number 1 in Great Britain, but sales fell flat in the United States.

Much debate has surrounded Ridgeley's importance to the duo he formed with his former schoolmate. It has been said that he contributed nothing to the band Wham! He did not really sing on their albums, he did not write much of the music, and he did not play many of the instruments. Others, including Michael, have been more charitable. They credit Ridgeley for providing Wham! with its all-important image. Be this as it may, Michael went on to a very successful solo career, while Ridgeley released only one unsuccessful album before retiring from music.

George Michael (AP/Wide World Photos)

Going Solo. Michael waited more than one year before launching his solo career with the album *Faith*; he felt it was important for memories of Wham! to fade a little in the minds of listeners. However, during the pause, he did contribute a song, "I Want Your Sex," to the sound track for the 1987 film *Beverly Hills Cop II.* The song's frank message proved extremely controversial. In fact, it incurred a British Broadcasting Corporation (BBC) ban, and many radio stations in the United States refused to play it. Nevertheless, it reached number 3 in the United Kingdom and, thanks to frequent airing on MTV, number 7 in the United States. The video for "I Want Your Sex" also unveiled Michael's new image, the chic playboy with three-day stubble growth.

Before *Faith* hit record stores, a second single, a duet with Michael's childhood idol Aretha Franklin, climbed to the top of both the pop and rhythm-and-blues charts. "I Knew You Were Waiting for Me" (1987) went on to win a Grammy Award for Best R&B Performance by a Duo. It also caused Michael problems, as some listeners took issue with a Caucasian winning awards for rhythm-and-blues music. He appeared genuinely hurt by charges of artistic imperialism but took comfort in the fact that record sales seemed to prove that many in the black community did like his music.

Faith finally appeared at the end of 1987. It was supported with a worldwide tour and heavy promotion by CBS/Columbia, and the album quickly reached number 1 in the United States and elsewhere. Five songs were released as singles, including the title track. All were picked up by radio and MTV, and four hit the top of the charts. In short order, Michael had achieved success even beyond that enjoyed by the duo he had just left. The crowning success was a Grammy Award for Album of the Year in 1988.

Withdrawal. All was not well with Michael, however. Extensive touring had left him exhausted, both physically and emotionally. As a result, he decided to do less personal promotion for his next album, *Listen Without Prejudice* (1990). He said that he also wanted fans to focus on the music rather than him. Indeed, the lyrics from *Listen Without Prejudice* hint at an artist trying to escape the sharp image that had been created for him.

Sony, who had bought CBS, did not appreciate Michael's passive approach to promotion and responded with little promotion of their own. In addition, the record-buying public did not respond as heartily to the more subdued sound and soul-searching lyrics heard on *Listen Without Prejudice.* "Praying for Time" and "Freedom '90" did reasonably well as singles but did not succeed like the hits from *Faith.* Lackluster sales led Michael to sue Sony. He felt the problem lay in their failure to promote *Listen Without Prejudice,* which he felt constituted an illegal restraint of trade. The courts did not agree, leaving Michael disappointed and bitter.

While his professional life may have been suffering, Michael's private life had blossomed. In 1991, he met Anselmo Feleppa, a Brazilian dress designer, at the "Rock in Rio" festival. Feleppa quickly became the love of Michael's life but died in 1993, crippling the singer emotionally.

Older. Michael worked his way through the depression that followed Feleppa's death by working on a new album, *Older* (1996). Michael has gone so far as to say that "bereavement tinges the whole album." It was released by Dreamworks, the entertainment corporation founded by Steven Spielberg, Jeffrey Katzenberg, and David Geffen, in 1995. It sold well in a number of countries but failed to achieve strong sales in the United States. Of the album's various songs about and for Feleppa, perhaps the most touching is the single "Like Jesus to a Child." It has been said that Michael's work is possibly the most autobiographical of any singer: *Older* reveals that he is deserving of that reputation.

Michael seemed to have put his life back together by 1997, but 1998 brought both embarrassment and scandal when Los Angeles police found him publicly engaging in lewd behavior. To his credit, Michael took quick and full responsibility for his misdeed and was punished with a fine and probation. Only time can assess the full impact of this incident on an artist Stephen Holden of *The New York Times* once called "the most talented heir to the tradition of pop craft that embraces Paul McCartney, Elton John, and the Bee Gees."

—David Lee Fish

SELECT DISCOGRAPHY

Wham!

■ ALBUMS

Fantastic, 1983
Make It Big, 1984
Music from the Edge of Heaven, 1986

George Michael

■ ALBUMS

Faith, 1987
Listen Without Prejudice, 1990
Older, 1996

SELECT AWARDS

Grammy Award for Best R&B Performance by a Duo or Group with Vocal for "I Knew You Were Waiting for Me," 1987 (with Aretha Franklin)

Grammy Award for Album of the Year for *Faith,* 1988

SEE ALSO: Franklin, Aretha.

For the Record

In the video for "Fastlove" from the album *Older,* George Michael shows contempt for his former label Sony with a shot of headphones bearing the name Fony.

Bette Midler

BORN: Honolulu, Hawaii; December 1, 1945
FIRST ALBUM RELEASE: *The Divine Miss M*, 1972
MUSICAL STYLE: Pop

Bette Midler was named after actress Bette Davis, but her parents, Fred and Ruth Midler, pronounced her name with a single syllable. She grew up in Aiea, a rural Hawaiian town, and was active in both music and theater during her high school years. She enrolled at the University of Hawaii, where she studied drama. In 1965, Midler earned a job as an extra in George Roy Hill's film *Hawaii.*

New York. After working on the film, she went to the continental United States and decided to settle in New York. After working as a singer and actress in nightclubs, restaurants, and Off-Broadway plays, Midler was given a part in the chorus of Jerry Bock and Sheldon Harnick's Broadway musical *Fiddler on the Roof.* She stayed with the production for three years, and was eventually chosen to play one of the leading roles (Tzeitel, Tevye's daughter). After she left the show in 1970, she wanted to emphasize her singing, so her manager found her work at the Continental Baths, a men's club. Appearing as the Divine Miss M, a stage name suggested by her makeup artist, she was very well received. Her act featured a wide variety of musical styles and genres, as well as a great deal of humor. She was accompanied by then-unknown Barry Manilow on piano, and her act often included a trio of female backup singers whom she named the Harlettes.

Bette Midler (Paul Natkin)

Stardom. Gradually, Midler became more popular and began to perform on television. In 1972, she signed a contract with Atlantic Records and released her first album, *The Divine Miss M.* The album reflected Midler's diverse musical interests and included pieces in 1940's swing style, soft rock, 1950's rock, and country. Several singles from this album became hits, including "Do You Want to Dance" and "Boogie Woogie Bugle Boy."

In 1973, she toured the United States, appearing with the Harlettes. Manilow, who was on the brink of becoming a star vocalist himself, was her musical director. He had played on Midler's first hit album, and before he left to produce his own show, he produced her second album, *Bette Midler* (1973). Although this album was not as successful as the first in terms of hit singles, it was still sold well, reaching gold status. In 1974, Midler won a Grammy Award for Best New Artist. The following year, she toured again with an act called the Clams in the Half-Shell Revue, which was very popular.

Temporary Decline. Midler's next album, *Songs for the New Depression*, was released in 1976, but it did not sell well. There were no hit singles from the release, which was disliked by music critics. A double album of her concert performances, *Live at Last*, was released the next year but was even less popular than the preceding album. Midler continued to tour and perform on television specials, and although they did not match the sales of her first recordings, her albums and singles managed to maintain her presence in the industry.

The Rose. A chance to revive her career came through the medium of film in 1979. She starred in *The Rose,* which was inspired by the life of singer Janis Joplin. Midler seemed an unlikely choice for this role, as she was known for her humor, not dramatic representations of tragic cultural icons. Her vocal style, while strong, was much softer than Joplin's hoarse, bluesy, shouting style. However, the film touched a nerve with the public as well as the critics, and Midler was nominated for an Academy Award for her performance. The sound-track album was a huge success, going platinum. The title single reached number 3 in the United States during 1980, and another track from the album, an updated version of Percy Sledge's "When a Man Loves a Woman," was also popular. Midler's book of memoirs, *A View from a Broad,* was published in 1980.

Second Slump. Midler released more films in rapid succession, but they were less popular. Although she continued to reap benefits from *The Rose,* which helped her earn a Grammy Award for Best Pop Vocal Performance in 1980, the film *Jinxed!* (1982) was not well received. She married Martin von Haselberg (of the Kipper Kids) in 1984 and continued recording, touring, and acting in films. As in 1979, it was her film career that led to a comeback in the years 1986 and 1987, with three films for Touchstone Pictures. In 1986, her daughter Sophie was born.

At the Top. When Midler started her own company, All Girls Production, her first venture, the film *Beaches* (1988), was a hit. The sound track was even more popular, with the single "Wind Beneath My Wings" reaching number 1 and the album reaching number 2 in 1989. Midler also won a Grammy for Record of the Year for "Wind Beneath My Wings" in 1989. Toward the end of that year, when the United States became involved in the Persian Gulf War, her single "From a Distance" expressed a resonant theme of world peace, and it reached number 2. In February of 1992, "From a Distance," which became Midler's second platinum single, won a Grammy for Best Song of the Year.

For the Record

"The worst part of having success is to try finding someone who is happy for you."
—*Bette Midler*

§

Midler won a lawsuit against the Ford Motor Company after one of their advertisements used a sound-alike vocalist singing one of her hits, "Do You Wanna Dance." She was awarded $400,000 in damages.

Later in 1992, she won an Emmy Award for her performance on the next-to-last *Tonight Show Starring Johnny Carson.* In the 1990's, Midler also returned to the screen, earning an Academy Award nomination for her role in 1991's *For the Boys,* and she remained active in social causes, including acquired immunodeficiency syndrome (AIDS) research, environmental concerns, diabetes research, and other issues. —*Alice Myers*

SELECT DISCOGRAPHY

■ ALBUMS

The Divine Miss M, 1972
Bette Midler, 1973
Songs for the New Depression, 1976
Broken Blossom, 1977
Thighs and Whispers, 1979
The Rose, 1979 (sound track)
Divine Madness, 1980
No Frills, 1983
Mud Will Be Flung Tonight! 1985
Beaches, 1988 (sound track)
Some People's Lives, 1990
Experience the Divine—Bette Midler: Greatest Hits, 1993 (compilation)
Bette of Roses, 1995

SELECT AWARDS

Grammy Award for Best New Artist, 1973
Golden Globe Awards for Newcomer of the Year and Best Actress for *The Rose,* 1979
Grammy Award for Best Pop Vocal Performance for "The Rose," 1980

Grammy Award for Record of the Year for "Wind Beneath My Wings," 1989
Emmy Award for Outstanding Individual Performance in a Variety or Music Program, 1992

SEE ALSO: Joplin, Janis; Manilow, Barry.

Midnight Oil

ORIGINAL MEMBERS: Rob Hirst, Jim Moginie, Andrew "Bear" James, Peter Garrett, Martin Rotsey
OTHER MEMBERS: Peter Gifford, Dwayne "Bones" Hillman
FIRST ALBUM RELEASE: *Midnight Oil*, 1978
MUSICAL STYLES: Rock and roll, punk rock

Formed in Sydney, Australia, in 1976, Midnight Oil created a uniquely Australian brand of issue-driven rock and roll. While selling more than twelve million records between 1978 and 1998, Midnight Oil passionately promoted nuclear disarmament, Aboriginal land rights, protection of rain forests, and social justice. Whether railing against corporate greed or environmental vandalism, the group did it with strong rock-and-roll hooks and fierce vocals.

Midnight Oil's Peter Garrett (Paul Natkin)

The Beginnings. In 1971, Jim Moginie, Rob Hirst, and Andrew "Bear" James formed the band Farm in Sydney, Australia. Moginie and Hirst had gone to school together. With Moginie on guitar and keyboards, Hirst on drums, and James on bass, Farm performed in Australian coastal towns during the summer holidays. The band placed a newspaper ad for a lead vocalist in 1975, and Peter Garrett was the only person who responded. Although a law student at the time, Garrett had been a member of the band Rock Island Line. With a shaved head and standing seven feet tall, Garrett cut an imposing figure. Along with Garrett, guitarist Martin Rotsey was asked to join the group. While performing in Sydney surf bars, the band used various names—including Farm, Ebb-tide and the Shore Breakers, and the Jerry Falwell Society—before deciding to change its name permanently to Midnight Oil in 1976. The band restricted its playing to the Sydney area while Garrett continued his law studies.

In the summer of 1977, Garrett received his law degree from the University of New South Wales. Midnight Oil began performing five nights per week and hoped that they would soon sign a recording contract. With the rise of punk rock in the late 1970's, Midnight Oil gained a loyal following. Since the band could not come to an agreement with any of the major labels, the band formed its own label, Powderworks. With Gary Morris as their manager, the band went into the studio and recorded their first album, completing it in ten days. Produced by Keith Walker and the band, *Midnight Oil* was released in November, 1978. While the album was part punk rock, part art rock, and part straight ahead rock and roll, the overall effect was one of a band searching for its own sound.

Midnight Oil eventually began to find its way out of the chaos of the first album. In 1978, the group played at a benefit for the Movement Against Uranium, a concert in support of Greenpeace, and a concert in support of the Tibet Council. Midnight Oil emerged as one of Australia's most articulate and poignant rock acts. While Garrett helped to write some of the group's songs, most of the songs were written by Hirst and Moginie. In 1979, the band released its second album, *Head Injuries.* Produced by Les Karski, the album was Midnight Oil's first gold album in Australia and included the hit single "Cold Cold Change."

Rocking with a Purpose. In a bold step, Midnight Oil formed its own booking agency that blacklisted clubs and halls that it believed overcharged the public for concerts. James left the band in 1980 because of the grueling tour schedule. He was replaced by Peter Gifford. In 1981, Midnight Oil traveled to England to record the album *Place Without a Postcard* with the legendary producer Glyn Johns. The album was hugely successful in Australia and led to a recording deal with Columbia Records. Toward the end of 1982, the group returned to England to record its next album. Working this time with producer Nick Launay, Midnight Oil made its most politically charged album to date. With such topical songs as "Power and the Passion," "Short Memory," and "US Forces," *10, 9, 8, 7, 6, 5, 4, 3, 2, 1* established Midnight Oil as superstars in Australia. The album spent two years on the Australian Top 40, and it was Midnight Oil's first album to be released in the United States.

After the release of *Red Sails in the Sunset* in 1984, Garrett ran for a seat in the Australian Senate as the Nuclear Disarmament Party (NDP) candidate. He received 200,000 votes and was narrowly defeated. In 1985, Midnight Oil participated in the Artists United Against Apartheid project. Determined to make a creative statement concerning the plight of Australia's Aboriginal population, the band recorded the ferocious album *Diesel and Dust* (1987). In addition to being an enormous hit in Australia, the album reached number 21 on the U.S. charts. The biting single "Beds Are Burning" was an international hit and reached number 17 on the U.S. charts. *Diesel and Dust* sold more than five million copies and made Midnight Oil famous throughout the world.

Staying True to the Cause. Gifford left the band in 1989 and was replaced by Dwayne "Bones" Hillman. Not wanting to repeat themselves, Midnight Oil experimented with their sound on *Blue Sky Mining* (1990). While the lyrics were just as pointed as those on the previous album, the songs had a more catchy sound. The album sold very well and climbed to number 20 on the U.S. pop charts. While on tour in 1990, Midnight Oil protested the *Exxon Valdez* oil spill in Alaska by giving a free concert outside of the Exxon Building in New York City.

When not touring or recording, the band could be counted on to involve itself in social causes. In 1992, Midnight Oil released the explosive live album *Scream in Blue,* and they finished a new studio album, *Earth and Sun and Moon,* in 1993. Although the album only reached number 43 on the U.S. pop charts, it contained some of the band's most focused performances. In 1997, Midnight Oil released the compilation album *20,000 Watt R. S. L.* In addition to the obvious selections, the album had two new songs, "What Goes On" and "White Skin Black Heart." These songs were included on the 1998 album *Redneck Wonderland,* which continued Midnight Oil's tradition of making music that is both hard hitting and thought provoking. —*Jeffry Jensen*

For the Record

The 1998 album *Redneck Wonderland* got its name from a graffiti map of Australia found in Melbourne that the graffiti artist had titled "Redneck Wonderland."

SELECT DISCOGRAPHY

■ ALBUMS

Midnight Oil, 1978
Head Injuries, 1979
Place Without a Postcard, 1981
10, 9, 8, 7, 6, 5, 4, 3, 2, 1, 1982
Red Sails in the Sunset, 1984
Diesel and Dust, 1987
Blue Sky Mining, 1990
Scream in Blue, 1992 (live)
Earth and Sun and Moon, 1993
Breathe, 1996
20,000 Watt R. S. L., 1997 (previously released material)
Redneck Wonderland, 1998

SEE ALSO: Clash, The; Lennon, John; R.E.M.; U2; Who, The; XTC; Young, Neil.

Luis Miguel

(Gallego Básteri)

BORN: Veracruz, Mexico; April 19, 1970
FIRST ALBUM RELEASE: *1+1=2 Enamorados,* 1982
MUSICAL STYLES: Pop, bolero, musica romantica

In 1982, when he was a mere twelve years old, Luis Miguel ignited his recording and film career. Miguel released four successful albums that year: *1+1=2 Enamorados* (1982), *Directo al Corazon* (1982), *Decidete* (1982), and *Palabra de Honor* (1982). On the strength of his album sales, Miguel embarked on his first international concert tour and made his film debut in *Ya Nunca Mas.* For his interpretation of songs featured in the film, Miguel received a gold record. At the end of 1983 he recorded a duet with Sheena Easton entitled "Me Gustas Tal Como Eres."

Early Success. In 1984, Miguel starred in his second film, *Fiebre de Amor.* The next year, he was honored with awards from three countries: Chile, Italy, and the United States (a Grammy Award for his duet with Sheena Easton). When Miguel was sixteen years old, he signed a long-term contract with Warner Music International. With this contract, Miguel began his association with producer Juan Carlos Calderon and recorded his fifth album, *Soy Como Quiero Ser* (1986). On the strength of its international sales, this album earned eight gold and platinum records.

Miguel recorded his sixth album in 1988, *Busca una Mujer,* and launched an extensive Latin American tour. Within one year of release the album yielded seven hit singles which together topped *Billboard*'s Hot Latin Tracks chart for more than one year. During 1989, Miguel accepted multiple gold and platinum awards on the strength of the album's international sales. Also that year, the President of Mexico presented the nineteen-year-old Miguel with an award recognizing a distinguished artistic career.

The 1990's. In 1990, Miguel recorded and released his seventh album, *20 Años.* This album yielded number 1 hits in Mexico, the United States, and throughout Latin America. Ultimately, the album had six single hits on Mexico's Top-100 record chart. On the strength of these record sales, Miguel conducted sold-out tours in Mexico, Venezuela, and Puerto Rico. He received the Excelencia Europea Award in Spain as well as the Best Latin American Singer Award at the World Music Awards in Monte Carlo.

Miguel completed a sold-out United States tour in 1991. Later that year, he recorded and coproduced his eighth album, *Romance.* For this album, Miguel worked with Bebu Silvetti and Armando Manzanero, sifting through more than one hundred songs to arrive at the fifteen on the album. *Romance* was an international success which showcased the Latin romantic ballad known as the bolero and shifted Miguel from Mexican and Latin American superstar to global superstar. The album sold 400,000 copies in the first 10 days of release and since then has sold

For the Record

At the end of 1996, Luis Miguel had four albums in the *Billboard* Latin Top 50 simultaneously.

more than 6,000,000 copies worldwide. The album earned fifteen platinum records, and with it, Miguel became the first Latin artist to be certified gold in the United States for a Spanish-language album. The album was a success not only in Spanish-speaking nations but also in Korea, Taiwan, and Brazil, where album sales achieved gold record status.

In 1992, Miguel made his Las Vegas debut as the highest-paid Latin performer. Later that year, Miguel won *Billboard*'s Music Awards for Top Pop Latin Artist, Top Pop Latin Album, and Top Hot Latin Tracks Album. Miguel ended 1992 by performing a benefit concert for Mexico's Children's Museum and enjoying unprecedented success on his Latin American tour.

Miguel recorded and made his production debut on his ninth album, *Aries* (1993). The album secured him a Grammy Award nomination in the United States and brought him Best Artist Awards in Korea, Venezuela, and Argentina. That year, according to the Amusement Business Top 100 list, Miguel was rated as having the sixth highest-grossing single-venue ticket sales. The year ended with *Aries* selling two million copies, and, for his Olympic Games tribute song, "America," Miguel won the MTV Music Video Award for the Best International Music Video.

In 1993, *Aries* won a Grammy Award for Best Latin Pop Album and *Billboard* magazine named Miguel Top Latin Male Artist of the Year and *Aries* Top Album of the Year. For *Aries*, Miguel earned twenty-four platinum and six gold records in the United States and in Latin America. In 1994, Miguel recorded and produced his tenth album, *Segundo Romance*, as a sequel to the *Romance* album.

Segundo Romance entered *Billboard*'s Top-200 chart at a record-breaking number 29, the highest entry ever for a Spanish-language album. Receiving both gold and platinum certification made it the first Spanish-language record to achieve that status without an English-language crossover. The hit single from the *Romance* album, "No Se Tu," was featured in the 1994 film *Speechless*.

In 1994, *Segundo Romance* earned Miguel a third Grammy in the category of Best Latin Pop Performance. In Mexico, the album also earned

Luis Miguel (AP/Wide World Photos)

several awards. Furthermore, *Segundo Romance* earned gold certifications in Brazil and Spain and platinum certifications in twelve nations. On October 17,1995, Miguel released his album *El Concierto* and closed the year by singing at the celebration of Frank Sinatra's eightieth birthday.

El Concierto was a worldwide success. Eleven nations reported international gold or platinum certification. Miguel was awarded a star on the Hollywood Walk of Fame, and he released his twelfth album, *Nada Es Igual* (1996). It debuted on the *Billboard* Top-200 chart at number 43, rivaling only his own record for first-week sales by a Spanish-language artist. Miguel ended 1996 with four albums within the top fifty on the *Billboard* album chart.

Contributions and Legacy. Luis Miguel is naturally associated with the bolero. Miguel did not create bolero music, but he has focused the tastes of an entire generation of new listeners on this musical genre. Through Miguel's vocal artistry, the bolero has made a dramatic comeback in Latin America, as well as gaining millions of fans in non-Spanish-speaking nations. Judging by the worldwide success of his eighth album, *Romance,* and the equally huge success of his tenth album, *Segundo Romance,* Luis Miguel could be viewed as the leading bolero artist. —*Albert Valencia*

SELECT DISCOGRAPHY

■ ALBUMS

1+1=2 Enamorados, 1982
Directo al Corazon, 1982
Decidete, 1982
Palabra de Honor, 1982
Soy Como Quiero Ser, 1986
Busca una Mujer, 1988
20 Años, 1990
Romance, 1991
Aries, 1993
Segundo Romance, 1994
El Concierto, 1995
Nada Es Igual, 1996
Romances, 1997

SELECT AWARDS

Grammy Award for Best Mexican/American Performance for "Me Gustas Tal Como Eres," 1984 (with Sheena Easton)
Grammy Award for Best Latin Pop Album for *Aries,* 1993
Grammy Award for Best Latin Pop Performance for *Segundo Romance,* 1994
Hollywood Walk of Fame, star awarded 1996
Grammy Award for Best Latin Pop Performance for *Romances,* 1997

SEE ALSO: Easton, Sheena; Gabriel, Ana; Iglesias, Julio; Selena.

Steve Miller

BORN: Milwaukee, Wisconsin; October 5, 1943
FIRST ALBUM RELEASE: *Children of the Future,* 1968
MUSICAL STYLE: Rock and roll, blues

Steve Miller was born into a musical family in Milwaukee, Wisconsin, and was exposed to blues and jazz greats from a very early age. During World War II, his father, Sonny Miller, a physician by day and a machine-shop foreman at night, began recording songs. Through his father, Miller met such great musicians as T-Bone Walker and Les Paul, the inventor of the solid-body electric guitar.

The Beginnings. Six years after his family moved to Texas in 1950, Miller founded his first band, the Marksmen Combo. He was in seventh grade, and the band was booked for an entire semester of college fraternity parties without anyone suspecting that Miller was only twelve years old.

After Miller entered the University of Wisconsin at Madison at age sixteen, the Marksmen Combo split up, but Miller continued to play guitar and formed a new band, the Ardells. While at home following his freshman year, Miller taught his friend William "Boz" Scaggs a few guitar chords. When Scaggs enrolled at the University of Wisconsin at Madison following next year, he joined the Ardells. Miller spent a senior semester at the University of Copenhagen, Denmark, and, after returning to the United States six credits short of earning his degree in literature, he decided to devote his life to music. He began playing backup guitar in Chicago with such artists as Muddy Waters, Howlin' Wolf, and Buddy Guy.

The Goldberg-Miller Blues Band. At this point, Miller was introduced to organist Barry Goldberg, and they founded the Goldberg-Miller Blues Band. The group played South Side Chicago clubs and eventually signed a contract with Epic Records, which released Miller's first single, "The Mother Song," in 1965. Later that year, after returning to Texas and being refused admission to the University of Texas at Austin music school, Miller bought a used Volkswagen bus and headed for San Francisco, California, where he began putting together a band in 1966. Following Buddy Guy's advice, Miller named the band the Steve Miller Blues Band. Their first performance was at the Avalon Ballroom in January, 1967, and their reputation spread rapidly.

The group played the Monterey Pop Festival in

June, 1967, and, shortly thereafter, a concert with Chuck Berry at the Fillmore Auditorium. In the same year, the band signed a contract with Capitol Records. The band's first songs with the new label were recorded in the basement studios of Hollywood's Capitol Tower, and the sessions did not go well. The band was not allowed to begin recording until after midnight, and the union recording engineers openly showed their contempt for the hippies.

The Steve Miller Band. Following this inauspicious debut, the band travelled to London, England, renamed themselves the Steve Miller Band, and began new recording sessions that led to the release of *Children of the Future* in 1968. Three months after this record was released, Capitol Records pressed Miller for another album. The result was *Sailor* (1968), which featured some of the band's finest work and introduced one of Miller's now-famous recording personas, the Gangster of Love.

The band was finally achieving some success. *Children of the Future* sold 150,000 copies and *Sailor* sold 200,000 copies. However, tensions began to break the group apart. Scaggs, tired of quarrelling with Miller and ready to branch out on his own, quit, and keyboardist Jim Peterman, sick of the constant touring, also left the band. The three remaining members, Miller, Lonnie Turner, and Tim Davis, were joined by Ben Sidran before they recorded 1969's *Brave New World*, their third album. The band spent almost all of 1969 on the road and paused only long enough to piece together a fourth album, *Your Saving Grace*. Despite the dreary sales results, Capitol Records pressed Miller for yet another album, and, despite problems within the group, 1970's *Number 5* was their biggest success to date.

The Steve Miller Band in 1967 (Archive Photos/John Platt Collection)

Miller was working constantly, having produced five albums in two years. He also went through a turbulent period in his personal life, having married and divorced in the course of a year. On top of all this, bassist Turner left the band after a backstage blowout with Miller in February, 1970. While a new musician was brought in to take Turner's place, Capitol put pressure on Miller to record a new album, which resulted in his apathetic 1971 album *Rock Love.* Miller was ashamed of the album and tried to make up for its shortcomings with *Recall the Beginning . . . A Journey from Eden* (1972). However, this album also failed to meet his expectations, and a frustrated Miller left for a European tour before finishing the redubs of his guitar solos. Guitarist Jesse Ed Davis was brought in to finish the record. On the way to the airport, Miller was injured in an automobile accident but continued on to Denmark. Despite the pain, he managed to complete the European portion of his tour before falling ill with hepatitis and cancelling his remaining American concerts. Exhausted and in poor health, Miller went to his parents' home in Texas to recuperate.

Success. At this point, Miller decided to produce a record himself. Channeling his anger and frustration, he went into the studio and emerged nineteen days later with *The Joker* (1973), which raced all the way to number 1 on the album charts. This was Miller's first major success. After recording eight albums and playing hundreds of live concerts in sixty-five months, *The Joker* finally turned Miller's luck around. The album sold more than one million copies, while the title track became his first gold record.

Exhausted from all this pressure, Miller took a year off and wrote the songs that would form the basis of his next two albums, the platinum *Fly Like an Eagle* (1976) and *Book of Dreams* (1977). *Fly Like an Eagle* produced six consecutive hit songs, and *Book of Dreams* continued this streak of hits with the song "Jet Airliner."

Miller's next album, *Circle of Love* (1981), went gold but proved to be a disappointment, having been recorded as his second marriage was ending. Again overcoming his setbacks, Miller moved to Seattle, Washington, and found the lyrics for a song he had held back from *Circle of Love.* This song became "Abracadabra," and the album of the same name became the third number 1 record of Miller's career.

Miller's three 1980's records, *Italian X-Rays* (1984), *Living in the 20th Century* (1986), and *Born 2B Blue* (1988), never matched the success of his mid-1970's albums. *Born 2B Blue,* a return to Miller's early roots, suffered particularly disappointing sales. The 1993 album *Wide River* was more successful and signaled a new productive period in Miller's life. Miller had again defied the odds and added to a solid repertoire of songs that had already earned him a place in the annals of rock and roll history. —*Gregory Weeks*

For the Record

Paul Ramon, who was credited with singing backup vocals and playing drums on the Steve Miller single "My Dark Hour," was really a pseudonym for Paul McCartney.

SELECT DISCOGRAPHY

■ ALBUMS

Children of the Future, 1968
Sailor, 1968
Brave New World, 1969
Your Saving Grace, 1969
Number 5, 1970
Rock Love, 1971
Recall the Beginning . . . A Journey from Eden, 1972
Anthology, 1972 (previously released material)
The Joker, 1973
Fly Like an Eagle, 1976
Book of Dreams, 1977
Greatest Hits 1974-1978, 1978 (previously released material)
Circle of Love, 1981
Abracadabra, 1982
Wide River, 1993
Steve Miller Band, 1994 (boxed set)

SEE ALSO: Scaggs, Boz; Waters, Muddy; Thorogood, George, and the Destroyers.

Milli Vanilli

ORIGINAL MEMBERS: Rob Pilatus (1965-1998), Fabrice Morvan (b. 1966)
FIRST ALBUM RELEASE: *All or Nothing*, 1988
MUSICAL STYLES: Pop, hip-hop, rap

The brainchild of producer Frank Farian, Milli Vanilli, during their brief existence, managed to win a Grammy Award, sell millions of records, and permanently upset the music world. Never a group so much as a pair of performers, Rob Pilatus and Fabrice Morvan did not sing even one note on their platinum-selling album.

Munich Days. Rob Pilatus was the illegitimate son of an African American soldier and a German stripper. He was born in New York and later adopted at age four and raised in Munich, Germany. Feeling alienated from his adoptive parents, he ran away during his teens. Fabrice Morvan was raised in Paris but fled to Munich in hopes of finding stardom. There he met Pilatus. The two were dancers in clubs, and, after meeting, they decided to pursue success together.

Since they were both good-looking and knew how to entertain, they devised an act singing songs and dancing. They were not spectacular singers, but their style had appeal. Dressed in spandex shorts, sporting colorful shirts and thin braids, they were an unmistakable presence. They made friends with many studio musicians and eventually were introduced to Frank Farian.

During the late 1980's, European dance groups reigned supreme at discos, clubs, bars, and concert halls. These bands were usually the creation of a producer and made up of recruited musicians. Farian, a German producer, was one of these men who hired studio musicians to perform his songs. In 1987, Pilatus and Morvan did a recording session with Farian, who judged it terrible.

Lip-Synching to Stardom. At the end of 1987, Farian recorded a song called "Girl You Know It's True." Its original studio singers, all middle-aged, were Charles Shaw, John Davis, and Brad Howe. The song had all the markings of a dance music hit, but its singers offered none of the image that Farian felt would market it. He brought Morvan and Pilatus back in, convinced their image could sell the record, and offered them an opportunity to perform the song without actually singing. Seeing an opportunity to win some quick fame and money, they agreed.

Lip-synching was nothing new; the act of moving one's lips along with a recording had been common for years, especially among dance acts. The late 1980's European dance groups Technotronic and Black Box used models who would lip-synch in their videos and live concerts in place of the less exciting actual vocalists. With Milli Vanilli, Pilatus and Morvan not only lip-synched the songs, but were credited with singing them as well, a grave misrepresentation. In May of 1988, they went on a European tour, lip-synching the song many times. "Girl You Know It's True" became a smash hit, reaching number 1 on the charts. This inspired Farian to record a whole album, *All or Nothing*, for Milli Vanilli. Pilatus and Morvan signed a contract that forced them to keep their lip-synching a secret, although Farian assured them they would eventually get to sing.

The duo appeared in several videos for their album's singles, including "Girl I'm Gonna Miss You," "Baby Don't Forget My Number," and "Blame It on the Rain." In January of 1989, they toured the United States. Milli Vanilli made appearances on everything from television sitcoms to dance shows. Three number 1 singles and a video compilation, *In Motion: The Video Hit Collection*, resulted from the album. Their popularity spread all over the world, and when touring they found legions of fans even in Africa and Australia. This success caused the duo a lot of strain, since the danger of being discovered as frauds became more of a threat as time wore on. With this pressure and a contract which swore them to secrecy, the duo slipped into drug usage.

Winning the Grammy Award. In July of 1989, Milli Vanilli were performing in Bristol, Connecticut, when their tape skipped during "Girl You Know It's True." While the fans did not seem to mind, this led to serious speculation among critics and reviewers. Meanwhile, record sales soared beyond ten million copies. To appease the fans, a

Milli Vanilli's Fabrice Morvan and Rob Pilatus (AP/Wide World Photos)

remix album was released—*Two x 2* (1990). In January of 1990, Milli Vanilli were awarded three American Music Awards, and one month later they won a Grammy Award for Best New Artist.

Due to spreading rumors and increasing scrutiny, suspicions regarding the duo's singing became serious. On November 14, 1990, producer Farian came clean, admitting that Pilatus and Morvan did not sing on their record. One week later, the duo appeared at a press conference to tell their side of the story. At the conference, they returned their awards.

Milli Vanilli were, at best, laughed at and, at worst, hated. Their record company offered rebates to those who had purchased Milli Vanilli's albums. Angry fans staged record burnings, and stores pulled Milli Vanilli merchandise. Their songs were removed from playlists, and books including Milli Vanilli passages were revised to exclude them.

A single was put out by *All or Nothing*'s studio musicians under the group name the Real Milli Vanilli. It did not sell. In 1991, Pilatus and Morvan were offered the opportunity to record an album themselves. During the course of these recordings, the two appeared in a self-mocking television commercial. Pilatus also attempted suicide during this period. However, by 1992 a record was completed, and they became known as Rob and Fab. They appeared on Arsenio Hall's popular late-night television show, performing to good response. However, their album failed and only sold two thousand copies. At this point, the two parted ways.

The End. Pilatus struggled with drugs and crime for the next few years. In 1997, after a major scrape with the law, Farian came to his aid and enrolled him in a drug rehabilitation program. Morvan continued to work on a musical career, performing his original compositions in Los Angeles clubs. In early 1998, the music video cable station VH-1 aired a special program that examined the Milli Vanilli story compassionately, creating positive exposure for the former duo. Just months later, on April 2, 1998, Pilatus was found dead in his hotel room in Frankfurt, Germany, due to a drug interaction. He was in the midst of creating new material for a comeback.

Although many people were wronged by the phenomenon of Milli Vanilli, they certainly made a mark on history. Since their days, a controversy has been waged over lip-synching. Dance acts would shrink from hiring performers who did not really sing on their recordings. For better or for worse, Milli Vanilli are one of the few groups remembered for something other than their music. —*Lawrence Ferber*

SELECT DISCOGRAPHY

■ ALBUMS

All or Nothing, 1988
Two x 2, 1989
The Remix Album, 1990

Charles Mingus

BORN: Nogales, Arizona; April 22, 1922
DIED: Cuernavaca, Mexico; January 5, 1979
FIRST ALBUM RELEASE: *Jazz at Massey Hall,* 1953
MUSICAL STYLE: Jazz

Charles Mingus is considered one of the most important figures in twentieth century music. His career developed in the late 1940's in a community of musicians who shared both jazz traditions and the technical discipline to improvise their own musical visions within a framework of complex compositions. Ahead of his time, Mingus believed that composition was the answer to moving jazz from its roots to art music. He was one of the first bass players to lead his own group, challenging the notion that bass players and drummers were only present to support the soloists.

Early Influences. Born in an army camp in Nogales, Arizona, in 1922, Mingus grew up in Watts, California. His mother died when he was an infant, and he was influenced by a stepmother who believed in the value of European classical music and encouraged his development in that direction. Only classical and religious music was allowed in the house, but Mingus remembers hearing Duke Ellington's band on the radio when he was seven or eight years old. Listening to brass instruments in his mother's church as well as in Ellington's band may have influenced Mingus, at age six, to choose a trombone when his father agreed to buy him an instrument.

Mingus was taught, as most poor black children were, by a music teacher who found it easier to teach his students to play by ear rather than how to read music. While Mingus was to say later in life that he felt this approach retarded his classical training, it helped his ability to improvise. By high school he had switched to the cello and played with the Los Angeles Junior Philharmonic. His high school friend Buddy Collette suggested he switch to the bass, because the school band

Charles Mingus in 1974 (AP/Wide World Photos)

needed a bass player, and it was a more appropriate instrument for an African American at a time when it would have been rare, if not impossible, for a black person to join a symphony.

The Making of a Composer. By the time Mingus was sixteen he was working out arrangements for the school jazz band and studying the piano to understand harmonies. Mingus still had little contact with black music (outside of the church and some Ellington pieces) and was encouraged by jazz trumpeter Roy Eldridge, who had stopped in Los Angeles on tour and was featured with Mingus's high school band, to learn more. His subsequent career was a constant struggle between his love and respect for the tradition of black music and his belief that its future lay in being fully integrated into something much broader.

After graduation, Mingus's father wanted him to go to work for the postal service, but Mingus knew that he wanted to make music his career. He worked in a variety of small jazz groups for the next few years with musicians who would migrate to California after World War II. Mingus also continued his classical studies with a former member of the New York Philharmonic who was then scoring films.

Mingus was becoming known as a promising bassist, and in the mid-1940's, he began to do studio work with a variety of jazz musicians and popular black artists while continuing to develop his own style. Bebop was being developed by this time on the East Coast, and he undoubtedly heard the proponents of this style when they toured the West Coast. He was ready for a major boost to his career by the time Lionel Hampton's band spent three months touring the West Coast. In 1947, upon a recommendation from Hampton's bassist, who decided to stay in Los Angeles, Mingus joined the band and stayed with them for about one year before the tour ended in San Francisco. He then left the music scene for a while, working full-time for the postal service, as his father had suggested. However, when vibraphonist Red Norvo returned to Los Angeles for a residency and needed to replace his bassist, Mingus answered the call.

Destination: New York. The trio did an East Coast tour, ending in New York. Mingus, then twenty-nine, decided to stay. He soon joined Charlie "Bird" Parker's band at Birdland. For the remainder of his life he was to be a New Yorker. Becoming the first jazz musician to do so, Mingus formed his own record company, Debut Records, and recorded his first album at age thirty. He had decided early in his career that it was important for a musician to control his own music. He also set up a publishing company with Max Roach, with whom he would have a lifelong musical and personal friendship. Besides their musical relationship, they had similar feelings about the position of African Americans and black music in American society. In the era of civil rights activism, a few black musicians were bringing protest to the ranks of jazz. Mingus's activities best exemplified this, from his founding of the Jazz Composers' Workshop in the 1950's to his staging of a hard-bop event outside the 1960 Newport Jazz Festival to protest its nostalgic and white-dominated tastes. Mingus also wrote works that attacked segregation, such as "Fables of Faubus."

His insistence on featuring his own compositions from the mid-1950's onward set an example for other musicians, as did his tenacity in running the longest lived of all the early attempts by musicians to own a record label. Mingus recorded more than one hundred albums and wrote more than three hundred scores.

In the late 1960's and early 1970's, Mingus organized a number of important concerts dubbed "Charles Mingus and Friends," which combined the musical energies of his peers and his protégés. He became one of the leaders of the avant-garde while continuing his interest in classical composition. His controversial autobiography, *Beneath the Underdog*, was also published that year. Mingus was unable to tour after 1977, when he was diagnosed with amyotrophic lateral sclerosis (Lou Gehrig's disease) and confined to a wheelchair; his last works were sung into a tape recorder. He died in Mexico in 1979 at the age of fifty-six. At his request, his ashes were scattered over the Ganges River in India, where, according to a biography, he believed his "spirit would be set free."

—*Jo Ann Collins*

SELECT DISCOGRAPHY

■ ALBUMS

Blues & Roots, 1959
Mingus Ah Um, 1959
Mingus Dynasty, 1960
Oh Yeah, 1962
Black Saint and Sinner Lady, 1963
Mingus Plays Piano, 1963
Let My Children Hear Music, 1972
Changes One, 1975

SEE ALSO: Kirk, Rahsaan Roland; Mitchell, Joni; Parker, Charlie.

Ministry

ORIGINAL MEMBERS: Al Jourgensen (b. 1958), Paul Barker (b. 1957)
OTHER MEMBERS: Bill Rieflin (b. 1960), Mike Scaccia (b. 1965), Roland Barker (b. 1957), others
FIRST ALBUM RELEASE: *Cold Life*, 1981 (EP)
MUSICAL STYLES: Industrial rock, synthesizer pop

During the 1970's, musicians experimented with new textures by melding synthesizer pop with abrasive noise. The result was a new genre called industrial music, pioneered by such bands as Throbbing Gristle, Cabaret Voltaire, SPK, and Einstürzende Neubauten. In the 1980's, the term "industrial" was redefined by musicians who infused electronic music with a strong dose of heavy metal guitars, and Ministry emerged as the seminal band for the new sound, laying the groundwork for future bands such as Nine Inch Nails. Cuban-born vocalist and guitarist Al Jourgensen and bassist Paul Barker remained at Ministry's core after they formed the group in 1981. Over the ensuing years, Ministry engineered a dramatic sonic transformation, shifting gears from a dance-music act to a band that married heavily distorted vocals and speed-metal guitar with angry, ominous lyrics.

A Short-Lived Pop Career. Ministry traces its roots back to Chicago, Illinois, where a local independent label called Wax Trax! helped put the band on the map in 1981. Ministry released an EP (*Cold Life*, 1981) and several singles under that label before signing with Arista Records in 1982. The band's first full-length album, *With Sympathy*, was released the following year, and it represented a debut that Jourgensen would prefer to forget. With catchy songs such as "Work for Love," the synthesizer-pop collection quickly established Ministry as a dance-club favorite. After touring with Front 242 in 1984, Jourgensen began to favor an edgier, more industrial sound. He later blamed Arista Records for Ministry's foray into synthesizer pop and has referred to *With Sympathy* as "an abortion." As Ministry's frontman, Jourgensen cultivated a dark, bad-boy image and was rarely without his trademark black cowboy hat.

The band briefly returned to Wax Trax! before signing with Sire Records in 1985. This led to Ministry's second full-length album, *Twitch* (1986), on which the band adopted the rapid-fire drum machine and blistering, "wall-of-sound" guitars that would become part of the band's signature. With *Twitch*, Ministry began to explore industrial territory, providing a distinct departure from the dance-pop of *With Sympathy*. Jourgensen and Barker also showcased their industrial thrust by producing numerous side projects through Wax Trax!, such as 1000 Homo DJs (with Nine Inch Nails' Trent Reznor), Lard (with Dead Kennedys vocalist Jello Biafra), and Revolting Cocks.

Embracing Industrial. Fueled by metallic riffs, ear-splitting samples, and accelerated tempos, Ministry delved deeper into the industrial genre with *The Land of Rape and Honey* (1988) and *The Mind Is a Terrible Thing to Taste* (1989). The band achieved unprecedented success in 1992 with the release of *Psalm 69: The Way to Succeed and the Way to Suck Eggs*, an album that eventually went platinum. *Psalm 69* garnered great critical acclaim, even from critics who had heretofore been detractors of industrial music. The group's widespread success was reinforced when they joined the 1992 Lollapalooza tour, a music festival established in 1991 by Jane's Addiction singer Perry Farrell. Ministry's kinetic energy reportedly stole the show from the Red Hot Chili Peppers and others in the Lollapalooza lineup.

For the Record

Ministry owes its name to literature. After Alain Jourgensen saw the 1944 film *Ministry of Fear,* based on a Graham Greene thriller, he became keen on giving the group a similar name. In addition to "Ministry of Fear," he also considered "Ministry of Truth," from George Orwell's dystopian novel *Nineteen Eighty-Four,* before settling on "Ministry."

§

A country music fan, Al Jourgensen has been known to play country songs at sound checks. When Ministry hosted a party to celebrate the completion of their Texas studio, Jourgensen asked country-swing artist Don Walser to perform.

Trouble In Texas. Seeking fresh surroundings for their next recording effort, Ministry relocated to Austin, Texas, in 1993. Their new home proved problematic: Technical difficulties abounded in the studio, and drummer Bill Rieflin quit (Rey Washam took his place). The band then ran into trouble with the law. In August, 1995, a narcotics team discovered heroin and cocaine in Jourgensen's home. As a result, he faced a two-year prison term and a $10,000 fine. Jourgensen pleaded guilty in December, 1995, which led to five years probation and a $1,000 fine.

Ministry emerged from that arduous experience to release *Filth Pig* in 1996. With less distortion than previous albums, listeners could hear Jourgensen's voice more distinctly. The collection probed deeper than ever before into Ministry's ominous, dark musings, as with the title track that declared, "I sleep with both eyes open." Also notable was the band's gritty cover of Bob Dylan's classic, "Lay Lady Lay." Not forgetting their roots, Ministry dedicated *Filth Pig* to the memory of Jim Nash, the former president and cofounder of Wax Trax! who died in 1995. *—Sandra Swanson*

SELECT DISCOGRAPHY

■ ALBUMS

Cold Life, 1981 (EP)
With Sympathy, 1983
Twitch, 1986
The Land of Rape and Honey, 1988
The Mind Is a Terrible Thing to Taste, 1989
Psalm 69: The Way to Succeed and the Way to Suck Eggs, 1992
Filth Pig, 1996

SEE ALSO: Dead Kennedys, The; Nine Inch Nails.

The Miracles. *See* Smokey Robinson

Joni Mitchell

BORN: Fort McLeod, Alberta, Canada; November 7, 1943
FIRST ALBUM RELEASE: *Joni Mitchell,* 1968
MUSICAL STYLES: Folk, pop, jazz, folk rock

If there is one characteristic to which Joni Mitchell's longevity as a popular singer can be attributed, it is her stylistic exploration—her transcendence and overlapping of the traditional boundaries placed between folk, rock, jazz, classical, and pop music. With a love for art and painting, Mitchell (born Roberta Joan Anderson) developed an artistic sensitivity when she was nine years old, recovering from a battle with polio. Three years later she was influenced by an English teacher who told her: "If you can paint with a brush, you can paint with words." The teacher drew out her potential for imagery and description, the most prominent characteristic of her music. Consequently, Mitchell wrote on her first album: "This album is dedicated to Mr. Kratzman, who taught me to love words."

Beginnings. Roberta Joan Anderson, a capable painter by her teen years, attended the Alberta College of Art (Calgary) from 1963 to 1964. Outside classes, she would play on her baritone ukulele, and with the encouragement of some friends, became a regular performer at a local club in Calgary called the Depression. Although she maintained an interest in painting (and later would use her own paintings on her album covers), she quit school after one year in order to be a folksinger, performing the music of others, particularly that of her idol, Judy Collins.

In 1965, on her way to attend the Mariposa Folk Festival in Toronto, Roberta wrote her first song, "Day After Day." She became intrigued with the folk scene in Toronto and decided to stay, building her reputation with more original contemporary folk songs. It was this same year that she married Chuck Mitchell and modified her middle name to Joni, using it as her stage name. She and her husband moved to Detroit in 1966, and although Joni and Chuck divorced shortly after the move, she retained the name Joni Mitchell.

After a brief move to the Chelsea district of New York City in 1967 (at which time she met David Crosby of the Byrds, who would become a significant influence on her career), Mitchell moved to Southern California in 1968 and became friends with a number of other pop groups and artists, including Stephen Stills and Graham Nash. She also got to know East Coast musicians and writers such as Carole King and James Taylor. (Later, Mitchell would contribute background vocals on Carole King's album *Tapestry* in 1971, tour as the opening act for Crosby, Stills, and Nash, and be featured on Taylor's 1971 album *Mud Slide Slim and the Blue Horizon.*) Mitchell has been romantically linked with a number of musicians. Among her most serious relationships of the late 1960's and early 1970's were those with Graham Nash and James Taylor.

Mitchell's first two albums (*Joni Mitchell*, 1968, and *Clouds*, 1969) can be classified as contemporary folk, with some unique features. The songs contain sophisticated poetry put to strikingly original melodies. The harmonies include segments of unusual chord progressions for guitar and piano accompaniments.

During this early phase of Mitchell's career, other artists were gaining recognition from her songs. Judy Collins, Buffy Sainte-Marie, Tom Rush, and others included Mitchell's songs in their repertoire. "Clouds," from Mitchell's second album, retitled "Both Sides Now," became a Top-10 hit for Judy Collins in 1968.

Joni Mitchell (Reprise/Gregory Heisler)

The Woodstock Festival. With her third album, *Ladies of the Canyon* (1970), Mitchell came to a stylistic turning point. One song on the album, "Woodstock," was both a chronicle and a testimony to the spirit of the August, 1969, Woodstock Music and Art Fair (which celebrated peace and love through music). A verse from "Woodstock" states: "By the time we got to Woodstock/ We were half a million strong/ And everywhere there was song and celebration/ And I dreamed I saw the bombers/ Riding shotgun in the sky/ And they were turning into butterflies/ Above our nation." Ironically, Mitchell was not at Woodstock but at a nearby hotel. She was scheduled to perform on the last day of the festival; however, her manager, Elliot Roberts, urged her not to go because he was afraid she would not be able to leave in time to make a scheduled television appearance on *The Dick Cavett Show* the next day. Although Mitchell was absent from the festival, her song "Woodstock" not only became a big hit for Crosby, Stills, and Nash the following year but also became a stylistic prototype of her new musical direction.

Mitchell Hits Her Stride. It was not until 1971, however, that the stylistic change intimated in "Woodstock" resulted in a new and different Mitchell that would make her a major success in her own right. In 1970, Mitchell decided to retire from performing, based in part on the unruly crowds she was encountering on tour and at festivals. (While opening for Crosby, Stills, and Nash, for example, Mitchell left the stage angrily at the Atlantic City Pop Festival because of an unruly crowd. The large crowds that came to hear a Crosby, Stills, and Nash concert were much different from the intimate gatherings at the clubs she was accustomed to playing.) Equally important, she believed that she needed new material. She took a year off to travel and produced a large number of songs, some of which were included in her next album, *Blue.*

Mitchell's next three albums, *Blue* (1971), *For the Roses* (1972), and *Court and Spark* (1974), were major artistic successes. Of the three, *Blue* and *Court and Spark* are generally regarded as her greatest; the two albums are a contrast in style. *Blue* is, in classical terminology, a song cycle, in which the songs are connected by common thematic material. The melodies are sometimes recitative, as the melody imitates the rhythms and inflections of speech. The background rhythms are subdued, a type of transformed rock beat. As much of her work does, it contains autobiographical reflections of her emotions and her personal relationships. *Court and Spark* is more lively and melodic than *Blue,* and it includes Mitchell's most successful single, "Help Me" (it went to number 11 on *Billboard*'s pop chart). *For the Roses* also included a successful single in "You Turn Me On (I'm a Radio)." *For the Roses* is an experimentation with poetry, philosophy, and music. The first song on *For the Roses,* "Banquet," sets the tone with a philosophical issue central to her work, a question that could be paraphrased as "What happens to the soul when the eye is cast honestly on a flawed but beautiful world?"

With the success of *Blue* in 1971, Mitchell returned to the stage, but not as an opening act for other artists. She had now earned recognition as a star. She went on her first major tour in 1974, accompanied by Tom Scott and the L.A. Express, who had played on and helped arrange *Court and Spark.* (Scott had also added subtle horn arrangements to *For the Roses.*) The collaboration with the L.A. Express resulted in a new jazz-pop-rock sound for Mitchell. With this approach she revisited some of her earlier folk hits. She released these new versions in 1974 on a double live album called *Miles of Aisles* and released a live version of "Big Yellow Taxi" as a single. *Court and Spark* and

For the Record

Joni Mitchell remembers that John Lennon, while recording across the hall from her in 1974, came into Mitchell's studio. After listening to a couple of tracks from *Court and Spark,* Lennon turned to her and said, "You want a hit, don't you? Put some fiddles on it. Why do you always let other people have your hits for you?"

Miles of Aisles probably marked the peak of Mitchell's popular success.

The albums from the middle to late 1970's range from jazz-rock to an avante-garde style of jazz, as Mitchell teamed up with jazz musicians such as bassist Jaco Pastorius, saxophonist Wayne Shorter (both from Weather Report), and drummer Don Alias. The 1976 album *Hejira* includes the songs "Coyote" and "Amelia," a haunting song with references to aviator Amelia Earhart. Mitchell's jazz phase culminated in a collaborative recording project with renowned jazz bassist Charles Mingus. Mingus was ill, and he died before the project was completed; however, the album (*Mingus*, 1979) is dedicated to him and features Mitchell's paintings of Mingus on the cover. (Mitchell has always devoted some of her time and creativity to painting, and this was especially true during the 1980's.) Through this period, Mitchell's pop following understandably dwindled. She retained a devoted, though smaller following.

In the 1980's she released albums that touched on a variety of styles, including more pop-oriented work than she had done since the early 1970's. She brought in guest performers as diverse as Michael McDonald, Peter Gabriel, Willie Nelson, actor Rod Steiger, and even Billy Idol to sing (or, in Steiger's case, talk) on her records. In the 1990's *Night Ride Home* and *Turbulent Indigo* both were well received by critics and, though not hits, sold respectably if modestly. Her live performances in the 1980's and 1990's were infrequent. In 1998 she did a short series of concerts in which she was co-billed with two other renowned singer-songwriters, Bob Dylan and Van Morrison.

It is her ability to change and experiment with style, her mastery of imagery, and her balancing of personal, social, and philosophical statements that make Mitchell unique. Her influence has been felt widely in pop and rock music; she is widely respected and listened to by other musicians. Chrissie Hynde of the Pretenders has cited Mitchell's influence, and it can be heard as well in the work of Rickie Lee Jones (who has used the Mitchell technique of creating dense harmonies by overdubbing her own voice repeatedly in the studio). Many other women musicians have noted that Mitchell was a pioneer and something of a role model in her feminist and no-holds-barred approach to her art. Numerous singer-songwriters, male and female, have listened to and been motivated, inspired, or influenced by her work.

—*Kerry Hart*

SELECT DISCOGRAPHY

■ ALBUMS

Joni Mitchell, 1968
Clouds, 1969
Ladies of the Canyon, 1970
Blue, 1971
For the Roses, 1972
Court and Spark, 1974
Miles of Aisles, 1974
The Hissing of Summer Lawns, 1975
Hejira, 1976
Don Juan's Reckless Daughter, 1977
Mingus, 1979
Shadows and Light, 1980
Wild Things Run Fast, 1982
Dog Eat Dog, 1985
Chalk Mark in a Rain Storm, 1988
Night Ride Home, 1991
Turbulent Indigo, 1994
Hits, 1996 (compilation)
Misses, 1996 (compilation)
Taming the Tiger, 1998

SELECT AWARDS

Grammy Award for Best Folk Performance for *Clouds*, 1969
Grammy Award for Best Arrangement Accompanying Vocalists for "Down to You," 1974 (with Tom Scott)
Canadian Music Hall of Fame, inducted 1981
Billboard Century Award, 1995
Grammy Awards for Best Pop Album and Best Recording Package for *Turbulent Indigo*, 1996
Rock and Roll Hall of Fame, inducted 1997
Nashville Songwriters Hall of Fame, inducted 1997

SEE ALSO: Byrds, The; Collins, Judy; Crosby, Stills, Nash, and Young; King, Carole; Pretenders, The; Taylor, James.

Thelonious Monk

BORN: Rocky Mount, North Carolina; October 10, 1917
DIED: Weehawken, New Jersey; February 17, 1982
FIRST ALBUM RELEASE: *Bean and the Boys,* 1944 (with Coleman Hawkins)
MUSICAL STYLE: Jazz

Thelonious Monk is considered one of the most influential jazz musicians of all time. Throughout his career, he suffered from being ahead of his time. His compositions were confusing to most musicians and difficult for his audience to understand. It was only midway through his career that his genius was recognized, and it took years of study and development by later musicians for his compositions to be truly appreciated. Many of Monk's songs have come to be among the most widely known and respected jazz compositions, including "Round Midnight," "Straight No Chaser," "Rhythm-a-Ning," and "Blue Monk."

Growing Up in the Capital of Jazz. Monk grew up in San Juan Hill in Manhattan, an area near the heart of Harlem with a thriving music scene. He liked to listen to his sister Marion's piano lessons and learned to play by ear by the time he was twelve. The music teacher recognized Monk's talent and suggested he take lessons rather than Marion, who was not interested.

Monk scored high on intelligence quotient (I.Q.) tests, but his academic record was sporadic, with the exception of his marks in music. He was already demonstrating some of the characteristics of a musical genius, and he developed a habit of staying home from school to listen to music and play the piano. He was indulged by his mother, who set aside an area in the kitchen for Monk's bed and piano. Monk eventually left school and began to play small gigs in town with other musicians.

Monk studied organ with the organist at his church and soon went on the road as the piano player for an evangelist. Mary Lou Williams, the well-known pianist and arranger, heard him in Kansas City during that time and recognized his talent even as a teenager. After a couple of years on the road, however, Monk missed New York and returned to his family's home, where he continued writing the music that was in his head and playing anywhere he could, regardless of the amount of money he was paid. His mother supported his decision to become a musician and also supported him financially during this period.

For the Record

Percy Heath, who would become famous as the bassist in the Modern Jazz Quartet, had been in New York for about six years in 1954 when he recorded with Miles Davis and Thelonious Monk for Prestige Records. It thrilled Heath to be "with all those great cats," he recalled. "My mother used to call Monk 'the onliest.' She got mixed up with his name Thelonious. I told her he sure was *the onliest.*"

Early Compositions. Before the end of the 1930's, Monk had already written many songs, including "Ruby, My Dear," written for his mother, and "Round Midnight," which became his most famous song. His first break came when he was hired as the house pianist for Minton's Playhouse, a small Harlem nightspot that became famous as the birthplace of bebop. Monk experimented with his ideas with other musicians at jam sessions. Other jazz musicians became familiar with Monk's music by the 1950's, but he remained fairly unknown out of that small circle. In fact, Monk's individual rhythmic style and dissonant harmonies were to lay the foundation for the coming change in the development of jazz, during which musicians such as Charlie Parker and Dizzy Gillespie would meet at jam sessions and share their ideas. Gillespie was known to comment that Monk was the most original and the least affected by what other musicians were doing at the time.

Monk continued to play off and on at Minton's, remaining in relative obscurity as a musician. Finally, in 1944, well-known saxophonist Coleman Hawkins asked Monk to join his group. By this time, Monk had received long-overdue credit for "Round Midnight" and had started claiming royalties. By the time he was first recorded with Hawkins, Monk was twenty-seven years old. He was beginning to develop a reputation for unreliability and inconveniencing others by showing up late whenever he got involved in his own composing or was not interested in the music that would be played. One admirer, however, was Miles Davis, who credited Monk with his rapid progress as a musician.

The Rain Before the Rainbow. The period from 1945 to 1954 was difficult for Monk. His reputation as an eccentric had led to periods of unemployment (he was known for wearing funny hats onstage), and his unusual rhythmic technique prompted some critics to label him an inferior pianist. Some of his compositions were so advanced that even some of the players (not Parker or Gillespie, however) thought he was crazy. Fortunately, he was still recorded extensively on Blue Note Records from 1947-1948 and 1951-1952, and was also recorded on Prestige, Verve, and Vogue Records.

Things changed when Monk was signed by Riverside Records in 1955. Producer Orrin Keepnews persuaded Monk to record an album of Duke Ellington songs and another one of standards that would make his music more accessible to jazz fans. The album, *Brilliant Corners* (1956), became a classic. Monk was booked for a long engagement at a club called the Five Spot, where he played with a quartet featuring tenor saxophonist John Coltrane. The audience and critics, ready to accept a change by 1957, finally recognized Monk's genius. He became a celebrity and remained so for the rest of his career. In 1964 he was featured on the cover of *Time* magazine, a monumental feat for a jazz artist.

Thelonious Monk (Archive Photos/Frank Driggs Collection)

Monk continued to tour extensively throughout the 1960's but suddenly retired in 1973. He was suffering from mental illness and lived his life in seclusion, playing only on rare occasions when he could be coaxed into appearing for a special event. He died of a stroke in 1982. Thelonious S. Monk, Jr., with the support of his aunt Marion, was appointed to assume charge of his father's estate. Eventually, he was asked to head a project to establish a lasting tribute to Monk, the Thelonious Monk Institute of Jazz. Established in 1986, the institute developed a reputation for launching the careers of young, aspiring jazz artists through its annual jazz competition. —*Jo Ann Collins*

SELECT DISCOGRAPHY

■ ALBUMS

Thelonious Monk Trio, 1952
Monk Plays Ellington, 1955
Brilliant Corners, 1957
Monk's Music, 1957 (with the Thelonious Monk Septet)
The Thelonious Monk Orchestra at Town Hall, 1959
The Thelonious Monk Story, Vols. 1 and 2, 1965
Thelonious Monk with John Coltrane, 1966 (recorded in 1957)
The Complete Genius, 1976 (recorded 1947-1952)

SEE ALSO: Davis, Miles; Mingus, Charles; Parker, Charlie.

The Monkees

MEMBERS: Michael Nesmith (b. 1942), Mickey Dolenz (b. 1945), Davy Jones (b. 1945), Peter Tork (b. 1944)
FIRST ALBUM RELEASE: *The Monkees*, 1966
MUSICAL STYLES: Rock and roll, pop

Unlike most rock bands, the Monkees were originally an artificial creation, fabricated to be a fictional band (similar to the Partridges of the 1970's) on a weekly television sitcom. The band's members were chosen more for their appearances, personalities, and acting abilities than their musical skills. Despite their artificial beginnings, the Monkees carved out a minor musical niche for themselves and defied all logic by lasting, on and off, three decades after their original television show ended.

Formation of the Band. Barely one year after Great Britain's Beatles made a triumphant visit to the United States in early 1964, Columbia Pictures producers Bert Schneider and Bob Rafelson got the idea of capitalizing on the group's phenomenal popularity by cloning an American version for television. The result was the Monkees, a band whose resemblance to the British "Fab Four" was so transparent that wags immediately dubbed its members the "Pre-Fab Four."

According to show business legend, the band's members were chosen from more than four hundred applicants who responded to an advertisement in the September 9, 1965, issue of *Variety* seeking musicians/singers it described as "4 Insane Boys, Age 17-21."

The four "insane boys" eventually selected had a collective physical resemblance to the Beatles, engaging personalities, and some entertainment experience and acting ability but comparatively little musical experience among them.

The Monkees' drummer, Mickey Dolenz, for example, came to the group with significant acting experience from having starred in the television series *Circus Boy* (1956-1958), in which he had been billed as Mickey Braddock. Dolenz also had some guitar experience, but he had to learn the drums from scratch. Davy Jones, the group's only British member, had stage experience in the Broadway production of *Oliver!*, but the only musical instrument he played before joining the Monkees was the tambourine. By contrast, Peter Tork (bass) and Michael Nesmith (guitar and vocals) came to the group with folk music experience. Tork could already play guitar and banjo, and Nesmith had serious musical aspirations that he would eventually realize in his post-Monkees career.

The Television Series. *The Monkees* debuted on September 12, 1966. It was an immediate hit. Similar in spirit and pacing to the Beatles film *A Hard Day's Night* (1964), *The Monkees* television series was an often anarchic comedy show tracing the lighthearted antics of a young rock band. Slapstick sketches connected by gossamer-thin plots were salted with music numbers. Don Kirshner was brought in to oversee the production of the music, and he engaged such top professional songwriters as Neil Diamond, Carole King, Harry Nilsson, Tommy Boyce and Bobby Hart, and Paul Williams to write fresh songs for each episode. Top studio musicians, including Glen Campbell and Stephen Stills, were among the session performers who played the instruments heard on the show.

The Monkees (Archive Photos)

As actors playing musicians, the members of the group sang the songs they performed on the show (lipsynching their own voices on camera), while only appearing to play the instruments they held. This was not unusual in acting jobs; however, the show's producers soon began issuing Monkees records, transforming the band from the realm of pure make-believe to something different. When the group's first two singles, "Last Train to Clarksville" and "I'm a Believer," shot to the top of the charts, the artificial band moved to the front rank of recording artists. A string of top-selling albums, beginning with *The Monkees* (1966) and *More of the Monkees* (1967), soon followed. As on the television show, however, the band's members sang on their recordings but did not play their instruments.

Crafted to meet the demands of the commercial market, Monkees songs were sprightly, upbeat tunes of the sort later known as "bubblegum" music. The opening stanza of "I'm a Believer," written by Neil Diamond, expresses their mood: "I thought love was only true/ in fairytales/ Meant for someone else/ but not for me." After finding love, however, the balladeer eventually declares, "Oh I'm a believer/ I couldn't leave her if I tried." Although the music lacked substance, it was so well made that only cynics could resist it.

For the Record

The Monkees made one lasting contribution to rock music. While touring England in 1967, they discovered an unknown musician named Jimi Hendrix and hired him as an opening act for their concerts. That arrangement did not last long, but it helped to launch Hendrix's own brief but spectacular career.

The Monkees took a further step toward becoming a real band when they were sent on concert tours, which required them to play their instruments. Adoring teenage audiences screamed so loudly that they might not have noticed if the Monkees played no instruments at all, but the band members—especially Nesmith—were embarrassed by the differences between how they sounded on stage and how they sounded on their highly polished recordings. At a press conference in New York, Nesmith revealed that although the Monkees could play their instruments, they had not played them on their recordings and were not allowed to do so. His pronouncement created a serious rift between the band and the production company, but the Monkees eventually prevailed and were allowed to play their instruments on future recordings.

The group's third album, *Headquarters* (1967), the first on which the Monkees played their own instruments, marked the group's beginning as a real band. Much of the music on that album was written and performed by the Monkees, but the only marked difference between this and earlier recordings was its less-polished sound. The Monkees wrote many of the songs and played their own instruments on later recordings but also continued to use established songwriters and session musicians.

After the Television Lights Went Out. The Monkees' television careers ended with the airing of their show's fifty-sixth and last episode in March, 1968. Toward the end of that year their only film, *Head* (written by producer Bob Rafelson and actor Jack Nicholson), was released. A chaotic attempt to capitalize on the "psychedelic" fad of the time, it flopped, doing nothing for the group's reputation. Shortly afterward, Tork left the group.

Nesmith, Jones, and Dolenz continued to perform as a trio, releasing several albums in 1969 and appearing in an unsuccessful television special. Nesmith then left the group to start a solo career, leaving Jones and Dolenz to complete their recording contract with a final album, *Changes*, in 1970. The group then ceased to exist. Later in the 1970's, Jones, Dolenz, and Tork combined with other musicians in new bands that performed Monkees music, but not under the Monkees name.

Fifteen years after the original Monkees disbanded, public interest in their music revived. After episodes of their television show were broadcast on the MTV cable channel in 1986, their original albums were rereleased, and there were calls for the band to reunite. By then Nesmith had become a respected country-rock artist and successful music video producer (he won the first Grammy in that field with *Elephant Parts* in 1981), and he ignored the calls for a reunion, but Jones, Dolenz, and Tork got together and put the band back on the road. They released a completely new album, *Pool It!* (1986).

Rhino Records eventually rereleased all the original albums, as well as videotapes of the television series. In 1996, Nesmith rejoined the group to record a new album, *Justus*, which contained new songs by all the band's original members. Nesmith himself mixed and produced the album while the other members of the band went back on tour. In November of that year, all four members of the band performed together onstage for the first time since the 1960's, in a Los Angeles club.

—R. Kent Rasmussen

SELECT DISCOGRAPHY

■ SINGLES

"Last Train to Clarksville," 1966
"I'm a Believer," 1966
"A Little Bit Me, a Little Bit You," 1967
"Pleasant Valley Sunday," 1967

"Daydream Believer," 1967
"Valleri," 1968

■ ALBUMS

The Monkees, 1966
More of the Monkees, 1967
Headquarters, 1967
Pisces, Aquarius, Capricorn & Jones, Ltd., 1967
The Birds, the Bees, and the Monkees, 1968
Head, 1968 (sound track)
Pool It!, 1986
Concert in Japan, 1996
Listen to the Band, 1991 (boxed set)
Justus, 1996

SELECT AWARDS

Emmy Award for Best Comedy Series, 1966-1967

SEE ALSO: Beatles, The; Diamond, Neil; Hendrix, Jimi; King, Carole; Milli Vanilli.

Bill Monroe and the Blue Grass Boys

ORIGINAL MEMBERS: Bill Monroe (1911-1996), Lester Flatt (1914-1979), Earl Scruggs (b. 1924), Chubby Wise (1915-1996), Howard "Cedric Rainwater" Watts

FIRST SINGLE RELEASE: "What Would You Give in Exchange (for Your Soul)," 1936 (as the Monroe Brothers)

MUSICAL STYLES: Bluegrass, country

Unlike most genres of music, bluegrass has a clearly recognized originator, the mandolin master and singer Bill Monroe. Monroe was also a prolific songwriter; some of the hundreds of his songs have gone on to become classics (such as Elvis Presley's first hit single in 1954, "Blue Moon of Kentucky"). Few performers have been more influential than Monroe, and bluegrass music, like jazz and blues, is now internationally recognized as a true American art form.

Before World War II. Musically, in the 1920's, the United States was regionally diverse. In the rural South, especially in the Appalachian Mountains and the Carolina Piedmont region, social activity centered on string-band and fiddle music, such as would be found at the traditional Saturday-night barn dance. This so-called mountain music was often based on old folk tunes brought over from the British Isles. Gospel music then dominated social life on Sundays, in contrast to the previous night's dance music. Radio and early recordings soon exposed the southerners to other music styles (such as northern pop music, midwestern jazz, and southern blues), and mail-order catalogs introduced new instruments (such as the mandolin, accordion, and guitar).

Radio and records did more than introduce new musical styles to different audiences. They also offered local southern musicians new opportunities to perform as true professionals or semiprofessionals, allowing many to make a living playing their unique brand of folk tunes. Southern radio stations found that broadcasting live local talent was an inexpensive way to entertain their listeners, while the performers found radio to be a way to increase attendance at their personal appearances. New York record company executives discovered that northerners also bought "hillbilly" music, believing it to be reflective of an authentic southern United States of earlier times. In short, by the late 1930's "hillbilly" music had definitely become commercialized, and many southern young men and women dreamed of using it to gain national fame and fortune. Charlie and Bill Monroe, two brothers in their twenties from a poor Kentucky farm family, had such ambitions.

The Old Southern Sound. Bill Monroe took up the mandolin because his older brothers had already laid claim to the household guitar and fiddles. The Monroe brothers left the farm to work in the oil refineries in Chicago and Gary, Indiana, and brought their instruments with them. With Charlie on rhythm guitar and Bill on lead mandolin, the Monroes eventually became known as one of the most sophisticated of the many country brother duos of the period, and they had recorded sixty songs by 1938. However, personal and musical differences caused them to go their separate ways early that year.

The breakup of the Monroe Brothers gave Bill an opportunity to develop musically in ways that the duo format had not allowed. He had a vision of creating a type of music that incorporated elements of African American blues, traditional gospel, and old string-band and fiddle tunes. This new form—eventually to be called bluegrass (after Monroe's home state)—was to be played at lightning speed, imitating some of the fast fiddle breakdowns of the rural dances. Thus, while it is widely believed that bluegrass is pure, uncontaminated country music, this is not quite true. Monroe certainly drew on traditional influences (perhaps more than any other country artist), but he had always been concerned with commercial success, and he intended his music to have wide appeal. Monroe formed his new band, calling them the Blue Grass Boys, in the late 1930's. In 1939 Monroe made his first appearance of many at the Grand Ole Opry in Nashville. In 1944 the best-known Blue Grass Boys lineup came together, including Lester Flatt (guitar and vocal) and Earl Scruggs (banjo). By 1945, Monroe had finally brought all the parts together to his liking. His first record to climb the charts was "Kentucky Waltz," released in 1946. The Blue Grass Boys were a popular performing and recording act through the late 1940's. Flatt and Scruggs left Monroe in 1948 to start their own band. (Their band, the Foggy Mountain Boys, also became very popular. Years later, Flatt and Scruggs had a big country hit in the 1960's with "The Ballad of Jed Clampett," the bluegrass theme song of *The Beverly Hillbillies.*)

Bill Monroe in 1941 (Archive Photos/Frank Driggs Collection)

Classic Bluegrass. Bill Monroe set the standard for the classic bluegrass ensemble. This consists of fiddle, banjo, and mandolin as lead instruments (playing improvised variations on the main melody during solos) with rhythm guitar and bass as backup. No drums or electric instruments would be allowed in a traditional bluegrass band. He also made the mandolin a significant instrument. Until this time, the mandolin provided chorded accompaniment for singers, or simply repeated the melody line of the song in single notes. With bluegrass, the mandolin became a lead instrument, and provided a drumlike chopping sound of chords between breaks or sung verses. In addition, Monroe created the style of high lonesome singing, typical of the bluegrass sound. In this style, the tenor voice is dominant, and songs are sometimes

For the Record

"I'd still rather listen to Bill and Charlie Monroe than any current record. That's what America's all about to me."

—*Bob Dylan*

§

"Rockabilly music is Bill Monroe and the blues tied together. That's it."

—*Carl Perkins*

sung in a key a little higher than the vocalist can sing. Below this are intricate vocal harmonies, sometimes in quartet fashion, reflective of old country church music.

Finally, Bill Monroe wrote (or popularized) the standard songs of the bluegrass repertoire. Many of these, such as "Uncle Penn" and "Kentucky Waltz," were actually penned by Monroe. Others were traditional mountain ballads adapted to bluegrass timing and instrumentation. Monroe recorded more than six hundred songs of both kinds. There was an unwritten rule that every bluegrass band pay homage to Bill Monroe by playing some of his tunes at a concert or recording session.

Bluegrass Music. Monroe's career had many highs and lows, partly due to his strict adherence to his singular musical vision. While other country musicians turned to electric instruments or crossed over to pop, Monroe held fast to his acoustic, traditional sound. In the 1960's and 1970's Monroe's music was rediscovered by a new generation of folk, county, and rock fans. The Grateful Dead's Jerry Garcia, Bob Dylan, Emmylou Harris, David Grisman, Ricky Skaggs, and Vince Gill are just a few of the many stars to have publicly acknowledged their musical debt to Monroe. While bluegrass now has a large international following, it is simply impossible to overestimate Monroe's influence on American music. He will no doubt be remembered as one the country's greatest composers, instrumental innovators, and musical stylists. —*James Stanlaw*

SELECT DISCOGRAPHY

■ ALBUMS

Master of Bluegrass, 1981
Bluegrass '87, 1987
Southern Flavor, 1988
Live at the Grand Ole Opry: Celebrating 50 years on the Grand Ole Opry, 1989
Cryin' Holy unto the Lord, 1991
The Essential Bill Monroe and His Bluegrass Boys 1945-1949, 1992
The Music of Bill Monroe from 1936-1994, 1994 (4-CD compilation)
Bill Monroe 16 Gems, 1996

SELECT AWARDS

Country Music Hall of Fame, inducted 1970
Nashville Songwriters Hall of Fame, inducted 1971
Society for the Preservation of Bluegrass Music, Bluegrass Hall of Fame, inducted 1984
Grammy Award for Best Bluegrass Recording, Vocal or Instrumental, for *Southern Flavor*, 1988
Grammy Award for Lifetime Achievement, 1993

SEE ALSO: Gill, Vince; Harris, Emmylou; Presley, Elvis; Skaggs, Ricky; Williams, Hank.

The Moody Blues

ORIGINAL MEMBERS: Denny Laine (b. Brian Hines, 1944), Ray Thomas (b. 1941), Mike Pinder (b. 1941), Graeme Edge (1941), Clint Warwick (b. Clinton Eccles, 1939)
OTHER MEMBERS: John Lodge (b. 1945), Justin Hayward (b. 1946), Patrick Moraz (b. 1948)
FIRST ALBUM RELEASE: *Go Now: Moody Blues #1*, 1965
MUSICAL STYLES: Art rock, classical rock

The Moody Blues are known for songs that express what might be called cosmic longing and for the lush sounds of their recordings. In the late 1960's and early 1970's they were influential both in creating an early version of what came to be called classical rock, art rock, and progressive rock, and in establishing that there was indeed an audience for this type of music.

The First Moody Blues. There were two distinct early versions of the Moody Blues, with two different musical approaches. The first incarnation of the band included Denny Laine and was essentially a "British-invasion" pop/rhythm-and-blues band. They had a hit called "Go Now," which was their cover version of a song first released, unsuccessfully, by an African American group. The Moody Blues were unable to follow up the success of "Go Now," however, and Laine and Warwick departed. (In the 1970's Laine played with Paul McCartney's Wings, and he frequently performed "Go Now" at their concerts.)

For the Record

Justin Hayward once explained why the Moody Blues had moved away from the blues toward progressive rock: "It was really because at that point we'd gone about as far as we could go singing about people's problems in the Deep South of America without knowing anything about it."

The Second Moody Blues. Two new players joined the Moody Blues—guitarist and singer Justin Hayward and bassist John Lodge—and the band's direction changed radically. A British record company offered them the chance to record, with an orchestra, a rock rendition of Anton Dvorak's New World Symphony. This project never came to completion; instead, it quickly evolved into the recording of Moody Blues material with an orchestra assembled especially for the recording sessions. The result was *Days of Future Passed* (1967), an album that went to number 3 on the U.S. charts and eventually produced two hit singles. It was an ambitious, if sometimes trite and melodramatic, attempt to present musical images of a passing day, from morning to night. Afternoon was depicted in "Tuesday Afternoon," the first single from the album. Night was represented by the love song "Nights in White Satin." With swelling orchestrations, lyrics such as "I'm looking at myself/ reflections of my mind," and occasional recitations of poetry, the album easily found a place in the psychedelic musical landscape of its time.

Recording Hits. The band continued to develop its songwriting and, most notably, its use of the recording studio, over the next few albums. A keyboard instrument called the Mellotron became central to their sound. Before the development of complex polyphonic synthesizers in the mid-1970's, the Mellotron used tapes to produce orchestral sounds—violins, cellos, flutes, and choruses of voices. The Moody Blues were not the only ones to use this instrument in the 1960's; it can be heard on the Beatles' *Magical Mystery Tour* (1967) and the Rolling Stones' *Their Satanic Magesties Request* (1967), for example. However, the Moody Blues used it as a central aspect of their sound, and it helped give their recordings a distinctive otherworldly feel. (They also set a precedent; the Mellotron was soon being used prominently by King Crimson, Genesis, and Yes.) The distinctive features of the Moody Blues' albums were a careful blending of Mellotron and real flute sounds (played by Ray Thomas), nicely blending harmony voices, and frequent use of acoustic guitar. Their songs explored love, loneliness, and yearning in quasi-mystical and science-fiction contexts.

The second album of the post-Laine Moody Blues was *In Search of the Lost Chord* (1968). It begins with the uptempo "Ride My Seesaw" and includes "Legend of a Mind," with its "Timothy Leary's dead" refrain and long flute solo section. Next came *On the Threshold of a Dream* in 1969, the year the band started its own Threshold record label. *To Our Children's Children's Children* (1969) concludes with the mysterious "Watching and Waiting."

A Question of Balance (1970) includes the successful (number 21) single "Question," with its slow, reflective middle section framed by an uptempo beginning and ending. The number 2 album *Every Good Boy Deserves Favour* (1971) contains "The Story in Your Eyes," one of their most effective songs and a number 23 single. Like many of their songs, it expresses feelings of love and hope yet has fearful, nearly despairing undertones. (The album's title is a mnemonic device that young music students use to learn the notes on the lines of the treble clef, EGBDF.)

In 1972 "Nights in White Satin" was finally released as a U.S. single, and the five-year-old-song became their biggest hit, going to number 2. *Seventh Sojourn* (1972), with simpler song arrangements than the previous albums, includes "I'm Just a Singer in a Rock and Roll Band" (a number 12 single). The song is a response to the sort of fan adulation a band of their popularity (and psychedelic leanings) would attract; inevitably some listeners would come to believe that musicians have mystical insights and secrets that ordinary folk do not. After this album, the band went on an extended break. Some members pursued solo projects, and Hayward and Lodge teamed in 1975 to record the Moody Blues-like album *Blue Jays.*

Continued Popularity. Eventually the group decided to record again, releasing *Octave* in 1978, *Long Distance Voyager* in 1981, and *The Present* in 1983. (Pinder left after *Octave,* replaced by former Yes keyboardist Patrick Moraz—who in turn left after 1986's *The Other Side of Life.*) The highlight of the Moody Blues' work in the 1980's was "Your Wildest Dreams," a bittersweet remembrance of long-lost love with no cosmic pretentions, from *The Other Side of Life.* The song was their first U.S. Top-10 hit since 1972. The popular video for the song good-naturedly conjured up nostalgia for a time long past.

In the 1990's the Moody Blues' primary success was in the performing arena. They began making concert appearances with local orchestras, performing orchestrated versions of their hits in such settings as the Hollywood Bowl and the Red Rocks amphitheater in Colorado—the latter the scene of a live album and concert video.

—*McCrea Adams*

SELECT DISCOGRAPHY

■ ALBUMS

Go Now: Moody Blues #1, 1965
Days of Future Passed, 1967
In Search of the Lost Chord, 1968
On the Threshold of a Dream, 1969
To Our Children's Children's Children, 1969
A Question of Balance, 1970
Every Good Boy Deserves Favour, 1971
Seventh Sojourn, 1972
Long Distance Voyager, 1981
The Other Side of Life, 1986
A Night at Red Rocks with the Colorado Symphony Orchestra, 1993
Time Traveller, 1994 (boxed set)

SEE ALSO: Genesis; King Crimson; Yes.

Alanis Morissette

BORN: Ottawa, Canada; June 1, 1974
FIRST ALBUM RELEASE: *Alanis,* 1991
MUSICAL STYLES: Rock and roll, pop

Canadian musician Alanis Morissette emerged in the mid-1990's as a dominant figure among young singer-songwriters. To fans in the United States she seemed to be an overnight sensation. In truth, she had already enjoyed a successful career as a pop star in Canada with dance-oriented hits such as "Too Hot." She debuted an edgier sound on her multiplatinum album *Jagged Little Pill* (1996), which contained a number of hit singles, including "You Oughta Know" and "Ironic."

Childhood Stardom. Morissette and her twin brother Wade grew up with their older brother Chad in Ottawa as children of a French-Canadian father and a Hungarian mother. Morissette began her career in the entertainment industry as a preteenage regular on Nickelodeon's television program *You Can't Do That on Television.* In 1987, the twelve-year-old Morissette sang a song she had written, "Find the Right Man," during an audition for Stephan Klovan, who was putting together a children's fashion show for Ottawa's annual Tulip Festival. Impressed with her precociousness, Klovan made Morissette the occasion's centerpiece. He remembers, "I sensed something right off the bat. . . . She definitely had an undefinable quality. I guess you could say star quality."

Klovan began booking Morissette to perform "O Canada" at major sports events. The experience gave her significant exposure and confidence as a performer. Morissette's performance of the national anthem at the opening ceremonies for the 1988 World Figure Skating Championships led to a meeting with Ottawa composer Leslie Howe. Soon, they were collaborating in Howe's home studio. Howe first arranged a version of the Osmonds' hit "One Bad Apple" for Morissette to sing during her audition for the television series *Star Search.* The pair then began collaborating on original material. At the same time, Klovan was grooming Morissette's image, even getting clothing retailers to sponsor the rising star. To attract record industry attention, Klovan took Morissette to Paris to record a video for a song she had written with Howe called "Walk Away," which Howe used to attract the attention of MCA Records representative John Alexander.

Alanis. In 1991, MCA Records of Canada released Morissette's debut album, *Alanis,* when the artist was still seventeen years old. It inspired comparisons with contemporary teenage singers such as Tiffany and Debbie Gibson and sold over 200,000 copies. The hit single from the album, "Too Hot," received extensive airplay and reached the Top 10 on the Canadian charts. The success of *Alanis,* along with Klovan's constant promotion, made Morissette a recognizable figure in the world of Canadian popular music. Honor followed fame when she brought home the 1992 Juno award for Most Promising Female Artist.

Morissette's second album, *Now Is the Time,* appeared in 1992 but did not sell as well as *Alanis.* It was less dance oriented than the artist's debut but too pop-oriented to reach the rock and roll audience. At the same time that her career was faltering, Morissette was experiencing personal problems. She had to cope with being a teenage pop sensation, which made school and dating very difficult. Furthermore, her perfectionist ways bedeviled her and made her feel that she was constantly letting herself down.

In 1993, John Alexander approached Scott Welch of Atlas/Third Rail Management in Los Angeles, California, about releasing Morissette's first two albums in the United States. Alexander's success in promoting Paula Abdul made him a natural choice for the job. He responded to Morissette as a singer but felt she needed a fresh start. At Alexander's suggestion, Morissette moved away from her family in Ottawa to Toronto. In the bigger city she attempted to collaborate with a number of other songwriters, but the efforts were futile; Morissette was trying to find a means of personal expression while her collaborators wanted to churn out hit songs.

Morissette finally found a musical partner she could work with by moving to Los Angeles. However, things did not start out well for her there. She was robbed at gunpoint soon after arriving and went through a good deal of cultural shock. She also went through a number of fruitless collaborations before meeting Glen Ballard. Ballard was already well-established within the Los Angeles music scene. He had been a producer for Quincy Jones and had worked with Aretha Franklin, Chaka Khan, George Benson, and Paula Abdul, but those in the music industry knew him best as the composer and arranger of Michael Jackson's hit "Man in the Mirror."

Alanis Morissette (Maverick/Michelle Lavrita)

Jagged Little Pill. Ballard and Morissette began collaborating in early 1994. Their work together resulted in the songs for Morissette's next album, *Jagged Little Pill* (1995), which was released by Madonna's Maverick Records. Morissette called the album her "true debut." Its rock-oriented sound was unlike anything heard on *Alanis* or *Now Is the Time*, and the songs on the album were those of an adult artist rather than a teenager.

Jagged Little Pill met with almost instant success, and Morissette immediately began touring with a newly formed band. Within six months she had performed at the MTV Video Awards in New York City and as a featured musical guest on *Saturday Night Live.* Hit singles from *Jagged Little Pill* included "You Oughta Know" and "Ironic." The album went multiplatinum and landed Morissette four Grammy Awards in 1996. Many in Canada remembered the teen pop star who had recorded *Alanis* and were both surprised and skeptical about the new Morissette. It did not help that her collaborator Welch was an established music industry figure. Critics charged that she was merely aping a musical trend.

Despite such criticism, Morissette displayed considerable talent as a singer on *Jagged Little Pill.* Her strong, expressive voice had a certain brash quality but could, by turns, also be quite intimate. Lyrically, the well-crafted "Ironic" stood out, as did "Right Through You," written by Morissette out of frustration with the sexist, profit-motivated executives she had encountered during her rise to stardom. In her own words, "Their very sort of money-hungry corporate way of thinking did not mesh at all with my purist, artistic outlook." She sang in a prophetic voice dripping with vitriol, "Now that I'm Miss Thing/ Now that I'm a zillionaire/ You scan the credits for your name/ And wonder why you're not there." *—David Lee Fish*

SELECT DISCOGRAPHY

■ ALBUMS

Alanis, 1991

Now Is the Time, 1992

Jagged Little Pill, 1995

Supposed Former Infatuation Junkie, 1998

SELECT AWARDS

Juno Award for Most Promising Female Artist, 1992

Grammy Awards for Album of the Year and Best Rock Album for *Jagged Little Pill*; for Best Female Rock Vocal Performance and Best Rock Song for "You Oughta Know," all 1995

SEE ALSO: Amos, Tori; Apple, Fiona.

Van Morrison

BORN: Belfast, Northern Ireland; August 31, 1945

FIRST ALBUM RELEASE: *Them*, 1965 (with Them)

FIRST SOLO ALBUM RELEASE: *Blowin' Your Mind*, 1967

MUSICAL STYLES: Rock and roll, blues, Celtic, pop, rhythm and blues

Van Morrison's career has spanned many decades, encompassing a wide variety of musical styles and influences and featuring songs ranging from earthy rock classics to traditional Celtic songs to literary spiritual musings.

The Belfast Years. George Ivan (Van) Morrison was born on Hyndford Street in a working-class neighborhood of Belfast, the only child of a shipworker father and a mother who had been a jazz singer. He grew up listening to his father's eclectic collection of music, featuring bluesmen such as Huddie Ledbetter (Leadbelly) and Muddy Waters, along with folk, country, jazz, and gospel artists. When he was eleven years old, Morrison was enrolled in the Orangefield School for Boys, which was notable for employing both Catholics and Protestants, but he was an indifferent student, primarily remembered later for his shyness and preference for books over sports. After playing guitar as a pre-teenager, Morrison learned the saxophone and played with several local groups. Morrison dropped out of school at fifteen years of age and worked briefly at a few menial jobs, most notably as a window cleaner, an experience later celebrated in his song "Cleaning Windows."

Music, however, was his focus and his love. His first band was the Thunderbirds, but its name

Van Morrison in 1979 (Paul Natkin)

changed several times according to the whims of the owners of the clubs at which it played local dances, covering such rhythm-and-blues numbers as "Whole Lotta Shakin' Going On." His shyness with people evaporated when he was on stage, and he became known as a riveting performer, whether playing saxophone or singing. After touring with a group called the Monarchs, Morrison and Monarchs guitarist Billy Harrison formed the band Them. Both sides of the group's second single—"Baby Please Don't Go" and "Gloria"—were hits in Europe and received some radio play in the United States. "Gloria," with its three-chord simplicity and catchy guitar part, soon became a standard part of the repertoire of many young rock bands, and it is still a staple of oldies radio stations.

A Solo Career in America. After leaving Them, Morrison flew to New York in 1966 and recorded eight songs with producer Bert Berns for the Bang label. When the single "Brown Eyed Girl" became a hit in 1967, Berns packaged all eight songs as *Blowin' Your Mind.* Morrison was displeased with the result and to placate him, Berns had him record eight more tracks, which he then released as *The Best of Van Morrison* (not to be confused with *The Best of Van Morrison* released in 1990). Morrison was even more unhappy with this album, and soon he left Bang for Warner Bros.

Morrison was given creative control on his first album for Warner Bros., *Astral Weeks* (1968), which contains few elements of a typical rock-and-roll album. Opening with the words, "If I ventured into the slipstream/ Between the viaducts of your dream . . . ," the album in many ways indicated the path that Morrison would travel in the music world: It used noted jazz musicians, such as Modern Jazz Quartet drummer Connie Kay and reed player John Payne; it featured horns and strings instead of electric guitar and bass; and its songs, such as the title song, "Cyprus Avenue," "Slim Slow Slider," and "Beside You," deal with childhood, rebirth, personal transformation, and redemption.

Astral Weeks would remain on the Top-10 lists of rock critics for decades, but it was not a commercial success. With little money, Morrison hoped to make a more commercial album and released *Moondance* in 1970. With songs ranging from the warmth of "Crazy Love" to the joyful, jazzy lilt of the title track, *Moondance* was Morrison's first million-selling album.

In 1968, Morrison secretly married Janet Planet, a young actress and singer. They settled in Woodstock, New York, before moving to California. They had a daughter, Shana, and seemed to have an idyllic life, pictures from which appear on the albums *His Band and the Street Choir* (1970) and the country-tinged *Tupelo Honey* (1971). However, Morrison's moodiness and reclusive behavior led to the breakup of his marriage in 1973.

Themes. Little of Morrison's work fits the standard definition of rock or pop music. Many of his songs incorporate Celtic themes and mythology, and he has recorded many traditional Irish songs with the well-known Irish group the Chieftains. He has set the poetry of William Butler Yeats to music and paid tribute to literary figures in "Rave On, John Donne." He has incorporated the names and lyrics of poets Yeats, William Blake, Walt Whitman, Patrick Kavanagh, and others into his music, alongside references to such earthy blues greats as Muddy Waters and Leadbelly.

Although he insists that little of his music is autobiographical, he often sang of his early musical influences and his continuing disdain for the music business and those he believed wronged him in his early days. Remembrances of his childhood and youth in Belfast, such as "On Hyndford Street," "And It Stoned Me," and "In the Days Before Rock and Roll," typify his ability to evoke a sense of place and time in a way seldom attempted in rock or pop music.

The spiritual is essential to much of Morrison's work, and spiritual healing is a recurrent theme. Over the years he has recorded "Till We Get the Healing Done," "Did Ye Get Healed?" and a song and album entitled "The Healing Game." Although he has immersed himself in a variety of religious traditions, including Buddhism, Christianity, and Scientology, he has drawn from all and subscribed exclusively to none. In interviews in the 1980's concerning his song "In the Garden," which contains the phrase, "No guru, no method, no teacher" (the title of the album on which it appears), Morrison spoke of his desire to lead his listeners through a meditative experience. The title phrase also explains Morrison's insistence that he not be seen as a cult figure or leader, and that he does not subscribe to a specific religion or philosophical standard.

Spiritual concerns do not dominate Morrison's work, however—religious songs such as "When Will I Ever Learn to Live in God" alternate in Morrison's repertoire with tender love songs such as "Tupelo Honey" and songs incorporating earthy references to "back-street jellyroll" (old blues slang for sexual activity), such as "And the Healing Has Begun."

While his 1980's releases often had a new-age sound to them, his 1990's albums returned to some of his early influences: the heavily blues-oriented live double compact disc, *A Night in San Francisco* (1994), a collection of jazz standards, *How Long Has This Been Going On?* (1995), and 1997's *The Healing Game*, which includes a 1950's-style doo-wop ditty entitled "It Used to Be My Life."

For the Record

When Van Morrison left Bang for Warner Bros., Bang still owned the rights to his next several songs. Morrison disdainfully recorded a series of brief nonsense ditties with titles such as "Shake and Roll," "Twist and Shake," "Big Royalty Check," and "Dumb Dumb George." Bert Berns's widow, exhausted after her husband's recent death, chose to accept these as fulfillment of Morrison's contract, although they were commercially useless.

Live Performances. Despite Morrison's enduring popularity in the United States, he performs only a few concerts a year in that country, preferring to perform at clubs, festivals, and concerts in Europe, primarily in Ireland, Northern Ireland, and England. Morrison is fiercely protective of his private life and shuns publicity, going years without granting interviews, seldom touring in support of the new albums he releases regularly, and rarely appearing on U.S. television.

Short, stocky, and balding, Morrison is still a commanding presence on stage. Although he was a temperamental performer in earlier years—at times walking off the stage after only a few songs if he were displeased with the audience or the band—Morrison has become a more consistent and relaxed performer. His backup bands comprise excellent musicians, often from the jazz world, and special guests are often blues greats such as John Lee Hooker (with whom Morrison has recorded on a number of occasions), Jimmy Witherspoon, and James Hunter.

Like a jazz scat singer, Morrison uses his voice like an instrument. Groans, growls, and breathy grunts punctuate many of his songs. Gospel-inspired call and response is often heard in long concert pieces, and at times he hypnotically repeats key phrases. Consistently defying the traditional expectations of the music business, Morrison has continued to make the music he wants and to touch the hearts, souls, and minds of his fans in a manner unique among rock and pop performers. —*Irene Struthers*

SELECT DISCOGRAPHY

■ SINGLES

"Brown Eyed Girl," 1967
"Domino," 1970
"Wild Night," 1971

■ ALBUMS

Blowin' Your Mind, 1967
The Best of Van Morrison, 1967
Astral Weeks, 1968
Moondance, 1970
His Band and the Street Choir, 1970
Tupelo Honey, 1971
It's Too Late to Stop Now, 1974
Into the Music, 1979
Common One, 1980
Live at the Grand Opera House Belfast, 1984
No Guru, No Method, No Teacher, 1986
Poetic Champions Compose, 1987
Irish Heartbeat, 1988 (with the Chieftains)
Avalon Sunset, 1989
The Best of Van Morrison, 1990
Hymns to the Silence, 1991
Too Long in Exile, 1993
A Night in San Francisco, 1994
How Long Has This Been Going On? 1995
The Healing Game, 1997

SELECT AWARDS

Rock and Roll Hall of Fame, inducted 1993
Grammy Award for Best Pop Collaboration with Vocals for "Have I Told You Lately That I Love You," 1995 (with the Chieftains)
Officer of the Order of the British Empire, named 1996
Grammy Award for Best Pop Collaboration with Vocals for "Don't Look Back," 1997 (with John Lee Hooker)

SEE ALSO: Hooker, John Lee; Leadbelly.

Morrissey. *See* The Smiths / Morrissey

Steve Morse

BORN: Hamilton, Ohio; July 28, 1954
FIRST ALBUM RELEASE: *Free Fall,* 1977 (with the Dixie Dregs)
MUSICAL STYLES: Rock and roll, country rock, southern rock, jazz fusion

If there were a decathlon for guitarists, Steve Morse would most likely be its gold medalist. His mastery of many styles—rock, fusion, classical, country—has been unequaled. He won *Guitar Player* magazine's Award for Best Overall Guitarist five years in a row (1982-1986), only to turn around and win Best Country Guitarist in

1986. An open-ears approach has allowed him to appear on recordings and stages with musicians as varied as Eddie Van Halen, John McLaughlin, Albert Lee, Liza Minelli, and reggae group Eek-a-Mouse.

In his three-decade career, Morse has earned a reputation as an unerring perfectionist in the studio, a guitarist's guitarist who combines head-spinning technical prowess with intelligence, taste, and finesse. He is usually included in the instrumental guitar bible of Joe Satriani, Steve Vai, and Eric Johnson and was elevated into *Guitar Player* magazine's Gallery of Greats in 1986.

Beginnings. Morse moved to Georgia with his family at age thirteen. After picking up the guitar, he quickly came under the influence of the reigning 1960's guitar heroes, Jimi Hendrix, Jeff Beck, Eric Clapton, Jimmy Page, and Ritchie Blackmore, whom he would later replace in Deep Purple. Morse began his professional career traveling the Georgia and Carolinas bar-band circuit in a band he and bassist Andy West put together called Dixie Grits.

It was not until he entered the guitar department at the University of Miami that his talent for sophisticated harmonies and melodic development beyond the standard 4/4 rock and boogie fare began to blossom. The turning point came the night he attended a recital in Atlanta, Georgia, by classical guitarist Juan Mercadal. Stunned by Mercadal's artistry and control, Morse asked for lessons. Mercadal told him he first had to learn the textbook rudiments of theory and technique, then apply to the University of Miami where the classical guitarist was a faculty member.

The Dixie Dregs. The famed Dixie Dregs were born at the school in 1974. The catalyst for the band came from a campus performance by John McLaughlin's original Mahavishnu Orchestra, which showed Morse a way to keep rock's intensity while advancing its vocabulary. The Dregs found a magical balance between McLaughlin's rhythmic and harmonic complexity and the straightforward southern boogie of the Allman Brothers Band, running the gamut from high-energy fusion suites to intricate chamber pieces to frenetic bluegrass breakdowns. With his blazing riffs over seamless, odd-time shifts at breakneck speeds, Morse was the centerpiece of the band.

For the Record

True to its title, Steve Morse began the album *Coast to Coast* in his garage in California, then finished it in his new garage after he moved to Florida, recording the guitar parts outside in a converted U-Haul trailer.

The Dixie Dregs (or Dregs, depending on the record label) released nearly a dozen albums, uniting and disbanding as inspiration and outside projects permitted. The guitarist would also front the Steve Morse Band, a harder, more rock-based trio, and release solo recordings.

His tenure with Kansas, for whom he also played violin, yielded two albums, 1986's *Power* and 1988's *In the Spirit of Things*. As he has admitted, the democratic approach of a band without a central figurehead ran contrary to the Morse code of total control over his projects.

Flying Fingers to Flying Planes. Between Kansas releases, the guitarist left the road and took to the sky to pursue another passion, flying. He ferried passengers around the southeastern United States for a commuter airline, a job that gave him regular hours (and a shorter haircut) and freedom from the pressures of supporting his own salaried band and road crew. Of course, though he would maintain his license and continue to own several small planes, music always beckoned. He was soon back on the road and in the studio with the Dixie Dregs, Kansas, the Steve Morse Band, and more recently, Deep Purple, where he followed in the footsteps of former guitarists Ritchie Blackmore, Tommy Bolin, and Joe Satriani. —*Tim Bradley*

SELECT DISCOGRAPHY

with the Dixie Dregs

■ ALBUMS

What If, 1978

Night of the Living Dregs, 1979

Unsung Heroes, 1981
Industry Standard, 1982
Bring 'em Back Alive, 1992
King Biscuit Presents Dixie Dregs, 1997

with the Steve Morse Band

■ ALBUMS
The Introduction, 1984
High Tension Wires, 1989 (solo)
Southern Steel, 1991
Coast to Coast, 1992
StressFest, 1996

with Kansas

■ ALBUMS
Power, 1986
In the Spirit of Things, 1988

SELECT AWARDS
Guitar Player magazine, named Best Overall Guitarist, 1982, 1983, 1984, 1985, 1986
Guitar Player magazine, named Best Guitar Album, 1982, 1989
Guitar Player magazine, named Best Country Guitarist, 1986

SEE ALSO: Deep Purple; Kansas.

The Mothers of Invention. *See* Frank Zappa / The Mothers of Invention

Mötley Crüe

ORIGINAL MEMBERS: Nikki Sixx (b. Frank Carlton Serafino Ferranno, 1958), Vince Neil (b. Vincent Neil Wharton, 1961), Tommy Lee (b. Thomas Lee Bass, 1962), Mick Mars (b. Robert Deal, 1956)
OTHER MEMBERS: John Corabi (b. 1959)
FIRST ALBUM RELEASE: *Too Fast for Love*, 1981
MUSICAL STYLES: Rock and roll, heavy metal

With leather clothes, makeup, teased hair, and an imposing, self-assured attitude, Mötley Crüe epitomized Los Angeles "glam metal." Their mission was to create escapist entertainment.

Coming Together. As a teenager, Frank Feranno's ambition was to move to Los Angeles from San Jose, California. Once there, he acquired a bass, christened himself Nikki Sixx, and, in 1979, formed a "glam" band called London. When London failed to secure a record deal, Sixx tried a new lineup. Seventeen-year-old drummer Tommy Lee had been a London fan eager to work with Sixx. An advertisement in a music newspaper seeking a Loud, Rude, Aggressive Guitarist Available introduced Mick Mars to the group. At the famed L.A. Starwood nightclub, the three saw a band called Rock Candy. As legend has it, Sixx and Lee cornered lead singer Vince Neil in the restroom and asked him to join their band. Sixx wanted to call the group Christmas until Mars came up with the name Mottley Krue. The spelling was modified and umlauts added for a formidable Germanic look.

Record Deal. An ornate stage show, complete with shocking props, built them a loyal following ready for the band's self-financed debut album, *Too Fast for Love*. An Elektra executive saw the album, attended a concert, and signed the group to a contract in 1981. Elektra remixed, reproduced, and rereleased *Too Fast for Love* in August, 1982.

Rock-and-Roll Excesses. Mötley Crüe's 1983 sophomore release, *Shout at the Devil*, featured an aggressive fist-in-the-air sound that was tempered by a top-notch producer. The band was living high during this period. However, liner notes extolling alcohol and drugs appeared to be both an explanation for their behavior and an omen of impending downfall.

Soon, high times took their toll. Sixx, Lee, and Neil were each involved in serious car accidents. Neil caused a collision that resulted in the death of Nicholas "Razzle" Dingley, the drummer of Finnish "glam" band Hanoi Rocks.

Narcotics became an even bigger factor during 1985, when *Theatre of Pain* was released. Lyrically, it was Sixx's cry for help; veiled drug references infiltrate most of the songs. The album includes a mix of anthems, quirky covers, and ballads. Among them is one of Mötley Crüe's most loved songs, "Home Sweet Home." The video for the song received extensive MTV airplay and helped make the album a quadruple-platinum success.

The 1987 album *Girls, Girls, Girls,* was dark in mood and lewd in subject matter. The videos were considered too distasteful for MTV (though the video channel did play them years later). On December 22, 1987, Sixx suffered a heroin overdose. His heart stopped beating for two minutes before doctors resuscitated him. Erroneously informed of Sixx's death, the rest of the band vowed to overcome their drug habits and eventually convinced Sixx to do the same.

Road to Recovery. The newly detoxified Mötley Crüe spent one year recording 1989's *Dr. Feelgood.* The album features Sixx's best lyrics, filled with colorful characters and thought-provoking subject matter. This was the first Mötley Crüe album to reach number 1 on the *Billboard* charts. In 1990, the album was nominated for a Grammy Award and an American Music Award. The videos gave fans their first glimpse of the new band—fit, trim, alert, but still cocky. The accompanying live shows featured pyrotechnics, lasers, scantily clad backup singers, and Lee and his drumset suspended from the ceiling.

Changes. In 1991, the band re-signed with Elektra for a reported twenty-five million dollars. A compilation album, *Decade of Decadence '81-'91*, marked Mötley Crüe's tenth anniversary. However, the celebration was short-lived. In February of 1992, Neil was abruptly fired from the band.

For the Record

"I absorb everything and it goes into my mind and comes out in some sick, demented way. How can you worry about rhyming? There's no soul in that. It just kind of happens. . . . I think escapism is really important. What I'm doing is something that, maybe, can change [a kid's] life. It's a little bit of escapism that allows a person to get on with the things they have to do in life." —*Nikki Sixx, 1990*

The vocalist quickly formed his own band and released an album, 1993's *Exposed.* Mötley Crüe regrouped with a young singer named John Corabi and released *Mötley Crüe* in 1994.

In 1997, Mötley Crüe reemerged with *Generation Swine* and lead singer Neil. In many ways the album reflected the group members' transistion into well-grounded family men. Though the album did feature a remake of "Shout at the Devil," somehow the sound was not the same as in the 1980's. Elektra quietly dropped the band from the label in 1998. —*Deirdre Rockmaker*

SELECT DISCOGRAPHY

■ ALBUMS

Too Fast for Love, 1981 (rereleased in 1982)
Shout at the Devil, 1983
Theatre of Pain, 1985
Girls, Girls, Girls, 1987
Dr. Feelgood, 1989
Decade of Decadence '81-'91, 1991 (compilation)
Mötley Crüe, 1994
Generation Swine, 1997

SEE ALSO: Aerosmith; Def Leppard; Guns n' Roses.

Anne Murray

BORN: Springfield, Nova Scotia, Canada; June 20, 1945
FIRST ALBUM RELEASE: *What About Me,* 1968
MUSICAL STYLES: Country, pop, folk

Anne Murray was Canada's first international female singing star. She is one of the foremost interpreters of contemporary pop music.

Background. The daughter of physician James Carson Murray and nurse Marion Margaret Murray, Anne Murray (full name Morna Anne Murray) was born in the coal-mining town of Springhill, Nova Scotia. The family's only daughter, Anne grew up with her five brothers. She always loved to sing and has said that she was singing all the time by the time she was seven years old. She took piano and vocal lessons. In high school, she enjoyed pop and folk music. At fifteen she sang in public for the first time. Murray has said she was absolutely terrified by the experience—but that she could not wait to do it again. She attended the University of New Brunswick and completed a bachelor's degree in physical education. While she was a sophomore, in 1964, she had her first professional audition for the Canadian Broadcasting Corporation's (CBC's) television show *Singalong Jubilee.* She was told that there were already enough altos in the cast. Although she was unsuccessful in getting the job, she did become a regular on the CBC musical program *Let's Go* in Halifax.

In 1966, two years after her *Singalong Jubilee* audition, the show's cohost and associate producer Bill Langstroth contacted her again and convinced her to join the show. At the time, Murray was working as a physical education teacher. She joined the show, and this is when her singing career began to blossom. In 1975 she married Langstroth, and they settled in Toronto, Ontario. Murray has always maintained that her family is her top priority, and when she and Langstroth had children, the whole family went on tour together.

Recording and Performing Career. Brian Ahern, who was the musical director of *Singalong Jubilee,* invited Murray to record an album for the little-known Arc Records, and in 1968 *What About Me* was released. Later she signed with Capitol Records, a partnership that was to last for the next twenty-two years. Murray's first major hit single, in 1970, was Gene McLellan's "Snowbird." With that song Murray became the first female artist from Canada ever to receive a gold record in the United States.

Murray released some thirty albums between 1968 and 1998. Her second big hit, in 1973, was her recording of Kenny Loggins's song "Danny's Song." Since then, her name has regularly appeared on both the pop and country charts. Worldwide, her album sales exceed twenty-four million copies. Her albums have attained multiplatinum status in North America and Australia and silver status in the United Kingdom. Murray has performed sold-out shows at venues such as Carnegie Hall and Radio City Music Hall in New York City, the Palladium in London, England, and the Royal Alexandra Theatre in Toronto. According to Murray, the high points of her career have included opening in Las Vegas and seeing Frank Sinatra's marquee on the other side of the street, and winning a Grammy Award for "You Needed Me" in 1978.

Murray says that she has always focused on what pleases her audiences the most. She has consistently worked on the range and the tone of her rich, velvety voice. She has also noted that she must be touched in some way by a song in order to interpret it in a way that affects others. Her "girl next door" image has also helped to endear her to her millions of fans. Among her hobbies, Murray is an avid golfer.

Through the 1990's Murray continued to be a very productive artist.

In 1993 she recorded the album *Croonin',* a collection of 1950's torch songs. In 1994 a three-disc boxed set retrospective of her career called *Now and Forever* was released. In 1996 she toured actively, playing thirty-one cities in the United States between August and October. Starting in November of that same year she held her first concert tour of Canada—a one-month, nineteen-city tour. Her first live album, *An Intimate Evening with Anne Murray,* was released in 1997.

Murray has received a huge number of awards, including four Grammys, three American Music Awards, three Country Music Association Awards, three Canadian Country Music Association

For the Record

Anne Murray's first brush with professional music came in 1964, when she auditioned for a Canadian television show, *Singalong Jubilee,* while she was attending college. Two years later she was surprised when the show's musical director approached her about making a record. "I thought they were crazy," she later said. "Singing was something you did in the bathtub and around bonfires. I felt there was no security in singing."

Awards, and almost thirty Juno (Canadian Music) Awards. In 1980 the Canadian Recording Industry Association honored her as its Female Recording Artist of the Decade. Her 1988 CBC Christmas Special was the most widely viewed program of the decade. In 1995 she was presented with the prestigious Canadian Governor General's Award, which is given to Canadians of "extraordinary talent and accomplishment." She is also an officer of the Order of Canada. In 1989 the Anne Murray Centre opened in her hometown of Springhill, Nova Scotia. —*Patricia L. Gibbs*

Anne Murray in 1974 (AP/Wide World Photos)

SELECT DISCOGRAPHY

■ SINGLES

"What About Me," 1968
"Snowbird," 1970
"Danny's Song," 1972
"What About Me," 1973
"You Needed Me," 1978
"Shadows in the Moonlight," 1979
"Could I Have This Dance," 1980
"If I Ever Fall in Love Again," 1989 (with Kenny Rogers)
"Bluebird," 1990

■ ALBUMS

What About Me, 1968
This Way Is My Way, 1969
Snowbird, 1970
Anne Murray/Glen Campbell, 1972
Annie, 1972
Danny's Song, 1973
Anne Murray's Greatest Hits, 1980
Something to Talk About, 1986
Anne Murray's Country Hits, 1987
As I Am, 1988
Croonin', 1993
The Best . . . So Far, 1994 (compilation)
Now and Forever, 1994 (boxed set)
The Best of the Season, 1994
Anne Murray, 1996
An Intimate Evening with Anne Murray, 1997

SELECT AWARDS

Juno Award for Country Female Vocalist of the Year, 1971; between 1971 and 1998 Murray won almost thirty more Juno Awards
Grammy Award for Best Country Vocal Performance, Female, for "Love Song," 1975
Officer of the Order of Canada, 1975
Grammy Award for Best Pop Vocal Performance, Female, for "You Needed Me," 1978
Canadian Recording Industry Association Female Recording Artist of the Decade, 1980
Hollywood Walk of Fame, star awarded 1980
Grammy Award for Best Country Vocal Performance, Female, for "Could I Have This Dance," 1980
American Music Award, Female Country Singer, 1982
Grammy Award for Best Country Vocal Performance, Female, for "A Little Good News," 1983
Country Music Association Award for Single of the Year for "A Little Good News" and for Album of the Year for *A Little Good News*, 1984
Canadian Country Music Association Award for Single of the Year for "A Little Good News," 1984

Country Music Association Award for Vocal Duo of the Year for "Nobody Loves Me Like You Do," 1985 (with Dave Loggins)
Canadian Country Music Association Awards for Single of the Year and Song of the Year for "Now and Forever (You and Me)," 1986 (wr. with David Foster, Jim Vallance, and Randy Goodrum)
Juno Hall of Fame, inducted 1993
Canadian Governor General's Award, 1995

SEE ALSO: Loggins and Messina / Kenny Loggins.

N

Rick Nelson

BORN: Teaneck, New Jersey; May 8, 1940
DIED: DeKalb, Texas; December 31, 1985
FIRST ALBUM RELEASE: *Ricky*, 1957
MUSICAL STYLES: Pop, country rock

When *Billboard* first introduced its Hot 100 chart on August 4, 1958, Ricky Nelson was at the top with "Poor Little Fool," his ninth Top-20 hit. This phenomenal success led writers to coin the term "teen idol" for Ricky Nelson, who was still only eighteen years old. Unlike other teen stars such as Frankie Avalon and Fabian, Nelson was a genuine musical talent whose cleancut image paved the way for middle-class acceptance of rock and roll in the United States.

Beginnings. Eric Hilliard Nelson came from one of the most famous families in the United States. His father, Oswald (Ozzie), was a bandleader who had a string of hits in the 1930's and 1940's. His mother, Harriet Hilliard, had been a singer and an actress since the early 1930's. Together they put together a radio program, *The Adventures of Ozzie and Harriet*, which went to television in 1952 and remained a staple of family programming until 1966. Ricky and his older brother David got their start in 1949, and the younger Nelson soon proved to be the most popular character on the program. Long before he released his first record, Ricky Nelson was a teen heartthrob and a star in his own right.

As a teen, Nelson became a fan of Sun Records rockabilly stars Carl Perkins and Jerry Lee Lewis. When a girlfriend once swooned over Elvis Presley, the sixteen-year-old Nelson declared that he too was making a record, and he used the television series' orchestra to back him on Fats Domino's "I'm Walking." Worked into the storyline, Nelson's singing debut aired on his television show on April 10, 1957, and the resulting single eventually went to number 4 on the pop charts. With ready-made video promotion, until *The Adventures of Ozzie and Harriet* went off the air in 1966, Nelson produced a remarkable string of thirty-three Top-40 hits between 1957 and 1964, including "Be-Bop Baby" (number 3, 1957), "Stood Up" (number 2, 1957), "Poor Little Fool" (number 1, 1958), "Lonesome Town" (number 7, 1958), "It's Late" (number 9, 1959), "Travelin' Man" (number 1, 1961), "Hello Mary Lou" (number 9, 1961), and "For You" (number 6, 1964).

Country Rock. As American rock and roll was eclipsed by the "British invasion" of the mid-1960's, Nelson struggled to find a new musical presence. He pioneered the emerging field of country rock (*Bright Lights & Country Music*, 1966; *Country Fever*, 1967), performing covers of material by Doug Kershaw, Willie Nelson, and Hank Williams, along with his own material. In 1969 he

Rick Nelson (Arkent Archive)

formed the Stone Canyon Band, which included former Poco bassist Randy Meisner (later of the Eagles), and had a minor hit with a cover of Bob Dylan's "She Belongs to Me" (number 33, 1969). Though the sound did not gain favor with the public, critics applauded it, and groups such as Fleetwood Mac and the Eagles acknowledged their debt to Nelson.

Nelson disliked carrying his teen-idol image into adulthood. He resisted typical teen-film roles to play in more serious films such as Howard Hawks's classic *Rio Bravo* (1959) with John Wayne. Later, when he headlined a rock-and-roll revival show at New York's Madison Square Garden in 1972, Nelson was booed when he played his later material. Out of this experience came his final hit record, "Garden Party" (number 6, 1972), with its famous lyric: "If you gotta play at garden parties/ I wish you a lotta luck/ But if memories were all I sang/ I'd rather drive a truck." In the midst of a bitter and protracted divorce, Nelson was penniless but still resisted a long-term offer to play in Las Vegas, Nevada.

Carrying On. Throughout the late 1970's and early 1980's Nelson toured incessantly, sometimes singing more than 250 nights per year. By 1985, he was performing more of his old material, plus many of the rockabilly classics he had cut his musical teeth on. While on tour in December, he closed his final performance with Buddy Holly's "Rave On." The next night his airplane crashed en route to Dallas, Texas, killing the original teen idol. Nelson was inducted into the Rock and Roll Hall of Fame in 1987. *—John Powell*

For the Record

The Nelsons are the only family to have produced three generations of chart-toppers. Ozzie Nelson had thirty-eight hits in the 1930's, including "And Then Some," which went to number 1 in 1935. Ricky Nelson hit the top with "Poor Little Fool" (1958) and "Travelin' Man" (1961). Ricky's twin sons, recording under the name Nelson, did the same with "(Can't Live Without Your) Love and Affection," which topped the charts in 1990.

SELECT DISCOGRAPHY

■ SINGLES

"A Teenager's Romance," 1957
"I'm Walking," 1957
"Be-Bop Baby," 1957
"Poor Little Fool," 1958
"Travelin' Man"/"Hello Mary Lou," 1961
"Teen Age Idol," 1962
"Fools Rush In," 1963
"Garden Party," 1972

■ ALBUMS

Ricky, 1957
Ricky Nelson, 1958
Songs by Ricky, 1959
Ricky Is 21, 1961
Album Seven by Rick, 1962
For Your Sweet Love, 1963
Bright Lights and Country Music, 1966
Country Fever, 1967
Another Side of Rick, 1968
Rick Nelson in Concert, 1970
Garden Party, 1972
Windfall, 1974
Playing to Win, 1981
Best of Rick Nelson, 1963-1975, 1990 (compilation)
Best of Rick Nelson, Vol. 2, 1991 (compilation)

SELECT AWARDS

Grammy Award for Best Spoken Word or Nonmusical Recording for *Interviews from the Class of '55 Recording Sessions*, 1986 (with others)
Rock and Roll Hall of Fame, inducted 1987

SEE ALSO: Everly Brothers, The; Presley, Elvis.

Willie Nelson

BORN: Abbott, Texas; April 30, 1933
FIRST SINGLE RELEASE: "No Place for Me"/"Lumberjack," 1956
MUSICAL STYLES: Country, pop

In addition to being one of the most popular and commercially successful musical artists of his time, Willie Nelson brought a fresh new attitude and sound to country music which changed it forever. With his long, braided hair and battered Martin classical guitar, Nelson did not fit the stereotypical image of a country-and-western star. He expanded the horizons of country music when he began releasing concept albums, and he widened its audience by appealing to a generation that usually listened to rock and roll.

Roots. Nelson was raised by his grandparents in a small farming town sixty miles outside Fort Worth, Texas. He received his first guitar at age six. While growing up, Nelson listened to African American blues, gospel, country standards broadcast over the radio, the western swing of Bob Wills, and popular music such as that of Hoagy Carmichael, which his older sister Bobbie practiced on the family piano. Nelson later recalled that his guitar influences included jazz great Django Reinhardt and Spanish flamenco guitarist Carlos Montoya. His exposure to different styles made Nelson open-minded and willing to cross musical boundaries, an element essential to his success as a musician.

Nelson formed his first band at age thirteen. Inspired by the music of Ernest Tubb, Nelson longed for success as a honky-tonk performer. During the 1950's he held various day jobs while playing the honky-tonks at night. He also honed his skills as a songwriter, writing classics such as "Family Bible" and "Night Life." Unfortunately, Nelson had to sell the rights to his songs for living expenses. He used the $150 he made from selling "Night Life," a song which was eventually recorded by more than seventy artists and sold more than thirty million copies, to buy a secondhand car.

In 1961 Nelson moved to Nashville, Tennessee, the recording capital of country music. During the 1960's he achieved success as a songwriter, penning the hits "Crazy," "Hello Walls," and "Funny How the Time Slips Away" for artists such as Patsy Cline. Nelson kept his rights to these songs and earned substantial royalties. He also recorded his own albums during this period, but he did not have any notable hits. His musical philosophy differed from that of the record company executives who dominated the country music industry. Using a technique he learned from listening to Frank Sinatra, Nelson often phrased his lyrics on the offbeat, a singing style contrary to the standard Nashville sound. Nashville record producers preferred a lush sound which often included bloated string arrangements, an approach Nelson did not like. They also insisted on using studio musicians, while Nelson wanted to work with his own band. Nelson's diverse musical interests contributed to his lack of recognition as a performer during the 1960's but would prove essential to his success in the coming years.

The Austin Sound. Frustrated with the Nashville music establishment, Nelson moved to the small town of Bandera, Texas, near the state capital of Austin, in 1971. Austin was a college town that tolerated long hair, unusual clothing, and discreet drug use. Nelson enjoyed the city's relaxed and progressive attitude. He became associated with a group of country musicians later known as outlaws (a tag Nelson disliked). The outlaws rejected the stale formulas of Nashville and returned to the honesty and simplicity of country music's roots. Their liberal attitudes and casual dress appealed to people who were not typically country music fans. During this period Nelson experimented with new approaches to country music. On the album *Yesterday's Wine* (1971), Nelson's songs told the story of a man remembering his life as he watches his own funeral. Rock groups such as the Who had released concept albums, but Nelson was the first country artist to do so. Although *Yesterday's Wine* was not a commercial success, Nelson enjoyed writing concept albums and would return to that format in the future.

The move to Texas coincided with a move from RCA to Atlantic Records. Nelson completed his first album with Atlantic, *Shotgun Willie* (1973), in less than two days. His next record, *Phases and Stages* (1974), was a concept album that examined a failing marriage. It sold more than 400,000 copies. The popularity of *Phases and Stages* allowed Nelson to start his own record label with a distri-

Willie Nelson in 1996 (Paul Natkin)

bution contract from CBS Records that allowed him complete artistic control. He chose an old country ballad, "Red Headed Stranger," as the centerpiece for his next album. Released in 1975, *Red Headed Stranger* told the story of a cowboy in the Old West who had lost his true love. The album sold more than one half million copies, and the single "Blue Eyes Crying in the Rain" reached number 1 on the charts. Willie Nelson, the outlaw musician who had turned his back on Nashville, had become the most popular country artist in America.

Stardom. Willie Nelson became an icon, representing both Texas and country music to most Americans. The album *Wanted: The Outlaws* (1976), a compilation featuring Nelson, Waylon Jennings, Tompall Glaser, and Jessi Colter, became the first Nashville album to sell one million copies. A duet with Waylon Jennings, "Good Hearted Woman," was one of the most popular country singles of 1976. The album *Waylon and Willie* (1978) debuted at number 1 on the country charts. Nelson, who loved life on the road, gave more than two hundred concerts each year. His annual Fourth of July picnics, which he began in 1973, became hugely popular, even though they earned a reputation for poor organization and rowdy crowd behavior.

Fame and fortune allowed Nelson to exercise his artistic freedom and explore the musical styles that had interested him in his youth. He recorded an album of standards that included the hit single "Georgia on My Mind." Entitled *Stardust* (1978), the album eventually sold more than five million copies, proving that his fans would follow him as he tested his musical skills. Nelson's duet with Spanish singer Julio Iglesias in 1984, "To All the Girls I've Loved Before," was an international hit. In addition to writing and performing music, Nelson began to act. He had a small part in the motion picture *Electric Horseman* (1979) and then starred in *Honeysuckle Rose* (1980), a film about a touring country music star. The soundtrack album included the hit single "On the Road Again," destined to become Nelson's signature piece. Nelson did not use his fame to pursue merely artistic interests. He drew attention to the economic plight of American farmers with his Farm Aid concerts, the first of which was held in 1985.

However, success had its downside. The constant touring put strains on Nelson's family life. Fans flocked to his home outside Austin, and Nelson decided to move his family to Colorado. His considerable income allowed him to make extensive real estate purchases, but he received poor financial advice, and in 1990 the Internal Revenue Service declared that Nelson owed $16.7 million in unpaid taxes and penalties. The bill was later reduced to $9 million, but Nelson lost many of his assets, including his Colorado home. Although he remained a popular performer, Nelson never matched his record sales of the late 1970's and early 1980's, and some critics complained that he had lost his creative spark.

Despite these problems, Nelson had secured his place in history as one of the greats in country music. Many of his compositions, including "Hello Walls" and "Night Life," had become country-and-western standards. Moreover, his willingness to take risks, to buck the music establishment, and to expand the boundaries of country music provided an inspiring example to young artists. —*Thomas Clarkin*

SELECT DISCOGRAPHY

■ ALBUMS

Yesterday's Wine, 1971
Shotgun Willie, 1973
Phases and Stages, 1974
Red Headed Stranger, 1975
Wanted: The Outlaws, 1976 (with Waylon Jennings, Tompall Glaser, and Jessi Colter)
To Lefty from Willie, 1977
Waylon and Willie, 1978 (with Waylon Jennings)
Stardust, 1978
Honeysuckle Rose, 1980 (sound track)
Always on My Mind, 1982
Who'll Buy My Memories, 1991
Across the Borderline, 1993
Teatro, 1998

For the Record

By 1997 Willie Nelson had released more than one hundred albums, including six collections of pop standards, and had appeared on the *Billboard* charts eighty times.

SELECT AWARDS

Nashville Songwriters Hall of Fame, inducted 1973
Grammy Award for Best Country Vocal Performance, Male, for "Blue Eyes Crying in the Rain," 1975
Country Music Association Album of the Year Award for *Wanted: The Outlaws* (with Waylon Jennings, Tompall Glaser, and Jessi Colter), Single of the Year Award for "Good Hearted Woman" (with Waylon Jennings), and Vocal Duo of the Year Award (with Waylon Jennings), 1976
Grammy Award for Best Country Vocal Performance by a Duo or Group for "Mamas Don't Let Your Babies Grow Up to Be Cowboys," 1978 (with Waylon Jennings)
Grammy Award for Best Country Vocal Performance, Male, for "Georgia on My Mind," 1978
Country Music Association Entertainer of the Year Award, 1979
Grammy Award for Best Country Song for "On the Road Again," 1980
Grammy Award for Best Country Vocal Performance, Male, for "Always on My Mind," 1982
Country Music Association Album of the Year Award for *Always on My Mind* and Single of the Year Award for "Always on My Mind," 1982
Country Music Association Vocal Duo of the Year Award, 1983 (with Merle Haggard)
Country Music Association Vocal Duo of the Year Award, 1984 (with Julio Iglesias)
National Farmers Organization Special Humanitarian Award, 1986
Grammy Living Legends Award, 1990
Country Music Hall of Fame, inducted 1993

SEE ALSO: Cline, Patsy; Frizzell, Lefty; Iglesias, Julio; Jennings, Waylon; Kristofferson, Kris; Tubb, Ernest; Wills, Bob and His Texas Playboys.

The Neville Brothers / Aaron Neville

The Neville Brothers

MEMBERS: Art Neville (b. 1937), Charles Neville (b. 1939), Aaron Neville (b. 1941), Cyril Neville (b. 1948)

FIRST ALBUM RELEASE: *Wild Tchoupitoulas*, 1976

Aaron Neville

BORN: New Orleans, Louisiana; January 24, 1941

FIRST ALBUM RELEASE: *Greatest Hits*, 1990

MUSICAL STYLES: Rhythm and blues, blues, funk, soul

The Neville Brothers are among the foremost ambassadors of New Orleans music. Born and bred in the city's Calliope projects, brothers Art, Charles, Aaron, and Cyril (in order of descending age), have been visible in popular music since the 1950's. Their music owes a debt to generations of New Orleans musicians, from brass bands to the earliest roots of jazz to the rhumba to the rhythm-and-blues piano of Professor Longhair. Steeped in these traditions, the brothers have moved their music forward by incorporating more contemporary traditions of disco, reggae, rock, rhythm and blues, and world music as they have gone along.

Beginnings. Art Neville (keyboards) played in the studio behind Little Richard, toured with Larry Williams, and was a member of the Hawketts, who had a regional hit with "Mardi Gras Mambo" in 1954. In the 1970's, Art's band the Meters was produced by New Orleans legend Allen Toussaint, made "Hey Pocky a-Way" popular, and opened for the Rolling Stones on their "Tour of the Americas." Charles (saxophone) did extensive session work in Memphis, Tennessee, playing with Big Joe Turner, Bobby "Blue" Bland, Wilson Pickett, B. B. King, and others. He also played in the house band at New Orleans' Dew Drop Inn, where the biggest stars of the blues and rhythm and blues would appear. He also taught saxophone at Goddard College in Vermont for a time. Aaron (vocals) performed in local New Orleans groups and had a solo hit with "Tell It Like It Is" in 1966. The first group which featured three of the brothers was the Neville Sounds, but they did not last long.

The Neville Brothers Band. In the mid-1970's, all four of the brothers recorded together for the first time on a project called *Wild Tchoupitoulas* (1976). This album, spearheaded by their uncle George "Chief Jolly" Landry commemorated the sights and sounds of the Mardi Gras Indians, specifically the time when runaway slaves were sheltered by Native Americans upon reaching their settlements. It was Landry who urged the brothers to record together under their own name to fulfill their parents' dreams. They worked together in New Orleans clubs and regionally for several years before realizing those dreams.

In 1981 they created *Fiyo on the Bayou*, which featured hot, danceable music. The group covered the Meters' "Hey Pocky a-Way," Jimmy Cliff's "Sitting in Limbo," the doo-wop classic "Ten Commandments of Love," and two New Orleans standards in a medley, "Brother John/Iko Iko." On the strength of this record, which Keith Richards called the best of the year, the Nevilles opened dates for the Rolling Stones on their "Tattoo You" tour. Even with this exposure, the album sold poorly.

The band then released albums on other labels in 1984 and 1987, the live *Neville-ization*, an attempt to capture the excitement of their concerts, and *Uptown*, referring to their home neighborhood. Neither of these brought the band to a nationwide audience or to stardom. *Neville-ization* included a version of Aaron's hit "Tell It Like It Is" and Professor Longhair's "Big Chief." Returning to their original label, A&M, in the late 1980's, they worked with producer Daniel Lanois on *Yellow Moon* (1989), which was their most successful studio effort. Combining engaging rhythms with social commentary, they more directly reflected their New Orleans and African American heritage with songs such as "Voodoo," "Congo Square," about the birthplace of American music, and "Sister Rosa," about Rosa Parks. The album *Brother's Keeper* (1990) featured an engaging song cycle about the trials and tribulations of urban life interspersed with unmistakable expressions of faith ("Steer Me Right," "Jah Love"), as well as a cover of "Mystery Train" and the title track from the 1990 film *Bird on a Wire.* 1992's *Family Groove* was anchored by a cover of Steve Miller's "Fly Like an Eagle" which received some crossover radio airplay on rock stations, but never climbed the sales charts.

Still Best Live. The double live release *Live on Planet Earth* (1994), is an excellent documentation of the band at its finest. Playing with the addition of a drummer, guitarist, bass player, and keyboardist, they showcased songs from all phases of their career and Aaron's solo work. What sets this recording apart are the stories and introductions which can only be found in the group's performances. The Nevilles show themselves as dedicated to a life guided by the Bible's Golden Rule, faith in God, the primacy of family, and the importance of human rights. It is this universal dimension of their message that drives their popularity worldwide, even as they remain a cult band at home. Some of their live dates have been billed as the Neville Brothers Featuring Aaron Neville, as there is a difference between the brothers' topical funk and the lighter vocal stylings of Aaron's solo work.

Aaron Neville Solo. Though his solo career began in the 1960's, Aaron Neville's solo career had many fallow years. He has worked on New Orleans docks, in steel mills, and at many other odd jobs, hoping his musical career would return full time. Neville's high falsetto is his trademark. His range and control often surprise, especially because of the broad physical package that is the source of the sound. Inspired by the yodeling of singing cowboys in films, notably Gene Autry and Roy Rogers, he began working on this skill at an early age.

Neville's solo career would be a 1990's phenomenon. It was rejuvenated by his featured performances on Linda Ronstadt's 1989 album *Cry Like a Rainstorm, Howl Like the Wind.* After extensive exposure of the duet hits "Don't Know Much" and "When Something Is Wrong with My Baby," the ground for his solo career became fertile again. Beginning with *My Greatest Gift* (1990), he returned with a remake of "Tell It Like It Is" and classic vocal tunes such as "Cry Me a River." 1991's *Warm Your Heart,* coproduced by Ronstadt and George Massenburg, served to bring his solo work to a mainstream audience. His cover of the Main Ingredient's "Everybody Plays the Fool" found his falsetto sound on middle-of-the-road radio stations. That album was followed by two albums in 1993, *Aaron Neville's Soulful Christmas* and *The Grand Tour,* which included "Don't Take Away My Heaven" and covers of the standard "These Foolish Things" and Bob Dylan's "Don't Fall Apart on Me Tonight," showcasing his vocal skill and interpretive style. His video of "Can't Stop My Heart from Loving You (The Rain Song)" from 1995's *The Tattooed Heart,* became highly visible on the VH-1 cable video network.

American Musical Treasures. All told, the Neville Brothers' music and Aaron Neville's solo recordings are gems of truly American music. Building on the varied and extensive traditions of their native New Orleans, the Nevilles, together and on their own, have made music that demands an open mind to truly feel the message and mindset the brothers are promoting. Not surprisingly, these men would never reach superstar status. The richness and complexity of what they do asks for much engagement by the audience. Their

For the Record

On two occasions, bands featuring one or more of the Nevilles opened concerts for the Rolling Stones: Art Neville's group, the Meters, in 1972 and 1973, and the Neville Brothers themselves in 1981.

§

Aaron Neville received the highest visibility of his career for his work on someone else's record, Linda Ronstadt's *Cry Like a Rainstorm, Howl Like the Wind.*

work is like buried treasure, waiting to be found by those seeking the heart and soul of American music.

—*Paul D. Fischer*

SELECT DISCOGRAPHY

■ ALBUMS

The Neville Brothers

Wild Tchoupitoulas, 1976
Fiyo on the Bayou, 1981
Neville-ization, 1984
Treacherous: A History of the Neville Brothers, 1988 (compilation)
Yellow Moon, 1989
Brother's Keeper, 1990
Treacherous Too! 1991 (compilation)
Live on Planet Earth, 1994

Aaron Neville

Warm Your Heart, 1991
The Grand Tour, 1993
Aaron Neville's Soulful Christmas, 1993
The Tattooed Heart, 1995

SELECT AWARDS

Grammy Award for Best Pop Instrumental Performance for "Healing Chant," 1989

Grammy Award for Best Pop Performance by a Duo or Group with Vocal for "Don't Know Much," 1989 (Aaron Neville solo with Linda Ronstadt)

Grammy Award for Best Pop Performance by a Duo or Group with Vocal for "All My Life," 1990 (Aaron Neville solo with Linda Ronstadt)

Grammy Award for Best Country Vocal Collaboration for "I Fall to Pieces," 1994 (Aaron Neville solo with Trisha Yearwood)

SEE ALSO: Ronstadt, Linda.

New Edition / Bobby Brown

New Edition

ORIGINAL MEMBERS: Bobby Brown (b. 1969), Michael Bivins (b. 1968), Ricky Bell (b. 1967), Ronnie DeVoe (b. 1967), Ralph Tresvant (b. 1968)
OTHER MEMBERS: Johnny Gill (b. 1965)
FIRST ALBUM RELEASE: *Candy Girl*, 1983

Bobby Brown

BORN: Boston, Massachusetts; February 5, 1969
FIRST ALBUM RELEASE: *Don't Be Cruel*, 1988
MUSICAL STYLES: Pop, soul, rhythm and blues

New Edition was the early 1980's version of the Jackson 5, a heavily produced and slickly packaged pop-soul band created to appeal to young teens. By the end of the decade each member of the group had proven himself an able musician in his own right, either achieving success with another group or as a solo act.

No Stopping Them. All of the members of New Edition attended junior high school in Boston's Roxbury district. Poor and often in trouble, they decided to become serious about music as a way to escape their surroundings. Their first performance, complete with choreographed steps, was "Ain't No Stoppin' Us Now." They were signed to a record deal with the hip-hop label Streetwise when producer Maurice Starr discovered them in 1981 at the "Hollywood Talent Night" at Boston's Strand Theater. Their first album, *Candy Girl* (1983), failed to make the Top 40 but did produce a number 1 rhythm-and-blues hit, "Candy Girl." Reminiscent of the early Jackson 5, some critics dismissed the song as "bubblegum" pop. Member Bobby Brown did not disagree, but he argued that they were just kids playing kids' music. "We might've grown up in a bad neighborhood, but there was still some sweetness there."

In 1983 New Edition left Starr to sign a major record deal with MCA. They released their self-titled debut album, which produced two number 1 rhythm-and-blues hits in "Cool It Now" (number 4, pop) and "Mr. Telephone Man" (number 12, pop). Written by Ray Parker, Jr., in the 1970's, "Mr. Telephone Man" was notable in affording Brown his first opportunity to sing lead vocals when lead vocalist Ralph Tresvant was unable to sing the high chorus. A string of Top-10 rhythm-and-blues hits followed, including "Lost in Love" (number 6, 1985), "Count Me Out" (number 2, 1985), "A Little Bit of Love (Is All It Takes)" (number 3, 1986), "With You All the Way" (number 7, 1986), "Earth Angel" (number 3, 1986), and "Once in a Lifetime Groove" (number 10, 1986).

Solo Careers. In 1986 Brown left New Edition for a solo career and was replaced by Johnny Gill. After New Edition's *Heart Break* album went double platinum in 1988, with the single "If It Isn't Love" peaking at number 7 on the pop charts, lead vocalists Gill and Tresvant left for solo careers, while the remaining members of New Edition were reincarnated as the group Bell Biv Devoe. All were successful, in part because they continued to assist one another in their various projects.

Between 1990 and 1993, former members of New Edition were ever-present on the rhythm-and-blues charts. Bell Biv Devoe had six Top-40 hits including "Poison" (1990), "B.B.D. (I Thought It Was Me)" (1990), and "The Best Things in Life Are Free" (1992), with Ralph Tresvant, Luther Vandross, and Janet Jackson, all of which topped the rhythm-and-blues charts. In the same period, Gill had five Top-40 hits, with "Rub You the Right Way" (1990) and "My, My, My" (1990), both number 1 rhythm-and-blues hits. In 1997 he joined soul stars Gerald Levert and Keith Sweat to produce *Levert-Sweat-Gill*, which rose to number 4 on the pop charts. Tresvant had three Top-40 singles. His "Sensitivity" (1990) topped the rhythm-and-blues chart, while Bobby Brown served as guest rapper on "Stone Cold Gentleman" (number 34, pop).

Bobby Brown (MCA/ Reisig & Taylor)

Bobby Brown. The most successful New Edition alumnus was Bobby Brown, who had nine straight Top-10 pop hits between 1988 and 1992, including number 1 pop hits with "My Prerogative" (1988) and "She Ain't Worth It" (with Glenn Madeiros, 1990). *Don't Be Cruel* (number 1, 1988) and *Bobby* (number 2, 1992) went multiplatinum and established Brown as a superstar. Brown, whose aggressive sexual image fostered a bad-boy reputation, created a sensation by marrying Whitney Houston in 1992. Despite constant tabloid rumors and Brown's 1998 conviction on drunk-driving charges, the couple stayed together and continued to work on each other's musical projects. Houston was featured on Brown's 1997 *Forever* album.

Reunion. In 1996, all six members of New Edition reunited for the much anticipated *Home Again* album and a 1996-1997 tour, both of which reflected the unique styles of the various members. Building upon the revived interest in the group, late in 1996 they released *New Edition's Solo Hits*, which included the biggest hits of Bobby Brown, Bell Biv DeVoe, and Ralph Tresvant as solo artists.

—*John Powell*

SELECT DISCOGRAPHY

New Edition

■ ALBUMS

Candy Girl, 1983

New Edition, 1984

For the Record

After Maurice Starr lost New Edition over a contractual dispute, he packaged, wrote for, and produced an even bigger group—New Kids on the Block.

All for Love, 1985
Christmas All Over the World, 1985
Under the Blue Moon, 1986
Heart Break, 1988
Greatest Hits, 1991 (compilation)
Home Again, 1996
New Edition's Solo Hits, 1996 (compilation)

Bobby Brown

■ ALBUMS
Don't Be Cruel, 1988
Bobby, 1992
Forever, 1997

SELECT AWARDS

Grammy Award for Best R&B Vocal Performance, Male, for "Every Little Step," 1989 (Brown)

SEE ALSO: Boyz II Men; Houston, Whitney; Jackson 5, The; New Kids on the Block.

New Kids on the Block

ORIGINAL MEMBERS: Donnie Wahlberg (b. 1969), Joe McIntyre (b. 1972), Jordan Knight (b. 1970), Jonathan Knight (b. 1968), Danny Wood (b. 1969)
FIRST ALBUM RELEASE: *New Kids on the Block,* 1986
MUSICAL STYLES: Pop, rap, hip-hop

A pop sensation in the late 1980's, the New Kids on the Block were wildly popular among a predominantly white, teenage, female audience—exactly the audience that songwriter and producer Maurice Starr hoped to reach when he created the group. Starr had previously managed New Edition, a black teenage group, and was aware of another musical act, Menudo, which served the same purpose for a Latino audience. Believing there was a void that he could fill, Starr shrewdly set out in 1984 to find several Boston-area white teenage boys with good looks and adequate talent. Within a few short years, Starr molded his discoveries into an incredibly profitable phenomenon.

Coming Together. The first New Kid recruited by Starr was Donnie Wahlberg, then fourteen years old. Talent agent Mary Alford had heard about Wahlberg from area neighborhoods' playground rappers and break-dancers and sent him to audition for Starr. Wahlberg performed a spontaneous rap routine for Starr and was quickly signed for the act. Wahlberg in turn recruited his younger brother, Mark, and his friends Jamie Kelly, Danny Wood, and brothers Jonathan and Jordan Knight. The younger Wahlberg and Kelly dropped out before the group made any recordings, however. To replace them, Starr asked Alford to find a younger, higher voiced boy to round out the group, and Alford brought in Joe McIntyre, who was only twelve years old.

Contrary to popular belief, the New Kids on the Block were not an instant success. Their first album, named after a Wahlberg-authored rap song from which the group took its name, was released in 1986 but did not earn much attention. It was not until 1988, when the New Kids released the album *Hangin' Tough,* that their single "Please Don't Go Girl" began to attract radio attention, leading to a national tour opening for established teen singer Tiffany. Eventually, *Hangin' Tough* sold several million copies, reviving interest in the group's debut album and leading to a Grammy Award nomination in 1989 for Best Music Video, Long Form. The group's reputation as clean-cut, antidrug teenagers endeared them not only to teenage girls, but also to those girls' parents.

Brief Time at the Top. By 1991, the New Kids on the Block had released two more albums and were listed by *Forbes* magazine as the highest paid

For the Record

The New Kids on the Block's success cannot be attributed to their music alone, which many critics considered mediocre. In *Time* magazine (1990), Jay Cocks stressed the marketing factor of the New Kids phenomenon, noting that "marketing and merchandising are integral parts of the pop machine, just as a movie's box-office receipts become part of its cachet."

New Kids on the Block (Archive Photos/Tom Gates)

entertainers in the world, earning an estimated $115 million in 1990 and 1991. This amount was not generated solely by album sales, but also by the related New Kids merchandise which Starr so adeptly promoted. Products varied from the usual T-shirts and posters to more unique items such as lunch boxes, sleeping bags, and even a line of dolls. The McDonald's restaurant chain sponsored the group's concerts, from which best–selling music videos were produced.

Not surprisingly, as the New Kids grew out of their teens, they found it more difficult to retain their teen-idol image and hold the attention of their target audience. In 1990, Donnie Wahlberg was accused of assaulting a fellow airplane passenger, while other group members were allegedly involved in separate barroom altercations. In 1992, the members took control of the group from Starr, but their frantic pace had left them exhausted, and they stopped touring and recording shortly thereafter. In 1994, they made one more attempt to regroup by changing to a more mature, abbreviated version of their name, NKOTB, and releasing a final album, *Face the Music*, which did not sell particularly well.

Grown-Up Kids. For the most part, the New Kids have enjoyed successful careers in other areas of the performing arts. Most notably, Donnie Wahlberg began producing records while still a New Kid; his projects included producing his younger brother Mark's debut rap album, *Music for the People* by Marky Mark and the Funky Bunch, and a solo album by Jordan Knight. Both Wahlbergs also added acting to their list of accomplishments, with Donnie appearing in the 1996 *Ransom* as a repentant kidnapper and Mark earning critical acclaim in the 1997 *Boogie Nights*. McIntyre also turned to acting, earning a role in the 1995 musical *The Fantastiks*. Like Donnie Wahlberg, Wood went into record production, leaving Jonathan Knight the only New Kid to leave show business altogether. —*Amy Sisson*

SELECT DISCOGRAPHY

■ ALBUMS

New Kids on the Block, 1986
Hangin' Tough, 1988
Merry Merry Christmas, 1989
Step by Step, 1990
Face the Music, 1994 (as NKOTB)

SEE ALSO: Jackson 5, The; Monkees, The; New Edition / Bobby Brown.

Randy Newman

BORN: Los Angeles, California; November 28, 1943

FIRST ALBUM RELEASE: *Randy Newman*, 1968

MUSICAL STYLES: Pop, rock and roll

Randy Newman has created darkly comical musical works that portray the American Dream as a nightmare. Unlike the confessional outpourings of most singer-songwriters emerging in the 1970's, his songs resemble character sketches. Newman has parlayed his storytelling ability into film scoring ranging from epic period pieces to animated children's stories.

Early Life. Randy Newman's involvement with music started early. His uncles, whom he remembers accompanying to film sound studios, were prominent in the Hollywood music industry: Uncle Lionel and Uncle Emil as conductors and Uncle Alfred as an Academy Award-winning composer of film scores. Newman, who started classical piano training at age four, performed weekly at family get-togethers.

Additional musical influences were jazz and rhythm and blues. He encountered jazz during nightly forays into the French Quarter during summertime visits to his mother's family in New Orleans. The hours he spent listening to such blues- and jazz-oriented artists as Fats Domino and Ray Charles apparently inspired Newman's drawling vocal style.

For the Record

Randy Newman says that he is proud of a parody of him on *SCTV*, the 1980's late-night comedy program, which portrayed him hunched over the piano, mumbling the lyrics to "Short People" until he is blown to bits.

In the early 1960's, as a counterpoint to his music studies at the University of California, Los Angeles, Newman began writing songs for Metric Music, a publishing division of Liberty Records. Newman terms these admittedly commercial efforts, recorded by such Top-40 bands as the Fleetwoods, "bad rock and roll."

Getting Noticed. The success of Judy Collins's 1966 recording of his wry ballad "I Think It's Going to Rain Today" brought Newman the attention of the music industry. Signing him for a debut album on their Reprise label, Warner Bros. apparently considered the raspy-voiced Newman a "prestige" artist, who would lend credibility to Reprise's reputation for progressiveness. Released in 1968, *Randy Newman* (originally titled *Randy Newman Creates Something New Under the Sun*) was an attempt to showcase Newman's talent for orchestrating and arranging as well as writing songs. While some critics found Newman's complex, full-orchestra arrangements at variance with his biting lyrics, he won near-unanimous praise as an original, thought-provoking artist.

Newman's second album, *Twelve Songs*, included "Mama Told Me Not to Come," a song the rock group Three Dog Night made a hit, reaching number 1 in July, 1970. Again revealing the perversity and paranoia at the underside of the American Dream, but this time featuring pared-down, blues-rock arrangements, *Twelve Songs*, like *Randy Newman*, garnered critical acclaim and lackluster sales. Following its release, Newman began playing club and concert dates, engaging audiences with his self-deprecating patter interspersed with his self-accompaniment on piano. Showcasing Newman as a performer, *Randy Newman Live* appeared in 1971.

Newman's next two albums, *Sail Away* (1972) and *Good Old Boys* (1974), escalated his attacks on bigotry and racism. Newman has stated that the "shock" of Los Angeles's 1965 Watts race riots precipitated some of his writing. Newman assumes the character of a slave trader on the title track of *Sail Away*, while he gives voice to unreconstructed Southerners in songs such as "Rednecks" on *Good Old Boys*. Contending that it is "too easy to say racism is horrible," he finds it "more interesting" to "let the other guy try and make his case." Newman had introduced this technique, which he describes as "setting up straw men and knocking them down," in "Davy the Fat Boy," the last track on his first album.

Newman's approach to satire has often led to misunderstanding. A number of short folk took offense to his sly assault on prejudice in "Short People," responding with bonfires of Newman's records and demands that record stations boycott the song. Despite such protests, the record reached the number 2 spot on the *Billboard* charts in 1977, and the album on which it appeared, *Little Criminals,* went gold.

Newman's next successful single, "I Love L.A.," has become that city's unofficial anthem. The album from which it was taken, *Trouble in Paradise* (1983), satirized the pretentiousness and excess of much of the rock scene in the early 1980's. As that decade wore on, Newman experienced disruptions in his personal life, including separation from his first wife, with whom he had three sons, and a debilitating fatigue and depression. Whether or not his subsequent diagnosis of infection with the Epstein-Barr virus was valid, holistic treatments apparently helped renew Newman's health. His probing, autobiographical album, *Land of Dreams,* was released in 1988.

Scoring. While it was the 1980's before Newman's successful career in film scoring gained momentum, this direction was not unexpected. Besides being influenced by his uncles, in 1970 he had served as music director for the film *Performance,* starring Mick Jagger. Additionally, as pointed out by journalist Steve Oney, Newman had demonstrated an ability to develop variations on a theme and convey the feel for a certain time and place beginning in *Good Old Boys.* In 1981, Newman scored the film version of E. L. Doctorow's novel *Ragtime* and received the first of numerous Academy Award nominations for Original Score. In 1984, Newman's Oscar-nominated score for *The Natural* won him a Grammy Award.

Randy Newman in 1983 (Paul Natkin)

Newman has also received a number of nominations under the Oscar category Original Song. On the 1995 Academy Award telecast, in a duet with alternative-country artist Lyle Lovett, Newman performed his nominated song, the jaunty "You've Got a Friend in Me," from Disney's *Toy Story. Toy Story*'s score was also nominated by the Academy, as was Newman's score for *James and the Giant Peach,* another animated film, the following year.

Newman's combined musical and narrative gifts have, in addition, produced the musical play *Faust,* which Newman calls "a total trashing of Goethe's great masterpiece" of nineteenth century Romanticism. Newman's protagonist is a slacker, a third-year college freshman caught in the rivalry between a bored and bumbling Devil and a golf-playing God. Having been worked on intermittently for a decade, *Faust* debuted in 1995 at the La Jolla Playhouse in Southern California, where a revue of Newman's songs, *Maybe I'm Doing It Wrong*, had played in 1981. After its libretto was retooled by playwright David Mamet, *Faust* was staged at Chicago's Goodman Theater. Although the theatrical *Faust* garnered mixed reviews, an album of the musical's songs performed by such pop luminaries as Elton John and Linda Ronstadt—with Newman taking the role of Satan—fared better, critically and financially.

Legacy. Newman has arguably contributed to expanding the scope and emotional complexity of the pop-rock song. His display of dry, devastating wit helped set a precedent for such singer-songwriters as Warren Zevon and Lyle Lovett. Critics have compared his satiric gifts with those of literary giants Jonathan Swift and Mark Twain. Newman, a prolific reader, remarks, "There's no reason why a songwriter should be limited any more than a short-story writer or a novelist."

—*Amy Allison*

SELECT DISCOGRAPHY

■ ALBUMS

Randy Newman, 1968
Twelve Songs, 1970
Randy Newman Live, 1971
Sail Away, 1972
Good Old Boys, 1974
Little Criminals, 1977
Ragtime, 1981 (sound track)
Trouble in Paradise, 1983
The Natural, 1984 (sound track)
Land of Dreams, 1988
Faust, 1995

SELECT AWARDS

Grammy Award for Best Instrumental Composition for "The Natural," 1984

SEE ALSO: Collins, Judy; Lovett, Lyle; Three Dog Night.

Olivia Newton-John

BORN: Cambridge, England; September 26, 1948
FIRST SINGLE RELEASE: "Till You Say You'll Be Mine," 1966
FIRST ALBUM RELEASE: *If Not for You*, 1971
MUSICAL STYLES: Country, pop, rock and roll

Although Olivia Newton-John's parents were academically oriented, they also loved music. Her Welch father was gifted with an operatic voice, and he and her German mother encouraged Newton-John to sing. When Newton-John was five, her parents moved to Melbourne, Australia, and at the age of fourteen, she and three friends formed a band known as the Sol Four. However, since Newton-John's parents felt that it interfered with schoolwork, the group was soon disbanded.

Establishing a Wholesome Image. At age fifteen, Newton-John made her first television appearance, singing "Summertime" on an Australian version of the United States program *The Gong Show*, and after winning a talent contest, Newton-John quit school and went to England, where she recorded her first single, "Till You Say You'll Be Mine," in 1966. After a two-year stint in a duo with Australian friend Pat Carroll, Newton-John joined Don Kirshner's short-lived musical group Toomorrow, a band developed to take the place of the disbanded Monkees. In 1970, Newton-John began touring with British superstar Cliff Richard, and she appeared regularly on his television series, which greatly boosted the sales of her first successful single, "If Not for You" (1971). Newton-John's next big single, "Banks of the Ohio" (1971), went silver in England and gold in Australia, and she released her first album in the United States, *If Not for You*, in November, 1971.

Her Popularity Skyrockets. Although Newton-John had gained popularity in England, her breakthrough in the United States did not come until 1973 with the release of "Let Me Be There," which reached number 6 on the U.S. charts and won Newton-John her first Grammy Award for Best Female Country Vocal Performance. Her next album, *If You Love Me (Let Me Know)* (1974), went gold and included her gold single, "I Honestly Love You," which won her Grammy Awards for Best Female Pop Vocal Performance and Record of the Year. Newton-John also won the Country Music Association's (CMA) Female Vocalist of the Year Award in 1974, but because some CMA members felt that Newton-John did not qualify as a country artist, they became enraged and formed the Association of Country Entertainers.

In 1975 Newton-John moved to Los Angeles, and her music continued to go gold. Hits such as "Have You Never Been Mellow" (number 1, 1975) and "Please Mr. Please" (number 3, 1975) reaffirmed Newton-John's ability to blend pop and country music with the greatest of ease. More awards and honors came from such renowned organizations as *Cashbox*, *Record World*, and the British Country Music Association, followed by another hit single, "Come On Over," and a successful album, *Don't Stop Believin'*, in 1976. Newton-John toured the United States and Great Britain in May of 1977, and her album *Olivia Newton-John's Greatest Hits* (1977) reached the Top-20 album chart, peaking at number 13 in January, 1978.

New Musical Image. Until 1978, Newton-John had a clean-cut, wholesome image, but that changed with the release of the hit film *Grease* (1978), in which she starred with John Travolta. The film yielded three gold singles: "You're the One That I Want" and "Summer Nights," both duets with Travolta, and "Hopelessly Devoted to You." Newton-John's new, leather-dressed look distanced her from her country beginnings.

In 1980, Newton-John and Cliff Richard had a duet hit, "Suddenly," and she also appeared in the film fantasy *Xanadu*. Although the film was not successful, the resulting album with the hit song "Xanadu" (1980) went double platinum. Newton-John's new, sexier image was reinforced with her platinum albums *Totally Hot* (1978) and *Physical* (1981), with the latter album boasting three hit singles, including the number 1 title track. "Physical" maintained the number 1 single status on the charts for ten weeks straight, and the *Olivia Physical* music video earned Newton-John her fourth Grammy in 1982 for Video of the Year.

For the Record

In 1959, Newton-John won a Hayley Mills look-alike contest when her sister Rona entered Olivia's picture into the contest without telling her.

New Directions. In 1984, Newton-John married actor Matt Lattanzi, and they had a daughter, Chloe Rose, in 1986. Newton-John's musical career slowed down significantly in 1984 when she decided to open the first of her Koala Blue chain of clothing stores in Hollywood. Her album *Soul Kiss*, released in 1985, revealed Newton-John in daring sultry poses and reflected her new rock-and-roll sound. From 1985 to 1987, Newton-John devoted most of her time to motherhood and to her Koala Blue chain, which had expanded worldwide.

In 1988, Newton-John released *The Rumour* and also appeared in a Home Box Office (HBO) cable special titled *Olivia Newton-John in Australia*. Her next album, *Warm and Tender* (1989), contained children's songs and lullabies, and she supported the album with many television appearances, including a special that highlighted her environmental concerns. (By then she had also become very involved in environmental causes.) In June of 1990, Newton-John was elected as the United Nations' first Goodwill Ambassador to the Environment, and she flew to Brazil that same year to report for the Fox television network on the devastation of the rain forest. From 1990 to 1991, Newton-John enjoyed some renewed success in England with the release of "The Grease Megamix" (1990) and "Grease: The Dream Mix" (1991).

In 1992, Newton-John's once-thriving Koala Blue chain was forced into bankruptcy, her father passed away, and she was diagnosed with breast cancer. She kept a positive attitude, underwent cancer treatments, and subsequently won her battle with the disease. In 1994, she released *Gaia: One Woman's Journey*, an album she wrote, produced, and financed herself, and in December of that year she released an album titled *Spirit of Christmas 94*. The following year, Newton-John wrote and recorded another Christmas song, "Christmas Never Felt Like This," which was included on the compilation album of various artists, *Mother and Child* (1995). In late 1997, Newton-John recorded a song with the Raybon Brothers titled "Falling," and the rerelease of the *Grease* sound track spent much of 1997 at the top of *Billboard*'s pop catalog chart. The film *Grease* was rereleased in 1998 and again experienced great success. In the late 1990's, Newton-John would devote most of her time to her daughter, to environmental causes, to her *Wild Life* television series that airs on the Animal Planet cable station, and to her music. —*Alvin K. Benson*

SELECT DISCOGRAPHY

■ ALBUMS

If Not for You, 1971
Olivia Newton-John, 1971
Olivia, 1972
If You Love Me (Let Me Know), 1974
Have You Never Been Mellow, 1975
Olivia Newton-John's Greatest Hits, 1977 (compilation)
Totally Hot, 1978
Physical, 1981
Soul Kiss, 1985
The Rumour, 1988
Gaia: One Woman's Journey, 1994

SELECT AWARDS

Grammy Award for Best Country Vocal Performance, Female, for "Let Me Be There," 1973
Grammy Awards for Record of the Year and Best Pop Vocal Performance, Female, for "I Honestly Love You," 1974
Country Music Association Female Vocalist of the Year Award, 1974
Grammy Award for Video of the Year for *Olivia Physical*, 1982
National Association of Women Business Owners Celebrity Businesswoman of the Year Award, 1989

SEE ALSO: Abba; Denver, John; Dylan, Bob; Electric Light Orchestra / Jeff Lynn; Reddy, Helen.

Nine Inch Nails

(Trent Reznor)

BORN: Mercer, Pennsylvania; May 17, 1965
FIRST ALBUM RELEASE: *Pretty Hate Machine*, 1989
MUSICAL STYLE: Industrial rock

Nine Inch Nails (NIN) is the creation of Trent Reznor. Reznor grew up in Mercer, Pennsylvania, where he began playing the piano when he was five years old. In adolescence he played the tuba and the saxophone and was a member of a band called Option 30. Reznor studied engineering at Allegheny College. After attending college, he moved to Cleveland, where he played in a succession of groups, including Problems, which performed "True Love Ways" in the 1987 Michael J. Fox-Joan Jett film *Light of Day*.

Launching Nine Inch Nails. Reznor wanted something different from the run-of-the mill rock-and-roll band. In 1988 he began using the name Nine Inch Nails, combining dance music with technology. Reznor was Nine Inch Nails from the beginning, doing nearly all the writing, performing, editing, and producing. However, through the years he has brought into the band other musicians to perform, particularly on tours.

In 1988 Reznor began to create music using the technology that he had studied as a computer engineering major. He wrote music that combined the anger and energy he admired in groups such as Skinny Puppy and Old Ministry with the sounds that could be created by synthesizers and computers. The album *Pretty Hate Machine* was released in 1989. In addition to writing and recording computer-generated music, Reznor wanted to perform the music live. He therefore had to tackle the problem of how to perform using sounds that were largely technologically created. He assembled groups of musicians who could play drums, guitar, and keyboards along with tapes of the sections of music that were computer generated.

In 1991 Reznor and other musicians—Richard Patrick on guitar, Chris Vrenna on drums, Jeff Ward on drums, and James Woolley on keyboards—played on the Lollapalooza tour as Nine

Inch Nails. On the tour Nine Inch Nails was extremely popular—for example, selling more T-shirts than any other group. Even before the Lollapalooza tour, however, Nine Inch Nails had established itself in the recording world and as a performing group. *Pretty Hate Machine* had, by the time of the Lollapalooza tour, become a commercial success. It had stayed on the *Billboard* charts for more than two years. The song "Head Like a Hole" from *Pretty Hate Machine* was a huge commercial and critical success, receiving considerable media attention. The song combined heavy metal, technology, and dance-club rhythms. Before Lollapalooza the group had gained performance experience by playing shows with Skinny Puppy, the Jesus and Mary Chain, and Peter Murphy.

Nine Inch Nails' Trent Reznor (Paul Natkin)

Later Work. Reznor had difficulty releasing an album after *Pretty Hate Machine* because of legal problems with his label, TVT. Eventually the problems were resolved, and in 1992 Nine Inch Nails released an extended-play single, *Broken.* "Wish" from the EP was extremely popular and won Reznor his first Grammy Award for Best Metal Performance.

In 1994 Nine Inch Nails released its second full-length album, *The Downward Spiral,* which debuted at number 2 on the *Billboard* charts. It sold more than two million copies. This album was released on the Nothing label, which had been created by Reznor and his manager, John Maim. Reznor created the label to sign groups that were doing the same sort of technologically oriented and angst-driven music that Nine Inch Nails was creating and performing. Nothing signed such groups as Marilyn Manson, Pop Will Eat Itself, and Coil. Reznor produced Marilyn Manson's first album, *Portrait of an American Family* (1994). Nine Inch Nails proved to be a crowd-pleaser at the Woodstock '94 festival.

Reznor produced the soundtrack for Oliver Stone's 1994 film *Natural Born Killers.* He weaved together songs, including Nine Inch Nails' "Something I Can Never Have" and "Bum" with dialogue from the film to create the sound-track album. Charlie Clouser, who became a Nine Inch Nails keyboardist, worked as an editor on the *Natural Born Killers* soundtrack. By the end of 1994 Nine Inch Nails was regarded as a mainstream group. *The Downward Spiral* was a great commercial success, and the group had been well-received at Woodstock. Reznor did not deny that he had entered the mainstream of American music, but he did maintain that he had not compromised and had become successful on his own terms.

For the Record

Trent Reznor once recalled being dragged into a strip show, where he realized, to his horror, that "the DJ was playing 'Hurt,' the last track on *Downward Spiral* and a song based on the most personal sentiments, the deepest emotions I have ever had. . . . We were crying when we made it, it was so intense. I didn't know if I even wanted to put it on the album. But there we were, and there it was, and girls were taking their clothes off to it."

Nine Inch Nails released the remix album *Further Down the Spiral* in 1995 and toured with David Bowie, whom Reznor has credited with being one of his chief influences. The tour was noted for its theatrical elements. In 1996 the Nine Inch Nails song "Happiness in Slavery" from the *Woodstock '94* album won Nine Inch Nails a Grammy for Best Metal Performance. Reznor then worked with David Lynch to create the soundtrack for Lynch's film *Lost Highway* (1997). Reznor reported that he wanted to work with Lynch because he was a great Lynch fan, especially enjoying the dark textures of Lynch's television series *Twin Peaks*. In February, 1997, Reznor and Lynch appeared together on the cover of *Rolling Stone.*

Controversy and Contribution. Nine Inch Nails has been criticized for the subject matter of its music and for its use of graphic language. Song titles such as "March of the Pigs" (1994) and "Suck," from the *Broken* extended-play single, as well as more graphic titles, have caused some people to criticize and condemn Nine Inch Nails without ever hearing its music. For example, William Bennett, former U.S. Secretary of Education, criticized the imagery in "Big Man with a Gun" (1994). Bennett and C. Delores Tucker demanded that Warner Bros. dissolve its relationship with Interscope, which was distributing Reznor's Nothing label. Reznor replied to Bennett's and others' charges by saying that they were concerned only with a few objectionable words and that they had not listened to the content of the music itself.

Pretty Hate Machine and *The Downward Spiral* were both platinum sellers, reaching millions of listeners. Thus, when Reznor says, "I focus on the pain/ the only thing that's real," he is striking a chord with many music fans and expressing feelings with which they empathize. Nine Inch Nails' ability to express the alienation, pain, and anger felt by many of its fans is part of its legacy.

Reznor has a talent for weaving computer-generated sounds into both his recordings and the band's stage performances. His use of tapes on stage to intersperse computer-generated sounds within live performances has influenced the music of other bands in his genre. His use of loops from rock-and-roll bands and film soundtracks, his use of tapes to intersperse computer-generated sounds, and his effective use of a drum machine all have influenced the recordings and performances of bands that play heavy metal abetted by technology.

A number of musicians other than the 1991 Lollapalooza group already mentioned have worked with Reznor. In 1995 Charlie Clouser replaced James Woolley on keyboard (although Woolley did the 1995 "Further Down the Spiral" tour. Richard Patrick was replaced on guitar by Robin Finck, who later left the band to play for Cirque de Soleil. Charlie Lohner has also worked with Nine Inch Nails, playing keyboards and bass, and Adrian Belew has played some guitar.

—Annita Marie Ward

SELECT DISCOGRAPHY

■ ALBUMS

Pretty Hate Machine, 1989
Broken, 1992
The Downward Spiral, 1994

SELECT AWARDS

Grammy Award for Best Metal Performance for "Wish," 1992

Grammy Award for Best Metal Performance for "Happiness in Slavery," 1996

SEE ALSO: Bowie, David; Manson, Marilyn.

Nirvana

ORIGINAL MEMBERS: Kurt Cobain (1967-1994), Aaron Burckhard, Chris "Krist" Novoselic (b. 1965)

OTHER MEMBERS: Dale Crover, Chad Channing, Dan Peters, Dave Grohl (b. 1969)

FIRST ALBUM RELEASE: *Bleach*, 1989

MUSICAL STYLES: Alternative, grunge, hard rock

Legendary as the finest example of grunge music and the Seattle sound, Nirvana's star burned brightly for only a short time. Innovative and introspective, they gave voice to the alienated culture of the post-baby-boom generation. Groundbreaking as their music was, Nirvana's image will always be marred and defined by the suicide of vocalist and songwriter Kurt Cobain at the age of twenty-seven.

The Wishkah's Muddy Banks. Nirvana's roots sprouted on February 20, 1967, with the birth of Wendy (O'Connor) and Donald Cobain's first child. Kurt came into the world in Hoquiam, Washington, in the heart of the Pacific Northwest's logging region. By the age of six months, Cobain had moved to the town with which his name is inextricably tied: Aberdeen.

Life in a logging town was difficult, with most Aberdeen residents' fortunes bound to the industry. Aberdeen was characteristic of other lumber centers in the region: rural, working-class or poor, and dreary most days of the year, due to the area's climate. Still, Cobain remembered his earliest years as happy. He was artistic and self-assured, and he loved music. His first influence was the Beatles; his aunts' record collections provided a thorough schooling. In his grade school years, Cobain would receive his second infusion of musical influences from his father's favorite bands: Led Zeppelin, Kiss, and Black Sabbath.

The turning point in Cobain's life was the divorce of his parents when he was eight. The breakup affected him deeply. Shuttled between his mother, father, and numerous other relatives, his sense of security was lost. Remarriage of both his parents introduced step-parents and the changes were disturbing for the young boy. Withdrawn and disillusioned, Cobain developed difficulty at school, and was placed on the drug Ritalin.

Struggling through school, always an outsider, Cobain's closest friends were girls and one gay male; both choices brought him taunts and threats from his male peers. He took to writing, especially poetry and short stories, and became a voracious reader. Eventually his isolation and refusal to keep up with schoolwork necessitated his admittance to a school specializing in gifted students who underachieved. At Grays Harbor Institute of Northwest Crafts, young Cobain met Chris Novoselic, also a self-defined misfit. The friendship blossomed during the groundswell of American interest in punk rock. Cobain and Novoselic loved the rebellious music, often trading tapes and records.

Unable to fit in even at the relatively lax school, Cobain quit two months short of graduation. His exasperated mother forced him out of the house, and he spent the next few weeks sleeping on friends' floors. Again living with uncertainty, Cobain was introduced to hardcore punk around this time, when a friend took him to see legendary San Francisco punk band Black Flag. With this revelation, Cobain knew what he wanted to do with his life: play music.

Formation. Soon, Cobain and Novoselic sought their fortunes in nearby Olympia, playing most of their dates at college parties, especially at Evergreen State University. As they built a name for themselves, the fledgling independent record label Sub Pop began to take notice. Sub Pop's founders, Bruce Pavitt and Jonathan Poneman, liked what they heard, and with founding drummer Dale Crover, Nirvana made its first recording. Taking the ten-song demo tape they had recorded in one day, Nirvana fashioned it into *Bleach* (1989), rerecording the tunes over six days at a cost of around six hundred dollars. *Bleach* would sell thirty-five thousand units, even before Nirvana became a national act.

Nirvana's potential was obvious. Sub Pop began casting around for a distributer for the band's second offering. The interest *Bleach* was generating reportedly caused a bidding war between major labels to sign Nirvana to a long-term contract.

In the midst of this flux, the band hired the last in a succession of drummers. Dave Grohl, of the Washington, D.C., band Scream, brought to the trio a driving power with his loud and fierce drumming. The match was perfect.

Recording Contract. Geffen Records signed Nirvana for $287,000, placing them with the alternative/punk division, DGC Records. Producer of their second album, Butch Vig, has said he instinctively knew the centerpiece of their sophomore effort would be an anthem for post-baby boomers. "Smells Like Teen Spirit" transfixed Americans in their twenties, especially those whose teen years had been as isolated as Cobain's. The single drove sales of *Nevermind* (1991), and the video for the single went into heavy rotation on MTV.

Fame was instantaneous. It was also deeply disturbing, particularly for Cobain. Under the crush of media attention and the pressure to be the new spokesman for his generation, Cobain relieved the madness with drugs. He had been a recreational user since his early teens, but with the influx of money, Cobain quickly developed a serious habit. Cobain and his peers used hard drugs with casualness. Heroin was the way the disaffected of Cobain's generation showed their fatalism. Reputedly, heroin was one of the things Cobain shared with the person about to become the most important woman in his life.

Love. Courtney Love was the name assumed by the vocalist and rhythm guitarist for the punk band Hole. She and Cobain wed on February 24, 1992, and their daughter, Frances Bean, was born in August of that year. This year also saw the birth of Nirvana's next album, *Incesticide.* The work was pieced together from outtakes from previous Nirvana recording sessions. Within the music industry, it was whispered that Nirvana released a record of outtakes because Cobain's addiction was taking its inevitable toll on him. The whispers grew to a shout when *Vanity Fair* magazine reported that Love had used heroin while pregnant.

Many feel that this was the beginning of the end of Cobain, and with him, Nirvana. Responding to the *Vanity Fair* article, Los Angeles County

Nirvana's Kurt Cobain (Ken Settle)

Children's Services started proceedings to take Frances from her parents. The sense of excitement and positivity Cobain had felt with his marriage and fatherhood was quickly dissipating. The couple immediately sued and won their case in 1993. Still, the damage had already been done.

Although the media focused on Cobain, Nirvana was an assemblage of talented peers. Toiling out of the spotlight, Grohl was establishing a reputation as a drummer's drummer, competent and creative, never resorting to mere volume. Meanwhile, bassist Novoselic was earning the praise of his peers and rediscovering a keen interest in his Croatian heritage. It was at this time that he returned to the more traditional spelling of his name (Krist).

Warning Signs. Nirvana's most sophisticated work, *In Utero*, was released in 1993. Serving up a brilliant mix of hard rock, soft introspection, and biting satire, *In Utero* garnered both critical and commercial success. The haunting song "All Apologies" included some insight into Cobain's growing sense of being trapped by all the institutions in his life. Plaintively, he sings "Married, buried," making the listener wonder if the securities he had so long sought had come to overwhelm him.

Despite *In Utero*'s debut at number 1 and Nirvana's heralded performance on MTV's *Unplugged* series, fame and success were turning sour for Cobain. He began to openly complain about the pressures of his life as a rock star. In 1994, Cobain made the first attempt on his life. In his hotel room in Rome, he took sixty sedatives, swallowing them with a full bottle of champagne.

When he emerged from a coma in an Italian hospital ten days later, Love by his side, Cobain's public statement was that the incident was an accidental overdose. Few family members, friends, or fans believed this. Privately, he vowed to Love to get treatment for his drug problem so he could be a decent father to Frances Bean. Back in Seattle, on March 20, 1994 (less than three weeks after the overdose), Cobain and Love quarreled. She called the police when he holed up in a bedroom with several guns. His longtime fascination with weapons was well known to friends, but Love feared that this night was particularly ominous. Eventually, Cobain left the bedroom, unhurt, and agreed to check into a drug rehabilitation clinic in California.

On March 28, 1994, the pair flew to Southern California, Love to work on Hole recording sessions, Cobain to enter the clinic. He stayed three days, leaving without contacting her, and flew back to their Seattle home alone. Worried, Love hired a private investigator to find him, but it was an electrician who chanced upon Cobain's lifeless body. Sometime around April 5, 1994, he had gone to the apartment above the garage of his Madrona, Washington, home. After arranging a number of personal effects around him, leaving a suicide note addressed to his childhood imaginary friend, and ingesting a large quantity of drugs, Cobain fatally shot himself with a rifle.

There was no question in the minds of Novoselic and Grohl that Nirvana had died with Cobain. Although each went on to success with other bands, they would carry the legacy of Nirvana into their subsequent efforts. Love, too, would continue her musical career, branching out to acting as well.

The live performance Nirvana rendered on MTV's *Unplugged* was released as a recording after Cobain's death in 1994. Two years later, DGC released *From the Muddy Banks of the Wishkah*, a compilation of live performances Nirvana recorded from 1992 to 1994. Dying young and tragically, Kurt Cobain became an icon for a generation, a man who had attained all fame and fortune had to offer and still found life wanting. In songs such as "Come as You Are," "All Apologies," and "Smells Like Teen Spirit," he gave voice to his generation's feelings of alienation.

—*Cynthia R. Kasee*

SELECT DISCOGRAPHY

■ ALBUMS

Bleach, 1989

Nevermind, 1991

In Utero, 1993

From the Muddy Banks of the Wishkah, 1996

SEE ALSO: Hole; Pearl Jam.

No Doubt

ORIGINAL MEMBERS: John Spence (b. 1970), Tony Kanal (b. 1970), Eric Stefani, Gwen Stefani (b. 1969)

OTHER MEMBERS: Adrian Young (b. 1969), Tom Dumont (b. 1968)

FIRST ALBUM RELEASE: *No Doubt*, 1992

MUSICAL STYLES: Alternative rock, ska, punk

No Doubt (Paul Natkin)

Formed in Anaheim, California, in early 1987, No Doubt was originally a two-tone ska band consisting of John Spence and Eric Stefani, with Eric's little sister Gwen teaming up with Spence on vocals. The Stefanis were obsessed with ska bands—Madness, Selector, and the Specials—and were mostly interested in duplicating the ska sound. As the lineup of the band changed, however, No Doubt became more heavily influenced by the tastes of its new members, and the band began to forge its unique sound—a mixture of ska, punk, pop, heavy metal, and modern rock. In the mid-1990's, No Doubt found a niche as an alternative pop-rock band and rose to popularity on the strength of vocalist Gwen's enigmatic persona—"alternately an embrace of little-girl-lost innocence and riot grrl feminism" (*All Music Guide to Rock*, 1997)—which found expression in the band's first big single, "Just a Girl."

The Beginnings. The lineup of the band changed radically in its first year. While playing for parties in Anaheim in early 1987, the trio picked up bassist Tony Kanal, a native of India. Later that year, founding member Spence committed suicide. The band, however, was able to resurrect itself. Gwen emerged as the lone vocalist, and two new band members were added: guitarist Tom Dumont and drummer Adrian Young. Success on the Anaheim party circuit generated a local following. Soon the band was opening for the Red Hot Chili Peppers and Ziggy Marley. Based on strong regional support and a growing reputation for great live shows, Interscope Records signed No Doubt in 1991, releasing the band's self-titled debut album in March of 1992.

For the Record

The words to "I'm Just a Girl," which Gwen Stefani wrote in 1994, are about being surrounded by boys. *Rolling Stone* reported that the phrase "just a girl" struck Stefani as funny, and she asked her friends and her sister for everyday examples of the way girls are patronized or diminished in society.

Despite No Doubt's punk influences, they were not included in the grunge boom of the early 1990's. This was largely because of the nature of their debut album, a polished production of heavily pop-oriented songs with new-wave keyboards and punchy brass inspired more by 1980's synthesized sounds than by the band's punk and ska heritage. Though the tour in support of the album was successful, the album itself was a commercial flop—it disappeared without a trace in the wake of the grunge movement—and Interscope Records refused to fund another album or tour. No Doubt responded by producing a second album with their own money. In *The Beacon Street Collection*, released in 1995, the band redefined its sound by pushing the synthesizer and new-wave influences to the background and returning to its punk roots with songs combining 1980's punk with 1990's grunge. At this juncture, keyboardist and principal songwriter Eric Stefani left No Doubt to pursue a career as a cartoonist for *The Simpsons*.

Tragic Kingdom. In 1994, Interscope Records allowed No Doubt to continue recording under their label and released the band's third album, *Tragic Kingdom* (1995). The recording served as an ironic commentary on the band's Anaheim roots—the Stefanis lived so close to Disneyland (the "Magic Kingdom") that ashes from the fireworks fell in their backyard—and also documented the breakup of a seven-year relationship between Gwen and bassist Kanal. The album was a crossbreed of 1990's punk, ska revival, and a new-wave pop sensibility.

The first single from *Tragic Kingdom*, "Just a Girl," was a modest pop hit but was played more widely on alternative radio and television video channels. With the second single, "Spiderwebs," No Doubt continued to get radio play. The third single, "Don't Speak," hit number 1. Like the reggae-flavored "Sunday Morning," an additional hit off the *Tragic Kingdom* album, "Don't Speak" recorded the sentiments of songwriter Gwen following her emotional breakup with Kanal. The heartfelt material and raw sound of the album resonated with American audiences. By the end of 1996, one year after its release, *Tragic Kingdom* hit number 1 on the pop charts. By 1997, eight million copies of the album had been sold in the United States. —*Amanda Walzer-Scott*

SELECT DISCOGRAPHY

■ ALBUMS

No Doubt, 1992

The Beacon Street Collection, 1995

Tragic Kingdom, 1995

SELECT AWARDS

California Music Award for Best Female Vocalist, Gwen Stefani, 1997

MTV Video Music Award for Best Group Video for "Don't Speak," 1997

SEE ALSO: Specials, The.

The Notorious B.I.G.

(Chris Wallace)

BORN: Brooklyn, New York; May 21, 1972

DIED: Los Angeles, California; March 9, 1997

FIRST ALBUM RELEASE: *Ready to Die*, 1994

MUSICAL STYLES: Rap, hip-hop

The Notorious B.I.G.'s debut album, *Ready to Die* (1994), immediately made him one of the most popular hip-hop performers of the mid-1990's. Unfortunately, the 280-pound rap artist gained even greater attention when he was murdered in March of 1997 in Los Angeles. His death set off a storm of media speculation about the apparently deadly rivalry between East Coast and West Coast rappers.

Hitting the Big Time. The Notorious B.I.G., born Chris Wallace and also known as Biggie Smalls, was raised in the tough Bedford-Stuyvesant section of Brooklyn, New York. Despite his status as an honor-roll student, he dropped out of school at the age of seventeen to sell crack cocaine. After being arrested in North Carolina and spending nine months in jail, he recorded a few rap songs in a friend's home studio. The tapes eventually led to a recording contract with Puff Daddy's Bad Boy Records.

The Notorious B.I.G. first came to the public's attention for work he did on a remix of Mary J. Blige's song "What's the 411?" in 1992. Real stardom would have to wait until 1994, however, when he released his platinum debut album *Ready to Die*. While the songs on the debut were reminiscent of the "gangsta" funk sound pioneered by Dr. Dre on *The Chronic* (1993), the Notorious B.I.G. used his deep voice and effective lyrics about urban street life to prove that he was an adept rapper capable

The Notorious B.I.G. in 1995 (Manny Hernandez/Archive Photos)

of taking hip-hop music to another level.

The Notorious B.I.G.'s success did not make him immune to trouble. In November of 1994, he and Puff Daddy were accused of plotting the robbery and shooting of rapper Tupac Shakur, a charge they heatedly denied but that seemed to support rumors that an intensely hateful rivalry had developed between West Coast and East Coast rappers. As the new star of the East Coast rap scene, the notorious B.I.G. became the primary target for much of the venom launched from the West Coast. The hefty rapper was also charged with beating several people over the next several years, including two fans who were trying to photograph him and the promoter of a cancelled show.

For the Record

Trouble continued to dog the Notorious B.I.G. even after his death. During his public funeral, fans who crowded around Bedford-Stuyvesant to see the hearse pass by began jumping on cars and scuffling with the police. The disturbance led to the arrest of ten people.

A Tragic End. The Notorious B.I.G. worked with several other artists after his debut album, including R. Kelly and Michael Jackson. In March, 1997, he traveled to Los Angeles to promote the release of his upcoming album, *Life After Death*, a title that, along with the title of the debut album, seemed to provide an eerie foreshadowing of future events. On March 9, he was shot and killed on his way from the Soul Train Awards ceremony to his hotel. Rumors and accusations immediately began to circulate, most of them centered on the belief that the Notorious B.I.G.'s murder was retribution for the September, 1996, murder of Tupac Shakur in Las Vegas, Nevada. The potential connection between the two murders set off a media blitzkrieg about the "rap war" between the coasts, and surviving rap stars met and called for a peaceful resolution to a problem that had gotten completely out of hand.

Life After Death was released three weeks after the death of the Notorious B.I.G. and lived up to the promise of the debut. Although the album was somewhat inconsistent, the better songs again showcased the Notorious B.I.G.'s prodigious musical and lyrical talents. The album debuted at number 1 on the charts and remained there for three weeks. *—Douglas Long*

SELECT DISCOGRAPHY

■ ALBUMS

Ready to Die, 1994

Life After Death, 1997

SEE ALSO: Blige, Mary J.; Dr. Dre; Jackson, Michael; Kelly, R.; Puff Daddy; Shakur, Tupac.

Ted Nugent

BORN: Detroit, Michigan; December 13, 1948
FIRST ALBUM RELEASE: *The Amboy Dukes*, 1967
FIRST SOLO ALBUM RELEASE: *Ted Nugent*, 1975
MUSICAL STYLE: Hard rock; rock and roll

Self-described "Motor-City Madman" Ted Nugent's cartoonish stage persona as a long-haired guitar-playing rock barbarian was coupled with a barrage of guitar sound and an unforgiving work ethic to forge a long string of commercially successful albums. Along with his music, Nugent's outspoken support of the National Rifle Association, unrepentant sexism, and vehement antidrug stance all contributed to Nugent's status as a unique rock icon.

Journey to the Center of the Mind. Having played guitar since the age of nine, Nugent was leading Detroit-area bands by his mid-teens. In 1965, he formed the Amboy Dukes, a psychedelic hard rock group. Signed by Mainstream Records, the Amboy Dukes' first release, a revival of the classic Them song "Baby Please Don't Go," was a local hit in 1967. The self-titled album *The Amboy Dukes* peaked at number 181 on the U.S. album charts in 1968. The follow-up album, *Journey To The Center of the Mind* (1968), reached number 74 and produced the band's only hit single, "Journey to the Center of the Mind," which topped out at number 16 on the U.S. singles chart. The Amboy Dukes engaged in a rigorous tour schedule, but their third album for Mainstream Records, *Migration* (1969), proved to be a commercial failure.

As the band continued to tour, their sound evolved from psychedelia to a Jimi Hendrix–inspired guitar barrage. Signed to a contract with Polydor Records, the band had minor success in 1970 with *Marriage on the Rocks/Rock Bottom* as well as with the live album *Survival of the Fittest* in 1971. The Amboy Dukes continued to tour heavily and, after a four-year silence and a switch to Frank Zappa's DiscReet Records, released their last two albums, *Call of the Wild* (1973) and *Tooth, Fang, and Claw* (1974).

Cat Scratch Fever. In 1975, Nugent signed a solo deal with Epic Records. In 1976, his first solo single, "Hey Baby," peaked at number 72 on the U.S. charts while his debut solo album, *Ted Nugent*, made a sixty-two-week run on the U.S. album charts, topping out at number 28 and achieving gold record status. The follow-up album, *Free for All* (1976), with vocals by Meat Loaf, became Nugent's first million-selling album. His second million seller came in 1977 with *Cat Scratch Fever*. These successes were followed by 1978's million-selling *Double Live Gonzo!* and *Weekend Warriors*. Nugent continued to tour and release commercially successful albums through the 1980's.

In 1989, Nugent, along with former Styx guitarist Tommy Shaw, formed the heavy metal combo Damn Yankees. Their self-titled album peaked at number 13 on the U.S. charts in 1991. In the same year, the band headlined Operation Rock n' Roll Storm, a concert in Norfolk, Virginia, to welcome U.S. troops back from Operation Desert Storm. Nugent continued to tour solo and with Damn Yankees through the 1990's.

In the 1990's, Nugent worked as hard offstage as he did onstage. He founded a monthly hunting magazine, *Ted Nugent's World Bow Hunters*, in 1990. He also participated in many charity events, cooking and serving venison at soup kitchens and homeless shelters. In 1994, Nugent was honored by Wyoming Senator Malcolm Wallop for his antidrug stance and for founding Wyoming's Hunters for the Hungry, who donate game to feed the hungry. *—B. Keith Murphy*

SELECT DISCOGRAPHY

■ ALBUMS

Amboy Dukes

The Amboy Dukes, 1967
Journey to the Center of the Mind, 1968
Migration, 1969
Marriage on the Rocks/Rock Bottom, 1970

For the Record

In 1974, Ted Nugent won the National Squirrel-Shooting Archery Contest.

Survival of the Fittest, 1971
Call of the Wild, 1973
Tooth, Fang, and Claw, 1974
Damn Yankees
Damn Yankees, 1990
Don't Tread, 1992
Ted Nugent solo
Ted Nugent, 1975
Free for All, 1976
Cat Scratch Fever, 1977
Double Live Gonzo! 1978 (live)
Weekend Warriors, 1978
State of Shock, 1979
Scream Dream, 1980
Nugent, 1982
Penetrator, 1984
Little Miss Dangerous, 1986
If You Can't Lick 'Em . . . Lick 'Em, 1988
Spirit of the Wild, 1995
Motor City Madness, 1996
Live at Hammersmith 1979, 1997 (live)

SEE ALSO: Meat Loaf; Styx.

N.W.A.

ORIGINAL MEMBERS: Ice Cube (b. O'Shea Jackson, 1969), Dr. Dre (b. Andre Young, 1965), Eazy-E (b. Eric Wright, 1973-1995), M.C. Ren (b. Lorenzo Patterson), D.J. Yella (b. Antoine Carraby)
OTHER MEMBERS: Arabian Prince, the D.O.C.
FIRST ALBUM RELEASE: *N.W.A. and the Posse*, 1987
MUSICAL STYLES: Hip-hop, rap

Gangsta rap originated in the 1980's with the help of artists such as Schoolly D, but N.W.A. (short for Niggaz With Attitude) made it a household word by the late 1980's. Gangsta rap was characterized by explicit lyrics, violent subject matter, and the image of an armed young black man rebelling against the oppression of white authority figures such as the police. N.W.A. in their brief career took the gangsta attitude and became a huge crossover success, surprisingly selling albums to Caucasians and African Americans alike.

Straight Outta Compton. Until N.W.A. became known, rappers tended to hail from New York. Compton, a district of Los Angeles, was the hometown of N.W.A., where several members gained experience as disc jockeys, studio engineers, and rappers on releases that did not sell well. Dr. Dre was a disc jockey for dance clubs, a host for a Los Angeles radio rap show, and a member of the rap group World Class Wreckin' Cru (which also featured rapper Coolio) for a brief time. With friends Ice Cube, from a rap group called CIA, Eazy-E, who had formed the Ruthless Records label and who was a fairly successful rap artist with one album under his belt, *Eazy-Duz-It* (1988), D.J. Yella, and M.C. Ren, they formed N.W.A. in 1988.

N.W.A.'s image was violent but not based on any particular black supremacist politics. They exuded anger and covered such controversial topics as police brutality, rape, pedophilia, and drug use. With a strong beat that occasionally referred to 1970's funk, the band's music was always second to their message. The songs included voice-overs, plenty of profanity, screams, gun shots, and sirens, with the band attempting to convey what life was

For the Record

N.W.A. is known for all three of their albums going platinum and multiplatinum. They were also one of the first hip-hop groups to see its members go on to successful solo careers. Dr. Dre, Ice Cube, and M.C. Ren all released albums that also went platinum and multiplatinum.

§

N.W.A. sold many albums despite the fact that their use of obscenity kept them off radio stations and MTV. The group recorded profanity-free tracks but claimed that the public preferred the obscenity. Each album sold well, but *Efil4zaggin* gained attention by entering the *Billboard* charts at number 2 and becoming number 1 in a week.

N.W.A. (Archive Photos/Fotos International)

like in the black inner city. N.W.A. concerts were a spectacle, with elaborate stage props, including crime-scene tape pulled across the stage on occasion.

Focus on N.W.A. N.W.A. was the first music group to receive a threatening letter from the Federal Bureau of Investigation (F.B.I.), in 1989, for a song that allegedly encouraged violence against the police. Police officers around the nation reacted when N.W.A. went on tour that year. Many tried to have the concerts canceled, but attendance was high. The media stressed the possibility of violence at the concerts, and in Chicago the police charged the stage. Ice Cube stated that the song in question was a protest against police harassing blacks on the assumption that they are all criminals and that it did not directly urge anyone to kill police officers.

Success and Breakup. Everything N.W.A. released quickly went platinum. However, even after the first album, members began to become dissatisfied with the group. Ice Cube left the band in 1989, citing difficulty with the group's white manager, Jerry Heller, and the financial situation that he claimed was cheating him out of royalties. He went on to produce best-selling albums, star in films, and even produce films. Dr. Dre remained with the group through the release of the extended-play single *100 Miles and Runnin'* (1990) and *Efil4zaggin* (1991, the title a mirror image of *Niggaz4Life*) but then left for a successful solo career, also starting his own record label, Death Row Records. M.C. Ren also went solo. Although he did not make a name for himself like Ice Cube and Dr. Dre, his albums sold well. D.J. Yella continued producing records at Ruthless. Eazy-E died from complications resulting from acquired immunodeficiency syndrome (AIDS) on March 26, 1995, at the age of thirty-one. —*Rose Secrest*

SELECT DISCOGRAPHY

■ SINGLES

100 Miles and Runnin', 1990 (extended-play single)

■ ALBUMS

Straight Outta Compton, 1989

Efil4zaggin, 1991

SEE ALSO: Coolio; Dr. Dre; Ice Cube; Public Enemy; Schoolly D; 2 Live Crew.

O

Oasis

ORIGINAL MEMBERS: Noel Gallagher (b. 1967), Liam Gallagher (b. William John Paul Gallagher, 1972), Paul "Bonehead" Arthurs (b. 1965), Paul McGuigan (b. 1971), Tony McCarroll
OTHER MEMBERS: Alan White (b. 1972)
FIRST ALBUM RELEASE: *Definitely Maybe*, 1994
MUSICAL STYLES: Pop, rock and roll

To some, they are the 1990's version of the Beatles: deserving superstars who singlehandedly brought new life and a new direction to the British pop music scene. To others, they are overhyped bad boys, destined to self-destruct because of ongoing clashes between the two brothers, Noel and Liam Gallagher, who stand at their musical core. Oasis's rise to fame that began in 1992 has unfolded with mixed results.

The Beginnings. England's Manchester-based Oasis got its start when Noel Gallagher, working as a guitar technician for the band Inspiral Carpets, decided to put his own band together. He approached younger brother Liam, who was already in a moderately successful group, originally called Rain, and offered his songwriting and guitar playing skills, provided he would have full artistic control over the band. Liam and his bandmates agreed, setting Oasis on the path to rapid stardom.

Early Success. Supported by growing music press interest generated by their live shows, the band's 1994 debut single, the coolly arrogant "Supersonic," made the charts in the United Kingdom at number 31. Oasis's follow-up single, "Shakermaker," which blatantly copied the 1970's pop ditty "I'd Like to Teach the World to Sing (in Perfect Harmony)," increased their popularity, and their third single, "Live Forever," marked the first time the group cracked the U.K. Top 10.

By then, the contrived arguments and brawls, usually peppered with a hearty dose of foul language between the Gallagher brothers, were becoming a trademark of the band, and other members said they had lost count of how many times one or the other brother had quit the band. Drummer Tony McCarroll, ironically, became the first casualty of the squabbling and was replaced by Alan White.

The First Album. By the time Oasis released its first album, *Definitely Maybe*, in the summer of 1994, they had the British press at their feet, who heralded the recording as an instant classic. Noel Gallagher's swaggering confidence only helped fuel the fire. Stardom, Gallagher said, was the brass ring the band was striving for: "I can't stand sniveling rock stars who complain about being famous. . . . There's no point in starting a band unless you want to be famous," he was quoted as saying.

The British press also had a field day with the supposed rivalry between Oasis and British pop stars Blur, as the two bands routinely swapped places on the charts during the second half of the year. *Definitely Maybe* went double platinum in the United Kingdom, and within a year of its release, it reached gold status in the United States.

The Climb Continues. By the time Oasis's second album, (*What's the Story) Morning Glory?*, was released in September, 1995, the band was poised to break through in the United States. That al-

For the Record

The squabbling between the brothers Gallagher is legendary. In 1996, a reporter kept his tape recorder running while the brothers had a verbal fight lasting nearly fifteen minutes. The tape was turned into a single, cleverly titled "Wibbling Rivalry," and reached the Top 40 on the British charts.

bum, which entered the U.K. charts at number 1, was a mix of Beatles-like pop rock and impassioned anthems, all sung by Liam Gallagher in his distinctive voice, simultaneously catchy and whiny.

The album reached the Top 5 in seventeen countries, hit number 1 in six of those countries, and sold nine million copies. In the United States, it went quadruple platinum on the strength of the singles "Champagne Supernova" and "Wonderwall."

Oasis (Express Newspapers/Archive Photos)

Bad Behavior. Almost from the start, Oasis seemed determined to revive the rock tradition of bad behavior, proudly indulging in pursuits such as drinking, using drugs, and wrecking hotel rooms. Their misogynistic comments proved that they were much more impudent than the Beatles ever were but did little to detract from their popularity. The band's appeal became so great in their native England, that in late August 1996, Liam Gallagher's decision to back out of their U.S. tour fifteen minutes before their plane was to depart made the front of nearly every newspaper in the country.

Third Album Released. While the band's third album, 1997's *Be Here Now,* also reached platinum status in the United States and in the United Kingdom, it was not as commercially or critically successful as *(What's the Story) Morning Glory?*, leading some critics to predict an Oasis backlash. In actuality, there would be a bit of a critical backlash against the band for some time, due in part to their rapid rise to fame and their brazen confidence.

—*Nicole Pensiero*

SELECT DISCOGRAPHY

■ ALBUMS

Definitely Maybe, 1994
(What's the Story) Morning Glory? 1995
Be Here Now, 1997
The Masterplan, 1998

SEE ALSO: Beatles, The.

Sinéad O'Connor

BORN: Dublin, Ireland; December 8, 1966
FIRST ALBUM RELEASE: *The Lion and the Cobra,* 1987
MUSICAL STYLES: Rock and roll, pop

Sinéad O'Connor was born in a lower-class suburb of Dublin, Ireland, on December 8, 1966. She was eight years of age when her parents separated; she and her siblings then lived with their mentally unstable mother for five years. During this time, O'Connor was abused by her mother, which led her to years of anger and self-loathing. Her father won custody of his children from their mother

Sinéad O'Connor at the 1993 WOMAD Festival (Archive Photos/ Howard Waggner)

when O'Connor was thirteen years of age; her mother died five years later.

Her Start. The troubled adolescent was sent to a home for wayward girls after being caught shoplifting. When she was sixteen years old, she ran away to Dublin, began singing in bars, and joined the group Ton Ton Macoute. By the age of eighteen, O'Connor was living in London and had a contract for a solo album.

Her first album, *The Lion and the Cobra*, was released in 1987 to critical acclaim on both sides of the Atlantic Ocean. Many of the songs, some written by O'Connor when she was in her teens, were angry, such as "Drink Before the War"; others were sexually charged, such as "I Want Your (Hands on Me)." O'Connor, with her wailing voice, shaved head, combat-style boots, and assertive opinions, captured the music world's attention.

Commercial Success. O'Connor's second album, *I Do Not Want What I Haven't Got*, was released in 1990. When her version of a Prince song, "Nothing Compares 2 U," was released as a single the same year, it became a number 1 hit in seventeen countries. Its appeal was enhanced by a dramatic music video, with its recurrant image of O'Connor's shaved head and a tear running down her cheek. Although the anger that dominated her first album could still be heard, there was the sense of movement toward a less confrontational stance—the opening song, "Feel So Different," starts with the serenity prayer used by many twelve-step groups: "God grant me the serenity to accept the things I cannot change/ Courage to change the things I can/ And the wisdom to know the difference."

Controversy. O'Connor's son, Jake, fathered by John Reynolds, the drummer on her first album, was born in June, 1987. The couple were married briefly after their son was born; after they separated, O'Connor moved to Hollywood, California. She became more politically outspoken: She refused to appear at a show in New Jersey because the U.S. national anthem would be played; she refused to attend a ceremony in England in which she was to receive the International Artist of the Year award; and she was regularly reviled in the British and Irish press for her opposition to the 1991 Persian Gulf War and her outspoken comments about child abuse, both in families and among a small number of Catholic priests. Her most notable public protest, however, came during her 1992 guest appearance on the U.S. television show *Saturday Night Live. After singing Bob Marley's "War," she stunned* the audience by tearing up a picture of Pope John Paul II, saying, "Fight the real enemy." Reaction was strongly negative, and copies of her albums were destroyed in protests. She eventually left the United States, donating her $800,000 home to the Red Cross.

O'Connor's third album seemed to be a radical departure from the first two. *Am I Not Your Girl?* (1992) was a collection of classic pop songs, including "Bewitched, Bothered and Bewildered" (Richard Rodgers and Lorenz Hart) and "I Want to Be Loved by You" (Herbert Stothart, Harry Ruby, and Bert Kalmar). However, the light, pleasant album, with O'Connor's emotive voice backed by a forty-seven-piece orchestra, ends startlingly with an angry speech.

Irish Roots. In 1993, while in Ireland working on the album *Universal Mother,* O'Connor suffered a nervous breakdown. After several months of illness, O'Connor joined a drug rehabilitation program and later entered treatment with a private therapist. *Universal Mother* is an apt name for an album that shows a more nurturing and less confrontational O'Connor. "John I Love You" is a warm love song, and "See Not His Simplicity," "My Darling Child," and "All Babies" speak tenderly of and to children. O'Connor, as the "universal mother," still exhibited righteous anger on behalf of her "children," in this case, the people of Ireland, with the stunning song "Famine." The song starts with O'Connor reminding her listeners that the Great Famine in nineteenth-century Ireland was not a famine at all, but a conscious attempt by England to destroy the Irish. She includes her goddess-centered beliefs in the lines, "We used to worship God as a mother/ Now look at what we're doing to each other," and ends her song with a plea for peace on the island: "We are all Irish in all our different kinds of ways/ We must not . . . show anything to each other except tolerance, forbearance, and neighborly love."

By 1997, O'Connor had repudiated *The Lion and the Cobra* to an extent, partly because she had grown beyond the feelings expressed, and also, she said, because on it she had tried to sing with an American accent because she had been brought up to be ashamed of who she was. After her return to Ireland, she began taking singing lessons and working to regain her Irish voice.

Peace. In 1987, O'Connor was projecting her anger in her voice, her songs, and her appearance. A decade later, however, she had worked through much of the anger that fueled her early music; no longer shaven-headed, she has said she wants to be a force for serenity and nonviolence, not anger. Her 1997 extended-play single, *Gospel Oak,* consists of love songs and lullabies, although her passion for Ireland infuses "This IS a Rebel Song."

In 1996, O'Connor and journalist John Waters had a daughter, Roisin. In 1998, she had her first major role in a film, Neil Jordan's *The Butcher Boy,* in which she played the Virgin Mary.

—Irene Struthers

SELECT DISCOGRAPHY

■ ALBUMS

The Lion and the Cobra, 1987
I Do Not Want What I Haven't Got, 1990
Am I Not Your Girl? 1992
Universal Mother, 1994
So Far. . . . The Best of Sinéad O'Connor, 1997 (compilation)

SELECT AWARDS

Grammy Award for Best Alternative Music Performance for *I Do Not Want What I Haven't Got,* 1990

SEE ALSO: Gabriel, Peter; Morrison, Van; Prince; U2.

For the Record

Sinéad O'Connor often sang "Don't Cry for Me, Argentina," from Andrew Lloyd Webber's score of *Evita,* as a teenager in Dublin pubs, and she won a number of talent contests singing the song. It was later included on her album of cover songs, *Am I Not Your Girl?*

The Ohio Players

BEST-KNOWN LINEUP: Billy Beck, Clarence "Satch" Satchell, Jimmy "Diamond" Williams, Leroy "Sugar" Bonner, Marvin Pierce, Marshall Jones, Ralph "Pee Wee" Middlebrook (d. 1997)
OTHER MEMBERS: Robert Ward, Joe Harris, Walter "Junie" Morrison, Richard "Dimples" Fields, Bobby Lee Fears
FIRST ALBUM RELEASE: *First Impressions*, 1968
MUSICAL STYLES: Funk, soul

The Ohio Players seemed to burst onto the U.S. music scene with five gold albums and two number 1 hits between 1974 and 1976. In fact, some members of the band had been playing together since their 1959 debut in Dayton, Ohio, as the Ohio Untouchables. After a brief and unsuccessful recording career with Detroit's Lu-Pine label, the group disbanded. In the mid-1960's the group reformed, when former Untouchables reedman Clarence Satchell and bassist Marshall Jones recruited other local musicians and christened themselves the Ohio Players. Working as the house band for Compass Records in 1967 gave them access to the recording studio and led to the signing of a contract with Capitol Records in 1969.

Releases. After an unsuccessful album, the Ohio Players pooled their resources for a whirlwind Nashville recording session with Westbound records which produced *Pain* (1972) in just four hours at a cost of four hundred dollars. Though it contained no hits, *Pain* did set the tone for the group's more successful ventures in the future. They had their first hit in 1973, when "Funky Worm" climbed to number 15 on the charts. Shortly thereafter, keyboardist Junie Morrison left to pursue a solo career.

By the mid-1970's, the Ohio Players had developed a signature, ultra-funk style that fed on the group's extensive talents and spontaneity and led to a string of hit singles and five gold albums. The group was unusual in that it relied upon the contributions of each band member on each song. According to Satchell, "We just jam and let things happen naturally. . . . Afterwards, when we feel that we've got something, we'll add the finishing touches, vocals, mixes, and effects. But first, it's gotta happen spontaneously." Although unconventional, the system clearly worked.

Skin Tight (1974), their first Mercury release, went to number 11 on the pop charts and produced "Jive Turkey" (number 47) and "Skin Tight" (number 13). The follow-up, *Fire* (1974), reached the top spot, with the title track reaching number 1 on the singles charts in February, 1975. The group resisted the temptation to develop a formula and deliberately waited to record their next album. After a forty-eight-date tour, they went back to the studio without prepared material, according to plan. The result was *Honey* (1975), which went to number 2 on the charts and produced the monster number 1 single, "Love Rollercoaster."

Death by Disco. By the late 1970's, disco ruled the airwaves, and the Ohio Players were unable to compete. Though they produced one more Top-40 album (*Contradiction*, 1976), they never managed to regain the spontaneous groove that had given them such a distinctive sound. Their last Top-40 single was "Who'd She Coo" (number 18, 1976). They continued to play into the 1980's, enjoying modest success with rhythm-and-blues hits such as "Try a Little Tenderness" (number 40, 1981), and "Let's Play (from Now On)" (number 33, 1988). —*John Powell*

SELECT DISCOGRAPHY

■ ALBUM

Observations in Time, 1969
Pain, 1972
Pleasure, 1972
Ecstasy, 1973
Climax, 1974

For the Record

In 1962, the Ohio Untouchables provided vocal backing for the Falcons hit "I Found a Love." The lead singer was nineteen-year-old Wilson Pickett.

Greatest Hits, 1975 (compilation)
Contradiction, 1976
Angel, 1977
Ouch! 1980
Graduation, 1984
Back, 1988

SEE ALSO: KC and the Sunshine Band.

Oingo Boingo

ORIGINAL MEMBERS: Danny Elfman (b. 1953), Steve Bartek (b. 1952), Kerry Katch, Johnny "Vatos" Hernandez (b. 1951), Sam "Sluggo" Phipps (b. 1953), Leon Schneiderman (b. 1954), Dale Turner (b. 1941), Richard "Ribbs" Gibbs

OTHER MEMBERS: John Avila (b. 1957), Warren Fitzgerald (b. 1968), and others

FIRST ALBUM RELEASE: *Oingo Boingo*, 1980 (EP)

MUSICAL STYLES: Pop, rock and roll, ska, new wave

During their development from a quirky "cult" band to a sophisticated pop outfit that defied categories, Oingo Boingo went through many changes in membership and musical style. Various band members also worked on side projects during the band's existence, which ended in 1995. Rather than simply disappearing, however, vocalist Danny Elfman and company staged a farewell tour and recorded a live album entitled *Farewell* (1996). With a healthy backlog of recordings, not to mention successful careers for its former members, Oingo Boingo stands to be recognized as one of the finest American new-wave bands.

Days of the Mystic Knights. Unlike many bands, Oingo Boingo began not in music, but in theater. The Mystic Knights of Oingo Boingo were a twelve-person theater troupe who performed around Los Angeles during the 1970's. Their routines were completely oddball, featuring slapstick humor and bizarre versions of ancient songs performed with weird sets, masks, costumes, and props. A healthy reputation spread until their shows were consistently sold out. Danny Elfman, always interested in music but never trained in the field, had studied for one year in West Africa during his teens. It was there that his taste for rhythm and percussion grew. As a member of the Mystic Knights of Oingo Boingo, he pushed the musical aspect of the performances further until the group eventually changed from a theater troupe to full-fledged band.

The late 1970's saw the birth of new wave music. Trading in their guitars for synthesizers, these bands kept the spirit of youthful rebellion alive but were usually less intense and more colorful than their punk predecessors. Adding another special element to the mix, the Mystic Knights of Oingo Boingo included a horn section, boosting the number of band members beyond that of most of their contemporaries.

As a foreshadowing of things to come, Elfman agreed, with the Mystic Knights group, to score his brother Richard Elfman's film *Forbidden Zone*. The sound track contained a series of eclectic, original Cab Calloway/Duke Ellington-style jazz numbers and an altered version of "Minnie the Moocher."

After dropping the "Mystic Knights" portion of their name to become Oingo Boingo, the band signed to I.R.S. Records and released a four-song recording called *Oingo Boingo* (1980). The album helped them gain new fans and a major-label deal with A&M Records, on which they released their first full-length album, *Only a Lad* (1981).

Oingo Boingo. With such quirky songs as "Only a Lad," which was about a violent adolescent, Oingo Boingo's records attracted a respectable portion of the new-wave youth rebellion market. This brought a critical backlash from those who accused the band of selling out. However, Elfman stood by his music, which was rather complex and addressed a number of social issues. The song "Imposter" took a vicious swing at some of these critics with the lyrics, "You never lived in the streets though you wish you had/ Not enough talent to play a guitar/ You failed as an artist 'cause you lacked in the confidence/ Now you're a critic and you're at the top/ (You're an imposter) you don't believe what you write." In 1982, their second album, *Nothing to Fear*, was released. A more melodic effort, the album helped the band gain a

Oingo Boingo (Lissa Wales)

following outside of Los Angeles. *Good for Your Soul* followed one year later.

In 1984, Danny Elfman released the solo album *So-Lo.* The album was essentially an Oingo Boingo record, with all the musicians included. One of its songs, "Gratitude," went on to be featured in the film *Beverly Hills Cop* (1984). In fact, the band had already contributed tracks to several youth-oriented films, including *Fast Times at Ridgemont High* (1982), *The Last American Virgin* (1982), and *Bachelor Party* (1984). One such sound track song would lead Oingo Boingo to their first serious success.

For the Record

Danny Elfman appeared as a devil in Richard Elfman's film *Forbidden Zone* (1980). Oingo Boingo can also be spotted in the film *Back to School* playing one of their songs.

Dead Man's Party. The song "Weird Science," written for a 1985 film of the same name, was the band's first Top-40 hit and was also included on their breakthrough album *Dead Man's Party* (1985). The only one of their albums to become certified gold in the 1980's, it was met with critical acclaim, launched four music videos, and included two other singles: "Stay" and "Just Another Day." The group's sound had become far more organized, refined, and accessible, factors that no doubt contributed to their newfound popularity.

That same year, Elfman was asked to score the film *Pee Wee's Big Adventure* and the television show *Amazing Stories.* Elfman and Steve Bartek, Oingo Boingo's lead guitarist, began spending time away from the band to work on film and television scores. Bartek acted as orchestral arranger for

Elfman's compositions. Their next few scores included the films *Back to School* (1986), *Wisdom* (1988), and *Beetlejuice* (1988). However, this was not the end of Oingo Boingo. In 1987, they released *BOI-NGO*, a moderately successful album that was more jazzy and varied in its musical styles, having by this point moved away from the new-wave sound entirely.

A double album of live recordings, *Boingo Alive*, followed in 1988. In 1989, a compilation of earlier hits, *Skeletons in the Closet*, was released, prompting rumors that the band had broken up. While Elfman continued to score films, including *Batman* (1989), other members formed secondary groups such as Food for Feet. In 1990, Oingo Boingo released the album *Dark at the End of the Tunnel* and set off on a tour to support it. This pattern of recording between side projects continued for the next five years. In that time, they released *The Best O' Boingo*, a greatest hits compilation, and 1994's *Boingo*, their final studio album.

Farewell. In 1995, Elfman and the others decided to disband Oingo Boingo. The band staged a final farewell concert on Halloween of that year, which led to the release of *Farewell*, a live double album recording, in 1996. Elfman went on to join the ranks of Randy Newman and Mark Knopfler as a respected pop musician/film composer. In 1993, he both scored and sang the role of Jack Skellington in *The Nightmare Before Christmas*. Bartek continued to work with Elfman on his scores while playing with other bands. Other members joined such bands as CID, Food for Feet, the Jazz Giants, and the Sam Phipps Jazz Quartet. Richard Gibbs, like Elfman, began scoring television shows. His credits include *The Tracy Ullman Show*.

—*Lawrence Ferber*

SELECT DISCOGRAPHY

■ ALBUMS

Oingo Boingo, 1980 (EP)
Only a Lad, 1981
Nothing to Fear, 1982
Good for Your Soul, 1983
Forbidden Zone, 1983 (sound track)
SO-LO, 1984 (Danny Elfman solo)
Dead Man's Party, 1985
BOI-NGO, 1987
Boingo Alive, 1988 (live)
Skeletons in the Closet, 1989 (previously released material)
Dark at the End of the Tunnel, 1990
Best O' Boingo, 1991 (previously released material)
Boingo, 1994
Farewell, 1996 (live)

The O'Jays

ORIGINAL MEMBERS: Bobby Massey, Walter Williams (b. 1942), Eddie Levert (b. 1942), Bill Isles, William Powell (d. 1977)
OTHER MEMBERS: Sammy Strain (b. 1941), Nathaniel Best (b. 1960)
FIRST ALBUM RELEASE: *Comin' Through*, 1965
MUSICAL STYLES: Soul, pop

One of the most popular black vocal groups of the 1970's began as a Canton, Ohio, doo-wop band. Elementary school friends Eddie Levert and Walter Williams had been a gospel singing duo before they decided to perform secular music. The Triumphs were formed in 1958 and began their recording career three years later as the Mascots, with the single "Miracles." Between 1963 and 1967 they enjoyed minor success with Imperial Records, with their highest charting single, "Stand in for Love" (1966), reaching number 12 on the rhythm-and-blues charts.

For the Record

After not going anywhere, first as the "Triumphs" and then as the "Mascots," the group took on Cleveland disc jockey Eddie O'Jay as their manager and began finding some success in the early 1960's. When O'Jay helped them get a new record deal, they changed their name to the "O'Jays" to show their gratitude.

The O'Jays (Freddie Patterson Collection/Archive Photos)

Success. Bill Isles left the group in 1965, and two years later a discouraged band, relegated to doing backup work for artists such as Nat "King" Cole and Lou Rawls, was contemplating retirement. The group's fortunes were transformed in the following year when producers Kenny Gamble and Leon Huff signed the O'Jays to their Neptune label. They had three chart singles for Neptune, but the label folded just as they were gaining momentum. Massey left in 1971 to become a record producer.

The O'Jays trio of Williams, Levert, and Powell turned down offers from the Motown and Invictus labels to return to work with Gamble and Huff's new label. It was a fruitful association. Between 1972 and 1979, the band produced nine albums for Philadelphia International, five going gold and four going platinum. One of the label's first releases was the O'Jay's *Back Stabbers* (1972), which peaked at number 10 on the album charts and included the group's two biggest singles, "Back Stabbers" (number 3) and "Love Train" (number 1). "Love Train" was both written and produced by Gamble and Huff. During this time they had eight number 1 rhythm-and-blues singles, six of which reached the Top 10 on the pop charts. In the middle of this incredible run, Powell was stricken with cancer and died in 1977. He was replaced by Sammy Strain, formerly of Little Anthony and the Imperials.

Rhythm-and-Blues Wonders. Though the O'Jays never regained their mainstream pop success of the 1970's, they continued to produce a steady stream of rhythm-and-blues hits throughout the 1980's and 1990's and remained a popular live act. "Lovin' You" (1987), "Let Me Touch You" (1987), "Have You Had Your Love Today" (1989), "Keep On Lovin' Me" (1991), "Don't Let Me Down" (1991), and Bob Dylan's "Emotionally Yours" (1991) all reached the Top 5 of the rhythm-and-blues charts, and the album *Emotionally Yours* (1991) was certified gold. In 1992 they participated in the Dylan tribute concert at New York's Madison Square Garden. —*John Powell*

SELECT DISCOGRAPHY

■ ALBUMS

Comin' Through, 1965
Greatest Hits, 1972 (compilation)
Ship Ahoy, 1973
Live in London, 1974
Survival, 1976
Family Reunion, 1976
Collectors' Items, 1977 (compilation)
Identify Yourself, 1979

The Year 2000, 1980
Love Fever, 1985
Seriously, 1989
Emotionally Yours, 1991
Heartbreaker, 1993
In Bed with the O'Jays: Their Greatest Love Songs, 1996 (compilation)

SEE ALSO: Booker T. and the MG's.

The Orb

ORIGINAL MEMBERS: Alex Paterson, Jimmy Cauty (b. 1954[?])
OTHER MEMBERS: Youth (b. Martin Glover, 1960), Thrash (b. Kris Weston), Thomas Fehlmann, Andy Hughes
FIRST ALBUM RELEASE: *The Orb's Adventures Beyond the Ultraworld*, 1991
MUSICAL STYLES: Ambient, electronic, house

Inspired by the progressive rock songs of the 1970's, disc jockey Alex Paterson and the KLF guitarist Jimmy Cauty began to produce electronically generated atmospheric music in the late 1980's. Together they pioneered a unique blend of beatless music, conceived as collage and sampling (digitally recording) everyone from Kiss and Minnie Riperton to the children's television program *Reading Rainbow* and the local church bells. Their best-known early piece was "A Huge Ever Growing Pulsating Brain That Rules from the Centre of the Ultraworld," a twenty-two-minute single that actually made the U.K. charts and earned them a chance to rerecord it on radio's *The John Peel Show* in 1989. According to one critic, it was "Pink Floyd-like space music . . . suited to those interested in psychedelia and the bizarre."

Gaining Notice. Working with Killing Joke's former bassist Youth, Paterson released "Little Fluffy Clouds" in November, 1990. Though it failed to make the charts, it became a big dance hit and further bolstered the growing Orb cult. Recruiting Kris Weston ("Thrash"), who had helped engineer "Little Fluffy Clouds," the Orb released their first album, the double *The Orb's Adventures Beyond the Ultraworld* (1991), which received enormous critical acclaim and broke into the U.K. Top 30. By 1992, they had made the charts again with *Aubrey Mixes: The Ultraworld Excursions*, which included work by Youth, Cauty, and Gong guitarist Steve Hillage.

Though no Orb release ever made the U.S. Top 40, their record-setting, thirty-nine-minute, fifty-eight-second, alien-abduction tale, "The Blue Room" (1992), reached the Top 5 in the United Kingdom, and their third album *U.F.Orb* debuted at number 1 later in the year. When their record label, Big House, initiated a controversial campaign to rerelease early singles, the Orb resisted and finally signed an international record deal with Island.

U.S. Recognition. After more than one year of legal wrangling, the Orb resurfaced in 1994 with the extended-play single *Pomme Fritz*. With 1995's epic *Orbus Terrarum*, featuring dense rhythms and natural samples, the group finally began to receive critical notice in the United States and thus packed venues for their road show. The Orb continued to evolve, however. Their next original album, *Orblivion* (1997), returned to its space-age atmosphere but included more drums and bass, sounds drawn from their live performances.

In between recordings, Paterson continued to

For the Record

The Orb's 1990 single "Little Fluffy Clouds" involved them in a lawsuit over the legality of sampling—digitally recording the work of other artists and reusing it in a new context. The song featured a sample of singer-songwriter Rickie Lee Jones speaking, describing fluffy clouds, on the television program *Reading Rainbow*. Jones sued the Orb for using it without permission, and she and their record label settled out of court. In 1998, a snippet of "Little Fluffy Clouds" featuring Jones was used in a Volkswagen television commercial.

disc jockey globally. Paterson, Fehlmann, and Hughes all became leading producers of electronic music, mixing and remixing for such diverse artists as System Seven, Mike Oldfield, the Cranberries, Tangerine Dream, Gong, and Nine Inch Nails. —*John Powell*

SELECT DISCOGRAPHY

■ ALBUMS

The Orb's Adventures Beyond the Ultraworld, 1991
Aubrey Mixes: The Ultraworld Excursions, 1992
U.F. Orb, 1992
Live 93, 1993
Orbus Terrarum, 1995
Auntie Aubrey's Excursions Beyond the Call, 1996 (compilation)
Orblivion, 1997
The U.F. Off: The Best of Orb, 1998

SEE ALSO: Chemical Brothers, The.

Roy Orbison

BORN: Vernon, Texas; April 23, 1936
DIED: Hendersonville, Tennessee; December 6, 1988
FIRST SINGLE RELEASE: "Ooby Dooby," 1956
MUSICAL STYLES: Rock and roll, rockabilly, country

Roy Orbison's career as a singer, songwriter, and guitar player spanned four decades, from the 1950's through the 1980's. His distinctions included an operatic three-octave vocal range and a flair for writing songs expressing melancholy, regret, and loss.

Getting Started. Orbison was raised in the small Texas town of Wink. He began playing the guitar at age six and by age thirteen dreamed of a career as a country singer. In high school, he formed the Wink Westerners and enjoyed regional fame through his own radio program. On the advice of Johnny Cash, Orbison sent a demonstration tape to Sam Phillips at Sun Records. On the strength of the single "Ooby Dooby," Phillips gave Orbison a contract. Orbison's work at Sun was a disappointment. After writing a hit song for the Everly Brothers, he bought out his contract and moved to the Monument label.

In September of 1959, Orbison released his first effort with Monument. One year later, he produced his first hit in three years with "Uptown," which reached number 72 on the *Billboard* charts. As the 1950's came to an end, many in the recording industry feared that Orbison's average looks, shy nature, and thick glasses (a necessity prompted by severe myopia and an astigmatism) would limit him to a career as a songwriter.

The Ballad Years. In 1960, Orbison wrote a ballad, "Only the Lonely," which taps into a profound pain. Orbison initially offered the song to Elvis Presley and subsequently to the Everly Brothers. They rejected it, no doubt finding it excessively gloomy. Orbison recorded it himself for Monument, and the result was an international success. The song topped the charts in Britain and reached number 2 in the United States. "Only the Lonely" afforded Orbison an opportunity to give voice to his doom-tinged vision of heartache. One of the highlights of the song is a dramatic climax demanding powerful falsetto singing. With the success of "Only the Lonely" came extensive touring dates. In concert, Orbison offered a striking contrast to other rock sensations of the day, as he engaged in no theatrics and allowed his vocal virtuosity to carry him.

From 1960 to 1965, Orbison cowrote and recorded numerous hits including "Running Scared," "Crying," "In Dreams," "Falling," and "Blue Bayou." These songs held their own on the charts against all competition. Even at the zenith of the Beatles' success, Orbison managed to reach the top of the charts twice with "It's Over" and "Oh, Pretty Woman." Throughout this period, Orbison remained amazingly well grounded. He and his wife Claudette lived in a modest home, he made cautious investments with his earnings, and he was reputed to have prudish attitudes toward the vices associated with life on the road.

Orbison's musical style was as distinctive as his unpretentious lifestyle. His songs from this period frequently employ unusual structures. A fine example is the surprising structure of "It's Over," which features a dramatic vocal climax on the title lyrics. This material does not function as a verse or a chorus. The song comes to an abrupt halt at its dramatic pinnacle.

Other distinctive features of Orbison's most outstanding songs include his penchant for ever more daring dramatic climaxes featuring an extremely high vocal range. These passages are no mere gimmick, but are used to express an urgent pathos. Orbison also possessed a gift for unusual instrumental touches such as the insistent snare drum repetitions in "Running Scared" and the simple and extremely effective single-line guitar material at the opening of "Oh, Pretty Woman." Orbison's best songs feature expansive and dramatic melodies requiring tremendous breath control. During the early 1960's, he fashioned some of the most enduring songs of the period.

Tragedies. In 1966, Orbison's wife Claudette was killed while riding her motorcycle. Orbison was devastated by the tragedy. Trying to cope, he filled his schedule with concert dates. He entered a fallow period, writing and recording no new songs. Upon returning to writing and recording and following a very brief career in Hollywood, Orbison found his new songs were not commercially successful, although his concerts were still typically sold out.

While touring in Britain in 1968, Orbison endured yet another catastrophe. Two of his sons were killed when his home burned to the ground. This second disaster in two years was much more

Roy Orbison in the 1970's (Fotos International/ Archive Photos)

For the Record

Monument Records signed Roy Orbison by accident. Fred Foster, founder of the fledgling record label, thought he was being offered the contract of Warren Smith when he accidentally signed a contract for Orbison.

§

During his first visit to London, Orbison donned his trademark sunglasses. He had forgotten his regular glasses on the airplane, so he had to wear his prescription sunglasses during the entire performance in order to see. The look remained a signature of his public image. At the time, some fans thought he might be blind.

§

In 1967 Orbison starred in a feature film called *The Fastest Guitar Alive.* He played a spy for the Confederacy who had a bullet-shooting guitar. The film was a failure, but critics were kind to the amateurish singer-turned-actor.

difficult for Orbison, and he suffered a period of depression. By the time he returned to recording less than one year later, his audience had lost interest in waiting for him.

The last years of the 1960's and the entirety of the 1970's were a bleak period for Orbison. Like so many rock-and-roll artists of the 1960's, he had failed to adapt to the tastes of a new generation of young fans. His prudish lifestyle was no longer a badge of distinction for a generation fascinated with challenging social conventions.

His older songs never lost their appeal, however. During the 1970's, Linda Ronstadt sold ten million copies of a cover of Orbison's "Blue Bayou," and Don McLean's rendition of "Crying" reached number 1 in Britain and number 5 in America. A compilation album, *The Best of Roy Orbison*, briefly topped the British charts in 1976.

Orbison underwent triple-bypass heart surgery in 1978 to clear severe arterial blockage. Soon afterward, he was primed for a comeback. He felt better than he had in a decade. His initial project, the 1979 album *Laminar Flow*, was at best a qualified failure.

Renaissance. From 1980 until the end of his life, Orbison enjoyed a steady increase in popularity. His rejuvenation began with a modest hit with the country single "That Lovin' You Feeling Again," a duet with Emmylou Harris. Orbison and Harris won a Grammy Award for their efforts.

In 1986, the song "In Dreams" was featured by director David Lynch in several fascinating scenes in his critically acclaimed film *Blue Velvet*. Following the tremendous artistic success of the film, Lynch produced a two-album release for which Orbison rerecorded all of his most celebrated songs. While most fans prefer the original recordings, these new versions demonstrated that Orbison was still every bit as formidable a singer as he was at the height of his career.

Orbison was not content to live off the celebrity of his older songs. In 1988, he joined Jeff Lynne, George Harrison, Tom Petty, and Bob Dylan to form the Traveling Wilburys. Together they recorded an album, *Traveling Wilburys, Volume One* (1988), posing as five fictional half brothers. Orbison, featured on the song "Not Alone Anymore," billed himself as Lefty Wilbury. The album became an instant classic.

Orbison would not live to enjoy the popularity of his final solo album, *Mystery Girl* (1989). He was aware of its promise, however, as the single "You Got It" was released one month before his death. While *Mystery Girl* is more an appendix to the Orbison career, it contains several fine songs indicating that Orbison's belated return to international attention was richly deserved. —*Michael Lee*

SELECT DISCOGRAPHY

■ SINGLES

"Ooby Dooby," 1956

"Uptown," 1960

"Only the Lonely," 1960

"Crying," 1961

"In Dreams," 1963

"It's Over," 1964

"Oh, Pretty Woman," 1964

"You Got It," 1989

■ ALBUMS

In Dreams: The Greatest Hits, 1987

The Traveling Wilburys, Volume One, 1988 (with the Traveling Wilburys)

Mystery Girl, 1989

SELECT AWARDS

Grammy Award for Best Country Performance by a Duo or Group for "That Lovin' You Feelin' Again," 1980 (with Emmylou Harris)

Rock and Roll Hall of Fame, inducted 1987

Grammy Award for Best Country Vocal Collaboration for "Crying," 1988 (with k. d. lang)

Grammy Award for Best Rock Performance by a Duo or Group with Vocal for *Traveling Wilburys, Volume 1*, 1989 (with the Traveling Wilburys)

Grammy Award for Best Pop Vocal Performance, Male, for "Oh, Pretty Woman," 1990

Tony Orlando and Dawn

ORIGINAL MEMBERS: Tony Orlando (b. Michael Anthony Orlando Cassivitis, April 3, 1944), Telma Hopkins (b. October 28, 1948), Joyce Vincent-Wilson (b. December 14, 1946)

FIRST ALBUM RELEASE: *Candida,* 1970
MUSICAL STYLES: Pop, rock and roll

Formed in 1970 in New York City, Tony Orlando and Dawn were a very successful group with one hit after another until they disbanded in 1977.

Early Years. Tony Orlando started his singing career at age sixteen. Don Kirshner of Aldon Music produced and Carole King wrote his early hits, including "Halfway to Paradise" and "Happy Times (Are Here to Stay)." In 1963, Orlando began working in music publishing, first with Robbins, Feist, and Miller, and then, in 1968, for April-Blackwood Music. Meanwhile, Telma Hopkins and Joyce Vincent-Wilson, a vocal duo who called themselves Dawn, were doing backup vocals for Edwin Starr, Freda Payne, and Johnnie Taylor.

In 1970, Dawn sent a demo tape to Bell Records producers Hank Medress and Dave Appell. Dissatisfied with the lead singer on the song "Candida" on the demo, they dubbed Orlando's voice over the original vocals. The song went on to become a number 3 hit in 1970. A second single called "Knock Three Times," written by Irwin Levine and L. Russell Brown, was recorded in a similar manner and reached number 1 in 1971. By most accounts, Orlando did not meet Hopkins and Vincent-Wilson until after the second single became a number 1 hit. In September, 1971, the newly formed trio made their concert debut in Manchester, England.

Success. The group toured successfully and had their own musical variety television program for two seasons. They recorded at least twenty hit songs, including "Tie a Yellow Ribbon 'Round the Ole Oak Tree" (1973), "Say, Has Anybody Seen My Sweet Gypsy Rose?" (1973), "He Don't Love You (Like I Love You)" (1975), and "Cupid" (1976). After his sister Rhonda died and his actor friend Freddie Prinze committed suicide, Orlando unexpectedly announced his retirement from show business during a concert in Cohasset, Massachusetts, on July 22, 1977. However, he started performing solo in Las Vegas in November of the same year. In 1979, Orlando signed with Casablanca Records and recorded "Sweets for My Sweet," which went to number 54 on the charts. He also embarked on an acting career, with roles in television movies and an appearance on *The Cosby Show.* In 1980, he joined the cast of *Barnum* on Broadway and played the leading role in 1981.

After the group broke up, Dawn continued performing for a short time. In September, 1979, Hopkins began a television acting career in *A New Kind of Family.* She later had regular roles in *Bosom Buddies, Gimme a Break,* and *Family Matters.* Vincent-Wilson went on to do backup vocals for Smokey Robinson. In 1988, Orlando, Hopkins, and Vincent-Wilson reunited as Dawn and performed live for a short period. In the 1990's, Orlando started his own theater in Branson, Missouri, called the Tony Orlando Yellow Ribbon Music Theater, with a stained-glass window showing a yellow ribbon. —*Alice Myers*

SELECT DISCOGRAPHY

■ SINGLES

"Candida," 1970
"Knock Three Times," 1971
"Tie a Yellow Ribbon 'Round the Ole Oak Tree," 1973
"Say, Has Anybody Seen My Sweet Gypsy Rose?" 1973
"He Don't Love You (Like I Love You)," 1975

■ ALBUMS

Candida, 1970
Dawn Featuring Tony Orlando, 1971
Tuneweaving, Dawn's New Ragtime Follies, 1973
Golden Ribbons, Prime Time, 1974
Tony Orlando and Dawn II, 1974
He Don't Love You (Like I Love You), 1975
Tony Orlando and Dawn: Greatest Hits, 1975 (previously released material)
Skybird, 1975
To Be with You, 1976

SELECT AWARDS

American Music Awards Favorite Pop/Rock Band, Duo or Group Award, 1976

Ozzy Osbourne. *See* Black Sabbath / Ozzy Osbourne

The Osmonds

ORIGINAL MEMBERS: Alan Osmond (b. 1949), Wayne Osmond (b. 1951), Merrill Osmond (b. 1953), Jay Osmond (b. 1955)

OTHER MEMBERS: Donny Osmond (b. 1957), Marie Osmond (b. 1959), Jimmy Osmond (b. 1963)

FIRST ALBUM RELEASE: *The Osmonds*, 1971

MUSICAL STYLES: Pop, rock and roll, country

The Osmond children grew up in a large Mormon family in Ogden, Utah, and were taught to sing and play musical instruments by their parents, George and Olive. In the early 1960's, the four older brothers, Alan, Wayne, Merrill, and Jay, began singing barbershop-quartet songs at a variety of functions. In 1962, they were invited to appear on *The Andy Williams Show*, and they made frequent appearances on the television show over the next decade. Joined by Donny in the mid-1960's, the Osmond Brothers appeared on Jerry Lewis's television program and toured with singer Pat Boone and comedian Phyllis Diller.

The Hits. In 1971, the Osmond Brothers had a gold hit with their first release, "One Bad Apple," which spent five weeks at number 1 on the national *Billboard* charts. Their 1971 albums, *The Osmonds* and *Homemade*, were both certified gold. During that year, Donny had two hits, "Sweet and Innocent" and the number 1 "Go Away Little Girl." The Osmond Brothers continued their string of hits in 1972 with "Down by the Lazy River," "Hold Her Tight," and "Crazy Horses," and Donny had hit singles with "I Knew You When," "Puppy Love," "Why," and "Too Young."

Marie Joins the Act. In late 1972, sister Marie and brother Jimmy joined the Osmond Brothers, and their group name was changed to the Osmonds. Their clean-cut image and good looks captured the hearts of teenagers everywhere, and they even had their own cartoon series. During the early to mid-1970's, the group had a number of hits, including "Going Home," "I Can't Stop," "Love Me for a Reason," and "The Proud One." Their 1973 album, *The Plan*, focused on songs attempting to express their beliefs as members of the Church of Jesus Christ of Latter-day Saints, and it reached the number 6 spot on the album charts in the United Kingdom. Marie had a number 1 country hit in 1973, "Paper Roses," followed by another big country hit, "Who's Sorry Now," while Jimmy had an international million

Marie and Donny Osmond in 1977 (AP/Wide World Photos)

For the Record

In the 1970's the Osmond Brothers were so popular that female fans went to extremes to reach them. On one occasion, two young women mailed themselves in a crate to the Osmonds' hotel room. Others occasionally rappelled down high-rise hotels to slip into the Osmonds' rooms.

seller with "Long-Haired Lover from Liverpool," which topped the British rock-and-roll charts for six weeks.

The television variety series *Donny and Marie* ran successfully from 1976 to 1979, and the Osmonds made several appearances on the program. During that time period, Donny and Marie had several hit duets, including "I'm Leaving It up to You," "Deep Purple," and "Morning Side of the Mountain." Due to their waning popularity, the Osmonds disbanded in 1980.

Different Directions. In 1982, the four original Osmond Brothers plus Jimmy formed a new Osmond Brothers group and moved into the country market, appearing regularly at the Country Music Festival in London, England. Donny's musical output lessened, and he turned to theater work, performing in Toronto, Chicago, and Salt Lake City in the successful musical revival *Joseph and the Amazing Technicolor Dreamcoat*, making his final appearance in 1998. Donny also recorded a number 2 hit, "Soldier of Love" (1989), as well as two other hits, "Sacred Emotion" (1989) and "My Love Is a Fire" (1990). Marie continued her country music success with three number 1 hits, "Meet Me in Montana" (1985), "There's No Stopping Your Heart" (1985), and "You're Still New to Me" (with Paul Davis, 1986).

The new Osmond Brothers group achieved success with country music, being named *Billboard*'s Top New Singles Group in 1992. They would own and operate the Osmond Family Theater in Branson, Missouri, performing twelve shows weekly. Marie and Donny would both remain active with national musical tours, and they began another *Donny and Marie* television series in 1998.

—*Alvin K. Benson*

SELECT DISCOGRAPHY

■ ALBUMS

The Osmonds, 1971
The Plan, 1973
The Proud One, 1975
Greatest Hits, 1992

SELECT AWARDS

Billboard, named Top New Singles Group, 1992 (Osmond Brothers)

SEE ALSO: Bennett, Tony; Carpenters, The; Jackson 5, The; Tillis, Mel.

Buck Owens

(Alvis Edgar Owens, Jr.)

BORN: Sherman, Texas; August 12, 1929
FIRST SINGLE RELEASE: "Down on the Corner"/"It Don't Show on Me," 1956
MUSICAL STYLE: Country

Buck Owens was one of the most influential and best-selling country artists of all time. Based in Bakersfield, California, a long way from the country capital of Nashville, Tennessee, Owens adhered to a pure vision of country music. When the trend was to add strings and vocal choruses to sweeten the country sound, Owens stayed with his trademark basic twangy style, an electric honky-tonk country that was often so raw it verged on rock and roll. In fact, he is credited, along with Merle Haggard, with creating the branch of country music known as the "Bakersfield sound."

Owens built a loyal audience that bought millions of his records—many made with his band the Buckaroos—and watched him week after week as a regular performer on the country television program *Hee Haw*. Owens retired for some time, but he found he could not stay away from the business, and with the urging of newcomer Dwight Yoakam, Owens made his way back into the limelight, as charismatic as ever.

Buck Owens (Archive Photos)

The Beginnings. When he was just three years old, Alvis Owens announced that he was renaming himself after his favorite horse, Buck. The nickname lasted, even after the Owens family moved to Mesa, Arizona, when Buck was seven. He picked cotton to help the family through the Depression, and he sang, sometimes in church, sometimes around the house. At age thirteen, he was given a mandolin and learned to play it, as he also did with the guitar and drums.

By age sixteen, Owens was able to earn money playing music. He loved the music that was then called country and western, especially artists such as Bob Wills, Roy Acuff, and Red Foley. He worked with other performers, giving live performances over the radio, and he married a girl who was in one of his groups. As Bonnie Owens, she later built up a music career of her own, as did the couple's son, who called himself Buddy Alan.

Owens soon decided that he needed to move to a larger city, so he settled in Bakersfield. There he found work with local country groups, and he played at recording sessions with established stars. By 1956 he was ready to make his own records, and he recorded his first few singles for the small Pep Records. In 1958 he was signed to the larger Capitol Records, and his long reign as a country superstar began.

Smash Hits and Buckaroos. Owens did not blaze his way up the charts immediately, but his fourth Capitol single, "Second Fiddle," established his name in 1959. That same year, "Under Your Spell Again" became his first big hit, reaching number 4 on the country charts. From then on, he had a string of hits.

By 1963, he was a national sensation, and he had his first number 1 country hit, "Act Naturally." Little did he know that thousands of miles from Bakersfield, in Liverpool, England, he was gaining new fans in a young rock group called the Beatles, who would record their own version of "Act Naturally," with Ringo Starr singing lead, in 1965.

Beginning with "Love's Gonna Live Here," which stayed at number 1 (country) for a staggering sixteen weeks, Owens became a country superstar. Nearly every single he released until the end of the 1960's went directly to number 1 on the country charts. Some of his records, particularly 1965's "I've Got a Tiger by the Tail," even crossed over to the pop charts.

Of course, Owens could not have accomplished this feat by himself, and a good part of his success can be attributed to his band, the Buckaroos. Joining him in 1962, the Buckaroos were one of the most creative and exciting bands in country music. In particular, guitarist Don Rich was a virtuoso, and the band gained such a devoted following that it was able to release its own singles and albums apart from Owens, winning several Country Music Association awards for Instrumental Group of the Year.

Buck Owens and the Buckaroos truly did buck traditional country trends. At the time that they were popular, country music had become urbanized. Artists and producers were looking to steer country away from its image as a rural music, and one of the ways to do that was to make country more like pop, by adding orchestration and vocal choruses to smooth out the music. Owens and his band preferred to keep the sound basic and driving, not unlike many of the later alternative country acts, and they found enough fans of their method to earn them a huge following. The Bakersfield sound, which Owens and Haggard popularized, was deliberately named to differentiate it from the more cosmopolitan Nashville sound.

Hee Haw. Country music was a phenomenon by the end of the 1960's, more popular than ever. There was enough interest in it to spawn a weekly television variety program built around country performers and the rural lifestyle. Although the nature of the show, which also starred Roy Clark, was basically comedic, it featured some good music. From 1969 until 1986, *Hee Haw,* as the show was called, was the place where one could find Buck Owens. Owens was so popular during this period that Capitol released nearly ten albums by him between 1969 and 1971, many of which reached number 1 on the country charts.

Owens continued to record for Capitol, and then Warner Bros., throughout the 1970's and the early 1980's, and although his records continued to sell well, he was no longer the force he once was. He had even given in to some of the Nashville trappings he had earlier sought to avoid. He influenced countless younger performers, though, among them Emmylou Harris, who recorded a duet with Owens in 1979, "Together Again." Others who have recorded his songs include Ray Charles and Garth Brooks.

By the late 1980's, Owens had virtually retired from the music business, preferring to concentrate on other business interests, such as radio stations he owned. In 1988, however, Dwight Yoakam, an upcoming new traditionalist country star who had been heavily influenced by Owens, convinced Owens to record a duet with him, a song called "Streets of Bakersfield," which Owens had originally recorded in 1972. The single went to number 1 on the country charts, and Owens was again in the public eye.

Although he would not record or tour as prolifically as he did in the 1960's, Owens would continue to appear onstage and on the charts. Such was the case in 1989, when former Beatles drummer Ringo Starr asked Owens to rerecord "Act Naturally," this time as a duet. —*Jeff Tamarkin*

SELECT DISCOGRAPHY

■ SINGLES

"Under Your Spell Again"/"Tired of Livin'," 1959

"Act Naturally"/"Over and Over Again," 1963

"Love's Gonna Live Here"/"Getting Used to Losing You," 1963

"My Heart Skips a Beat"/"Together Again," 1964

"I Don't Care (Just as Long as You Love Me)"/"Don't Let Her Know," 1964

"I've Got a Tiger by the Tail"/"Cryin' Time," 1965

"Before You Go"/"(I Want) No One but You," 1965

"Waitin' in Your Welfare Line"/"In the Palm of Your Hand," 1966

"Streets of Bakersfield," 1988 (with Dwight Yoakam)

"Act Naturally"/"The Key's in the Mailbox," 1989 (with Ringo Starr)

For the Record

In the 1990's, Buck Owens opened a theater/restaurant/museum complex in his hometown of Bakersfield, California, called Buck Owens's Crystal Palace.

■ ALBUMS

I've Got a Tiger by the Tail, 1965

Carnegie Hall Concert, 1966

The Buck Owens Collection (1959-1990), 1992 (3-CD boxed set, compilation)

SELECT AWARDS

Academy of Country Music Male Vocalist of the Year Award, 1965

Capitol Records Artist of the Decade Award, 1970

Academy of Country Music Pioneer Award, 1988

Country Music Hall of Fame, inducted 1996

SEE ALSO: Beatles, The; Brooks, Garth; Charles, Ray; Clark, Roy; Haggard, Merle; Harris, Emmylou; Wills, Bob, and His Texas Playboys; Yoakam, Dwight.

P

Robert Palmer

BORN: Batley, Yorkshire, England; January 19, 1949

FIRST ALBUM RELEASE: *Sneakin' Sally Through the Alley*, 1974

MUSICAL STYLES: Pop, reggae, rock and roll

Robert Palmer, one of the most popular artists of the middle and late 1980's, made his mark in the music industry with hit singles that were boosted in the charts by music videos of the well-dressed singer performing his songs with a band composed of beautiful women. The videos proved very popular on cable music television networks and were eventually recognized as some of the best ever produced. Although Palmer has recorded many styles of music during his career, he is most identified with his pulsating rock recordings of the 1980's.

Beginnings. Born Alan Palmer, Robert Palmer spent much of his youth living on the island of Malta in the Mediterranean Sea where his father served in the British Royal Navy. As a teenager, he experimented with rhythm-and-blues music, actually joining a band known as the Mandrakes at the age of fifteen. Preferring a music career to his original employ as a graphic designer, he returned to England in 1968 to sing with the Alan Brown Set. The following year he joined DaDa, a twelve-piece soul group that evolved and eventually changed its name to Vinegar Joe. The group produced three albums during the brief two-year period that Palmer played rhythm guitar and alternated vocals with Elkie Brooks as a member of Vinegar Joe. He left the group in 1974 to start his solo career, debuting that year with *Sneakin' Sally Through the Alley*, which was recorded with members of Little Feat and the Meters. The album, recorded in New York, New Orleans, and England, peaked at number 107 on the U.S. charts and marked the beginning of a very successful solo career for Palmer.

In 1975, Palmer released *Pressure Drop*, which reached number 136 on the U.S. charts. The album contained a much more rhythmic reggae feel than his previous work, a trend evidenced by a move to the Bahamas. *Double Fun* (1978), featuring Palmer's first hit single, "Every Kinda People," introduced Palmer to a much broader American audience. The self-produced *Secrets* (1979), his most successful album of the 1970's, was more indicative of his shift toward mainstream rock, as evidenced by his single "Bad Case of Loving You (Doctor, Doctor)." Palmer's dramatic stylistic experimentation continued with *Clues* (1980), a collaboration with Gary Numan and Talking Heads' Chris Frantz. Ironically, while the album became his best-selling yet in England, the stylistic shift failed to appeal to his fans in the United States. *Maybe It's Alive* (1982), which mixed live tracks from a 1980 concert with new studio recordings, was even less popular with his U.S. fans than *Clues*. *Pride* (1983) was equally disappointing.

Stardom. In an effort to revive his failing career, Palmer teamed up with Andy and John Taylor of Duran Duran to form the group Power Station. A commercial success with hit singles "Some Like It Hot" and "Get It On," the group's album peaked at number 6 on the U.S. charts. Encouraged by his recent success, Palmer left the group prior to a planned Live Aid appearance to continue his solo career. His 1985 album, *Riptide*,

For the Record

Robert Palmer has been recognized as one of the most fashion conscious and stylish male performers in the music industry. In 1989, *Rolling Stone* named Palmer the Best Dressed as part of its music awards.

went to number 1 with the hit single "Addicted to Love." Perhaps most interesting about the hit single was the accompanying music video that became an instant hit on cable television. It was to be the first of several hit singles, including "I Didn't Mean to Turn You On," accompanied by video releases featuring Palmer flanked by a stage full of undulating beautiful women. "Simply Irresistible," the first hit single from his 1988 platinum album *Heavy Nova,* was also boosted by a sexually charged video that received much play on MTV.

Don't Explain (1990), Palmer's first release of the 1990's, was a move away from his music and videos of the 1980's to material similar to his earlier releases. The collection did not sell as well as his 1980's releases. Undaunted, Palmer released *Ridin' High* in 1992, a collection of big band standards that only reached number 173 on the U.S. charts. *Honey,* recorded in Milan and released in 1994, failed to achieve the chart success of his earlier albums. *—Donald C. Simmons, Jr.*

SELECT DISCOGRAPHY

■ ALBUMS

Sneakin' Sally Through the Alley, 1974
Some People Can Do What They Like, 1976
Double Fun, 1978
Secrets, 1979
Clues, 1980
Pride, 1983
Riptide, 1985
Honey, 1994

SELECT AWARDS

Grammy Award for Best Rock Vocal Performance, Male, for "Addicted to Love," 1986
Grammy Award for Best Rock Vocal Performance, Male, for "Simply Irresistible," 1989

SEE ALSO: Duran Duran; Talking Heads.

Charlie Parker

BORN: Kansas City, Kansas; August 29, 1920
DIED: New York, New York; March 12, 1955
FIRST RECORDINGS: "Swingmatism" and "Hootie Blues," 1941 (with the Jay McShann Band)
FIRST ALBUM RELEASE: *Charlie Parker's Beboppers,* 1945
MUSICAL STYLE: Jazz

Charlie "Yardbird" Parker, sometimes known as Bird, is considered by many people to be the greatest single musician in the history of jazz. He has influenced almost every jazz soloist since the 1940's with the unique style he developed during his brief career. Unfortunately, Parker's achievements and accomplishments as a gifted and talented musician were often marred by his addiction to drugs and alcohol. Nonetheless, although many musicians contributed to the development of bebop jazz in the 1940's, critics continue to point to Parker, as well as John Birks "Dizzy" Gillespie, as the main architects and perpetuators of this music.

Early Background. Parker was born on August 29, 1920, in Kansas City, Kansas, but his family moved across the Kaw River to Kansas City, Missouri, when Parker was seven years old. Parker's first experience with music was playing baritone horn in the Lincoln High School band in 1933. Realizing that her son did not like playing the cumbersome baritone horn, Parker's mother, Addie, purchased an alto saxophone for him. His affinity and interest toward his music began to grow, and Parker quit school in 1935 to pursue a professional career with the Deans of Swing led by pianist Lawrence "88" Keyes.

In 1935, Kansas City was a mecca for fine musicians, especially saxophonists. Parker was exposed to some of the finest saxophonists of the day, such as Ben Webster with the Clouds of Joy and Lester Young and Buster "Professor" Smith with Count Basie's newly formed band. However, because there was no one available to teach him the saxophone, Parker had to learn to play his instrument by emulating the established jazz players of the time.

As a young musician, Parker participated in informal late-night performances or jam sessions in order to develop his craft. Unfortunately, his first experiences at these jam sessions were embarrassing because Parker had not yet understood the music and was not yet prepared to play more

Charlie Parker (Freddie Patterson Collection/ Archive Photos)

than two compositions (the first eight bars of "Lazy River" and "Honeysuckle Rose"). On one occasion Parker was laughed off the bandstand because he unknowingly played one composition while the band played another. Although the immediate result of this incident was humiliation, it also served as a motivational tool for Parker's development.

The Developmental Years. In the summer of 1937, soon after his humbling experience during the Kansas City jam session, Parker joined a band led by George E. Lee. The band performed in various resorts in the Ozark Mountains. During his time off, Parker was said to have practiced diligently by listening to recordings of the Count Basie band and imitating his musical mentor, tenor saxophone soloist Lester Young. Later that year he returned to Kansas City and joined a band led by one of his first influences and mentors, Buster "Professor" Smith. After a short time with Smith's band and the Jay McShann band, Parker traveled to New York City, via Chicago, to hone his talents. He spent the final years of the 1930's in New York listening to the great jazz musicians of the day, including the virtuoso pianist Art Tatum, and participating in jam sessions in Harlem with other young, developing jazz musicians. It was during these developmental years that Parker began to hear and formulate the new sounds that were soon to change the way jazz musicians played their music. The new music that was developing in Harlem clubs, later called bebop, was to include faster tempos, colorful harmonies, intricate rhythmic nuances, and virtuoso solo improvisations.

Spreading the Word. Parker returned to Kansas City in 1940 and rejoined the Jay McShann band as he continued to develop his explorations in jazz. His earliest recordings were made with the Jay McShann band in 1940 during a Wichita, Kansas, radio broadcast of several compositions from the band's repertoire in which Parker had several solos. On April 30, 1941, Parker recorded with the Jay McShann band and was featured on two of the three selections, "Swingmatism" and "Hootie Blues." Parker's solos during these compositions portrayed a mature jazz musician whose improvisations were to pave the way into modern jazz and the bebop era.

Parker left the Jay McShann band in 1942 and returned to New York to spread the word of the new music by playing in various jam sessions throughout the city. In 1943, Parker was asked to play tenor saxophone in a band led by the well-known pianist Earl Hines. This band was composed of many fine young jazz musicians, including trumpeter Dizzy Gillespie, and afforded Parker the opportunity to continue his development and the perpetuation of bebop. From the Hines band, Parker joined the newly formed big band led by Billy Eckstine in June, 1944. Again Parker was teamed with Gillespie and a host of other young, rising jazz musicians. Parker's experience with these musicians on and off the bandstand provided the final foundation for his transformation into a major jazz innovator.

Leading the Way. After leaving the Eckstine band in the latter part of 1944, Parker began leading his own bebop band, mainly a quartet, in New York. Between the end of 1944 and November, 1945, Parker recorded several albums as a sideman with guitarist Tiny Grimes (September, 1944), Gillespie (February and May, 1945), and, along with Gillespie, an all-star group of jazz musicians from the earlier big band swing era (June, 1945).

It was not until November 26, 1945, that Parker recorded as a leader for the first time under the session name of Charlie Parker's Beboppers. This was an important recording not only because Parker was the leader of the session but also because the personnel constituted the ideal bebop band (Parker on alto saxophone, Gillespie on trumpet and piano, Miles Davis on trumpet, Argonne Thorton on piano, Curly Russell on bass, and Max Roach on drums) and the compositions recorded were examples of the standard bebop repertoire, including "Now's the Time," "Billie's Bounce," "Koko," and "Warming Up a Riff."

At the end of 1945, Parker and Gillespie traveled to the West Coast to perform their music. Despite a successful debut, the music did not attract audiences as it did in New York, and the group disbanded soon after. While Gillespie returned to New York, Parker remained in California to perform and record. In July of 1946, Parker's addiction to narcotics worsened, and he was eventually committed to Camarillo State Hospital for treatment. After sixteen months of rehabilitation and psychiatric care, Parker was released from Camarillo and returned to New York.

Furthering the Legend. Upon his return from California, Parker began his most productive and arguably his most creative period. From 1947 to 1949, Parker recorded extensively and performed with a variety of ensembles, including his own bebop quintet, throughout the United States as well as Europe. Other than performing with his own quintet, Parker thoroughly enjoyed his performances with strings in 1949 and 1950. The earlier recordings produced such classics as "Just Friends," "April in Paris," and "Summertime." Parker made such an impact on the way jazz was played that he influenced almost every jazz musician, regardless of instrument.

For the Record

In the 1950's, pianist Lennie Tristano once commented on the extent of Parker's influence on jazz musicians by saying, "If Charlie Parker wanted to invoke plagiarism laws, he could sue almost everybody who's made a record in the last ten years."

The last five years of Parker's life were erratic and unpredictable, ranging from such periods of genius as the historic concert on May 15, 1953, with his good friend Gillespie to moments of absurdity and tragedy. His body worn down from his addiction to narcotics, Parker died on March 12, 1955, in the home of Baroness Pannonica de Koenigswarter (a wealthy patron who assisted many jazz musicians in the 1940's and 1950's).

Parker's virtuoso skills as a performer, his warmth and beauty of tone on the saxophone, and his expressiveness as a musician all contributed to his stature as an important figure in jazz. More important, Parker brought the art of improvisation to a higher level with his innovative approach to harmony, rhythm, and melodic manipulation. —*Frank J. Bongiorno*

SELECT DISCOGRAPHY

■ ALBUMS

The Immortal Charlie Parker, c. 1945
The Genius of Charlie Parker, 1945
Bird: The Complete Charlie Parker on Verve, 1988

SELECT AWARDS

Down Beat Hall of Fame, inducted 1955

SEE ALSO: Adderly, Julian "Cannonball"; Davis, Miles.

Graham Parker

BORN: London, England; November 18, 1950
FIRST ALBUM RELEASE: *Howlin' Wind*, 1976
MUSICAL STYLES: Rhythm and blues, new wave, punk

Graham Parker was one of the original "angry young men" who emerged in the 1970's to pioneer the iconoclastic music generally known as new wave. Although new wave quickly became a broad genre with myriad strains and a measure of mass appeal, Parker was seen as a new wave "traditionalist" in that he kept his music grounded in earthy rock rhythms and traditional rock-and-roll instrumentation.

The 1970's. Graham Parker has never achieved great commercial success, but his music has earned critical acclaim, and he has a loyal following. Parker's music is soulful, impassioned, and steeped in rhythm and blues. His earlier work in particular demonstrated a revivalist quality. It was Parker's lyrics, however, that were most distinctive. Bristling with cynicism and snide social criticism, his songs exuded a feeling of alienation. Parker's whiskeyed singing voice and energetic, anxious attitude seem well suited to his combination of rhythm-and-blues music and sardonic wit. His somewhat strained delivery and fluid articulation emphasize a careless urgency. His trademark dark glasses added an air of aloofness and mystique in concert performances and publicity photographs.

Parker's first album was *Howlin' Wind* (1976), produced by Nick Lowe. It captured the "pub-rock" qualities of Parker's music. Critics praised the record for its raw energy, engaging lyrics, and rock-revival melodies—qualities that were increasingly rare in the 1970's. His second album, *Heat Treatment* (also 1976), continued in the same vein. At the same time it demonstrated Parker's depth and versatility. There was a vast reservoir of energy, wit, emotion, and intelligence that Parker

Graham Parker (Paul Natkin)

presumably could draw upon for dozens of albums. Critics praised the combination of new rhythm-and-blues tunes, clever and urgent lyrics, a soulful and biting voice, and a tight brass-backed band called the Rumour.

That formula was not commercially popular, however. Wearing one's political heart on one's sleeve did not lead to successful pop music in the late 1970's. Worse, Parker's temper, partly exacerbated by heavy drinking, caused friction with recording executives. As a result, he was constantly switching record labels—from Mercury to Arista to Electra to Atlantic to RCA to Capitol to the independent label Razor and Tie. His falling out with Mercury was especially unpleasant, and it was the subject of one of his bitterest songs, "Mercury Poisoning."

Squeezing Out Sparks, released in 1979, was the only one of Parker's albums to achieve widespread recognition and commercial respectability. The album reached number 18 in Britain and number 40 in the United States, and it established Parker as a major influence on new wave and rock music. Music critics, who had been cool to *Stick to Me* (1977), were back in the fold. Comparisons to Elvis Costello were made, though Parker generally was able to stand on his own as a significant artist in the genre. It has also been noted that Parker himself probably influenced Costello, as Parker was performing and recording before Costello was.

The 1980's. Within a few years, Parker would be heading back into relative obscurity, save for a small clutch of loyal fans. Any of a number of factors could have been responsible. Parker got married and strived to cut back on his drinking. Many among Parker's core following believed that Parker had lost much of his edge. Musically, Parker's *The Real Macaw* (1983) did not deviate greatly from his previous album, *Another Grey Area* (1982). Many of the lyrics of the new album were uncharacteristically upbeat, however—the less generous of his critics would call them vapid. While the 1982 album included songs entitled "Temporary Beauty," "No More Excuses," "Dark Side of the Bright Lights," and "Big Fat Zero," the new album seemed to reflect Parker's focus on his newfound love: "Life Gets Better," "Can't Take Love for Granted," "Miracle a Minute," "Anniversary," and "Last Couple on the Dance Floor."

Another reason for the quick decline of Parker's commercial success could be his stubbornness—a quality that prevented him from working amiably with record companies, from tailoring his work to be more in sync with popular tastes, and from successfully utilizing the increasingly important format of rock videos.

Graham Parker's subsequent albums never achieved the success or critical recognition of *Squeezing Out Sparks. Steady Nerves* (1985) did include the only of Parker's songs to make the Top 40 "Wake Up (Next to You)," number 39 in 1985). The album was a commercial disappointment, however, and his record label, Elektra, quickly dropped Parker. He tried to rebound with yet another record label—Atlantic—but Parker once again found himself at odds with the company over the issue of creative control. He left Atlantic without an album to show for it and spent some time without luck trying to find a receptive label. Finally he managed to secure the means and an acceptable measure of artistic autonomy for recording a relatively low-budget album with RCA. The result was *The Mona Lisa's Sister* in 1988.

Although it did not propel Parker back to the cutting edge of pop music, where he had found himself in the late 1970's, *The Mona Lisa's Sister* was hailed by critics as a welcome return to Parker's Rumour-era style. Indeed, the musicians on *The Mona Lisa's Sister* included two original members of the Rumour: Brinsley Schwartz playing guitar and Andrew Bodnar on bass. The musical

For the Record

Graham Parker has tried his hand at writing novels as well as music. In the late 1970's he wrote *The Great Trouser Mystery* (published only in Britain). In 1997 he was searching for a publisher to take his second novel, *The Thylacine's Nest.*

arrangements were simplified from his recent albums' tendency to be overproduced. The lyrics were once again biting and nervous, observing such topics as societal nihilism, the hypocrisy and vapidity of the music industry, and a father's anxiety about the too-early awakening of his daughter's sexuality. The opening lines from "OK Hieronymus" is typical of Parker's return to acerbity: "I break your heart in a thousand places/ She makes a slur against other races/ He rejects all of the unpretty faces/ Sticks them full of knives." Still, Parker proves that he is not all bile and sneers by ending the album with a version of Sam Cooke's wistful 1961 hit "Cupid."

The 1990's. After *The Mona Lisa's Sister* Parker completed several more albums for RCA, including *Struck by Lightning* (1991) and *Burning Questions* (1992). Then, in 1995, he released *12 Haunted Episodes* on yet another label, Razor and Tie. This album is notable for its almost complete lack of irony. Still without a hit, Parker turned back to his punk roots and released *Acid Bubblegum* in 1996 and toured with the Figgs the following year. —*Steve D. Boilard*

SELECT DISCOGRAPHY

■ ALBUMS

Howlin' Wind, 1976
Heat Treatment, 1976
Stick to Me, 1977
Squeezing Out Sparks, 1979
The Up Escalator, 1980
Another Grey Area, 1982
The Real Macaw, 1983
Steady Nerves, 1985
The Mona Lisa's Sister, 1988
Struck by Lightning, 1991
Burning Questions, 1992
12 Haunted Episodes, 1995
Acid Bubblegum, 1996

SEE ALSO: Costello, Elvis.

Parliament. *See* George Clinton / Parliament / Funkadelic

The Alan Parsons Project

ORIGINAL MEMBERS: Alan Parsons (b. 1949), Eric Woolfson (b. 1945)

FIRST ALBUM RELEASE: *Tales of Mystery and Imagination*, 1976

MUSICAL STYLES: Pop, rock and roll, progressive rock

A unique experiment in studio music, the Alan Parsons Project employed more than one hundred musicians and various vocalists over its ten-album career. Formed by two record producers as a way to free themselves from the traditional confines of recording albums, they established an unusual and creative niche in modern music.

The Beginnings. Alan Parsons was born in Great Britain on December 20, 1949. In school he learned traditional instruments such as the piano, flute, and guitar and also developed an interest in electronics. While working at EMI's tape-manufacturing plant, Parsons heard the album that would chart his future career: *Sgt. Pepper's Lonely Hearts Club Band* (1967) by the Beatles. Parsons was so impressed with the highly innovative and experimental album that he became determined to work at Abbey Road studios to learn how the Beatles created their sound. Within ten days he was working at Abbey Road.

Parsons eventually worked with the Beatles on their last two albums, *Abbey Road* (1969) and *Let It Be* (1970). To Parsons's surprise, the Beatles used every nonconventional sound technique they could think of to produce the sounds they wanted, such as blowing bubbles through a straw for "Octopus's Garden." This lesson would remain with Parsons throughout his career. During the next several years Parsons worked as both a producer and an engineer on what would be the signature albums of many artists, most notably Pink Floyd. Pink Floyd's 1973 album *Dark Side of the Moon* was as much a testament to Parsons's abilities as a studio engineer as it was to the band's creative brilliance.

The "Producer Album." It was around this time that Parsons met Eric Woolfson, a fellow studio engineer who was trying to make an album

For the Record

Pink Floyd and Alan Parsons began work on an album following *Dark Side of the Moon.* They intended to use objects such as rubber bands, tin cans, and wine glasses to produce all the music. The process was so painstaking, however, that after one month only two minutes' worth of music had been produced. The project was abandoned, to Parsons's disappointment.

based on the writings of Edgar Allan Poe. Parsons had both the credibility and writing ability to pull off a project of this magnitude, and with the 1976 release of *Tales of Mystery and Imagination,* the Alan Parsons Project was born. The album proved to be groundbreaking because it was the first album to be created by producers rather than musicians. This meant that the musicians were not permanent but could be changed with each album as needed, creating greater musical possibilities. (Parsons was a keyboardist and occasional vocalist for the Project, but often employed other vocalists such as Arthur Brown, the Hollies' Allan Clarke, and former Zombie Colin Blunstone.) This allowed Parsons to experiment and, via experimentation, discover his compositions. An interesting and unique debut album, *Tales of Mystery and Imagination* was the first of what would become a series of theme albums.

While their debut album had been a combination of traditional rock sounds and studio wizardry, *I Robot* (1977) featured the sweeping orchestration and electronic composition that would become the recognized sound of the Alan Parsons Project. Taking its theme of technology (and its title) from science fiction author Isaac Asimov, *I Robot* featured the hit single "I Wouldn't Want to Be Like You," a song which can be interpreted as either a man talking to a machine or as a machine talking to a man.

Pyramid (1978), the first of several gold albums, explored mythologies and their religious metaphors, while *Eve* (1979) dealt with women, particularly the many personas women have embodied in literature and society. While *Eve* contained one of Parsons's most challenging themes, some critics thought Parsons's writing was cold and possibly misogynistic. Gambling was the theme of 1980's *The Turn of a Friendly Card,* a platinum album that produced two hit singles: "Time" and "Games People Play."

Eye in the Sky. Criticized for being pretentious because of their theme albums, Parsons and Woolfson decided to produce their next album without a specific theme. In spite of their attempt, *Eye in the Sky* (1982) focused on the George Orwell novel *1984*'s theme of government intrusion into everyday life. Released in 1982, this album also went platinum and was the project's most successful album.

The Alan Parsons Project continued to produce albums regularly for the rest of the 1980's, but none attained the success of *Eye in the Sky.* With the departure of Woolfson in 1992, Parsons decided to continue working under his own name.

—Kelly Rothenberg

SELECT DISCOGRAPHY

■ ALBUMS

Tales of Mystery and Imagination, 1976
I Robot, 1977
Eve, 1979
Eye in the Sky, 1982

SEE ALSO: Beatles, The; Pink Floyd.

Gram Parsons

(Ingram Cecil Connor III)

BORN: Winter Haven, Florida; November 5, 1946
DIED: Yucca Valley, California; September 19, 1973
FIRST ALBUM RELEASE: *GP,* 1973
MUSICAL STYLE: Country rock

Gram Parsons was a rare figure in popular music. Though he never had a hit record, he was perhaps the most important pioneer of the country-rock sound that emerged in the late 1960's. His work with the Flying Burrito Brothers and the Byrds helped bridge the gap between traditional country harmonies and instrumentation and standard rock-and-roll arrangements. His legacy lived on after his untimely death at the age of twenty-six, with stars as diverse as the Rolling Stones, Emmylou Harris, Elvis Costello, Dwight Yoakam, and the Eagles keeping his musical heritage alive.

Early Days. Born to the heiress of a Florida citrus magnate and a part-time country singer, Ingram Cecil Connor had a difficult childhood. His father committed suicide when his son was twelve. When his alcoholic mother remarried a New Orleans, Louisiana, businessman two years later, the teenager was adopted and his name changed to Gram Parsons. Parsons began learning the piano and guitar before he entered his teens, and he decided on a career in music at a young age. By the age of fourteen, he was playing with local rock-and-roll bands. One, the Legends, included Jim Stafford and Kent Lavoie, who would later have eight Top-40 hits under the name Lobo. By 1964, Parsons's group, the Shilohs, already had recorded two unheralded singles and toured Florida. On the day that he graduated from high school in 1965, his mother died of alcohol poisoning.

Parsons attended expensive preparatory schools and eventually spent a semester at Harvard University, but he dropped out to pursue the music business in New York City. While at Harvard he formed the International Submarine Band. Though commercially unsuccessful, they made their mark in Los Angeles by introducing the pedal steel guitar and a playlist of country songs to an essentially rock format. Their rare *Safe at Home* album (1967), recorded for the small LHI label before it folded, anticipated the work of the Nitty Gritty Dirt Band and other country-rock groups.

The Byrds. While in Los Angeles, he met Chris Hillman of the Byrds and was invited to join the group. Because of Hillman and Parsons, the band embraced the country-rock sound, producing the classic *Sweetheart of the Rodeo* (1968), recorded in Nashville one year before Bob Dylan's *Nashville*

Gram Parsons (Archive Photos/John Platt Collection)

Skyline. Sweetheart of the Rodeo included bluegrass and country arrangements and even a truck-driving song. Though a commercial failure, the album featured two Parsons songs, including "Hickory Wind." Parsons's lead vocals were supposed to be prominent but had to be erased when a contractual disagreement with LHI could not be resolved.

Flying Burrito Brothers. Late in 1968, Parsons and Hillman left the Byrds to form the Flying Burrito Brothers. With Sneaky Pete Kleinow on pedal steel guitar, Chris Ethridge on bass, and, later, former Byrd Michael Clarke on drums and future Eagle Bernie Leadon on guitar, banjo, and Dobro, the Flying Burrito Brothers produced their best work. *The Gilded Palace of Sin* (1969) and *Burrito Deluxe* (1970) were neat fusions of rock arrangements, pop harmonies, and old-time country songs and instrumentation taken from the songbooks of Merle Haggard, George Jones, and the Louvin Brothers. Though *The Gilded Palace of Sin* only sold forty thousand copies, it earned the band a devoted following throughout Southern California. The Rolling Stones arranged for the Burrito Brothers to play at the ill-fated Altamont festival.

Parsons sometimes led the Flying Burrito Brothers onstage wearing a white cowboy suit with embroidered marijuana leaves, according to critic Bill Malone, vividly illustrating "the fusion of country music and youth-culture motifs." It also represented the rock culture excesses which limited his musical production and eventually led to his death. After leaving the group in 1970, supported by money from his trust fund, Parsons began using drugs more heavily. He spent much of his time with friend Keith Richards and the Rolling Stones, touring with them in England in 1971. His influence is evident on their albums of the period, *Sticky Fingers* (1971) and *Exile on Main Street* (1972).

Fallen Angel. In 1973 Parsons put together a new group, the Fallen Angels, which included Rick Grech (of Blind Faith), Barry Tashian, and three sidemen from Elvis Presley's touring band, Glen D. Hardin, Ronnie Tutt, and James Burton. Working with vocalist Emmylou Harris, he recorded two solo albums, *GP* (1973) and *Grievous Angel* (1974). Shortly after the completion of *Grievous Angel*, Parsons died of an overdose of drugs and alcohol near Joshua Tree National Monument in California. Though Parsons enjoyed little commercial success (*Grievous Angel* only reached number 195 on the *Billboard* charts), his music was kept alive, most notably by Harris, who routinely covered his material, and Hillman, who continued his country-rock legacy in the Desert Rose Band.

—*John Powell*

SELECT DISCOGRAPHY

■ ALBUMS

with the Byrds

Sweetheart of the Rodeo, 1968

with the Flying Burrito Brothers

The Gilded Palace of Sin, 1969

Burrito Deluxe, 1970

Gram Parsons solo

GP, 1973

Grievous Angel, 1974

Sleepless Nights, 1976

Gram Parsons: The Early Years, 1963-1965, 1979 (compilation)

Gram Parsons and the Fallen Angels—Live 1973, 1982

Warm Evenings, Pale Mornings, Bottled Blues: A Country Rock Career 1963-1973, 1991 (compilation featuring Parsons with each of his bands)

Cosmic American Music, 1995

SEE ALSO: Byrds, The; Eagles, The; Harris, Emmylou; Rolling Stones, The.

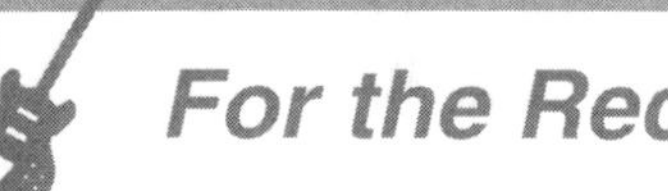

For the Record

While Gram Parsons's body was being returned to New Orleans for burial, it was commandeered, returned to the Southern California desert, and cremated by his manager, Phil Kaufman. Apparently before his death Parsons had expressed a wish for a Joshua Tree cremation.

Dolly Parton

BORN: Locust Ridge, Tennessee; January 19, 1946
FIRST SINGLE RELEASE: "Puppy Love"/"Girl Left Alone," 1960
MUSICAL STYLES: Country, pop, rockabilly

Singer, actress, and composer Dolly Rebecca Parton was the fourth child of Robert Lee Parton. Parton worked as a sharecropper and at whatever jobs he could find. Dolly's mother, Avie Lee Owens Parton, married at fifteen and by age thirty-five had borne twelve children. Born in a cabin in East Tennessee's Great Smoky Mountains, Parton spent her childhood in poverty; the walls of the cabin were newspaper-lined, and there were no telephones, running water, indoor plumbing, or electricity.

In her 1994 autobiography, *Dolly: My Life and Other Unfinished Business*, Parton recalled a passionate need to bring beauty into her life; she found this beauty in books, songwriting, and religious faith. She was later to record songs of her childhood such as "Little Rosewood Casket," which her mother had sung to her, as well as songs written by her aunt Dorothy Jo Hope, a gospel songwriter and evangelist. With Hope, Parton later wrote a song, "Daddy Was an Old Time Preacher Man," about Parton's uncle Jake. Some of these songs were recorded on Parton's *Golden Streets of Glory* album (1971).

Beginnings. As a child, Parton invented substitutes for the cosmetics she saw in magazine illustrations and dreamed of the tight and flashy clothes that she was later to adopt. She constructed a microphone from a tin can and a tobacco stake, singing for her family and herself. The Partons became a family singing group who performed in area churches. An uncle, Bill Owens, recognized Dolly's talent and helped her get her first job, singing on radio station WIVK in Knoxville. At thirteen, Parton made her first record, recording her own rockabilly song, "Puppy Love," at a Louisiana studio her uncle had rented. Owens, with whom she collaborated, also took her to Nashville in hopes of finding work with the Grand Ole Opry. She was sixteen when Mercury Records issued her "(It May Not Kill Me But) It's Sure Gonna Hurt," also in rockabilly style.

In 1964, she became the first person in her family to graduate from high school. The next day she left for Nashville. Living on food scraps that she sometimes took from trays left in hotel corridors, she was finally signed by Monument Records. Owner Fred Foster helped her develop a wardrobe and booked her on television's *American Bandstand* and elsewhere. In the meantime, she met Carl Dean, whom she married on May 30, 1966.

Success. Parton's first major success came when "Put It Off Until Tomorrow," cowritten by Owens, was named Broadcast Music Incorporated (BMI) Song of the Year in 1966. On January 21, 1967, she first appeared on the *Billboard* country charts with "Dumb Blonde." She was invited to join the successful Porter Wagoner on the Grand Ole Opry, making her first appearance on October 16, 1967. On stage, on tour, and on records, the two artists performed hits ranging from romantic ballads to comic songs of working-class couples fighting over money. They won a Music City News (MCN) award as a duet in 1970 and Country Music Association (CMA) Awards as Vocal Duo of the Year in 1969 and 1970. Together, Wagoner and Parton reached the *Billboard* charts more often than any other duo. Their tumultuous professional relationship lasted until April 21, 1974, ending in a lawsuit.

On her own, Parton performed the assertive songs that brought her a feminist audience, such as "Just Because I'm a Woman" (1968), which condemns the double standard, and "My Blue Ridge Mountain Boy" (1969), which deals with prostitution. Her songs also show a strong identification with working-class people of all backgrounds and races; in 1969, she recorded Mac Davis's "In the Ghetto," a song about the inner-city poor. Wagoner helped Parton obtain an RCA recording contract; her song "Mule Skinner Blues" was a hit in 1970, and her next single, "Joshua," was a top country hit in 1971. "Jolene" was among *Billboard*'s Top-100 hits in 1974; for the first time, Parton crossed over from country to pop.

Dolly Parton at the 1993 Country Music Association Awards (AP/Wide World Photos)

Hollywood. Parton found new management in Hollywood. She had cultivated a glitzy image with tight, glittering clothes, enormous blonde hair, and high heels, but she carried this image off with humor and self-mockery that attracted mainstream as well as country audiences, as did her willingness to deal directly with women's issues. She appeared as a guest on such shows as *The Tonight Show with Johnny Carson, Hee Haw, Today,* and *Mary Hartman, Mary Hartman.* Her 1977 crossover hit, "Here You Come Again," topped the country chart for five weeks and rose to third place on *Billboard's* Hot 100. In 1977, she also successfully appeared at New York's Bottom Line, a Greenwich Village club known as the home of East Coast rock. She repeatedly returned, however, to her roots. *New Harvest . . . First Gathering* (1977) was named Favorite Country Album at the American Music Awards (AMA) in 1978. In 1983 Parton teamed with Kenny Rogers; their single "Islands in the Stream" (written by the Bee Gees) reached number 1 on the pop, country, and adult contemporary charts. *Trio* (1987), which she recorded with Emmylou Harris and Linda Ronstadt, was a major hit. Her 1996 release, *Treasures,* showed her loyalty to traditional country songs such as "Behind Closed Doors," "Satin Sheets," and "For the Good Times," as well as her willingness to experiment. Guest performers include John Popper of Blues Traveler, Ladysmith Black Mambazo, and David Hidalgo.

Parton also branched out into other media and enterprises. She became the first female country music singer to have her own syndicated television show, *Dolly!* (1976 and 1987-1988), although her shows were not successful. She established a publishing company and marketed a successful Dolly doll; she began a series of Las Vegas appearances.

Her first film, for which she also wrote and sang the songs, was the hit comedy *9 to 5* (1980), with Lily Tomlin and Jane Fonda, about the revenge of three oppressed women office workers. The title song was part of a concept album, *9 to 5 and Odd Jobs* (1980), featuring working people's songs. It included "Dark as a Dungeon," about miners; "Deportee," about migrant workers; and "The House of the Rising Sun," about prostitutes.

In 1982, she starred opposite Burt Reynolds in *The Best Little Whorehouse in Texas,* an adaptation of a Broadway hit for which she wrote additional songs. In *Steel Magnolias* (1989), she joined Sally Field, Shirley MacLaine, Daryl Hannah, Olympia Dukakis, and Julia Roberts in a powerful drama based on the problems of southern women; her performance as the operator of the beauty shop that is the center of the action was critically acclaimed. Parton's other films, which include *Rhinestone* (1984) and *Straight Talk* (1992), were less successful, but her made-for-television film, *A Smoky Mountain Christmas* (1986), set a two-year viewer record for the ABC network, and her production company, Sandollar, received an Academy Award for the 1989 AIDS quilt documentary, *Common Threads: Stories from the Quilts.*

Parton's theme park, Dollywood, opened in 1986 in Pigeon Forge, Tennessee. It was designed to display mountain life and culture and to offer employment to people in the economically deprived area. In 1988, the Dollywood Foundation was established as a nonprofit foundation designed to improve education and the quality of life in Parton's native Sevier County.

—*Betty Richardson*

SELECT DISCOGRAPHY

■ ALBUMS

Home for Christmas, 1963
Hello, I'm Dolly, 1967
The World of Dolly Parton, 1967
Just Because I'm a Woman, 1968
Just the Two of Us, 1969 (with Porter Wagoner)
My Blue Ridge Mountain Boy, 1969
The Fairest of Them All, 1969
Coat of Many Colors, 1971
Joshua, 1971
Golden Streets of Glory, 1971
My Tennessee Mountain Home, 1973
Jolene, 1974
Here You Come Again, 1977
New Harvest . . . First Gathering, 1977
9 to 5 and Odd Jobs, 1980
Greatest Hits, 1982
Trio, 1987 (with Emmylou Harris and Linda Ronstadt)
Home for Christmas, 1990
Eagle When She Flies, 1991
Honky Tonk Angels, 1993 (with Loretta Lynn and Tammy Wynette)
Heartsongs: Live from Home, 1994
Treasures, 1996

For the Record

Dolly Parton's Dollywood amusement park attracted more than one million visitors in its first year and by 1997 had provided more than $1,500,000 in funding for projects such as college scholarships, computer labs, teacher assistants, guidance counselors for Sevier County schools, and a graduation incentive program.

SELECT AWARDS

Broadcast Music Incorporated Song of the Year Award for "Put It Off Until Tomorrow," 1966
Billboard, named Best Female Songwriter, 1971, 1975
Cash Box, named Best Female Vocalist, 1975
Country Music Association Female Vocalist of the Year Award, 1975, 1976
Academy of Country Music Entertainer of the Year Award, 1977
Country Music Association Entertainer of the Year Award, 1978
Grammy Award for Best Country Vocal Performance, Female, for "Here You Come Again," 1978
Academy of Country Music Female Vocalist of the Year Award, 1980
Grammy Awards for Best Country Song and Best Country Vocal Performance, Female, for "9 to 5," 1981
Academy of Country Music Single Record of the Year Award and Vocal Duet of the Year Award for "Islands in the Stream," 1983 (with Kenny Rogers)
Academy of Country Music Album of the Year Award for *Trio*, 1987 (with Emmylou Harris and Linda Ronstadt)
Grammy Award for Best Country Performance by a Duo or Group with Vocal for *Trio*, 1987 (with Emmylou Harris and Linda Ronstadt)
Ms., named Woman of the Year, 1987

SEE ALSO: Gill, Vince; Harris, Emmylou; Lynn, Loretta; Rogers, Kenny; Ronstadt, Linda; Wynette, Tammy.

Sandi Patti

BORN: Oklahoma City, Oklahoma; July 12, 1956
FIRST ALBUM RELEASE: *Sandi's Song*, 1979
MUSICAL STYLES: Christian pop, gospel

Sandi Patti was one of the biggest stars of Christian music between 1980 and 1992, when she divorced her husband and manager. During that time she won five Grammy Awards and an incredible thirty-three Dove Awards. With such vocal range and distinction that she came to be known simply as "the Voice" of contemporary Christian music, Patti articulated in song the spiritual ideals of millions of middle-class Americans.

Beginnings. Like many Christian artists, Patti, born Sandi Patty, began her career in church singing "Jesus Loves Me" and other standards. Her vocal talent was evident even then, and as a youngster she developed her gift by singing in area churches with the family group the Ron Patty Family. While majoring in music at Anderson College in Indiana, she earned money by singing commercial jingles. It was also there that she met her future husband and manager, John Helvering. Helvering encouraged her to record a self-produced album, *For My Friends*, which would be important to her career in two ways. First, her surname was misspelled Patti on the sleeve, the spelling she would use professionally until the mid-1990's. Second, a recording executive heard the album and offered her a contract.

In the wake of *Sandi's Song* (1979), her notoreity grew rapidly, leading to an invitation to sing backup for the Bill Gaither Trio. Her 1982 album, *Lift Up the Lord*, earned Patti the first of her thirty-five Dove awards, and her third album, *Sandi Patti Live: More than Wonderful* (1983), went gold and helped her win a Grammy Award for Best Gospel Performance. With the success of her first major solo tour in 1984, Patti confirmed her position as the leading figure in popular Christian music.

For the Record

Sandi Patti's self-produced first album was made with the insurance settlement from an automobile accident.

Successful Ventures. Over the next eight years, virtually every project earned professional accolades and led to her four-time selection as Inspirational Artist of the Year by *Billboard*. Patti never strayed far from her hallmark ballads and ringing crescendos, but with *Make His Praise Glorious* (1988) she began to introduce occasional rock and jazz licks. She further demonstrated her versatility by releasing *Sandi Patti and the Friendship Company* (1989), a classic children's album in which she promoted self-esteem by encouraging young listeners to believe in themselves and their purpose in God's plan.

As Patti began to appeal to a broader fan base in the late 1980's, she was more frequently in the public eye. The three major television networks included her in televised holiday celebrations, and she frequently performed on programs such as *The Today Show*, *The Tonight Show*, and *Good Morning America*. She also sang at the 1988 Republican National Convention and at President George Bush's 1989 inauguration.

Setback. At the peak of her popularity, Patti shocked the Christian community when she announced in June, 1992, that she was filing for divorce. After publicly suggesting a wholesome family life, then divorcing Helvering without stating biblical grounds, Patti angered many who had looked to her for spiritual inspiration. Several stations stopped playing her music, and a few retailers refused to sell her records. Though most of her fans were nominally supportive, particularly after she publicly declared in 1993 her childhood sexual abuse at the hands of a family friend, record sales dropped, and Patti stopped touring.

Find It on the Wings (1994), Patti's first regular studio album in almost four years, found her working with a wide range of vocalists (Peabo Bryson on "Make It 'Til Tomorrow"), songwriters (Michael W. Smith and Bob Farrell), and producers (the legendary Phil Ramone). After recording the album, Patti planned her first tour (with 4HIM) since 1991 and began to make appearances as a guest soloist with major symphony orchestras across the country, singing old standards, Broadway tunes, big-band hits, and gospel favorites.

Scandal. Just when it seemed that the furor over her divorce was subsiding, in December, 1994, it was learned that she had conducted two extramarital affairs before her divorce. In the wake of this news, along with her August, 1995, marriage to a former backup singer in her band, Word Records delayed release of her Christmas album for one year (*O Holy Night,* 1996). Patti withdrew from most public commitments as she pondered the best way of proceeding in the morally conscious Christian music world.

She began her public comeback with the nationally televised singing of the U.S. national anthem at President Bill Clinton's inauguration in January, 1997. Late in the year she returned to the charts with *Artist of My Soul,* which spent five weeks in the contemporary Christian Top 10. At the same time she spoke openly about her marital problems on television's *Prime Time Live.* With "Breathe on Me" gaining significant airplay on Christian stations nationally in 1998, Patti appeared to be regaining some of the audience that she had lost. —*John Powell*

SELECT DISCOGRAPHY

■ ALBUMS

Sandi's Song, 1979
Love Overflowing, 1981
Sandi Patti Live: More than Wonderful, 1983
Song from the Heart, 1984
Morning Like This, 1986
Make His Praise Glorious, 1988
Sandi Patti and the Friendship Company, 1989
Finest Moments, 1989
Another Time, Another Place, 1990
Hymns Just for You, 1991
Le Voyage, 1993
Find It on the Wings, 1994
Artist of My Soul, 1997

SELECT AWARDS

Grammy Award for Best Gospel Performance by a Duo or Group for "More than Wonderful," 1983 (with Larnelle Harris)
Grammy Award for Best Gospel Performance by a Duo or Group for "I've Just Seen Jesus," 1985 (with Larnelle Harris)
Grammy Awards for Best Gospel Performance, Female, for *Morning Like This* and Best Gospel Performance by a Duo or Group, Choir or Chorus, for "They Say" (with Deniece Williams), 1986
Grammy Award for Best Pop Gospel Album for *Another Time, Another Place,* 1990

SEE ALSO: Grant, Amy.

Les Paul

(Lester Polfus)

BORN: Waukesha, Wisconsin; June 9, 1915
FIRST SINGLE RELEASE: "Just Because"/"Deep Elm Blues," 1936
MUSICAL STYLES: Pop, jazz, country

Les Paul was a guitar virtuoso and musical inventor. He pioneered much of the technology and techniques of modern pop and rock recording: the solid-body electric guitar, amplification, multitrack recording, echo, close microphone positioning, and sound-on-sound taping. As a pop star, his recordings with his wife, vocalist Mary Ford, were huge hits in the 1950's.

From Country to Pop. Paul grew up in the 1920's as a guitar prodigy and tireless explorer of technical innovations in music. He could play guitar, harmonica, and banjo by the age of thirteen and soon performed on the radio in Chicago, becoming known as Rhubarb Red, a country guitarist and singer. At the same time in the 1930's, he started to explore jazz and in 1936 formed a jazz trio with Jimmy Atkins (Chet Atkins's brother) and bass player Ernie Newton. They played with Fred Waring's big band for three years over a nationally broadcast radio show and became quite well known. Around 1939 Paul started to experiment with a solid-body electric guitar design that did away with the traditional hollow-body natural amplification and sound-box design. Paul had been experimenting with electric pickups on acoustic

For the Record

In 1948, just as his first multitrack recording hit, "Lover," was released, Les Paul severely injured his right arm in an automobile accident. Doctors debated whether to amputate the arm or try to mend it. Paul insisted that they try to restore it by grafting bone and inserting a metal plate at the elbow. They did succeed in saving his arm, but it had to be permanently positioned at a guitar-playing angle.

guitars for years and went to the next step of constructing a guitar body that served solely as a platform for electrical circuitry that controlled volume, tone, string tension, and timbre.

He moved to California in the early 1940's and became a backup musician for performers such as Bing Crosby and the Andrew Sisters. In the late 1940's he met country singer Colleen Summers. They fell in love, got married, and decided to form a duo to record pop songs. Summers became Mary Ford, and together they created a string of pop hits from 1951 through the late 1950's: "How High the Moon" (number 1, 1951), "Mocking Bird Hill" (1951), and "Vaya con Dios" (number 1, 1953). Ford's pretty voice was recorded over Paul's multitracked guitar (and sometimes over other instruments he alone played) to give the effect of a small combo. Paul also had hit singles featuring his own overdubbed guitar playng: "Lover"/"Brazil" (1948) and "Nola" (1950).

Technical Innovator. Paul loved to improvise on standards, and all of his recordings reveal his creative jazz stylings. Before and after his pop success with Ford (they divorced in 1963), he worked hard in his home studio to expand the capacities of recording voices and instruments. Even Ford's voice was overdubbed to sound like two or three voices on their pop hits.

Paul experimented initially with eight-track technology as well as with echo effects and speed variability to raise or lower the pitch of sounds on records. Beginning in 1952, the Gibson guitar company finally recognized Paul's innovations in solid-body guitar design. They had been unimpressed with his idea back in 1941, but with the success of Leo Fender's electric solid bodies in the intervening years, they realized that the future lay in building more electrically sophisticated instruments. The Les Paul guitar models from Gibson have become classics. They have been played by legions of rock guitarists, Led Zeppelin's Jimmy Page being one of many. The Gibson Les Paul is a versatile instrument that produces strong solo sounds and has a variety of controls for modifying the tone.

In the 1970's Paul recorded a hit album with Chet Atkins and has since become a sort of elder statesman for aspiring guitar players. In the 1980's and 1990's he has continued to play in small clubs and to be honored as a pioneer of modern guitar playing and design. —*Frederick E. Danker*

SELECT DISCOGRAPHY

■ SINGLES

"Lover"/"Brazil," 1948
"Nola"/"Jealous," 1950
"How High the Moon," 1951 (vocal by Mary Ford)
"Vaya con Dios," 1953 (vocal by Mary Ford)

■ ALBUMS

Chester and Lester, 1977 (with Chet Atkins)
Les Paul: The Legend and the Legacy, 1991 (four-CD boxed set, compilation and original material)

SELECT AWARDS

Grammy Award for Best Country Instrumental Performance for *Chester and Lester*, 1976 (with Chet Atkins)
Grammy Trustees Award, 1983
Rock and Roll Hall of Fame, inducted 1988

SEE ALSO: Atkins, Chet.

Pearl Jam

ORIGINAL MEMBERS: Jeff Ament (b. 1963), Stone Gossard (b. 1965), Dave Krusen, Mike

McCready (b. 1965), Eddie Vedder (b. Edward Louis Seversen III, 1965)
OTHER MEMBERS: Dave Abruzzese (b. 1968), Jack Irons, Matt Chamberlain
FIRST SINGLE RELEASE: "Alive"/"Once," 1991
FIRST ALBUM RELEASE: *Ten*, 1991
MUSICAL STYLES: Hard rock, grunge, alternative

Known for their introspective lyrics merged with hard-rock music, Pearl Jam has defied simple categorization. Their catalog includes ballads ("Daughter"), quasi-heavy metal ("Evenflow"), and true-life narratives ("Jeremy"). Overshadowed by the critical acclaim of fellow Seattle, Washington, bands Nirvana and Soundgarden, their contributions have often been unappreciated.

Pearl Jam's Eddie Vedder (Ken Settle)

The Great Northwest. In the late 1980's, the Pacific Northwest music scene was a national phenomenon. Dubbed grunge, the main theme of the music was disillusionment of young people raised in broken families, impermanence everpresent. This mélange gave birth to innovators such as the Melvins, Malfunkshun, and Green River. From the unlikely roots of 1970's glam-metal band Kiss and the effects of the amphetamine ecstasy came one of these Seattle bands. Green River was the brainchild of Jeff Ament (bass), Mark Arm (guitar), Steve Turner (lead guitar), and Alex Vincent (drums). They played loud, droning music that had a near-therapeutic effect. The fact that the prolific Green River Killer of the 1980's remained at large gave the band a special, grim mystique.

Formed in 1984, Green River first recorded on 1984's compilation *Teriyaki Asthma Vol. 1* with other Seattle vanguard bands. In 1986, Turner left the band, replaced by Bruce Fairweather; Stone Gossard (guitar) was also added to the lineup. One of independent label Sub Pop's first releases was Green River's 1986 extended-play single, *Dry as a Bone*. It received a North American Music Awards nomination in July, 1987. Arm left, and the remaining members of Green River, joined by vocalist Andy Wood, became Mother Love Bone. Mother Love Bone's only album, *Apple*, was released in 1990.

Setback. On March 19, 1990, Wood's girlfriend found him overdosed on heroin. After three days in a coma, Wood died. Certain it would be an affront to carry on without their singer and friend, bandmates Fairweather, Ament, Gossard, and current drummer Greg Gilmore decided to disband. Ament went back to commercial art, but it no longer satisfied his creative urge. He performed with friends, one of whom was talented guitarist Mike McCready. McCready was leery of joining another band after the breakup of his group, Shadow. Still, he enjoyed playing with Ament and Gossard at Gossard's house. Gossard had already written the major portions of songs such as "Alive." All the group needed was a drummer and a singer. They were hoping to find a good lyricist who did not mind being a front man.

Trying to recruit Matt Chamberlain, they took his advice when he suggested a former acquaintance, Dave Krusen, although neither he nor Chamberlain had been the group's first choice. That distinction belonged to Jack Irons, who declined, but suggested a singer from San Diego, California, Eddie Vedder.

Pearl Jam Forms. Virtually unknown, a singer who fronted San Diego's Bad Radio, Vedder was born Edward Seversen to parents who separated soon after his birth. His mother married a man named Mueller who raised Vedder as his own. It was not until he was a young adult that Vedder learned, from his mother, that Mueller was not his real father. Never meeting his own father profoundly affected the young writer.

So it was that in 1990, Vedder received a copy of the demo tape Irons had passed on. Listening to it, he wrote reams of lyrics. The story of Vedder's mother's revelation became the basis of "Alive." Vedder also created cover art for the album, sending it back to Seattle. Gossard and Ament were astounded. Within days, Vedder was in Seattle with the band, soon to be called Pearl Jam. The name allegedly is derived from a preserve that Vedder's great-grandmother, Pearl, made from hallucinogenic plants. The group excelled at the now familiar grunge drone, and Vedder's lyrics lent the music a ceremonial quality.

For the Record

If Pearl Jam had not been afraid of being sued, they would have kept their original name, Mookie Blaylock—the name of a professional basketball player whom they liked almost as much as they liked his unusual name. They decided to call themselves "Pearl Jam" after a special kind of jam made by Eddie Vedder's grandmother, Pearl—it was allegedly laced with peyote. Meanwhile, they did not forget Blaylock, whose uniform number, 10, they later used for an album title.

They played their first show December 22, 1990, opening for Alice in Chains, and were signed by Epic in 1991. After the departure of Krusen, the band found drummer Dave Abruzzese. "Alive," the band's first video, featured Vedder's antics of diving into the audience from the stage. The video became wildly popular, going into heavy rotation on MTV.

Ten, Pearl Jam's first album, was released in October, 1991. Nirvana's Kurt Cobain derided Pearl Jam, much to Pearl Jam's chagrin. For Epic Records, the commercial success of *Ten* seemed unending. It spawned "Alive," "Once," "Evenflow," and "Jeremy." Another source of promotion for *Ten* was the 1992 film *Singles*, in which Pearl Jam appeared. Their third released single and video, "Jeremy," is the true story of a Texas teen, pushed to despair by family and peers, who commited suicide in front of his class. It won *Rolling Stone*'s Best Video of the Year Award.

Acclaim. In 1992, they won three Northwest Music Awards, appeared on MTV's popular *Unplugged* series, and played the Lollapalooza tour. *Ten* was named *Billboard*'s best hard-rock album of 1991, and *Spin* called it one of the top ten albums of the 1990's. Commercial expectations for their follow-up album, *Vs.*, were realized. In the first week after its 1993 release, *Vs.* sold 950,000 units, going multiplatinum by its fifth month of release. Pearl Jam held *Vs.* from release for two weeks in order not to coincide with the release of Nirvana's *Nevermind*, a nod of respect toward their detractors. Press-shy, Pearl Jam's silence fueled rumors they were on the verge of splitting. Over the next three years, they toured and embarked on side projects.

David and Goliath. Pearl Jam, upset by high service fees charged by industry agency Ticketmaster, filed a memo with the Department of Justice on May 6, 1994. They alleged that Ticketmaster held a virtual monopoly on concert ticket sales. Gossard and Ament testified before the House Government Operations Sub-Committee, further alleging that Ticketmaster pressured venues not to book Pearl Jam. The resulting investigation lasted several years, and the band eventually called a truce.

When the third album, *Vitalogy*, was released in 1994, it met with criticism from reviewers. Pearl Jam fans were happy to have new music from their favorite group, the constant rumors of the band's demise finally dispelled. On April 8, 1994, Nirvana's Cobain was found dead, the victim of a self-inflicted gunshot wound. Vedder's erratic behavior created rumors that he would be the next victim, but Pearl Jam carried on the business of writing and playing music. They joined with "Godfather of Grunge" Neil Young for many of the songs on his 1995 album, *Mirrorball*. On his European tour, Young played with Pearl Jam instead of his longtime band, Crazy Horse.

Amid rumor and hope, Pearl Jam released *Yield* in 1998. An eclectic mix of styles, *Yield* divided fans on its merits, but confident, quirky, and enigmatic, Pearl Jam would keep playing.

—*Cynthia Kasee*

SELECT DISCOGRAPHY

■ ALBUMS

Ten, 1991
Vs., 1993
Vitalogy, 1994
Yield, 1998

SELECT AWARDS

Rolling Stone, named Best New American Band and Best Video for "Jeremy," 1993

SEE ALSO: Nirvana; Soundgarden, Stone Temple Pilots.

Teddy Pendergrass

BORN: Philadelphia, Pennsylvania; March 26, 1950
FIRST ALBUM RELEASE: *Teddy Pendergrass*, 1977
MUSICAL STYLE: Soul

Teddy Pendergrass became one of the premier vocal stylists of the late 1970's and early 1980's with a string of seven gold or platinum albums between 1977 and 1984. As a boy he taught himself to play several instruments, practicing on equipment from a Philadelphia club where his mother worked. After playing with local groups as a teen, in 1970 he joined Harold Melvin and the Blue Notes as their drummer and soon succeeded John Atkins as lead singer.

Teddy Pendergrass (Paul Natkin)

Record Deal. Though the Blue Notes had been playing for fifteen years when Pendergrass joined, they were primarily a club act with only two rhythm-and-blues Top-40 hits to their credit. The group's direction changed dramatically in 1972 when they signed with Kenny Gamble and Leon Huff's Philadelphia International Records. Gamble and Huff wrote most of the group's hits and provided them with seasoned producers such as Thom Bell, Martin Harris, and Norman Harris. With the move to Philadelphia International, Pendergrass's raspy baritone became the focal

For the Record

Pendergrass was ordained a Christian minister when he was ten years old.

point of the Blue Notes' music, covering richly textured tracks characterized by dramatic orchestrations.

In 1975 they released two albums which eventually went gold, including *Wake Up Everybody* (number 9). With a string of Top-40 hits between 1972 and 1976, Pendergrass established a reputation as a classic stylist, most notably in the popular "If You Don't Know Me by Now" (number 1, rhythm and blues; number 3, pop).

Solo Act. In 1976 Pendergrass took his sex appeal solo. His steamy love songs included "Close the Door" (number 25, pop; number 1, rhythm and blues, 1978) and "Turn Off the Lights" (number 48, pop; number 2, rhythm and blues, 1979). Female fan reaction was so intense that a series of "For Women Only" concerts were marketed, in which stuffed teddy bears (Pendergrass's fan nickname) were distributed at the door. By 1980 he had produced four platinum and two gold albums. His 1979 platinum *Teddy* went to number 5 on the album charts. As a bona fide star, he also was recruited to act in the 1982 film *Soup for One* and to sing "Dream Girl" on the sound track, produced by Nile Rodgers and Bernard Edwards of Chic.

Tragedy struck on March 18, 1982, when Pendergrass was paralyzed from the waist down after an automobile accident outside Philadelphia. However, after months of physical therapy, he went back into the studio to record *Love Language* (1984), which included "Hold Me" (number 5, rhythm and blues), featuring the vocals of Whitney Houston. Though Pendergrass never regained the pop mainstream limelight, he did have a series of rhythm-and-blues hits in the 1980's and 1990's. He made a notable live appearance, his first after the accident, at the Live Aid benefit concert in 1985.

—John Powell

SELECT DISCOGRAPHY

■ ALBUMS

with Harold Melvin and the Blue Notes

To Be True, 1975
Wake Up Everybody, 1975

Teddy Pendergrass solo

Teddy Pendergrass, 1977
Life Is a Song Worth Singing, 1978
Teddy Live! Coast to Coast, 1979
TP, 1980
It's Time for Love, 1981
This One's for You, 1982
Heaven Only Knows, 1983
Greatest Hits, 1984 (compilation)
Workin' It Back, 1985
Joy, 1988
Truly Blessed, 1990
A Little More Magic, 1993

SEE ALSO: Chic.

Carl Perkins

BORN: Tiptonville, Tennessee; April 9, 1932
DIED: Jackson, Tennessee; January 19, 1998
FIRST SINGLE RELEASE: "Movie Magg"/"Turn Around," 1955
MUSICAL STYLES: Rock and roll, rockabilly, country

Carl Perkins was born into a cotton sharecropping family in western Tennessee near the Mississippi River. Picking cotton alongside African Americans, he heard their spirituals and their call-and-response style at an early age. John Westbrook, a local black guitarist, taught him how to bend guitar strings for blues effects, a style he later used on electric guitar. Perkins also heard country music from Nashville's Grand Ole Opry. He came to like Bill Monroe's new string-band music called bluegrass. Perkins also liked to take slower country songs and speed up the tempo. He began to blend the music he was hearing into a sort of hybrid made up of elements of spirituals, gospel songs, blues, country, and bluegrass.

Having moved east near Jackson, Tennessee, to farm independently, Perkins and his brothers Jay and Clayton decided, in 1946, to form a band to earn extra money in local clubs, with Carl on an amplified guitar, Jay on rhythm guitar, and Clayton on upright string bass. By 1954 Perkins had a fully electric guitar and had created rockabilly music. This white country music with a black rhythm featured ringing electric guitars with bluesy licks and solos, a slapped bass with a heavy beat, a percussive rhythm guitar, and, eventually, drums which stressed the offbeats. The vocal style tended to vary from plaintive country to exuberant shouts, yelps, and hiccups, mingled with bluesy slurred syllables and scat singing. With drummer W. S. Holland added to the group, Perkins could develop a virtuostic solo style as he improvised on licks and the melody. He played lead guitar on breaks and sang in the manner of a blues singer.

Perkins heard Elvis Presley's first record on the radio in 1954, "Blue Moon of Kentucky," at a faster tempo than Bill Monroe's original. This was the same kind of rockabilly the Perkins Brothers were working on. Perkins felt he too could make a record and follow in Presley's footsteps.

"Blue Suede Shoes." Presley recorded at Sun Records, started in 1952 by owner Sam Phillips to record both black and white Delta talents who had never had the chance to work their way beyond amateur status. Prior to 1952, Phillips had leased recordings he had made to larger independent companies which served the African American market. The stunning success of Jackie Brenston's 1951 rhythm-and-blues song on Chess Records, "Rocket 88," (which is often considered the first rock-and-roll record) alerted Phillips to the potential of upbeat rocking songs, and he decided to purchase his own label rather than lease work to other companies. However, many of his black artists were lured away by bigger companies in the North or on the West Coast. By 1954 Phillips was looking for a white artist with a feel for black music who could sell in different markets. He found Elvis Presley. When Carl Perkins arrived at his tiny studio in Memphis in October, 1954, Phillips did not at first see him as a rock-and-roll artist. Perkins was—and is—a hard-edged country singer in the vein of Hank Williams, and Phillips was looking for another rockabilly performer. Then Perkins came into the studio with his own rocker, "Blue Suede Shoes." Released in January, 1956, it climbed to the top rungs of the the three major record charts: a number 1 country hit, and number 2 on both the rhythm-and-blues and pop charts. Here was something never achieved before by a nominally country record. It became Sam Phillips's first million seller.

However, Presley covered the song on RCA almost immediately and also had a hit with it. He performed it on national television in March, leading many people to associate the song with Presley alone. Perkins had a chance to make his

Carl Perkins (Archive Photos/Frank Driggs Collection)

national television debut singing the song on *The Perry Como Show,* but again fate intervened. On the way to New York City in 1956 for the show, he and his brothers were injured in a car accident and missed their chance to expose the song on television at the peak of the song's rise on the charts.

In the Afterglow. Momentum for his career was lost. "Blue Suede Shoes" would remain his biggest hit. Other fine rockabilly songs on Sun include: "Boppin' the Blues," "Honey Don't," and "Dixie Fried," all his own compositions. His brother Jay never fully recovered from his injuries in the 1956 car accident and died in 1958. His ace drummer, W. S. Holland, departed for the Johnny Cash band, where he would permanently reside. In 1958, with sagging sales and Sam Phillips's increasing attention to his new star, Jerry Lee Lewis, Perkins signed with the major label Columbia Records. Although he had some chart success with two of his own teen-oriented rockers on Columbia, "Pointed Toe Shoes" and "Pink Pedal Pushers," the Nashville studio musicians assigned to him could not fully handle his rockabilly and blues orientation.

Renewing a Career. Convinced to tour England in 1963 and 1964, Perkins found part of his salvation at this low point in his life. The fans loved him and still admired his original hits and style. There he ran into a group of four lads just starting out: the Beatles. They admired his music and wanted to jam with him to understand his licks and rhythms. They met and soon after, the Beatles went on to record several of Perkins's songs. Their admiration and the revival of his songs for a new, worldwide audience gave him a renewed sense of his own worth. In later years, Perkins would become good friends with Paul McCartney in particular and would record with him.

Legacy. After finding this new appreciation for his work, Perkins traveled with the Johnny Cash touring troupe for a decade, 1965 to 1975, and began to accept his role as a sort of elder statesman of rock and roll. After leaving Cash, he formed a band with his two sons that would continue through the 1990's. Celebrated everywhere, he has appeared on television documentaries and music shows, taken part in rock-and-roll tribute concerts and reunions, and recorded on various labels, all the while revealing not only that he could recreate his original hits with the same fervor but also that his new songs were worthy successors. A rural poet, he is remembered as a triple threat: singer, guitarist, songwriter.

—*Frederick E. Danker*

For the Record

It was fellow Sun artist Johnny Cash who suggested that Carl Perkins write a song about blue suede shoes. When Cash was in the Air Force in Germany, a friend had told him not to step on the blue suede shoes he was wearing. Perkins was not convinced until a few weeks later at a dance; then he heard a young man whose girlfriend had scuffed his shoes say, "Don't step on my suedes." That night at about 3:00 A.M., Perkins, unable to sleep while thinking about the incident, went downstairs to his kitchen. He emptied a potato sack and scribbled the lyrics for "Blue Suede Shoes" on it.

SELECT DISCOGRAPHY

■ ALBUMS

Dance with Carl Perkins (also known as *The Dance Album of Carl Perkins*), 1957
Original Sun Greatest Hits, 1986 (compilation)
Carl Perkins: Born to Rock, 1989
Restless: The Columbia Recordings, 1992 (compilation)
Silver Eagle Presents Carl Perkins Live, 1997

SELECT AWARDS

Grammy Award for Best Spoken Word or Non-Musical Recording for *Interviews from the Class of '55 Recording Sessions,* 1986 (with others)
Rock and Roll Hall of Fame, inducted 1987

SEE ALSO: Beatles, The; Cash, Johnny; Lewis, Jerry Lee; McCartney, Paul; Monroe, Bill, and the Blue Grass Boys; Orbison, Roy; Williams, Hank.

Peter, Paul, and Mary

MEMBERS: Peter Yarrow (b. 1938), Noel Paul Stookey (b. Paul Stookey, 1937), Mary Allin Travers (b. 1937)
FIRST ALBUM RELEASE: *Peter, Paul, and Mary*, 1962
MUSICAL STYLE: Folk

Peter, Paul, and Mary joined forces in Greenwich Village at the beginning of the 1960's when folk music was becoming popular, and their enormous success in 1963 proved to be the high point of the folk revival. Yet they retained their popularity through the mid-1960's, even when rock and roll ended the dominance of folk music. The group was one of the era's most distinctive acts and played a crucial bridging role between two contrasting generations of folk music.

The Beginnings. Paul Stookey was an early fan of rock and roll and played the electric guitar in a rock band to help pay tuition at Michigan State University. After graduation he held many odd jobs before he moved to New York to try a career in show business. He went through months of near starvation and worked in a chemical company while trying to break into comedy. By the end of 1960, he was known as a stand-up comic in Greenwich Village.

Mary Travers's family moved to New York when she was a child, where she became interested in folk music in elementary school. In high school she sang with teenage folk groups, appearing at Carnegie Hall twice with a group called the Songswappers. After school she worked in the chorus of a Broadway show that eventually failed, and she, too, worked at daytime jobs while making contacts in the music field at nights and on weekends. She met Stookey and a former music teacher and folk-singer named Milt Okun who was managing new talent in New York. He encouraged Travers and Stookey to form a team, which they did in 1961, but Okun felt the act would work better as a trio.

Peter Yarrow grew up in New York City. He was adept at guitar and violin by the time he entered Cornell University, where he played in local clubs while earning a degree in psychology. When he returned to New York City, he worked with various folk groups and was chosen as a cast member for a television special, *Folk Sound, U.S.A.* That exposure gained him a spot in the 1960 Newport Folk Festival, and by the time he joined forces with Stookey and Travers in 1961, he had decided to make folk music his life.

For the Record

When Peter Yarrow was still a Cornell student, he invited a freshman friend, Lenny Lipton, to dinner at his apartment. While Yarrow was making spaghetti in the kitchen, Lipton idly scribbled some fanciful verses on the back of an envelope. After Yarrow joined Stookey and Travers, he set the verses to music. The song was "Puff (the Magic Dragon)," which eventually sold more than a half million singles.

Riding the Wave. The trio made their performing debut in New York City in 1962 and were ranked among the most promising newcomers on the Manhattan folk scene. They signed a recording contract with Warner Bros., which was still their company at the end of the 1970's. In May, 1962, their debut album was released. Titled simply *Peter, Paul, and Mary*, it was one of the top debut releases of the year.

The rising tide of interest in folk music was still swelling, and the trio had an even better year in 1963. Their second album, *Peter, Paul, and Mary—Moving*, issued in March, was a chart hit as well as their next album, *Peter, Paul, and Mary—In the Wind*, released in December. The group had four major hit singles that year, "Puff (the Magic Dragon)," "Stewball," and two Bob Dylan songs: "Blowin' in the Wind" and "Don't Think Twice, It's Alright." Peter, Paul, and Mary were one of the most popular acts in music and were featured on major television shows and concerts throughout the United States and Canada. Their music is smooth, the delivery slickly paced. Yet their great popularity was perhaps due to what Yarrow called

Peter, Paul, and Mary (AP/Wide World Photos)

with their rendition of his "Early Morning Rain."

One of their best collections came out in 1967 with *Album 1700*, and two singles from that album made the charts: "I Dig Rock 'n' Roll Music" and "Great Mandela." As the 1960's progressed, the trio became synonymous with folk's liberal traditions, but they were increasingly perceived as old fashioned. However, they released an album each year from 1967 to 1970 and enjoyed their greatest success in 1969 with their gold-record version of "Leaving on a Jet Plane," written by a then unknown troubador, John Denver.

On Their Own. By this time, the group was on its way to breaking up, due partly to the natural desire of the artists to try new creative directions and partly to the pressures of stardom. Stookey began to feel he was neglecting his family, and he wanted to develop a closer relationship with Christianity. He eventually settled in Maine in 1973, where he wrote three albums on biblical parables and worked on recording and animation projects in his own studio.

involvement. Each member of the trio manages to convey a sense of intense conviction to the audience.

The trio headlined many major folk festivals and some rock festivals during the 1960's. Many of the songs in their repertoire in those years were written by one or more of them, sometimes in collaboration with Okun. The group kept adding to its credits through the decade, although the folk music phenomenon was fading. In 1964, "Tell It on the Mountain" was a hit single, and they released three albums in 1965. That year they brought Gordon Lightfoot, a Canadian songwriter, to attention in the United States

Yarrow, who went through an unsettled period after the breakup, married Marybeth McCarthy, a niece of Senator Eugene McCarthy, and settled in Malibu. He remained active in the folk movement throughout the 1970's, appearing on folk radio shows and in concerts and festivals.

Travers also continued to be active after the breakup. She had her own radio and interview program in Los Angeles, performed in numerous college concerts, and was featured with symphony orchestras. She lectured in colleges on society and its effect on music and devoted much of her time to her two daughters.

Legacy. Many performers who came to prominence in the 1970's, such as Maria Muldaur, James Taylor, Jackson Browne, and Woody Guthrie's son, Arlo, owed much to the folk movement. Perhaps the most enduring legacy of the folk revival for the rock scene, however, was an attitude of self-consciousness that stemmed from the keen anticommercialism of the folk world. Reflecting on the folk scene in connection with their successful 1978 reunion tour, Travers said: "We are the children of Pete Seeger. We came from the folk tradition in a contemporary form where there was a concern that idealism be a part of your music and the music a part of your life."

—*Sheila Golburgh Johnson*

SELECT DISCOGRAPHY

■ ALBUMS

Peter, Paul, and Mary, 1962
Peter, Paul, and Mary in Concert, 1964
Peter, Paul, and Mary Album, 1966
Album 1700, 1967
Reunion, 1978

SELECT AWARDS

Grammy Awards for Best Folk Recording and Best Performance by a Vocal Group for "If I Had a Hammer," 1962

Grammy Awards for Best Folk Recording and Best Performance by a Vocal Group for "Blowin' in the Wind," 1963

Grammy Award for Best Recording for Children for *Peter, Paul, and Mommy*, 1969

SEE ALSO: Baez, Joan; Dylan, Bob; Guthrie, Woody; Kingston Trio, The; Seeger, Pete.

Tom Petty and the Heartbreakers

ORIGINAL MEMBERS: Tom Petty (b. 1952), Ron Blair (b. 1952), Mike Campbell (b. 1954), Benmont Tench (b. 1954), Stan Lynch (b. 1955)

OTHER MEMBERS: Howie Epstein (b. 1955)

FIRST ALBUM RELEASE: *Tom Petty and the Heartbreakers*, 1976

MUSICAL STYLES: Rock and roll, pop

When they appeared on the music scene in 1976, Tom Petty and the Heartbreakers were both new and familiar. Influenced by everyone who came before but sounding like no one else, they were southern rockers who did not fit the Allman Brothers mold, American rockers making British-style rock, and punk rockers. No one knew quite what to make of the band from Gainesville, Florida. Petty did not want to be labeled; in the liner notes to his 1995 boxed set, he said it would be more challenging to work in the mainstream, playing to everybody, rather than seeking out one small niche of listeners.

The Beginnings. In 1961, an uncle took ten-year-old Petty to the set of Elvis Presley's latest film, *Follow That Dream*. Petty was fascinated. Using a Beatles songbook, he taught himself guitar and at thirteen formed his first band, the Sundowners. Petty's partner in the band was Tom Leadon, younger brother of future Eagle Bernie Leadon. The Sundowners evolved into the Epics, and by the time Petty graduated from high school, they had a large local following.

The Epics soon became Mudcrutch. Their search for a new drummer led them to Randall Marsh, whose roommate, Mike Campbell, played some guitar. A college student, Campbell was not looking for a full-time band, but his skillful rendition of "Johnny B. Goode" impressed Petty and Leadon. Mudcrutch began playing larger venues, sometimes sharing the bill with another local band, Lynyrd Skynyrd. Using their own money, they went to Miami and recorded two songs in the studio Eric Clapton used to record "Layla."

Local keyboard player Benmont Tench sometimes sat in with the band when he was home from college. By this time, Leadon had left the group and followed his older brother to California, where he later became part of Linda Ronstadt's band. Tench wavered between music and school, until Petty convinced Tench's father that Tench was wasting his musical talent.

California. In 1974, Petty, new Mudcrutch guitarist Danny Roberts, and road crew member Keith McAllister took a tape of their best material to California and started knocking on record company doors. They had several offers, but the best one came from London Records. They returned to Florida just long enough to gather their belongings and for Tom to marry his girlfriend, Jane Benyo. However, the return to California was interrupted by a telephone call from Denny Cordell of Shelter Records. He had heard the demo tape and invited the band to stop at Shelter's Tulsa, Oklahoma, studio. An offer of a place to stay clinched the deal, and by the time they eventually reached the West Coast, Mudcrutch was signed to Shelter.

Unfortunately, Mudcrutch could not reproduce in the studio what they performed on the stage, and the band eventually dissolved. The project became a Tom Petty solo album, with Mike Campbell on lead guitar. Cordell brought in an impressive list of session musicians, and while the results were promising, Petty missed being part of a band. At loose ends, Tench recruited his roommate, drummer Stan Lynch, and another former Gainesville resident, Ron Blair, on bass to record a demo. They invited Campbell to play guitar, and when Petty arrived, everything fell into place. Petty invited them all into the studio, and the Heartbreakers were born.

Heartbreakers. Their 1976 self-titled debut album, *Tom Petty and the Heartbreakers*, attracted little attention in the United States, but an English tour as Nils Lofgren's opening act put the album on the British charts. Sensing a good thing, the U.S. distributor, ABC, rereleased the single "Breakdown," which made the U.S. charts nearly one year after its initial release. Their second album, 1978's *You're Gonna Get It*, went gold and featured

Tom Petty and the Heartbreakers (Freddie Patterson Collection/Archive Photos)

the singles "Listen to Her Heart" and "I Need to Know," both of which reached the charts.

Breakdown. Petty and his manager Tony Dimitriades attempted to renegotiate his contract when MCA Records bought ABC in 1979. It took nine months of litigation and Petty filing for bankruptcy to work out a new deal. The third Heartbreakers album, *Damn the Torpedoes* (1979), was produced by Jimmy Iovine and released on MCA affiliate Backstreet Records. It sold more than two million copies and produced the band's first smash hit, an old Mudcrutch song called "Don't Do Me Like That."

However, Petty's record company troubles were just beginning. When MCA announced its intention to price the Heartbreakers next album, *Hard Promises* (1981), at an industry high of nine dollars and ninety-eight cents, Petty threatened to retitle the album *$8.98.* MCA relented and *Hard Promises,* priced at eight dollars and ninety-eight cents, went platinum. The 1981 single "The Waiting" went to number 19 on the charts, but the Heartbreakers reached number 3 on a duet with Stevie Nicks of Fleetwood Mac, "Stop Draggin' My Heart Around."

Personnel Changes. The first defection came in 1982 when bass player Ron Blair grew weary of band life. His replacement, Howie Epstein, had played with John Hiatt and Del Shannon. The bleak *Long After Dark* (1982) reflected the turmoil in the band and between Petty and Iovine, who had seemed intent on making a replica of *Damn the Torpedoes.* Petty was bored with the formula, and though the album spawned one Top-20 hit, "You Got Lucky," it did not match the success or sales of *Hard Promises.*

The next album, *Southern Accents* (1985), was three years in the making. The combination of multiple sounds, multiple producers, and recording in his own home so frustrated Petty that he punched a wall and broke his left hand. The injury, which nearly ended his guitar-playing days, forced him to settle back and focus on his original intent—to make an album about his roots. The result, *Southern Accents,* is considered by many to be Tom Petty and the Heartbreakers' signature album. It also featured an unlikely collaboration between Petty and Dave Stewart of the Eurythmics, "Don't Come Around Here No More."

> **For the Record**
>
> Tom Petty called himself Charlie T. Wilbury and Muddy Wilbury in the band the Traveling Wilburys.

The "Southern Accents" tour resulted in a 1985 double live album, *Pack Up the Plantation,* and an appearance at the first Farm Aid benefit concert, backing folk legend Bob Dylan. This led to a two-year collaboration, a world tour, and the Heartbreakers' appearance on Dylan's 1986 album, *Knocked Out Loaded.* Playing live with the mercurial legend brought new life to the Heartbreakers' sound, and their 1987 album, *Let Me Up (I've Had Enough),* was one of their loosest. It was also the first album produced internally, with Petty and Campbell doing the honors.

Side Projects. In 1988, Petty began what was to become an extended vacation from the Heartbreakers. Petty and his current producer Jeff Lynne (formerly of the Electric Light Orchestra) joined music legends Bob Dylan, George Harrison, and Roy Orbison in creating the Traveling Wilburys. The fictitious band of brothers' debut release, *The Traveling Wilburys, Volume 1,* reached number 3 on the U.S. charts. In 1989, a meeting with Lynne led to an impromptu recording session in Campbell's garage. The result, "Free Fallin'," set the stage for Petty's first solo album. *Full Moon Fever* (1989) featured appearances by all of the band members except Lynch, who made no secret of his unhappiness at being left out. He did not sit idle though, contributing heavily to Don Henley's 1989 *End of the Innocence* album. The other Heartbreakers also remained busy; Epstein produced albums for John Prine and Carlene Carter, and Tench did session work for artists such as U2, Elvis Costello, and the Replacements.

Reunion. Petty and the Heartbreakers got back together in 1991 for *Into the Great Wide Open,* an unhappy collaboration between the band and producer Lynne. Too many artists aiming for too many directions led to an uneven effort, and all of the band members felt the strain. A 1993 *Greatest Hits* album produced the hit single "Mary Jane's Last Dance." Lynch made a few concert appearances with the band, then he and Petty had their final disagreement, and he left the band for the last time.

After a second solo album by Petty in 1994 (*Wildflowers*), the Heartbreakers recorded the sound track to the 1996 film *She's the One*. Drummer Steve Ferrone, who appeared on *Full Moon Fever* and *Wildflowers*, filled in for the departed Lynch, but was not listed as one of the Heartbreakers on the liner notes. In 1997, the group provided backup to country legend Johnny Cash on his album *Unchained*. —*P. S. Ramsey*

SELECT DISCOGRAPHY

■ ALBUMS

Tom Petty and the Heartbreakers, 1976
You're Gonna Get It, 1978
Damn the Torpedoes, 1979
Hard Promises, 1981
Long After Dark, 1982
Southern Accents, 1985
Pack Up the Plantation, 1985
Let Me Up (I've Had Enough), 1987
Into the Great Wide Open, 1991
Songs and Music from the Motion Picture "She's the One," 1996 (sound track)

SELECT AWARDS

Grammy Award for Best Rock Performance by a Duo or Group with Vocal for *Traveling Wilburys, Volume 1*, 1989 (Tom Petty with the Traveling Wilburys)

SEE ALSO: Cash, Johnny; Dylan, Bob; Electric Light Orchestra; Henley, Don; Orbison, Roy.

Phish

ORIGINAL MEMBERS: Ernest "Trey" Anastasio (b. 1964), Mike Gordon (b. 1965), Jonathan Fishman (b. 1965), Jeff Holdsworth
OTHER MEMBERS: Page McConnell (b. 1963)
FIRST ALBUM RELEASE: *Junta*, 1989
MUSICAL STYLE: Rock and roll

Phish's unique musical language has been sculpted by a dedication to composing and performing original material and an openness to all musical styles. The band's laid-back attitude, which extends to their philosophy of music, has resulted in the inclusion of everything from bluegrass tunes to jazz standards in their totally unpredictable, highly improvised live shows. Although every member has contributed pieces to the band's song list, guitarist Trey Anastasio is Phish's most prolific composer and songwriter.

The Beginnings. Phish's origins began in the dormitory halls of the University of Vermont at Burlington in the fall of 1983. After meeting rhythm guitarist Jeff Holdsworth and drummer Jonathan Fishman, freshman music student Trey Anastasio found bassist Mike Gordon by hanging signs around campus. The band played its first performance for a Reserve Officers' Training Corps (ROTC) Halloween dance under the temporary name Blackwood Convention. They played classic rock standards such as "Heard It Through the Grapevine" and used duct taped hockey sticks as mike stands. During the first break, the unimpressed crowd seized the chance to play Michael Jackson's album *Thriller* over the audio system. Taking a hint, the band left early, realizing their first show was a failure.

After a short hiatus, the band reformed in the fall of 1984 under the new name Phish. Although numerous stories circulate about the origin of the name, most sources claim the band simply chose a silly variant on Fishman's last name. Slowly the band began acquiring jobs at local bars and college parties. Set lists included covers and original songs such as "Fluffhead" and "Slave to the Traffic Light," which would long remain favorites among fans.

Addition and Loss. While playing at Goddard College's annual Springfest in April, 1985, the band caught the attention of Springfest organizer and pianist Page McConnell. McConnell later joined the band, and Phish became a quintet that May. McConnell was impressed by the band's commitment to composing and performing original material, a factor that eventually led to Holdsworth's leaving the band in early 1986.

Phish began to fill their sets with more original songs, most of which were written by Anastasio with lyrics provided by his childhood friend Tom Marshall. During this period, Anastasio composed several more of the most popular Phish songs, including "David Bowie," "Divided Sky," and "Harry Hood." As they continued to play, Phish's popularity grew, as word of their epic jams and eccentric sense of onstage fun spread around New England.

Gordon and McConnell graduated in the spring of 1987 followed by Anastasio in 1988 (Fishman would not graduate until 1990). For his senior thesis at Goddard College, Anastasio composed a musical fairy tale entitled *The Man Who Stepped into Yesterday*. Originally intended to be staged as a musical, it contains many popular Phish songs, such as "Wilson," "Lizards," and "AC/DC Bag." The spring of 1988 saw the band playing its first out-of-state performances in New Hampshire and western Massachusetts.

Albums and New Directions. In April of 1989, the band completed its independent first album, *Junta* (pronounced Joon-ta), which was sold at concerts. By that summer the band had an entire staff in place, including soundmen, lighting crews, and management, which would remain with them throughout their ascension to larger venues in the 1990's.

In September of 1990, the band released its first commercial album, *Lawn Boy*. With such popular songs as "Reba," "Run Like an Antelope," and "Bouncin' Around the Room," the album sold all of its ten thousand copies for Absolute A-Go-Go Records. However, the distributing company, Rough Trade Records, went out of business, and the band made no money from the deal.

The devoted fan loyalty eventually caught the attention of Elektra, which signed Phish to a record deal in November, 1991. In the spring of 1992 the band released *A Picture of Nectar*, which exemplified the band's ability to play in a variety of musical styles, a fact that eventually led the band to remark that the album lacked cohesion. The summer of 1992 found the band on the road with other relatively obscure touring bands such as Blues Traveler, the Spin Doctors, and Widespread Panic in the first HORDE (Horizon of Rock Developing Everywhere) tour. The band spent the second half of the summer opening for guitar legend Carlos Santana. Still lacking any serious airplay on radio stations and a video on MTV, the band continued to grow in popularity due to the trading of live bootleg cassettes among fans and their Internet Web site. The year 1992 ended well for the band when they played New Year's Eve to a record six thousand fans at a sold-out Matthew's Arena in Boston.

Rift, a concept album in which each song reflects a dream dreamed by a man throughout a restless night, was released in early 1993. Following the release of *Rift*, the band did a seventy-date spring tour of the United States. That summer the band moved from late night, indoor clubs and theaters into most of the major amphitheaters on the East Coast. By the end of the year the band had played to 14,500 fans at the Worcester Centrum, selling out the show in less than one day. Despite the bigger venues, the band still took time out to interact with their fans to discuss new songs, the night's shows, or the tour in general.

Hoist, released in the spring of 1994, was extremely controversial among the band's possessive fans. They felt its shorter, more marketable songs and the first MTV video signaled a commercial change in direction for the band. Gordon, a University of Vermont film student, directed the video for "Down with Disease." It received little

For the Record

Billboard magazine listed Phish's Clifford Ball as the top-grossing single-band concert of 1996.

§

The band broke the record for most balloons dropped on an indoor audience during its show on New Year's Eve, 1996.

airtime from MTV and was generally played in the early hours of the morning, until it was finally dropped from rotation. For Halloween that year, Phish played the entire double album *The Beatles* (known as the White Album) as their set. The band let the fans pick, through a mail-in vote before Halloween, the album they wanted to hear covered. This tradition continued for the next two years, with the band covering the Who's *Quadrophenia* in 1995 and Talking Heads' *Remain in the Light* in 1996.

Onstage Magic. In the summer of 1995 the band released *A Live One*, a double album that included six previously unreleased songs and six others recorded during the fall tour of 1994. The band felt that *A Live One* was their best commercial release, capturing the true Phish experience. July of 1996 found the band in Europe opening for Carlos Santana and headlining a few of their own shows. In the fall of 1996 the band released its sixth studio album, *Billy Breathes*. This album marked a return to basics for the band, with no guest artists and a number of acoustic songs. The high point of 1996 was the Clifford Ball, held in Plattsburgh, New York, in August. More than eighty thousand fans attended the ball for two days of camping, activities, and six shows by Phish. The band again returned to Europe in the summer of 1997, playing at many festivals and headlining all other performances. *Slip, Stitch, or Pass*, a live album recorded on that tour in Europe, was released in the winter of 1997.

Devoted Phish "phans" often travel hundreds of miles, following Phish across the continental United States in search of the ultimate show. The magic that Phish produces is the result of these four musicians' dedication to their art.

—Douglas Dixon

SELECT DISCOGRAPHY

■ ALBUMS

Junta, 1989 (rereleased 1992)
Lawn Boy, 1990 (rereleased 1992)
A Picture of Nectar, 1992
Rift, 1993
Hoist, 1994
A Live One, 1995
Billy Breathes, 1996
Slip, Stitch, or Pass, 1997
The Story of the Ghost, 1998

SEE ALSO: Blues Traveler.

Wilson Pickett

BORN: Prattville, Alabama; March 18, 1941
FIRST ALBUM RELEASE: *In the Midnight Hour*, 1965
MUSICAL STYLES: Soul, rhythm and blues

Along with Otis Redding and Aretha Franklin, Wilson Pickett was one of the premier soul singers of the 1960's. Performing songs ranging from gritty ballads to up-tempo dance tunes, Pickett personified the Memphis soul sound of the period with screams, swaggering bravado, and sexual innuendo. He was also one of the most influential performers of his time, with his hit songs such as "In the Midnight Hour," "Mustang Sally," and "Ninety-Nine and a Half (Won't Do)" recorded by numerous other artists.

The Beginnings. Alabama-born Pickett moved to Detroit, Michigan, in 1955 and, influenced by his deeply religious family, was a gospel singer before being asked to join rhythm-and-blues group the Falcons after one of its members, Willie Schofield, heard him singing on the front porch of his home. The Falcons had already had a hit in 1959 with "You're So Fine," and after Pickett became their lead singer, they had another in 1962 with "I Found a Love," cowritten by Pickett. Although the song deals with romantic success, Pickett sings with a plaintive wail that would become emblematic of his slow ballad style.

In 1963, Robert Bateman, the Falcons' producer, convinced Pickett to become a solo performer. He was signed by singer Lloyd Price's Double L label and recorded three soul singles, including "It's Too Late" and "If You Need Me," written by Bateman and Pickett and later recorded by Solomon Burke and the Rolling Stones. In 1965, Atlantic Records purchased Pickett's contract, and after two unsuccessful singles, he was turned over to producer Jerry Wexler.

Memphis Soul. Pickett recorded at the Stax studio in Memphis with Booker T. and the MG's as instrumentalists. "In the Midnight Hour," written by Pickett and MG's guitarist Steve Cropper, is one of the Memphis soul classics of the period. Driven by Cropper on lead guitar, Donald "Duck" Dunn on bass, Al Jackson on drums, and especially Wayne Jackson on trumpet and Floyd Newman, Andrew Love, and Packy Axton on saxophone, "In the Midnight Hour" is typical of Pickett's best work, being both a catchy dance tune and an ode to sexual passion yet to be fulfilled. Pickett's other Memphis-based hits included "634-5789" and "Ninety-Nine and a Half (Won't Do)," both of which feature Isaac Hayes on piano. The prominence of the horn section on these recordings is a perfect complement to Pickett's raw, braying vocals.

Muscle Shoals. After his enormous Memphis success, Pickett and Wexler moved in 1966 to another legendary recording site, Rick Hall's Fame Recording Studio in Muscle Shoals, Alabama. Here they recorded another of Pickett's best-known and most lasting successes, "Mustang Sally," as well as distinctive versions of previously recorded songs such as "Land of 1,000 Dances," a hit for Cannibal and the Headhunters, and "Funky Broadway," which had been a minor hit for Dyke and the Blazers.

Pickett returned to Memphis in 1968 to work with soul pioneer Bobby Womack. The best of the songs he wrote for Pickett is the ballad "I'm in Love," on which Womack plays lead guitar and King Curtis, the great soul-blues saxophonist, also performs. Womack and Curtis wrote "Jealous Love," one of Pickett's most haunting ballads. Back in Muscle Shoals in 1968, Pickett had an unexpected success with his version of the Beatles' "Hey Jude," recommended by the Allman Brothers' Duane Allman, who played guitar on the recording. Pickett took a sad song and made it truly mournful.

Throughout his career, Pickett usually improved an established song when he recorded it. His "Bring It on Home to Me" is much closer to the blues than the Sam Cooke original. His version of "You Keep Me Hangin' On," the oft-recorded classic by Eddie Holland, Lamont Dozier, and Brian Holland, is considerably more anguished than the slick original by the Supremes. In the tradition of jazz and blues vocalists such as Billie Holiday and Etta James, Pickett is a master of nuance.

Final Successes. While a soul version of "Hey Jude" may not seem all that farfetched, Pickett raised many eyebrows with a soul version of the ultimate pop tune, the Archies' "Sugar Sugar," recorded at Criteria Studios in Miami in 1969. Such a recording indicates that Pickett could imbue style and passion into almost any type of song. While many interpreters of popular music polish their rough edges, Pickett explored and even added to the roughness of the original.

Moving on to Philadelphia in 1970 and working with producers Kenny Gamble and Leon Huff, Pickett recorded one of his last great soul songs, "(Get Me Back on Time) Engine Number 9," again combining funky dance rhythms with a lament for lost love. Gamble, Huff, and arranger Lenny Pakula were also behind "Don't Let the Green Grass Fool You," Pickett's first million-selling single.

A brief return to Muscle Shoals in 1971 indicated the beginning of a decline for Pickett. Randy Newman's "Mama Told Me Not to Come," previously recorded by Three Dog Night, is the kind of hard, aggressive song that suited Pickett, but the result was an unnecessarily upbeat mediocrity. Shortly after that release, Pickett left Atlantic, with which he had been feuding, for RCA, for whom he made three unsuccessful albums. He reached his low point in 1979, after disparaging the negative influence of disco on soul, with two poorly received disco-influenced albums for EMI. Pickett recovered somewhat from this failure by returning to music from his successful period while touring with veterans Solomon Burke, Don Covay, former Falcon Eddie Floyd, Ben E. King, and Joe Tex, performing as the Soul Clan. By the 1990's, however, the once electrifying performer became known for indifferent stage work, often abandoning songs before finishing them.

Legal Troubles. Pickett had well-publicized run-ins with the law as early as 1974, when he was

For the Record

Pickett received new popular-culture immortality through Alan Parker's 1991 film, *The Commitments*, adapted from the Roddy Doyle novel. It celebrates Pickett as a soul pioneer. The title characters' Dublin band reaches its apex with a performance intended for their idol, Pickett, who arrives (unseen in the back of a limousine) too late. Initially he was upset about being portrayed in the film as an unapproachable star, but Pickett later performed on stage with the actors when they toured the United States as the Commitments, doing such Pickett standards as "Mustang Sally."

arrested in Andes, New York, after drawing a gun during an argument. The 1990's witnessed one embarrassing episode after another, including a conviction for driving while intoxicated and aggravated assault after hitting an eighty-six-year-old man with his truck; hospitalization after a fight with a fellow inmate at the Bergen County Jail in Hackensack, New Jersey, while serving a year's sentence; threats made against the mayor of his adopted hometown of Englewood, New Jersey, after driving across his lawn; a domestic violence complaint by his live-in girlfriend; and an arrest for cocaine possession.

Legacy. While Pickett has never quite achieved the stature of Redding, Franklin, Ray Charles, or James Brown, he recorded at least one dozen memorable songs during a decade of solid, unpretentious work. Singing in a distinctively robust style, he could balance exuberant shouting with much quieter moments that seem all the more poignant for the contrast. More than any other male soul performer—though he was easily outdone by the young Tina Turner—he made the sexual side of soul overt. Fittingly nicknamed the "Wicked Pickett," the braggadocio of "A Man and a Half" might seem ridiculous from any other singer but Pickett. At the same time, Pickett, at his best, conveys pain and vulnerability. For a generation, he, along with Redding, best expresses the essence of soul. —*Michael Adams*

SELECT DISCOGRAPHY

■ SINGLES

"In the Midnight Hour," 1965
"Land of 1000 Dances," 1966
"Mustang Sally," 1966
"Funky Broadway," 1967
"Engine Number 9," 1970
"Don't Knock My Love," 1971

■ ALBUMS

In the Midnight Hour, 1965
The Exciting Wilson Pickett, 1966
The Wicked Pickett, 1966
The Sound of Wilson Pickett, 1967
I'm in Love, 1968
Wilson Pickett in Philadelphia, 1970
A Man and a Half: The Best of Wilson Pickett, 1992 (compilation)

SELECT AWARDS

Rock and Roll Hall of Fame, inducted 1991

SEE ALSO: Brown, James; Charles, Ray; Cooke, Sam; Franklin, Aretha; Hayes, Isaac; James, Etta; Redding, Otis; Turner, Ike and Tina / Tina Turner; Wilson, Jackie; Womack, Bobby.

Pink Floyd

ORIGINAL MEMBERS: Syd Barrett (b. 1946), Roger Waters (b. 1944), Nick Mason (b. 1945), Richard Wright (b. 1945)
OTHER MEMBERS: David Gilmour (b. 1944)
FIRST ALBUM RELEASE: *The Piper at the Gates of Dawn*, 1967
MUSICAL STYLE: Psychedelic rock, rock and roll

The name "Pink Floyd" was derived from the first names of two American bluesmen, Pink Anderson and Floyd Council. Formed in London in 1965, the band initially contained two singer-songwriters, Syd Barrett and Roger Waters, childhood friends from Cambridge. Barrett was one of the band's principals until he was institutionalized, most likely at least partially as a result of his extensive LSD use. Roger Waters and new guitarist David Gilmour then assumed the group's leadership. Despite (or because of) Pink Floyd's subsequent massive success, issues of control caused quarrels among the group's members.

In the mid-1970's Pink Floyd became known for their garish stage show as much as their music. The musicians themselves only stood (or sat) and played, but elaborate sound and lighting effects were used, an inflated jet appeared to crash into the stage, and gigantic animal-shaped helium balloons hovered over the audience. Eventually, for *The Wall*, a huge wall was constructed piece by piece that eventually obscured the stage.

The Beginnings. Pink Floyd's early music, written largely by Barrett, is heavily psychedelic. The band became a popular "underground" attraction in the London scene of 1966 and 1967 and was among the first bands in England to use a light show. After the band's first album came out in 1967, two Pink Floyd songs were banned by the BBC: "Arnold Layne" because it was about cross-dressing, and "Let's Roll Another One" because it was about smoking marijuana. The biggest success of the Barrett-era Pink Floyd was the 1967 single "See Emily Play," which hit number 6 on the British charts. Barrett's songwriting exhibited a whimsical sense of humor that rapidly disappeared from Pink Floyd after he departed. Unfortunately, however, Barrett's drug use made his performances increasingly erratic. When the band went on their first American tour, at some shows he would drool and repeatedly play the same guitar chord. At other times he ignored the concert altogether and would not leave the tour bus. Such problems lost the band bookings and cost them a great deal of money. Barrett left in 1968.

After Barrett. Between 1968 and 1973 Pink Floyd was a modestly successful band that was

Pink Floyd in the early 1970's: Richard Wright, David Gilmour, Roger Waters, Nick Mason

slowly building its audience. They recorded, toured, and managed (barely) to pay their bills. In 1969 they released a sound-track album, *More*, and a double album entitled *Ummagumma* that contained two sides of very atmospheric, spacy live performances and two sides of uneven studio work that included some imaginative use of sound and stereo effects. In 1970 came *Atom Heart Mother*, in 1971 *Meddle*, with an entire side devoted to a song suite called "Echoes." Another sound-track album, *Obscured by Clouds*, came out in 1972. Pink Floyd from 1967 to 1972 was influential in the art-rock and psychedelic communities primarily for their use of sound as such. Their concerts featured an eerie effect of footsteps echoing across the ceiling of the hall, for example, and the song "Alan's Psychedelic Breakfast" from *Atom Heart Mother* set acoustic guitar passages against a recording of the sound of one of their roadies cooking breakfast. Then, in 1973, everything changed.

In 1973 the band released *Dark Side of the Moon*. The phenomenal success of this album, produced by Alan Parsons, probably surprised Pink Floyd itself as much as it did the rest of the music world. Its songs are bridged by instrumental and sound-effects sections, resulting in an album that plays continuously from beginning to end. It included the single "Money." On both the album and tour, the band used a saxophone player and female backup singers. The album is in some ways an unlikely hit, with its lyrics being almost entirely reflective and gloomy. Yet all members of the band had matured artistically. In particular, Waters had become an accomplished lyricist, and Gilmour a well-respected and fluid guitarist. *Dark Side of the Moon* topped the charts in England and America and stayed on the charts for four years. It eventually sold more than thirty million copies.

After the album's success and a long tour on which they played *Dark Side of the Moon* in its entirety, the band had difficulty working on their next album. In later interviews, they implied that its title, *Wish You Were Here* (1975), carried the subtext that they wished they were *not* there. Nonetheless, the album went to number 1. The album is dedicated to Syd Barrett, the "crazy diamond" mentioned in one of the songs. The undistinguished album *Animals* was released in 1977. Another major achievement was still ahead, however. In 1978, Pink Floyd began work on *The Wall*.

Waters wrote the lyrics for *The Wall* partially as autobiography, and in many respects it can almost be considered a Waters solo album. During the long, grueling process of recording this double album, conflicts within the band erupted with new force. Waters and Gilmour, in particular, were frequently at loggerheads. One example involves Gilmour approaching Waters with a completed instrumental song that he had already played for the rest of the band. Waters said that he did not want it on the album. The rest of the band stood up for the song, however, and Waters gave in. He put together the lyrics in less than half an hour. The song, "Comfortably Numb," became one of the album's most popular cuts. Only two weeks after this confrontation, Waters fired keyboardist Richard Wright, and the band officially became a trio.

The Wall was released in 1979 and met with worldwide success, as did the film of the same name. A massive tour followed, as did breakup rumors in the media. In 1983, amidst turmoil within the band and rumors of a split, Pink Floyd released *The Final Cut*. Some people, Pink Floyd members included, considered it a Waters "solo" album, much like *The Wall*. All the songs were

For the Record

In February, 1981, Pink Floyd's album *Dark Side of the Moon*, released eight years earlier, became the longest-charting rock album in U.S. history, with 402 weeks on the *Billboard* charts. Only a Johnny Mathis greatest-hits album and the original cast recording of the Broadway show *My Fair Lady* had spent more weeks on the chart. By mid-1985, however, the Pink Floyd album was undisputed champion, with a total of 560 weeks on the charts.

written solely by Waters, and much of the sound and emotion that previously held the band sound's together seemed to be missing. After the band did a short tour and a United Kingdom film, no one heard much from Pink Floyd for two years. Then, in late 1985, Waters left the band.

The next year he sued the remaining band members for exclusive rights to the works of Pink Floyd, including the name and stage effects. Waters claimed to be the major creative force behind the band's success and wanted the rights to continue the band himself. The fight was long and messy, lasting over a year. Finally, in 1987, a judge ruled that Waters had left the band of his own free will and that, since the band had never entirely broken up, the rights to the name and most of the material belonged to what was left of the band. However, Waters did receive a partial victory: He was to receive royalties for anything that he had worked on. Neither side was entirely satisfied, but the legal battle was over and both sides could move on.

After Waters. In September of 1987, Pink Floyd (Gilmour and Mason, with Wright as a paid sideman) released *Momentary Lapse of Reason.* Originally intended as a solo album for Gilmour, the album was released as a product of the entire band. Some fans embraced the album, saying that the spirit of the band was still alive. Others turned their backs on the project. A very successful tour followed, and it seemed that the band was as popular as ever. Waters was having modest success of his own. He released *Radio K.A.O.S.* in 1987 and *Amused to Death* in 1992. When the Berlin Wall came down in 1989, Waters orchestrated a star-studded performance of *The Wall* in a now unified Germany. Performers for this gala event included Van Morrison, Joni Mitchell, Bryan Adams, and Cyndi Lauper. In 1994 Pink Floyd released *The Division Bell,* which topped the American charts.

—Melissa R. Grimm

SELECT DISCOGRAPHY

■ ALBUMS

The Piper at the Gates of Dawn, 1967
A Saucerful of Secrets, 1968
Ummagumma, 1969
Relics, 1971 (previously released material)
Meddle, 1971
Dark Side of the Moon, 1973
Wish You Were Here, 1975
Animals, 1977
The Wall, 1979
The Final Cut, 1983
A Momentary Lapse of Reason, 1987
Delicate Sound of Thunder, 1988
The Division Bell, 1994

SELECT AWARDS

Grammy Award for Best Rock Instrumental Performance for "Marooned," 1994

The Platters

ORIGINAL MEMBERS: Tony Williams (1928-1992), David Lynch (1929-1981), Herb Reed (b. 1931), Alex Hodge (b. c. 1931)

OTHER MEMBERS: Zola Taylor (b. 1934), Paul Robi (1931-1989), Charles "Sonny" Turner (b. 1939)

FIRST ALBUM RELEASE: *The Platters,* 1956

MUSICAL STYLES: Rhythm and blues, pop, rock and roll

The Platters were one of the top vocal groups of the 1950's and were one of the most popular African American groups of their time. They had a lengthy string of hits between 1955 and 1960, including four singles that reached the number 1 spot on the pop charts.

Getting Together. The Platters were originally organized by businessman and songwriter Buck Ram in Los Angeles in 1952, and the group made its first recording in 1953. After some unsuccessful efforts in 1953 and 1954, Ram made some personnel changes in the group. A lineup stabilized around five members in 1955 with Tony Williams (lead tenor), David Lynch (tenor), Herb Reed (bass), Paul Robi (baritone), and Zola Taylor (contralto). The group signed with Mercury Records and released their first big hit, "Only You," which rose to number 5 on the pop charts in 1955. Although Ram felt that "Only You" was not one of

The Platters (Archive Photos/Frank Driggs Collection)

his better songs, it gained popularity because of its simple, meaningful lyrics and the crooning, harmonious style of the group of four males and a female.

Four Number 1 Hits. With Mercury, the Platters became one of the nation's top vocal groups and a major nightclub attraction. Their first number 1 hit, "The Great Pretender," was recorded in late 1955 and reached number 1 on the pop charts in early 1956. Later in 1956, "My Prayer" rose to number 1 on the pop charts and to number 2 on the rhythm-and-blues charts, followed by three more big hits, "The Magic Touch," "You'll Never Know," and "I'm Sorry."

Success continued for the Platters in 1958, with two more major hits, "Twilight Time" and "Smoke Gets in Your Eyes," rising to the number 1 pop spot. "Smoke Gets in Your Eyes" became an international hit, reaching number 1 in England and Australia. The Platters' increasing popularity landed them in a number of rock films, including *Rock Around the Clock* (1956) and *The Girl Can't Help It* (1956). "Enchanted" was a top hit for the group in 1959, but they suffered a major setback later that year when the four male members were accused of having sexual relations with four female minors. Although the men were acquitted, the popularity of the group declined for some time. Their last single to reach the Top 10 was "Harbor Lights" in 1960.

New Faces, Same Sound. The lead singer, Tony Williams, left the group for a solo career in 1961 and was replaced by Charles "Sonny" Turner. More changes occurred in 1962 when Sandra Dawn replaced Taylor and Nate Nelson replaced Robi. With the new personnel embracing a more contemporary singing style, the group made a limited comeback with "I Love You 1000 Times" (1966) and "With This Ring" (1967), both singles making it into the Top 40. During the late 1960's, Sonny Turner and Herb Reed formed their own version of the Platters, and Tony Williams did likewise.

When Turner left his version of the group in 1970, he was replaced by Monroe Powell, who had sung with both the Dominoes and the Ink Spots. By 1998, this version of the Platters was made up of Powell, Wilson Williams, Kenn Johnson, Allen Holland, and Verceal Whitaker, and they continued to deliver the same Platters sound as the group did in the 1950's and 1960's. Another version of the Platters was formed in the late 1990's by Robi's daughter, Franchesca. Although the faces have changed, the Platters' unique sound would remain unchanged. The original Platters were inducted into the Rock and Roll Hall of Fame in 1990. —*Alvin K. Benson*

SELECT DISCOGRAPHY

■ SINGLES

"Only You," 1955
"The Great Pretender," 1955
"The Magic Touch," 1956
"My Prayer," 1956
"I'm Sorry," 1957
"Twilight Time," 1958
"Smoke Gets in Your Eyes," 1958
"Enchanted," 1959
"Harbor Lights," 1960
"Apple Blossom Time," 1960
"With This Ring," 1967
"Who's Sorry Now," 1970

■ ALBUMS

The Platters, 1956
The Very Best of the Platters, 1991

SELECT AWARDS

Rock and Roll Hall of Fame, inducted 1990

SEE ALSO: Coasters, The; Cole, Nat "King"; Drifters, The; Four Seasons, The / Franki Valli; Supremes, The.

For the Record

When the Platters were rehearsing "Only You" in 1955, Tony Williams's voice cracked on a high note, and manager Buck Ram insisted it be recorded that way. It established the unique sound of the Platters.

The Pointer Sisters

ORIGINAL MEMBERS: Bonnie Pointer (b. 1950), Ruth Pointer (b. 1946), Anita Pointer (b. 1948), June Pointer (b. 1954)

FIRST ALBUM RELEASE: *The Pointer Sisters*, 1973

MUSICAL STYLES: Rhythm and blues, rock and roll, country, pop

Raised in the ghetto of Oakland, California, the four Pointer sisters were the children of minister Elton Pointer and his wife, Sarah. Growing up in a strict household, the girls sang in church but were not allowed to listen to secular music until they reached high school. The girls rebelled against their parents and moved toward careers in popular music after becoming interested in jazz, blues, and rhythm and blues.

Roots. Bonnie studied piano and African and modern dancing, and, for a time, she worked as a topless dancer. In the late 1960's, Bonnie and June teamed to sing at parties and clubs before joining Dorothy Morrison's Northern California State Youth Choir. After the choir disbanded, the four sisters traveled to Houston, Texas, prompted by their first manager to seek work. With no money, the girls were rescued by producer David Rubinson who paid for their tickets home. He found them work as backup singers for Cold Blood, Boz

Scaggs, Grace Slick, Esther Phillips, and Dave Mason, who took them on his 1969 European tour. The sisters posed for an album cover for Taj Mahal and sang backup for blues singer Elvin Bishop who took them on tour in 1971.

That year, Atlantic Records executive Jerry Wexler saw the group backing Bishop and offered them a contract. In September, they recorded "Don't Try to Take the Fifth," their first imitation of vocal groups such as Lambert, Hendricks, and Ross and the Supremes. In 1973, the Pointer Sisters appeared at the Los Angeles club the Troubadour, impressing audiences with their camp 1940's wardrobe and their stage act of burlesques, similar to the act Bette Midler was performing in New York.

Hits. After moving to Blue Thumb Records in 1973 and appearing on local television, Rubinson produced their first album, which included the Allen Toussaint composition "Yes We Can Can," which reached number 11. This success was followed by the sisters' remake of Willie Dixon's "Wang Dang Doodle" and Anita and Bonnie's "Fairytale," a country ballad which earned a Grammy Award in 1975 before being covered by Elvis Presley and Tammy Wynette. "Live Your Life Before You Die," another country song, was also nominated for a Grammy in 1975. After being the first black female group to perform at the Grand Ole Opry, later that year the group capitalized on the popularity of funk music with their next single, "How Long (Betcha Got a Chick on the Side)"

The Pointer Sisters (American Stock/Archive Photos)

which reached number 1 on the rhythm-and-blues charts.

Dance Queens. After a three-year-long popularity slide and lack of direction, June quit the group in November, 1975, after a nervous breakdown, but returned just after Bonnie permanently departed for a solo career with Motown Records. Beginning their long association as a trio with producer Richard Perry and Planet Records, the sisters reformulated their sound focusing on crossovers between rock and soul music. Dropping the nostalgic costumes, their next success was Bruce Springsteen's "Fire" (1979) followed by another country ballad, "Slow Hand," also recorded by country singer Conway Twitty the same year.

The next Perry-produced album, *Black and White,* was a deliberate attempt to imitate the 1960's Motown style of girl-group harmonies in songs such as "He's So Shy" (1981). The follow-up, 1983's *Breakout,* reworked 1970's disco themes and contained four Top-10 singles, "Automatic," "Jump (for My Love)," "Neutron Dance," and "I'm So Excited." Capitalizing on the new MTV video market and deliberately reaching for a younger black audience, the album reached number 8 on *Billboard's* album charts.

After this success, in 1985 the sisters revamped their stage show, began playing larger arenas, and released their last Top-20 hit, "Contact." Their popularity declined until 1994 when their song with country star Clint Black, "Chain of Fools," was another crossover country hit. In 1995 and 1996, the trio took time off from touring to participate in the cast of Thomas Wright "Fats" Waller's *Ain't Misbehavin',* a revival of the Broadway musical in which the sisters returned to their pre-World War II wardrobe. As a result, many critics determined the group had gone full circle and was moving back to their roots in more traditional black music. —*Wesley Britton*

SELECT DISCOGRAPHY

■ ALBUMS

The Pointer Sisters, 1973
That's a Plenty, 1974
Steppin', 1975
Black and White, 1981
Breakout, 1983
Fire: The Very Best of the Pointer Sisters, 1996 (compilation)

SELECT AWARDS

Grammy Award for Best Country Vocal Performance by a Duo or Group for "Fairytale," 1974

Grammy Awards for Best Pop Performance by a Duo or Group with Vocal for "Jump (for My Love)" and Best Vocal Arrangement for Two or More Voices for "Automatic," 1984

SEE ALSO: Black, Clint; Midler, Bette; Springsteen, Bruce.

The Police

MEMBERS: Stewart Copeland (b. 1952), Sting (b. Gordon Sumner, 1951), Andy Summers (b. 1942)

FIRST ALBUM RELEASE: *Outlandos d'Amour,* 1978

MUSICAL STYLES: Rock and roll, pop, reggae rock, new wave, punk rock

Formed in London in 1976, the Police was a group whose individual members' drive and musical ability came together to create one of the most successful and popular bands of the 1980's. At their height they were the top rock band in America, Europe, and, arguably, the world.

Beginnings. The Police formed at a time when rock music was purging itself of the indulgent musicianship of the progressive rock movement of the early 1970's. Polished pop and dance bands remained the big sellers on the charts, but the fresh blood and vitality in rock was emerging from the raw new genre known as punk.

Drummer Stewart Copeland was finishing up his time as drummer for the progressive band Curved Air and wanted to start a more aggressive-sounding band. Copeland had already decided to name his new group the Police and had written a few songs, but he was looking for strong musicians with whom to collaborate. He joined with a young musician named Sting, who had just moved to London. At age twenty-four, Sting was a semi-professional musician with his own group, a rock-jazz quartet called Last Exit, which he had formed in his hometown of Newcastle. When two members of Last Exit decided not to move to London, Sting lost his reservations about joining a punk band and came on board. The initial trio of the band was completed by Henri Padovani, a Corsican guitarist. Padovani's limited skills made him the weak link in the group.

The band's first single, a raw, energetic Copeland number called "Fallout," was recorded in February of 1977. After a few quick rehearsals the trio began to perform on the punk circuit. Their entire set consisted of about thirteen songs, mostly written by Copeland, which took the band only a half hour to blitz through on stage. Gigs became difficult to find, however, because the hard-core punk audience felt that the Police were both too old and too "musical" to be true punk rockers.

While playing with a band called Strontium 90 in May of 1977, Sting and Copeland met Andy Summers. Summers was a top-notch guitarist whose musical career had included stints with Soft Machine and Zoots Money's Big Roll Band as well as experience with a host of other groups as a session musician. The three were interested in working together, but Summers insisted that if he joined the band Padovani would have to go. Sting and Copeland decided to give up the thrashings of Padovani's three-chord guitar talents, and the classic Police trio was born.

The new lineup gave their first performance in Birmingham in August of 1977. This band fit into the punk scene even less than the earlier version had, however, and soon the only gigs they could get came when another band canceled. While the trio could empathize with the anger and dissatisfaction of the punk movement, the fact remained that their musical background made them far more sophisticated than the average punk band.

Down on their luck, the band borrowed money from Copeland's brother Miles so they could record a full album at a budget studio. Produced by the studio's owner, Nigel Grey, the recording took place sporadically over the course of six months. It was during one of these sessions that Miles, at that time a manager and agent for a number of bands on the punk circuit, came by and heard a rough version of a Sting composition called "Roxanne." Excited by what he heard, Miles maneuvered himself into the position of the band's manager. He quickly went out and sold first "Roxanne," then "Can't Stand Losing You" as singles to A&M Records. Though the songs received good reviews, they failed to chart.

The finished album was called *Outlandos d'Amour*, a play on words meaning "bandits of love." The album, certainly rough when compared with the group's later work, is full of the energy and angst of the punk spirit. The songs are propelled mostly by the frenzied drive of Summers's guitar riffs, but the singles written by Sting stand out as the beginning of something new: a style that takes its inspiration from rock, but adds elements from the styles and syncopations of world music, notably reggae.

With the album finished, the Police set out on a short but punishing tour of America, where they were virtually unknown. They traveled together in a rented van. Their playlist was short, so in concert they jammed, riffing off the chords and rhythms of individual songs to lengthen the set. In doing so they made great strides in developing their own sound. The difficult tour did more than expand their unique musical style; it also helped make them a very tight band. Sting later claimed that the 1978 tour was "the most exciting time of our musical life. . . . We were a real band—brothers." On the road in the United States they became, in the words of Miles Copeland, a "fighting unit."

In February of 1979 the Police began recording their second album. Working again with Nigel Grey, this second foray clearly showed their growth. The more sophisticated compositions allowed them to move away from the raw punkish sound of their earliest efforts. The album, called *Regatta de Blanc*, or "white reggae," expanded on the loose and open reggae style that had started on the most successful songs from *Outlandos d'Amour* and developed in their live set. Each individual member's talents had room to shine. The album highlighted Copeland's ability to play complex polyrhythms, Summers's muted jazz chordings and swirls of atmospheric sound, and Sting's solid bass lines, vocals, and growing songwriting skills. *Regatta de Blanc* delivered three songs that were British hits and received airplay in the United States, Sting's "Message in a Bottle," "Walking on the Moon," and "The Bed's Too Big Without You."

The "Fighting Unit" Attacks. In 1979, after a second short U.S. tour during the recording of *Reggata de Blanc* to encourage American airplay, things suddenly began to go the Police's way. "Roxanne" climbed to number 32 on the singles charts in the United States, and a re-release of the song in Britain found its way to number 12. Following the song's success, *Outlandos d'Amour* went to number 6 in Britain and number 23 in the United States. Soon after, a re-released "Can't Stand Losing You" hit number 2 in Britain just as *Regatta de Blanc* hit the shelves.

Like any good fighting unit, the Police responded by mounting a major offensive. The band started with their first headlining tour across Britain and Europe, which finished with a show as one of the three top-billed acts at Britain's Reading Festival. The year's tour did not end there, for as "Message in a Bottle" and "Walking on the Moon" each rose to number 1 in England in September and December respectively, manager Miles Copeland devised an ambitious plan.

With a barely established reputation in

The Police: Sting, Stewart Copeland, Andy Summers (Paul Natkin)

Europe, Miles booked the band on a comprehensive nineteen-country world tour which included not only the usual American and European legs but also unusual stops such as Hong Kong, Thailand, New Zealand, Mexico, India, and Egypt. His idea was to treat the entire world as a potential audience. Countries such as India and Egypt had never even seen concerts by an international rock band, and he believed that the seeds of recognition and acceptance planted by the band's trailblazing shows would blossom into something larger. Once a certain "critical mass" was achieved, he hoped, the entire world would become the band's market.

Though the tour was an arduous, logistical nightmare, the trio's powerful live set gained converts to their music across the world—and the unusual tour created excellent publicity back home. When at last they returned to England, the coverage they had received on the road resulted in forty thousand people vying for the four thousand available seats at the tour's final show. Miles Copeland's "critical mass" had been achieved, and the world seemed to be theirs.

Top of the World. In July of 1980 the trio cut their third album with Nigel Grey, *Zenyatta Mondatta.* A made-up name which roughly meant "on top of the world," *Zenyatta Mondatta* was another step forward in the Police's sophistication, both musically (in the use of more overdubs and unique rhythmic and harmonic arrangements) and in a new depth in the themes of the lyrics. As Sting said in one interview "The songs on the previous albums were about the individual—about alienation and loneliness. The songs on this album are more about the problems of society as a whole."

Another hard tour followed, and the hits "Don't Stand So Close to Me" and "De Do Do Do, De Da Da Da" rose up the charts (both reached number 10 in the U.S.) as the album went platinum. However, the difficult cycle of album, tour, album, tour was taking its toll. Even above the challenge of keeping the egos of three very individual spirits in check during the rigors of a long tour, the stress and time away on the road had made casualties of both Sting's and Summers's marriages. The tour ended early.

The title of the Police's fourth album, *Ghost in the Machine* (1981), refers both to a book by Arthur Koestler and to the fact that the volume controls ("faders") on the mixing console they were using could be programmed to slide up and down by themselves in a somewhat eerie manner. Taking advantage of the growing technology in music recording, this album more than any other saw the Police using overdubs of multiple vocal harmonies, keyboard and guitar synthesizers, horns (played by Sting), and a host of odd percussion sounds. Working with new producer/engineer Hugh Padgham, the Police filled up the space that had been left bare in their earlier work with washes of layered sound. The album produced new hits for the trio with Sting's dark songs "Spirits in the Material World" and "Invisible Sun" as well as the lighter smash hit "Every Little Thing She Does Is Magic" (a number 3 U.S. single).

The fifth album, *Synchronicity* (1983), produced once again with Hugh Padgham, saw all three members stretch out in new musical directions. Widely lauded as their best album, *Synchronicity* returned to the more open arrangements of their work before *Ghost in the Machine.* Though the album yielded great hits for the band

For the Record

While starting out, the Police landed a part playing a punk band in a Wrigley's gum commercial. Done solely for the money, it required all three of them to bleach their hair blond, a look that became a signature for the band.

§

Sting claimed to have written the hit "Every Breath You Take" in one night. He recalled that he "woke up in the middle of the night in Jamaica and went straight to the piano and the chords and song just came out within ten minutes. Wrote the song. Went back to bed."

with Sting's songs "Wrapped Around Your Finger," "King of Pain," and "Synchronicity II," it was Sting's composition "Every Breath You Take" that proved to be the trio's biggest success. The single held number 1 in the U.S. for eight weeks and propelled the album to number 1 for an amazing seventeen weeks—and this in the year of Michael Jackson's *Thriller*. Even before a remix of "Every Breath You Take" became a huge success for Puff Daddy (Sean "Puffy" Combs) in 1997, the album had garnered a 1991 award for having received two million plays on the air.

The Group Disbands. After pursuing individual projects for two years, in July of 1986 the Police came together to record their sixth album. In reality, though, the group had already broken up in all but name. Not only had Sting found success with his first solo album, *The Dream of Blue Turtles* (1985), but more significantly, he brought with him no new songs for the group to record. In the end, one last song was recorded, a new version of "Don't Stand So Close to Me" that later became the basis for a greatest hits album. It was a richly overproduced track for which Copeland could only program his drum parts electronically—his collarbone had been broken, an injury officially reported to be from a fall in a polo game. (Other sources have maintained that it was the result of a wrestling tussle between him and Sting.) With tempers on edge, each member recorded his parts alone and bypassed the band's previous vehement tug-of-war method that had slimmed down the songs to tight compositions. With obvious personal differences and the financial freedom to pursue their own interests, the group disbanded after finishing the single song.

Beyond the Police, Stewart Copeland and Andy Summers achieved moderate success on their own, while Sting went on to a very successful solo career; he had released eight albums by 1998. Copeland has recorded two solo albums and two albums with the group Animal Logic. He has also written music for two operas and a host of film and television sound tracks. Summers has produced widely respected instrumental albums both in collaboration with Robert Fripp and John Etheridge, and has released five albums as a solo artist.

A rare joining of individual talents, the Police hold a firm place in the history of popular music. Aside from their Grammy Award-winning instrumentals, the band rarely openly displayed their full musical virtuosity, instead letting their skills surface more subtly. As a result, each member is known and respected for his unique contributions in popularizing new techniques and sounds on bass, guitar, and drums. Though a few bands (such as Men at Work) have attempted to mimic their sound, the strength of these three members individual abilities has kept any band from following them into the same musical territory.

—*Todd Elhart*

SELECT DISCOGRAPHY

■ ALBUMS

Outlandos d'Amour, 1978
Reggatta de Blanc, 1979
Zenyatta Mondatta, 1980
Ghost in the Machine, 1981
Synchronicity, 1983
Message in a Box, 1993 (4-CD compilation)
Police Live! 1995

SELECT AWARDS

Grammy Award for Best Rock Instrumental Performance for "Reggatta De Blanc," 1981
BRIT Award for Best British Group, 1982
Grammy Award for Best Rock Performance By a Duo or Group for "Don't Stand So Close to Me," 1982
Grammy Award for Best Rock Instrumental Performance for "Behind My Camel," 1982
Grammy Awards for Song of the Year and Best Pop Performance by a Duo or Group for "Every Breath You Take" and for Best Rock Performance by a Duo or Group for "Syncronicity II," all 1984
BRIT Career Award for Outstanding Contribution to British Music, 1985

SEE ALSO: Puff Daddy; Sting.

Porno for Pyros. *See* Jane's Addiction / Porno for Pyros

Elvis Presley

BORN: Tupelo, Mississippi; January 8, 1935
DIED: Memphis, Tennessee; August 16, 1977
FIRST SINGLE RELEASE: "That's All Right"/"Blue Moon of Kentucky," 1954
MUSICAL STYLES: Rock and roll, rockabilly, country, pop

The first real rock-and-roll star, Elvis Presley combined country, blues, and gospel music to astound a huge audience of young people. His full-throated singing and hip-swiveling onstage manner perplexed or outraged older fans of both country and pop music who were accustomed to more sedate styles of performing. Presley became a role model for young white singers and, in essence, started the worldwide dominance of rock and roll and later rock music. For the next two decades, he was the symbol of youth music and the coming together of white and black styles in the mass marketplace. He and the Beatles remain the top sellers of records in popular music.

Tupelo to Memphis. Born into poverty in Tupelo, Mississippi, as an only child (his twin brother died at birth), Presley showed an early interest in music. He won a prize for singing the country standard "Old Shep" at a local fair in 1945 and got his first guitar soon after. Times remained hard for his parents, Gladys and Vernon, after the end of World War II, so the family decided to move north to Memphis, Tennessee, the nearest big city, in 1948. While attending the all-white Humes High School in Memphis, Presley began to practice his singing with the accompaniment of his simple acoustic guitar.

Presley's musical influences were quite varied. He had grown up in Tupelo with gospel music in the Pentecostal church he attended, and he had learned some basic guitar chords and country songs from a local singer. In Memphis, however, the music was even more diverse. With its many radio stations and large population of both Caucasians and African Americans, Memphis was a melting pot of American musical styles and performers. The city had long been a blues center, both for recording and for live performances. Presley lived near Beale Street, which was famous across the United States as a center for clubs and the black culture of the teeming city. On the radio he heard blues, rhythm and blues, country, and pop played by local disc jockeys who advertised local acts and amateur contests. He came to like the pop sounds of singers such as Dean Martin and, for a time, was an usher at a downtown movie house where he saw the glamour of Hollywood films for the first time. It was a heady world he was being exposed to after his down-home, small-town youth. He sang a bit at high school shows but took working-class jobs after graduation in 1953, most notably driving a truck for Crown Electric.

Sun Records. Sam Phillips, the founder of Sun Records, was a key figure in the development of modern American popular music. Growing up in northern Alabama, he heard black blues as a young man and eventually moved to Memphis to act as a sound engineer for a radio station. Aware that Memphis seemed to do little to record black artists in the 1940's and 1950's, he set up the Memphis Recording Service in 1950 and began to record local blues artists such as B. B. King, Howlin' Wolf, Little Milton, Junior Parker, and Rosco Gordon, all of whom later became major blues musicians. In the little studio on 706 Union Avenue, close to Beale Street, he captured the raw sounds of small combo blues and the newer rhythm-and-blues style with its brasher uptempo sounds. He leased all these recordings to other record labels on the West Coast and in Chicago. Many sold so well that Phillips decided in 1952 to start his own label, Sun Records. Phillips had a good sense of the market and realized that white teenagers were starting to tune in the local radio stations that played black music. Here was a po-

For the Record

"Anybody who sees Elvis Presley and doesn't want to be like Elvis Presley has got to have something wrong with him."

—*Bruce Springsteen*

Elvis Presley (Imapress/Archive Photos)

tential market for a white singer who might have the sound and feel of black music.

Presley had not given up on music after graduating from high school. He sang to friends informally, doing songs made popular by black vocal groups, country singers, and pop stylists such as Dean Martin. He was exploring a variety of styles on his own. He listened to local radio, bought records, and dressed in a hip style with sideburns, greased-back hair, and colorful clothes bought at Lansky Brothers, the premier clothing shop for African Americans on Beale Street. Presley stood out even in high school as different, as a rebel of sorts from middle-class norms of decorum.

In the summer of 1953, just after he graduated from high school, Presley went to Sun Records and made a private recording of two songs, "My Happiness" and "That's When Your Heartaches Begin." These were slow ballads sung in a high tenor voice with just his guitar as accompaniment. The secretary at Sun took notice. Presley indicated that he could sing any kind of song, so she kept his name on file. These songs were supposedly for his mother's birthday, but that was months away. Presley was, in reality, testing his potential as a musician. He had the ambition now to go beyond his job as a truck driver. He recorded two more slow songs in early 1954 and was soon called by Phillips himself to try out a new song, "Without You." Although nothing came of this attempt, Phillips wanted to push Presley further. He heard in his voice what he was looking for—a white kid who could perform songs in the same style as black musicians.

Phillips soon teamed Presley with two local musicians who had a good sense of different styles: electric guitarist Scotty Moore and stand-up bassist Bill Black. They practiced together and found that Presley knew an incredible number of songs from many sources. In early July, they went into the Sun Records' studio to try to work up something that could be recorded for release. The first session moved slowly, with Presley doing too many slow ballads made popular by others in a crooning style. In a session break, Presley started to sing the recent blues song released by bluesman Arthur Crudup, "That's All Right." Black and then Moore joined in to get into a rocking groove appropriate to the original. Phillips heard them and egged them on, quickly sensing that this kind of uptempo blues song with the combo punch of rhythm and blues—sung by a white man—was what he had been looking for and had believed that Presley could get out of himself. Phillips recorded the song and rushed a test copy to a local disc jockey who emceed a black music show. The song got a great response from listeners, which convinced Phillips to press it as a single. They needed another song to fill the other side of the record, so they again worked on a jumping arrangement of "Blue Moon of Kentucky," a waltz-time bluegrass song written and recorded by Bill Monroe. With this matching of songs, Presley could appeal to listeners and record buyers of both races. He was on his way in mid-July, 1954, as a regional sensation.

In 1955 Presley did four more singles for Sun Records that had regional success. His versions of black uptempo songs such as "Good Rockin' Tonight," "Baby, Let's Play House," "Milkcow Blues Boogie," and "Mystery Train" became the classics that defined rockabilly music. Presley's shouted

For the Record

Elvis Presley scandalized many television viewers on the June 5, 1956, *Milton Berle Show* with his suggestive movements while singing his new song "Hound Dog." His hip swivels and leg gyrations prompted producers to tone down his appearance on *The Steve Allen Show* on July 1 of the same year. Allen introduced him as the "new Elvis Presley." Dressed in a tuxedo with blue suede shoes and dragging his guitar beside him, Presley looked very uncomfortable. He performed "Hound Dog" without the guitar, standing beside a motionless, expressionless basset hound. Nevertheless, on July 2, Presley recorded the song, which became one of his biggest hits.

vocals and wide vocal range owed much to African American vocal styles, just as the small combo of electric guitar and slapped upright bass was drawn from jump blues recordings laced with country music boogie woogie models from the 1940's. This kind of uptempo country music was itself inspired by black music traditions. Some songs were slower, and some were newly composed by white songwriters. By the end of 1955, Presley had signed with RCA Records and a new, high-powered manager, Colonel Tom Parker, and was ready for national exposure and a mass audience.

National Fame and Hollywood. Throughout 1956, Presley appeared on primetime television variety shows and made such enduring recordings as "Heartbreak Hotel," "Hound Dog," "Don't Be Cruel," and "Love Me Tender," all number 1 pop hits. He was no longer just a country singer. Television gave him the opportunity to introduce these new recordings and develop a performing style that could handle all types of songs, including the slow ballads he had always liked but that Phillips at Sun Records had tried to avoid releasing. His band was augmented with drums and the backup group, the Jordanaires. In the studio, a piano was sometimes added to the mix. However, Presley kept his rocking style over the years and did not resort to using such add-ons as strings until the 1970's.

Hollywood beckoned in 1956. Presley soon became a popular singing actor in such successful films as *Love Me Tender* (1956), *Loving You* (1957), *Jailhouse Rock* (1957), *King Creole* (1958), and *Blue Hawaii* (1961). In 1957, Presley purchased Graceland, a twenty-three-room mansion that had been converted from a church, where he would live until his death in 1977. His time in the Army between 1958 and 1960 barely slowed the momentum of his career, although his service was interrupted by the death of his mother in August of 1958, a tragedy that Presley would later refer to as the greatest trauma of his life.

Priscilla Beaulieu, whom Presley had met while in the Army in Germany, moved into Graceland in 1961, one year after Presley's discharge from the Army. Several years later, on May 1, 1967, the couple married in Las Vegas, Nevada. The following year Priscilla gave birth to their only child, Lisa Marie, on February 1. During this time, Presley had turned his attention to making a series of high-grossing but increasingly mediocre films. These formula love plots featured Presley as a sort of all-American hero who righted wrongs and always won the girl while warbling mostly forgettable movie ditties. By 1968, however, he was fed up with his Hollywood career and yearned to return to live performing.

Comeback and Return to Touring. Although he had many million-selling singles through the early 1960's as well as successful sound track albums from his films (*Blue Hawaii* in 1961 was his best-selling album release, with twenty weeks at the top of the pop charts), sales of recordings and the popularity of his films began to slack off. With the arrival of the Beatles and other British rock groups, the American musical scene changed greatly from the mid-1960's on. The earlier rock and roll style disappeared, and a new and eventually more sophisticated style of music and songwriting emerged. Presley felt the competition and believed that he could match the excitement of the new, young musicians by getting out in public after nearly a decade without performing live.

Presley chose to do a television special to signal his reentry into the music scene. Shown in December, 1968, it was a phenomenal success and unveiled the musical style and repertory that Presley was to follow for the rest of his career. On the one-hour show, he displayed all that he had learned while making movies: smooth and choreographed dancing, sophisticated moves and gestures (the old and controversial hip-swiveling had been so stylized that no one could object), and a command of vocal and song styles unrivalled in American popular music. The television show gave Presley the opportunity to perform the gospel songs he had always loved, revisit his old hits, take part in production numbers with dancers, and most impressively, just sit down with members of his band and old friends and jam on blues, rhythm and blues, and country songs many thought he had abandoned for weak movie songs. He sang rockers, love ballads, and blues, and he performed a new contemporary inspirational song about the hope for a more peaceful world called "If I Can Dream."

The show changed his life. He now knew he could successfully play live again because the television show had been performed in front of a live audience in Burbank, California. In 1969, he started an eight-year series of shows in Las Vegas and a touring schedule that took him to large arenas and auditoriums all over the United States right up to the time of his death in 1977. His recording career was renewed also. Hits such as "In the Ghetto," "Suspicious Minds," "Don't Cry Daddy," "Kentucky Rain," and "Burning Love" showed he was still a master. The live shows featured an orchestra in addition to rock band and backup singers. Presley dressed in elaborate jump suits and displayed a dynamic stage presence. New songs and old hits let him keep abreast of changing tastes and allowed him to interpret the whole range of American popular music.

Unfortunately the demands of endless travel and nightly shows over eight years wore Presley down. His physical appearance began to deteriorate as he struggled with obesity. His worries were compounded by financial difficulties brought on by the bad business advice he had received over the years and by his habit of giving away cash and expensive gifts. After Presley died on August 16, 1977, it was revealed that he had been abusing prescription drugs for quite some time and that they may have played at least a partial role in his death, which had originally been attributed to congestive heart failure. —*Frederick E. Danker*

SELECT DISCOGRAPHY

■ SINGLES

"Heartbreak Hotel," 1956
"Don't Be Cruel," 1956
"Hound Dog," 1956
"Love Me Tender," 1956
"All Shook Up," 1957
"(Let Me Be Your) Teddy Bear," 1957
"Jailhouse Rock," 1957
"A Big Hunk o' Love," 1959
"It's Now or Never," 1960
"Are You Lonesome Tonight?" 1960
"Surrender," 1961
"(Marie's the Name) His Latest Flame"/"Little Sister" 1961
"Can't Help Falling in Love," 1961
"Good Luck Charm," 1962
"Return to Sender," 1962
"(You're the) Devil in Disguise," 1963
"Viva Las Vegas," 1964
"In the Ghetto," 1969
"Suspicious Minds," 1969
"Kentucky Rain," 1970
"Burning Love," 1972

■ ALBUMS

Elvis Presley, 1956
Elvis, 1956
Blue Hawaii, 1961 (sound track)
Elvis TV Special, 1968
From Elvis in Memphis, 1969
The Complete Sun Sessions, 1987 (previously released material)
The King of Rock 'n' Roll: The Complete 50's Masters, 1992 (boxed set)
From Nashville to Memphis: The Essential 60's Masters, 1993 (boxed set)
Amazing Grace: His Greatest Sacred Songs, 1994 (boxed set)
Walk a Mile in My Shoes: The Essential 70's Masters, 1995 (boxed set)

SELECT AWARDS

Grammy Award for Best Sacred Performance for "How Great Thou Art," 1967
Grammy Lifetime Achievement Award, 1971
Grammy Award for Best Inspirational Performance for "He Touched Me," 1972
Grammy Award for Best Inspirational Performance for "How Great Thou Art," 1974
Rock and Roll Hall of Fame, inducted 1986

SEE ALSO: Beatles, The; Cash, Johnny; Domino, Fats; Haley, Bill; Lewis, Jerry Lee; Little Richard; Perkins, Carl.

The Pretenders

ORIGINAL MEMBERS: Chrissie Hynde (b. 1951), Martin Chambers (b. 1952), James Honeyman-Scott (1957-1982), Pete Farndon (1953-1983)

OTHER MEMBERS: Malcolm Foster, Robbie McIntosh (b. 1950), Adam Seymour, Andy Hobson, Blair Cunningham (b. 1957), others
FIRST ALBUM RELEASE: *Pretenders*, 1980
MUSICAL STYLES: Rock and roll, punk rock

At the age of forty-three, Pretenders' lead singer, guitarist, and songwriter Chrissie Hynde told an interviewer before starting a new concert tour, "Some women need a man; I need a band!" Having once said that she prefers living out of a suitcase to child rearing, Hynde nearly wrote the book on how to be a female rock and roller. A woman leading an all-male band, an American leading an all-English band, a solid rhythm guitarist and excellent singer-songwriter, Hynde is the godmother of rock and roll women.

Emerging from the rich, chaotic musical subculture of the mid-1970's London punk scene, the Pretenders fused punk's aggressive energy with pop melodies and song craft to create a charged erotic mix that produced two classic albums and a series of hits. When guitarist James Honeyman-Scott and bassist Pete Farndon met drug-related deaths in a nine-month period beginning in mid-1982, the band lost its original sound. For the next decade, the band was composed of Hynde and a changing set of studio musicians, makeshift units that never generated the creative, collective intelligence of a great rock band. The return of original drummer Martin Chambers stabilized a new band lineup in 1994 and resulted in the album *Last of the Independents.*

The Pretenders' Chrissie Hynde (Ken Settle)

London Punk Beginnings. "I always wanted to be a hobo," Hynde once said, comparing the sound of a train outside her childhood Akron, Ohio, window to that of great rock and roll. Both sounded wild and free and gave off the sound of adventure. Equally influenced by the Beatles and Iggy Pop, Hynde played in local bands but became bored and unhappy with American society. As a self-admitted hippie in the late 1960's, Hynde refused to become involved in the corporate nine-to-five lifestyle. As a student at Kent State in 1970, she witnessed the shooting deaths of four anti-Vietnam War protesters by the National Guard. She became quite militant on the issues of vegetarianism and animal rights. In 1974, Hynde packed a suitcase and moved to London, arriving just as the punk scene began. She wrote rock criticism for *New Musical Express* and landed a job at Sex, the infamous boutique owned by punk entrepreneur Malcolm McLaren, the manager of the Sex Pistols. Hynde met and played with many rising stars of punk and new wave, including Mick Jones of the Clash and songwriter and producer Nick Lowe.

Bassist Pete Farndon met Hynde in 1978, and they decided to form a band after playing together a few times. Farndon recruited guitarist James Honeyman-Scott, and when drummer Martin Chambers came on board, the band clicked immediately. Nick Lowe produced their first single, a cover of the Kinks' "Stop Your Sobbing," which became a Top-40 hit in England. Hynde's tough

For the Record

Chrissie Hynde got the idea of naming her band the Pretenders when she was spending time with a white motorcycle tough. One day the fellow took her to his room and bolted his door shut. He wanted to play his favorite record for her but did not want any of his white "brothers" to hear it. The record was "The Great Pretender," by the African American group the Platters. Hynde recalls looking at "this white supremacist lowlife, with his hand on his heart and his eyes shut, swaying to that clear, black voice." She knew then that she wanted to make music that had that kind of power.

independence and driving rhythm guitar separated her from previous female rock and rollers. For a woman to coolly and unemotionally tell her male lover to be strong or be gone ("There's one thing you gotta do/ to make me/ still want you/ [you] gotta stop your sobbing now") was something of a new-wave sexual throwdown. Hynde's influence extended to Madonna, who saw her perform in the early 1980's. Madonna called Hynde's performance "awesome," adding, "It gave me courage, inspiration, to see a woman with that kind of confidence in a man's world."

Two Classic Albums. *Pretenders* (1980) featured well-crafted songs that were intelligent and erotic, melodic and explosive. Hynde's vocals combined jazz phrasing with punk attitude, while her rhythm guitar work added rock and roll drive. Honeyman-Scott's quick, bright rhythm guitar riffs commented on Hynde's vocals; the rhythm section provided either steady grooves to ground Hynde's punk aggression or a frantic, thrash-type backbeat. "Brass in Pocket" was a slow, reggae-flavored pop ballad whose musical power derived from Hynde's slow attempt to wear a reluctant lover down with all her charms. In "Precious," Hynde narrated the story of a relationship between two explosive people in a half-spoken, half-sung whisper.

That kind of controlled passion was absent from *Pretenders II* (1981), a set of songs that played up Hynde's tough sexuality to the point of caricature. There were still two classics: "Talk of the Town," a lilting ballad buoyed by jangling guitars, and "Message of Love," a rocking celebration of earthy sexuality with a powerful keyboards-and-guitar electronic beat. After drug-related deaths claimed Honeyman-Scott and Farndon in June, 1982, and April, 1983, respectively, Hynde admitted that she had a drinking problem. She cut down on her drinking while pregnant with her first daughter (born in January, 1983), the product of a tumultuous four-year relationship with the Kinks' Ray Davies.

The Pretenders took that chaotic series of events and produced an impressive, eclectic set of songs on *Learning to Crawl* (1984). The album featured the tough, don't-mess-with-me revenge song "I Hurt You" sitting side by side with "2000 Miles," a beautiful, Christmas-like hymn about a lover's return. The Motown-style hit "Back on the Chain Gang" was a tribute to Honeyman-Scott, Hynde's closest musical partner. "Thumbelina" was about an imaginary cross-country train ride with her daughter powered by a shuffling steam-engine rhythm. The album's masterpiece was "Middle of the Road," a riff-driven rocker in which Hynde faced up to the temptation of success, the responsibility of her age, and her new roles ("I'm not the cat I used to be/ I got a kid/ I'm 33, Baby") yet still exclaimed, "I'm hitting the road." When the guitars crunched down, Hynde erupted into a perfectly timed cat snarl that rolled into a powerful guitar solo that reaffirmed the sense of freedom and adventure that rock and roll had always held for her and her audience.

Hynde toured often and recorded a hit reggae version of Sonny and Cher's "I Got You Babe" with UB40. In May of 1984, Hynde had a whirlwind romance with James Kerr of Simple Minds that resulted in a short-lived marriage and a second daughter. Hynde's priority in the late 1980's was raising her daughters, and the joys and challenges of parenting dominated *Get Close* (1987). *Packed!*

(1990) was the band's least focused collection but contained a few gems, such as the deep reggae groove of "How Do I Miss You." Drummer Martin Chambers's return did not make *Last of the Independents* (1994) a great record, but "Night in My Veins" and "Revolution" were two of the band's best songs in years. Many of the best songs on these three albums received excellent acoustic treatments on the live set, *Isle of View* (1995).

The Mother of All Riot Girrls. Hynde's tough exterior has always been the mainstay of the Pretenders' image, and her style remains virtually unchanged since her punk beginnings. Black bangs nearly cover her eyes, and massive black eye shadow turns her eyes into targets. Favoring leather jackets, skin-tight jeans, boots, and ripped T-shirts, she emanates a hard, wiry, street-tough strength that is somehow highly feminine and somewhat androgynous. She combines the danger and allure of bikers, derelicts, Vampirella, and Cher. Tough and vulnerable, sexually aggressive and man-crazy, maternal and bitchy, Hynde at times portrays herself as all women within one woman. In the beautiful ballad "Hymn to Her" (1986), she sang to her daughter about the continuum of female life cycles, from daughter to lover to mother to grandmother: "she will always carry on/ something is lost/ but something is found/ they will keep on speaking her name/ some things change/ some stay the same." In "I'm a Mother" (1994), Hynde's shrieks reflected brute female force as exerted in the roles of queen, lover, femme fatale, and old crone. Yet for all this self-conscious female identification, Hynde has never called attention to her pioneering role as a female rocker.

On "Sense of Purpose" (1990), she began a seductive ode to a gentle man by showing how easily she wore her female strength: "Bully boys don't bother me/ I purse my lips and they run away," she sang sweetly. However, she has yet to solve the dilemma of the middle-aged rock and roller. How does one contribute to a musical form based on rebellion and attitude once wisdom and experience replace the unchanneled anger and raw sexuality of youth? Hynde's voice has matured into a subtle and supple instrument, and she is one of rock and roll's finest songwriters. Yet when she sings to that same gentle man, "Give me a sense of purpose/ a real sense of purpose now," she seems to be looking less for love than musical direction. —*Joel Dinerstein*

SELECT DISCOGRAPHY

■ ALBUMS

Pretenders, 1980
Pretenders II, 1981
Learning to Crawl, 1984
Get Close, 1986
The Singles, 1987 (previously released material)
Packed!, 1990
Last of the Independents, 1994
Isle of View, 1995 (live)

SEE ALSO: Clash, The; Kinks, The; Sex Pistols, The.

Charley Pride

BORN: Sledge, Mississippi; March 18, 1938
FIRST ALBUM RELEASE: *Country Charley Pride*, 1966
MUSICAL STYLES: Country, gospel, pop

Charley Pride was reared in a family of ten children on a cotton farm in Mississippi, and he started working in the fields at the age of five, chopping and picking cotton. Whenever possible, Pride would listen to country music on the radio, especially the *Grand Ole Opry* on Saturday nights. His idol was Hank Williams, and he memorized all the lyrics to Williams's songs, as well as songs of Ernest Tubb, Roy Acuff, and Eddy Arnold. At the age of fourteen, he purchased a cheap guitar, and being a very observant, good listener, he taught himself how to play it by following what he heard on the radio.

Baseball over Music. Although music was very important to Pride, he initially concentrated on a professional baseball career, seeing it as a way to escape picking cotton. His early dream was to play for the Brooklyn Dodgers and later pursue a singing career. When he was fifteen, his parents signed a contract for him to play in the farm system of the New York Yankees, and he left school to play for the Yankees minor league affiliate in Lodi,

California. However, due to a pulled tendon in his shoulder, he soon returned home.

In 1955 at the age of seventeen, he left home to play for the Memphis Red Sox in the Negro American League. He also played for Detroit and for Birmingham in that league. Two years spent in the U.S. Army, from late 1956 to 1958, put his baseball career on hold. He returned to the Memphis baseball club in 1958 and played with them until 1959, when he quit due to a salary dispute. He tried out for the Missoula Timberjacks, but, failing to make the team, Pride went to work as a zinc smelter for Anaconda Mining Company in Helena, Montana, and played semi-professional baseball for the East Helena Smelterites and the Helena Amvets.

Still ambitious to play in the major leagues, Pride went to the spring training camp of the Los Angeles Angels, a major league expansion team, in 1961. He tried out as a pitcher and an outfielder and lasted with the team for two and one half weeks. In 1964, he gave major league baseball one more try, traveling to the training camp of the New York Mets in Tampa, Florida. When Mets manager Casey Stengel rejected him, Pride finally accepted the fact that he would not have a major league career.

First Recordings. While playing semi-professional baseball in Montana, Pride began developing his musical talents singing in nightclubs and bars. One night, country singing stars Red Sovine and Red Foley heard Pride singing in Great Falls, Montana. They were so impressed with his talent that they encouraged him to visit Nashville for an audition.

After failing to make it with the Mets in 1964, Pride stopped in Nashville on his way back to Montana and woke up Red Sovine in the middle of the night to let him know that he was ready for an audition. Pride recorded a tape that was listened to by Nashville record producer Jack Clement, who then took Pride to see Chet Atkins, head of RCA in Nashville. Atkins liked Pride's rich, smooth, slightly baritone voice, which sounded more like that of a white man, and signed Pride to a long-term recording contract with RCA in 1965. Worried about the reception of a black country singer by white listeners, RCA released Pride's first three records without any of the usual publicity or photographs.

In 1965, Pride's first single release, "The Snakes Crawl at Night," was a success, and at the Country Music Convention in Nashville in 1966, he sang before his peers and received a standing ovation and an encore. His second release near the end of 1966, "Just Between You and Me," reached the Top 10 in 1967. On January 7, 1967, Ernest Tubb introduced him at the Grand Ole Opry, and Pride enjoyed a successful debut as the Opry's first African American singing star.

Country Charley Pride. In the summer of 1969, Pride had his first number 1 hit, "All I Have to Offer You." In the same year, he recorded his first gold album, *The Best of Charley Pride.* Pride has had thirty-five number 1 records on the U.S. country charts, including six consecutive top hits between 1969 and 1971. In addition to "All I Have to Offer You," some of his most significant top singles are "Is Anybody Goin' to San Antone," "Afraid of Losing You Again," "Kiss an Angel Good Morning," "She's Too Good to Be True, "Someone Loves You Honey," "Night Games," and "Honky-Tonk Blues." His 1970 hit, "Kiss an Angel Good Morning," became a million seller and earned Pride his first gold record.

Pride won two Grammy Awards in 1971 when his album *Did You Think to Pray?* was named Best Sacred Performance, and his single record "Let Me Live" was named Best Gospel Performance. Another Grammy came in 1972 for Best Country Vocal Performance for his 1971 album *Charley Pride Sings Heart Songs.* Pride has sold more than twenty million records and more than forty albums, thirty-one of which have attained gold status, and four of which have gone platinum. In the 1997 *Book of Lists,* he is listed as one of the top fifteen all-time worldwide record sellers.

—Alvin K. Benson

SELECT DISCOGRAPHY

■ ALBUMS

Country Charley Pride, 1966
Pride of Country Music, 1967
Songs of Pride . . . Charley, That Is, 1968

The Best of Charley Pride, 1969
Just Plain Charley, 1970
Did You Think to Pray? 1971
Charley Pride Sings Heart Songs, 1971
Pride of America, 1974
Someone Loves You Honey, 1978
Night Games, 1983
The Power of Love, 1984
I'm Gonna Love Her on the Radio, 1988
Classics with Pride, 1991
My 6 Latest & 6 Greatest, 1993

SELECT AWARDS

Grammy Awards for Best Sacred Performance for *Did You Think to Pray?* and Best Gospel Performance (Other than Soul Gospel) for "Let Me Live," 1971

Country Music Association Entertainer of the Year and Male Vocalist of the Year Awards, 1971

Grammy Award for Best Country Vocal Performance, Male, for *Charley Pride Sings Heart Songs*, 1972

Country Music Association Male Vocalist of the Year Award, 1972

American Music Award for Favorite Male Vocalist in Country Music, 1976

SEE ALSO: Arnold, Eddy; Atkins, Chet; Haggard, Merle; Kristofferson, Kris; Nelson, Willie; Parton, Dolly; Tubb, Ernest; Williams, Hank.

Prince

(The Artist; ♀︎)

BORN: Minneapolis, Minnesota; June 7, 1958
FIRST ALBUM RELEASE: *For You*, 1978
MUSICAL STYLES: Pop, rock and roll, rhythm and blues, funk

Prince has been an innovator, a prolific songwriter, and one of the most dynamic performers in rock and roll. An amazing musician, producer, and versatile music visionary, he has written songs for such diverse artists as George Clinton, Chaka Khan, Miles Davis, Madonna, Celine Dion, Kenny Rogers, and Paula Abdul. Though by the late 1990's his eccentric behavior often received more attention than his creative output, his legacy will be that he shocked listeners with his mixed messages of sexuality and spiritual devotion and ignited passion in a time when popular music desperately needed it.

Humble Beginnings. Prince Rogers Nelson was born to swing-band leader Roger Nelson and named after his father's jazz band, the Prince Rogers Trio. When Prince was seven, his parents separated. His father left behind his piano, and Prince taught himself to play. "At thirteen I went to live with an aunt," Prince said. "She didn't have room for a piano so my father bought me an electric guitar, and I learned how to play that." Prince also taught himself to play bass, saxophone, and drums, eventually learning more than twenty instruments. Soon after, Prince formed his first band, Champagne.

In 1976 Champagne made its first recording in a small Minneapolis, Minnesota, studio, Moon Sound. Young Prince's natural talent in the studio was discovered, and he was offered a job as a tape operator. It would be in that studio that he would hone his producing expertise and develop skills that would influence what would become known as the Minneapolis sound. Local lawyer Owen Husney became his first manager, and with the superior demo that nineteen-year-old Prince provided him, Husney secured him an unheard-of three-record contract at Warner Bros. that included producing rights.

Impressive Debut. Prince wrote, produced, and performed all the instruments on his 1978 debut album, *For You*. From that album, he scored a modest rhythm-and-blues hit, "Soft and Wet." His second album, *Prince* (1979), produced a modest hit on the soul charts with "I Wanna Be Your Lover."

In 1980 he recorded *Dirty Mind*. Using local Minneapolis musicians, it was submitted as a demo with the intention of rerecording all the songs later in California. However, the songs' unpolished rawness was edgy and spirited, and it was decided to release the album in its original state. *Rolling Stone* magazine and *The Village Voice* both included it on their top-ten album lists of the year. The sexually explicit lyrics caused radio stations to shy away from playing its tracks, and while it did not yield any hit singles, it still sold well enough to go platinum. "I only write from experience," Prince said. "I don't plan to shock people. I write about things I guess people are afraid to talk about. *Dirty Mind* was written totally from experience."

Superstardom by *1999*. His 1982 double album, *1999*, crossed over beyond the soul and rhythm-and-blues charts to the rock and pop charts, reaching a more diverse audience. The title track was a hit dance tune, though originally intended as a group vocal. Prince and band members Lisa Coleman and Dez Dickerson sang the entire song together, but when Prince mixed it, he divided the vocals so all three sang solo lines, creating a likable party effect. "1999" went to number 9 on the pop charts and was followed by "Little Red Corvette," which reached number 6.

Both songs were also hit videos on MTV, and *Rolling Stone* named *1999* Album of the Year. Prince supported the album with a national tour to sold-out concert venues with his band the Revolution. Certifiably a superstar, by the age of twenty-five Prince had earned over thirty million dollars and sold more than nine million albums.

The Artist Formerly Known as Prince (Paul Natkin)

***Purple Rain*.** Based on that success, Prince pressured his managers to secure him a film deal with Warner Bros. A few weeks after the "1999" tour, Prince rented an industrial warehouse where he and his band had drama classes, dance classes, and music rehearsals. The resulting semi-autobiographical film *Purple Rain* (1984) was sexual, playful, and filled with popular songs, including some from other Minneapolis-based Prince-sponsored bands, the Time and Vanity 6. It was a success, even with critics: *Rolling Stone* called it "the most spiritual rock-and-roll movie ever made."

The album of the same name, released in 1984, included the single "When Doves Cry," a haunting song that dealt with the seldom breached subject of spousal abuse. It would be Prince's first song to reach number 1. "Let's Go Crazy," which featured some of Prince's fine but underutilized guitar playing, also reached number 1. The film's title track later made it to number 2 on the charts.

After the film's success and another sold-out concert tour, the prolific Prince returned to Minneapolis, where he produced and wrote the hit song "Sugar Walls" for Scottish singer Sheena Easton. His next album, *Around the World in a Day*, was released in 1985 and contained music influenced by the psychedelic sounds and lyrics of the 1960's. Prince then opened Paisley Park, a state-of-the-art recording studio in Minneapolis, in September and started a record label of the same name, which was to be distributed by Warner Bros.

Prior to *Around the World in a Day*, Prince announced he would retire from live performances to solely be a recording artist, as the Beatles did at one point in their career. His fans were shocked and saddened by the news but then confused when he performed in St. Paul, Minnesota, two months later, with more live performances to follow.

Prince's next film, *Under the Cherry Moon*

(1986), a frivolous romantic comedy, was a critical and commercial disappointment. Yet Prince was still writing many songs for other artists, and in 1986 the Bangles had a hit with his "Manic Monday," which rose to number 2 on the charts.

The 1986 album *Parade—Music from the Motion Picture Under the Cherry Moon* went to number 1 and had two hit singles: "Kiss" and "Girls and Boys," the latter steeped in Prince's classic sexual innuendo. The tour of the same name, backed by his band the Revolution, was spectacular and included Sheila E., a percussionist and singer who would later become a star in her own right.

Various Styles. In the 1987 double album *Sign '☮' the Times*, Prince's lyrics addressed drug-related violence and urban decay. Following that, Prince recorded *The Black Album*. Shortly before its scheduled release in late 1987, Prince changed his mind and ordered the copies that had been printed to be destroyed. The album was widely bootlegged, and in 1994 Prince released the album officially. *Lovesexy* (1988) was the opposite of the *Black Album*: fun and funk-inspired. A song from that album, "Nothing Compares 2 U," was later covered by Sinéad O'Connor, and her version reached number 1 in 1988.

Prince next recorded the sound track to the hit 1989 film *Batman*. One of the most memorable scenes featured Jack Nicholson dancing to a new Prince song while vandalizing a museum. (Nicholson, a Prince fan, had lobbied for Prince to record the film's score.) The album was a commercial success.

Graffiti Bridge was released in 1990 with his new band, the New Power Generation (NPG). A concert film was made of this tour. In 1991, with the NPG, he released the album *Diamonds and Pearls*, which marked a return to his early 1980's sound. In 1992 he released an album whose title was a symbolic combination of the male and female symbols (referred to as the *Symbol* album). He then announced that he was retiring from recording. Like his announcement that he would not perform live again, this statement proved premature. In 1992, Prince signed a $100 million record deal with Warner Bros., making him one of the world's highest-paid pop performers.

The Artist Formerly Known As. Like many complicated and talented artists, Prince has displayed eccentric behavior and made outrageous comments that have garnered bad press and have been mocked by late-night comedians. As he has granted only one major print interview and one television interview in his entire career, Prince has inadvertently allowed his public persona to be defined by others.

He in part is to blame, however, for his reputation of being odd and difficult. He was responsible for a long line of impromptu firings of popular mangers and band members. From the beginning of his career he has sported unusual, sexy clothes: In 1991 he appeared on the MTV Video Music Awards ceremony wearing yellow pants that exposed his backside.

Prince has also been notorious for last-minute performance cancellations. He has backed out of performing live on popular television shows such as *Saturday Night Live* and *The Tonight Show* several times. In 1985, Prince first committed to the USA for Africa benefit project "We Are the World," then backed out at the last minute, allegedly because Michael Jackson had more recording time than Prince.

His most infamous act came in a 1993 feat when he legally changed his name to an unpronounceable symbol (identical to the [symbol] album that year). When asked what people were supposed to call him, he made it known that the Artist For-

For the Record

Tipper Gore, wife of future Vice President Al Gore, credited Prince's sexually explicit lyrics in "Darling Nikki" for inspiring her to form the Parents Music Resource Center (PMRC) and launch the Senate hearings on offensive rock lyrics. The PMRC would eventually force the record industry into an unpopular voluntary album-stickering policy warning against possible offensive lyrics.

merly Known as Prince would be appropriate (later shortened to simply the Artist). He became a laughingstock with the mainstream media.

Alienation. Warner Bros. abruptly dropped Prince's distribution deal, effectively closing his recording company. During the bickering that followed Prince wrote the word "slave" on his cheek for a photo session. Warner Bros. responded by delaying the release of his next album until fall of 1995.

On February 14, 1996, he married dancer Mayte. He opened the wedding reception to the public for a twenty-five-dollar fee and then did not attend. His 1998 album, *Crystal Ball*, was to be released directly to prepaying fans for sixty dollars, but delays and problems with his organization caused it to hit the record stores first at a price of forty dollars, further alienating his fan base.

—Kevin M. Mitchell

SELECT DISCOGRAPHY

■ ALBUMS

For You, 1978
Dirty Mind, 1980
1999, 1982
Purple Rain, 1984
Sign '☮' the Times, 1987
Lovesexy, , 1988
Graffiti Bridge, 1990
Diamonds and Pearls, 1991
⚥, 1992
The Black Album, 1994
Crystal Ball, 1998

SELECT AWARDS

Grammy Awards for Best Album of Original Score Written for a Motion Picture or a Television Special and Best Rock Performance by a Duo or Group with Vocal (with the Revolution) for *Purple Rain*; for Best New R&B Song for "I Feel for You," all 1984

National Association for the Advancement of Colored People (NAACP) Image Award, 1984

Academy Award for Original Song Score for *Purple Rain*, 1984

Grammy Award for Best R&B Performance by a Duo or Group with Vocal for "Kiss," 1986 (with the Revolution)

SEE ALSO: E., Sheila; Easton, Sheena; Khan, Chaka; O'Connor, Sinéad.

John Prine

BORN: Maywood, Illinois; October 10, 1946
FIRST ALBUM RELEASE: *John Prine*, 1971
MUSICAL STYLES: Folk, country, rock and roll, pop

A unique American singer-songwriter, John Prine has built an enduring body of work from the simplest of tools: a steady narrative rhythm, a few bluegrass licks, a raspy, expressive voice, a storyteller's grasp of human foibles, and the ability to turn a phrase. Prine's story songs mix a primal, self-effacing appreciation of life's small pleasures (such as dancing, whistling, and swimming in the local lake) with deep emotional understanding and offbeat humor. Emerging in the singer-songwriter boom of the early 1970's as one of many "new [Bob] Dylans," Prine distinguished himself with four straight excellent albums that mixed the rhythms of rock and roll, English ballads, Appalachian hymns, and country laments into an American folk pastiche. With the advent of disco and new wave, however, Prine's character-driven social commentary—his narratives of lost souls looking for connection—fell completely out of favor, and he found himself abandoned by the recording industry. After a six-year dry spell, he released three albums on his own label in the mid-1980's that spoke of a quiet satisfaction with his personal life. The bigger, more electric sound of *The Missing Years* (1991) brought Prine a new generation of young musical disciples and the commercial success that had long eluded him.

The Classic First Album. Prine's self-titled first album features the songs for which he is still most famous: "Hello in There" (about old age), "Angel from Montgomery" (about a lonely marriage), "Paradise" (about strip-mining) and "Sam Stone" (about a heroin-addicted Vietnam War veteran). Despite an ode to the escapist joys of marijuana ("Illegal Smile") and a satire of blind patriotism ("Your Flag Decal Won't Get You into Heaven Anymore"), Prine was less a hippie rebel than a small-town midwestern boy with little tolerance for pretense. Prine learned his musical essentials at home: His grandfather had played in a country-western band with Merle Travis, and his brother taught him a few rudimentary finger-picking patterns when he was fourteen. After a few unambitious years in college and two more in the Army, Prine worked as a postman for five years. At age twenty-three he was working steadily enough at small clubs around Chicago to attract the attention of country singer-songwriter Steve Goodman and Atlantic Records.

Then, bursting with songs, Prine wrote about characters who either wanted a little more peace or a little less. The characters on his second and third albums display his range of sympathies: a Vietnam War veteran who quietly pleads with his family not to ask about the war; a convict's letter reporting on the merits of "Christmas in Prison"; a barfly's drunken report of romantic rejection (with the alcohol-soaked title, "YesIThinkTheyOughtaNameADrinkAfterYou"); a husband who blames himself for his wife's departure with a salesman and promises to do better next time; and a personal tribute to his carpenter grandfather. Prine rarely judged his characters, but focused instead on the hard emotional choices they made, simply singing these minor characters to life. If he occasionally fell victim to sentimentality, he more often provided a fresh perspective on unusual topics. A song such as "Come Back to Us, Barbara Lewis Hare Krishna Beauregard" could easily dissolve into parody; instead, this open request to a young runaway to return home from a life of cult worship and drug use is as touching as it is funny.

A Storyteller's Themes. Prine's songs of yearning would be the ones most often covered by other singers, but his recurrent themes include hippie fantasies, parables of love, and playful religious meditations. In fact, his songs could be direct, deep, and goofy at the same time; it seems all three qualities are necessary to find meaning in Prine's world. In "Fish and Whistle" (1978), the narrator strikes a deal with a higher power: "Father forgive us for what we must do/ You forgive us and we'll forgive you/ We'll forgive each other 'til we both turn blue/ Then we'll whistle and go fishin' in Heaven." A song such as "It's a Big Old Goofy World" seems lightweight on paper, but Prine's bemused delivery turns it into a life-affirming meditation on accepting the terms of the human condition. That's also how Prine described the evolution of the easy-going mood that pervades "That's the Way the World Goes Around": "Originally a sad song," he wrote in the liner notes of his live album, "it only got happy after I started singing it."

For the Record

Singer and guitarist Bonnie Raitt once said about John Prine: "He's a true folksinger in the best tradition, cutting right to the heart of things, as pure and simple as rain."

The Comeback. Prine recorded three competent but unremarkable albums for his small audience of fans in the 1980's, the best of which (*German Afternoons*, 1986) featured two strong lyrics that floated gracefully on buoyant rhythmic grooves: "Speed of the Sound of Loneliness" and "I Just Wanna Dance with You." It was *The Missing Years* (1991), however, that put Prine back on the musical map; his first big-budget recording in more than ten years, the album became his biggest commercial success. With the assistance of a new producer, bassist Howie Epstein of Tom Petty and the Heartbreakers, Prine assembled a new band of studio musicans. The band's firepower and musical tone helped rejuvenate Prine's songwriting (and singing), while Epstein's studio knowledge and rock-and-roll sensibility led to a bigger sound featuring dense rhythmic textures. The album led to a tour with the Cowboy Junkies, which helped turn Prine into a respected musical elder; live recordings of duets with Bonnie Raitt and Nanci Griffith brought him to an even larger audience.

A comparison of Prine's two live albums, recorded ten years apart, is revealing. On *John Prine Live* (1988), Prine comes off as a wry, mellow, wise hippie, adept at conducting the audience through a ritualistic set of old songs that have lost their edge. *Live on Tour* (1997) opens with a banging guitar riff, and Prine's sandpaper-grained voice rides in on the sonic roar of a rock band with arena-sized ambitions. In "Quit Hollerin' at Me," Prine sings of a man who can not quiet the noise in his brain; his delivery is answered by a searing electric guitar solo, some quirky keyboard stylings, and a hard backbeat. In the more upbeat "You Got Gold," the band's harmonies blend with its steady-rolling rhythmic power to create a sound almost orchestral in its fullness. Prine alternates between songs in which he slams his voice up loud and hard against the steady backbeat and those in which he gently weaves it between the sounds of the accordions, keyboards, and guitars.

Prine's philosophy is perhaps best summed up in two lines from "Humidity Built the Snowman" (1995): "The fundamental story/ of the contemporary man/ is to walk away/ and someday understand." In 1970, songwriter Kris Kristofferson walked away stunned from seeing Prine at a small Chicago club and wrote in the liner notes of his first album, "He's 24, but he writes like he's 224." Once wise beyond his years, he became wise within his years, perhaps an even more impressive artistic achievement. —*Joel Dinerstein*

SELECT DISCOGRAPHY

■ ALBUMS

John Prine, 1971
Diamonds in the Rough, 1972
Sweet Revenge, 1973
Common Sense, 1975
Bruised Orange, 1978
Storm Windows, 1980
German Afternoons, 1986
John Prine Live, 1988
The Missing Years, 1991
The John Prine Anthology: Great Days, 1993 (compilation)
Lost Dogs and Mixed Blessings, 1995
Live on Tour, 1997

SELECT AWARDS

Grammy Award for Best Contemporary Folk Album for *The Missing Years,* 1991

SEE ALSO: Kristofferson, Kris; Petty, Tom, and the Heartbreakers; Raitt, Bonnie.

Procol Harum

ORIGINAL MEMBERS: Gary Brooker (b. 1945); Keith Reid (b. 1945); David Knights (b. 1945); Robin Trower (b. 1945); Matthew Fisher (b. 1945); B. J. Wilson (1947-1989)

OTHER MEMBERS: Chris Copping (b. 1945); Dave Ball (b. 1950); Mick Grabham; Pete Solley; others

FIRST ALBUM RELEASE: *Procol Harum,* 1967

MUSICAL STYLES: Rock and roll, art rock; blues

British band Procol Harum's central claim to fame is the hit song "A Whiter Shade of Pale," released in 1967. The band went on to release ten albums between 1967 and its breakup in 1977. After its first single, the band had only modest commercial success, but it was influential beyond its sales figures. Its work between 1967 and 1970, in particular, helped define the classical rock or art rock genre that led in such differing directions as the Moody Blues, Yes, and, later in the 1970's, Supertramp. Unlike many other practitioners of the genre, however, their sound always maintained a connection with bluesy rock.

Beginnings. In the early 1960's, singer and pianist Gary Brooker was playing in a band called the Paramounts that specialized in covers of American rhythm-and-blues songs. The group also included future Procol Harum members Robin Trower, B. J. Wilson, and Chris Copping. The Paramounts recorded a few singles but had no real success. After they disbanded in 1966, Brooker focused on songwriting and soon met a lyricist named Keith Reid. The two wrote a number of songs, and Brooker assembled a group to do some recording. The group was first called the Pinewoods, then Procol Harum, although only three of its five members would go on to record Procol Harum albums. The name is roughly Latin for "beyond these things."

Producer Denny Cordell recorded their first song, "A Whiter Shade of Pale," and liked the result enough to send a copy to a major offshore "pirate" radio station. (These stations had sprung up to serve the growing English rock audience that the conservative BBC radio still largely ignored). The song was an immediate hit, and it was soon number 1 on the British charts, where it stayed for six weeks. It reached number 5 in the United States.

It is a remarkable record, with its combination of stately, haunting organ, obscure but evocative lyrics, and Brooker's powerful singing. Brooker derived the melody from a Johann Sebastian Bach piece ("Air on a G String"). No one, not even writer Reid, could say what the song *meant* exactly, but phrases such as "We skipped the light fandango," "the room was humming harder," and the "sixteen vestal virgins" who "are leaving for the coast" were appropriately psychedelic and conjured up odd mental images. The song also contains one of the few passing references to Geoffrey Chaucer's *Canterbury Tales* in rock and roll in the line "when the miller told his tale." Matthew Fisher played the slow, descending chord progression on a Hammond organ, and though the chords do bear a resemblance to Percy Sledge's soul hit "When a Man Loves a Woman" of the year before, "A Whiter Shade of Pale" was a sound that no one had heard before. The song also came out at an exciting time; hits by the new groups Jefferson Airplane and the Doors were on the charts, as was the Beatles' masterpiece, *Sgt. Pepper's Lonely Hearts Club Band.*

Procol Harum had a problem, however: They had only a few songs they could play live, and they had not yet recorded an album. The single's runaway success had taken everyone by surprise. Two members of the band were quickly replaced by guitarist Robin Trower and drummer B. J. Wilson from the old Paramounts lineup. The group recorded a second single, "Homburg" (modestly successful), and then their first album. All the lyrics on the album, and nearly all on following albums, were written by Reid. They are filled with puns and wordplay and contain strings of images that do not make literal sense but are intended to create subconscious emotional connections. Reid's approach undeniably owed a strong debt to the mid-1960's work of Bob Dylan. His lyrics helped

Procol Harum in 1970: Gary Brooker, Robin Trower, Chris Copping, Keith Reid, B. J. Wilson (Archive Photos/John Platt Collection)

make the group distinctive, but they also probably helped keep it from being a major commercial success.

The album *Procol Harum* came out late in 1967, many months after the success of "A Whiter Shade of Pale." This loss of momentum was only one of many setbacks, including serious problems with managers, that would hamper the band in the coming years. The second album, *Shine on Brightly* (1968), continued the pattern of the first, with sounds both bluesy and vaguely classical and with contrasting keyboard and distorted guitar textures. Side 2 included a long suite of songs entitled "In Held Twas in I" (the title makes no sense; it consists of the first word of each section). The songs are bridged by sound effects, and the piece ends with a slow choral finale.

The third album, *A Salty Dog* (1969), produced by Fisher, is often cited as their best overall record. It begins with the orchestrated title track, whose lyrics are a variation on the "Flying Dutchman" motif; when the song's sailors finally row ashore they find "a sand so white/ a sea so blue/ no mortal place at all." The song is moody, even spooky (the only spookier Procol Harum song is Trower and Reid's "Song for a Dreamer" on *Broken Barricades*). The rest of the album contains an almost Beatles-like variety of moods and sounds, including orchestration on two tracks, offbeat percussion, marimba, and a blend of acoustic and electric instruments. "Juicy John Pink" is a short blues tune with Brooker's singing accompanied only by Trower's guitar lines. "Wreck of the Hesperus" is another nautical tale, this one sung by Fisher (who also wrote the music) and containing a brilliantly simple but powerful guitar figure by Trower.

Fisher and bassist Knights left the band after *A Salty Dog*, and Chris Copping joined, playing both organ and bass. This lineup recorded the next two albums, *Home* and *Broken Barricades*, both produced by Chris Thomas. Reid's lyrics were taking on an increasingly downbeat, gothic, and occasionally morbid tone. The music and production were simplified from the ambition of *A Salty Dog* but continued to be effective, a bit quirky, and uniquely Procol Harum. The lead song on *Home*, a bluesy Trower rocker called "Whisky Train," received some airplay—as, to a lesser degree, did "Simple Sister" from *Broken Barricades*—but the band was not breaking through to a higher level of success.

Trower's writing and guitar work—he could wring considerable emotion out of his solos—had come into their own, and after *Broken Barricades* he left to pursue a solo career. He formed a trio that released a number of successful, if very Jimi Hendrix-influenced, albums. The second, *Bridge of Sighs* (1974), was probably Trower's solo high-water mark. He continued to record and tour into the 1990's.

Procol Harum's next album was a live recording with the Edmonton (Alberta, Canada) Symphony Orchestra, and it finally produced another hit for the band—"Conquistador" (number 16), an orchestrated version of a song from their first album. The next studio album was *Grand Hotel* (1973), again produced by Thomas. It featuring new guitarist Mick Grabham, who fit perfectly because he sounded much like Trower. Brooker had told Reid that he needed to write some less gruesome lyrics, and the album is a blend of playful images (in the title song, "the waiters dance on fingertips") and upbeat and downbeat themes. The lively "Bringing Home the Bacon" and "Toujours L'Amour," both with propulsive drumming by Wilson, received some airplay, but the album had no hits. As always, the band's material was not accessible enough to attract a wide audience. Nevertheless, the album itself rose briefly to number 21 on the *Billboard* album chart.

More albums followed, but the band was running out of steam. Their last album of the 1970's, *Something Magic* (1977), was produced by Jerry Leiber and Mike Stoller, famous as American rhythm-and-blues songwriters and producers of hits by the Coasters. The collaboration was unsuccessful, and Procol Harum disbanded.

Brooker released two solo albums in the 1980's and played on Eric Clapton's *Another Ticket* (1981). In the early 1990's, Brooker formed a new version of Procol Harum for a recording project. Both Fisher and Trower came on board for the album, entitled *The Prodigal Stranger* (1991).

Drummer B. J. Wilson had died from a drug overdose in 1989. Wilson, virtually unknown outside a small clique of admirers, was a creative player with a unique approach to rock drumming—sometimes playful, sometimes powerfully dramatic, often using unusual syncopations and accents. His absence certainly contributed to the lackluster sound of *The Prodigal Stranger*, a disappointment both musically and lyrically. The music sounded bland and generic (even Trower's guitar work sounded anonymous), and Reid's lyrics were equally uninteresting. The band toured in the early 1990's (with Fisher but without Trower). Uninteresting as the newer material was, Brooker's singing remained strong and distinctive.

—*McCrea Adams*

SELECT DISCOGRAPHY

■ ALBUMS

Procol Harum, 1967
Shine on Brightly, 1968
A Salty Dog, 1969
Home, 1970
Broken Barricades, 1971
Live in Concert, 1972
Grand Hotel, 1973
Exotic Birds and Fruit, 1974
Procol's Ninth, 1975

SELECT AWARDS

British Phonographic Industry Britannia Award for Best British Pop Single of the Last 25 Years for "A Whiter Shade of Pale," 1977 (with Queen's "Bohemian Rhapsody")

Grammy Hall of Fame, "A Whiter Shade of Pale" inducted 1998

SEE ALSO: Band, The; Dylan, Bob; Emerson, Lake, and Palmer; Moody Blues, The; Supertramp; Yes.

The Prodigy

ORIGINAL MEMBERS: Liam Howlett (b. 1971), Keith Flint, Leeroy Thornhill

OTHER MEMBERS: Maxim Reality (Keith Palmer)

FIRST ALBUM RELEASE: *Experience*, 1992

MUSICAL STYLE: Electronica

During the late 1990's, the American music industry was looking for a new sound to sell. They found it in a new style of British dance music. The genre heralded as the next big thing was "electronica": electronic art-dance music driven by keyboards and drums. Essentially, electronica is an extension or evolution of the techno genre, which mixes dance and punk elements. Buoyed by electronica publicity, the Prodigy produced chart-topping albums and singles, and some industry insiders looked to the band's approach as pointing the way to the future of rock and roll.

Riding the Rave. The Prodigy emerged from Britain's rave scene in 1991 in Braintree, England. (Early 1990's raves were dance parties that were often accompanied by the psychedelic drug ecstasy.) Liam Howlett, the band's primary architect, was working as an acid-house DJ when he met Keith Flint and Leeroy Thornhill—both dancers in London's club scene. "Charly" (1991), their first single, included a recorded (sampled) British children's public-safety announcement. Before long, it topped the U.K. dance charts. *Experience* followed in 1992.

The Prodigy became the leading band of the rave scene. In 1993, Maxim Reality joined the mix. For Howlett, however, the band's popularity soon became a dubious honor. He grew tired of the rave scene's predictability and was upset that his band was so often dismissed as being lightweight. Searching for a new sound, he found inspiration in the grittier tones of groups such as Rage Against the Machine and Smashing Pumpkins.

Howlett incorporated that sound in the Prodigy's 1994 album, *Music for the Jilted Generation*, which blended hard-core dance music with pop. While the album immediately claimed the top spot on the U.K. charts, it peaked at number 198 on the *Billboard* 200. America, it seemed, was not quite ready for the Prodigy.

Welcome to America. Yet in a few short years, the U.S. music industry changed significantly. As the electronica craze swept the nation, it bolstered the Prodigy's mainstream popularity. The result was that *The Fat of the Land* not only debuted at number 1 on the U.S. charts in July of 1997 but also hit the top spot in twenty-two countries

For the Record

Britain's most-watched music television show, *Top of the Pops*, reportedly received a record number of complaints about the video for "Firestarter." Viewers were disturbed by Keith Flint's appearance, which included spiked, multicolored hair and a bolt through his nose.

§

Liam Howlett, the driving force behind Prodigy's hard-edged sound, is a classically trained pianist.

around the world, including Germany, the Netherlands, Australia, Canada, and Hong Kong. The album, which sold three million copies worldwide in one week, contains the hit single "Firestarter," Keith Flint's vocal debut.

In addition to resounding success, controversy followed the band. Howlett has said that the lyrics for "Firestarter" were intended to convey Flint's persona: "I'm the self-inflicted mind detonator . . . I'm the bitch you hated." Some British citizens saw danger in the song's lyrics and tried to have it banned, fearing the song would prompt an arson outbreak.

Prodigy also came under fire for "Smack My Bitch Up," another song from *The Fat of the Land.* MTV received criticism for airing the video for the song, which shows women who are beaten and who inject drugs. The National Organization for Women protested vehemently, and after playing the video for ten days in an early-morning rotation MTV stopped airing it. The lyrics of "Smack My Bitch Up" concerned decision makers at Kmart and Wal-Mart, prompting both retailers to pull *The Fat of the Land* album from their shelves.

Still, electronica has caught the attention of several prominent pop artists. Madonna incorporated the sound in her *Ray of Light* album (1998); U2 and David Bowie have borrowed from electronica as well. All three artists tried to recruit the Prodigy to help with their electronica projects—and all three were turned down. Howlett's decision not to produce Madonna's album is particularly notable because the Prodigy is signed to her label, Maverick. —*Sandra Swanson*

SELECT DISCOGRAPHY

■ ALBUMS

Experience, 1992
Music for the Jilted Generation, 1994
The Fat of the Land, 1997

SELECT AWARDS

Brit Award for Best Dance Act, 1997

SEE ALSO: Chemical Brothers, The; Orb, The; Rage Against the Machine; Smashing Pumpkins.

The Psychedelic Furs

ORIGINAL MEMBERS: Richard Butler (b. 1956), Roger Morris, John Ashton (b. 1957), Duncan Kilburn, Tim Butler (b. 1958)

OTHER MEMBERS: Vince Ely, Phil Calvert, Mars Williams, Joe McGinty, Knox Chandler, Keith Forsey, Paul Garisto, Don Yallech

FIRST ALBUM RELEASE: *The Psychedelic Furs,* 1980

MUSICAL STYLES: Pop, new wave

The Psychedelic Furs were a study in contradictions. Despite their psychedelic name, this London-based band's sound originated with punk. The song the group became most closely associated with, however, "Pretty in Pink," was very far from punk.

Beginnings. Formed in London in 1978 by singer-songwriter Richard Butler, his younger brother Tim, Duncan Kilburn, and Roger Morris, the Psychedelic Furs took their name because they thought it would stand out from other punk and new-wave bands, as well as allow them to pay homage to their idols of the psychedelic era, such as the Velvet Underground, the Doors, and the Stooges. The Psychedelic Furs' sound, in fact, has often been called an updated version of the Velvet Underground with a hint of 1970's-era David Bowie.

A Voice Like No Other. Richard Butler, an art college graduate, decided to pursue a career in music upon graduating, although he knew little about it. Never the most talented singer—he was always known as a better songwriter than vocalist—Butler, with his flat vocals, sounded so unlike anyone else that it hardly mattered. An incisive lyricist whose music could be either testosterone laden ("I Just Wanna Sleep with You") or poetic ("The Ghost in You"), Butler was certainly an original. Although their early loyalties were to the punk movement, the Furs were never a true punk band—their music was far more complex, lyrically and sonically, than much of their contemporaries'.

Early Efforts. British disc jockey John Peel lent support to the Psychedelic Furs' early efforts and, combined with word-of-mouth enthusiasm, the band obtained a record contract with Columbia. The band's self-titled debut, produced by Steve Lillywhite and Howard Thompson, included their first U.K. hit, "Sister Europe," and was embraced by listeners and critics alike as a compelling and challenging record.

The Psychedelic Furs' 1981 follow-up, *Talk, Talk, Talk*—produced solely by Lillywhite—is considered by some critics to be the high-water mark of their career. To fans, this record is best known for the song "Pretty in Pink," which later inspired the 1986 teen-angst John Hughes film of the same name. Despite receiving plenty of play on MTV and college radio stations, the Psychedelic Furs sold only moderately in their homeland and abroad, earning their well-deserved reputation as a cult band.

For the Record

The Psychedelic Furs can count a number of musicians as fans. Bob Dylan is said to have written a song for the Psychedelic Furs, "Clean Cut Kid," which they turned down. Counting Crows recorded a cover of "The Ghost in You" as a B side; Buffalo Tom did the same with "Heaven," and Elvis Costello has been known to perform an acoustic version of "Pretty in Pink" in concert.

The band's third record, the Todd Rundgren-produced *Forever Now* (1982) did a little better on the charts, reaching gold status, and was their first recording to include brass and strings. It featured the Furs' first U.S. (albeit minor) hit, "Love My Way" (number 44). Two years later, the album *Mirror Moves* went one notch higher on the charts and included the U.K. hit "Heaven." In 1987, the band released its highest charting album, *Midnight to Midnight*, which reached the number 29 spot on the charts. The album contained "Heartbreak Beat," its only Top-30 U.S. single. Despite the fact it sold well, Butler was said to have disliked it.

A Film of the Same Name. The band rerecorded "Pretty in Pink" for the John Hughes film of 1986; this new version was included on both the film sound track and their career retrospective, 1988's *All of This and Nothing*. Still, a major hit record eluded the band. The Fur's last two albums, 1989's *Book of Days* and 1991's *World Outside*, hardly made a dent on the charts, though the latter featured an alternative radio hit, "Until She Comes." The Psychedelic Furs were in a career freefall and decided to end the group in 1991, with the Butlers going on to form Love Spit Love.

—*Nicole Pensiero*

SELECT DISCOGRAPHY

■ ALBUMS

The Psychedelic Furs, 1980
Talk, Talk, Talk, 1981
Forever Now, 1982
Mirror Moves, 1984
Midnight to Midnight, 1987
All of This and Nothing, 1988 (compilation)
Book of Days, 1989
World Outside, 1991

SEE ALSO: Bowie, David; Cars, The; Echo and the Bunnymen; Velvet Underground.

Public Enemy

ORIGINAL MEMBERS: Chuck D (b. Carlton Ridenhour, 1960), MC Flavor Flav (b. William Drayton, 1959), Professor Griff (b. Richard Griffin), Terminator X (b. Norman Rogers, 1966)

OTHER MEMBERS: James Norman, Sister Souljah
FIRST ALBUM RELEASE: *Yo! Bum Rush the Show*, 1987
MUSICAL STYLES: Rap, hip-hop

Public Enemy quickly became popular, as well as controversial, when they entered the rap scene in the late 1980's. Their music was notorious for its fast beats and incredibly complex blend of sounds, but it was their overtly political lyrics that distinguished them from other dance bands. Dealing with issues often deemed important by young African American males, Public Enemy's songs presented comments that disparaged all kinds of discrimination, from refusal to play rap music to reluctance to treat black hospital patients. Based on the Nation of Islam religious movement, with a nod to leader Malcolm X, Public Enemy has been accused of being anti-gay, misogynist, and racist (anti-white). Despite this, their music has become popular among Caucasians and people outside of the inner city.

The Reluctant Rapper. Public Enemy was the result of a collaboration of disk jockeys who, in 1982, worked together on a rap radio show at Adelphi University in Garden City, New York. Chuck D and MC Flavor Flav provided the rap and commentary, while sound engineers Hank and Keith Shocklee were responsible for putting together the show. At this time, the group produced a few singles and played them on the show. One was called "Public Enemy Number One," a song that pointed out the feelings of oppression felt by

Public Enemy (Paul Natkin)

For the Record

As a graphic design major at Adelphi University, leading rapper of Public Enemy Chuck D became the first black student to write and draw his own comic series, which he called "Tales of the Skind."

§

When asked about including radio broadcasts as samples in Public Enemy's tracks, Chuck D answered that rap is "black America's CNN." He explained later, "Our music is filled with bites, bits of information from the real world, a real world that's rarely exposed. Our songs are almost like headline news. We bring things to the table of discussion that are not usually discussed, or at least not from that perspective."

young black males, the "target" of white society's fear and hatred.

Fellow student Bill Stephney, who had also worked at the college radio station, secured a position in 1986 with the Def Jam record company. His first assignment was to sign Chuck D and form a rap group. Chuck D was reluctant, presumably because of the limited success of his earlier releases and because of possible restrictions on his political agenda. After persistent persuasion on the part of Def Jam's co-owner Rick Rubin, Chuck D relented, deciding on the name Public Enemy and using his graphic design ability to come up with the group's logo: a silhouette of a black man in the crosshairs of a rifle.

Public Enemy's sound was the result of band members who signed on with Chuck D: Flavor Flav, Terminator X, and Professor Griff. However, it was also necessary to form a team of sound engineers who worked with Chuck D to produce complex, "noisy" (highly distorted) music with as many as seventy tracks. The Shocklee brothers and Eric "Vietnam" Sadler formed the production Bomb Squad. By 1987, Public Enemy's first album, *Yo! Bum Rush the Show* was available, with respectable sales of 150,000 copies. Their second album, however, established Public Enemy as a successful group, as *It Takes a Nation of Millions to Hold Us Back* (1988) went platinum. This album was unusual in that it had no dead space between singles. Instead, it was fifty-eight minutes of a pseudo-radio show. The listener would hear music, certainly, but the songs were surrounded by live concert excerpts from the group, deliberate static, bits of spoken broadcasts, and even the sound of a bored listener tuning back and forth across the dial.

Professor Drops Out. Success was quickly followed by controversy, however, when the group's selected publicist, or Minister of Information, Professor Griff, made anti-Semitic remarks in a published interview. Accusing Jews of "wickedness," Professor Griff aroused the Jewish community to protest Public Enemy's existence, and Chuck D fired him soon afterward. He went on to form his own group, Professor Griff and the Last Asiatic Disciples.

A Touch of Hollywood. Public Enemy survived the Professor Griff controversy to briefly dabble in the new interest Hollywood had in black films. "Fight the Power" appeared in Spike Lee's *Do the Right Thing* (1989) and became the biggest-selling twelve-inch disk in the history of Motown Records at the time. Continuing controversy surrounded the group's use of security guards at concerts who carried fake Uzis. Called the Security of the First World, or S1W, their use was pointed out as a sign of Public Enemy's avowed black supremacist ideals.

Collaborations. Chuck D followed up the unusual *It Takes a Nation of Millions to Hold Us Back* with yet another album full of samples from earlier rap music as well as excerpts from broadcasts relating to Professor Griff's anti-Semitic remarks on the single "Welcome to the Terror Dome." *Fear of a Black Planet* (1990) also went platinum. The next year a two-record set, *Apocalypse 91 . . . The Enemy Strikes Black*, followed as yet another platinum success story. At this time rap activist Sister Souljah went from appearing as a cameo in their videos to become a full-fledged member of the group. Another collaboration on *Apocalypse 91...The Enemy Strikes Black* was a nod to an earlier

Run-D.M.C./Aerosmith collaboration. White thrash-metal band Anthrax appeared on the single "Bring the Noise."

Public Enemy spoke to young African Americans, yet their influence carried over to the white audience. Duran Duran confirmed this by doing a cover of the song "911 Is a Joke" soon after its release. Written to protest the practice of delayed ambulance service to black neighborhoods, "911 Is a Joke" presented a societal problem about which all people could get angry. Chuck D also collaborated with Sonic Youth on their 1990 album *Goo.*

Influence and Later Hits. Chuck D claimed, after the release of Public Enemy's first album, that the Federal Bureau of Investigation (FBI) was wiretapping his phone. Public Enemy did appear in an FBI file called "Rap Music and Its Effects on National Security." No other direct influence has been claimed for the band's music.

The Bomb Squad, Public Enemy's sound engineers, went on to work on albums by other artists, including Vanessa Williams. Keith and Hank Shocklee established Shocklee Entertainment in 1993, a record label and production firm. Public Enemy released two greatest-hits albums in the early 1990's and released *Muse Sick-N-Hour Mess Age* (a play on "music and our message") in 1994. Chuck D formed a hip-hop clothing company called Rapp Style in 1992 and formed a multimedia company in 1995, with plans to produce a hip-hop talk show. A brief hiatus in 1995 following Flavor Flav's serious motorcycle accident in Europe was not any indicator of the group's breakup. Public Enemy, despite other ventures by individual members, has stayed together. In 1998, Public Enemy reformed, along with Professor Griff, to do the sound track for the Spike Lee film *He Got Game.* —*Rose Secrest*

SELECT DISCOGRAPHY

■ ALBUMS

Yo! Bum Rush the Show, 1987
It Takes a Nation of Millions to Hold Us Back, 1988
Fear of a Black Planet, 1990
Apocalypse 91 . . . The Enemy Strikes Black, 1991
Greatest Misses, 1992 (compilation)
Twelve Inch Mixes, 1993 (compilation)
Muse Sick-n-Hour Mess Age, 1994

SEE ALSO: N.W.A., Run-D.M.C.

Puff Daddy

(Sean "Puffy" Combs)

BORN: New York, New York; November 4, 1969
FIRST ALBUM RELEASE: *No Way Out,* 1997
MUSICAL STYLES: Rap, hip-hop

In just a few short years, Puff Daddy catapulted himself from an ambitious party promoter to the reigning monarch of an entertainment empire. Known in the popular music community as a producer with the Midas touch, Puff Daddy launched his own career with a platinum debut album. However, his swift ascent to the pinnacle of the hip-hop scene was riddled with personal tragedy.

Moving up at Uptown. Sean "Puffy" Combs was born in Harlem in 1970. His father, a reputed street hustler, was shot to death when Puff Daddy was only three years old. It would not be the last time that violent death would impact his life. His mother moved the family to Mount Vernon, New York, when Puff Daddy was twelve. At that time, the popularity of hip-hop music was gaining momentum, driven by musicians such as L. L. Cool J and Run-D.M.C.

When Puff Daddy enrolled at Howard University, he aspired to a career as a rapper. First, however, he established a career as an entrepreneur, selling tickets for rap and dance parties that he hosted (he reportedly sold term papers as well). He moved a step closer to achieving his dreams for a music career when he landed an internship at Uptown Records in 1990. Andre Harrell, the head of Uptown Records, took Puff Daddy under his wing and even provided him with room and board. A self-professed workaholic, Puff Daddy was determined to earn his keep; within one year, he became vice president of promotion.

In 1991, nine people died in a riot at a celebrity

basketball game that Puff Daddy had promoted. He struggled with bouts of severe depression as a result but eventually returned to Uptown Records and continued his reputation as a producer of multiplatinum albums for artists such as Mary J. Blige and Jodeci. However, his overwhelming successes fostered an arrogance that became intolerable for Harrell. In 1993, he fired Puff Daddy.

Birth of an Empire. While the experience left Puff Daddy shaken to the core, it forced him to move in a new direction with even greater opportunities for achievement. That same year, he signed a fifteen million dollar distribution deal with Arista Records for his Bad Boy Entertainment label. One of the artists he signed was a street hustler from Brooklyn known for vivid narratives and effortless rhymes named Christopher "the Notorious B.I.G." Wallace, who would become one of Puff Daddy's closest friends. By 1994, the label had sold more than twelve million albums.

Puff Daddy accepting a World Music Award in 1998 (AP/Wide World Photos)

In the years that followed, Puff Daddy branched out into other business ventures as well, including a clothing line, Bad Boy Films, and a restaurant in lower Manhattan named after his son, Justin.

Death of a Friend. In March, 1997, tragedy struck. The Notorious B.I.G. was shot to death in Los Angeles. Several months earlier, a rival rapper, Tupac Shakur, had also been murdered. Rumors abounded, and many blamed the murders on tensions that had escalated between the East and West Coast rap scenes, represented by Bad Boy and Death Row Records respectively.

In the aftermath of the Notorious B.I.G.'s death, the spotlight seemed to shine even brighter on Puff Daddy. After years of contributing to the work that fueled the careers of other artists, Puff Daddy finally made his solo debut in 1997 with *No Way Out.* With guest appearances by artists such as the late Notorious B.I.G. and Busta Rhymes, the album quickly went platinum and provided two number 1 singles: "Can't Nobody Hold Me Down" and a tribute to the Notorious B.I.G. called "I'll Be Missing You."

No Way Out was more musical than most rap records and even used a choir on "I'll Be Missing You." Puff Daddy, who does not play an instrument, received some criticism for using recycled melodies of familiar pop songs. "I'll Be Missing You," for example, borrowed its melody from the Police hit "Every Breath You Take." Rappers such as Mase and Busta Rhymes collaborated with Puff Daddy on every song and ultimately did more rapping than he did. This was not surprising, since Puff Daddy admitted that rapping and lyric-writing did not represent his forte. While Puff Daddy incorporated plenty of gritty, obscenity-

For the Record

While playing on his school's football team, Sean Combs reportedly earned the nickname "Puffy" for his tendency to "puff" out his chest to create an appearance of greater strength.

laced street talk on the album, he also used it as vehicle to contemplate his mortality. On the song "Is This the End," he rapped, "Folks think I'm gonna die/ I be concealed up in my room, knowing that it could happen." After the death of the Notorious B.I.G., Puff Daddy went on to produce artists such as Mariah Carey and L. L. Cool J.

—*Sandra A. Swanson*

SELECT DISCOGRAPHY

■ SINGLES

"I'll Be Missing You," 1997

"Can't Nobody Hold Me Down," 1997

"Come with Me," 1998 (from the *Godzilla* sound track)

■ ALBUMS

No Way Out, 1997

SELECT AWARDS

Grammy Awards for Best Rap Performance by a Duo or Group for "I'll Be Missing You" (with Faith Evans featuring 112) and for Best Rap Album for *No Way Out,* 1997

SEE ALSO: Blige, Mary J.; Notorious B.I.G., The; Shakur, Tupac.

Queen

ORIGINAL MEMBERS: Freddie Mercury (b. Frederick Bulsara, 1946-1991), Brian May (b. 1947), Roger Taylor (b. Roger Meddows-Taylor, 1949), John Deacon (b. 1951)
FIRST ALBUM RELEASE: *Queen*, 1973
MUSICAL STYLES: Hard rock, disco, rockabilly

Begun in London in 1971, Queen blended intricate vocal harmonies, heavy metal, and touches of opera with a stage show that featured elaborate stage setups, state-of-the-art light shows, and outrageous costumes. Lead singer Freddie Mercury's powerful multitracked vocals and onstage theatrics combined with Brian May's complex guitar work created a signature presence that remains unique. Queen led the glamour rock movement and became one of the most popular bands worldwide.

Queen's Freddie Mercury (Paul Natkin)

The Beginnings. In 1968, Brian May, Roger Taylor, and Tim Staffell were in a local band named Smile. Staffell was taking art classes at Ealing College of Art with Fred Bulsara. The two became friends, and Bulsara became a fan of Smile. When Smile was disbanded, Bulsara left his band, Wreckage, and joined forces with May and Taylor. Bulsara legally changed his last name to Mercury and named the band Queen. After three temporary bass players, John Deacon joined the band in 1971. At first, the band played very few performances, while the members finished their studies (Mercury earned a degree in graphic design, Taylor in biology, Deacon in electronics, and May holds a Ph.D. in astronomy).

The band began to tour in April of 1973, opening at the Marquee Club in London. Their first album, *Queen*, was released in July of 1973. The band's first big break came when they were offered the opportunity to open for Mott the Hoople in England. In 1974, *Queen II* was released, and they toured the United States with Mott the Hoople.

Breakthrough. Later in 1974, Queen released their third album, *Sheer Heart Attack*, which remained on the U.S. album charts for more than forty weeks. The single "Killer Queen" proved to be the band's first single to reach the Top 10 in the United States. While *Sheer Heart Attack* remained on the charts, Queen went back to the studio to record *A Night at the Opera* (1975), which has become one of their most famous albums. *A Night at the Opera* also produced one of the greatest rock singles of all time, Queen's signature song, "Bohemian Rhapsody."

"Bohemian Rhapsody." At nearly six minutes in length, "Bohemian Rhapsody" made the band's management uneasy because it was nearly twice as long as the average single of the day. However, due in part to London disc jockey Kenny Everett, who gave the song a great deal of advance airplay, "Bohemian Rhapsody" became a colossal hit.

Bohemian Rhapsody was written by Mercury and produced by Roy Thomas Baker. Recording sessions lasted nearly three weeks. The operatic interlude alone took one week of studio time to produce. The band sang the term "Galileo" for up to twelve hours per day to produce the 180 vocal overdubs in the segment. The investment in time paid off with a number 1 single in the United Kingdom and Queen's first platinum record. "Bohemian Rhapsody" remained number 1 on the U.K. charts for nine weeks. In 1977, "Bohemian Rhapsody" won the unique honor of receiving the British Phonographic Industry's Britannia Award for Best British Pop Single of the Last Twenty-Five Years (shared with Procol Harum's "A Whiter Shade of Pale"). More than a decade later, in 1992, "Bohemian Rhapsody" would be prominently featured in the film *Wayne's World* (1992) and would finally reach number 1 in the United Kingdom and number 2 in the United States.

"Bohemian Rhapsody" was also one of the first singles to be promoted through the use of a music video. While others had used short films to promote singles and albums, Queen and director Bruce Gowers used state-of-the-art video effects and a feature quality video to introduce "Bohemian Rhapsody" to the world. The video predated the inception of MTV by five years and is credited with creating the music video genre.

"We Are the Champions." Queen rode their wave of popularity with their next album, *A Day at the Races* (1976). Advance orders for *A Day at the Races* were in excess of 500,000, the highest EMI had ever received. *A Day at the Races* produced the hit single "Somebody to Love" which made it to number 2 on the British charts. *A Day at the Races* was followed in 1977 by *News of the World*, which went double platinum in the United States on the strength of the double A-sided single "We Will Rock You"/"We Are the Champions," anthems which have become part of the standard repertoire of major U.S. athletic events.

The Game. After the release of *Live Killers* (1979), Queen returned to the studio with a new producer. These sessions produced *The Game* (1980), in which the band moved away from their extravagant richly produced trademark style and explored new genres. This eclectic approach was a success, as the rockabilly "Crazy Little Thing Called Love" and the camp disco "Another One Bites the Dust" both reached number 1 in the United States. *The Game* proved to be a phenomenal success worldwide. It went platinum five times in Canada alone. "Another One Bites the Dust" became an enormous crossover hit topping charts in disco, rock, and soul.

The popularity of "Another One Bites the Dust" may have brought more harm than good. As disco began to lose popularity in the United States, Queen's only disco hit cost them popularity and credibility in the eyes of the loyal U.S. fans of the classic Queen sound. In 1980, Queen composed and performed the sound track to the film *Flash Gordon*. *Flash Gordon* did not see enough sales to earn even gold-record status. *Hot Space* (1982) saw a move to recapture loyal Queen fans as one side of the album was filled with songs that displayed the classic Queen sound. The other side of the album were funky follow-ups to "Another One Bites the Dust." *Hot Space* did not sell well. Only the single "Under Pressure," a collaboration with David Bowie, was a success.

After one year of rest and pursuit of solo ventures, the band released their thirteenth album in 1984. *The Works* led to a resurgence in popularity. "Radio Ga Ga," the single released from *The Works*, became a number 1 hit in nineteen countries. The follow-up single, "I Want to Break Free," created

For the Record

In 1982 the members of Queen were listed in the *Guiness Book of World Records* as Great Britain's highest paid executives.

more controversy than sales in the United States and stalled Queen's U.S. comeback. The video for the song featured the band members dressed in drag, satirizing a popular British soap opera. MTV refused to air the video, and conservative Americans believed that the video confirmed that Queen was a gay band.

In 1985, Queen continued their resurgence with their stage-stealing performance at the Live Aid benefit concert. Queen then recorded film scores for 1986's *Highlander* (released as *A Kind of Magic*) and *Iron Eagle*. In 1991 Queen released the successful album *Innuendo* and the single of the same name. This was followed by the haunting "These Are the Days of Our Lives" single. Queen seemed to be on the road to recovering their former glory when, on November 23, 1991, Mercury announced that he had acquired immunodeficiency syndrome (AIDS). He died the next day. As a tribute to Mercury, a double A-sided single pairing "Bohemian Rhapsody" and "These Are the Days of Our Lives" was released to raise money for what was to become the Mercury Phoenix Trust, an AIDS charity. The single entered the U.K. charts at number 1, eventually raising more than one million British pounds for the charity.

Four years later, in November of 1995, the album *Made in Heaven* was released. It was Queen's twentieth and final album. Taylor, May, and Deacon finished vocal tracks that Mercury had recorded in the last months of his life. *Made in Heaven* was dedicated to the "immortal spirit of Freddie Mercury." In 1997, production began on a ballet entitled *Le Presbytère* (The Rectory), which is a tribute to Mercury (and dancer Jorge Donn). The score is composed of Queen classics with pieces by Wolfgang Amadeus Mozart. For the opening night of the ballet, Queen reunited (with Elton John stepping in for Mercury) to play "The Show Must Go On." —*B. Keith Murphy*

SELECT DISCOGRAPHY

■ ALBUMS

Queen, 1973
Queen II, 1974
Sheer Heart Attack, 1974
A Night at the Opera, 1975
A Day at the Races, 1976
News of the World, 1977
Jazz, 1978
Live Killers, 1979 (compilation)
The Game, 1980
Hot Space, 1982
The Works, 1984
A Kind of Magic, 1986
The Miracle, 1989
Innuendo, 1991
Classic Queen, 1992 (compilation)
Made in Heaven, 1995

SELECT AWARDS

Billboard Award for Top Crossover Single for "Another One Bites the Dust," 1980
Billboard Award for Top Crossover Single for "The Days of Our Lives," 1991
British Phonographic Industry Award for Outstanding Contribution to British Music, 1991

SEE ALSO: Bowie, David; John, Elton.

Queen Latifah

(Dana Owens)

BORN: Newark, New Jersey; March 18, 1970
FIRST ALBUM RELEASE: *All Hail the Queen*, 1989
MUSICAL STYLES: Rap, hip-hop, reggae, rhythm and blues

With a flamboyant wardrobe and a sassy attitude, Queen Latifah burst onto the music scene at a time when sexism and violence in rap music were headline news. Her outspoken feminist-rap style helped pave the way for women in a male-dominated genre. In addition to recording three albums, Latifah has also become a successful entrepreneur and actress.

Early Breaks. Queen Latifah was born Dana Owens in Newark, New Jersey, the daughter of Lance Owens, a police officer, and Rita Owens, a high school art teacher. When she was eight, her parents divorced, and she moved with her mother and only brother, Lancelot, to the High Court housing project in East Newark. Determined to improve the family's prospects, her mother

Queen Latifah in 1992 (AP/Wide World Photos)

worked two jobs and put herself through school, eventually landing a job teaching art at Irvington High School.

As a girl, Owens was given the nickname "Latifah" (Arabic for "delicate and sensitive") by a Muslim cousin. When she began rapping in high school with a group called Ladies Fresh, she adopted the title "Queen" as a reference to the rich heritage of black history. Her most important contact from these years was Mark James, known as DJ Mark the 45 King. He recorded her first demo, entitled "Princess of the Posse," in the summer of 1987. That fall, Latifah enrolled at the Borough of Manhattan Community College to study communications. Meanwhile, DJ Mark gave the demo to Fred Brathwaite, host of cable show *Yo! MTV Raps*, who played it for Dante Ross, an A&R representative at Tommy Boy Records.

Latifah was immediately signed by the label, which released the single "Wrath of My Madness." It sold forty thousand copies, considered a big success for a first release with no video accompaniment. Her debut album, *All Hail the Queen* (1989), sold 400,000 copies, hit number 6 on *Billboard*'s rhythm-and-blues chart, and was nominated for a Grammy Award. It also secured Queen Latifah a reputation as the queen of rap.

Reigning Queen. Although the commercial success of Queen Latifah's debut was modest, *All Hail the Queen* attracted a great deal of media attention. The album was released only one year after N.W.A.'s controversial hit "F— tha Police" prompted calls for industry regulation of violent rap music and an F.B.I. investigation. Dressed in regal, African-inspired costumes, the statuesque Latifah stood for pride and confidence. She used the boasting tradition of rap to demand respect for herself and women in general, but especially black women.

For example, "Ladies First," a duet with British rapper Monie Love, challenges sexist attitudes with rhymes such as "Some think that we can't flow/ Stereotypes they got to go/ I would mess around and flip the scene into reverse/ With what?/ With a little touch of ladies first." In the video, Latifah tackles racism as well. Images of prominent black women activists such as Angela Davis, Sojourner Truth, and Harriet Tubman are mixed with shots of ordinary South African women resisting soldiers. Dressed in a variety of funky African outfits, Latifah plays a mock game of chess on a map of Africa, replacing symbols of white power with black ones.

Although Queen Latifah is often described as a feminist rapper, she dislikes the term and has refused to criticize any of her male counterparts specifically. Indeed, her ability to confront racism and sexism in a positive way has been widely admired as both politically savvy and morally virtuous.

Needless to say, expectations for her second album were extremely high. Perhaps not surprisingly, *Nature of a Sista'*, released in 1991, disappointed many fans and critics who felt it was aimed at a more mainstream audience. When Tommy Boy released her from her contract, she moved to Motown for her third album, *Black Reign* (1993).

Musical Flavor. Even on *All Hail the Queen*, Latifah's music is not hardcore rap. Synthesized and sampled (digitally recorded) sounds are mixed with live music. In her own words from "Come into My House," "It's a new fusion I'm usin' / You ask what is it I'm doin' / Hip-hop house, hip-hop jazz / With a little pizazz." Her later albums experiment even more with reggae beats, tinges of Latin disco, and jazzy riffs, sometimes shifting styles within an individual tune. Latifah also sings, which is unusual for a rap artist. Her sultry voice on the jazzy "How Do I Love You" (from *Nature of a Sista'*) has been compared to Madonna's. In *"Weekend Love" (Black Reign)* she switches to a more traditional rhythm-and-blues sound.

On *Nature of a Sista'*, Latifah worked with a number of different producers, which led to criticism that the album lacked cohesiveness. Some critics also complained that the album lacked the critical edge of *All Hail the Queen*. However, she was praised for her work as a producer on "How Do I Love You," and "Fly Girl" was nominated for a Grammy Award for Best Rap Performance.

In *Black Reign*, Queen Latifah traded in her regal style for a tougher "gangsta" image and vocabulary. Guest artists included Treach, Heavy D., and KRS-One. The angrier tone of this album also expresses Queen Latifah's grief at the death of her brother in a motorcycle accident in 1992. Latifah pays tribute to her brother in "Winki's Theme," which she produced. The album, which sold 500,000 units, made Latifah the first female solo rap artist to earn a gold record. The single "U.N.I.T.Y.," which returns to the theme of "Ladies First" in a more aggressive mood, won Latifah a Grammy Award for Best Solo Rap Performance.

New Directions. By the time *Black Reign* was released, Queen Latifah had already begun to explore other career opportunities, such as acting and business. In the early 1990's, she began to take small roles in films including *Jungle Fever* (1991), *House Party 2* (1991), and *My Life* (1993). In 1993, she began playing Khadijah James on the popular Fox television sitcom *Living Single*. In 1996, she was praised for her leading role in the gritty film *Set It Off*, about four women struggling to get out of the ghetto.

Motivated by her firsthand knowledge of the difficulties of the music business, Queen Latifah formed her own management company, Flavor Unit, in 1991. Based in New Jersey, Flavor Unit was run by many of Latifah's high school friends and has represented prominent rap groups including Naughty by Nature, Nikki D, and Fu-Schnickens. Latifah's willingness to represent Apache, whose rough lyrics include "Gangsta Bitch," seems to contradict her dislike of violence. She explains it this way: "[Rappers] aren't the problem. We simply reflect what is going on in our society. Plus, if I believe in an artist and I sign them, I don't feel it's my place to tell them how to make their music." In 1993, Flavor Unit also became a recording label in connection with distributor Epic Records. Their first release, *Roll Wit tha Flava* (1993), featured Flavor Unit talent in a compilation album.

Although Queen Latifah seemed to have shifted her energies away from music in the late 1990's, the book had not closed on her musical career. The woman who once predicted she would "do everything" by the age of thirty began work on a new album. *—Rebecca Green*

SELECT DISCOGRAPHY

■ ALBUMS

All Hail the Queen, 1989
Nature of a Sista', 1991
Black Reign, 1993

SELECT AWARDS

Grammy Award for Best Solo Rap Performance for "U.N.I.T.Y.," 1994

Soul Train Sammy Davis, Jr., Entertainer of the Year Award, 1995

SEE ALSO: Public Enemy; Salt-n-Pepa.

For the Record

In one of her first performances, Queen Latifah played Dorothy in a production of *The Wiz* at Saint Anne's Roman Catholic School in New Jersey.

R

Radiohead

ORIGINAL MEMBERS: Philip Selway (b. 1967), Edward O'Brien (b. 1968), Thomas Yorke (b. 1968), Colin Greenwood (b. 1969), Jonathan Greenwood (b. 1971)
FIRST ALBUM RELEASE: *Pablo Honey*, 1993
MUSICAL STYLE: Alternative rock

The first U.S. single from Radiohead, "Creep," rocketed the Oxford, England, band to success. However, "Creep" was not representative of either the band's sound or their direction; it was seen as a paint-by-numbers jump onto the grunge bandwagon, complete with self-deprecating lyrics, distorted guitars, and an undeniably catchy chorus.

On a Friday. "Creep" and its accompanying album, 1993's *Pablo Honey*, were not particularly exceptional. The album contained some good songs, including "Ripcord" and "Anyone Can Play Guitar," but it was ultimately bogged down by the fact that the band did not seem particularly enthused about it. Some of singer Thom Yorke's lyrics were particularly trite ("I wanna be Jim Morrison"), and the songs themselves were only slightly better than average. The instant success that came with "Creep" nearly broke up the band.

Immediate success in the United States was not even a consideration for five teenagers at a private boys' school in England in the early 1980's. Yorke formed a band called On a Friday with bassist Colin Greenwood, drummer Phil Selway, and guitarists Ed O'Brien and Jonny Greenwood. The band played on and off until the members went to separate universities in the late 1980's. All five found themselves back in Oxford in 1991 and, after much rehearsal and gigging, decided to become professional musicians. Major record labels began scrambling after them almost immediately.

"Creep" was actually Radiohead's second single in England, and it sold relatively poorly. Only after the song's success in the United States and other areas in Europe did it become a Top-10 single at home. The band was not there to enjoy the success, however, because the demands of their American record label, Capitol Records, were keeping them busy in the United States. Yorke found the pressures of an American hit single difficult to handle. He remarked to *New Musical Express*, "When I got back to Oxford I was unbearable. You start to believe you're this sensitive artist who has to be alone . . . this melodramatic, tortured person, in order to create wonderful music. The absolute opposite is true."

Luckily, Yorke had that revelation before Radiohead began work on their second album, 1995's *The Bends*. Self-reflection and infighting—followed by reconciliation and songwriting—caused a huge artistic leap for the band. Where *Pablo Honey* wallowed in transparent self-pity, *The Bends* twisted cynicism and doubt into something almost beautiful. The feeling throughout *The Bends* is one of a band driven to the edge but determined to push its way back.

"Fake Plastic Trees," the first U.S. single from *The Bends*, was accompanied by a stunning video, with Yorke driving a shopping cart around a futuristic supermarket while singing sadly of his "fake plastic love." The video helped propel the song to a certain degree of success, as did the mysterious, subtitled video for "Just," one of *The Bends*' strongest tracks. Those two songs, along with "High and Dry" and "Street Spirit (Fade Out)," served as cornerstones for a solid, if not quite perfect, album. The band members were happier with it, and *The Bends* earned Radiohead a stronger fan base and more critical respect.

Radiohead also found an important fan in R.E.M. singer Michael Stipe; much of Radiohead's touring in support of *The Bends* occurred while opening for R.E.M. in huge arenas around the United States and Europe. They also spent about two weeks in an odd pairing, opening for Alanis Morissette. In spite of these obviously helpful boosts in exposure, *The Bends* was not massively successful.

Come Together. Radiohead started recording a third album with the intention of making a pop record, but the result was something quite different than they expected. *OK Computer* (1997) was the album that Radiohead had longed to make since their inception. Combining the band's trademark depression with a new sense of both the paranoid and the absurd, *OK Computer* had all the trappings of a masterwork. New to Radiohead's formula was a dark sense of humor permeating the lyrics.

OK Computer begins with "Airbag," a song with a guitar line stronger than any they had ever recorded, and the power continues throughout the album. Yorke's lyrics develop as an indictment of technology as he runs through discussions of a "Paranoid Android," a "Subterranean Homesick Alien," and "The Tourist." The music itself is unlike anything fashionable in the late 1990's; rather, it looks back to records with more classic sensibilities without sounding dated.

Critics and the public came to the same conclusion: *OK Computer* is a classic album made by a group no one expected to make it. The album made many "best of 1997" lists. Even the notoriously conservative Grammys gave *OK Computer* their approval—it was nominated for Album of the Year and won the Grammy for Best Alternative Music Performance. The band, probably not expecting to win, did not attend the ceremony.

In 1998 Radiohead began a unique tour in which the band played only a handful of dates in venues they knew would sell out quickly. In conjunction with the tour, the band released the *Airbag: How Am I Driving* EP, which contained "Airbag" from *OK Computer* and six tracks that had previously been available only on import singles. This recording is notable not only for its *OK Computer* outtakes such as "Pearly" and "Palo Alto" but also for its bizarre packaging, which further explores the band's uneasy relationship with technology. The booklet serves as a mock questionnaire, with statements such as "Oxygen should be regarded as a drug" and "I am bad. I am to blame." Even more overt is an invitation to Radiohead's web site: "Why visit www.radiohead.com when you can go for a stroll in the sunshine instead?"

—*Josh Modell*

SELECT DISCOGRAPHY

■ ALBUMS

Pablo Honey, 1993

The Bends, 1995

OK Computer, 1997

Airbag: How Am I Driving, 1998 (EP; compilation of import material)

SELECT AWARDS

Grammy Award for Best Alternative Music Performance for *OK Computer*, 1997

Rage Against the Machine

ORIGINAL MEMBERS: Zack de la Rocha (b. 1970), Tom Morello (b. 1964), Tim "Tim Bob" Commerford (b. 1968), Brad Wilk (b. 1968)

FIRST ALBUM RELEASE: *Rage Against the Machine*, 1992

MUSICAL STYLES: Heavy metal, punk rock, rap, hip-hop

Rage Against the Machine has used a hard-hitting combination of punk rock, heavy metal, and hip-hop to deliver a political message expressed in lyrics shouted in an angry rap style. Surprisingly successful for a band with an uncompromisingly radical political viewpoint, they have sold millions of albums and made numerous live appearances around the world.

Early Years. Vocalist Zack de la Rocha and guitarist Tom Morello, the founders of Rage Against the Machine, came from very different backgrounds. De la Rocha was the son of Beto de la Rocha, a Mexican American artist whose work often had political content. His parents divorced when he was thirteen. De la Rocha spent weekdays with his mother, an Irish German Mexican American anthropology student, in Orange County, California. He spent weekends with his father in Los Angeles. Beto de la Rocha suffered a nervous breakdown in 1981 and destroyed much of his artwork. He also began fasting and forced his son

For the Record

The members of Rage Against the Machine rarely discuss their music without also discussing politics. When asked to name his favorite guitar player, Tom Morello named Joe Hill instead of a rock guitarist. Joe Hill was a folksinger and radical labor union organizer who was executed for murder in 1915. Hill's role in the crime for which he was executed is still a matter of controversy.

to fast along with him. De la Rocha has acknowledged that his difficult childhood influenced his political beliefs. Musically, he was influenced by the politically radical rap music of bands such as N.W.A. and Public Enemy.

Unlike de la Rocha, who has admitted that he had difficulty getting through high school, the other founder of Rage Against the Machine had a successful college career. Morello's father was Kenya's first representative to the United Nations. When his parents divorced one year after he was born, he lived with his mother, a white high school teacher, in Libertyville, Illinois. Morello's experience as the only child of mixed race in Libertyville contributed to his political viewpoint.

Morello went on to graduate with honors from Harvard University in 1986. While in college, he constantly practiced guitar, influenced by heavy-metal bands such as Black Sabbath. After graduation he moved to Los Angeles to organize a band. He also worked for California Senator Alan Cranston, an experience that made him cynical about the role of money in U.S. politics.

Fame and Controversy. Together with bassist Tim Commerford and drummer Brad Wilk, de la Rocha and Morello formed Rage Against the Machine in 1991. Blending de la Rocha's interest in rap and hip-hop and Morello's interest in heavy metal with a shared interest in punk-rock artists such as the Sex Pistols and Black Flag, the band developed a highly energetic style of performance. Based on impressive live shows and a demonstration tape, Rage Against the Machine signed a contract with Epic Records that allowed the band creative control.

The band's self-titled first album was a critical and popular success, selling nearly four million copies. Rage Against the Machine spent the next two years playing live shows. In 1994 they moved to Atlanta, Georgia, in an attempt to record new music, but tensions among the band members delayed the next album, *Evil Empire*, until 1996. When the album was finally released, it was another success.

Message. All of the music of Rage Against the Machine has a strong political content. Their behavior in concert was no less controversial. In Philadelphia, Pennsylvania, during the multiband music festival Lollapalooza, the band stood naked onstage with their mouths taped shut to protest censorship. During an appearance on the *Saturday Night Live* television show, they were allowed to perform only one song after attempting to hang U.S. flags upside down on their equipment.

—*Rose Secrest*

SELECT DISCOGRAPHY

■ ALBUMS

Rage Against the Machine, 1992
Evil Empire, 1996

SEE ALSO: Black Flag / Henry Rollins; Black Sabbath / Ozzy Osbourne; N.W.A.; Public Enemy; Sex Pistols, The.

Bonnie Raitt

BORN: Burbank, California; November 8, 1949
FIRST ALBUM RELEASE: *Bonnie Raitt*, 1971
MUSICAL STYLES: Rhythm and blues, blues, rock and roll, folk, pop, country

Whereas many successful music artists achieve fame in their young-adult years, Bonnie Raitt did not. She began her career in the 1970's, revered by a devoted group of fans who respected her voice and guitar playing, but she only became popular with the release of her tenth album, *Nick of Time*, in 1989. It was one of the year's most acclaimed and best-selling releases. Raitt was forty years old.

Early Career. Born to talented musicians—a father (John Raitt) who starred in Broadway musicals and a mother who was an accomplished pianist—Raitt was perhaps destined to become a musician. She began playing guitar during her preteen years, and she dropped out of Radcliffe College to pursue an education within the walls of old clubs where musicians such as Sippie Wallace, Fred McDowell, Son House, and Muddy Waters instructed her in the blues. She started performing, and at age twenty she was part of an act consisting of Buddy Guy and Junior Wells, which opened for the Rolling Stones in concert. Warner Bros. released her first album two years later. On this blues album, which was favorably reviewed, she performed songs by Wallace and Robert Johnson and featured instrumental contributions from Junior Wells and A. C. Reed.

Bonnie Raitt (Paul Natkin)

Raitt, however, was interested in more than just the blues, and in her next several albums she experimented with a mix of musical styles, including rock and country as well as the blues. Many of these albums were successful. In *Give It Up* (1972), her second release, Raitt marked herself as a talented interpreter of other writers' songs with her rendition of Jackson Browne's "Under the Falling Sky" and Eric Kaz's "Love Has No Pride." Her third album, *Takin' My Time* (1973), in which she received assistance from Lowell George and Bill Payne of Little Feat, was her first to make the Top 100. *Sweet Forgiveness* (1977), her first major success, went gold and made the Top 30; it included a hit single, Raitt's version of Del Shannon's "Runaway," which just missed making the Top 40.

In spite of Raitt's successes, her work received little commercial attention, in part because her songs were difficult to categorize and therefore received little radio play. Raitt also released a streak of albums—*The Glow* (1979), *Green Light* (1982), and *Nine Lives* (1986)—which were reviewed unfavorably and sold poorly. In 1986, after fifteen years with the label, she was dropped by Warner Bros. Raitt began using drugs and drinking heavily. In the mid-1980's she wrestled with personal problems as well as a career slump.

Moving Up. Although it was Raitt's own resolve that turned her life and career around (she adopted what she called a healthier lifestyle when she considered doing a video with Prince), Don Was, the producer of her watershed album, *Nick of Time*, certainly helped. The album, released by Capitol Records in 1989, won three Grammy Awards and sold three million copies; it was her first album to reach number 1. Raitt finally won commercial success, and, amazingly, she did it her way, without sacrificing her artistic integrity. Two years later, *Luck of the Draw* followed in the successful footsteps of its predecessor. This album, also produced by Was, reached number 2, sold more than three million copies, and won three Grammy Awards. Both albums contained a variety of musical styles and feature material by John Hiatt, Bonnie Hayes, and Raitt. One of her songs, "One Part Be My Lover," on *Luck of the Draw,* was cowritten by Martin O'Keefe, an Irish poet and actor who married Raitt in 1991.

One might think that with her personal life seemingly in order Raitt might stop singing about her favorite topic—love, especially disappointment in love—or that she might stop singing altogether. Instead she completed a trilogy of sorts with the successful release of *Longing in Their Hearts* in 1994. This album also featured Raitt's talents as a singer, musician, and lyricist. She, in fact, wrote five songs for the album, including the title song, which were stronger songs than many she had written in the past. The album sold two million copies and won a Grammy for Best Pop Album. Throughout her low periods and her high periods, two things about Raitt's work would remain consistent: her wonderful voice, "bluesy," rich, and emotional, and her ability to play bottleneck or slide guitar extremely well.

Raitt's Philanthropic Side. Perhaps because her parents were Quakers, Raitt has always liked protest music and frequently participated in benefit concerts on behalf of different political causes. During the 1970's she played five concerts at New York's Madison Square Garden in support of the antinuclear movement; in 1979 she was, along with John Hall, Jackson Browne, and Graham Nash, a founding member of Musicians United for Safe Energy (MUSE). During the 1980's she appeared at Farm Aid and Amnesty International concerts. She also participated in the 1987 joint Soviet/American peace concert staged in Moscow. At the end of the 1980's, Raitt began serving on the Board of Trustees of the Rhythm and Blues Foundation, an organization involved in documenting the history of rhythm and blues as well as awarding money to rhythm-and-blues artists in need of financial assistance; this merger of music and politics, which gives her a chance to thank the aging artists who have influenced her, seems to be her biggest philanthropic interest.

—*Cassandra Kircher*

For the Record

"I belong to the A.A. and the Triple A. I'm pretty disgustingly healthy. I'm a vegetarian. I don't eat dairy. I work out. My vice is torturing myself. My mind is my own trap. It is not easy to be awake with this brain all the time."

—*Bonnie Raitt* in the 1990's

§

While in her early twenties, Bonnie Raitt played in coffeehouses and associated with blues musicians. As Raitt said, "I was hanging out with seventy-year-old blues guys who drank at ten in the morning. My parents were a little concerned."

SELECT DISCOGRAPHY

■ ALBUMS

Bonnie Raitt, 1971
Give It Up, 1972
Takin' My Time, 1973
Streetlights, 1974
Home Plate, 1975
Sweet Forgiveness, 1977
The Glow, 1979
Green Light, 1982
Nine Lives, 1986
Nick of Time, 1989
The Bonnie Raitt Collection, 1990 (compilation)
Luck of the Draw, 1991
Longing in Their Hearts, 1994
Road Tested, 1995

SELECT AWARDS

Grammy Awards for Album of the Year and Best Rock Vocal Performance, Female, for *Nick of Time*; for Best Pop Vocal Performance, Female, for "Nick of Time"; for Best Traditional Blues Recording for "I'm in the Mood" (with John Lee Hooker), all 1989

Grammy Awards for Best Pop Vocal Performance, Female, for "Something to Talk About"; for Best Rock Vocal Performance,

Solo, for *Luck of the Draw*, for Best Rock Performance by a Duo or Group with Vocal for "Good Man, Good Woman" (with Delbert McClinton), all 1991

Grammy Award for Best Pop Album for *Longing in Their Hearts*, 1994

SEE ALSO: Browne, Jackson; Guy, Buddy; Hiatt, John; Little Feat; Prince; Waters, Muddy.

The Ramones

ORIGINAL MEMBERS: Joey Ramone (b. Jeffrey Hyman, 1952), Johnny Ramone (b. John Cummings, 1951), Dee Dee Ramone (b. Douglas Colvin, 1952), Tommy Ramone (b. Tom Erdelyi, 1952)

OTHER MEMBERS: Marky Ramone (b. Marc Bell, 1956), C. J. Ramone (b. Christopher John Ward, 1965), Richie Ramone (b. Richard Reinhardt)

FIRST ALBUM RELEASE: *Ramones*, 1976

MUSICAL STYLE: Punk rock

Forming a band in Queens, New York, in 1974 to play for a private party, schoolmates Jeffrey "Joey" Hyman, Johnny Cummings, Dee Dee Colvin, and Tommy Erdelyi named their band the Ramones and took the name as their own surnames. The original lineup consisted of Dee Dee and Johnny on guitars, Joey on drums, and Tommy as manager. They soon changed to their best-known configuration with Joey on vocals, Johnny on guitar, Dee Dee on bass, and Tommy on drums. Despite several personnel changes over the years, the Ramones were one of the most enduring and most successful punk bands rock and roll has ever produced.

The Beginning. Punk music was born of the no-frills garage bands of the 1960's such as the MC5, Count Five, and the Seeds. They played simple three-chord rock and roll with buzz-saw guitars, pounding drums, and often angry lyrics. The musical form was in opposition to the "British invasion," which the Beatles and the Rolling Stones led with a more sophisticated, pop-oriented form of rock. New York City was the center of the punk movement in the early 1970's, with a nightclub in the Bowery called CBGB presenting such bands as Television, the Talking Heads, and soloist Patti Smith to the public for the first time. CBGB was also the venue for the Ramones's first public performance.

Showing up for their audition wearing black leather jackets, torn jeans, and dirty T-shirts, the Ramones had the manager of CBGB thoroughly confused. She thought they were street hoodlums trying to steal band equipment. Even after their eight-song, seventeen-minute set, she was not completely sure of their intentions, but she offered them a job anyway. At their first show, they played for five people and the bartender's dog. However, things would change rapidly for this hardworking punk band.

The New York City music scene in general, and the bands playing CBGB in particular, soon caught the attention of the entertainment press. The CBGB Rock Festival Showcase in mid-1975 was instrumental in attracting national attention to punk music. Representatives from various record labels rapidly descended upon the club, anxious to sign bands from this new, potentially profitable punk sound. Sire was successful in signing contracts with several of these bands, including the Ramones, only the second punk group to earn a contract (after Patti Smith).

Punk Finds Commercial Success. In 1976, Sire Records released the band's debut album, *Ramones*. It contained fourteen songs and ran barely thirty minutes, in typical Ramones style. The album gave the musical world its first punk hit single, "Blitzkrieg Bop." The song bore the words "Hey ho, let's go!" which became the anthem for fans awaiting Ramones performances. Oddly, the album *Ramones* was released in Great Britain several months before it was issued in the United States. The Ramones's appearance at the Roundhouse in London for a Fourth of July musical tribute to the American bicentennial gave the English punk scene the boost it needed to emerge as its own powerful musical movement. Meanwhile, the band's second album, *Leave Home* (1977), was released stateside to an enthusiastic

The Ramones in 1979 (Paul Natkin)

reception by fans, who could now be found worldwide.

The year 1977 also saw the release of the band's third album, *Rocket to Russia*, which contained the songs "Rockaway Beach" and "Sheena Was a Punk Rocker," both very popular with Ramones fans. The songs showed quite clearly that the band's roots were deeply imbedded in the "bubblegum" and surf music traditions of the 1960's.

Tommy left the band in late 1977 to pursue his love of record producing, using his real name. He was replaced by Marc Bell, who had been the drummer for punk pioneer Richard Hell's band, the Voidoids. He immediately became Marky Ramone. The band's first album with this new lineup was *Road to Ruin* (1978). Despite the slick production sound, courtesy of T. Erdelyi (the former Tommy Ramone), the album nearly lived up to its name. The massive fan base, which the Ramones had cultivated during nearly two years of incessant touring, was not impressed by this release. It was the first Ramones album to run longer than a half hour, and it featured actual guitar solos and acoustic passages. The album's two singles, "Needles and Pins," a cover of a song made famous by the "British invasion" band the Searchers, and "Don't Come Close," failed to dazzle the public. The band was featured in the 1979 film *Rock 'n' Roll High School*, but this appearance, too, failed to generate much approval.

Tough Times. The decade of the 1980's opened with the Ramones enlisting the assistance of renowned record producer Phil Spector. His famous wall-of-sound production style ensured the success of such acts as the Crystals, the Ronettes, and the Righteous Brothers in the 1960's. Spector's contribution to the Ramones legacy, the album *End of the Century* (1980), garnered few followers. Their next effort, the 1981 album *Pleasant Dreams,* was produced by Graham Gouldman, formerly of the band 10cc and writer of the smash hit "Bus Stop" for the "British invasion" band the Hollies. Unfortunately, this album also failed to recapture the band's success of the mid-1970's. After their 1983 release, *Subterranean Jungle,* Marky quit the band and was replaced by Richard Reinhardt, known as Richie Beau, previously the drummer for the band Velveteens. As Richie Ramone, he was drummer for the Ramones on four albums, until Marky returned in 1987.

The album *Too Tough to Die* was released in 1984, announcing to the world that the Ramones were not about to give up. Produced by Dave Stewart of the Eurythmics, the album contained the hit single "Howling at the Moon," which helped recapture some of the band's earlier momentum. In 1986, *Animal Boy* gave Ramones fans one of the band's most successful singles, "Bonzo Goes to Bitburg."

The year 1989 was pivotal for the band. They gained wide exposure by recording the title track to the 1989 film *Pet Sematary,* yet the year also saw the band's most disruptive personnel change. Dee Dee left the band to record a rap album and then to form his own band, Chinese Dragons. Always the band's definitive punk rocker, Dee Dee had been a heroin addict for many years. His departure from the band truly marked the end of a punk era, yet the band persevered. Dee Dee was replaced by C. J. Ramone, whose real name was Christopher Joseph Ward. C. J. was fourteen years younger than Ramones cornerstones Joey and Johnny, and he was reportedly absent without leave from the Marine Corps at the time he joined the band, but his youthful energy contributed to their ultimate survival. In 1989 they released their next album, ironically titled *Brain Drain.* All in all, the 1980's were not kind to the Ramones, but the decade did not mourn the band's demise. The Ramones persevered.

Renewed Success. The decade of the 1990's was ushered in with the release of two volumes of the Ramones' greatest hits, titled *All the Stuff (and More).* Although they were not chart-toppers, the albums did help acquaint a new generation with the basic, no-frills quality of the Ramones. In 1992, the band released the album *Mondo Bizarro* on Radioactive Records. It featured guest appearances by Vernon Reid, guitarist for the band Living Colour, and Flo and Eddie, formerly of the band the Turtles and sound-track composers for the *Strawberry Shortcake* children's videos. The songs on *Mondo Bizarro,* much longer and more complex by Ramones standards, attacked such contemporary issues as drug abuse and censorship. One song in particular targeted Tipper Gore, wife of Vice President Al Gore, and her campaign to have parental warnings and age limits placed on recordings containing questionable lyrics. The single release from the album was "Poison Heart," which enjoyed considerable radio play.

Their 1994 release, *Acid Eaters,* showed the world that the Ramones still harbored a deep respect for the music of the 1960's, which was the wellspring of their own sound. The album featured punk renditions of a dozen late 1960's hits, such as "Somebody to Love" by the Jefferson Airplane, "Can't Seem to Make You Mine" by the Seeds, "7 and 7 Is" by Love, and "Surf City" by Jan and Dean. Their version of "Substitute" featured a guest appearance by Pete Townshend of the Who, the band that originally recorded the song. The following year, the album *Adios Amigos* was released, announcing to the world that the Ramones were ready to retire. The band signed on for the Lollapalooza tour in 1996 as part of their farewell concert series. *—David A. Clark*

For the Record

After attending a Ramones concert, author Norman Mailer said, "For me, it was like I was an old car and I was being taken out for a ride at one hundred miles an hour."

SELECT DISCOGRAPHY

■ ALBUMS

Ramones, 1976
Leave Home, 1977
Rocket to Russia, 1977
Road to Ruin, 1978
End of the Century, 1980
Pleasant Dreams, 1981
Subterranean Jungle, 1983
Too Tough to Die, 1984
Animal Boy, 1986
Halfway to Sanity, 1987
Ramones Mania, 1988
Brain Drain, 1989
All the Stuff (and More), Volume 1, 1990 (compilation)
All the Stuff (and More), Volume 2, 1991 (compilation)
Loco Live, 1991
Mondo Bizarro, 1992
Acid Eaters, 1994
Adios Amigos, 1995

SEE ALSO: Sex Pistols, The; Smith, Patti.

The Rascals

ORIGINAL MEMBERS: Felix Cavaliere (b. 1944), Eddie Brigati (b. 1946), Dino Danelli (b. 1945), Gene Cornish (b. 1945)

OTHER MEMBERS: Buzzy Feiten, Robert Popwell, Ann Sutton

FIRST SINGLE RELEASE: "I Ain't Gonna Eat Out My Heart Anymore"/"Slow Down," 1965

MUSICAL STYLES: Rock and roll, soul

The Rascals made striking contributions to both rock and soul music. They successfully integrated soul and rock into a sound that earned the band considerable success on pop and rhythm-and-blues radio formats with such songs as "Good Lovin'," "Groovin'," and "People Got to Be Free."

The Beginnings. The Rascals came together in New York City in 1964, after Felix Cavaliere, Eddie Brigati, and Gene Cornish left Joey Dee and the Starliters and formed a white soul quartet with Dino Danelli. Cavaliere, Danelli, and Brigati grew up in and around New York City and had considerable experience as sidemen before they began the Rascals; Cornish was a guitarist from Canada.

Cavaliere began taking classical piano lessons as a boy. However, when he began listening to the recordings of such rhythm-and-blues greats as Ray Charles and Otis Redding, he knew he wanted to play rhythm and blues. In high school he became the only white member of a soul group from Pelham called the Stereos. He left the group and started school at Syracuse University in New York. However, whenever he could, he returned to New York City and spent time at such clubs as the Peppermint Lounge. After leaving Syracuse University, Cavaliere moved to New York City, where he met Danelli, and the two moved to Las Vegas to perform with a casino house band. On their return to New York, Cavaliere joined Joey Dee and the Starliters, which featured Brigati and Cornish.

Danelli learned to play drums before he reached his teens and started playing professionally at age fifteen. His first interest was jazz, not rhythm and blues. In his mid-teens, he took a job with Lionel Hampton, and later worked with a band on Bourbon Street in New Orleans, Louisiana. In New Orleans he changed his musical direction from jazz to rhythm and blues. Danelli returned to New York City and found work as a sideman and session performer; by the time he met Cavaliere, he was playing in support of rhythm-and-blues artists such as Little Willie John. A short time before, while playing with a band in a New Jersey club, Danelli had met Eddie Brigati, a young singer who sat in with rhythm-and-blues groups when he could.

As Cavaliere, Brigati, Cornish, and Danelli spent more of their spare time together, the idea for beginning their own group took hold. During the winter of 1965 they locked themselves in Cavaliere's house and produced a repertoire of twenty-five songs, many of them written by Cavaliere and Brigati, who jointly wrote many of the group's later hits, with Cavaliere writing the music and Brigati writing the lyrics.

In February of 1965, the band opened in a small New Jersey roadhouse, the Choo Choo.

For the Record

The term "blue-eyed soul," which has been applied to such artists as the Righteous Brothers and Hall and Oates, was allegedly coined for the Rascals, although none of them had blue eyes.

Later that year they became the regular band at the Barge, a floating nightclub in Westhampton, Long Island. The Young Rascals, as they were called until 1967, became one of the most talked-about groups in the New York area during that summer. After Sid Bernstein, the promoter who brought the Beatles to America, heard them, he became their manager.

Success. Soon after acquiring Bernstein as their manager, the Rascals signed with Atlantic and released their first single, "I Ain't Gonna Eat My Heart Out Anymore" (number 52, 1965), sung by Brigati. They followed with another great success, "Good Lovin'" (number 1, 1966), sung by Cavaliere, one of the year's biggest hits. During 1966 and 1967, the group had nine more Top-20 hits, including "You Better Run" (number 20, 1966), "(I've Been) Lonely Too Long" (number 16, 1967), "Groovin'" (number 1, 1967), and "A Girl Like You" (number 10, 1967), most of them written by Cavaliere and Brigati.

The Young Rascals gained an international reputation in 1966. They performed in England at such major rock clubs as the Scotch and Sybylla's. Hardly anyone knew the quartet when they arrived, but after their first performance, their fans included the elite of English rock music: members of the Beatles, the Animals, and the Rolling Stones, among others.

As established hit makers, the group tried to portray a more serious image by dropping "Young" from their name in 1967 and the Edwardian knickers from their onstage wardrobe. With *Freedom Suite* (1969), the Rascals' music took on elements of jazz, but the quartet continued to score with "How Can I Be Sure" (number 4, 1967), "A Beautiful Morning" (number 3, 1968), and "People Got to Be Free" (number 1, 1968). Cavaliere and Brigati wrote the latter song shortly after the 1968 assassinations of Civil Rights leader Martin Luther King, Jr., and politician Robert F. Kennedy. Though they never brandished their politics like some bands, the Rascals truly lived theirs, demanding that an African American group appear on the bill at each of their concerts.

The Rascals continued to rank as one of the best in their field at the start of the 1970's, but there were internal strains among the members, and there was little chart action for the band's recordings in 1970. In 1971 the group moved from Atlantic to Columbia and also changed personnel.

The Reorganized Group. After the changeover from Atlantic to Columbia, Brigati and Cornish left the group before their label debut. Filling their shoes were guitarist Buzzy Feiten, formerly of the Butterfield Blues Band, bassist Robert Popwell, and vocalist Ann Sutton. Feiten's talents included playing lead guitar, piano, and bass, as well as singing and songwriting. He had been working with instruments since his youth. Popwell learned to play drums while he was in grade school. At age twelve he had his first professional job and played with a number of local groups in his teens. At age seventeen, he took up the bass guitar and became a popular studio guitarist. Sutton began taking voice lessons for opera while she was attending high school in western Pennsylvania. She majored in music at the University of Pittsburgh, but soon became interested in rhythm and blues and sang with soul and jazz groups.

The new group's debut album, *Peaceful World*, was released in the summer of 1971. It moved onto the charts in June and remained there through the summer. The group's next album, *The Island of Real*, issued in the spring of 1972, was also on the charts for a time. However, it was obvious that the audience for the band had diminished. The Rascals disbanded in 1972. Danelli later joined Cornish in a group called Bulldog, then in Fotomaker. Cavaliere continued as a solo artist and producer, and the three reunited in 1988 for a U.S. tour.

—Inoke F. Funaki

SELECT DISCOGRAPHY

■ SINGLES

"Good Lovin'," 1966
"(I've Been) Lonely Too Long," 1967
"Groovin'," 1967
"How Can I Be Sure," 1967
"A Beautiful Morning," 1968
"People Got to Be Free," 1968

■ ALBUMS

The Young Rascals, 1966
Collections, 1967
Groovin', 1967
Once upon a Dream, 1968
Time Peace: The Rascals' Greatest Hits, 1968
Freedom Suite, 1969
See, 1969
Search and Nearness, 1970
Peaceful World, 1971
The Island of Real, 1972

SELECT AWARDS

Rock and Roll Hall of Fame, inducted 1997

SEE ALSO: Buffalo Springfield; Clinton, George / Parliament / Funkadelic; Crosby, Stills, Nash, and Young; Donovan; Mitchell, Joni; Monroe, Bill, and the Blue Grass Boys; Righteous Brothers, The; Three Dog Night.

Lou Rawls

BORN: Chicago, Illinois; December 1, 1935
FIRST SINGLE RELEASE: "Bring It on Home to Me," 1962 (with Sam Cooke)
MUSICAL STYLES: Rhythm and blues, soul, pop

Lou Rawls was reared on the South Side of Chicago by his grandmother, and he began singing in church as a young boy. Rawls was greatly influenced by visits to Chicago's Regal Theater, where he enjoyed the entertainment of Billy Eckstein, Arthur Prysock, and Joe Williams. Those early experiences laid the foundation for Rawls's own unique style that invites audiences to lift their spirits by sharing, laughing, and reflecting with him.

Putting the Pieces Together. For a brief period of time in the mid-1950's, Rawls sang with the acclaimed gospel group the Pilgrim Travelers, before joining the U.S. Army in 1956. After his military stint, Rawls moved to California in 1958 and toured with Sam Cooke. While traveling to a concert, Cooke and Rawls were involved in a serious auto accident. Rawls was initially pronounced dead at the scene, but after lying in a coma for five days, he began to recover.

Lou Rawls (Archive Photos/Lynn McAfee)

In 1959, Rawls began singing rhythm and blues in Los Angeles nightclubs, and he signed a contract with Capitol in 1961. At Capitol, his singing style was molded to appeal to the fans of Nat "King" Cole. In 1962, Rawls's first single was the classic duet with Sam Cooke, "Bring It on Home to Me."

Establishing His Style. In the mid-1960's, Rawls had a succession of big hits, including his first number 1 rhythm-and-blues single, "Love Is a Hurtin' Thing" (1966), followed by the Grammy Award-winning "Dead End Street" (1967) and "Your Good Thing" (1969). *Lou Rawls Live* (1966) was his first of several gold albums, followed by *Soulin'* (1966), *Carryin' On* (1967), and *That's Lou* (1967). Rawls's success guaranteed him a spot on the cabaret circuit, and he appeared regularly on television variety shows and in Las Vegas nightclubs during the late 1960's.

Rawls released his popular Grammy Award winner "A Natural Man" in 1971, but his popularity declined over the next five years. However, in 1976, Rawls came back with his second number 1 rhythm-and-blues hit, "You'll Never Find Another Love Like Mine," as well as his only platinum album, *All Things in Time.* Four more big hits, "Groovy People" (1976), "See You When I Git There" (1977), the classic "Lady Love" (1977), and "Let Me Be Good to You" (1979), followed. Rawls won his third Grammy Award in 1977 for Best Male R&B Vocal Performance for *Unmistakably Lou.*

The 1980's brought several new albums, including *Now Is the Time* (1982), *When the Night Comes* (1983), *Close Company* (1984), and *Love Blues All the Way* (1986). Rawls's "I Wish You Belonged to Me," recorded on his own Blue Note label, made the rhythm-and-blues charts in 1987. In 1989, Rawls's Grammy Award-nominated album, *At Last,* featured a host of jazz musicians, such as George Benson, Ray Charles, Stanley Turrentine, Cornell Dupree, and Richard Tee, but Rawls's appeal was again declining.

Budweiser and Garfield. From the late 1970's through the early 1990's, Rawls provided the voice for several Budweiser beer commercials and subsequently became known as the voice behind Budweiser ads. Rawls even recorded an album with the title based on Budweiser's slogan, *When You Hear Lou, You've Heard It All* (1977). Rawls also provided his voice for the cartoon cat Garfield, recording three Garfield television specials. In the 1990's, Rawls sponsored the annual *Lou Rawls' Parade of Stars* telethon, which raises money for black colleges and the United Negro College Fund.

In 1993, Rawls combined with guests Phoebe Snow, Joe Williams, and Buddy Guy on *Portrait of the Blues,* and *Spotlight on Lou Rawls* was released in 1996. *Ballads* was recorded in 1997, featuring vocals by Rawls and Dianne Reeves, accompanied by jazz musicians Stanley Turrentine, Cornell Dupree, Richard Tee, David Newman, and Joe Lovano. Rawls would maintain a very active tour schedule through the 1990's. —*Alvin K. Benson*

For the Record

Rawls's popularity soared beyond the Earth when the first African American in space, Lieutenant Colonel Guion Bluford, Jr., took Rawls's album *When the Night Comes* on a space shuttle *Challenger* voyage in 1983.

SELECT DISCOGRAPHY

■ ALBUMS

Lou Rawls Live, 1966
Unmistakably Lou, 1977
At Last, 1989
Portrait of the Blues, 1993
Ballads, 1997

SELECT AWARDS

Grammy Award for Best R&B Vocal Performance, Male, for "Dead End Street," 1967
Grammy Award for Best R&B Vocal Performance, Male, for "A Natural Man," 1971
Grammy Award for Best R&B Vocal Performance, Male, for *Unmistakably Lou,* 1977

SEE ALSO: Benson, George; Charles, Ray; Cole, Nat "King"; Cooke, Sam.

The Red Hot Chili Peppers

ORIGINAL MEMBERS: Anthony Kiedis (b. 1962), Michael "Flea" Balzary (b. 1962), Hillel Slovak (1962-1988), Jack Irons (b. 1962)

OTHER MEMBERS: Cliff Martinez, Jack Sherman, John Frusciante (b. 1970), Chad Smith (b. 1962), D. H. Peligro, Dewayne "Blackbyrd" McKnight (b. 1954), Jesse Tobias, Arik Marshall (b. 1967), Dave Navarro (b. 1967)

FIRST ALBUM RELEASE: *The Red Hot Chili Peppers*, 1984

MUSICAL STYLES: Alternative, rock and roll, punk, funk, heavy metal

Anthony Kiedis, Michael "Flea" Balzary, Hillel Slovak, and Jack Irons began playing music together as early as 1978. Known around Los Angeles, California, as Los Faces and Anthym, they eventually evolved into the Red Hot Chili Peppers.

Getting Started. Kiedis's family left Grand Rapids, Michigan, when he was eleven years old. He met Flea in Los Angeles and attended Fairfax High School. Flea was born in Melbourne, Australia, and moved to New York at the age of five. At age eleven, he moved with his family to the West Coast. Kiedis (vocals), Flea (bass), Slovak (guitar), and Irons (drums) played together in the late 1970's until Kiedis quit to pursue a political science degree at University of California at Los Angeles in the early 1980's. Flea joined the hardcore punk band Fear. In 1983, Kiedis and Flea asked Slovak and Irons if they were interested in restarting the Red Hot Chili Peppers.

The First Album. Some of the early attention the Red Hot Chili Peppers received had more to do with their on-stage antics than their music. At one Los Angeles club, the band appeared on stage wearing nothing more than socks to cover their genitals. While building a following in Los Angeles, however, the Red Hot Chili Peppers began to fall apart internally. The lack of a recorded album within the first few months led to the separation of Irons and Slovak, who tried to attain success with the band What Is This?, with whom they had a commitment prior to the reestablishment of the Red Hot Chili Peppers. Flea and Kiedis looked to Jack Sherman and Cliff Martinez (guitar and drums, respectively) to fill in, and the first Red Hot Chili Peppers album was recorded with EMI Records in 1984.

The following year Sherman was replaced with Slovak, and the second album, *Freaky Styley* (1985), was recorded. Funk legend George Clinton produced the album. In 1986, Irons returned to the band, replacing Martinez and reuniting the original lineup for the recording of the third album, *Uplift Mofo Party Plan* (1987). A successful tour followed.

Tragedy Strikes. In 1988, the Red Hot Chili Peppers recorded *The Abbey Road EP* in the United Kingdom. However, tragedy struck only a few weeks after the band returned to the United States when Slovak died of a drug overdose. Finding the weight of this loss too much to bear, Irons left the Red Hot Chili Peppers (he would later reappear with Pearl Jam). Kiedis, who was also known to experiment with drugs, attempted to rehabilitate himself before returning to California to rebuild the band with Flea's help.

Dewayne "Blackbyrd" McKnight (guitar) joined the Red Hot Chili Peppers for a brief period, only to be replaced by eighteen-year-old John Frusciante. After auditioning dozens of drummers, the band rounded out their new lineup with the addition of Chad Smith, a Minnesota native, and recorded *Mother's Milk* (1989), their first certified gold album.

The 1990's. In 1990, Flea and Smith ran into legal trouble in Florida and were arrested on charges of battery for sexually harassing a woman in Daytona. The two band members eventually paid a combination of fines and apologized for their behavior.

The Red Hot Chili Peppers' next album, *BloodSugarSexMagik*, produced in 1991, was tremendously successful. This multiplatinum album reached markets formerly untouched by the alternative sound, eventually selling over four million copies in the United States alone and winning a Grammy for the song "Give It Away." Despite this success, the lineup changed again. Frusciante left the band, only to be replaced by Arik Marshall and then by Jesse Tobias. Guitarist Dave Navarro, formerly of Jane's Addiction, eventually became the permanent replacement for Frusciante. Rick Rubin produced *BloodSugarSexMagik* as well as the 1995 follow-up, *One Hot Minute.* In between, EMI Records issued a retrospective album, *What Hits!?,* which became a platinum best-seller following its 1992 release. The appeal of the Red Hot Chili Peppers never slowed during the mid-1990's. *One Hot Minute* also went platinum.

The Red Hot Chili Peppers (Paul Natkin)

The years 1996 and 1997 proved to be challenging for the band. A fall performance in 1996 would be their last until the summer of 1997. Side projects and solo ambitions took time away from the band's pursuits. In late July of 1997, fans at Mount Fuji, Japan, witnessed the final live performance of the band for the year. Even that performance was cut short because of inclement weather in the form of a typhoon.

Other problems included Flea's and Navarro's tour with Jane's Addiction for a substantial part of 1997. Kiedis admitted to having a heroin problem and sustained injuries to his wrist that required surgery and prevented him from performing during his recovery. Smith dislocated his shoulder in a motorcycle accident. No stranger to accidents, Smith had also broken his wrist in 1995, causing a number of tour dates to be rescheduled. In April of 1998, Navarro announced that he, too, would be leaving the Red Hot Chili Peppers to work with his own band, Spread. Within days of Navarro's departure, former Red Hot Chili Pepper guitarist Frusciante declared he would return to fill the vacated spot.

—Donna Addkison Simmons

SELECT DISCOGRAPHY

■ ALBUMS

The Red Hot Chili Peppers, 1984
Freaky Styley, 1985
The Uplift Mofo Party Plan, 1987
The Abbey Road EP, 1988 (EP)
Mother's Milk, 1989
BloodSugarSexMagik, 1991
What Hits!? 1992
One Hot Minute, 1995

SELECT AWARDS
Grammy Award for Best Hard Rock Performance with Vocal for "Give It Away," 1992

SEE ALSO: Jane's Addiction / Porno for Pyros.

Otis Redding

BORN: Dawson, Georgia; September 9, 1941
DIED: Madison, Wisconsin; December 10, 1967
FIRST SINGLE RELEASE: "These Arms of Mine," 1962
MUSICAL STYLE: Soul

Though he was born in Dawson, Georgia, Otis Redding's parents moved to Macon in 1944; there Otis spent the remainder of his childhood. His father, who was working on a local Air Force base, came down with tuberculosis. Otis dropped out of school at age fifteen and worked as a well digger and gas station attendant. His love for music, however, led him to tour with a band called the Upsetters, a group formerly associated with Little Richard. This job afforded Redding the opportunity to send twenty dollars home to his family each week. Redding's musical talents had surfaced when he was a child. He sang with a gospel group at his church, played drums with his school band, and took an interest in piano and composition. His interest in becoming a professional musician was stimulated by the rich musical tradition of Macon, which, during Otis's childhood, had already seeded the careers of Little Richard and James Brown.

The first signs of Redding's greatness occurred when he began appearing on a Saturday morning talent show hosted by local disc jockey Hamp Swain. The show was broadcasted over WIBB and housed at the Douglas Theater. Redding won this event consistently each week. While at the Douglas Theater Redding met and befriended Phil Walden. Under the management of Walden and his brother Alan, Redding began playing the college fraternity circuit. During this time Redding was the driver and occasional backup singer with the Pinetoppers, a group led by guitarist Johnny Jenkins.

Otis Redding (Freddie Patterson Collection/ Archive Photos)

The First Stax Session. Redding's career began to blossom when he became affiliated with Stax Records in 1962. At the behest of Phil Walden, the Pinetoppers were invited to record at Stax's studio in Memphis. The invitation was engineered by Joe Galkin, a regional promotions executive for Atlantic Records. The session was originally designed to showcase the talent of Johnny Jenkins. As an afterthought, Redding was given recording time at the end of the session. The results were "Hey, Hey, Baby" and "These Arms of Mine."

Galkin recognized Redding's potential from the beginning, and he supported a single that resulted from the session. John Richbourg, a prominent Nashville disc jockey, also recognized Redding's genius, especially in "These Arms of Mine." He promoted the single for six months, after which it began to generate strong sales. The record went to number 20 on the rhythm-and-blues chart. On the strength of "These Arms of Mine," Redding was invited back to Stax for additional recordings. These recordings marked the beginning of Redding's ascent to stardom.

Success. By 1965 Redding had established himself as a major force among soul singers. That year saw the release of "Respect," his biggest hit to date at number 4 on the rhythm-and-blues chart (the song later became a signature song for Aretha Franklin). He also went on a successful European tour. After the tour Redding expanded his repertoire to include his versions of songs by the Rolling Stones ("Satisfaction") and the Beatles ("Day Tripper"). Redding's expanded repertoire also featured versions of Smokey Robinson's "It's Growing" (1966) and perennial pop classics such as Irving Berlin's "White Christmas" (1967). The conventional Otis Redding, however, continued with hits such as "Fa-Fa-Fa-Fa-Fa" (1966), "I've Got Dreams to Remember" (1967), and "(Sittin' on) The Dock of the Bay" (1968).

For the Record

Redding often got lyric ideas from his daily life. The inspiration for "Mr. Pitiful" was a disc jockey's comment on the pleading nature of Redding's lyrics and singing. The title for "Fa-Fa-Fa-Fa-Fa," according to Steve Cropper, was originally syllables Redding sang to describe the sound of a saxophone riff. "I'm Sick Y'All" was the excuse Redding asked his wife to give to those who complained that he was spending too much time developing the career of his protégé Arthur Conley. (Redding produced the song "Sweet Soul Music" for Conley in 1967.)

Mainstream audiences became increasingly interested in Redding after 1965. This interest, however, did not lead to any major changes in Redding's style. His language, both as a singer and songwriter, remained distinctively his own throughout his seven-year career. The evolution of his style reflected the trends of soul music during the 1960's. In 1967 Redding appeared at the Monterey Pop Festival along with a number of primarily white pop and rock-and-roll acts. His passionate performance won over the audience on his own terms. "(Sittin' on) The Dock of the Bay," written and recorded later in 1967, became Redding's biggest hit in the following year, hitting number 1 on both the pop and rhythm-and-blues charts.

Early Influences. "These Arms of Mine" was Redding's first hit but not his first recording. In 1960 he had left Macon and traveled to Los Angeles, where he recorded the songs "She's All Right" and "Getting Hip." These early recordings show clearly the influence of Sam Cooke on Redding's early vocal style. This influence is evident in Redding's use of melodic embellishments, turns, verbalisms, vocal rhythms, and pentatonic pitch patterns. Cooke's influence also helped motivate Redding to aspire to the same type of entrepreneurial independence that Cooke himself acquired.

The arranging methods of Cooke and Redding were similar. Cooke conceived much of his band's material and then communicated his ideas to his arranger, Rene Hall. Bass lines, horn lines, and vocal background parts were all part of Cooke's conception. Redding did not write songs at the prolific rate that Cooke did, and he did not come to sessions with finished products as Cooke often did. However, with his voice, his guitar, and sometimes the piano, Redding communicated to his band the musical ideas he had in mind. He was particularly creative in his conception of horn parts.

Though Cooke's influence on Redding was stronger than that of any other artist, it was not exclusive. In Redding's 1960 "Shout Bamalama," for example, the influence of Little Richard is noticeable in the arrangement and in Redding's singing. The quasi-screams sporadically delivered in Redding's "Mary Had a Little Lamb" (1963) are reminiscent of the vocal technique of Jackie Wilson. The influence of James Brown is noticeable in some of Redding's compositions after 1966. In "I'm Sick Y'All" (1966), for example, the harmony is unusually static—consisting essentially of only two harmonies. Also, the melodic parts provided by the bass, the guitar, and the voice are strikingly independent and distinctive, yet strongly interactive. These attributes reflected the emerging funk sound cultivated principally by James Brown.

Vocalist and Composer. Redding was a great vocal stylist, not a crooner. His approach was earthy, deeply emotional, and shaped by the blues and gospel traditions of the South. His singing featured an extemporized delivery, poignant embellishments, added words, and spontaneous verbalisms. "Let Me Come on Home" opens with the line "Baby, I wanna come home to ya," but Redding's delivery renders the line as "Oh ba-by, yeah . . . babe, wanna come home to ya." Elsewhere Redding enriches the lyric with words that transform it into a highly emotional and dramatic plea: "Baby, yeah . . . girl . . . huh . . . lawd . . . said, I got to get home to ya."

Redding's writing process resulted generally from interchanges between Redding and his studio musicians during recording sessions. Redding generally came to sessions with attractive but incomplete ideas. He hummed or played his ideas to the members of the group. The ideas would then be creatively reworked until a finished song emerged. Songs were generally worked out and recorded the same day. In this way Redding, his group, and collaborators constructed some of the most enduring soul pieces in the canon of 1960's soul music. Among Redding's cowriters were guitarist Steve Cropper and Jerry Butler.

Redding's harmonic language was not innovative, but it suited his emotionalism. Likewise, his use of form was conventional but served his emotional and aesthetic expression. Introductions often opened the songs. Lyric improvisation sections, often called vamps (sections with repeated harmonic phrases underscoring an improvised, sermonistic vocal), generally closed them. He seldom used background singers. The pentatonic scale pervades Redding's work, and his vocal melodies were strongly influenced by the pentatonic and blues scales.

Birth of a Legend. On December 10, 1967, Otis Redding's plane crashed in Lake Monona, a few minutes short of the airport in Madison, Wisconsin. This tragedy took place only three days after Redding recorded "(Sittin' on) The Dock of the Bay," so he never knew how popular the song became in the following year. Despite his early death, Redding's artistic significance has endured. Of all the soul artists of the 1960's only James Brown exerted a greater impact on later artists. Redding's works have been covered by artists such as Aretha Franklin, the Rolling Stones, and, later, Michael Bolton. Most important, since the 1960's Redding has earned the adoration and respect of fans all over the world. —*Earl L. Stewart*

SELECT DISCOGRAPHY

■ ALBUMS

Pain in My Heart, 1964
Complete and Unbelievable . . . The Otis Redding Dictionary of Soul, 1966
The Dock of the Bay, 1968
Otis Redding/Jimi Hendrix Experience, 1970
Otis! The Definitive Otis Redding, 1993 (compilation)

SELECT AWARDS

Grammy Awards for Best R&B Song (wr. with Steve Cropper) and Best R&B Vocal Performance, Male, for "(Sittin' on) The Dock of the Bay," 1968
Rock and Roll Hall of Fame, inducted 1989

SEE ALSO: Brown, James; Cooke, Sam; Franklin, Aretha; Little Richard; Wilson, Jackie.

Helen Reddy

BORN: Melbourne, Australia; October 25, 1941
FIRST ALBUM RELEASE: *I Don't Know How to Love Him*, 1971
MUSICAL STYLES: Pop, country

After starting her career as a child performer in her native Australia, Helen Reddy became best known for her early 1970's anthem "I Am Woman" and a string of other country-pop hits such as "I Don't Know How to Love Him" and "Delta Dawn." In later years she continued to make concert appearances but focused on acting, appearing in theater productions in London and throughout the United States.

The Beginnings. Helen Reddy began performing when she was a child. When she was two years old, her parents, who were also performers, held her up to a microphone during their radio show in her native Australia. Reddy later made her stage debut when she was four, dancing in a chorus line at the Tivoli Theatre in Perth. After leaving boarding school at age fifteen, she joined a road show in which she sang and acted. This latter experience led to her own program on Australian television, *Helen Reddy Sings.*

In 1966, Reddy won a trip to New York through an Australian Bandstand International contest, which was sponsored by Philips-Mercury Records. New York City was not exactly welcoming to the young Australian singer, but her trip did lead to her introduction to Jeff Wald, an agent with the William Morris talent agency. He became her husband one year later and, in 1970, set up her first appearance on *The Tonight Show.*

The next year, Reddy, who had signed with Capitol Records, scored her first hit, "I Don't Know How to Love Him," written for the musical *Jesus Christ Superstar.* The song, the first pop hit for a then-unknown composer named Andrew Lloyd Webber, went to number 13 and was soon followed by a string of other hits. These included the number 1 hits "I Am Woman" (1972), "Delta Dawn" (1973), and "Angie Baby" (1974), as well as several Top-10 successes, including "Leave Me Alone" (number 3, 1973), "You and Me Against the World" (number 9, 1974), and "Ain't No Way to Treat a Lady" (number 8, 1975). Her other chart hits included "Peaceful" (number 12, 1973), "Keep On Singing" (number 15, 1974), "Emotion" (number 22, 1975), and "You're My World" (number 18, 1977).

Her recording success brought her television exposure, including a 1973 variety show and a long-time stint as host of the late-night rock show *The Midnight Special.* Her television specials over the years have been seen in forty countries.

For the Record

Helen Reddy has a good sense of humor about the fleeting nature of fame. "You know, you look like a good-looking Helen Reddy," she was told by a woman who approached her in a restaurant in the mid-1990's. "I've decided to take it as a compliment," Reddy said.

The Big Screen Beckons. As the hits dried up for Reddy in the mid-1970's, she focused more on acting. Her movies include *Airport 1975* (1974), *Pete's Dragon* (1977), for which she also sang on the sound track, and *Sgt. Pepper's Lonely Hearts Club Band* (1978). In the early 1980's she divorced Wald, and in 1983, she married Milton Ruth. That marriage also ended in divorce. During the 1980's, Reddy continued to make live concert appearances and record, although her albums did not sell nearly as well as they had in her heyday the decade before. She began to appear onstage as an actress in theater productions in the United States, Canada, and London. She also served as parks commissioner for her adopted home state of California. *—Rob DiGiacomo*

SELECT DISCOGRAPHY

■ ALBUMS

I Don't Know How to Love Him, 1971
Helen Reddy, 1971
I Am Woman, 1972
Long Hard Climb, 1973
Free and Easy, 1974
No Way to Treat a Lady, 1975
Helen Reddy's Greatest Hits, 1975
Music, Music, 1976
Ear Candy, 1977
Pete's Dragon, 1977 (sound track)
We'll Sing in the Sunshine, 1978

Live in London, 1978
Reddy, 1979
Imagination, 1983
Lust for Life, 1984
Helen Reddy Greatest Hits (and More), 1987 (previously released material)
Feel So Young, 1991
All-Time Greatest Hits, 1992 (previously released material)

SELECT AWARDS
Grammy Award for Best Pop Vocal Performance, Female, for "I Am Woman," 1972

SEE ALSO: Murray, Anne.

Lou Reed

(Louis Firbank)

BORN: Brooklyn, New York; March 2, 1942
FIRST SINGLE RELEASE: "So Blue," 1957 (with the Shades)
FIRST SOLO ALBUM RELEASE: *Lou Reed*, 1972
MUSICAL STYLE: Rock and roll

Lou Reed has few serious rivals for the mantle of outstanding musical poet for society's most marginalized people. His songs celebrate, albeit in a despairing way, the struggles of drug addicts, transvestites, homeless people, and sadomasochists. His work has benefited from his deeply rooted understanding of rhythm and blues, his fine guitar playing, his singular and melancholy voice, his surprising and original lyrics, and his willingness to take career-threatening risks at seemingly every turn.

Suburban Roots of an Urban Poet. Lou Reed was born in Brooklyn, New York, and his family moved to Long Island's suburban enclave of Freeport. His father owned an accounting firm. When, as a teen, Reed evinced an interest in a life as a rock-and-roll musician, his parents counseled him to consider learning to type so he would have a marketable skill, in case his musical ambitions could not earn him a steady income. During his high school years, he formed and joined several bands. He made his first records with a band of teenaged musicians called the Shades. Their single "So Blue" was a brief local success.

Reed's ambitions as a creative writer and his parents' hopes for a secure future for their son took him to Syracuse University. Reed's rebellion against his roots began early in his college career. He was dismissed from the Reserve Officers' Training Corps (ROTC) for insubordination. Reed was trained instead as a poet. His haunting and rueful lyrics form a hallmark of his style. In Syracuse, Reed continued to make music a priority in his life. While a student, he met several musicians with whom he would later form the influential band the Velvet Underground. These included Sterling Morrison and Angus MacLise.

After completing his work at Syracuse, Reed went to work for Pickwick Records as a songwriter. Reed's most talked-about success at Pickwick was a parodic gibe aimed at that 1960's rock-and-roll staple, the dance song; it was entitled "The Ostrich." This song constitutes his first collaboration with experimental musician John Cale, who provided an electric viola line. Pickwick encouraged Reed to form the Primitives in order to record the song and expolit its commercial potential. The Primitives would undergo numerous personnel changes and changes of name before evolving into the Velvet Underground.

The Velvet Underground. From 1966 until his departure from the band in 1970, Lou Reed worked with the Velvet Underground. The band's lineup eventually settled into Reed (guitar and vocals), John Cale (various instruments, but often viola), Sterling Morrison (bass), and Maureen "Moe" Tucker (drums). Together this group released four studio albums recorded in New York City from 1966 through 1970. They were the favored band of pop artist Andy Warhol, who produced the band's first album, *The Velvet Underground and Nico* (1967). Reed wrote most of the band's material and was the backbone of their sometimes aggressive, sometimes sparse, and always interesting sound. Perhaps more important than his work in crafting the group's sound were Reed's lyrics. In his songs written for the group, Reed explored a host of difficult issues. He celebrated the life of drug addicts in "Heroin" and

"I'm Waiting for My Man." His rich characters created in his lyrics include sadomasochists ("Venus in Furs"), transvestites ("Sister Ray"), and drug dealers. Reed and the group failed to win commercial success, in part because Reed's dark poetic vision was doomed to marginalize the group along with the marginalized characters about whom he sang.

Reed experienced difficulties working with Cale on the band's second album, *White Light/White Heat* (1968). Cale was the chief instigator of the band's wholly uncommercial sound. Reed, who harbored hope for some commercial success, encouraged Cale to leave the group. The band's next two albums, *The Velvet Underground* (1969) and *Loaded* (1970), explore a much more accessible musical landscape. Gone are the shrill drones, repetitive musical structures, and manic improvisations associated with Cale's participation. In 1970, with the band's most commercially motivated album on the verge of release, Reed left the band and returned to Long Island, where he worked for his father for nearly two years.

"Walk on the Wild Side." When Reed emerged from his self-exile from music, he was armed with a host of interesting new songs. Some had been written for the Velvet Underground and never been performed, others were born of fresh inspiration. RCA was attracted to these creations, and Reed was sent to London to record them. The resulting album, *Lou Reed* (1972), marked the beginning of Reed's long solo career. While the album constitutes his solo debut, it was not made alone. Rick Wakeman, among others, offered able assistance. His second solo album, *Transformer* (1972), was produced by David Bowie, who has always described himself as a great supporter of Reed. *Transformer*, like *Lou Reed* before it, is considered by many to be uneven effort, but it contains Reed's most heroic single, "Walk on the Wild Side." This song was configured as a homage to the dark aspects of New York City's outcasts drawn together around the chaotic artistic energy of Andy Warhol and the avant-garde of the 1960's. Despite its grim and gritty lyrics, the song became the kind of hit that the Velvet Underground had never achieved. "Walk on the Wild Side" made the Top 20 in the United States and made the Top 10 in the United Kingdom.

Just as Reed seemed on the verge of tremendous commercial success, he pulled back. His next three albums were uneven and failed to catapult him to the

Lou Reed (Reprise/Timothy Greenfield-Sanders)

forefront of his field. The third of these, *Metal Machine Music* (1975), was a harsh and acidic atonal work spanning two albums. Hailed as a breakthrough among a tiny assemblage of avant-gardists, the album was resoundingly disliked by mainstream critics. *Metal Machine Music* can only be seen as Reed's most profound attempt to eschew the fame associated with a commercially successful popular musician.

Reed ended his walk through the 1970's with unpredictable work ranging from the uninspired album *Rock and Roll Heart* (1976) to the often brilliant album *Street Hassle* (1978). With the latter, Reed found himself once again in the company of his fictional creations from the margins of society.

New York. The 1980's showed Reed continuing in the tradition of chief songwriter on the topic of the downtrodden. His solo work during the decade included four fine albums: *The Blue Mask* (1982), *Legendary Hearts* (1983), *Mistrial* (1986), and *New York* (1989). This last collection is filled with powerful and startling imagery and frequent touches of bitter humor. The lyrics and stripped-down guitar/bass/drums instrumentation work perfectly together. *New York* offers a darkly pessimistic vision that reveals Reed at his best.

Reed achieved peace with his old friend John Cale as the two collaborated on *Songs for Drella* (1990). This album provided a poignant love letter to the legacy of Andy Warhol. It paved the way for a reunion and triumphant tour of the Velvet Underground in 1993, coupled with the release of a live album, *MCMXCIII.*

The 1990's would see Reed's solo career continue to flourish. His albums *Magic and Loss* (1992), *Set the Twilight Reeling* (1996), and *Perfect Night: Live in London* (1998) demonstrated Reed's ranking among the foremost singer-songwriters working in popular music. —*Michael Lee*

For the Record

Lou Reed was apparently not cut out for military life. While studying at Syracuse University, he was enrolled in the Reserve Officers' Training Corps (ROTC) program. He was dismissed, however, for his ill-advised threat to shoot a superior officer.

SELECT DISCOGRAPHY

■ ALBUMS

Lou Reed, 1972
Transformer, 1972
Berlin, 1973
Rock 'n' Roll Animal, 1974
Sally Can't Dance, 1974
Metal Machine Music, 1975
Lou Reed Live, 1975
Coney Island Baby, 1976
Rock and Roll Heart, 1976
Street Hassle, 1978
The Bells, 1979
Growing Up in Public, 1980
The Blue Mask, 1982
Legendary Hearts, 1983
New Sensations, 1984
Mistrial, 1986
New York, 1989
Magic and Loss, 1992
Set the Twilight Reeling, 1996

SEE ALSO: Vega, Suzanne; Velvet Underground.

Martha Reeves and the Vandellas

ORIGINAL MEMBERS: Martha Reeves (b. 1941), Annette Beard, Rosalind Ashford (b. 1943)

OTHER MEMBERS: Betty Kelly (b. 1944), Lois Reeves, Sandra Tilley (d. 1981)

FIRST SINGLE RELEASE: "I'll Have to Let Him Go," 1963

MUSICAL STYLES: Pop, rhythm and blues

The Motown Records girl group Martha and the Vandellas recorded some of the biggest hits of the 1960's, including "Heat Wave," "Dancing in the Street," and "Nowhere to Run." The creative team of Brian Holland, Lamont Dozier, and Eddie Holland developed a wave of percussive formula hits for the group, featuring the distinctive lead vocals

Martha Reeves and the Vandellas (Fotos International/Archive Photos)

of Martha Reeves, and forged them into one of the most successful recording groups in Motown's first generation of stars. The upbeat, urban music of Martha and the Vandellas, along with the songs of other African American Motown artists such as Smokey Robinson and the Miracles, the Temptations, and the Supremes, crossed over racial lines, appealing to black and white teenagers with danceable rhythms and nonthreatening lyrics about young love.

The Early Days. The three founding members of the group, Martha Reeves, Annette Beard, and Rosalind Ashford, began their singing career in high school. Reeves, who had also been performing professionally under the name Martha LaVaille, took an office job at Detroit's Motown Records. She was discovered there by Motown head, Berry Gordy, Jr. Along with Beard and Ashford, Reeves took the first steps on the road to fame singing backup on Motown studio sessions. In 1963, the three young women recorded their first hit, "Come and Get These Memories," taking their name from Van Dyke Street in Detroit and Reeve's favorite performer, Della Reese.

The Motown Sound. This first hit was followed by a streak of dance records written for the group by the Holland-Dozier-Holland creative partnership. The writing team refined and perfected the distinctive Motown style and production techniques. "Heat Wave" (1963), the first song written by them for Martha and the Vandellas, reached number 4 on the ppop charts and number 1 on the rhythm-and-blues charts, inaugurating a three-year run of hits launching both Martha and the Vandellas and the Motown sound. "Heat Wave" is a classic example of the Holland-Dozier-Holland style, which rejected the standard song forms of the day, pioneering a cyclical pattern and using the hook line in a repetitive refrain. Boosted by Reeves's high-octave, gospel-inspired vocals and backed by pounding tambourines, the song achieved huge popularity as a crossover hit.

Gordy exercised a tight reign over his artists. All were carefully groomed and marketed to conform to the Gordy-manufactured image of the Motown hit factory. His female performers in particular, Mary Wells, the Marvelettes, Martha and the Vandellas, and the Supremes, were carefully mentored and controlled. Motown provided these young entertainers with everything needed to launch their careers, from dance lessons to tour bookings. In an interview with *Rolling Stone* in 1974, Reeves recalled the etiquette lessons given to the young performers by a local Detroit beauty school owner, Maxine Powell, who lined up Martha and the Vandellas, along with the other girl groups, and drilled them on how to dress, walk, sit, and stand properly.

In addition to molding their stage image, Motown restricted Martha and the Vandellas to formula follow-up recordings which varied only slightly from the hits which preceded them. Only after their third song failed to reach higher than number 42 on the charts did the group have the opportunity to vary their style. The group had little control over what they would record. Their biggest hit, the hugely popular teen anthem of 1964, "Dancing in the Street" was given to Martha and the Vandellas only after having been turned down by other Motown artists. The group's other major hits, "Nowhere to Run" (1965), "I'm Ready for Love" (1966), and "Jimmy Mack" (1967) were all written for them by the Holland-Dozier-Holland producing team. The team stopped composing for the group in 1967, and consequently, their run of hits came to an end.

In 1967, the group began to be billed as Martha Reeves and the Vandellas, accentuating the role of the lead vocalist. Betty Kelly from the less successful Motown group the Velvelettes replaced Annette Beard, who retired in 1963. When Kelly left four years later, Reeve's younger sister Lois came aboard. This version of the group remained intact through 1969, when Sandra Tilley, who had sung with both the Velvelettes and the Orlons, replaced original member Rosalind Ashford. After a farewell performance in Detroit in late 1972, the group broke up. Reeves pursued a solo career, and her sister Lois went on to perform with soul singer Al Green. Tilley later developed a brain tumor and died in 1981.

For the Record

Martha Reeves began her career at Motown Records as a secretary in the artist and repertoire (A&R) department. When Motown head Berry Gordy, Jr., needed backup singers for a hastily arranged recording session for Marvin Gaye, he called her over. Reeves brought in two of her high school friends, Beard and Ashford. Recognizing a good thing when he saw it, Gordy quickly formed the trio into a new recording group, Martha and the Vandellas.

Conflicts. Motown Records had evolved into the largest African American-owned corporation in the country, and the only one with African Americans in control of technical, musical, and artistic departments. Despite this success, the company's history is rife with conflicts between management and artists. In Reeves's 1994 autobiography, *Dancing in the Street: Confessions of a Motown Diva*, she revealed the professional rivalry that existed between the Vandellas and Gordy's supergroup, the Supremes, and her personal rivalry with the Supremes's popular lead singer, Diana Ross. Reeves blamed Gordy for sabotaging the Vandellas at the height of their popularity in favor of the smoother, less earthy sound of the Supremes. Gordy's obsession with Ross and the Supremes propelled them to stardom at the expense of the already well-established Vandellas. The group's last big hit for Motown, the infectiously peppy but nonformulaic "Jimmy Mack," was kept from release for more than two years because of its similarity to singles being produced for the Supremes. Gordy expected his troupe of young entertainers to yield to him on both financial and creative decisions, but Reeves questioned Gordy's management, conflicting with him over business questions as well as artistic decisions. It was not until 1989, however, that Reeves, along with original members Beard and Ashford, sued Motown for back royalties.

After the Breakup. After she left Motown, Reeves faced a number of personal struggles. She continued to pursue a busy recording and performing schedule, signing a solo contract with MCA in 1974. That same year, the single "Power of Love," produced for Reeves by Richard Perry, rose to minor success on the charts but her subsequent solo releases were less well received critically and commercially. Reeves had acquired an addiction to prescription drugs and suffered at least two nervous breakdowns. Institutionalized for a time with emotional problems made more acute by her drug dependency, Reeves struggled through most of the 1970's as she tried to build her solo career. Drug-free since 1977, she would continue to tour, sometimes solo and sometimes with later incarnations of the Vandellas, which have included the Reeves sisters Lois and Delphine. Inducted into the Rock and Roll Hall of Fame in 1995, Reeves and the original Vandellas, Beard and Ashford, have occasionally reunited for special performances.

Legacy. Martha Reeves and the Vandellas are pioneers of early rock and roll, creating the most popular dance music of the 1960's and helping to define the distinctive Motown sound. One of the first groups to appeal to African American and crossover white audiences, Martha and the Vandellas represented a unique addition to the Motown girl groups. Their sound and look were more earthy and aggressive than the girl-next-door image presented by the Supremes. A staple of Top-40 radio stations in the 1960's, their songs have enjoyed considerable airplay on oldies stations.

—Janice Monti-Belkaoui

SELECT DISCOGRAPHY

■ SINGLES

"Come and Get These Memories," 1963
"Heat Wave," 1963
"Dancing in the Street," 1964
"Nowhere to Run," 1965
"I'm Ready for Love," 1966
"Jimmy Mack," 1967
"Honey Chile," 1967

■ ALBUMS

Dance Party, 1965
Martha & the Vandellas Live! 1967
Martha Reeves & the Vandellas Anthology, 1974 (compilation)

SELECT AWARDS

Rock and Roll Hall of Fame, inducted 1995

SEE ALSO: Four Tops, The; Gaye, Marvin; Robinson, Smokey; Ross, Diana; Supremes, The; Temptations, The.

R.E.M.

ORIGINAL MEMBERS: Bill Berry (b. 1958), Peter Buck (b. 1956), Mike Mills (b. 1958), Michael Stipe (b. 1960)
FIRST ALBUM RELEASE: *Murmur*, 1983
MUSICAL STYLES: Alternative, pop, rock

Music genres are often defined by the musicians who create them. While new wave was the dominant musical style in the early 1980's, it would be the group R.E.M. that would create the next great genre in rock music, the alternative music style that would come to be known as the Athens sound. This sound would dominate college alternative music until the early 1990's and the advent of the Seattle sound pioneered by Nirvana and Pearl Jam. As their success grew, R.E.M. came to embody every garage band's dreams of making it big.

Small-Town Roots. The Athens sound, so named because the musicians that played it were from the Athens, Georgia, area, had already been developing for several years before R.E.M. made its debut. Groups such as the B-52's and Indigo Girls helped call attention to the Athens music scene, which primarily appealed to the underground, college crowd. Bill Berry and Mike Mills had known each other since high school and played in local bands together. Peter Buck, originally from California, worked in a local record store, where he met Michael Stipe. The four musicians were brought together by a mutual friend and they began playing together under the name Twisted Kites. By the summer of 1980 they had settled on the name R.E.M., chosen after randomly flipping through the dictionary.

Within the following two years R.E.M. became famous both for the amount of local touring they did and for the sound they were creating. Stipe had begun writing the often mysterious lyrics that would typify the band, and Buck was developing his signature jangly guitar style. In 1981 at the Hib-Tone record label, R.E.M. recorded their first single, "Radio Free Europe," which *Village Voice* rated as the Top Independent Single of the Year. The single built up their following and led to a recording deal with I.R.S. Records in 1982. R.E.M. cut their first extended-play single, *Chronic Town,* that same year and released their debut album, *Murmur,* in 1983. *Rolling Stone* would vote *Murmur* Best Album of the Year (beating Michael Jackson's *Thriller*) and later the eighth most important album of the decade. *Murmur* made it into Top-40 radio airplay and caused the group's following to grow substantially.

The Athens Sound Spreads. With Buck's recognizable guitar sound, Stipe's mumbled and cryptic lyrics, and the band's refusal to make videos, R.E.M. became the favorite band to imitate, which they supported wholeheartedly. In this way the Athens sound began to proliferate outside the southern college region.

Another R.E.M. trait was the often mysterious artwork and graphic designs used on their albums. Their third album, released in 1985, was known as either *Fables of the Reconstruction* or *Recon-*

R.E.M. in 1984 (Paul Natkin)

struction of the Fables, depending on how the title was read (the title was designed circularly with no discernable beginning or end). On this much darker album, Stipe's unclear enunciation was at its most incomprehensible, making parts of the album even harder to understand than usual. Nonetheless, it became R.E.M.'s best-selling album to date in the United States.

R.E.M. teamed with John Mellencamp's producer, Don Gehman, for *Life's Rich Pageant* (1986), a more accessible album with a cleaner sound and a deliberate attempt on Stipe's part to enunciate his vocals. A few months later the group released a collection of rare tracks and B-sides called *Dead Letter Office* (1987), one of their most interesting collections. *Dead Letter Office* featured covers of songs as diverse as Aerosmith's "Toys in the Attic" and Roger Miller's "King of the Road," each done in R.E.M.'s trademark style.

For the Record

R.E.M. may hold a record for having played under the most different names. Before adopting "R.E.M." in 1980, the band used such names and pseudonyms as—to list only a few—Fat, Drunk, and Stupid; Hornets Attack Victor Mature; It Crawled from the South; Male Nurses; Neon Mud Men; Pink Pajamas; and Twisted Kites. Its members finally settled on "R.E.M.," not because it had anything to do with the well-known expression "rapid eye movement," but because it was short and they liked its sound

§

"It's so much easier to write about angst and anger and fear and darkness . . . than to write about intense happiness. Happiness just sounds dorky." —*Michael Stipe*

Politics and Popularity. R.E.M.'s popularity continued to grow with *Document* (1987), their fifth album, which became a hit quickly after it was released. A semipolitical album (song titles included "Welcome to the Occupation" and "Exhuming McCarthy"), it featured one of their most recognizable songs, "It's the End of the World as We Know It (and I Feel Fine)." The band's major breakthrough came in 1988 when they signed a multimillion dollar contract with Warner Bros. Records that allowed them total artistic freedom. *Green* was released later that year and went double platinum. Songs such as "Stand," "Pop Song 89" and "Orange Crush" would become standards on pop radio stations and help propel R.E.M. into their first stadium shows in the U.S. The album's success also pushed the band into a massive international tour that physically drained the group. When the tour ended in 1989 the members took an extended break.

The group reunited and released *Out of Time* in 1991, which would prove to be another commercial success. Still drained from their previous tour, they decided not to tour again but instead concentrated on working in the studio. Even without a tour, *Out of Time* would be their biggest selling album and would produce their biggest single, "Losing My Religion," which became a mainstay on Top-40 radio stations. While the album still retained R.E.M.'s lyrical style, it was clear and easy to understand and catchy in a pop style. It also featured a duet with fellow Athens musician Kate Pierson of the B-52's on "Shiny Happy People."

The critically acclaimed *Automatic for the People* was released in 1992. A subdued, introspective album that at times was almost acoustic in sound, *Automatic for the People* also went quadruple platinum, aided largely by the single "Man on the Moon," a tribute to late comic Andy Kaufman. The album also featured string arrangements by former Led Zeppelin bassist John Paul Jones, which was a continuation of the band's expanded sound begun on *Out of Time*.

The *Monster* Tour. Their long-promised rock album came with the release of *Monster* (1994), which Stipe was said to have described as punk music, only loud. An album that typified many things that R.E.M. had come to represent, it also featured prominent distortion and a return in part to Stipe's mumbled singing and quirky pop-culture references. "What's the Frequency, Kenneth?" referred to an attack on news anchorman Dan Rather in 1986, while the song "Let Me In" was a plea to Nirvana's late Kurt Cobain that came too late. Lyrically smarter than the majority of the rock and pop albums released that year, *Monster* nonetheless seemed to copy the European discotheque sound that was becoming popular in rock music. Having been predated by U2's *Achtung Baby* and *Zooropa* albums several years earlier, *Monster* at times did not seem as original as other R.E.M. works. The *Monster* tour, the band's first in six years, became as famous for its problems as the songs it was supporting. During the tour, Stipe needed an emergency hernia operation, Mills had an intestinal tumor removed, and Berry suffered a brain aneurysm onstage (he recovered and resumed touring two months later).

New Adventures. In spite of all this, the group recorded a new album during the tour and released it in 1996. *New Adventures in Hi-Fi* came just after the band had re-signed their contract with Warner Bros. for a record eighty million dollars. Somewhat ironically, the album did not sell well, even though it received good reviews. The album would also begin a new phase in the band's career; shortly after it was released, drummer Berry announced that he was retiring from the band. The remaining members decided to continue, with a new album scheduled to be released in 1998.

R.E.M. always set standards and paved the way for their fellow musicians while at the same time adhering to their inner visions without regard to commercial success or failure. Despite the changes in their musical style over the years, it is this adaptability and willingness to follow their instincts that allowed them to survive and thrive while so many other bands fell by the wayside. —*Kelly Rothenberg*

SELECT DISCOGRAPHY

■ ALBUMS

Murmur, 1983
Document, 1987
Green, 1988
Out of Time, 1991
Automatic for the People, 1992
Monster, 1994
Up, 1998

SELECT AWARDS

Grammy Awards for Best Alternative Music Album for *Out of Time*; for Best Pop Performance by a Duo or Group with Vocal and Best Music Video, Short Form, for "Losing My Religion," 1991

SEE ALSO: B-52's, The; Indigo Girls, The.

REO Speedwagon

ORIGINAL MEMBERS: Gary Richrath (b. 1949), Neal Doughty (b. 1946), Alan Gratzer (b. 1948), Terry Luttrell, Greg Philbin

BEST-KNOWN LINEUP: Gary Richrath, Kevin Cronin (b. 1951), Neal Doughty, Alan Gratzer, Bruce Hall (b. 1953)

OTHER MEMBERS: Dave Amato (b. 1953), Bryan Hitt (b. 1954), Michael Murphy

FIRST ALBUM RELEASE: *REO Speedwagon*, 1971

MUSICAL STYLES: Rock and roll, pop

Formed in a dormitory room at the University of Illinois in Champaign, REO Speedwagon began as a hard-rocking party band but ultimately came to be the epitome of the "power-ballad" band in the late 1970's and early 1980's. Their middle-of-the-road style never challenged, nor was it meant to be more than it was: decent songwriting complemented by good hooks and catchy melodies.

Campus Bar Band. Drummer Alan Gratzer and keyboardist Neal Doughty were college roommates when they formed a band in 1967. The two got the name REO Speedwagon from an early type of fire engine designed by Ransom E. Olds. Playing mostly cover songs, the band went through changes before arriving at the lineup of Greg Philbin (bass), Terry Luttrell (vocals), and Gary Richrath (guitar).

Richrath was key to moving the band in the direction of original music. Not only was he an excellent guitarist, but he also had good songwriting skills. In 1971, the group recorded their first album, *REO Speedwagon*. Although they did not gain national fame with this album, it received good reviews and was a solid effort.

Soon after, Luttrell left the band and was replaced by Kevin Cronin, whom Richrath found through a musician's referral service in Chicago. A mediocre vocalist with limited songwriting talent, Cronin left after the second album, *REO TWO* (1972), to pursue a solo career. He was replaced by Mike Murphy, and REO recorded their first gold-selling album, *Ridin' the Storm Out* (1973). The title track was a modest hit.

National Prominence. In 1976 Murphy left and Cronin rejoined, his songwriting skills having matured. Shortly afterward, the more aggressive Bruce Hall replaced Philbin on bass. The band's live shows improved greatly, and their fun, rocking style was captured on their 1977 live album, *You Get What You Play For.* It went platinum, and Cronin's version of "Ridin' the Storm Out" became a hit again. Their hard work at building a grassroots fan base was beginning to pay off. It helped that Irving Azolf, who later managed the Eagles and Steely Dan, was their manager and made sure they opened for such acts as Bob Seger, Kansas, and Ted Nugent—all popular midwestern acts with similar appeal.

You Can Tune a Piano, but You Can't Tuna Fish (1978) also went platinum and included more of Cronin's power-ballad songwriting. Their next album, *Hi Infidelity,* was released in 1980 and was their best-selling album. It included four Top-100 hits, including "Keep On Lovin' You," which went to number 1, and "Take It on the Run," which went to number 2.

As their popularity rose, their critical success waned. An article in *Rolling Stone* magazine during this time mockingly suggested that REO Speedwagon was so faceless they could trade individual members with such other power-pop acts as Styx, Kansas, and Foreigner, and no one would notice the difference.

Album Highs and Lows. Their next album, *Good Trouble,* released in 1982, was one of their least successful. Disappointed in themselves, they rented a warehouse in Los Angeles for six months to provide a creative, laid-back environment in which to write and record. It worked, because 1984's *Wheels Are Turnin'* proved to be almost as successful as *Hi Infidelity* and featured another number 1 hit in "Can't Fight This Feeling."

The next two albums, *Life as We Know It* (1987) and *The Earth, a Small Man, His Dog and a Chicken* (1990), were both commercial disappointments. Richrath's departure, brought about by continuous feuds with Cronin, no doubt contributed to the band's downfall (he was replaced by Dave Amato, former lead guitarist for Ted Nugent).

New Incarnation. The band produced a new album in 1995 called *Building the Bridge.* In the liner notes of the album, they said that they were "building a bridge from the old REO to the new REO." Never short on ego, on their Website they also contended that the album's title track inspired President Bill Clinton to use the "building a bridge" theme as part of his 1996 reelection campaign, a dubious claim at best. (Cronin did perform the song at some benefits during that election, however.) Based in Los Angeles in the late 1990's, the band would continue to perform live and assemble greatest-hits collections of their older material. —*Kevin M. Mitchell*

For the Record

REO Speedwagon has the distinction of having been the first band to perform a live concert on MTV. On August 8, 1981, the recently begun cable channel broadcast the band's concert from Denver, Colorado.

SELECT DISCOGRAPHY

■ ALBUMS

REO Speedwagon, 1971
Ridin' the Storm Out, 1973
You Get What You Play For, 1977
You Can Tune a Piano, but You Can't Tuna Fish, 1979
Hi Infidelity, 1980
Wheels Are Turnin', 1984

SEE ALSO: Foreigner; Kansas; Nugent, Ted; Styx.

Trent Reznor. *See* **Nine Inch Nails**

Charlie Rich

BORN: Colt, Arkansas; December 14, 1932
DIED: Hammond, Louisiana; July 25, 1995
FIRST SINGLE RELEASE: "Whirlwind"/"Philadelphia Baby," 1958
MUSICAL STYLES: Country, blues, soul, rhythm and blues, rockabilly, pop

Charlie Rich became a superstar only in the 1970's, after years of experimenting with a wide variety of styles. He was one of the most versatile and talented musicians of his generation.

The Arkansas Delta. Rich grew up in eastern Arkansas in the Delta region. His family operated a farm around Colt, Arkansas, and Rich early on picked up the blues from C. J. Allen, a black sharecropper on his family farm. Allen was a piano player and inspired Rich to make that instrument his own. His family sang gospel music, another source of Rich's inspiration. He also loved jazz and further developed his singing and piano playing from this source. While attending college, he played saxophone in a band.

After military service, he started to play in local clubs in the Memphis, Tennessee, area, married, and tried farming. His wife, Margaret, encouraged him to try music as a full-time profession. She took a tape of his music to Bill Justis, a new producer at Sun Records, in 1957. Justis knew jazz and sensed that Rich had the makings of a commercial performer. He and label head Sam Phillips decided to hire him as a session pianist and songwriter as well as a potential solo recording artist.

Rich worked hard at Sun, writing songs for Johnny Cash, Jerry Lee Lewis, and others. He played piano on many recordings before having his own records released. Only one really succeeded in making the charts: "Lonely Weekends" (his own song) in 1960. At Sun he performed all kinds of roots music: blues, rhythm and blues, jazz stylings, country. He seemed too talented to fit into any one style. Thereafter, he drifted from one record label to another, scoring only one pop hit in 1965 with "Mohair Sam." Songs such as his own "Who Will the Next Fool Be" (which became a country standard), "Sittin' and Thinkin'," "Stay," "Don't Put No Headstone on My Grave," and his wife's "Life's Little Ups and Downs" remain notable achievements.

Superstar in the 1970's. At Epic Records in the 1970's, Rich worked with Billy Sherrill, an old friend from his Sun days who understood his many sides better than most producers, and who had developed in Nashville a lush style of record making that stressed strings and choruses. This style, when applied to Rich's music, made him a superstar in the mid-1970's with crossover songs that started out as country and then became pop hits. Songs such as "Behind Closed Doors" and "The Most Beautiful Girl" (a number 1 pop hit) made him a national star. Yet, he was, and had always been, a shy and reluctant performer. He valued his family life over the allure of pop stardom. His musical tastes were too varied for pigeonholing, and his stylings were often too moody and brooding for sustained mass success. He disliked touring, and in the 1980's he retired for a decade. Returning in 1992 with a masterful album, *Pictures and Paintings*, he was finally able to work through his many styles with a small combo.

"Feel Like Going Home." In many of Rich's songs the theme is a longing to return home to family or a loved one. He often sang of failed love and regrets, about relationships spoiled or beyond easy recapture. He could croon or shout with a wide ranging and expressive voice capable of soaring or putting across the most subtle emotions in intimate tones, akin to a white soul singer. Phillips believed that with the exception of Elvis Presley, Rich had the most potential of the Sun artists of his era. Perhaps the core of his music resided in the words of his own song "Feel Like Going Home," whose finest version perhaps is the one he recorded on his last album in 1992, with a choir. There he paints a sad portrait of perceived failure in the larger world and the desire to go back to peace at home, enhanced by the call-and-response singing of the choir. The song became a spiritual of great and aching power, a testimony to the muted greatness of its singer-songwriter.

—Frederick E. Danker

SELECT DISCOGRAPHY

■ SINGLES

"Lonely Weekends," 1960
"Mohair Sam," 1965
"Behind Closed Doors," 1973
"The Most Beautiful Girl," 1973

■ ALBUMS

Set Me Free, 1968
Behind Closed Doors, 1973
The Silver Fox, 1974
Pictures and Paintings, 1992
Feel Like Going Home: The Essential Charlie Rich, 1997 (compilation)

SELECT AWARDS

Country Music Association Single of the Year for "Behind Closed Doors," Album of the Year for *Behind Closed Doors*, and Male Vocalist of the Year Awards, 1973

Country Music Association Album of the Year for *A Very Special Love Song* and Entertainer of the Year Awards, 1974

Grammy Award for Best Country Vocal Performance, Male, for "Behind Closed Doors," 1974

SEE ALSO: Cash, Johnny; Lewis, Jerry Lee; Wynette, Tammy.

Lionel Richie

BORN: Tuskegee, Alabama; June 20, 1949
FIRST ALBUM RELEASE: *Lionel Richie*, 1982
MUSICAL STYLES: Funk, pop

The velvet-voiced singer-songwriter Lionel Richie scored a number of hits in the 1980's, mainly with ballads such as "Say You, Say Me" and "Hello." He began as a saxophonist and later became the lead singer of the popular funk band the Commodores, but his greatest success came as a solo artist. Indeed, only Michael Jackson, with whom Richie wrote the memorable song "We Are the World," was a bigger pop-music figure during the first half of the 1980's.

Tuskegee Roots. Lionel Brockman Richie, Jr., grew up in Tuskegee, Alabama, home to the famed Tuskegee Institute. Richie enjoyed a double connection with the college through his paternal grandparents: His grandfather worked in the business office, and his grandmother taught piano at the school. The latter gave the young Richie his first lessons on the instrument. As a boy, Richie also sang in his church choir and played saxophone in the school band. It was only natural for Richie to go on to study at the Tuskegee Institute after graduation from high school. In 1967, the young economics major met fellow student and guitarist Thomas McClary in a registration line.

Richie and McClary, along with Milan Williams, formed the Commodores. In 1969, the group signed to Atlantic Records and recorded a number of singles that did not go anywhere. Later in 1969, the Commodores were hired to open for the Jackson 5's world tour. Three years later, at the end of the tour, the Commodores signed a contract with Motown Records as recording artists in

Lionel Richie (Paul Natkin)

their own right. The Commodores went on to reign as Motown's most successful male group of the 1970's, but it took them until 1975 to score their first number 1 hit, "Slippery When Wet," from their second album, *Caught in the Act* (1975). The Commodores alternated between being soulful balladeers and a funk band. As funk masters, the band's biggest hit was 1977's "Brick House," but their biggest single of all came with Richie's ballad "Three Times a Lady" (1979).

The early 1980's was a time of increasing friction between Richie and the rest of the Commodores. While still ostensibly a member of the Commodores, Richie released the 1982 hit single "Truly," which earned him a Grammy Award for Best Pop Male Vocal Performance. The eponymous debut solo album from which "Truly" came sold close to four million copies and became one of Motown's best-selling albums ever.

Goodbye to the Commodores. Richie had obviously outgrown the Commodores, but it took the 1982 death of manager Benjamin Ashburn to precipitate his leave-taking. The group continued without Richie but only scored one more hit, 1985's "Nightshift." Meanwhile, Richie continued to mine gold from his solo efforts. His second album, *Can't Slow Down* (1983), yielded a number of Top-10 singles, including "All Night Long" and "Hello." Together, they helped make *Can't Slow Down* the biggest album in Motown's history.

During this period Richie topped both the singles and album charts, a feat only Michael Jackson had achieved before him. In August of 1984, Richie performed for millions of people tuned into the Los Angeles Olympic Games. Things only got better in 1985. Richie began the year by winning two more Grammies and cowriting the humanitarian anthem "We Are the World" with Jackson. His theme song for the movie *White Nights* (1985), "Say You, Say Me," quickly reached the top of the charts, making it the ninth straight number 1 hit Richie had written. The song also landed Richie Academy and Golden Globe Awards for best song.

In 1986, Richie released the album *Dancing on the Ceiling* and seemed poised to reach even higher levels of success. Richie, however, needed time away from the spotlight. According to him, "I walked offstage one night with the Oscar in my hand, 'We Are the World' playing on the radio, and me having sung at the Olympics with 1.5 billion people watching: Mr. Household Word. If there was ever a time to take a vacation, now was the time." Richie did not record another full-length album until 1996's *Louder than Words,* which met with moderate success. It seemed, however, as if the man who helped define music in the 1980's had not fully made the transition into the 1990's. This dedication to the style that had produced so many hits was appreciated by many of Richie's devoted fans. As Edna Gundersen wrote in *USA Today,* "Richie's voice is as smooth and luscious as aged brandy, not an unwelcome alternative to the carbonated pop of his younger peers."

—David Lee Fish

For the Record

Lionel Richie has made his most indelible mark in the pop music record books as a writer. He wrote hits that reached number 1 during nine consecutive years:

1978 "Three Times a Lady" (Commodores)
1979 "Still" (Commodores)
1980 "Lady" (Kenny Rogers)
1981 "Endless Love" (Richie and Diana Ross)
1982 "Truly" (Richie)
1983 "All Night Long" (Richie)
1984 "Hello" (Richie)
1985 "We Are the World" (all-star group)
1986 "Say You, Say Me" (Richie)

SELECT DISCOGRAPHY

■ SINGLES

"We Are the World," 1985
"Say You, Say Me," 1985

■ ALBUMS

Lionel Richie, 1982
Can't Slow Down, 1983

Dancing on the Ceiling, 1986
Louder than Words, 1996

SELECT AWARDS

Grammy Award for Best Pop Vocal Performance, Male, for "Truly," 1982

Grammy Awards for Album of the Year for *Can't Slow Down* and for Producer of the Year (Non-Classical; with James Anthony Carmichael), 1984

Academy Award for Best Song for "Say You, Say Me," 1985

Grammy Award for Song of the Year for "We Are the World," 1985 (with Michael Jackson)

Tuskegee Institute, awarded Honorary Doctorate 1985

SEE ALSO: Commodores, The.

The Righteous Brothers

ORIGINAL MEMBERS: Bill Medley (b. 1940), Bobby Hatfield (b. 1940)

FIRST SINGLE RELEASE: "Little Latin Lupe Lu"/"I'm So Lonely," 1963

MUSICAL STYLES: Soul, easy listening, rock and roll

Although they were not brothers in real life, the Righteous Brothers' voices blended so well when they sang together that it was easy to believe that they had spent their entire lives perfecting their act. One of the greatest duos in the history of rock and roll, Bill Medley and Bobby Hatfield, who came together in 1962, are identified with the style called blue-eyed soul, a term affectionately given to white artists who sang rhythm-and-blues and soul music in the 1960's.

If they had done nothing else but record "You've Lost That Lovin' Feelin'," their biggest hit, in early 1965, they still would have had a place in history. Broadcast Music Incorporated (BMI), which keeps track of radio airplay, has confirmed that this song is the most often played in radio history, having aired more than seven million times. (Although this tally includes other versions of the song, the Righteous Brothers' is undoubtedly the one most often heard.) However, the Righteous Brothers were anything but one-hit wonders. They recorded numerous times before and after releasing their best-known song.

The Beginnings. Medley, the baritone, first sang in church, although he grew up listening to the rhythm-and-blues and rock-and-roll records that were popular in Southern California in the 1950's. Ray Charles was a particular influence. Late in that decade, Medley joined a duo called the Romancers, and in the early 1960's he joined a group called the Paramours, who recorded two singles for the Chicago-based Smash label.

By 1962, the Paramours were recording for Moonglow Records, by which time Bobby Hatfield had joined the group. His high voice was not used to its best effect on the Paramours' recordings, but it is unmistakable on "Little Latin Lupe Lu," the first single credited to the Righteous Brothers, who got their name when someone who heard them singing commented on their sound, "That sure is righteous, brothers."

Hatfield had first been in a group called the Variations, who were rivals of the Paramours in the Orange County, California, rock-and-roll scene. A friend of both bands suggested combining members. They did, briefly, but then Medley and Hatfield decided to form a duo. While signed to Moonglow, the pair recorded both together and individually. As the Righteous Brothers, they reached the singles and albums charts but were not an instant success.

Phil Spector. In 1964, the Righteous Brothers were performing in San Francisco at the Cow Palace when Phil Spector heard them and was impressed by their dynamic stage show and the perfect mix of their voices and personalities. Spector was the biggest record producer in the United States at the time, having released a string of hits by such groups as the Ronettes, the Crystals, and Bob B. Soxx and the Blue Jeans. Spector had created a production technique called the wall of sound, which often utilized dozens of instruments and voices to create a larger-than-life sound, never before heard on rock-and-roll records. He also had his own record label, Philles, and believing the Righteous Brothers to be ideal for it, he signed them to a contract.

The Righteous Brothers (Archive Photos)

The duo's first record for Spector was "You've Lost That Lovin' Feelin'," written by the New York team of Barry Mann and Cynthia Weil. With its layers of voices, crescendos of orchestration, and the Brothers' disparate voices delivering an emotional reading of the lyrics, it went to number 1 in early 1965. It would remain one of the most popular songs in history, the first ever to be played on the air or otherwise performed more than seven million times. Nearly every time a poll is taken to determine the greatest songs of all time, this one invariably places high on the list.

"You've Lost That Lovin' Feelin'" was a hard act to follow, but the Righteous Brothers came close twice in 1965. "Just Once in My Life" took a very similar approach to "You've Lost That Lovin' Feelin'" and reached number 9, but "Unchained Melody" was completely different in that only one of the Brothers, Hatfield, sang on the record. The song had existed since about 1955, as the theme from the film *Unchained,* and had been recorded in many different styles, both balladic and uptempo. The Righteous Brothers stripped it to its basics, Hatfield's tenor riding the lyric slowly and steadily with a soft intensity, until it exploded. The single peaked at number 4 in 1965, but it would resurface decades later.

The duo followed with a song called "Hung on You," but the next major hit, "Ebb Tide," in late 1965, was another old song done as a Hatfield solo, and it fared nearly as well as the earlier one, rising to number 5 nationally. The two also appeared regularly on one of the most popular rock music television shows of the era, *Shindig.*

On Their Own. After their string of hits with Spector, the Righteous Brothers left Philles and signed with Verve Records, a jazz label that was trying to branch out into rock and roll. Their first single for the company, "(You're My) Soul and Inspiration," was very much like "You've Lost That Lovin' Feelin'" and followed its route to number 1, but it was the last time the Righteous Brothers would make it to the top. In 1967, Medley and Hatfield went their separate ways. Hatfield tried to keep the act going by hiring Jimmy Walker, but the public lost interest. Both he and Medley spent the next seven years working on separate projects.

In 1974, though, they decided to reunite. Hatfield and Medley recorded a song called "Rock and Roll Heaven," a tribute to several dead rock stars. The maudlin song managed to make it to number 3 and reestablished the Righteous Brothers. The regrouping only lasted a couple of years, however; when Medley's wife was murdered by an unknown assailant in 1976, he retired for several years.

One More Time. The Righteous Brothers came together again in the early 1980's, and continued to work together intermittently. Medley had one great success outside of the group, in 1987, when he teamed with singer Jennifer Warnes on the ballad "(I've Had) The Time of My Life," the theme from the film *Dirty Dancing*. The record went to number 1 and earned a Grammy Award, but there was no follow-up.

In 1990, another film brought the music of the Righteous Brothers to the fore when "Unchained Melody," their 1965 hit, was used prominently in the hit film *Ghost*. The twenty-five-year-old record went back up to number 13, and a new version recorded by the Brothers did well also, going to number 19. That was the last time the Righteous Brothers came close to reliving their past glories, but given their history, another return is not unquestionable. —*Jeff Tamarkin*

SELECT DISCOGRAPHY

■ SINGLES

"Little Latin Lupe Lu"/"I'm So Lonely," 1963
"You've Lost That Lovin' Feelin'"/"There's a Woman," 1964
"Just Once in My Life"/"The Blues," 1965
"Unchained Melody"/"Hung on You," 1965
"Ebb Tide"/"(I Love You) For Sentimental Reasons," 1965
"(You're My) Soul and Inspiration"/"B-Side Blues," 1966
"Rock and Roll Heaven"/"I Just Wanna Be Me," 1974

■ ALBUMS

Some Blue-Eyed Soul, 1964
Soul and Inspiration, 1966
Anthology (1962-1974), 1989 (compilation)

SELECT AWARDS

Grammy Award for Best Pop Performance by a Duo or Group with Vocal for "(I've Had) The Time of My Life," 1987 (Bill Medley with Jennifer Warnes)

SEE ALSO: Charles, Ray; Ronettes, The.

For the Record

The Righteous Brothers almost turned down "You've Lost That Lovin' Feelin'." When they first heard the song, they did not think it was right for them. They thought it would be perfect for another set of rock-and-roll brothers, the Everly Brothers.

LeAnn Rimes

BORN: Jackson, Mississippi; August 28, 1982
FIRST SINGLE RELEASE: "Blue," 1996
MUSICAL STYLES: Country, pop

With her debut single, "Blue," and an album of the same title in mid-1996, LeAnn Rimes created a sensation in country music and also became a crossover artist on the pop music charts. For a thirteen-year-old, this was remarkable. Some critics dismissed her as a novelty act who would fade quickly, but this was not the case. With four albums released in two years and several hit singles, she has regularly placed records on country, pop, and contemporary Christian music charts and has even had singles on dance listings. From her record debut, her voice, a basic alto with strength through several octaves, has been that of an woman able to handle adult songs.

The Singing Girl. For the first six years of her life, Rimes lived near Jackson, Mississippi, in the small town of Pearl. Both parents sang, and her father, Wilbur, played guitar. From age the of two, Rimes sang, taped by her father who sensed her potential. At five, she was winning local talent contests with her dancing and singing. To further her chances of performing as a singer, the family moved to Dallas in 1988. There her father became an even more determined advocate of his daughter's talent, procuring engagements on local country music shows.

Rimes had a broad taste in music. She liked show tunes, Judy Garland, and Barbra Streisand, but she began to listen to country singers Patsy Cline, Reba McEntire, and Wynonna. In particular, she liked Cline's rendition of the Willie Nelson song "Crazy." Cline had been a notable success in crossing over from country to pop music with her bluesy and subtle pop stylings in the early 1960's. She had demonstrated that a female country singer could adjust her style to reach a broader audience than that normally listening to country music. It was a matter of both material sung and backing instruments: less steel guitar and fiddle, more backup choruses and a touch of strings.

Young Professional. Rimes's parents believed their daughter had no limits to her talents. Her voice was stunning people even when she was eight and nine years old. Although she did not win an audition for the cast of the Broadway musical *Annie II* in 1988, she did win twice on the television show *Star Search* in 1990, singing a country ballad. Rimes had also become a local sensation in the Dallas area by singing "The Star-Spangled Banner" a cappella at rodeos and other events. She then gained unmeasurable experience on the Arlington, Texas, Johnnie High Revue from 1989 to 1995, performing on more than three hundred Saturday nights. It is this professionalism and experienced vocal style that she later brought to the Nashville music scene. Her father also wanted to further capitalize on and promote his prodigy by having her record an album.

LeAnn Rimes at the 1998 Academy of Country Music Awards (AP/Wide World Photos)

The album, *All That* (1994), on a local label, did well and revealed her already amazingly mature voice and eclectic choice of songs. She opens some songs a cappella with her clear voice and soars to a falsetto or drops for low rhythm-and-blues cadences. The album was a well-produced debut, suggesting the kind of mix of country and pop she would continue to feature in later albums.

Novelty to Superstar. In 1995, Nashville record executives heard her sing live, and soon a contract with Curb Records was sealed, and her first album and single were set for release in 1996. Her first release was a single of a song she had sung for some time and put on her first album, "Blue," a thirty-year-old song originally intended for Patsy Cline which she never recorded. This became Rimes's signature song. The mature theme about a lonely woman was sung in a rich voice backed with a heavy walking bass and steel guitar, with an echo of Cline's style. The public was astonished to learn that the singer was just thirteen.

The single was released in March and built great expectation for the album, which came out in July. Those expectations were more than met; Rimes proved to be more than a novelty. All the songs dealt with adult themes; some rocked, some soothed with the quiet singing Rimes could handle with equal aplomb. Another hit song came from the album, the powerful "One Way Ticket (Because I Can)." Its shouting vocal celebrates a woman's desire for freedom with a one-way railroad ticket. It was Rimes's first number 1 hit. The

For the Record

Bill Mack, a Fort Worth, Texas, disc jockey, wrote "Blue" around 1960 in a style fit for Patsy Cline, to whom he sent it. Cline died in a plane crash before she had a chance to record the song. When Mack heard Rimes singing Cline's hit "Crazy," he realized that she had a voice like Cline's, even as a teenager. He sent it to her, and she recorded it but added a little yodel and soon made it her signature, career-breaking song.

album debuted at the top of the country charts and went to number 3 on the pop charts, selling more than five million copies. Her two 1997 albums, *Unchained Melody/The Early Years* (a reissue of her first album with the addition of a soaring performance of "Unchained Melody") and *You Light Up My Life: Inspirational Songs* debuted at the top of both country and pop charts and would remain there for more than one year, also selling in the multiple millions. Both "You Light Up My Life" and "How Do I Live" were hits from the album, with the latter available in a dance club extended mix. Her fourth album, *Sittin' on Top of the World*, released in May, 1998, debuted near the top of both charts. Two singles from this album (released earlier) were hits, "Commitment" and "Looking Through Your Eyes." Again, Rimes extends her eclectic musical style with some big production numbers, but she also sings three heartfelt ballads that reveal her country and soulful style at its best: "These Arms of Mine," "When Am I Gonna Get over You," and "More than Anyone Deserves." —*Frederick E. Danker*

SELECT DISCOGRAPHY

■ ALBUMS

Blue, 1996

Unchained Melody/The Early Years, 1997

You Light Up My Life: Inspirational Songs, 1997

Sittin' on Top of the World, 1998

SELECT AWARDS

Grammy Awards for Best New Artist and Best Female Country Vocal Performance for "Blue," 1996

American Music Award for Best New Country Artist, 1996

SEE ALSO: Cline, Patsy; Judds, The / Wynonna Judd; McEntire, Reba; Streisand, Barbra.

Marty Robbins

BORN: Glendale, Arizona; September 26, 1925

DIED: Nashville, Tennessee; December 8, 1982

FIRST SINGLE RELEASE: "Love Me or Leave Me Alone," 1952

MUSICAL STYLES: Blues, country, pop, rockabilly

Marty Robbins wanted to be remembered as a good entertainer and, more important, a good person. He was more than good entertainer: Robbins was King of the Balladeers, one of country music's most successful superstars and the quintessential entertainer, whose music has delighted audiences everywhere. His achievements were legendary; winner of the first-ever Grammy Award for a country song ("El Paso," one of the "Top 100 Country Songs of All Time"), winner of the Artist of the Decade Award from the Academy of Country Music in 1969, a member of the Country Music Hall of Fame, the first Nashville superstar to appear in Las Vegas, and one of the first crossover artists. He was also an entrepreneur, a comedian, a film star, a lover of the Old West and cowboys such as Gene Autry, a stock-car racer, and a family man.

The Beginnings. The entertainer was born Martin David Robinson on September 26, 1925, in the desert near Glendale, Arizona. His family was large (he had nine siblings) and poor. He said he was in trouble often and only went to high school for three years, without ever passing a single subject. Robbins began writing songs when he was sixteen years old. At the age of seventeen, he quit school and joined the Navy. It was while in the Navy that he became serious about being a singer-songwriter. To help pass the time while on duty in the Solomon Islands, he played the guitar and wrote songs. He also fell in love with Hawaiian music.

Discharged in 1945, Robbins returned to Arizona and worked odd jobs. His first job in music was playing the guitar in a bar band. One day, he stopped at a roadside stand and heard a mediocre singer broadcasting over KTYL-radio in nearby Mesa, Arizona. Feeling he could do better, he dropped by the station the next day and sang the cowboy tune "Strawberry Roan." The station fired the other singer and hired Robbins.

Robbins's big break came in 1951, when national country music star Little Jimmy Dickens appeared on Robbins's radio show to publicize a concert. Dickens was impressed and recommended Robbins to Columbia Records, which signed him to a contract. Robbins's first recording, "Love Me or Leave Me Alone," was released in 1952. A second big break occurred the same year when songwriter-publisher Fred Rose of Acuff-Rose Publishing heard one of Robbins's early recordings and signed him to a contract. Robbins made his first tour in 1952. In 1953, he became a permanent member of the Grand Ole Opry.

From the start of his career, many of Robbins's recordings were of his own compositions. He valued simplicity and stories in his music. He was winning "favorite artist" polls by the mid-1950's. He was an early writer and singer of rockabilly songs, which mixed country music with rock and roll. Then-newcomer Elvis Presley served as Robbins's opening act. Robbins wrote a number of hit songs during this period, including "Singing the Blues." In 1957, he enjoyed his first big hit with his own composition "A White Sport Coat (and a Pink Carnation)." During the 1950's, he acted and sang in several motion pictures, westerns, and is often credited with keeping cowboy songs alive when no other performer would sing them. Robbins's first western hit was "The Hanging Tree," the theme for a 1958 film starring Gary Cooper and George C. Scott. In 1959, he released the album *Gunfighter Ballads and Trail Songs* and the legendary single "El Paso." The song won the first Grammy ever awarded to a country song. In 1961, Robbins helped make musical history during the recording of "Don't Worry," which was a number 1 hit for ten weeks. As musician Grady Martin played his six-string bass guitar solo, a pre-amplifier in the mixing board malfunctioned, distorting every note. Robbins and the band liked the sound so much they left it in the song. This sound would later be harnessed and became known as the "fuzz tone." Robbins enjoyed continuing success in the 1960's with songs such as "Devil Woman" in 1962 and "Ribbon of Darkness" in 1965.

Racing. Stock-car racing was a passion for Robbins. In 1966, he began racing stock cars for the National Association for Stock Car Auto Racing (NASCAR). He never won a race and was involved in three near-fatal crashes in the mid-1970's, but he continued racing anyway. Robbins said he came close to death so many times that he should have been dead. He raced for fun and to be with racing stars. In August of 1969, Robbins suffered his first of three heart attacks. He wrote "My Woman, My Woman, My Wife" in 1970 as a tribute to his wife, Marizona, who nursed him back to health. He won his second Grammy for the song in 1970.

Robbins the high-energy performer was a superb showman, even though he often said he was just a singer. At his concerts, he often wore brightly embroidered and sequined costumes he had designed himself. He played the guitar, piano, Dobro, harmonica, and a little Spanish guitar. His concerts were fast-paced and filled with clowning and the kind of silly jokes told by comedians Red Skelton and Flip Wilson. Robbins was even known to imitate fellow musicians Merle Haggard, Hank Snow, and Johnny Cash during his concerts.

Legacy of a Legend. Robbins claimed that he knew at least one thousand songs by heart. He loved to sign autographs and talk to his fans, who were often referred to as Marty's Army. His fans loved the fact that he frequently stayed on stage far longer than his contract required. Tributes to Robbins continued even after his death. In 1983, CBS Records and NASCAR paid tribute to him with the running of a special race, the Marty Robbins 420 in Nashville. In 1986, a television special, *Marty Robbins—Super Legend*, was produced and syndicated around the United States.

Robbins is remembered as a good entertainer and one of country music's superstars. He had eighteen number 1 hits, only two of which were country. His talent and devotion won acceptance for country music among people of all musical tastes. He was one of the last of the cowboy singers and loved to sing about the Old West. Perhaps the best tribute of all is that his songs are still played, sung, and appreciated. Marty Robbins would have liked the fact that fans are still buying and playing his music. *—Fred Buchstein*

SELECT DISCOGRAPHY

■ SINGLES

"Love Me or Leave Me Alone," 1952
"A White Sport Coat (and a Pink Carnation)," 1957
"El Paso," 1959
"Devil Woman," 1962
"Ruby Ann," 1962
"Ribbon of Darkness," 1965
"My Woman, My Woman, My Wife," 1970
"El Paso City," 1976

■ ALBUMS

Gunfighter Ballads and Trail Songs, 1959

SELECT AWARDS

Grand Ole Opry, became member 1953
Grammy Award for Best Country and Western Performance for "El Paso," 1960
Grammy Award for Best Country Song for "My Woman, My Woman, My Wife," 1971
Rookie of the Southern 500 Award, 1972
Nashville Songwriters Hall of Fame, inducted 1975
Country Music Hall of Fame, inducted 1982

For the Record

The only major music award that Marty Robbins did not win was the Entertainer of the Year Award from the Country Music Association.

SEE ALSO: Cash, Johnny; Haggard, Merle; Presley, Elvis.

Smokey Robinson

BORN: Detroit, Michigan; February 19, 1940
FIRST ALBUM RELEASE: *Hi . . . We're the Miracles*, 1961
FIRST SOLO ALBUM RELEASE: *Smokey*, 1973
MUSICAL STYLES: Rhythm and blues, soul, pop

In January, 1958, William "Smokey" Robinson, a college freshman, yearned to hear his first record played on the radio. His wish came true when a disc jockey in Detroit, Michigan, Robinson's hometown, played "Got a Job." Smokey Robinson went on to attain legendary status as the lead singer of the Miracles, one of the twentieth century's most successful pop and rhythm-and-blues groups, as a gifted, prolific writer of hit songs for the Miracles and other well-known entertainers, and as an extraordinary solo recording artist.

From Chimes to Miracles. Robinson's phenomenal musical career began in 1954. While in high school, he formed a singing group called the Five Chimes. In addition to Robinson, the group included Warren "Pete" Moore, Clarence Dawson, James Grice, and Donald Wicker. When Wicker and Dawson left the group, they were replaced by Ronnie White and Emerson "Sonny" Rodgers. The group won a local television talent contest before Grice left, and Bobby Rodgers replaced him. The group then changed its name to the Matadors. When Sonny Rodgers joined the Army, his sister Claudette, a member of the girl group the Matadorettes, joined. Robinson sang lead, Bobby Rodgers sang tenor, White sang baritone, and Moore sang bass. In 1957, the group auditioned for the manager of famed rhythm-and-blues singer Jackie Wilson. Although he was unimpressed with the Matadors, songwriter and record producer Berry Gordy recognized their talent and became the group's manager. They were the second act signed to Gordy's management/production company.

The group's first record was "Got a Job," a song

written by Robinson as an answer to the Silhouettes' "Get a Job." Public reaction to the Matadors' song was encouraging, yet Gordy was not satisfied with the group's name. Names were placed in a hat, and the one selected was Miracles, Robinson's choice. Other significant changes were made. Marv Tarplin, the talented former guitarist for the Primettes (who would later become the Supremes) began an association with the Miracles that continued into Robinson's years as a solo artist. In 1959 Robinson and Claudette were married. That same year, "Bad Girl," the Miracles' first national hit, was recorded. The success of "Bad Girl," along with Robinson's urging, convinced Gordy to form his own record company.

Motown: Hitsville U.S.A. Gordy envisioned Motown, his record company, as "the sound of young America." His goals were to use the Motown sound to abolish barriers between black and white popular music and to make good music that people of all races would enjoy. Barrett Strong's song "Money (That's What I Want)" and the Miracles' "Shop Around" marked the establishment and distribution of Gordy's national label. "Shop Around," written by Robinson in half an hour, was the first million seller for the Miracles. The record's B-side, "Who's Loving You," was the first of a number of two-sided hits for the Miracles (decades later it was recorded by Terence Trent D'Arby and En Vogue). "Shop Around" elevated the Miracles to the status of Motown's first "star" group. The group was now known nationwide for its exquisite harmony and Robinson's distinctive lead vocals.

Although Robinson was kept busy writing new songs, recording, and performing with the Miracles, he played an invaluable role in promoting other Motown acts. Robinson wrote hit records for Mary Wells, including "The One Who Really Loves You," "You Beat Me to the Punch," "Two Lovers," and "My Guy"; the Marvelettes, including "Don't Mess with Bill"; The Four Tops, including "Still Water (Love)"; and Marvin Gaye, including "I'll Be Doggone" and "Ain't That Peculiar." Robinson also composed songs recorded by Martha and the Vandellas, the Isley Brothers, the Contours, and the Supremes. However, his most successful collaboration was with the Temptations, who recorded such hits as "The Way You Do the Things You Do" and "My Girl." In 1965, the Temptations recorded an album of songs composed by Robinson called *The Temptations Sing Smokey*. In all, Robinson wrote more than four thousand songs. During the 1960's and 1970's, Motown artists dominated the music industry. The Miracles recorded hit after hit, including "You've Really Got a Hold on Me," "Ooo Baby Baby," and "The Tracks of My Tears." These songs, along with songs Robinson wrote for other artists, are now regarded as pop and rhythm-and-blues classics.

In 1965 Claudette stopped touring with the Miracles in order to start a family but continued recording with them. With the release of the *Going to a Go-Go* album the same year, the group changed its name to Smokey Robinson and the Miracles in order to capitalize on Robinson's increasing popularity. "The Tears of a Clown," a song Robin-

Smokey Robinson in 1986 (Paul Natkin)

son wrote in 1967, became the group's biggest hit in 1970. In 1972, Robinson made his last public appearance with the group at the Carter Barron Amphitheater in Washington, D.C. He was replaced by Billy Griffin, and the Miracles' new hits included "Do It Baby" and "Love Machine." Another transition occurred in 1986 when Robinson and Claudette divorced. In the early 1990's, the Miracles still toured occasionally.

A Stellar Solo Career. Robinson's 1973 debut solo album, *Smokey*, included "Sweet Harmony," the song he wrote and dedicated to the Miracles, and "Baby Come Close," his first solo single and first solo hit. One year later, Robinson released the immensely popular *Quiet Storm*, a landmark album that led to an innovation in radio programming. Influenced by Robinson's melodious falsetto and tenor as well as his captivating lyrics, radio stations began airing programs of romantic rhythm-and-blues songs. Such programming remained a radio favorite for more than twenty-five years. Robinson's biggest hit of the 1970's was "Cruisin.'" In the 1980's, Robinson's hit records included "Let Me Be the Clock," "Tell Me Tomorrow," "Ebony Eyes" (a duet with Rick James), "Being with You," "Just to See Her," "One Heartbeat," and "We've Saved the Best for Last" (with Kenny G playing soprano sax).

In 1983 Robinson and the Miracles, along with other Motown entertainers, appeared on the Emmy-winning television special, "Twenty-Five Years of Motown." In 1989 his candid autobiography *Smokey: Inside My Life*, highlighting the successes and pitfalls of his musical career, was published. Robinson began the 1990's with the hit solo "Everything You Touch." In 1998 he led a cast of Motown performers in Super Bowl XXXII's halftime show, which celebrated the fortieth anniversary of Motown.

Robinson has been hailed by fellow pop legend Bob Dylan as "America's greatest living poet" and identified by others as the "poet laureate of soul music." Robinson has recorded approximately twenty-four albums with the Miracles and more than seventeen albums as a solo artist. His enduring lyrics and voice continue to appeal to legions of fans of various generations. —*Linda M. Carter*

SELECT DISCOGRAPHY

■ SINGLES

The Miracles

"Bad Girl," 1959
"Shop Around," 1960
"You've Really Got a Hold on Me," 1962
"Mickey's Monkey," 1963
"Ooo Baby Baby," 1965
"The Tracks of My Tears," 1965
"My Girl Has Gone," 1965
"Going to a Go-Go," 1965
"The Love I Saw in You Was Just a Mirage," 1966
"More Love," 1967
"I Second That Emotion," 1967
"The Tears of a Clown," 1970

Smokey Robinson solo

"Cruisin,'" 1979
"Being with You," 1981
"Just to See Her," 1987
"One Heartbeat," 1987

SELECT AWARDS

Rock and Roll Hall of Fame, inducted 1987
Songwriters Hall of Fame, inducted 1987
Grammy Award for Best R&B Vocal Performance, Male, for "Just to See Her," 1987
Grammy Legend Award, 1990
Motor City Music Lifetime Achievement Award, 1992

SEE ALSO: Four Tops, The; Gaye, Marvin; Supremes, The; Temptations, The.

Jimmie Rodgers

BORN: near Meridian, Mississippi; September 8, 1897
DIED: New York, New York; May 26, 1933
FIRST SINGLE RELEASE: "The Soldier's Sweetheart"/"Sleep, Baby Sleep," 1927
MUSICAL STYLES: Traditional country, blues

Jimmie Rodgers is generally considered by most scholars and musicians to be the father of American country music. Though obviously a bit of an overstatement, there is little doubt that he was the most influential country artist of his time, and he changed forever the way country music would be performed, recorded, and marketed. Known by many nicknames—"the Singing Brakeman," "the Blue Yodeler," and "Jimmie the Kid," among others—he was country music's first superstar, often selling five or ten times the amount of records sold by his closest competitors. Though mass-marketing techniques and modern advertising were still in their infancy—and the star himself preferred small venues to large concert halls—he reached national and international fame with his output of 110 songs. In 1933, when tuberculosis took his life at the age of thirty-five, Rodgers was loved by millions of Americans, especially those in the South and the Southwest.

The Early Years. James Charles Rodgers was born in rural Pine Springs near Meridian, Mississippi, in 1897. His father (with whom Rodgers had a very close relationship, and who was the source of some of his songs) was a railroad worker, a job that Rodgers himself would take up later in his teens. His mother died when he was only six years old. Rodgers began performing publicly after winning a talent contest when he was twelve, singing "Bill Bailey" and "Steamboat Bill." By 1920, the thirty dollars per week he earned as a brakeman on the New Orleans & Northeastern Railroad allowed Rodgers to follow his favorite pursuits: "girlfriends, sporty clothes, phonograph records, and [music] theater tickets more or less in that order," as one biographer once said. After a brief first marriage after World War I lasting only a few months, he married his second wife, Carrie Williamson of Meridian, Mississippi, but immediately contracted pneumonia. Respiratory problems would plague him for the rest of his life. Knowing he would soon have to give up his railroad job, in the early 1920's he began to take his amateur music career more seriously, playing in dance bands, blackface minstrel shows, and Hawaiian roadshows, or singing southern folk and popular songs on local radio programs.

Jimmie Rodgers (Archive Photos/Frank Driggs Collection)

Between the World Wars. Before World War I, the popular music industry in the United States was largely an urban affair, dominated by live vaudeville shows and various household entertainments: sheet music, phonograph records, or parlor musical instruments. Radio and the automobile changed this, bringing the latest city stars and songs out to the farms, as well as giving urban dwellers a nostalgia for simpler rural times and tunes. In the 1920's there was still no such thing as a clearly defined country music, at least as it is known today. In the South, rural white mountain folk songs and black Delta blues intermingled with the latest Tin Pan Alley novelty hits from the cities in the North.

Ralph Peer, an independent record producer for the Victor Talking Machine Company from New York, discovered there was a national audience for authentic old-time southern "hillbilly" music and made one of the earliest country music recordings of Fiddlin' John Carson in 1923. In 1927 he visited the Appalachian town of Bristol, Tennessee, on a field trip, in search of local talent on the Tennessee-Virginia border. In what has often been described as the most seminal event in country music history, he recorded six songs by the Carter Family and two by a bandleader without a band, the twenty-nine-year-old Jimmie Rodgers (his backup singers decided to try and audition without him). Both these artists would go on to national stardom and change the direction of country music.

Recording. Rodgers's two songs, an old Spanish-American war ballad (adapted for the first World War) called "The Soldier's Sweetheart" and "Sleep, Baby, Sleep," a lullaby recorded three years earlier by another fledgling country artist, Riley Puckett, did not make Rodgers into an overnight success. Though they sold moderately well considering the little publicity given for the first release of an unknown singer, Peer's new electric recording process, which was a vast improvement over existing technology at the time, probably contributed to sales as well. Undaunted and determined, and at his own expense, Rodgers drove his old car to New York for several more sessions with Peer. Rodgers's first hit record and trademark tune, "Blue Yodel No. 1 (T for Texas)," was recorded at this time, even though Peer was actually unimpressed and only included it to finish the session. Fame and fortune followed, and Peer went on to record, publish, and manage Rodgers until his death in 1933.

Stardom and Musical Style. Rodgers's career as a major entertainer only lasted some six years, but in that time his unique style of the "blue yodel" made an immediate impact on country music. He was one of the most versatile singers in American music history, covering popular vaudeville numbers, cowboy laments, rustic mountain ballads, Mississippi blues, and songs of the rail. In 1929 Rodgers made what was probably the first country music video, shooting the *Singing Brakeman*, a ten-minute short film (and the first Hollywood film to feature a country artist). When the Depression hit, Rodgers played in a series of Red Cross relief concerts for drought-stricken southern farmers with the famous humorist Will Rogers, anticipating some of the Farm Aid extravaganzas made by country singers in the 1980's.

Though a well-known star in the 1930's, Rodgers' health and the Depression made it increasingly difficult for him to find work. It was obvious to all that tuberculosis was taking its toll, and Rodgers knew his days were numbered. Against his doctor's advice, he traveled from Texas to New York for a final recording session with Peer in order to provide money for his family after his death. The day after finishing a marathon week-long session of thirteen songs, Rodgers passed away due to a severe hemorrhage.

The Jimmie Rodgers Legacy. It is impossible to overestimate the influence of Jimmie Rodgers's work on today's country artists. Most of the famous first generation of country stars, including Gene Autry, Bill Monroe, Hank Snow, and Bob Wills, either directly imitated his vocal style (at least for a while) or covered his songs. Ernest Tubb even played Rodgers's guitar, which he received from his widow when he visited her in 1936. Lefty Frizzell is said to have learned to sing by sticking his head in a Victrola speaker as Rogers's songs were playing. Merle Haggard's 1969 tribute album was only the most obvious tip of a very deep iceberg; hardly a year goes by without some major country or popular artist reinterpreting a Rodgers tune.

More important, however, Jimmie Rodgers did more than anyone else in his day to commercialize

For the Record

"In the days when a steak cost forty cents and a phonograph record cost seventy-five cents, southerners, it would appear, were prepared to sacrifice a great deal to purchase the latest Rodgers recording."

—authors Chris Comber and Mike Paris on Rodgers's popularity at the height of the Depression

§

"Dolly Parton gets $350,000 a week in Las Vegas; even when adjusted for inflation, that's more than Jimmie Rodgers earned in a lifetime."

—Rodgers biographer Nolan Porterfield

country music, and he helped bring it nationwide attention. The star-centered orientation of urban northern popular music became applied to hillbilly music largely through the work and lifestyle of Rodgers. (Rodgers never played the country hick, hayseed, or buffoon; though he sometimes posed for publicity stills in a cowboy or railroad engineer's outfit, he performed in a suit, bow tie, and straw hat.) Rodgers, in short, took country music out of its regional and rural roots and brought it to national prominence, combining the various southern musical styles with northern popular music, touching them with his own unique techniques and expressions. Before Rodgers arrived, country music was an undefined and unspecified genre. Before Rodgers, there was little in country music to imitate; after him, it became hard for modern country musicians not to imitate him, at least in some way. His Country Music Hall of Fame plaque probably best describes the significance of this small, scrawny Texas yodeler on one of America's most important musical styles: "Jimmie Rodgers's name stands foremost in the country music field as 'The man who started it all.'" —*James Stanlaw*

SELECT DISCOGRAPHY

■ ALBUMS

First Sessions, 1927-1928, 1991
The Early Years, 1928-29, 1991
America's Blue Yodeler, 1930-31, 1991
Last Sessions, 1933, 1991
Jimmie Rodgers, 1991
Train Whistle Blues, 1992
Jimmie Rodgers: The Singing Brakeman, 1994
American Legends #16: Jimmie Rodgers, 1996
The Essential Jimmie Rodgers, 1997

SELECT AWARDS

Country Music Hall of Fame, inducted 1961
Nashville Songwriters Hall of Fame, inducted 1970
Rock and Roll Hall of Fame, inducted 1986

SEE ALSO: Frizzell, Lefty; Haggard, Merle; Monroe, Bill, and the Blue Grass Boys; Tubb, Ernest; Williams, Hank; Wills, Bob, and His Texas Playboys.

Kenny Rogers

BORN: Houston, Texas; August 21, 1938
FIRST ALBUM RELEASE: *New Kick!* 1966
FIRST SOLO SINGLE RELEASE: "Love Lifted Me," 1976
MUSICAL STYLES: Country, pop, country rock, folk

Kenny Rogers grew up with little money and became the first member of his family to graduate from high school. He sang with a high school band, the Scholars, and joined a jazz group when he attended the University of Houston. In 1966, Rogers joined the New Christy Minstrels and appeared on their 1966 album, *New Kick!*. Later in 1967, Rogers joined the First Edition, which was made up of former members of the New Christy Minstrels, and he sang lead vocals on their first major hit, "Just Dropped In" (1968).

In 1969, Rogers and the First Edition had two country hits with "Ruby, Don't Take Your Love to Town" and "Reuben James," followed by a rock-and-roll hit, "Something's Burning." From 1971 to 1973, Rogers and the First Edition had a syndicated television show, *Rollin' on the River*, and they released two successful albums, *Kenny Rogers and the First Edition's Greatest Hits* (1971) and *The Ballad of Calico* (1972).

Going Country. After the First Edition broke up in 1974, Rogers had a string of top country solo hits, including "Lucille" (1977), "The Gambler" (1978), "Coward of the County" (1979), "I Don't Need You" (1982), "Through the Years" (1982), and "Love Will Turn You Around" (1982). Rogers's first number 1 hit was "Lady" (1982), and he had numerous duet hits, including "Every

For the Record

One day in 1978 Rogers ran into singer Dottie West in a recording studio in Nashville. On the spur of the moment, they recorded a duet, "Every Time Two Fools Collide," which became a top country hit.

Time Two Fools Collide" (1978) with Dottie West, "Don't Fall in Love with a Dreamer" (1980) with Kim Carnes, "We've Got Tonight" (1983) with Sheena Easton, and "Islands in the Stream" (1983) with Dolly Parton. "Islands in the Stream" remains the best-selling country single of all time, logging more than four million single sales.

Although Rogers's popularity waned somewhat in the mid-1980's, he continued to score big hits. He had number 1 hits in "Crazy" (1984), "Morning Desire" (1985), and "Tomb of the Unknown Love" (1986), as well as two number 2 hits with "Twenty Years Ago" (1986) and "I Prefer the Moonlight" (1987). His albums *Love Will Turn You Around* (1982) and *We've Got Tonight* (1983) were certified gold, and *Eyes That See in the Dark* (1983), *Twenty Greatest Hits* (1983), and *What About Me?* (1984) were all certified platinum.

Rogers won a Grammy Award for Best Country Male Vocal Performance for "Lucille" in 1977, followed by a Grammy Award for Best Country Male Vocal Performance for "The Gambler" in 1979. As one of music's biggest crossover successes, Rogers has won three Grammies, eleven People's Choice awards, eight Academy of Country Music awards, and five Country Music Association awards; his album sales have exceeded ninety million units.

Diversity. In 1980, Rogers began his acting career, starring in the television film *The Gambler*, and by the end of the 1994, he had appeared in four more *Gambler* episodes. Rogers portrayed a photographer in the 1989 television drama *Christmas in America: A Love Story*, and he starred in the television western *Rio Diablo* with Naomi Judd and Travis Tritt in 1993. Rogers served as the narrator of the highly rated television series *The Real West*, and played the lead detective, MacShayne, in 1994 television films.

In 1990, Rogers received the Horatio Alger Award for overcoming personal hardships and succeeding in his field through hard work and integrity. By the mid-1990's, Rogers had completed two books, *Kenny Rogers' America*, a compilation of scenic landscapes revealing his photographic skills, and *Kenny Rogers: Your Friends and Mine*, a collection of portraits of his celebrity friends. Rogers would continue to perform at his theater in Branson, Missouri, as well as make several tours each year. In 1997, seven more of Rogers's albums became certified gold, making a total of twenty-nine gold albums, and he released the album *Across My Heart*. —*Alvin K. Benson*

Kenny Rogers (Paul Natkin)

SELECT DISCOGRAPHY

■ ALBUMS

Kenny Rogers, 1975
The Gambler, 1978
Gideon, 1980
Eyes That See in the Dark, 1983
What About Me? 1984
Love Is Strange, 1990

SELECT AWARDS

Grammy Award for Best Country Vocal Performance, Male, for "Lucille," 1977

Grammy Award for Best Country Vocal Performance, Male, for "The Gambler," 1979

Country Music Association Album of the Year for *The Gambler*, Vocal Duo of the Year (with Dottie West), and Male Vocalist of the Year Awards, 1979

Academy of Country Music Vocal Duet of the Year and Single Record of the Year Awards for "Islands in the Stream," 1983 (with Dolly Parton)

Grammy Award for Best Country Vocal Performance, Duet, for "Make No Mistake, She's Mine," 1987 (with Ronnie Milsap)

SEE ALSO: Bee Gees, The; Campbell, Glen; Easton, Sheena; Gayle, Crystal; Ingram, James; Parton, Dolly.

The Rolling Stones

ORIGINAL MEMBERS: Mick Jagger (b. 1943), Brian Jones (1942-1969), Keith Richards (b. 1943), Ian Stewart (1938-1985), Charlie Watts (b. 1941), Bill Wyman (b. 1936)

OTHER MEMBERS: Mick Taylor (b. 1948), Ron Wood (b. 1947)

FIRST SINGLE RELEASE: "Come On," 1963

MUSICAL STYLES: Rock and roll, rhythm and blues, blues, country, psychedelic rock, reggae, disco

Formed in London in 1962, the Rolling Stones soon established themselves as one of the most dynamic and influential groups of the period. Vocalist Mick Jagger and guitarist Keith Richards have written a body of successful songs rivaled only by the John Lennon-Paul McCartney team of the Beatles. Along with drummer Charlie Watts, bassist Bill Wyman, and guitarist Brian Jones (and his successors), they have set a standard of high-energy live performance matched only by the Who. Within just a few years of their formation, they were calling themselves "the World's Greatest Rock and Roll Band"—a title that few groups have challenged and that most fans and critics have echoed.

The Beginnings. The early 1960's found most of the musicians who would later become members of the Rolling Stones playing with British bands specializing in rhythm and blues (R&B), the African American forerunner of rock. The group's original core consisted of vocalist Mick Jagger, guitarist Keith Richards, rhythm guitarist Brian Jones, and pianist Ian Stewart. By late 1962 bassist Bill Wyman had joined the group, while drummer Charlie Watts signed on at the end of 1963.

From the beginning, the Rolling Stones presented a clear contrast to the enormously popular Beatles. The two groups not only played differing musical styles but also cultivated sharply differing images. Where the Beatles played pop-oriented rock and roll, the Rolling Stones emphasized their roots in R&B and, to a lesser extent, country. Where the Beatles projected an almost "cuddly" image, the Rolling Stones cultivated a scruffy, aggressive stance that they maintained throughout the ensuing years. In fact, the talented Stewart would soon be forced out of the lineup partly because he looked too clean-cut, but he continued as a trusted adviser, road manager, and occasional pianist.

As they coalesced, the Rolling Stones played such London-area clubs as the Marquee and the Crawdaddy and recorded several demo tapes. The first to be released appeared on June 7, 1963, and featured a cover of rhythm-and-blues great Chuck Berry's "Come On." Later that year the group released "I Wanna Be Your Man," written for them by John Lennon and Paul McCartney of the Beatles, backed with "Stoned," a modest composition of their own.

The group's aggressive playing was earning them a large and often raucous following. They made their first appearance on British television in mid-1963 and by the end of the year were touring Britain with the Everly Brothers, Bo Diddley, and Little Richard. They played three short British tours in early 1964 as headliners, and, in mid-1964, embarked upon their first North American tour, making them one of the components of the first "British invasion." As they became better known on both sides of the Atlantic, they came to symbolize the spirit of rebellion so characteristic of the 1960's.

Early Classics. The albums that the Rolling Stones recorded in quick succession between 1964 and 1972 are their strongest claim to fame and were backed with increasingly long and elaborate tours. Their first EP and LP releases (both in 1964) were self-titled *The Rolling Stones*. These and succeeding albums consisted primarily of covers, but some songs achieved such close identification with the Rolling Stones that most listeners assumed they were originals. In fact, "It's All over Now" (by Bobby Womack) became a 1964 British number 1 hit—their first in an impressively long string of chart-topping songs.

By the time *Out of Our Heads* (1965) was released, the Rolling Stones (meaning in most cases Jagger and Richards) were writing more of their own material. That album yielded the hits "The Last Time" and "(I Can't Get No) Satisfaction." The latter was destined to become the Rolling Stones' signature number, and the tension it established between the seeming uncertainty and frustration of its lyrics and the taunting insistence of its beat would become a hallmark of their best work. *December's Children (and Everybody's)*, released in 1965, produced the hit "Get off of My Cloud." *Aftermath* (1966) followed with the despairing hit "Paint It, Black." The latter album also featured "Goin' Home," which ran almost twelve minutes and for the first time exhibited the Rolling Stones' ability to extend a song beyond its usual recording length.

The group's next two albums—*Between the Buttons* and *Their Satanic Majesties Request* (both 1967)—marked time, although the former yielded the hit "Ruby Tuesday." The latter album proved

The Rolling Stones in 1963: Mick Jagger, Brian Jones, Charlie Watts, Bill Wyman, Keith Richards (Archive Photos/Popperfoto)

to be a weak echo of the Beatles' psychedelic *Sgt. Pepper's Lonely Hearts Club Band* (1967). With the 1968 *Beggar's Banquet*, however, the Rolling Stones came into their own. Almost every song—from the ominous opening cut "Sympathy for the Devil" to the resigned but oddly euphoric closing cut "Salt of the Earth"—was destined to become a classic.

By now the group was playing together seamlessly. Watts and Wyman provided a hard-driving rhythm line, while Richards made a dependable foil for Jagger's drawling, insinuating voice and increasingly flamboyant stage presence. Jones' experimentation on such instruments as sitar and mandolin had contributed much to the Rolling Stones' distinctive early sound, but he was growing increasingly dissatisfied—and surely jealous of Jagger's charisma. By mutual agreement, Jones left the band in mid-1969, only to be found less than one month later drowned in his swimming pool. The Rolling Stones quickly replaced him with Mick Taylor, formerly of John Mayall's Bluesbreakers.

The End of an Era. *Let It Bleed* (1969) surpassed the success of *Beggar's Banquet*, rising to number 1 in Britain and number 3 in the United States. Outstanding individual cuts included the menacing "Gimme Shelter," the sardonic "Let It Bleed," and the chilling "Midnight Rambler," in which Jagger aped "Boston Strangler" Albert de Salvo. The London Bach Choir joined in on the concluding number, "You Can't Always Get What You Want."

As bad luck would have it, the Rolling Stones had scheduled a free concert at the Altamont Speedway in Livermore, California, on the night of December 6, 1969—one day after the release of *Let It Bleed*—to conclude their sixth North American tour. Groups such as the Jefferson Airplane had agreed to open, and the Rolling Stones had been talked into hiring a local contingent of the Hell's Angels motorcycle gang to maintain security. As it turned out, the Rolling Stones began playing late—by which time the Hell's Angels and apparently most of the enormous, impatient audience were under the influence of drugs or alcohol. As violence broke out again and again, the Rolling Stones were forced to stop and restart their set. The entire disaster—including the stabbing death of a spectator by a member of the Hell's Angels—was captured on film by cinematographers David and Albert Maysles and released as the motion picture *Gimme Shelter*. It was clear that the 1960's—ostensibly the decade of love and tolerance—were over.

The Rolling Stones' 1971 album *Sticky Fingers* proved to be a Taylor showcase, with the guitarist's work on "Wild Horses," "Can't You Hear Me Knocking," and "Moonlight Mile" lifting already strong material to an exhilarating level. The album peaked at number 1 in both Britain and the United States. The 1972 double album *Exile on Main Street* marked a high point of high points. The work's energy was relentless, and its lyrics were sometimes unintelligible. However, it yielded the hits "Tumbling Dice" and "Happy," in which Jagger and Richards respectively dramatized the public roles they had adopted. Dismissed or misunderstood by many fans and critics, *Exile on Main Street* nevertheless reached number 1 in both England and the United States and eventually came to be recognized as the Rolling Stones' most outstanding album—the fitting culmination of their first decade.

Fame and Fortune. As the Rolling Stones continued to record and tour, one of the factors they had to contend with was their own reputation. Were new releases worthy of "the World's Greatest Rock and Roll Band"? Their 1973 album *Goats Head Soup*, for instance, was relaxed and lyrical, leading many to complain about its lack of energy. Despite the reviews, the album reached number 1 in both Britain and the United States and produced a hit in the anguished ballad "Angie." *It's Only Rock 'n' Roll*, released in 1974, also drew less-than-enthusiastic reviews but reached number 2 in Britain and number 1 in the United States.

It was at this point that Taylor, probably the most talented guitarist ever to work in the group, resigned. He was replaced by Ron Wood, until then a member (with Rod Stewart) of the Faces. Wood lacked Taylor's skill as a soloist, but his loose, happy-go-lucky style melded perfectly with Richards's style, bringing a fresh burst of energy to his fellow guitarist and the group as a whole.

For the Record

Mick Jagger is instantly identifiable as one of the most famous figures that rock has produced, but his distinctive looks were not always an advantage. Soon after the Rolling Stones appeared for the first time on British television in 1963, the producer of the show advised their manager to drop "that vile-looking singer with the tire-tread lips."

The title of their first album with the new lineup, *Black and Blue* (1976), signaled a return to their roots in African American music—R&B and blues—as well as an interest in Jamaican reggae. However, billboards for the album picturing a battered woman suggested a different meaning and provoked strong controversy. Like its predecessor, the album made number 2 in Britain and number 1 in the United States.

In early 1977 the Rolling Stones flew to Toronto, Canada, to play and record in the small El Mocambo Club for an upcoming live album. When suspicious authorities searched Richards's luggage, they found enough heroin to charge him with trafficking. Although various members of the group had faced drug charges over the years, this was clearly the most serious and could have resulted in a life sentence. Richards quickly checked into an addiction treatment program and was eventually given a suspended sentence for possession with the stipulation that he continue treatment and give a charity concert—all in all a wildly lucky outcome.

With the release of their 1978 album *Some Girls*, the Rolling Stones won renewed critical favor. Many saw the work as a response to the challenge of a new wave of musicians—punk groups such as the Sex Pistols and the Clash—who made no secret of their belief that the Rolling Stones were past their prime. Whatever impulse lay behind it, the album was lean and aggressive—clearly their most ambitious work since *Exile on Main Street.* The disco-inspired single "Miss You" was the group's most successful single in the United States to date, although controversy flared over many of the other songs' racist and sexist lyrics. Two years later, *Emotional Rescue* displayed much the same energy and directness but was panned as an imitation.

Tattoo You (1981) marked a return to form. The rousing single "Start Me Up" was as good as any song that Jagger and Richards had written, recalling their big hits of the late 1960's, and the sweet-tempered ballad "Waiting on a Friend" was further enhanced by the playing of jazz saxophonist Sonny Rollins. The group went on to conduct highly successful tours of the United States in 1981 and of Europe in 1982.

The following two albums, *Undercover* (1983) and *Dirty Work* (1986), divided listeners. They were raw, dark, and angry, and by the time the latter album was released Jagger and Richards were publicly feuding. The band did not tour to support either release, which was taken by fans and critics as an ominous sign. Yet *Dirty Work* proved to be the equal of *Some Girls*—a direct, stripped-down album that echoed the frustration the group had immortalized in "(I Can't Get No) Satisfaction." Richards's moving vocals in the concluding cut, "Sleep Tonight," underscored the increasingly important role he had come to play in the band. *Dirty Work* was dedicated to original Rolling Stone Ian Stewart, who had died in late 1985.

A Working Band. The Rolling Stones' 1989 North American tour was their first in seven years and signaled not only a reconciliation between Jagger and Richards but also a renewed commitment to touring—the primary requirement of any working band. The tour backed the 1989 album *Steel Wheels* and proved to be the Rolling Stones' most profitable to date. A European tour followed early the next year. The 1991 live album *Flashpoint* featured their best recorded performances since the early *Get Yer Ya-Ya's Out!* (1970).

In early 1993 Bill Wyman, the oldest Rolling Stone, announced his retirement from the group. Unofficial replacement Darryl Jones was picked to play on *Voodoo Lounge* (1994) and *Bridges to Babylon* (1997) and took part in the long, highly successful world tours that followed. The driving

Voodoo Lounge even won a Grammy Award for Best Rock Album of the Year. —*Grove Koger*

SELECT DISCOGRAPHY

■ SINGLES

"Time Is on My Side," 1964
"(I Can't Get No) Satisfaction," 1965
"Get off of My Cloud," 1965
"19th Nervous Breakdown," 1966
"Paint It, Black " 1966
"Mother's Little Helper," 1966
"Ruby Tuesday," 1967
"Jumpin' Jack Flash," 1968
"Honky Tonk Women," 1969
"Brown Sugar," 1971
"Tumbling Dice," 1972
"Angie," 1973
"Miss You," 1978
"Emotional Rescue," 1978
"Start Me Up," 1981
"Harlem Shuffle," 1986
"Mixed Emotions," 1989

■ ALBUMS

The Rolling Stones, 1964
12 X 5, 1964
Out of Our Heads, 1965
December's Children (and Everybody's), 1965
Aftermath, 1966
Between the Buttons, 1967
Their Satanic Majesties Request, 1967
Beggars Banquet, 1968
Let It Bleed, 1969
Get Yer Ya-Ya's Out! 1970 (live)
Sticky Fingers, 1971
Exile on Main Street, 1972
Goats Head Soup, 1973
It's Only Rock 'n' Roll, 1974
Black and Blue, 1976
Some Girls, 1978
Emotional Rescue, 1980
Tattoo You, 1981
Undercover, 1983
Dirty Work, 1986
Steel Wheels, 1989
Flashpoint, 1991 (live)
Voodoo Lounge, 1994
Bridges to Babylon, 1997

SELECT AWARDS

New Musical Express Best British R&B Band Award, 1968
Billboard Best Band Award, 1972
Rolling Stone Critics' Picks for Best Artists and Best Album for *Some Girls*, 1978
Rolling Stone Readers' Picks for Best Band, Best Male Vocalist (Mick Jagger), Best Album (for *Tattoo You*), Best Single (for "Start Me Up"), Best Songwriters (Mick Jagger and Keith Richards), and Best Instrumentalist (Keith Richards), 1981
Rolling Stone Critics' Picks for Best Artist, Best Album (for *Tattoo You*), and Best Single (for "Start Me Up"), 1981
Grammy Lifetime Achievement Award, 1986
Rock and Roll Hall of Fame, inducted 1989
Rolling Stone Critics' Picks for Best Artist, Best Tour (for the Steel Wheels tour), and Best Drummer (Charlie Watts), 1989
Billboard Lifetime Achievement Award, 1994
Grammy Award for Best Rock Album for *Voodoo Lounge*, 1994
Grammy Award for Best Music Video, Short Form, for "Love Is Strong," 1994 (with others)

SEE ALSO: Beatles, The; Berry, Chuck; Stewart, Rod; Who, The.

Henry Rollins. *See* Black Flag / Henry Rollins

The Ronettes

ORIGINAL MEMBERS: Veronica Bennett (b.1943), Estelle Bennett (b. 1944), Nedra Talley (b. 1946)

FIRST ALBUM RELEASE: *Presenting the Fabulous Ronettes Featuring Veronica*, 1964

MUSICAL STYLES: Rock and roll, pop

The Ronettes were a classic early rock-and-roll girl group. Of all the girl groups, including the Chantels, the Shirelles, the Crystals, and the Supremes, they were the most feminine, projecting an image that was refreshingly flirtatious. Pretty, heavily made-up, and vivacious, the Ronettes were no shrinking violets. Apart from their stage image, the Ronettes had an important association with the greatest record producer of the 1960's, Phil Spector.

The Beginnings. Before they were the Ronettes, the Bennett sisters and their cousin Nedra Talley called themselves the Dolly Sisters and worked as dancers in New York City in the Joey Dee Revue at the Peppermint Lounge. In 1961, they toured with disc jockey Clay Cole's rock-and-roll show and appeared in the film *Twist Around the Clock*. After recording several unsuccessful songs, they signed a contract with Spector, released "Be My Baby" as the Ronettes, and had a number 2 break-out hit. Although their next six releases were profitable, they never reached the sales of this first Spector release. "Baby I Love You," one of their finest songs, went to number 24 in 1963, but "The Best Part of Breaking Up" barely broke into the Top 40. "Walking in the Rain" made it to number 23 and "Do I Love You," from 1964, went no further than number 34. These songs had the misfortune of going up against the first of the Beatles' singles released in America. By 1965, the "British invasion" had driven the Ronettes' joyful, catchy tunes further down the charts, as had the increasing popularity of soul music, particularly from Motown. "Is This What I Get for Loving You?" reached no higher than number 75, and the ecstatic "I Can Hear Music" finished last in the Hot 100 of 1966. Although "Beatlemania" had made success elusive for the Ronettes, the Beatles were among their most avid fans, taking them on their U.S. tour in 1966 and also getting to know Phil Spector, who would later remix their last album *Let It Be* (1970).

Phil Spector. After apprenticing with Lester Sill, Lee Hazlewood, Jerry Leiber, and Mike Stoller, the twenty-year-old Phil Spector teamed with Sill in 1961 to form his own production company, Philles. He was revolutionary, the first to make the producer the senior partner in the craft of record making, the first to make the producer a performer and the studio his instrument. Often writing the songs, arranging them, supervising the final mix of tracks, and handling business affairs with a toughness that belied his years, Spector at twenty-one was one of the youngest self-made millionaires in American history.

His first act was the Crystals, a girl group for whom Spector produced the hit "There's No Other (Like My Baby)" in 1962, followed by "Uptown" and the ill-considered "He Hit Me (and It Felt Like a Kiss)," which many radio stations refused to play. With "He's a Rebel," also in 1962, Spector and the Crystals earned Philles its first chart topper, and followed up with a number 3 hit in 1963, "Da Doo Ron Ron." Despite their success, the Crystals lost Spector's attention when he became infatuated with the Ronettes' Ronnie Bennett. They married in 1968, but it was a stormy union, musically and romantically.

The Spector Wall of Sound. During the 1950's and early 1960's, most recordings featured a small instrumental ensemble and vocals, usually recorded simultaneously on a single track and during a single take at a brief and inexpensive recording session. Consequently, the production aimed to be as transparent as possible. By contrast, Spector called attention to the production, making it the focal point. His method was time-consuming and expensive; a two-and-a-half-minute song could take weeks to record and cost much money. Built up by dozens of musicians laboriously overdubbed in many layers and then mixed down to a single track to which echo was added, Spector's wall of sound comprised a thundering, rhythmic backdrop to songs of remarkable simplicity but great heart. Yet Spector's music—he labeled it "blues pop" and "little symphonies for the kids"—was never highbrowed. Melodically simple ("Da Doo Ron Ron" employs only the first three notes of the diatonic scale), lyrically uncomplicated, and rhythmically propulsive, it was pop-inflected rock and roll, slightly suggestive and meant for dancing. Even slow-tempo songs, like the Righteous Brothers' "You've Lost That Lovin' Feelin'," were best heard on the dance floor.

Recording Classics. Arguably the finest of Spector's earliest albums was *A Christmas Gift for You from Phil Spector* from 1963, which suffered the

The Ronettes (Archive Photos)

burden of being released just after the assassination of President John F. Kennedy. Caught in the most depressing Christmas season since 1941, after the Japanese bombing of Pearl Harbor in World War II, the album was not a big seller. Spector assembled a crew of brilliant studio musicians (among them Leon Russell, Sonny Bono, Glen Campbell, Steve Douglas, and Hal Blaine) to build the wall of sound behind the Ronettes and other Philles acts. The Ronettes contributed memorable versions of "Frosty the Snowman," "Sleigh Ride," and "I Saw Mommy Kissing Santa Claus" to the album. The highlights of the album, however, were an energetic "Santa Claus Is Coming to Town" from the Crystals and Darlene Love's astonishingly soulful "Christmas (Baby Please Come Home)." The latter number revealed Spector at his most inspired and most technically dazzling. In 1966 he consciously set out to bring his unique sound to its epitome with "River Deep, Mountain High," featuring Ike and Tina Turner. Despite exhaustive labors, the song was not successful in the United States, although it was a huge hit in Great Britain. Spector always considered it his masterpiece, but it proved to be turgid and overdone, the predictable result of trying too hard to be profound.

Legacy. Angry and depressed after the failure of "River Deep, Mountain High" and burned out after years of hard work and business frustrations, especially over battles with record distributors, whom he considered no better than racketeers, Spector abandoned the music business for several years in the mid-1960's. In his absence the Ronettes' career stagnated. After marrying Ronnie Bennett in 1968, Spector tried to recapture the group's brief day in the sun, producing "You Came, You Saw, You Conquered" in 1969, but this, too, failed to find a large audience. In 1971, Ronnie struck out without the Ronettes, recording George Harrison's "Try Some, Buy Some."

After Ronnie's marriage to Spector ended in 1974, she divorced his label as well, moving to Buddah Records and teaming with Denise Edwards and Chip Fields to form Ronnie and the Ronettes. They recorded "Lover Lover," a disappointment, then renamed themselves Ronnie Spector and the Ronettes to release "I Wish I Never Saw the Sunshine" (1976). After this last failed attempt to capitalize on past success, Ronnie abandoned the Ronettes and pursued a solo career. During the 1970's a number of artists claimed her as an influence, among them Billy Joel and Bruce Springsteen. Joel even wrote "Say Goodbye to Hollywood" for her. She then recorded an album called *Siren* (1980) and seven years later another, *Unfinished Business.*

As for Phil Spector, his approach to producing exerted an enormous influence on the major talents of the era: Brian Wilson of the Beach Boys made the epochal *Pet Sounds* (1966) to outclass the Beatles musically but also to pay tribute to Spector, while George Martin's producing of the Beatles' *Sgt. Pepper's Lonely Hearts Club Band* (1967) and *Abbey Road* (1969) would have been unthinkable without Spector's influence. In fact, no one would produce records in the same way after Spector.

In the early 1970's Phil Spector and George Harrison made two albums with studio technology far surpassing anything available one decade earlier, when Spector was producing the Ronettes. Created by the most disciplined all-star bands in the history of popular music, *All Things Must Pass* (1970) and *Concert for Bangla Desh* (1972) revealed walls of sound of unsurpassed clarity and emotional power. —*David Allen Duncan*

SELECT DISCOGRAPHY

■ SINGLES

"Be My Baby," 1963

"Baby I Love You," 1964

"Walking in the Rain," 1964

■ ALBUMS

A Christmas Gift for You from Phil Spector, 1963 (with others)

Presenting the Fabulous Ronettes Featuring Veronica, 1964

The Ronettes Featuring Veronica, 1965

Phil Spector Wall of Sound, Volume 1: The Ronettes, 1975 (compilation)

The Ronettes Sing Their Greatest Hits, 1975 (compilation)

SEE ALSO: En Vogue; Go-Go's, The; LaBelle, Patti; Reeves, Martha, and the Vandellas; Pointer Sisters, The; Supremes, The.

Linda Ronstadt

BORN: Tucson, Arizona; July 15, 1946

FIRST ALBUM RELEASE: *Hand Sown . . . Home Grown*, 1969 (with the Stone Poneys)

FIRST SOLO ALBUM RELEASE: *Don't Cry Now*, 1973

MUSICAL STYLES: Country rock, soft rock, folk rock, pop, folk, rock and roll, Latin, reggae, light opera

A prolific singer and the daughter of a professional musician, Linda Maria Ronstadt was influenced by Mexican ballads, country music, big-band music, and rock and roll. She is of upper-class Mexican and German descent and was born in Tucson, Arizona. Her mother, known as "La" Ronstadt, played the ukelele, and her father sang Mexican songs while playing the guitar. As part of the Three Ronstadts, Linda obtained her first singing experience with her brother Pete and sister Suzie at a young age.

In 1964, Ronstadt moved to California, where she helped form the trio the Stone Poneys with Bob Kimmel and Ken Edwards. They recorded the Capitol single "Some of Shelley's Blues"/"Hobo (Morning Glory)," which was released in 1965 from their first album, *We Five Sounds* (1967). It was not until the release of their second album, *Evergreen*, that their first single reached the charts with the Top-20 hit "Different Drum." The third and final album released under the name the Stone Poneys was *Linda Ronstadt, Stone Poneys, and Friends, Volume III* in 1968, which was recorded by session musicians.

Bleak Years. Ronstadt refers to her early years as a soloist during the late 1960's and early 1970's as her "bleak years." During this time, she opened for Alice Cooper and the Mothers of Invention and was on the road, "in a coma for about eight years." She also experienced a personal identity crisis and professional insecurity during this time.

Her early solo albums, *Hand Sown . . . Home Grown* (1969) and *Silk Purse* (1970), were conservative, with more country-flavored material. The one song Ronstadt liked on *Silk Purse* was Gary White's "Long, Long Time," which was a modest hit. Her third solo album, *Linda Ronstadt* (1971), featured such excellent musicians as Andrew Gold, who became a solo star, and Glenn Frey, Don Henley, Bernie Leadon, and Randy Meisner, who went on to form the Eagles. The album's content emphasized a contemporary approach with songs by Neil Young, Jackson Browne, and Eric Anderson.

Success. Ronstadt was able to overcome her "bleak years" identity crisis when she began to work with Peter Asher. They collaborated on *Don't Cry Now* (1973) for Asylum. However, it was not until Asher became her manager and record producer in 1974 that Ronstadt scored her first hit album with *Heart Like a Wheel* (1974). This platinum album established her as the most popular female rock singer of the 1970's. "You're No Good" and "When Will I Be Loved" became top singles. The dramatic version of Hank Williams's "I Can't Help It" won her a Grammy Award for Best Female Country Vocal. Due to the success of this album, many of her future releases were aimed to please both the rock and country audiences.

Prisoner in Disguise (1975) and *Greatest Hits* (1976) also sold more than one million copies each. In view of her success, Ronstadt released *Hasten down the Wind* (1976), which became her fourth straight platinum album. Among the cuts were Buddy Holly's rock classic "That'll Be the Day," the title song by Warren Zevon, two reggae-folk-rock songs, and several songs by Karla Bonoff. Ronstadt wrote "Lo Siento, Mi Vida" and "Try Me Again" in collaboration with guitarist Albert Gold.

Linda Ronstadt (Express Newspapers/Archive Photos)

In January of 1977, Ronstadt had the honor of singing at President Jimmy Carter's inauguration. In February of that year, she received her second Grammy for Best Female Pop Vocalist for her album *Hasten down the Wind.*

Released by Asylum in October, 1977, *Simple Dreams* was Ronstadt's twelfth album, the fifth to go platinum. This album included Roy Orbison's tune "Blue Bayou," J. D. Souther's title song, Eric Kaz's "Sorrow Lives Here," the Rolling Stones' "Tumbling Dice," Warren Zevon's "Poor, Poor, Pitiful Me," and a duet with Dolly Parton, "I Never Will Marry."

The 1980's and 1990's. Ronstadt's work during the 1980's became more divergent as she developed her soprano extension. She obtained very favorable reviews with her work as Mabel in Joseph Papp's production of Gilbert and Sullivan's *The*

Pirates of Penzance (1980-1981), a role she reprised in the 1983 film. However, her 1984 role in Giacomo Puccini's opera *La Bohème*, at the Public Theater in New York, received less praise.

The album *What's New?* (1983) was devoted to American popular songs of the pre-rock era. It reached number 3 on the charts. Its sequels, *Lush Life* (1984) and *For Sentimental Reasons* (1986), also became successful due to Ronstadt's collaboration with veteran arranger-conductor Nelson Riddle.

In 1987, Ronstadt produced a duet with James Ingram, "Somewhere out There," for the film *An American Tail*. This song became number 2 in the United States and a Top-10 hit in the United Kingdom. Her collaboration with Dolly Parton and Emmylou Harris, *Trio* (1987), and a selection of mariachi songs, *Canciones de Mi Padre* (1987), became successes in the late 1980's. *Canciones de Mi Padre* brought her her third Grammy. In 1991, *Mas Canciones* was released due to the overwhelming success of *Canciones de Mi Padre*.

"Don't Know Much," a duet with Aaron Neville from her album *Cry Like a Rainstorm, Howl Like the Wind*, became another number 2 hit in 1989. The emotional album *Winter Light* (1993) was produced by Ronstadt and George Massenburg. Her releases *Feels Like Home* (1995) and *Dedicated to the One I Love* (1996) demonstrated once more Ronstadt's versatility.

Linda Ronstadt speaks often on behalf of domestic violence awareness since she has experienced domestic violence within her own family. Although many have criticized her changing singing style, she is one of the few singers who can take another person's song and make it into a hit. She is considered by many to be the reigning torch singer of country rock music. *—José A. Carmona*

For the Record

"When I left Tucson, I thought it would be a big deal to have your name on the marquee of a club. That was the pinnacle of success. I never dreamed I'd have a number 1 record." *—Linda Ronstadt*

SELECT DISCOGRAPHY

■ ALBUMS

Hand Sown . . . Home Grown, 1969
Silk Purse, 1970
Linda Ronstadt, 1971
Don't Cry Now, 1973
Heart Like a Wheel, 1974
Prisoner in Disguise, 1975
Greatest Hits, 1976 (compilation)
Hasten down the Wind, 1976
Simple Dreams, 1977
Mad Love, 1980
Greatest Hits, Volume 2, 1980
What's New? 1983
Lush Life, 1984
For Sentimental Reasons, 1986
Trio, 1987 (with Emmylou Harris and Dolly Parton)
Canciones de Mi Padre, 1987
Cry Like a Rainstorm, Howl Like the Wind, 1989
Mas Canciones, 1991
Winter Light, 1993
Feels Like Home, 1995
Dedicated to the One I Love, 1996

SELECT AWARDS

Grammy Award for Best Country Vocal Performance, Female, for "I Can't Help It (If I'm Still in Love with You)," 1975
Grammy Award for Best Pop Performance, Female, for *Hasten Down the Wind*, 1976
Grammy Award for Best Mexican/American Performance for *Canciones de Mi Padre*, 1988
Grammy Award for Best Pop Performance by a Duo or Group with Vocal for "Don't Know Much," 1989 (with Aaron Neville)
Grammy Award for Best Pop Performance by a Duo or Group with Vocal for "All My Life," 1990 (with Aaron Neville)
Grammy Awards for Best Tropical Latin Album for *Frenesi* and Best Mexican/American Album for *Mas Canciones*, 1992

SEE ALSO: Eagles, The; Gabriel, Ana; Henley, Don; Ingram, James; Parton, Dolly; Williams, Hank.

Diana Ross

BORN: Detroit, Michigan; March 26, 1944
FIRST ALBUM RELEASE: *Diana Ross*, 1970
MUSICAL STYLES: Pop, rhythm and blues, soul

Before the female groups of the 1990's such as En Vogue and the Spice Girls, there was the 1960's Motown group the Supremes. Their first hit record was "Where Did Our Love Go" in 1964. By 1965, the Supremes were international celebrities. In 1967, the trio's name was changed to Diana Ross and the Supremes in order to capitalize on the lead singer's charisma and popularity. Twelve of the group's songs soared to the number 1 position on *Billboard*'s Top 100 before Ross left the Supremes in 1970 in order to begin a successful solo career. Decades later, Diana Ross remained a musical, television, and film superstar.

Ross on Her Own. After eleven years as a Supreme, Ross found even greater success as a solo artist. Her first single was "Reach out and Touch (Somebody's Hand)" in 1970. Since then, she has recorded such number 1 hits as "Ain't No Mountain High Enough," "Touch Me in the Morning," "The Theme from *Mahogany* (Do You Know Where You're Going To)," "Love Hangover," "Upside Down," "Endless Love" (the biggest hit of her career thus far), "Why Do Fools Fall in Love," and "Missing You." Her distinctive renditions of "Ain't No Mountain High Enough," "Endless Love," and "Muscles" earned Grammy Award nominations, while "The Theme from *Mahogany* (Do You Know Where You're Going To)" and "Endless Love" earned Academy Award nominations. Among her best-selling albums are *Lady Sings the Blues* (1972), which sold 300,000 copies during its first eight days in release; *Diana Ross* (1976); *The Boss* (1979); *Diana* (1980); and *Why Do Fools Fall in Love* (1981). Ross has also recorded hit duets with some of the recording industry's most talented and famous male entertainers, including Marvin Gaye, Michael Jackson, Lionel Richie, and Julio Iglesias, and she was one of many pop and rhythm-and-blues artists who, united in their efforts to end hunger in Africa, recorded "We Are the World" as USA for Africa in 1985.

Diana Ross's recording career was at its peak in the 1970's and 1980's. In the early 1980's, Ross, while still enjoying phenomenal recording success, left Motown Records and signed a recording contract with RCA Records for approximately twenty million dollars. RCA allowed Ross opportunities to produce her own records. During her RCA years Ross recorded several hit albums, including *Why Do Fools Fall in Love* and *Swept Away* (1984). In 1987 Ross returned to Motown as a part owner as well as a recording artist. Since the late 1980's, Ross's recording career has not generated big hits, but her superstar status remained secure because of her highly successful concerts and world tours.

The Central Park Concerts. In 1983, motivated by her desire to build a playground in New York City, Ross scheduled a free outdoor concert in New York's Central Park. Anticipated sales from concert souvenirs would provide the necessary funds for the playground. Approximately 400,000 people attended the July event, billed as "For One and for All—Diana Ross! in Central Park." Rain began to fall twenty minutes after the show started. The shower turned into a downpour, but Ross, performing on an open-air stage, did not stop the show. The rainstorm raged on with strong winds, as the drenched superstar told the concertgoers, "It took me a lifetime to get here; I'm not going anywhere." However the thunderstorm grew more severe, and Ross was forced to end the show forty-five minutes after it began. Central Park was overflowing the following night with 400,000 fans who witnessed Ross's rescheduled show that included songs from her days with the Supremes, her earliest hits as a solo artist, and her current hits. The two nights' performances, simulcast around the world, confirmed Ross's status as a legendary entertainer. These 1983 concerts, which broke Central Park attendance records, were arguably the best concerts of her career.

Television and Film Work. Ever since her years with the Supremes, Diana Ross's appearances on television have continued to endear her to generations of fans. As a solo artist, she has appeared on a wide range of television programs. She has hosted or cohosted a number of television specials, including the 1974 Academy Awards ceremony, "The Thirteenth Annual American Music Awards" (1987), and "Motown 40: The Music Is Forever" (1998). In 1976 Ross sang the Academy Award-nominated song "The Theme from *Mahogany* (Do You Know Where You're Going To)" during the awards program; her live-via-satellite performance in Holland was the first of its kind for the Academy Awards. As a solo artist, Ross had starred in seven television specials by the mid-1990's, including "An Evening with Diana Ross" (based on her one-woman show at the Broadway Palace Theater, 1977), "For One and for All—Diana Ross Live! in Central Park" (1983), and "Christmas in Vienna" (also starring tenors Plaçido Domingo and José Carreras, 1992).

Diana Ross made her film debut in *Lady Sings the Blues* (1972) and was nominated for an Academy Award for her portrayal of jazz great Billie Holiday. In 1975's *Mahogany*, Ross portrayed a successful fashion model and designer. *The Wiz* (1978) was Ross's third film and was a cinematic version of the highly successful Broadway play based on the children's film classic *The Wizard of Oz*. Ross starred as Dorothy, and one of her costars was Michael Jackson, who played the Scarecrow. In the 1994 made-for-television film *Out of Darkness*, Ross portrayed a schizophrenic who is repeatedly institutionalized.

Legacy. As lead singer of the Supremes, Ross helped paved the way for groups such as the Pointer Sisters, En Vogue, and the Spice Girls. As a soloist, Ross was one of the first major female crossover artists to appeal to people of all races. In a recording industry in which most singers have one or several hit records and then disappear from the public eye, Ross has thrived over the decades and become a musical icon. As an actress, Ross has helped expand the African American presence on film, and today's younger black actors and actresses continue to benefit from her efforts.

Diana Ross, the mother of three daughters, remarried in 1985. She and Norwegian shipping tycoon Arne Naess have two sons. Ross published her autobiography, *Secrets of a Sparrow: Memoirs* in 1993. One of the most influential women in the entertainment industry, she would continue to record as well as tour more than four decades after

Diana Ross (Paul Natkin)

her musical debut, remaining the "First Lady of Motown." —*Linda M. Carter*

SELECT DISCOGRAPHY

■ SINGLES

"Reach out and Touch (Somebody's Hand)," 1970
"Ain't No Mountain High Enough," 1970
"Good Morning Heartache," 1972
"Touch Me in the Morning," 1973
"The Theme from *Mahogany* (Do You Know Where You're Going To)," 1975
"Love Hangover," 1976
"Boss, The," 1979
"Upside Down," 1980
"Endless Love," 1981 (with Lionel Richie)
"Why Do Fools Fall in Love," 1981
"Mirror, Mirror," 1981
"Muscles," 1982
"Swept Away," 1984
"Missing You," 1984
"Workin' Overtime," 1989

■ ALBUMS

Surrender, 1971
An Evening with Diana Ross, 1977
Red Hot Rhythm and Blues, 1987
Forever Diana Ross: Musical Memoirs, 1993 (four-CD compilation)

SELECT AWARDS

Billboard, named Number 1 Female Vocalist, 1971
Billboard, named Female Entertainer of the Century, 1976
Rock and Roll Hall of Fame, inducted 1988 (with Supremes)

SEE ALSO: Richie, Lionel; Supremes, The.

For the Record

The first album issued by Motown that had Diana Ross's name without the Supremes was actually not a Ross recording but the 1969 recording *Diana Ross Presents the Jackson Five.*

Roxy Music / Bryan Ferry

Roxy Music

ORIGINAL MEMBERS: Bryan Ferry (b. 1945), Andy Mackay (b. 1946), Brian Eno (b. 1948), Graham Simpson, Dexter Lloyd, Roger Bunn

BEST-KNOWN LINE-UP: Bryan Ferry, Andy Mackay, Brian Eno, Phil Manzanera (b. Philip Targett-Adams, 1951), Paul Thompson (b. 1951)

OTHER MEMBERS: Eddie Jobson (b. 1955), Gary Tibbs (b.1958), Paul Carrack (b. 1951), John Porter, John Gustafson

FIRST ALBUM RELEASE: *Roxy Music*, 1972

Bryan Ferry

BORN: Washington, England; September 26, 1945

FIRST ALBUM RELEASE: *These Foolish Things*, 1973

MUSICAL STYLES: Art rock, pop, disco

After an innovative early period that wed avant-garde music to high fashion, Roxy Music moved to the commercial mainstream with a string of international hits. Though successful in the United States, the group became forerunners of a distinctly European pop music; front man Bryan Ferry's doomed romantic persona has influenced such performers as David Bowie, Simon LeBon, and Morrissey.

Classic Period. Singer Bryan Ferry assembled Roxy Music in London in 1971. He did so in seemingly random fashion, seeking to create not so much a cohesive musical unit as an experimental ensemble made up of disparate parts. Andy Mackay, a classically trained reed player, brought a knowledge of synthesizers and recording wizard Brian Eno to the group. Former dockworker Paul Thompson (quickly replacing Dexter Lloyd) supplied a hard-driving drumbeat that owed more to 1950's rock and roll than to the avant-garde pretensions of his bandmates. Graham Simpson was the first of a series of bass players, and after several personnel changes (eliminating Roger Bunn and David O'List), progressive jazz-rock guitarist Phil Manzanera rounded out the lineup.

To evoke the glamour of Hollywood's golden age, Ferry and Mackay chose Roxy from a list of film house names; since a U.S. band was already using that name, the group added a second word to their title and, to underscore the postmodern self-consciousness of the act, added quotation marks to become "Roxy Music." Prior to signing a label deal, the group developed a strong following on the London dance-club circuit as much for their glam-rock look as for their music.

Albums. Their first album, *Roxy Music* (1972), showcased the group's experimentalism with innovative dance numbers such as "The Bob (medley)" and "Ladytron." At the same time, "Virginia Plain," a released single not on the album, reached number 4 on the British pop charts. The follow-up album, *For Your Pleasure* (1973), solidified the band's sound and codified its chief theme, the alienation and disillusionment of a modern culture devoted to the pursuit of pleasure. Its stylish cover underscored the point, depicting a leather-clad model leading a panther on a leash while Ferry, in chauffeur's outfit, admires from a distance. Ferry's musical personae on the album are constantly in pursuit of a pleasure that they can never attain. "Editions of You" finds the singer lusting after a cover girl tantalizingly beyond his reach, while "In Every Dreamhome a Heartache," perhaps the definitive Ferry lyric, is a love song directed to an inflateable doll ("I blew you up but you blew my mind"). The album's high point is the nine-minute "Bogus Man," a Ferry song about a fetishistic Frankenstein's monster set against a musical stew of Eno's tape loops and Mackay's Ornette Coleman-inspired saxophone riffs.

Stranded (1973) and *Country Life* (1974) continued to work the ground broken in *For Your Pleasure.* The cover models changed, but the themes remained essentially the same. (The models' outfits did, however, become increasingly revealing: *Country Life,* featuring a pair of underwear-clad women, was censored in the United States.) A major change in the group's direction, though, was the loss of Brian Eno, who had left the band increasingly dominated by Ferry. Keyboardist-violinist Eddie Jobson replaced him, and the production became slicker, if more predictable. *Stranded*'s opening track, "Street Life," very much in the vein of previous singles "Virginia Plain" and "Do the Strand," mixed a danceable beat with wry social commentary. The album's "A Song for Europe" transformed the persona of "In Every Dreamhome a Heartache" into an isolated aristocrat keening the death of the *ancien régime.* However, songs such as "Psalm" and the tour-de-force "Mother of Pearl" revealed a more autobiographical Ferry willing to give a glimpse of himself behind the ironic poses.

Solo. In the meantime Ferry had embarked on a solo career in which he adopted the role of tuxedo-clad lounge lizard that he had toyed with in Roxy Music. *These Foolish Things* (1973) established his solo formula, in which the singer brought his idiosyncratic phrasing and stylized romantic lilt to an odd gamut of cover songs ranging from Bob Dylan's "A Hard Rain's a-Gonna Fall" to Lesley Gore's "It's My Party." Ferry's interpretation of the Dylan classic, released as a single, epitomized his postmodernist approach as he transformed the gloom-and-doom ballad of the 1962 Cuban Missile Crisis into a snappy soul number, complete with female backing vocals—effectively decontextualizing it from any historical reference. Ferry's message was simple and ironic: every pop song, even one aspiring to social significance, is still a only pop song. Ferry employed many of his Roxy associates on the solo albums, including follow-ups *Another Time, Another Place* (1974) and *Let's Stick Together* (1976), making it hard at times to differentiate a Ferry solo project from a Roxy Music album.

Roxy Music's next release, *Siren* (1975), included the single "Love Is the Drug," the band's first Top-30 hit in the United States. To fans of the early Roxy Music, the album seemed a disappointment, the songs lyrically thinner, the production more glossy. In fact, the unfairly maligned record included some of the band's best work. Ferry curbed his habitual wordiness on lyrically incisive songs such as "Both Ends Burning" and "Just Another High"; moreover, the band's accompaniment tended to support rather than distract from the songs (a number of which were coauthored by Manzanera and Mackay).

Breakup, Reformation, Breakup. Unfortunately, the group disbanded just as it seemed to have found its niche, both artistically and commercially. The poorly recorded live album *Viva!* (1976), issued after the breakup, sounded less like an encore than a contractual expediency that would allow Ferry to pursue a solo career. After a public affair and breakup with model Jerry Hall (who had sported blue body paint and ankle-wings for the memorable *Siren* cover), the distraught Ferry released *The Bride Stripped Bare* (1978), an uninspired effort except for a good Ferry original, "Sign of the Times," and an interesting remake of Al Green's "Take Me to the River" (a hit for the Ferry-inspired Talking Heads).

A chastened Ferry reassembled Roxy Music for the commercially successful *Manifesto* (1979), which included the memorable tale of disco ennui, "Dance Away," but at times left the group sounding like its new-wave imitators. *Flesh + Blood* (1980) continued the comeback with a string of modest hits and an interesting reading of the Byrds' "Eight Miles High." The international hit *Avalon* (1982), which included the blockbuster singles "More than This" and the samba-laced title track, suggested that something of the group's original magic had returned.

Unfortunately, history repeated itself and the group disbanded just as it had found its stride. *The High Road* (a 1983 extended-play single), issued after the band's second breakup, contained wonderful renderings of John Lennon's "Jealous Guy" and Neil Young's "Like a Hurricane" and showed the band's capabilities. Ferry continued to release listenable albums much in the vein of his earlier solo efforts, though with considerably less wit and spontaneity. —*Luke A. Powers*

SELECT DISCOGRAPHY

Roxy Music

■ ALBUMS

For Your Pleasure, 1973
Stranded, 1973
Siren, 1975
Avalon, 1982

Bryan Ferry

■ ALBUMS

These Foolish Things, 1973
Another Time, Another Place, 1974
Bête Noire, 1987

SEE ALSO: Bowie, David; Eno, Brian; Talking Heads / David Byrne.

Rufus. *See* Chaka Khan

Run-D.M.C.

ORIGINAL MEMBERS: Run (b. Joseph Simmons, 1964), D.M.C. (b. Darryl McDaniels, 1964), Jam Master Jay (b. Jason Mizell, 1965)
FIRST ALBUM RELEASE: *Run-D.M.C.*, 1984
MUSICAL STYLES: Rap, hip-hop

Rap existed by the late 1970's, yet no major black artist crossed over to white audiences or became a major success in that era. Run-D.M.C. in the mid-1980's changed the style of rapping to quickly become a hugely successful group and a role model for later rap artists to imitate. Run-D.M.C. rejected the 1970's rappers' flamboyant stage costumes and succinct rapping over dance music. Instead, they initiated the baggy clothing style and tough, lengthy rapping songs of the 1980's. Wearing street clothes, short afros, and untied tennis shoes and setting up a turntable and drum machine to rap with, Run-D.M.C. practically invented rap culture.

Homeboys. All three members of Run-D.M.C. grew up together in Queens, New York. Run's older brother Russell Simmons was cofounder of the Def Jam record label, which specialized in rap music. As a teenager, Run worked with him at sound engineering, also becoming adept at turntable playing and rap-lyric writing. Not content to back up Russell's prodigies in live concerts, Run asked his brother to produce a record featuring only Run. The demo of the song went nowhere. In 1983, however, with D.M.C., Run wrote the lyrics for the single "It's Like That"/"Sucker M.C.'s." A small independent record label accepted it, and it sold twenty thousand copies in one month.

Run took his nickname from his ability to quickly take cuts in the recording studio, though rumors ascribe it to his talking too much and too fast. D.M.C., a play on the name Darryl McDaniels, has also been called an abbreviation for Darryl Makes Cash or Devastating Mic[rophone] Control. Run and D.M.C. were the rappers, and they promised their friend Jam Master Jay the job of disc jockey once they made a record. Together, they produced a single, "Hard Times," which reached number 1 on *Billboard*'s black singles charts. An album soon followed.

Rap Recognition. Along with successful albums, Run-D.M.C. became known through their live performances, with appearances in the SwatchWatch New York City Fresh Fest in 1984 and an anti-apartheid rally at Columbia University in 1985. Run-D.M.C. were the first rappers to be considered for Steven Van Zandt's anti-apartheid single and video titled "Sun City." They were the only rap performers at the Live Aid benefit concert. Run-D.M.C. also appeared in the films *Krush Groove* (1985), the story behind Def Jam, and *Tougher than Leather* (1988). Run-D.M.C. had their share of talk-show appearances and public service announcements asking black youths to refuse drugs and stay in school. They also held "street seminars" to discuss intergang violence. Run-D.M.C. was also responsible for the single and video "King Holiday" (1985) in honor of Martin Luther King, Jr.

Rock and Rap. A collaboration with Aerosmith in 1986 on the hit song "Walk This Way" familiarized Run-D.M.C. with white audiences. Run-D.M.C. claimed to be a rock-rap band. Their songs were three to four minutes long, had a chorus, and had a theme, much like popular songs in rock. They focused more on the music and the

RUN-D.M.C. (Paul Natkin)

message than on having a beat people could dance to. Run and D.M.C. collaborated on the rapping, but, instead of alternating stanzas as the more conventional rappers did, they harmonized so well that they could trade lines and even converse. This timing led to the pair finishing each other's lines in a tribute to repartee.

Burn Out. Run-D.M.C. continued to make it big. Their biggest album, *Raising Hell* (1986), sold three million copies in the United States and made it to number 1 on the rhythm-and-blues charts. The single "My Adidas" from the album led to an endorsement contract with Adidas athletic wear, thanks to the appearance of the company public relations director at a Run-D.M.C. concert. While the trio sang the praises of their favorite athletic shoes, members of the audience raised their Adidas sneakers in tribute.

After the release of *Tougher than Leather* in 1988, however, the band members began to suffer from personal problems as well as the public's preference for new kinds of rap. Run-D.M.C.'s concerts, despite the group's community centered efforts, had always been plagued with outbreaks of violence in the audience. Run had a nervous breakdown, was seriously depressed, and admitted to feelings of inadequacy over his much rewarded talent. He smoked marijuana constantly. D.M.C. drank excessive amounts of malt liquor daily, leading to alcoholic pancreatitis and an extended hospital stay. Jam Master Jay fared better. He went on to form his own record label, JMJ. In 1988 Run and D.M.C. followed suit, with the record label JDK/MCA. They then announced themselves to be born-again Christians and became involved with televangelist Robert Tilton.

Comeback. In 1989 Run-D.M.C. accepted the opportunity to rap for the film *Ghostbusters II*, releasing the single "Pause." They quickly released their fifth album, *Back from Hell* (1990). The new songs partially dealt with street life and partially with the group's newfound Christian beliefs. After an album of greatest hits in 1991, Run-D.M.C. remained together to put out the album *Down with the King* in 1993. KRS-1 and Neneh Cherry provided guest appearances on the album. Working with hot new rap artists made sense to Run-D.M.C., because the new album was directly influenced by the new sounds of the 1990's. Sampling became more evident, and sound effects such as sirens, guns firing bullets, and screams added to the tough messages of the songs. Competing with such groups as N.W.A. and rappers such as Ice Cube, however, was not a successful venture on Run-D.M.C.'s part. Like the rappers of the 1970's who Run-D.M.C.'s new, widely imitated style had displaced, they, as rappers of the 1980's, had to step down for the artists of the 1990's. One feature remained constant, however. Run-D.M.C. continued to be active in the Christian community, working with televangelist Dr. E. Bernard Jordan. —*Rose Secrest*

For the Record

Run-D.M.C. was the first black rap band to make it big. They were the first to have a gold record with *Run-D.M.C.*, the first to have a platinum album with *Raising Hell*, the first to have a double-platinum album, the first to appear on *American Bandstand*, the first to appear on MTV, and the first to appear on the cover of *Rolling Stone.*

§

Run-D.M.C.'s version of "Walk This Way" helped lead to Aerosmith's revival in the 1980's, after the two groups teamed for a video that received much play on MTV.

SELECT DISCOGRAPHY

■ ALBUMS

Run-D.M.C., 1984
King of Rock, 1985
Raising Hell, 1986
Tougher than Leather, 1988
Back from Hell, 1990
Together Forever: Greatest Hits 1983-1991, 1991 (compilation)
Down with the King, 1993

SEE ALSO: Aerosmith; Grandmaster Flash.

The Runaways

ORIGINAL MEMBERS: Ann "Cherie" Currie (b. 1959), Rossana "Lita" Ford (b. 1958), Joan Jett (b. Joan Marie Larkin, 1958), Sandy West (b. Sandy Pesavento, 1959)

OTHER MEMBERS: Jackie Fox (b. Jacqueline L. Fuchs, 1959), Micki Steele (b. Sue Thomas, 1954), Laurie McCallister (b. 1958), Vicki Tischler Blue (b. 1959), Kari Krome

FIRST ALBUM RELEASE: *The Runaways* (1976)

MUSICAL STYLES: Punk rock, heavy metal, rock and roll

Former Runaway Lita Ford (Ken Settle)

The Runaways were part of the rock-and-roll renaissance that swept Great Britain and the United States in the mid-1970's. Led by Joan Jett and Lita Ford, both of them strong guitarists and vocalists, the Runaways mixed punk and heavy metal elements to create their own original musical style.

The Beginnings. In 1975, seventeen-year-old Joan Jett and her fourteen-year-old friend Kari Krome approached producer Kim Fowley at an Alice Cooper party about forming an all-girl band. According to legend, Fowley told them that if they could find a third person he would manage the group. Shortly afterward, Jett and Krome met Sandy West in the parking lot of Los Angeles's Rainbow Bar, and the Runaways were born. Their first known concert was held at a private residence in Torrance, California, in 1975.

Fowley, true to his word, began making changes in the group's lineup to insure their success. After Jett, Krome, and West played together on August 5, 1975, Fowley quickly realized that Krome was a good lyricist but not lead-singer material, so he brought in Micki Steele to be the new vocalist. However, the band was also in desperate need of a lead guitarist and a bass player, and, when Fowley was unable to find either, he paid someone to teach Jett to play lead and arranged for Steppenwolf's Nick St. Nicholas to teach Steele how to play bass.

The new threesome—Jett, Steele, and West—recorded a demo album with Jett on guitar, Steele on bass, and West on drums, while all of them shared vocals. The album was not released at the time, although it appeared in 1991 under the title *Born to Be Bad*. At this point, Fowley realized that even further changes would need to be made if the band was to be successful, so guitarist Lita Ford was auditioned through *Backdoor Magazine*, a music industry trade publication. Since Steele was now the bass player, Fowley began searching for a new lead singer and found Cherie Currie at the Sugar Shack, a San Fernando Valley teen club. Steele quit the band shortly after Currie joined. Some accounts say she was fired, while others claim she was opposed to the band's "tough" image. Jackie Fox became the band's new bassist.

A few weeks before Fox joined the Runaways, a tentative recording deal was made with an independent label called Bomp Records. Before the

For the Record

When asked by *New Musical Express* in April, 1982, about why the Runaways failed, Joan Jett delivered a fitting epitaph when she said, "I think the Runaways were just too honest."

deal was finalized, however, Mercury Records became interested after one of their scouts heard the Runaways play at a Cedar Grove, California, nightclub in November, 1975. Shortly thereafter, the band signed a contract with Mercury Records, and their first album, *The Runaways,* was recorded in May, 1976.

Jailbait Rock. The Runaways quickly established a reputation as "jailbait rockers" because they were young, their song lyrics dealt with teenage sex, and Currie appeared onstage in stockings, a garter belt, and lingerie. The Runaways' songs were statements of teenage rebellion and spoke for a generation of young American women who wanted to play rock and roll loud, fast, and hard. The pulsating rhythm section of Jett, West, and Fox provided the perfect backdrop for Ford's aggressive guitar playing and helped promote the band's hard-rocking, bad-attitude image.

Earle Mankey, the Beach Boys' producer, was brought in to coproduce the band's second studio album, the appropriately titled 1977 *Queens of Noise.* This album, combined with their 1977 promotional tour in Japan, established the Runaways as major players on the music scene. Although the Runaways were never very popular in the United States, they were a smash hit in Japan, where an all-girl rock band was readily accepted. The group's tour through Japan was a huge success, and their 1977 *Live in Japan,* an album that was not released in the United States, contained some of their best recorded material.

The Breakup. The tour of Japan also spelled the beginning of the end for the group. After a series of mishaps and differences with other band members, Fox became frustrated and decided to leave the band. Despite evidence to the contrary, rumors persisted that Fox had been admitted to the hospital after she tried to commit suicide or because of drug addiction. After Fox's departure, Vicki Tischler Blue became the group's new bassist and stayed with the band until its dissolution a year and a half later.

In 1978, the band parted ways with Fowley and brought in Blondie's manager Toby Mamis. Mamis offered the group to producer Kenny Laguna, who refused to work with them. After this rebuff, Mamis brought in producer John Alcock, who had previously worked with Thin Lizzy, to produce the group's fourth studio album, *And Now . . . The Runaways* (1978). It was during these recording sessions that major differences in musical taste and personality began to tear the band apart. Ford and West wanted the band to pursue a heavy metal path, while Jett preferred punk rock. The band divided itself into two major camps and slowly disintegrated as the members failed to agree on what music they should write and play. The Runaways' final concert was on New Year's Eve, 1978, in San Francisco. The band's total dissolution occurred in early 1979.

Further Careers. After the band's breakup, Jett set out on a solo career with a backing band called the Blackhearts. The Runaways' lack of a hit song and unfavorable critical reception made it difficult for Jett to find a major label interested in her music. When she finally did, her first solo album, *Bad Reputation* (1981), was well received by critics but did not sell well. Two years later, however, she released the Kenny Laguna-produced album *I Love Rock 'n' Roll,* which included the number 1 title track and two other Top-20 songs. After that, Jett's albums varied greatly in popularity. Platinum-certified *Up Your Alley* (1988), with "I Hate Myself for Loving You" and "Little Liar," was one of the highlights. Ford also formed her own band after the breakup of the Runaways. After two unsuccessful albums, she released *Lita* in 1988. The album went platinum and included "Close My Eyes Forever," a duet with Ozzy Osbourne that entered the Top 10, and "Kiss Me Deadly," which reached number 12 on the pop charts.

—Gregory Weeks

SELECT DISCOGRAPHY

■ ALBUMS

The Runaways, 1976
Queens of Noise, 1977
Waitin' for the Night, 1978
And Now . . . The Runaways, 1978
The Best of the Runaways, 1982 (previously released material)
Born to Be Bad, 1991 (demos recorded in 1975)

SEE ALSO: Benatar, Pat; Clash, The; Go-Go's, The; Black Flag / Ozzy Osbourne; Ramones, The; Sex Pistols, The; Steppenwolf.

Todd Rundgren

BORN: Upper Darby, Pennsylvania; June 22, 1948
FIRST SOLO ALBUM RELEASE: *Runt*, 1970
MUSICAL STYLES: Pop, rock

Throughout his long, eclectic career, Todd Rundgren has proven himself to be a true individualist, unwilling to compromise his vision—except when he is producing some other recording artist's hit album. His work as a solo artist and with the rock group Utopia has created some wonderful music that features multilayered musical arrangements, catchy pop melodies, and simple, if slightly naive, lyrics. A master in the studio and a talented musician and songwriter, Rundgren has always been more interested in innovation than in building on his early pop-star stature.

A Wizard, a True Star. Rundgren grew up in a Philadelphia, Pennsylvania, suburb and taught himself guitar in high school. He left home at age eighteen and played in a blues band before forming the Nazz in 1967. Rundgren has referred to the Beatles-influenced Nazz as a "power-pop flash in the pan," but the quartet achieved two minor hits from their two albums before breaking up in 1969.

Rundgren's first solo album, *Runt* (1970), featured the Top-20 hit "We Got to Get You a Woman" and was critically acclaimed for its strong pop melodies and excellent production and engineering, which Rundgren did himself. In 1972 he released his breakthrough album, *Something/Anything?* The two-record set featured Rundgren playing all the instruments and singing all the vocals on three of the sides. The fourth side featured great jazz musicians such as Michael and Randy Brecker, among others.

Something/Anything? was filled with catchy pop and rock songs, amazing guitar solos, and soulful Philadelphia-inspired harmonies. It also had several hit singles, including "Couldn't I Just Tell You," "I Saw the Light," and a keyboard-based pop styling of one of the Nazz's hits, "Hello, It's Me." A brief comic monologue, snippets of banter from the musicians, and a parody of a show tune were also included. It was to become his best-selling album.

On the Road to Utopia. Of Rundgren's 1973 album, *A Wizard, a True Star*, Rundgren said, "I wanted to get far away from what I had just done." The concept album was a mix of diverse styles and oddities, including more hard-edged rock mixed in with the Walt Disney-like "Never Never Land" and a medley of classic soul songs. Rundgren had indeed gotten "far away" from *Something/Anything?*—alienating many fans and critics of his previous work in the process.

In 1975 he formed Utopia, a progressive rock group that experimented with long, art-rock songs with often mystical overtones. By the 1980's, the group included Rundgren, John Wilcox on drums, Kasim Sulton on bass, and Roger Powell on keyboards. While Utopia developed a devout following, they never achieved great critical or commercial success. During his time with Utopia, Rundgren also continued to release solo projects that often produced the hit singles that seemed to elude Utopia albums.

Rundgren was to provide a song for the sound track to the 1980 film *Roadie*, starring Meat Loaf. When the song Utopia furnished was refused on the grounds that it sounded too much like the Beatles' music, Rundgren decided to do an entire album in the style of the Beatles. Each song on the quirky, original *Deface the Music* (1980) sounds like a Beatles song, but it is usually difficult to tell which one. A fun album that is half tribute, half parody, it well represents Rundgren's ability to capture the essence of pop music in humorous ways.

Though often his lyrics would include shades of social commentary, he never addressed politics as directly as in the 1982 Utopia album *Swing to the Right.* A reaction to the U.S. embrace of the policies of President Ronald Reagan, it featured a startling cover: a picture of a book-burning from the 1940's, doctored to show a child holding the cover of *Swing to the Right,* about to throw it on the flames.

By the mid-1980's, Utopia had run out of steam. *POV,* released in 1985, was their last album. They performed a reunion tour in Japan in 1992, and Rundgren would continue to use members of the group for his solo projects (especially Sulton), but by the late 1980's, he focused solely on his own projects.

Rundgren Sans Utopia. In 1978, his *Hermit of Mink Hollow* included the hit piano ballad "Can We Still Be Friends," which was later covered by Robert Palmer. In 1983, his *The Ever Popular Tortured Artist Effect* also featured some great pop music, including the catchy "Bang the Drum All Day," which became a minor hit for him as well as a concert favorite. In 1985 he released *A Cappella,* an album consisting only of sounds made by the human voice. While not much of a commercial success, it was certainly innovative.

In 1989 his *Nearly Human* showed his old Philadelphia soul roots and was critically acclaimed. *Rolling Stone* magazine called it "simple, superb white pop soul with no heavy intellectual strings attached." In 1997, again being predictably unpredictable, he released *With a Twist,* which was a greatest-hits collection redone with a bossa-nova beat (including a third recording of his biggest hit, "Hello, It's Me").

Rundgren's offbeat sense of humor and creative music skills made him perfect for sound-track work. Highlights include the theme and background music to the early *Pee Wee's Playhouse* television show in 1986 and the sound track to the 1994 hit film *Dumb and Dumber.*

In Concert. Rundgren's live shows were varied. In the 1970's, with Utopia, they would include big

Todd Rundgren in 1983 (Deborah Feingold/Archive Photos)

For the Record

"I have never made records trying to calculate what the listener is going to respond to or how he's going to respond to it," Todd Rundgren has said. "I know as a producer what is popular and, in some respects, the reasons why it's popular. But as an artist myself, those considerations are put in a box somewhere and forgotten."

set pieces, such as a glass pyramid taking up the entire stage, from which Rundgren would swing down at the concert's climactic end. In the 1980's, during his solo shows, he would play and sing along with video, include a comic monologue, and bring audience members onstage to play percussion instruments on his "Bang the Drum All Day." In the 1990's, he experimented with interactive shows which were more confusing than successful. He also toured with a bossa-nova band in support of *With a Twist.*

Producer and Innovator. When Rundgren left the Nazz, he first made his living as an engineer working with such diverse artists as Bette Midler and the Band. His reputation as a studio expert grew, and throughout his career he was often in demand as a producer. By far the most successful of his productions was Meat Loaf's *Bat out of Hell,* one of the best-selling albums of all time. Rundgren not only produced the album, but his signature lead guitar playing, along with that of other members of Utopia, is on every song. The album proved that while Rundgren had mostly forsaken his pop sensibility for himself, he was certainly willing to exploit his talents to their fullest with other artists. In addition to *Bat out of Hell,* Rundgren also produced best-selling albums for a diverse group of artists, including Patti Smith, Grand Funk Railroad, Hall and Oates, the Tubes, the Psychedelic Furs, and Shaun Cassidy, to name just a few.

Rundgren and Technology. From the beginning, Rundgren was fascinated by technology. In the 1970's, he was one of the first artists to experiment with music videos, long before the advent of MTV. In the 1990's, he became fascinated by computers and the Internet. Considered one of the experts in the field of music and computer technology, Rundgren would often lecture and perform at computer shows and conventions.

In 1993, Rundgren released a CD-I version of *No World Order.* It was the first of its kind: an interactive compact disc that allows the listener to choose different mixes of each song. While a noteworthy achievement, it was one of his worst-selling albums, as taking full advantage of the program required a special, obscure compact-disc player.

Typical of many artists who are unwilling to compromise, Rundgren spent most of his career in battles with his record company. Constantly disappointed in the lack of support for his work, Rundgren went straight to the public and started the Web site www.tr-i.com in 1995. With this interactive Web site, he planned to produce albums directly online, which subscribers could then download and hear songs as Rundgren worked on them, effectively allowing the fan to act as producer. As of 1998, he was still working on that project; given Rundgren's history, it will not necessarily be commercially successful, but it will be another interesting first for this often overlooked, brilliant rock innovator. —*Kevin M. Mitchell*

SELECT DISCOGRAPHY

■ ALBUMS

Runt, 1970
Something/Anything? 1972
A Wizard, a True Star, 1973
Todd, 1974
RA, 1977 (with Utopia)
Hermit of Mink Hollow, 1978
Deface the Music, 1980 (with Utopia)
Swing to the Right, 1982 (with Utopia)
The Ever Popular Tortured Artist Effect, 1983
A Cappella, 1985
Nearly Human, 1989
With a Twist, 1997

SEE ALSO: Hall and Oates; Meat Loaf; Palmer, Robert; Psychedelic Furs, The; Smith, Patti.

Rush

ORIGINAL MEMBERS: Geddy Lee (b. 1953), Alex Lifeson (b. 1953), John Rutsey

BEST-KNOWN LINEUP: Geddy Lee, Alex Lifeson, Neil Peart (b. 1952)

FIRST ALBUM RELEASE: *Rush*, 1974

MUSICAL STYLES: Progressive rock, hard rock, heavy metal

Rush has achieved a level of success and longevity that few rock bands can even hope to duplicate. The Canadian trio has accomplished this success without the benefit of either hit singles or a great deal of media support. Instead, the group has relied on uncompromising devotion to their own musical beliefs and the unswerving loyalty of their large number of fans throughout North America and Europe.

The Beginnings. Rush began as a weekend band for Geddy Lee (bass and vocals), Alex Lifeson (guitar), and John Rutsey (drums) while they were still in high school. In 1972, they began to play regularly in numerous bars throughout southern Ontario, Canada. One of their first big breaks was performing as the opening band for the New York Dolls in Toronto in 1973.

Initially, Rush had little success in getting a contract with a major record label. Strongly influenced by groups such as Led Zeppelin, Cream, and Jimi Hendrix, the band was not considered to be commercially viable. However, the band members managed to save enough money to fund the recording of their first album, *Rush*, in 1974. A radio station in Cleveland began playing the new recording frequently, attracting considerable attention in the United States.

Citing health reasons, Rutsey quit the band about the same time that this first album was released. The change in personnel was also a result of Lee and Lifeson wanting a different sound and direction for the band than Rutsey. After auditioning several drummers, Lee and Lifeson settled on Neil Peart just six weeks before their U.S. debut opening for Manfred Mann's Earth Band and Uriah Heep. Peart was not only an inspiring drummer but also a literary scholar who was to become the lyricist of the group.

During the next several years, the trio toured almost constantly. Their skills as musicians and their fan support eventually led to a recording contract with Mercury Records. Rush recorded two albums for the major label in 1975: *Fly by Night* and *Caress of Steel*. Both albums were certified gold in Canada and did well in the United States. The band opened for such acts as Blue Öyster Cult, Aerosmith, and Kiss, and attracted enough attention to headline a number of shows in their native Canada.

Coming of Age. The release of their fourth album, *2112*, in 1976 was a turning point in Rush's career. Although it was panned by critics and had virtually no radio airplay, the album sold well in both North America and England. Fresh from this success, the band recorded a live album entitled *All the World's a Stage* (1976) at Toronto's Massey Hall. After this, Rush began headlining their own shows at larger venues throughout the United States, Canada, and England.

Beginning with *A Farewell to Kings* (1977), the band gradually moved toward a more complex sound, both musically and technologically. Lee, in addition to playing bass and singing, began to use synthesizers in many of Rush's compositions. Always faithful to their loyal fans, the band maintained a frequent touring schedule throughout most of the 1980's and released numerous albums. Of their twenty albums, the three live recordings serve to demonstrate the various stages through which Rush progressed: *All the World's a Stage* documents their early style and influences, *Exit . . . Stage Left* reveals their interest in technology, synthesizers, and other electronic devices, and *A Show of Hands* showcases their maturation into a band with highly developed technical and song-writing skills.

Aside from their first recording, Rush never followed any commercial trends. Their early albums featured songs of mammoth length such as "By-Tor and the Snow Dog" and "The Fountain of Lamneth." The lyrics for many of these early works were heavily inspired by Peart's interest in fantasy and science fiction themes. In the early to mid-1980's, their sound became more textured and technology based as synthesizers became a common element in many of the songs. Starting with *Signals* (1982), Rush gradually moved away from epic-length compositions. Peart turned to a variety of other literary resources for inspiration, including Dylan Thomas, Ernest Hemingway, and T. S. Eliot. As the 1990's advanced, the trio gradually moved back to a more traditional bass, guitar, and drum sound.

Recording with Rush. Although the band is famous for their lengthy (normally over two hours), high-energy performances that typically include an impressive light and video show, Rush places a high emphasis on creativity in the recording studio. Their system of recording is defined by their respect for each other as artists and friends. Typically, Peart writes the lyrics in one end of the building and then relays them to Lifeson and Lee in the other end, who then begin composing the music to fit the words. The three revise, refine, and frequently reject lyrics and music before settling on the final product. The band typically writes most of the music in this manner and then play it in concert for a period of time before actually recording the material in the studio.

—*Jeffrey E. Bush*

For the Record

In addition to his literary work as lyricist of Rush, drummer Neil Peart is also a published author. *The Masked Rider,* released in 1997, describes his bicycle odyssey with several friends through West Africa.

SELECT DISCOGRAPHY

■ ALBUMS

Rush, 1974
Fly by Night, 1975
Caress of Steel, 1975
2112, 1976
All the World's a Stage, 1976
A Farewell to Kings, 1977
Hemispheres, 1978
Permanent Waves, 1980
Moving Pictures, 1981
Exit . . . Stage Left, 1981
Signals, 1982
Grace Under Pressure, 1984
Power Windows, 1985
Hold Your Fire, 1987
A Show of Hands, 1989
Presto, 1989
Chronicles, 1990
Roll the Bones, 1991
Counterparts, 1993
Test for Echo, 1996
Different Stages, 1998

SELECT AWARDS

Juno Award for Group of the Year, 1977
Juno Award for Group of the Year, 1978
Juno Award Best Heavy Metal Album, 1991
Juno Award for Best Hard Rock Album, 1992
Juno Award Hall of Fame, inducted 1993

SEE ALSO: Emerson, Lake, and Palmer; Morse, Steve / The Dixie Dregs; Yes.

S

Sade

(Helen Folasade Adu)

BORN: Ibadan, Nigeria; January 16, 1959
FIRST ALBUM RELEASE: *Diamond Life*, 1984
MUSICAL STYLES: Pop, rhythm and blues, light jazz

During the 1980's, Sade (pronounced *shar-day*) became popular internationally with her exotic beauty and sultry musical style that can best be described as part pop, part jazz, and part rhythm and blues. Having been inspired by such legendary singers as Nina Simone and Billie Holiday, Sade created a distinctive sound that became popular around the world. Between 1984 and 1998, she sold nearly thirty million albums worldwide.

The Beginnings. Born Helen Folasade Adu, she took the last four letters of her middle name to construct Sade as her stage name. Sade is the daughter of a Nigerian father and an English mother. During the 1950's, her parents met in England when her father was a graduate student at the London School of Economics. After getting married, Sade's mother gave birth to a son. The family relocated to the village of Ibadan, Nigeria, where Sade's father had secured a teaching position. In 1959, Sade was born in Ibadan. Eventually, her parents separated and, in 1963, Sade's mother returned to England with Sade and her brother. In 1969, Sade's mother remarried, and the family moved to the English seaside town Clacton-on-Sea.

By the time Sade was fourteen, she fell in love with the soul music she heard at dance clubs. She was drawn to the music of Marvin Gaye, Aretha Franklin, Al Green, and Smokey Robinson. At seventeen, Sade moved to London to study fashion design at St. Martin's College of Art. While struggling to make a living designing men's clothes, Sade helped to support herself by modeling. Over the years, she had written some songs, but it was not until 1980 that she got the chance to perform any of them. She joined the group Arriva, and one of its most popular live songs became "Smooth Operator," which she wrote with Ray St. John. In 1981, Sade joined the jazz-funk group Pride. Managed by Lee Barrett, he allowed Sade and some of the musicians from Pride to perform a set of their own between Pride's own sets.

By 1983, it was obvious to Barrett that Sade was becoming the focal point of the performances. She quit Pride and formed her own group, which included Stewart Matthewan on saxophone and guitar, Paul Denman on bass, Andrew Hale on keyboards, and Paul Cook on drums. Matthewan and Sade decided to become a songwriting team. With Barrett as Sade's manager, she signed a recording contract with CBS/Epic Records as a solo artist in 1984. The band members then signed a deal with her. In July, 1984, Sade's first album, *Diamond Life*, was released in the United Kingdom. It rose to number 2 on the English pop chart. The album's first single, "Your Love Is King," had been released in February of 1984 and peaked at number 6 on the English pop singles chart. The second single, "When Am I Gonna Make a Living," went to number 36. The third single, "Smooth Operator," reached number 19 and also became a huge success in Europe. *Diamond Life* was not released in the United States until 1985.

Success in the United States and Around the World. With the release of *Diamond Life* in the United States, Sade became an international celebrity. The album rose to number 5 on the U.S. *Billboard* pop chart and sold more than six million copies worldwide, while the single "Smooth Operator" climbed to number 5. At the twenty-eighth annual Grammy Awards ceremony held on February 25, 1986, Sade was named Best New Artist for 1985. The exotic and cool jazz-tinged pop of Sade had found a large audience as well as critical acclaim. In late 1985, Sade's second album, *Promise*, was released. It rose to the top of both the *Billboard* and the English pop charts. Such singles from the album as "The Sweetest Taboo" and

"Never as Good as the First Time" also became huge hits. The album sold more than four million in the United States alone. Sade's third album, *Stronger than Pride*, was released in May, 1988. Although criticized for sounding emotionally cold, the album went to number 7 on the *Billboard* pop chart and to number 1 on the rhythm-and-blues chart.

On February 11, 1989, Sade married Spanish music video producer Carlos Scola in Spain. Although the couple had been together for years prior to the marriage, the marriage itself lasted for less than two years. It was not until October, 1992, that Sade released another album. *Love Deluxe* was generally well received and sold more than four million copies. In 1994, a *Best of Sade* compilation was released. After the release of the compilation, Sade took time off to concentrate on taking care of her daughter Ila. During the late 1990's, the other members of the band recorded on their own. —*Jeffry Jensen*

SELECT DISCOGRAPHY

■ ALBUMS

Diamond Life, 1984
Promise, 1985
Stronger than Pride, 1988
Love Deluxe, 1992
Best of Sade, 1994 (previously released material)

SELECT AWARDS

Grammy Award for Best New Artist, 1985
British Phonographic Institute Best Album Award for *Diamond Life*, 1985
Grammy Award for Best R&B Performance by a Duo or Group with Vocal for "No Ordinary Love," 1993

SEE ALSO: Baker, Anita; Cole, Natalie; Dion, Celine; Houston, Whitney; Richie, Lionel; Vandross, Luther.

Salt-n-Pepa

ORIGINAL MEMBERS: Salt (b. Cheryl James, c. 1964), Pepa (b. Sandy Denton, c. 1961), Pamela Greene
OTHER MEMBERS: Spinderella (Deidre "Dee Dee" Roper)
FIRST ALBUM RELEASE: *Hot, Cool and Vicious*, 1986
MUSICAL STYLES: Rap, hip-hop, pop

This pioneering female rap group was formed in Queens, New York, in 1985, when Cheryl James's boyfriend, Hurby Azor, asked James and Sears coworker Sandy Denton to rap for a project he was doing for an audio production class at the Center for Media Arts. "The Show Stoppa," eventually released as a single by Pop Art Records and credited to the band Super Nature, reached number 46 on the rhythm-and-blues charts.

Reaching New Plateaus. Changing their name to Salt-n-Pepa, the group signed with the independent rap label New Plateau. Azor wrote and produced their platinum debut, *Hot, Cool and Vicious* (1986). "Chick on the Side," "My Mike Sounds Nice," and "Tramp" all did moderately well on the rhythm-and-blues charts. *Hot, Cool and Vicious* became a hit, however, when San Francisco disc jockey Cameron Paul remixed "Push It" (the flip side of "Tramp"). "Push It" soared to number 1 on the rhythm-and-blues and rap charts, peaked at number 19 on the pop charts, and earned a Grammy Award nomination.

The follow-up, *A Salt with a Deadly Pepa* (number 38, 1988), produced no hits but did contain a reworking of the Isley Brothers' "It's Your Thang" (as "Shake Your Thang") and "Twist and Shout." Their third album, *Blacks' Magic* (number 38, 1990), had a better critical reception and saw the introduction of Steevee-O and Salt as producers alongside Azor. After being accused by some rap fans of sacrificing their originality for commercial gain, Salt-n-Pepa paid explicit tribute to their African heritage in *Blacks' Magic* and loaded it with hit singles. "Expression" topped the rap charts for eight weeks and eventually went to number 26 on the pop charts. "Do You Want Me" went to number 21 and the controversial "Let's Talk About Sex" went to number 13.

Charity. With the country waking up to the acquired immunodeficiency syndrome (AIDS) epidemic in the wake of Earvin "Magic" Johnson's 1992 announcement that he was HIV-positive,

Salt-n-Pepa (Paul Natkin)

television news anchor Peter Jennings approached Salt-n-Pepa about the idea of rewriting and rerecording the song. The result was the new single, "Let's Talk About AIDS" (1992), with its proceeds going directly to the T. J. Martell Foundation for AIDS research.

After splitting with Azor over creative differences, Salt-n-Pepa released the smash album *Very Necessary* (1993), which played upon an explicit sexuality. Driven by singles such as "Shoop" (number 4) and "Whatta Man" (number 3) with En Vogue, *Very Necessary* shot to number 4 on the pop charts in 1993, selling more than four million copies. The final single from the album, "None of Your Business" (number 32) earned them a Grammy Award for Best Rap Performance by a Duo or Group. In keeping with their longtime AIDS activism, Salt-n-Pepa ended the album with a public service announcement about AIDS by a group of Boston actors. Salt-n-Pepa performed "Start Me Up" on the *Stay Tuned* sound track (1992), and Salt starred in *Who's the Man?* in the following year.

Continued Success. For two years, Salt-n-Pepa produced singles, but no albums. "Ain't Nuthin' but a She Thing" (1995), the title track for an all-female charity album, peaked at number 38. They also recorded "Champagne" for the 1996 film *Bulletproof* and "Upside Down" for *Space Jam* (1996). A desire for greater creative control, however, led to a new record deal with MCA Records. Salt-n-Pepa returned with their much anticipated *Brand New* album (1997), the first in which they had a major hand in production. Working with an eclectic group of stars, from Queen Latifah to Sheryl Crow, they produced their most diverse album. The first single, "Gitty Up," peaked at number 9 on the rap charts. —*John Powell*

For the Record

In 1993 Salt-n-Pepa played at President Bill Clinton's Inaugural Youth Ball, where they met fan Chelsea Clinton.

SELECT DISCOGRAPHY

■ ALBUMS

Hot, Cool and Vicious, 1986
A Salt with a Deadly Pepa, 1988
Blacks' Magic, 1990
A Blitz of Salt-n-Pepa Hits, 1991 (compilation)
Very Necessary, 1993
Brand New, 1997

SELECT AWARDS

Grammy Award for Best Rap Performance by a Duo or Group for "None of Your Business," 1994

SEE ALSO: En Vogue; Queen Latifah.

Sam and Dave

ORIGINAL MEMBERS: Sam Moore (b. 1935), Dave Prater (1937-1988)

FIRST SINGLE RELEASE: "I Need Love"/ "Keep Walkin'," 1962

MUSICAL STYLE: Soul

Sam and Dave helped define soul music in the 1960's. Their 1967 hit "Soul Man" was an anthem of black pride. The song reached the top of the rhythm-and-blues charts and number 2 on the pop charts, a triumph for the southern, Memphis-based sounds of the premier soul label, Stax. Sam and Dave had developed a dynamic church- and gospel-influenced performance style that enthralled audiences for the rest of the decade. Their exuberant, shouting, call-and-response singing, as well as the sounds produced by the studio band at Stax (featuring heavy bass and powerful horn section blasts with an often syncopated beat), struck African Americans as more authentic and less compromising than the more crossover oriented and generalized music coming from Motown.

Florida Beginning. Sam Moore grew up in Miami, Florida, and started singing gospel music in church. Later he joined several gospel quartets in the area. His singing style was founded on the shouting and ecstatic religious singing he loved so much. The use of melisma (the breaking of a single syllable of a word into several notes), slurs connecting rising or falling notes, falsetto notes added at the end of vocal phrases to emphasize emotional intensity, and the call-and-response pattern of voices trading words and phrases back and forth were inspired by black gospel music.

Moore was also intrigued by the rhythm and blues he heard in local clubs and on records. In the 1950's he started to hear vocal groups such as the Five Royales, the Ravens, and the Orioles, all classic black groups who were nationally successful. In the mid-1950's the famous Soul Stirrers gospel group came to Miami with their brilliant lead tenor, Sam Cooke. Moore became acquainted with Cooke who was about to leave for his meteoric career as a soul singer. Moore was invited to join the group and was tempted to follow a professional gospel career. Then the charismatic rhythm-and-blues and soul singer Jackie Wilson came to town. Moore's life was changed. Wilson was one of the most dynamic performers in black music. Like James Brown, he never stopped moving and worked himself into a sweat with each song. The fans were ecstatic, and Wilson was approached by dozens of fans after each show. Moore was impressed.

He started to play more amateur nights at clubs, performing Sam Cooke and Ray Charles songs. One night in 1961, Moore was joined on stage by Dave Prater. Prater, two years younger than Moore, was from the south Georgia town of Ocilla and had come to Miami to start a gospel music career. Like Moore, he had been brought up in chuch music. His lower and rougher voice fit nicely with Moore's soaring voice in the call-and-response style they both knew.

They decided to team up, sing secular music in clubs, and make a record. In 1962 they released "I Need Love" and "Keep Walkin'" on a small local record label that soon had its releases reissued by the much larger Roulette Records. This first release and a couple of others were unsuccessful, and their work largely remained in the clubs and black theater circuit.

For the Record

While performing in 1961, Sam Moore got tangled up in the microphone cord and slipped on the waxed stage floor, tangling himself even more. Dave Prater, with Moore, fell to his knees to try to pick up the microphone. They both grabbed the microphone stand as it was falling over, Prater with his legs spread wide, and rose back up, all the time shouting and singing. The club audience thought this mishap was part of their planned act and shouted its approval. From then on the action became part of the show.

Soul Stars. In 1964 the head of Atlantic Records heard them and gave them a contract but sent them to Memphis, Tennessee, to record on the Stax label that Atlantic distributed. Working with the Stax house band, which was interracial, they found their mature style. Generally working with Isaac Hayes and David Porter as writers and arrangers in the studio, Sam and Dave had a series of rhythm-and-blues hits over the rest of the decade. "You Don't Know Like I Know" was a 1966 number 7 hit, but it was "Hold On! I'm Comin'" in 1966 that made them national stars, topping the rhythm-and-blues charts and going to number 20 on the pop charts.

Style. Most of their songs are up-tempo shouting songs, in the gospel tradition but concerned with the troubles and joys of male-female relationships. Moore claims they never really sang harmony; rather, they joined and split their voices almost at will as they improvised, answering and calling back and forth while repeating key phrases over and over. Moore compares this style to the testifying style of black gospel. Their songs build in intensity as their voices wail, moan, and cry out in the imploring kind of songs in which they specialized. "Hold On! I'm Comin'" typifies the Stax style itself. Heavily rhythmic on electric bass and drums, the band mix has a timbral integration so that a groove is set up and maintained throughout a song. Different instruments are blended with pulsing horns (often in staccato bursts), a choppy piano, and terse electric guitar licks. To get these effects, the Stax house band would play with loosening and tightening snare drum heads to get a dampened sound and use rubber mouthpieces on the horns to get a fat sound. This kind of percussive blended sound with cross rhythms helped define funk music, as exemplified by James Brown's music.

Sam and Dave (Archive Photos/Frank Driggs Collection)

Hit followed hit in the next few years: "Said I Wasn't Gonna Tell Nobody," "You Get Me Hummin'," "When Something Is Wrong with My Baby," "I Thank You," and their biggest, "Soul Man," a top rhythm-and-blues hit that went to number 2. This 1967 hit, like "Soul Sister, Brown Sugar" in 1969, is an anthem of black pride and defines the genre of soul music. Unlike the older blues, this music was more upbeat and celebratory and captured the more affirmative and hopeful mood of the civil rights era of the 1960's.

Separate Ways. By the time of their last release in 1971, Sam and Dave had gone their separate ways. Personal tensions and differences in lifestyle brought their act to an end. Though they occasionally reunited over the next decade, their kinetic stage style and no-holds-barred singing style no longer dominated the black music charts.

Dave Prater died in an automobile accident in 1988. Moore continued to sing alone and record with others, including a stirring rendition of "Rainy Night in Georgia" with country singer Conway Twitty on his last recording in 1993. He recorded three songs with Bruce Springsteen for his album *Human Touch* in 1992. There Moore injected the cries and shouts that he had brought to his recordings with Prater, urging and affirming Springsteen's lead vocals, while confirming his own great voice. —*Frederick E. Danker*

SELECT DISCOGRAPHY

■ SINGLES

"Hold On! I'm Comin'," 1966

"Soul Man," 1967

"I Thank You," 1968

■ ALBUMS

Sam and Dave, 1966

Soul Man, 1967

Sam and Dave: Sweat 'N' Soul (Anthology, 1965-1971), 1993 (compilation)

SELECT AWARDS

Grammy Award for Best R&B Group Performance, Vocal or Instrumental (Two or More), for "Soul Man," 1967

Rock and Roll Hall of Fame, inducted 1992

SEE ALSO: Brown, James; Cooke, Sam; Hayes, Issac; Wilson, Jackie.

Carlos Santana

BORN: Autlán de Navarro, Jalisco, Mexico; July 20, 1947

FIRST ALBUM RELEASE: *Santana*, 1969

MUSICAL STYLES: Blues, soul, jazz fusion, psychedelic rock

After beginning his career in San Francisco during the 1960's, Carlos Santana, with his band, became the first to merge electric rock with the percussive rhythms of Africa and Latin America. He is one of the few guitar virtuosos of that era who has enjoyed uninterrupted fame and success. His attempts to fuse rock and roll with jazz resulted in a compelling format that inspired and uplifted his listeners to Santana's spiritual sense of humanity. The remarkable consistency of his guitar work is Santana's legacy.

Origins. Carlos Santana was born in central Mexico in 1947 to José and Josefina Santana. His father became Santana's first musical influence. José Santana was a street musician who played in local bars. In the mid-1950's, the family moved to Tijuana. José Santana migrated to San Francisco while the family remained in Mexico. He bought Carlos his first guitar, a Gibson. Although observers have credited Santana as having deep roots in Latin and African-Cuban music, the musicians that most influenced him were African American blues artists, particularly Jimmy Reed, Bobby Bland, Bo Diddley, and Chuck Berry. However, it was B. B. King who made the greatest impact. Santana often played in Tijuana strip clubs with black patrons who performed in order to earn money to recross the border.

The Santana family moved to San Francisco in the early 1960's. Carlos worked by washing dishes to help support his large family as he attended school. He also attended concerts at Fillmore West and began to jam with musicians such as Mike Bloomfield on Sundays.

Early Success. In 1966, Santana became a recognized musician. He had been influenced by white blues acts such as Eric Clapton, the Paul Butterfield Blues Band, and the Spencer Davis Group, although B. B. King remained his favorite artist. In 1966, Santana teamed with Mike Carabello (percussion), Gregg Rolie (organ), and Tom Frazier (guitar) to form the Santana Blues Band. In 1967 Frazier left, while David Brown (bass) and Marcus Malone (percussion) were added to the band. Malone was responsible for adding the Afro-Cuban sound for which the band, now known simply as Santana, became famous. After Malone was convicted of manslaughter, José Areas joined the band in 1969 to continue this Afro-Cuban influence.

The original Santana band: Michael Shrieve, David Brown, Mike Carabello, José "Chepito" Areas, Gregg Rolie, Carlos Santana (Columbia Legacy/Coni Night Loon Beeson)

The Santana band debuted at San Francisco's celebrated Fillmore West in 1968 with resounding success. Their local popularity earned them a trip to the Woodstock festival in 1969. Santana's rousing triumph and the resulting documentary film baptized them as rock-and-roll stars. The Woodstock performance also garnered Santana a contract with Columbia, which released their first album, *Santana*, in November, 1969. This album achieved the number 1 spot in in the United States and was honored with a double platinum award. The music can be characterized as cosmic and psychedelic yet braced with jazz as well as Latin influences. The band was tight and sharp, spreading a psychedelic culture to working-class and minority youth. A Latin American performer, Willie Bobo, inspired Santana's first single, "Evil Ways." Of Bobo, Carlos recalls that he was one of the first to merge Latin music and blues together on record, a style of performance that required emotion and energy.

Santana followed the success of their first album with *Abraxas* (1970) and *Santana III* (1971). The former yielded two big hits in "Black Magic Woman" and "Oye Como Va." *Abraxas* is the album most identified with this incarnation of the band.

Jazz and Spiritual Directions. Santana became disenchanted with the direction of his band and began experimenting with jazz, influenced by greats such as John Coltrane and Miles Davis. The result was *Caravanserai* (1972), widely considered Santana's best work. Santana followed in this mode with *Welcome* (1973) and *Borboletta* (1974). *Borboletta* is notable for the appearance of Brazilian musicians Airto Moreira and Flora Purim. Also during this period, Santana entered the solo arena and produced the jazz-fused albums *Love, Devotion, Surrender* (1973), *Illuminations* (1974), and *The Swing of Delight* (1980). These efforts did not result in the commercial success of Santana's earlier rock efforts, but Santana philosophized that integrity and true artistry were more fundamental to his needs.

In 1972, Santana adopted the Asian religious teachings of Sri Chinmoy and changed his name to Devadip Carlos Santana. During the 1970's, Santana continued to record rock, blues, and Latin pieces. He even delved into disco and recorded a version of Buddy Holly's "Well All Right" which emphasized the tremendous diversity of Santana's tastes. Santana once explained about his style: "It's what America is, a melting pot." By this time his self-confidence was complete. He continued to spread a message of light, love, joy, and peace. Santana became a born-again Christian with his wife Deborah in Santa Cruz, California, in 1992.

The Legacy. By the early 1980's, rock historians could gauge the influence of Santana. Perhaps his greatest impact was to encourage rock as well as soul musicians to use percussion to enhance their music. Santana and various versions of his Santana band continued to perform and record well into the 1990's. When Latin American dignitaries visited Washington, D.C., President Bill Clinton invited Santana to perform at the White House. Santana declined, maintaining his nonpolitical stance. When Mexican president Ernesto Zedillo visited the White House and requested that Santana perform, Clinton again extended an invitation. Santana again refused. He explained that "I would have liked to perform but I haven't seen him make progress toward civil rights for the Indians in Chiapas and until he does, I can't feel oneness with him."

The Latin heritage of Carlos Santana is often overemphasized as the primary characteristic of his music, but the Afro-Cuban rhythms brought into the band by Marcus Malone and José Areas also define Santana's style. Furthermore, Santana's roots lie deep in the blues. He does not reject his Mexican heritage (he sponsors a charity organization named Ciudad de los Niños in Tijuana), yet he does not perceive himself as a Latino or Mexican role model. "The illusion of separation to me is a European indoctrination that started with Caesar, to divide and conquer. I don't believe in flags or borders. We're all one family."

—Douglas W. Richmond

SELECT DISCOGRAPHY

■ ALBUMS

Santana, 1969 (Santana band)
Abraxas, 1970 (Santana band)
Santana III, 1971 (Santana band)
Caravanserai, 1972 (Santana band)
Welcome, 1973 (Santana band)
Borboletta, 1974 (Santana band)
Amigos, 1976 (Santana band)
Festival, 1976 (Santana band)
Oneness, 1979 (solo)
The Swing of Delight, 1980 (solo)
Zebop!, 1981 (Santana band)
Havana Moon, 1983 (solo)
Blues for Salvador, 1987 (solo)
Brothers, 1994 (solo)

SELECT AWARDS

Grammy Award for Best Rock Instrumental Performance (Orchestra, Group, or Soloist) for *Blues for Salvador*, 1988

SEE ALSO: Berry, Chuck; Clapton, Eric; Coltrane, John; Davis, Miles; Diddley, Bo; King, B. B.

Boz Scaggs

BORN: Ohio; June 8, 1944
FIRST ALBUM RELEASE: *Boz*, 1965
MUSICAL STYLES: Rhythm and blues, soul, pop, disco

Born in Ohio, William Royce "Boz" Scaggs moved with his family to Plano, Texas, very early in his life. His father was a salesman, and his mother was a housewife. Scaggs went to school at St. Mark's Preparatory School in Dallas, Texas, where he met Steve Miller, who would later found the very influential Steve Miller Band. While at St. Mark's, Miller would teach Scaggs how to play the guitar. As teenagers, they organized a group called the Marksmen Combo and played at school dances in the Dallas area.

Making Things Happen. The two friends headed north to attend the University of Wisconsin in the early 1960's. There they met Ben Sidran, a Chicagoan who had contacts with the city's blues community. The three musicians formed a group, called the Ardells, that played at clubs in the Madison, Wisconsin, area. Scaggs left Madison after a few years, without graduating, and returned to Dallas. There, he joined a new band called the Wigs. The group decided to leave Texas and try to find fame in England, but success never materialized. The Wigs fell apart, and Scaggs headed to the European continent, where he made a living by singing on street corners and in public squares. In the mid-1960's he settled down in Stockholm, Sweden, where he made and released his first album, *Boz* (1965), for Karusell Records, a Swedish company. It contained mostly American folk songs and was well received in Europe, though it was rarely heard in the United States and sold only a few copies.

The Psychedelic Scene. One day in Stockholm, Scaggs received a telegram from his old friend Miller, who had left Madison and was living in San Francisco. In the late 1960's, San Francisco had become the center of an entirely new music scene. Miller wanted Scaggs to join the newly organized Steve Miller Band, one of California's first psychedelic-rock groups. Miller's band had just signed a major record contract, and he wanted his friend to help make their first album a success. Scaggs played on the group's first two albums, which many critics consider to be the best ever released by the Steve Miller Band, *Children of the Future* and *Sailor* (both 1968). He then abruptly quit the band and headed out on his own again.

Scaggs released his first album made in the United States, *Boz Scaggs,* in 1969. It was produced by Jann Wenner, founder of *Rolling Stone* magazine, and featured the then-unknown guitarist Duane Allman. It contained blues, ballads, and some rock songs Scaggs had written. Despite good reviews it did not sell very well except in California. Apparently, Scaggs's audience was still too narrow and limited to the San Francisco Bay area.

Over the next few years Scaggs smoothed out the rougher edges of his blues style in three albums, *Boz Scaggs and His Band* (1971), *My Time* (1972), and *Slow Dancer* (1974), all released on the Atlantic label. Critics found his music and lyrics gifted and aggressive, but he still had not found a large audience. His first real success did not come until 1976 with *Silk Degrees,* an album that sold more than five million copies. Critics labeled it urban pop and described it as elegant and passionate; the album made Scaggs a real star. It included his first number 1 single and Grammy Award winner, "Lowdown." Scaggs called *Silk Degrees* a blend of his favorite styles: rock, soul, and disco. The success of this album quickly led to two more that sold millions of copies around the world, *Down Two Then Left* (1977) and *Middle Man* (1980). Four of his singles became Top-20 sellers in 1980, and he gave sold-out performances in Europe and the United States.

Dropping Out Again. Then, at the peak of his success, Scaggs shocked his fans by announcing that he was leaving music for an indefinite period of time. He and his wife, Carmella, were having problems that led to a bitter divorce and battle over custody of their two sons. Family trouble had a major impact on his decision to drop out of music for what he said would be only a short while.

For the Record

Boz Scaggs dropped out of the music business in 1981 at the height of his fame, saying that he was very uncomfortable being a sex symbol and a worldwide celebrity. "Fortune and fame aren't what they appear to be," he told *Rolling Stone.*

The singer was also troubled by his new image as a laidback singer of disco songs, with blow-dried hair and fancy clothes. He had given up his blue jeans, long hair, and rough blues and had achieved celebrity status and financial success with his new style, but that was not enough. So, from 1981 until 1985 he played only rarely in public, usually at benefit concerts such as one he gave for prisoners at San Quentin Prison in California.

He began work on a new album in 1985, but it was not completed until 1988. His record company, Columbia, decided, however, that it was not ready for release and told him it would have to be almost completely redone. Finally, late in 1988, *Other Roads* was released, containing original ballads, some dance music, and a few cuts containing the harder-edged blues he had been singing in the early 1970's. One song, "Heart of Mine," reached the Top-20 list, but the album itself was a financial failure, selling only a few thousand copies. Scaggs said he liked it, but few other record buyers did.

New Directions. Scaggs turned most of his attention, after the failure of *Other Roads*, to running his restaurant in San Francisco, the Blue Light Cafe. In 1994 he recorded another album, *Some Change*, for Virgin Records. Scaggs wrote all the songs for this release and also played the guitar and piano on the album. Songs on the album included a cajun-country track, "Fly Like a Bird," and a blues piece called "I'll Be the One." Critics liked *Some Change* and thought that it had brought Scaggs back to his roots. *Rolling Stone* found the songs "lit by the fire at the heart of cool." Sales, however, did not indicate that the public had yet rediscovered the virtues of Scaggs's music. He would give only a few concerts in the mid- to late 1990's, but he would maintain an intensely loyal, though very small, following.

—Leslie V. Tischauser

SELECT DISCOGRAPHY

■ ALBUMS

Boz, 1965
Boz Scaggs and His Band, 1971
My Time, 1972
Slow Dancer, 1974
Silk Degrees, 1976
Down Two Then Left, 1977
Middle Man, 1980
Other Roads, 1988
Some Change, 1994
Come On Home, 1997

SELECT AWARDS

Grammy Award for Best R&B Song for "Lowdown," 1976 (with David Paich)

SEE ALSO: Allman Brothers Band, The; Miller, Steve.

Schoolly D

(Jesse B. Weaver, Jr.)

BORN: Philadelphia, Pennsylvania; June 22, 1966
FIRST ALBUM RELEASE: *Schoolly D*, 1986
MUSICAL STYLE: Rap

Schoolly D's merits as a rapper have always been debated. He is generally regarded, however, as a pioneer "gangsta" rapper who paved the way for more talented rappers.

Auspicious Debut. Schoolly D's self-titled first album introduced the world to Philadelphia, Pennsylvania's vicious side. Along with DJ Code Money (Lance Allen), Schoolly D early in his career featured violence, vendettas, and guns in his lyrics. Included on his first self-produced album was an unsentimental description of the Parkside Killers (a Philadelphia gang) in "PSK—What Does It Mean?" Schoolly D also recorded the rap anthem "I Don't Like Rock 'n' Roll." Long before there was a national debate over the value of "gangsta" rap, Schoolly D had city officials calling for the removal of his albums from record stores.

Saturday Night (1987) and *Smoke Some Kill* (1988) continued in the same tradition, with pointed comment on the inner-city drug culture and lewd descriptions of genitalia. Schoolly D moved toward African philosophizing in *Am I Black Enough for You?* (1989) and *How a Black Man Feels* (1991), though without much success. *Welcome to America* (1994) is his best album, and a return to his "gangsta" roots. He was backed on

For the Record

Though he virtually disappeared in the late 1990's, Schooly D did contribute a hip version of "This Old Man" to *Rudy's Rockin' Kiddie Caravan* in 1997.

Welcome to America by a band which included session player Mike Tyler and bassist Chuck Treece.

Gangsta Pioneer. Schoolly D is an unusual figure. A rapper with limited lyrical grace, and who never had a commercial hit, he nevertheless was a widely respected pioneer of the "gangsta" style in the late 1980's. The *Jive Collection Series, Vol. 3* (1995) captures the elusive quality of his fame by including the underground sensations of the early 1980's, along with representative singles and album tracks. —*John Powell*

SELECT DISCOGRAPHY

■ ALBUMS

Schoolly D, 1986
Saturday Night, 1987
The Adventures of Schoolly D, 1987 (compilation)
Smoke Some Kill, 1988
Am I Black Enough for You?, 1989
How a Black Man Feels, 1991
Welcome to America, 1994
Reservoir Dog, 1995
Gangster's Story, 1996 (compilation)

SEE ALSO: Ice-T; N.W.A.; Snoop Doggy Dogg.

Seal

(Sealhenry Olumide Samuel)

BORN: London, England; February 19, 1963
FIRST ALBUM RELEASE: *Seal*, 1991
MUSICAL STYLES: Pop, pop rock, funk

Sealhenry Samuel became an international sensation in the summer of 1995 when a seven-year-old song and a hit action film magically collided. "Kiss from a Rose," written around 1988 while he lived in a London council flat, was chosen off his second album for inclusion in the sound track to 1995's *Batman Forever.* After racing to the top of the charts, this song awakened the interest of fans worldwide.

Early Days. The son of Nigerian and Brazilian parents, Seal first began performing at his school at the age of eleven, and joined his first group, Stay Brave, at age fifteen. After earning a degree in architecture and working several jobs, Seal began singing in London pubs. He was invited by the funk band Push to join them on their tour of Japan, and he briefly joined a Thai blues band. Having always loved travel, he spent several months exploring India and would credit his musical success in part to the calm and serenity he experienced there. Returning to England's Summer of Love House Explosion led to his first big break in the music industry. Through rap artist Chester he was introduced to the techno musician Adamski, who was looking for lyrics to what would become one of the hottest dance tracks of the 1990's. "Killer" (1990), with Seal on vocals, went to number 1 in the United Kingdom.

With a number 1 hit, Seal marketed his demo for "Crazy" but found record companies reluctant to offer him a deal. He eventually signed with producer Trevor Horn's ZTT label, and together they delivered a magnificent self-titled debut album (1991), recorded with former Prince bandmates Wendy and Lisa. *Seal* produced the pop hit "Crazy" (number 7) and eventually rose to number 24 on the album charts. It was widely acclaimed for its originality in laying strong melodies and structures over dance-floor grooves. The video for "Crazy" also introduced the public to Seal's mysterious persona. In part because his music reflected an unusual mixture of folk, soul, pop, and rock influences, the public was also intrigued by Seal's physical presence—six feet, four inches tall, black, with dreadlocks and heavy, half-moon facial scars under his eyes. He hinted at mysterious rites and rituals which many took to be natural to his African Caribbean heritage, though the truth was more mundane. The scars had resulted from severe blistering caused by a childhood disease, lupus.

For three years Seal toured, worked on his next album, and had several brushes with death. A major car accident near his new home in Los Angeles left him questioning his direction in life. In 1992 he taped an environmental-awareness public service announcement with Madonna for MTV, and the following year he joined Jeff Beck to deliver "Manic Depression" for the Jimi Hendrix tribute album *Stone Free.*

New Look, New Sound. His long awaited follow-up album, also entitled *Seal* (number 20, 1994), featured both a new look and a new sound. The dreadlocks were gone in favor of a shaved head, and the music moved into quieter and more nuanced grooves, though the insistent funk beat of the first single, "Prayer for the Dying" (number 21), proved that he had not altogether abandoned his dance roots. Slightly uncomfortable with the dance path he had traveled to stardom and personally preferring the folk rock of Joni Mitchell and Crosby, Stills, Nash, and Young to Chicago house music, he invited Mitchell to join him for a duet on "If I Could."

Despite the critical acclaim for the second *Seal*, his status as an international superstar was not fixed until the release of "Kiss from a Rose," which was featured in the sound track to *Batman Forever.* In the summer of 1995 "Kiss from a Rose" became the number 1 pop hit in the United States and spent twelve weeks on top of the adult contemporary charts. On the strength of the single, the parent album reentered the charts, and by the summer of 1996 it had sold more than four million copies.

Outside Projects. In September, 1997, Seal broke with longtime producer Trevor Horn and ZTT Records, signing with Warner Music and enlisting Stu Levine (Simply Red, Joe Cocker, Genesis) to produce his third album. Late in 1997 he contributed covers of classic tracks to two notable projects. Seal covered Peter, Paul, and Mary's "Puff (the Magic Dragon)" for the Pediatric AIDS Foundation album *For Our Children, Too* and the Steve Miller Band's "Fly Like an Eagle" (number 10, 1998) for the *Space Jam* sound track. *—John Powell*

SELECT DISCOGRAPHY

■ ALBUMS

Seal, 1991

Seal, 1994

Human Being, 1998

SELECT AWARDS

Grammy Awards for Record of the Year, Song of the Year, and Best Male Pop Vocal Performance for "Kiss from a Rose," 1995

SEE ALSO: Mitchell, Joni.

Seal at the 1996 Grammy Awards (AP/Wide World Photos)

Seals and Crofts

ORIGINAL MEMBERS: Jim Seals (b. 1941), Dash Crofts (b. Darrell Crofts, 1940)
FIRST ALBUM RELEASE: *Seals and Crofts*, 1970
MUSICAL STYLES: Pop, country, folk, jazz, soft rock

In the 1950's it was not uncommon for junior high school friends to form rock bands for fun. For Jim Seals and Dash Crofts, music was serious business. They were two musically talented teens who, from their junior high school years, would remain together for a long and fruitful musical career.

The Beginnings. Four-year-old Jim Seals was so intrigued by the fiddler in his grandfather's country music group that his grandfather ordered him a fiddle from a Sears catalog. Unable to play the instrument immediately, Seals, out of frustration, stored the fiddle under his bed for one year. After having a dream in which he could play, he took the fiddle out of storage, and the dream came true. Seals was playing both the fiddle and the guitar at age five, and by the time he was nine he had won the Texas State Fiddle Championship. Before long, he was playing with country bands traveling through Texas. By the time Seals was in high school, he was playing saxophone as well, and would later display his versatility on all three instruments as a professional musician.

Dash Crofts also showed an interest and ability in music when four years old; however, his first instrument was the piano, and his mother provided classical training for him until he was nine. Giving up the piano in order to play baseball, Crofts was influenced by rhythm-and-blues broadcasts from a Memphis radio station, which rekindled his musical interests. Instead of returning to the piano, Crofts began playing drums. He remained a drummer until his discovery of the mandolin in the late 1960's.

A few years after Seals and Crofts met in junior high school, Seals had the opportunity to work with Dave Burgess of the Champs ("Tequila"), who persuaded Seals to join him in Los Angeles. Seals in turn persuaded Dean Beard, owner of the Champs, to hire his drummer friend, Dash Crofts. From 1958 to 1965, Seals and Crofts toured and performed with the Champs until the group disbanded. Seals and Crofts then teamed up with guitarist Louie Shelton (later to become Seals and Crofts' producer) and bassist Joey Bogan (later to become Seals and Crofts' engineer) to form a group called the Mystics, performing other artists' material in clubs in the Los Angeles area.

With the formation of the Mystics, their manager, Marcia Day, brought the group through a series of transformations as the members tried to succeed as recording artists. With the first (unsuccessful) contract with Valiant Records, the name Mystics was changed to the Mushrooms. Three of Day's daughters who were performing as a trio in Las Vegas then joined the group, and the new seven-member group became known as the Dawnbreakers, performing in Las Vegas from 1967 to 1969. It was during this time that Marcia Day introduced Seals and Crofts to the Baha'i faith (an independent world religion whose central tenet proclaims the necessity of the unification of the human race), and after some investigation, both made separate decisions to become members of the faith in 1969.

Although the Dawnbreakers disbanded in 1969, all seven members had become Baha'is and remained deeply involved in their newly discovered religion. Seals and Crofts began performing as a duo with songs that often reflected teachings and principles of the Baha'i faith. Symbolic of the Baha'i principle of unity, for example, their music took on a mixture of different genres, blending country, folk, jazz, rock, and occasionally classical, and they experimented with new vocal harmonies, some Oriental in flavor, which would become the trademark sound of Seals and Crofts. Generally, their music became softer,

For the Record

"Summer Breeze," the song from the album of the same name, remained on the *Billboard* charts for two years, making it the longest-charting single in pop history.

sounding more like folk than rock. Seals concentrated on guitar, and Crofts learned to play mandolin and guitar. Some of the lyrics were inspired by the writings of Baha'u'llah, prophet and founder of the Baha'i faith, and from that point on, Seals and Crofts would be known as much for their association with the Baha'i faith as they would for their music.

A Career-Threatening Controversy. Shortly after Seals and Crofts became members of the Baha'i faith, their career moved quickly. They officially began performing as a duo called Seals and Crofts in 1969, recorded their first two albums in 1970 (*Seals and Crofts* and *Down Home*), and from 1972 to 1976, produced five gold albums: *Summer Breeze* (1972), *Diamond Girl* (1973), *I'll Play for You* (1975), *Seals and Crofts Greatest Hits* (1975), and *Get Closer* (1976). However, there was one album in this period, *Unborn Child* (1974), that became controversial and temporarily damaged their careers.

Although the title song of the album, "Unborn Child," reached number 14 on the *Billboard* charts, it became subject to an ongoing abortion debate. Nonjudgmental in its position on abortion, the lyrics to "Unborn Child" simply stated that life is the beginning of the soul. The issue of abortion, however, was so controversial that many radio stations banned the playing of Seals and Crofts' music; and once, while on tour in Wisconsin, protesters lined the streets outside the concert hall. At that particular concert, Seals stated that out of respect for those protesters who stood in the snow, "Unborn Child" would not be performed. Notwithstanding the public debate and controversy over *Unborn Child,* Seals and Crofts received more personal letters and flowers from their fans regarding *Unborn Child* than from any other recording.

Recording Classics. On tour in the Boston area after the release of their fourth album, *Summer Breeze,* Seals and Crofts were scheduled to perform an outdoor concert. The impending cancellation of the concert due to rainy weather precipitated more bad news. Manager Marcia Day received a call from Warner Bros. indicating that *Summer Breeze* was "dead," and they should abandon the tour. "Over my dead body," was Day's reply, and she proceeded to call radio stations explaining that Seals and Crofts were in town and would perform a free concert if an indoor auditorium could be obtained. A hall at Harvard University was acquired, and in the process of publicizing the performance, radio stations began playing the music of Seals and Crofts. Two concerts were given that day, and both were flooded by the media. The publicity resulted in an immediate success of the title song, "Summer Breeze," which would remain on the *Billboard* charts for two years.

Legacy. In the early 1980's, growing weary of the concert tours, Seals and Crofts decided to take some time off, and they simply never recorded again, although they embarked on a short reunion tour in 1991 and 1992, and they would occasionally perform for special Baha'i events. Seals and Crofts are considered by many to have been among the most underappreciated pop musicians. They never had a number 1 hit, nor did they receive a Grammy Award; however, surveys consistently reveal that the most often played group on oldies and light-rock radio programs is Seals and Crofts. Their music and influence is evident in the music of other artists as well as in the heightened spiritual awareness of those who listen to their music, an influence which has received recognition particularly in the international Baha'i community. —*Kerry Hart*

SELECT DISCOGRAPHY

■ ALBUMS

Seals and Crofts, 1970
Down Home, 1970
Year of Sunday, 1972
Summer Breeze, 1972
Diamond Girl, 1973
Unborn Child, 1974
I'll Play for You, 1975
Seals and Crofts Greatest Hits, 1975
Get Closer, 1976
Sudan Village, 1976
Takin' It Easy, 1978
The Longest Road, 1980

SEE ALSO: Bread; Simon and Garfunkel.

John Sebastian. *See* The Lovin' Spoonful

Jon Secada

BORN: Havana, Cuba; October 4, 1962
FIRST ALBUM RELEASE: *Jon Secada*, 1992
MUSICAL STYLES: Latin, pop

With a smooth blend of Latin, pop, and rhythm and blues, Jon Secada was one of the biggest adult-contemporary artists of the 1990's. Along with early protégés Gloria and Emilio Estefan, he paved the way for mainstream pop with Latin roots. Secada's recordings, often released in both English and Spanish versions, routinely charted on the pop, Latin, and adult contemporary charts.

Beginnings. Secada was born in Havana, Cuba. When his parents applied to leave the island legally in 1969, his father was sent to a work camp for a year and a half. The family finally was allowed to leave Cuba in 1971 and resettled in Miami Beach, Florida. Secada was a good student, but he came late to music, first demonstrating his talent as the young Ebenezer Scrooge in an eleventh-grade rendition of Charles Dickens's *A Christmas Carol.* He went on to earn a masters degree in jazz vocal performance from the University of Miami, then took a teaching job at Miami Community College.

In the mid-1980's, Secada was introduced to Emilio Estefan, Jr., by mutual friends. Estefan was then influential in the Miami pop scene, producing the Miami Sound Machine and other south Florida acts. He had been a founding member of the disco group Miami Sound Machine, and his wife, Gloria, continued to be their lead singer. Estefan hired Secada as a songwriter and for five years mentored him in every aspect of the music business, including production, songwriting, industry protocol, and marketing. Secada worked closely with Estefan as he turned the Miami Sound Machine from a novelty Latin disco band into a mass-market vehicle for Gloria Estefan. Between 1986 and 1989, all three Miami Sound Machine albums went multiplatinum.

Secada's big break as a performer came in 1990 when he was invited to sing backup on Gloria Estefan's "Into the Light" tour, a natural development considering his smooth vocals and the fact that he had cowritten six songs on the multiplatinum *Into the Light* (1991) album, including the number 1 pop hit "Coming out of the Dark." At one point halfway through the tour, Estefan turned the stage over to the publicly unknown Secada, who became an instant star. Following the tour, Emilio Estefan was convinced that Secada was ready for his first solo release.

Popularity. Secada's intimate debut album, *Jon Secada* (1992, number 15) was an instant hit, with four Top-40 singles: "Just Another Day" (number 5), "Do You Believe in Us" (number 13), "Angel" (number 18), and "I'm Free" (number 27). *Jon Secada* spent thirty-one weeks in the Top 40 and within five years had sold more than six million copies. When three tracks from *Jon Secada* went to the top of the Latin charts, it was decided to release a Spanish version. *Otro Dia Mas Sin Verte* (1992) topped the Latin album charts and earned Secada his first Grammy Award, for Best Latin Pop Album. Despite the success, Estefan continued to market Secada heavily around the world in order to guard against a perception that he was simply a Latin phenomenon. They promoted the album overseas and encouraged Secada to tour Europe and Asia. Early in 1993 he gave more than eighty interviews to press agents from twenty-two countries and received a complete makeover from former model Ingrid Casares.

With the public primed for his second album, *Heart, Soul & a Voice* (1994), Secada continued to deliver the smoldering pop love ballads that made him famous, but he echoed more of his early pop and rhythm-and-blues influences such as Earth, Wind, and Fire, Stevie Wonder, Chic, and Marvin Gaye. "If You Go" reached number 10 on the pop charts, and the album went platinum. The English version differed substantially from its Spanish counterpart (*Si Te Vas*), incorporating more hip-hop rhythms and soul strains.

More Releases. Secada released *Amor* in October, 1995, which earned him another Grammy for

For the Record

Jon Secada appeared live onstage with tenor Luciano Pavarotti in 1996, performing "Angel" and "Granada."

Best Latin Pop Performance. Also in 1995, he starred in the Broadway production of Jim Jacobs and Warren Casey's *Grease*, fueling rumors that he intended to pursue an acting career. Through 1997, however, he had only made minor guest appearances, including one on television's *Melrose Place*. Early in 1997 he recorded "Somewhere" for *Dave Grusin Presents West Side Story*, whose release coincided with the fortieth anniversary of the Leonard Bernstein/Stephen Sondheim Broadway premiere. Produced by Phil Ramone, the album is a fusion of Jazz, Latin, and classical music that features Secada, Gloria Estefan, Arturo Sandoval, Michael Brecker, and Lee Ritenour. His fourth album, *Secada* (1997), marked a return to the style of his monster debut album, featuring emotional ballads and midtempo pop tunes. —*John Powell*

SELECT DISCOGRAPHY

■ ALBUMS

Jon Secada, 1992
Heart, Soul & a Voice, 1994
Amor, 1995
Secada, 1997

SELECT AWARDS

Grammy Award for Best Latin Pop Album for *Otro Dia Mas Sin Verte*, 1992
Grammy Award for Best Latin Pop Performance for *Amor*, 1995

SEE ALSO: Estefan, Gloria.

Neil Sedaka

BORN: Brooklyn, New York; March 13, 1939
FIRST SINGLE RELEASE: "The Diary," 1958
MUSICAL STYLES: Pop, rock and roll

Neil Sedaka's interest in music began around age four, after listening to music programs on the radio. By age eight, Sedaka was playing the piano five hours per day, and by age thirteen, he was playing classical piano music at a hotel resort in the Catskill Mountains of New York. In late 1952, Sedaka and his Brooklyn friend Howard Greenfield began writing songs together, and Sedaka became strongly attracted to popular music. He formed a high school band known as the Tokens in 1956 and was also selected that year as one of the seven best classical pianists in New York high schools. As a result, he received a two-year scholarship to the prestigious Juilliard School of Music.

From Classical to Pop. In early 1958, song publishers Al Nevins and Don Kirshner contracted Sedaka and Greenfield as professional

Neil Sedaka (Archive Photos)

songwriters, and their song "Stupid Cupid," sung by Connie Francis, became an international hit in the summer of 1958. At the end of 1958, Sedaka was signed to sing for the Radio Corporation of America (RCA), and he quickly released his first hit, "The Diary." It was followed by one of his most famous songs, "Oh! Carol," which was written in honor of his former girlfriend Carole King.

Writing and Singing Major Hits. Sedaka's great voice and memorable tunes resulted in a string of big hits in the early 1960's. "Stairway to Heaven" rose to number 9 on the pop charts in 1960, and "Calendar Girl" and "Happy Birthday, Sweet Sixteen" rose to number 4 and number 6, respectively, in 1961. Sedaka's first number 1 hit came in 1962 with his classic "Breaking Up Is Hard to Do," followed by "Next Door to an Angel," which rose to the number 5 spot.

With the increasing popularity of British pop groups, Sedaka's singing career began to wane in 1963, but he still had three moderate hits in "Let's Go Steady Again," "Alice in Wonderland," and "Bad Girl." By 1964, Sedaka had abandoned his pop-star role, and he concentrated on songwriting with Greenfield. Over the next ten years, the two friends wrote numerous hits, including "Venus in Blue Jeans" for Jimmy Clanton, "Workin' on a Groovy Thing" for the Fifth Dimension, "Puppet Man" for Tom Jones, and "Is This the Way to Amarillo?" for Tony Christie. By the end of 1973, Sedaka and Greenfield had written more than five hundred songs that had sold more than twenty million records.

A Successful Comeback. Between 1971 and 1972, Sedaka began his singing comeback and relocated to England. By 1973, he was on the British charts with "That's When the Music Takes Me" from his album *Solitaire*, and Elton John accelerated Sedaka's comeback by signing him to his Rocket Records label. In 1974, "Laughter in the Rain" was a number 1 hit in England and the United States, completing a remarkable international comeback for Sedaka. "Love Will Keep Us Together," cowritten by Sedaka and Greenfield, was a number 1 hit for the Captain and Tennille in 1975, and won the Record of the Year Grammy Award. By the end of 1975, Sedaka's *The Hungry Years* was certified gold, and "Bad Blood" was a number 1 hit on the U.S. pop charts.

A ballad reworking of "Breaking Up Is Hard to Do" took Sedaka to number 8 on the pop charts in 1976, and "Love in the Shadows" reached number 16. That same year, Sedaka performed his first television special, followed by another in the summer of 1980. Also in 1980, Sedaka and his daughter Dara recorded "Should've Never Let You Go," which reached number 19 on the pop charts. In the late 1980's, Sedaka intensified his song lyrics, concentrating on inspirational, spiritual themes. Using a seventy-five-piece symphony orchestra, he produced a successful compact disc titled *Classically Sedaka*, and he would continue to have a very active touring schedule, performing hits from three decades. —*Alvin K. Benson*

For the Record

While Sedaka was traveling incognito on a tour bus in Beijing, China, the tour guide said that because there were so many Americans on board, he would sing a famous American song. After the guide sang "Oh! Carol," Sedaka exclaimed, "That's my song!"

SELECT DISCOGRAPHY

■ SINGLES

"Calendar Girl," 1961
"Happy Birthday, Sweet Sixteen," 1961
"Breaking Up Is Hard to Do," 1962
"Next Door to an Angel," 1962
"Laughter in the Rain," 1974
"Bad Blood," 1975

■ ALBUMS

Neil Sedaka Sings His Greatest Hits, 1962
Sedaka's Back, 1974
The Hungry Years, 1975
All-Time Greatest Hits, 1991 (compilation)

SEE ALSO: Captain and Tennille; Carpenters, The; Everly Brothers, The; Fifth Dimension, The; John, Elton; Jones, Tom; King, Carole.

Pete Seeger

BORN: Patterson, New York; May 3, 1919
FIRST ALBUM RELEASE: *Songs for John Doe*, 1941 (with the Almanac Singers)
MUSICAL STYLE: Folk

Pete Seeger was born into a musical family; his father, Charles, was a musicologist and a professor at the University of California at Berkeley, and his mother was a pianist. Charles Seeger lost his professorship as a result of his radical activities and returned to the family estate in upstate New York. Pete attended a private high school in Connecticut on a scholarship and was accepted on scholarship into Harvard University. He spent two years there studying sociology. However, he was dissatisfied with the abstract and academic approach to social issues. His father was drawn to the significance of folk and protest songs during the Great Depression of the 1930's, and Seeger learned some of these songs from his father. Seeger wanted to go among the people and learn their songs, then sing them at meetings of labor unions. He hopped freight trains and traveled all over the country one summer after meeting Woody Guthrie, and he learned more about people and their songs. He played banjo and, later, twelve-string guitar. In 1941 he met Lee Hays, and they formed a folk singing group called the Almanac Singers. The group performed at union halls where they sang radical songs and adaptations of traditional ballads. Seeger was becoming more adept at playing the five-string banjo after listening to folk musicians in the South. He was, however, still inexperienced in performing; he could play or sing but not do both at the same time. His voice was very high; he called it a split tenor, although it was close to a countertenor. His high voice was balanced by the very deep bass of Lee Hays and the baritone of Mill Lampell. The Almanac Singers achieved local fame and were offered a record contract in 1941. Their record label, Keynote, was afraid to put its name on the record due to its radical content, but it was released as an Almanac record in June of 1941. The Almanac Singers recorded two other albums with Folkway Records and continued to have limited success. However, the United States was by this time involved in World War II, and Seeger was drafted in 1942, which meant the end of the Almanac Singers.

The Weavers. Seeger continued to sing at union halls and other gatherings after he was discharged from the Army. In 1949, he founded a new group, the Weavers, with Lee Hays singing bass, Fred Hellerman baritone, and Ronnie Gilbert soprano. The group tried to maintain the folk purity that embodied their ideals. However, their phenomenal success in clubs and in record sales threatened that purity. At one point, they had the number 1 and number 2 songs in the country with "Goodnight Irene" and "Tzena, Tzena." Gordon Jenkins, who arranged "Good Night Irene," added a melancholy set of violins to the song written by Huddie Ledbetter (Leadbelly). The manager of the Weavers also booked the group dates at fancy supper clubs and nightclubs, where they felt out of place singing protest songs in formal clothes. More significant, Decca records censored the selections of the Weavers and refused to allow them to sing the radical songs that had originally inspired the group. When Seeger wanted to continue singing at union meetings, his manager refused to allow it. In addition, the group's enormous popularity was threatened by their identification with radical and communist causes, and they lost club dates, the Decca contract, and radio and television appearances. This was especially a problem for Seeger since he challenged the authority of the House Un-American Activitites Committee. Subsequently, he was not allowed to appear on television for more than ten years. As a result of these pressures, the Weavers broke up, although various versions of the group still recorded. The Weavers performed a reunion concert to a nostalgic audience in May, 1963, at New York's Carnegie Hall. The record of this concert, *The Weavers at Carnegie Hall*, was treasured by fans of the group and gained new converts.

Seeger's Solo Career. After the breakup of the Weavers, Pete Seeger traveled around the country appearing at high schools and small auditoriums. Often his appearance was preceded by some con-

In 1969 Pete Seeger stands on the bow of the boat he and other volunteers would sail to rally people to the cause of fighting pollution on the Hudson River (AP/Wide World Photos)

troversy because of his political views or his reputation. It was a difficult period for him, but he perfected his art as a banjo and guitar player and as a singer. He became more proficient in relating to his audience and getting them to sing and join in the performance. He found that he needed that contact with an audience to make him feel whole and alive. He claimed that he was not much of a vocalist but that he could get any audience to sing along with him. A natural audience for him would have been the viewers of the television program *Hootenanny*; however, he was not able to appear on the program because of his radical political views. He did find a larger audience at the Newport Folk Festival in 1959 and in subsequent years there. The creation of the festival was a tribute to the proselytizing for folk music that Seeger had done over the years. The record *Folk Festival at Newport, Volume 1* contains a number of songs performed by Seeger.

During this period, Seeger recorded a number of solo albums. He recorded *The Rainbow Quest* in 1960, *Gazette, Volume 1* in 1958, *Gazette, Volume 2* in 1961, and *The Bitter and the Sweet* in 1963. He recorded "Where Have All the Flowers Gone" (it appears on *The Bitter and the Sweet*) in 1956 and forgot about the song. However, when the Kingston Trio recorded the song and made it a hit record, they claimed to have written the song. When Seeger called their attention to his earlier record, they were forced to admit the song was Seeger's. It is ironic and unfortunate that a number of folk groups were first influenced by the records and appearances of Pete Seeger and then prospered while Seeger remained blacklisted. Seeger had his first solo hit with "Little Boxes." It was a satiric rather than a true folk or protest song, and this may have accounted for its popularity.

Seeger became deeply involved with the civil rights protests in the 1960's. He appeared at Birmingham in 1963 when Martin Luther King, Jr., was in prison. He was also in Selma, Alabama, in 1965 when King made one of his most significant marches. Seeger was the one to bring the song "We Shall Overcome" to the attention of civil rights groups, and he sang the song, adding verses, all through this difficult period.

Pete Seeger finally was allowed to appear on television on *The Smothers Brothers Comedy Hour.* However, there was another controversy about Seeger's insistence on singing "Waist Deep in the Big Muddy," a protest song about the Vietnam War. Seeger sang the song, but when the program was broadcast, it was cut out. He was enraged at this duplicity, and he continued to refuse to compromise his principles, even though it continued to cause him difficulties and cost him a good deal of money.

Folk's Elder Statesman. Pete Seeger became discouraged after the assassinations of Martin Luther King, Jr., and Robert Kennedy in 1968. He decided to stop singing in public. However, he found a new cause; he brought a group of people together, determined to clean up New York's Hudson River. The river had been deeply polluted for a number of years, and most people thought the effort to clean it was folly. Seeger did rally people to this cause, however; he built a boat to sail the river and did succeed in cleaning large sections of the river. He recorded "Clearwater" in 1974 to raise money and to rally more people to the cause.

During this period, a number of Seeger albums appeared. *The Essential Pete Seeger* was issued in 1978. Later, the Weavers performed a final farewell concert at Carnegie Hall, and a film and an album of the concert, both titled *Wasn't That a Time,* were issued. This marked the end of the Weavers, but Seeger kept recording and making appearances, never losing his enthusiasm for a song or a cause. —*James Sullivan*

SELECT DISCOGRAPHY

■ ALBUMS

Talking Union and Other Songs, 1941 (with the Almanac Singers)
The Weavers on Tour, 1958 (with the Weavers)
Gazette, Volume 1, 1958
Pete Seeger's Greatest Hits, 1967
Rainbow Race, 1973

SELECT AWARDS

Grammy Award for Lifetime Achievement, 1993

SEE ALSO: Dylan, Bob; Guthrie, Woody; Leadbelly.

Bob Seger

BORN: Dearborn, Michigan; May 6, 1945
FIRST ALBUM RELEASE: *Ramblin' Gamblin' Man,* 1968
MUSICAL STYLES: Rock and roll, pop

Bob Seger is a heartland rocker with one of the most remarkable voices in popular music. During the latter half of the 1970's, his no-frills, hard-edged, garage-band sound with its hints of rhythm and blues and soul helped keep alive the spirit of rock and roll during the reign of Bee Gees-style disco. Seger enjoyed seven Top-10, platinum selling albums in a row, beginning with 1976's *Live Bullet.*

Early Life. The foundation of Seger's musical identity can be found in his midwestern, blue-collar roots. He was the son of a dance-band leader and medic for Ford Motor Company. His father influenced Seger to take up music but then deserted the family before Bob was a teenager. Seger formed his first band, a trio called the Decibels, when he was still in high school. He soon found himself playing with the Town Criers in the Ann Arbor area as well as with Doug Brown and the Omens. Under the name the Beach Bums, the latter group recorded a parody of the then-popular novelty song, "The Ballad of the Green Beret." It was removed from the market when the creator of its inspiration, Sergeant Barry Sadler, threatened a lawsuit.

Seger went on to record several songs for the independent label Cameo, bringing him one or two years of regional success before the label declared bankruptcy. In 1968, he formed the Bob Seger System and signed with Capitol Records. The band's debut did well, its title track, "Ramblin' Gamblin' Man," reaching number 17 on the national charts, but their second album fizzled. Dejected, Seger abandoned music in 1969 in favor of college.

Road to Success. Seger's early retirement from music was short-lived. By the end of 1969, he had formed a new band and soon released another album, *Mongrel* (1970). However, it failed to sell well—a fate shared by other Seger albums released in the early 1970's. However, constant touring did help him create a strong fan base. Seger's support during this period mainly came from the Midwest, where he was quickly becoming something of a homegrown rock-and-roll icon. Seger would later reveal the personal cost of this incessant touring in one of his best known songs, "Turn the Page."

Seger returned to Capitol Records in 1975 to record *Beautiful Loser* with a new ensemble, the Silver Bullet Band. The group featured Drew Abbott on guitar, Robyn Robbins on keyboard instruments, Alto Reed on saxophone, Chris Campbell on bass, and Charlie Allen Martin on drums, and it was to become closely associated with Seger and his music. Signing with Capitol was a move in the right direction for Seger's career, but it did not result in instant success. *Beautiful Loser* did produce one regional hit, "Katmandu." The song would eventually become much better known, but it was the extensive touring by Seger and the Silver Bullet Band in support of *Beautiful Loser*, more than record sales, which laid the foundation for the national acclaim that was to soon follow.

The Big Time. Seger finally reached national attention with a live double album released in 1976, *Live Bullet*. This was recorded in Detroit, the city with which Seger is most closely associated. Only a few other artists, most notably Peter Frampton, have first seized the public ear with a live effort. The fact that Seger emerged nationally in this way testifies to his ability as a concert performer. So great was the success of *Live Bullet* that it spent more than three years on the charts and eventually went quadruple platinum. Seger followed it with a studio effort, *Night Moves*. Released late in 1976, it became one of the most popular albums of 1977. Capitol issued several songs from *Night Moves* as singles that quickly climbed the charts, including the album's title track.

By the late 1970's, Seger had hit his stride as both a recording artist and songwriter. His 1978 effort, *Stranger in Town*, contained the hard driv-

Bob Seger (Paul Natkin)

ing hits "Still the Same," "Hollywood Nights," and "Old Time Rock & Roll." Shifting gears somewhat, Seger next released *Against the Wind* in 1980, the album reaching number 1 on the album charts with the help of three memorable ballads, "Fire Lake," "Against the Wind" and "You'll Accomp'ny Me." Upbeat or slow and tender, each hit helped establish Seger's rough-hewn, down-to-earth persona in the minds of the record-buying public. Following up on the success of *Live Bullet*, Seger released a second live album, *Nine Tonight*, in 1981. It too went multiplatinum.

Seger's career then took a downturn. He recorded *The Distance* in 1982, but it only sold one million copies and generated only one single, a cover of Rodney Crowell's "Shame on the Moon." The album's use of studio musicians also led to guitarist Drew Abbott leaving the Silver Bullet Band. Perhaps in response to these setbacks, Seger began touring and recording less. He released only one other album during the decade, 1986's *Like a Rock*. Its title track became one of the best-known Seger songs, due in large part to its extensive use in Chevrolet commercials.

Contributions. "Like a Rock" highlighted Seger's two contributions to popular music. First, it once again demonstrated his ability to compose a hit with lasting appeal. Second, it showcased his remarkable voice. Concerning Seger the songwriter, his most popular numbers have fallen into two broad categories. There are the straightforward, hard-rocking numbers "Fire down Below" and "Katmandu." Several of these have become rock-and-roll anthems and sound almost as fresh today as when first recorded. Seger has also shown a knack for writing wistful rock ballads, such as "Like a Rock" and "Against the Wind." Tough and tender at the same time, they look back nostalgically in a way that continues to resonate with American baby boomers.

Seger's talent as a singer has been as great as his gift as a songwriter. Few other rock vocalists have been blessed with such a powerful instrument. It blasts forth from speakers, threatening to melt down their cones. Actually, Seger possesses three distinct voices. The first is a full, rich, conversational baritone; the second is higher and more rock oriented, full of grit; and the third is a high-altitude shriek that is even more powerful. Seger uses these voices in different combinations to create a remarkably broad range of musical expression.

For the Record

Seger showed that he had not forgotten his blue-collar roots by donating royalties from the Chevrolet ads that used his "Like a Rock" to groups supporting American autoworkers.

"Shakedown." Seger enjoyed his first chart-topping single in 1987 with "Shakedown," from the sound track of the hit film *Beverly Hills Cop II* (1987). Seger's career would remain rather static from that point. *The Fire Inside* (1991) sold fairly well but contained nothing memorable in comparison to earlier albums. *It's a Mystery*, released in 1995, fared worse, becoming the first album since *Live Bullet* to not go platinum. However, Seger would maintain a strong fan base through live performances. His concerts continued to sell out, making him one of the most popular older artists on the so-called Jurassic rock circuit. The number of Websites established by Seger fans also testifies to his continued popularity.

—David Lee Fish

SELECT DISCOGRAPHY

■ ALBUMS

Live Bullet, 1976
Night Moves, 1976
Stranger in Town, 1978
Against the Wind, 1980
Like a Rock, 1986

SELECT AWARDS

Grammy Award for Best Rock Performance by a Duo or Group with Vocal for "Against the Wind," 1980 (with the Silver Bullet Band)

SEE ALSO: Petty, Tom, and the Heartbreakers; Springsteen, Bruce.

Selena

BORN: Lake Jackson, Texas; April 16, 1971
DIED: Corpus Christi, Texas; March 31, 1995
FIRST ALBUM RELEASE: *Selena y los Dinos*, 1984
MUSICAL STYLES: Latin, rhythm and blues, rock and roll, country

With her special blend of Latin cumbia (the polka style popular along the Texas-Mexican border), rhythm and blues, country, and rock, Selena was a superstar of tejano music. She also served as a role model for young Latina women. She was on the verge of a successful crossover career with the recording of her first English-language album when she was shot to death by her friend and business associate Yolanda Saldivar on March 31, 1995.

Early Years and Career Successes. Selena was born Selena Quintanilla in 1971. She first began performing in 1980. In 1982 she recorded two singles in Spanish, but these were never released. Her first album recording came in 1984 with *Selena y los Dinos* and included such songs as "Ya Se Va," "Ya Lo Se Que Tu Te Vas," "Tres Veces No," and "Give Me One Chance." In the same year, she also recorded twelve songs on cassette, but they were never released. Under the management of her father, Abraham Quintanilla, she traveled and performed with the family band, Los Dinos, which included her sister Suzette and her brother A. B.

In 1987, Selena received her first Female Vocalist of the Year and Performer of the Year awards at the Tejano Music Awards, produced by the Texas Talent Musicians Association. She signed on with EMI Latin in 1989. That year, *Selena*, her first EMI Latin album, was released. She married Chris Perez, a musician in her band, on April 2, 1992.

Live won her a Grammy Award for Best Mexican/American Album in 1993. Also in that year, Selena won the Female Vocalist of the Year award at the ACE Awards in New York and was chosen as *Billboard*'s number 1 Latin artist, and *Entre a Mi Mundo* was named *Billboard*'s number 1 Latin album. Selena also started a clothing manufacturing business, *Selena Etc.* She opened a factory in

Selena (Archive Newsphotos/Percy Hawke)

Monterrey, Mexico. In 1994 she opened two *Selena Etc.* boutiques in Corpus Christi and San Antonio, Texas. Yolanda Saldivar, the president of Selena's fan club, was hired to help with the clothing boutiques, and she often accompanied Selena on trips to Monterrey. That year, the band performed in Los Angeles, New York, Puerto Rico, and Argentina.

In 1995, Selena won six Tejano Music Awards. One of these was her eighth Top Female Vocalist award. She had previously won this award in 1987 and in each year from 1989 to 1994. Selena was also nominated for a second Grammy for the album *Amor Prohibido* (1994), which sold approximately 500,000 copies before her untimely death. In February, over 62,000 fans attended her concert at the Astrodome in Houston, Texas. This was her last concert. On March 31, 1995, Selena was shot to death by Saldivar outside a motel in Corpus Christi. It was believed that Saldivar and Selena had argued over business records. Saldivar later testified that she had intended to kill herself, but her gun accidentally went off and killed Selena instead. Saldivar went to trial, and, on October 23, she was convicted of the murder. She was sentenced to life imprisonment in a state prison.

Selena's Legacy. Some critics believe that at the time of her death, the popular Mexican-American singer was well on her way to achieving the success of a Gloria Estefan, Julio Iglesias, or Jose Feliciano. She was about to embark on a true crossover career with her first English-language album. It is generally agreed that Selena was a charismatic and talented role model with whom fans could identify. She represented hard work, family devotion, and wholesome cultural values.

Hispanic fans were pleased by her success in mainstream popular culture because she was able to achieve this success without sacrificing the elements of Mexican-American traditional music in her style. Although she projected strong family values, Selena also had a sensual side that attracted many listeners. To some extent, the tension between these aspects of her personality served to enhance the public's fascination with her. As with Jim Croce, Glen Miller, Janis Joplin, John Lennon, Jimi Hendrix, and other similar figures in popular music, her early death only served to increase her fame.

Posthumous Recognition. Governor George W. Bush of Texas proclaimed April 16, 1995, "Selena Day." On May 29, 1995, 30,800 people attended the Memorial Day Tribute to Selena at the Astrodome in Houston, Texas. *People* magazine's special tribute issue sold out its first printing's 600,000 copies immediately, and 350,000 additional copies had to be printed. *Selena!* (1995), a bilingual biography written by Clint Richmond, debuted at number 1 on *The New York Times* best-seller list. Her first English-language album, *Dreaming of You* (1995), released five months after her death, debuted on the *Billboard* Top 200 album charts at number 1, with 331,000 copies purchased in the first week. *Selena*, a movie written and directed by the Mexican-American Gregory Nava (*El Norte/The North*, 1984), opened in U.S. theaters in March, 1997, with two versions available: one in English and one with Spanish subtitles. The film starred the Puerto Rican actress Jennifer Lopez as Selena from ages eighteen to twenty-three and Academy Award nominee Edward James Olmos (*Stand and Deliver*, 1988; *American Me*, 1992; *Mi Familia/My Family*) as Selena's father. Newcomer Becky Lee Meza, a ten-year-old Texan, portrayed the younger Selena at age eight. Selena's father was the executive producer.

—Alice Myers

For the Record

In 1978, when Selena was seven, Johnny Herrera recorded her singing with guitar accompaniment on an audiocassette recorder. This was the very first known recording of the future superstar. The next year, Selena recorded "Si Quieres Verme Llorar" in English, but the two-inch master tape was never pressed.

SELECT DISCOGRAPHY

■ ALBUMS

Los Dinos

Selena y los Dinos, 1984
Baile Esta Cumbia, 1992

Selena Solo

Ven Conmigo, 1990
Entre a Mi Mundo, 1992
Live, 1993 (live)
Amor Prohibido, 1994
Dreaming of You, 1995
Siempre Selena, 1996
Selena, 1997 (motion picture sound track)
Anthology, 1998 (previously released material)

SELECT AWARDS

Grammy Award for Best Mexican/American Album for *Live*, 1993.

SEE ALSO: Croce, Jim; Estefan, Gloria; Feliciano, José; Gabriel, Ana; Hendrix, Jimi; Iglesias, Julio; Joplin, Janis; Lennon, John.

Brian Setzer. *See* The Stray Cats / Brian Setzer

The Sex Pistols

ORIGINAL MEMBERS: Johnny Rotten (b. John Lydon, 1956), Steve Jones (b. 1955), Paul Cook (b. 1956), Glen Matlock (b. 1956)

OTHER MEMBERS: Sid Vicious (b. John Simon Ritchie, 1957-1979)

FIRST SINGLE RELEASE: "Anarchy in the U.K."/"I Wanna Be Me," 1976

MUSICAL STYLE: Punk rock

Formed by sex shop and boutique owner Malcolm McLaren in 1975, the Sex Pistols were composed of McLaren's shop assistant Steve Jones; two customers, Jones's friends Paul Cook and Glen Matlock; and John Lydon, who was selected by McLaren as the group's front man for his ability to pose and sneer. Although they were not the first punk-rock group, the Sex Pistols managed to exploit and spread the punk image worldwide.

Beginnings. McLaren's sex emporium had various names, including Let It Rock, Seditionaries, and Sex. Thus, the name Sex Pistols was a reference to McLaren's shop as well as to the male genitalia. The core of the group, Jones, Cook, and Matlock, originally had worked together in their own band called Swankers, with a lead singer named Wally Nightingale, whom McLaren replaced with Lydon (christened Johnny Rotten by Jones for his poor hygiene) after becoming manager. Putting Jones on guitar, Cook on drums, Matlock on bass, and leaving the vocals to Rotten, McLaren succeeded in creating and propagating a "bad-boy" image for the band. Due to McLaren's successful marketing, the group's reputation preceded its first album release.

Shock Value. The Sex Pistols' first concert was on November 6, 1975. At this and many other concerts, Rotten shouted insults at the audience, hurled empty beer bottles, blew his nose, and made obscene gestures. During performances, other members of the group often spat in the air or vomited. In addition, the members of the group openly bragged about their drug and alcohol abuse and their sexual prowess. Sporting black leather and hairstyles that looked as if they had been blown dry in a wind tunnel, the Sex Pistols served as models for the punk movement and epitomized the punk look. With their dress and actions, they were able to shock and terrorize audiences more than any other previous punk-rock group had done.

Reports of the group's strangely dressed following and early live concerts, which were frequently punctuated by brawls, had previously circulated in the press, but it was a television appearance on December 1, 1976, that established the group's reputation. A provocative interview by Bill Grundy on London Weekend Television's *Today* show ended in a flurry of four-letter words, prompting endless telephone complaints to the station and coverage of the band in the national press.

The group's guitarist Steve Jones later admitted that the antisocial posturing of the Sex Pistols was a sham. He said that he joined the group in order to meet girls and get drunk, stating bluntly, "I was really a football hooligan. I went to matches and bashed people. Punk was the perfect way to do what I wanted to do—cause trouble—and get paid for it."

Buzz and Blast. In its January 16, 1978, issue, *Time* magazine called the Sex Pistols' music a return to "basic buzz and blast" rock and roll. This judgment could not have been more fitting since this was exactly the aim of punk, to breathe life back into a boring music industry. The music was

For the Record

When the legendary Bo Diddley was told that members of the Sex Pistols occasionally vomited during their performances, he was not impressed: "This group . . . pukes onstage? I don't necessarily like that. That's not showmanship. . . . They gotta get themselves an act."

ear shattering and brutal and showed extreme cynicism toward popular culture, public policy, and the establishment in Britain. Some observers found this primitive, purposely repetitive music simplistic and entirely lacking in artistic value. However, others, especially fans of the group, argued that this was exactly what the music industry and the public at large required to jar them out of their complacency.

Steve Jones's wall-of-noise guitar, the breakneck speed of the music, and audience abuse became trademarks of the group. Their music is not only full of energy but also is aggressive and self-destructive, as in the lyrics to "Anarchy in the U.K.": "I am an Antichrist/ I am an Anarchist/ Don't know what I want/ But I know how to get it/ I want to destroy. . . . I wanna be—anarchy!"

The Sex Pistols in 1976 (Express Newspapers/Archive Photos)

Recordings. The group's antisocial stance brought them financial gain. Manager McLaren negotiated recording contracts with EMI and A&M, both of which were subsequently cancelled by the record companies. The reason given by both was the revoltingly obnoxious behavior of the group. McLaren received a payment of fifty thousand British pounds from EMI to allow the company to withdraw its contract and avoid legal action by the Sex Pistols. After signing with A&M, the group's contract was cancelled due to their antics after only one week, and McLaren once again collected a five-figure sum.

The group then signed with Virgin Records and released the single "Anarchy in the U.K." (1976). A later song with the same label, "God Save the Queen," which appeared on the group's first album, *Never Mind the Bollocks, Here's the Sex Pistols* (1977), attacked Queen Elizabeth II as a "moron" during the celebration of her Silver Jubilee. Even worse was the album's cover, which depicted the Queen with a safety pin through her cheek. The British Broadcasting Corporation (BBC) forbade airplay of the song. Despite (or because of) this censorship, the song rose to number 3 on the British charts. In this instance, the Sex Pistols functioned as a mouthpiece for the lower working classes who were dissatisfied with the policies of the monarchy and the British government. Whether intentionally or unintentionally, the Sex Pistols embodied the unhappiness, dissatisfaction, and anger of a generation.

The revolution produced by the Sex Pistols led to the establishment of numerous punk bands in Great Britain. The Sex Pistols' 1976 "Anarchy in the U.K." tour with the Damned, the Clash, and others motivated fans to form their own bands. For instance, Sex Pistols fans Siouxie Sioux (Susan Dallion) and Steve Severin (Steve Baile) formed the group Siouxie and the Banshees after meeting at a Sex Pistols concert in 1975. In addition, Billy Idol was motivated to begin his recording career after attending a Sex Pistols concert.

The Breakup. The first member to leave the band over differences with manager McLaren was bassist Glen Matlock, who was replaced by John Simon Ritchie (Sid Vicious) in 1977. On the group's 1978 U.S. tour, Rotten disagreed violently with McLaren, left the group on January 14, and changed his name back to Lydon. Just prior to the disintegration, he and the other Sex Pistols completed material for the film *The Great Rock 'n' Roll Swindle* (1979), one of McLaren's last attempts to keep the group in the public eye. Shortly after storming off, Lydon formed a new band called Public Image Ltd. (PiL), with which he released several successful songs in an eighteen-month period following the split of the Sex Pistols.

On October 11 of the same year, Sid Vicious murdered his American girlfriend Nancy Spungen and died of a heroin overdose on February 2, 1979, while out of jail on bail awaiting his trial. Both events are depicted in Alex Cox's 1986 film *Sid and Nancy.* Vicious's death spelled the end of the band since without him and Rotten, the two attention-getting personalities of the group, it was impossible for Jones and Cook to carry on. McLaren recruited two new singers, Jimmy Pursey and Tenpole Tudor, but the group collapsed.

In 1986, Lydon and the other former Pistols successfully sued their former manager McLaren for substantial back royalties. Ten years later, however, they reconciled with him and staged a reunion tour together. The tour, "Filthy Lucre Live," certainly was not a major success musically, but it was financially. When asked in an interview what the Sex Pistols stood for in 1996, Johnny Rotten responded with the one word answer: "Money!" The tour received immense publicity, but offered little to revolutionize music the way the group's first recordings had done.

Sphere of Influence. Despite their limited original repertoire of approximately twenty-five songs, the Sex Pistols have left their mark musically on almost every major rock band that has followed, influencing groups as varied as U2, Guns n' Roses, and Green Day. This is evidenced by the wide range of groups that have covered their material, and in their continued reputation as one of the most controversial bands in rock history. Moreover, the Sex Pistols' brand of shock rock has exerted an immense influence on musical styles as diverse as rap, grunge, house, and hip-hop. —*Gregory Weeks*

SELECT DISCOGRAPHY

■ ALBUMS

Never Mind the Bollocks, Here's the Sex Pistols, 1977
Great Rock 'n' Roll Swindle, 1979
Some Product, 1979
Filthy Lucre Live, 1996

SEE ALSO: Anderson, Laurie; Clash, The; Ramones, The; Runaways, The / Joan Jett / Lita Ford; Talking Heads / David Byrne; Velvet Underground; Zappa, Frank / The Mothers of Invention.

Tupac Shakur

BORN: Brooklyn, New York; June 16, 1971
DIED: Las Vegas, Nevada; September 13, 1996
FIRST ALBUM RELEASE: *2Pacalypse Now,* 1991
MUSICAL STYLES: Rap, rhythm and blues

Tupac Shakur began his career in 1989 as a member of the short-lived rap group Strictly Dope before joining the San Francisco Bay area rap group Digital Underground as a dancer and rapper in 1990. Dressed in wild costumes that recalled and mocked George Clinton and his 1970's Parliament and Funkadelic bands, Digital Underground was a throwback to 1980's rap when "old school" beats and lyrics exhorted concertgoers and record buyers to dance the night away. Yet, in his short career as a rapper and actor, Shakur's flirtation with party music, socially aware ruminations, and "gangsta" rap put-downs paralleled the various roles he played in the six films he completed before his death. As such, Shakur's career embodied the contradictions, tensions, and irreconcilable desires of hip-hop culture as a whole.

The Beginnings. Growing up in the 1970's and 1980's, Tupac Shakur was subject to two major developments in American political and cultural life. His childhood was embroiled in the fiery flameouts of failed black nationalist movements, embodied in his own mother, former Black Panther Afeni Shakur. Her spiral into poverty, drugs, and a parade of boyfriends and households diminished the prodigious enthusiasm for art and theater displayed by her young son. Later, the Ronald Reagan and George Bush presidential administrations that defined the 1980's as an era of rollbacks in civil rights initiatives confirmed for many black Americans, including Shakur, that political and cultural backlash was inevitable after the destruction of black revolutionary potential in the previous decade.

It was against this backdrop that rap music developed, and Shakur, like almost all his teenage peers, was fascinated by the music that seemed to articulate their confusion, anger, and fear. Settling in northern California with his mother, Shakur formed the New African Panthers in 1989, a political group dedicated to the original goals of their predecessors, the Black Panthers. Then, in 1990, he became a member of the rap party ensemble Digital Underground. These divergent interests—radical nationalist politics and hormone-driven party music—point to the diverse passions of a black teen male on the cusp of adulthood. These divisions would only deepen over the remaining six years of Shakur's life.

Top Ten with a Bullet. Shakur's debut recording, *2Pacalypse Now,* was released in 1991 and eventually went gold, selling more than half a million units. The rap lyrics reveal all too typical teen anger and angst, naïveté and frustration, with a black male slant. Riven with contradictory emotions, these lyrics suggest that Shakur's semi-precocious education was warped by his unsettled childhood and adolescence, if not the distorted legacies of the Black Panthers. His lyrics, though impassioned, are finally simply brash validations of black anger. Shakur willfully misread both Malcolm X and Martin Luther King, Jr. ("Wordz of Wisdom"), acknowledged teenage pregnancy as a problem by blaming teenage mothers, not fathers ("Brenda's Got a Baby"), and began the first of several troubled confrontations with his parental figures by attacking his mother ("Part Time Mutha").

Two years later in 1993, having survived a few altercations with the law and other rappers, Shakur released his second album, *Strictly for My N.I.G.G.A.Z.* This album went platinum, largely on the strength of the hit video, "Keep Your Head Up." Despite—or perhaps because of—his run-ins with the law prior to the release of *Strictly for My N.I.G.G.A.Z.*, the success of the song demonstrated how easily the hip-hop audience wanted to believe in the possibility of a world in which women were respected and blacks were unified. That the album also contained songs that undercut the message of "Keep Your Head Up"—for example, "I Get Around," a typical playboy fantasy of limitless access to cars, cash, and women, or "Papa'z Song," the just-as-bitter other side of "Part Time Mutha"—seemed irrelevant to those that needed to believe in rap's redemptive powers. There would be only two more full-length recordings, including his first and only one for Death Row Records, before Shakur would be fatally wounded in a drive-by shooting.

Dead Man Talking. Talented enough to have forged the politics of Public Enemy with the swagger of N.W.A. and the charisma of R. Kelly, Shakur succumbed to his own hype and the romance of

For the Record

At age ten, Tupac Shakur was a member of the House of the Lord church in Brooklyn, New York. The Reverend Herbert Daughtry remembers that Shakur told him that he "wanted to be a revolutionary."

violence of "gangsta" rap in general and Death Row Records in particular. The confusions and contradictions of Shakur were evident not only between (and sometimes within) individual songs on his albums. The public outbursts, ill-advised statements, shooting incidents, sexual assault charges, and gangland tauntings of real and supposed rap rivals were often at odds with, or confused with, the Tupac Shakur who attempted to organize black youths into political cadres, promoted black self-respect and unity, and envisioned a life—with credible reasons—as an up-and-coming serious actor.

The turning point seems to have occurred during Shakur's four-and-a-half-year prison sentence for sexual assault in 1995. His third full-length album, *Me Against the World*, had just been released. The bravado and confusion of the first two albums was supplemented with rage ("Ghetto Bastard") and self-pity ("It Ain't Easy" and "Heavy in the Game"), making it one of the most narcissistic rap records ever released. Although it debuted at number 1 on the *Billboard* charts, this recording might have been just another mediocre commercial success were it not for the song that is, unlike "Part Time Mutha," a loving tribute to his mother. Yet "Dear Mama" is not without its ambivalence. Given the reverence, even deification, of mothers in African American culture, especially by African American males, it is not surprising that "Dear Mama" carried *Me Against the World* to multiplatinum sales. Yet, in true Shakur fashion, this tribute to his activist mother was also his plea for absolution, for forgiveness for his sins.

Nonetheless, in prison, Shakur watched other rappers adopt and revise his tough, slick style and became increasingly resentful of their success. Since most of the new sound derived from the advent of what would eventually be dubbed "gangsta" rap, Shakur decided to sign with the record company that practically invented the new tough image: Death Row Records. Death Row president Suge Knight visited Shakur in prison, contract and bail money (reportedly one million dollars) in hand. The monster of a record that came out of that deal, the two-album *All Eyez on Me* (1996), was yet another grandstanding act by the young rapper, as if he wanted to outdo his arch rival, East Coast rapper Biggie Smalls (also known as the Notorious B.I.G.).

Recording Classics. Given that Shakur's full-length recordings were as inconsistent as he was divided and confused, his major contributions to rap may well be his singles. The irony is that his crossover singles, "Dear Mama" and "I Ain't Mad at Cha," showcase a reflective but uncompromising man that is unrepresentative of Shakur himself. Still, for all its self-aggrandizement, *All Eyez on Me* was significant as "gangsta" rap's first two-album recording, a sprawling work that contains as many gems as it does failures. Despite multiplatinum sales of his final three albums, Shakur is probably etched in the American cultural consciousness more for his promising acting roles in films such as *Juice* (1992), *Poetic Justice* (1993), and *Above the Rim* (1994) than for his rapping and recordings. His last album, *Makavili: The Don Kil-*

Tupac Shakur in the film Poetic Justice (Archive Photos/Fotos International)

luminati the 7-Day Theory, was released posthumously under a new pseudonym, Makaveli. It too contains far more lows (the incoherent and illogical "Blasphemy") than highs ("Krazy").

Legacy. No doubt the advent of the Reagan administration's attacks on civil rights initiatives, the proliferation of felonious crimes in Southern cities (including Baltimore), and Afeni Shakur's inability to escape the death throes of drugs or find a stable male role model for her son all conspired to misshape the idealized moralism and adolescent ambitions of Tupac Shakur. All Shakur had as resistance, as legacy, was his mother's former associates, the Black Panthers. In another tragic irony of history, however, the Panthers' infighting would only prefigure the East Coast-West Coast rivalries in rap music, rivalries initially disdained but eventually endorsed by Shakur.

The fallout from the Black Panthers' implosion—the alleged murders of Panthers by Panthers and Federal Bureau of Investigation marksmen, the imprisonment of the surviving leaders, the spiral into petty crime and drug abuse by Huey Newton, Afeni Shakur, and others—was Shakur's inheritance. It was no surprise then that he would both attempt to inflame and stamp out the smoldering ashes of the Panthers. It was also no surprise that the lesson he drew from the Panthers' debacle—the possibility of change and the impossibility of consensus—replicated itself in the soldier-Souljah model of socially engaged rap music. Shakur himself embodied these East Coast-West Coast tensions as he struggled to reconcile unresolved, conflicting feelings toward his mother, his father, and his fellow rappers.

—*Tyrone Williams*

SELECT DISCOGRAPHY

■ ALBUMS

2Pacalypse Now, 1991

Strictly for My N.I.G.G.A.Z., 1993

Me Against the World, 1995

All Eyez on Me, 1996

Makaveli: The Don Killuminati the 7-Day Theory, 1996

SEE ALSO: Dr. Dre; Notorious B.I.G., The; Snoop Doggy Dogg.

Sheila E. *See under* E.

Carly Simon

BORN: New York, New York; June 25, 1945

FIRST ALBUM RELEASE: *Carly Simon*, 1971

MUSICAL STYLES: Folk, pop, rock

The popular singer-songwriter Carly Simon was blessed from the outset with a strong and appealing voice, a distinctive song style, and the talent for capturing the many nuances of love (and the lack of it) in a way that rings true to a broad audience. Stylistically, she has ventured from folk and children's songs into rock, pre-rock popular standards, and the torch song ballads heard in piano bars and cabarets.

Early Recognition. Carly Simon, the daughter of a prominent book publisher (the Simon of Simon and Schuster), was born on June 25, 1945, in New York City. There was much music in the home, and two daughters besides Carly would make music their careers. At her private school, Simon learned of American folk music from one of its foremost artists, Pete Seeger. She then attended Sarah Lawrence College for several years before drifting away to pursue music. Billing themselves as the Simon Sisters, Carly and sister Lucy began to sing in the folk clubs of Greenwich Village. By 1964, they had impressed record producer Dave Kapp, for whom they recorded two albums of folk and children's songs. The single "Winkin' Blinkin' and Nod" gave Simon her chart debut at number 73.

When the sisters' professional partnership ended in 1965, Simon was obliged to consider a number of career options. In 1966 she met both Bob Dylan and his manager Albert Grossman, who intrigued her with the idea of becoming a "female Dylan." The association was shortlived but did lead to some creative collaborations with Dylan and the Band. Two other contacts proved more enduring. In 1966 she reconnected with childhood friend Jacob Brackman, with whom she composed a long string of hits beginning with

Carly Simon in 1997 (George Dabrowsky/Archive Photos)

"That's the Way I've Always Heard It Should Be" in 1970. The second contact was with Jac Holzman, founder of Elektra Records, under whose contract Simon would release all of her successful albums of the 1970's.

The debut of the album *Carly Simon* (1971) came at a time when solo singers were in high demand. As a gifted singer and songwriter with a broadly appealing musical persona, Simon was destined for considerable success. While many of her songs are collaborations, they project a personal view of life, love, and lovers that has encouraged speculation as to their real-life inspirations.

The conflict between a young girl's dreams and a young woman's reality in "That's the Way I've Always Heard It Should Be" reflects common experience. The pulse-quickening thrills of love voiced in "Anticipation," however, were traced by some to her brief liaison with Kris Kristofferson. Likewise, the triumphant mockery of an egotistical lover's self-absorption in "You're So Vain" has been viewed as her response to either actor Warren Beatty or singer Mick Jagger (who sang backup on the song). Name-dropping aside, such songs were novelties in their day, whose expressive power was heightened by Simon's full-ranged strong alto voice, which was equally adept at the low-pitched opening verses delivered in a confessional tone and the soaring, affirmative choruses.

Marriage and Movies. Carly Simon and James Taylor met backstage at one of her concerts in 1971 and were married the next year in her New York apartment. Soon two sets of fans were treated to joint efforts appearing on the two artists' respective albums from the mid-1970's. Their first song collaboration was "Forever My Love" from the 1974 album *Hotcakes*. Their most successful duet, also from *Hotcakes*, was "Mockingbird," a cover of an old Charlie and Inez Foster hit that reached number 5 in 1974. Simon began a modest film career with a cameo appearance in the 1972 film *Taking Off*. In 1977, she sang her first film theme song, "Nobody Does It Better," written by Marvin Hamlisch and Carole Sager for the score of the James Bond film *The Spy Who Loved Me*. In the next year Simon saw her album *Boys in the Trees* reach number 10 and its hit single, "You Belong

For the Record

To her list of such illustrious sidemen as James Taylor, Mick Jagger, and Stevie Wonder, Carly Simon could add President Bill Clinton, who performed saxophone on the song "Dream" at a private get-together on Martha's Vineyard in 1994.

To Me" (cowritten with Doobie Brother Michael McDonald), reach the number 6 spot. However, her album *Spy* of 1979, her last for Elektra, achieved only a number 45 spot.

The 1980's and later. During the 1980's, Simon's vocal and creative versatility enabled her to take a number of creative risks. In 1981, the year that she filed for divorce from Taylor, she released *Torch,* an album of popular standards lavishly accompanied by a large studio orchestra. Despite an onstage collapse in 1980, she continued to risk public appearances at benefit concerts and more rarely on brief promotional tours. Two more successful theme songs followed: "Coming Around Again" for the romantic comedy *Heartburn* (1986) and "Let the River Run" for *Working Girl* (1988). The latter won her a Grammy Award, an Academy Award, and the chance to compose a complete film score for *Postcards from the Edge* (1990). In her albums and songs of the 1980's, Simon continued to explore how to bridge the gap between dreams and reality, frequently focusing on the ingredients necessary to make love last for adults who have had their share of good and bad relationships. The ingredients in the song "The Stuff That Dreams Are Made Of" are found not in a bright and shiny new love interest but in the "slow and steady fire" of an old familiar one. "Coming Around Again" chronicles the cyclic return of a love strong enough to survive change and human fallibility.

In the third decade of her singing career, Carly Simon pursued established paths and two new ventures: the composition of a short opera and the writing of four children's books. The opera, entitled *Romulus Hunt,* concerned the efforts of a young boy to bring his separated parents back together. Its premiere at New York's John Jay Theatre on February 23, 1993, was followed by a move to the Kennedy Center in Washington, D.C., and the release of a full-length recording. To her old themes, Simon added nostalgia and reminiscences, most vividly in the albums *Have You Seen Me Lately* (1990) and *Letters Never Sent* (1994). The former album was also notable for occasioning a reunion between Simon and her sister Lucy. A second album of standards, *My Romance* (1990), was followed in 1997 by *Film Noir,* containing atmospheric original songs backed by a studio orchestra, meant to evoke American cinema at its moodiest. *—David Haas*

SELECT DISCOGRAPHY

■ ALBUMS

Carly Simon, 1971
Anticipation, 1971
No Secrets, 1972
Hotcakes, 1974
Playing Possum, 1975
Boys in the Trees, 1978
Spy, 1979
Torch, 1981
Greatest Hits Live, 1988
My Romance, 1990
Have You Seen Me Lately, 1990
Romulus Hunt—A Family Opera, 1993
Letters Never Sent, 1994
Film Noir, 1997

SELECT AWARDS

Grammy Award for Best New Artist of the Year, 1972
Grammy Award for Best Song Written Specifically for a Motion Picture or Television for "Let the River Run," 1989
Academy Award for Best Song for "Let the River Run," from *Working Girl,* 1989
Nashville Songwriters Hall of Fame, inducted 1994

SEE ALSO: King, Carole; Seeger, Pete; Taylor, James.

Paul Simon

BORN: Newark, New Jersey; October 13, 1941
FIRST ALBUM RELEASE: *The Paul Simon Songbook,* 1965
MUSICAL STYLES: Folk, pop

Paul Simon's solo career, spanning many decades, has surpassed even the phenomenal success of his career with Art Garfunkel as the duo Simon and Garfunkel. Incorporating such diverse musical traditions as reggae and "township jive" into his musical style, Simon has become one of the most significant artists in American popular music.

Rhymin' Simon. The album that Simon released in 1972, titled simply *Paul Simon*, carried a tremendous burden. It was his first solo effort in seven years, and his first album since his split with Garfunkel. (He had released a little-heard solo album in 1965 while the two were still together but before they attained success.) While Simon had written all of their songs, he knew he could not equal the vocal mastery of his former partner, and the possibility of individual failure after so much shared success loomed menacingly over the thirty-year-old singer. Fortunately, Simon's fans realized that he was not attempting to repeat his earlier success but was moving in a new direction musically. The reggae-inspired sound of "Mother and Child Reunion" and "Me and Julio Down by the Schoolyard" was new to American listeners. The desire to expand beyond the limits of the Simon and Garfunkel repertoire had been a major factor in Simon's decision to work alone, and would continue to motivate him throughout his career.

In September of 1972, Simon's wife, Peggy, gave birth to their first child, Harper. Simon's next album, *There Goes Rhymin' Simon* (1973), included the hits "Kodachrome" and "Loves Me Like a Rock," as well as the melancholy "American Tune." The most charming song on the album, "St. Judy's Comet," depicts Simon as he struggles to put his son to bed, confessing to the child that, "If I can't sing my boy to sleep, well it makes your famous daddy look so dumb." Sales of *There Goes Rhymin' Simon* were helped by Simon's return to the concert tour, which produced the album *Live Rhymin'*. The singer would not emerge from the shadow of Simon and Garfunkel, however, until 1975's *Still Crazy After All These Years*. Ironically, the album included a new song with Garfunkel, "My Little Town." The album's biggest hit, however, began as a nonsense rhyme for Harper. "You just slip out the back, Jack/ Make a new plan, Stan/ You don't need to be coy, Roy/ Just get yourself free" made "Fifty Ways to Leave Your Lover" Simon's first number 1 hit since "Bridge Over Troubled Water" in 1970. *Still Crazy After All These Years* won Simon a pair of Grammy Awards, affirming his stature as a solo performer.

For the Record

At the conclusion of one of his concert tours, Paul gave a speech in which he wished he could do more for the audience than simply sing them a few songs. When a member of the crowd shouted, "Buy us a drink, then!" he did so, paying for drinks for three thousand people.

Foray into Films. Simon decided that he wanted his next album to be part of a more complete artistic work. "I wanted to do something other than just record an album. I felt my choices were either to write a Broadway show or a movie." Unsatisfied with writing music for others to perform, he chose to make a film in which he could record the music himself. *One Trick Pony*'s protagonist Jonah Levin is a rock musician whose life has gone the way Simon's might have gone; traveling from town to town, performing long–forgotten songs for audiences who prefer punk rock, Jonah is a music lover who has been jilted by rock and roll. By the end of the film, however, he salvages his self-respect by refusing to compromise his principles for commercial success. Film critic Roger Ebert called it "a wonderful movie, an affectionate character study with a lot of good music in it." However, the filmgoing public ignored it.

Musically, *One Trick Pony* (1980) scored with the lively hit "Late in the Evening," but the real treasures on the sound-track album are more subdued. "Nobody," for example, begins like one of Simon's trademark songs of loneliness and isolation, asking, "Who took my two hands and made them four?/ Who is my heart, who is my door?/ Nobody." It is transformed, however, into a song of love and redemption with the addition of two unexpected words: "Nobody . . . but you." Even if the film was a commercial failure, it was part of the creative process behind an outstanding album.

Think Too Much. Disappointed by the reception of *One Trick Pony,* Simon turned to a project guaranteed to please his fans: a reunion concert with Art Garfunkel. On September 19, 1981, half a million people crowded into Central Park to hear the two sing together again. Spurred by the concert's success, they decided to record an album together, to be entitled *Think Too Much.* The strain of working together again after ten years proved too great, however, and the album, retitled *Hearts and Bones* (1983), carried no trace of Garfunkel's distinctive harmonies.

Considering the personal nature of the songs on the album, perhaps it is better that it remained a solo effort. "Train in the Distance" tells the story of Simon's relationship with Peggy, who was "beautiful as southern skies the night he met her/ but . . . married to someone." Their divorce is the subject of "Think Too Much," which begins: "The smartest people in the world had gathered in Los Angeles/ To analyze our love affair and finally unscramble us." Simon's relationship with Carrie Fisher, whom he married in 1983 and divorced the following April, was the inspiration for several songs on the album, including "Hearts and Bones." Even the superficially lighthearted "Cars Are Cars" contains the confession "If some of my homes had been more like my car/ I probably wouldn't have traveled this far."

Days of Miracle and Wonder. After the extreme introspection of his previous two albums, Simon turned outward for inspiration once again, this time to South African "township jive." In the summer of 1984, a friend gave Simon a copy of *Gumboots: Accordion Jive Hits, Volume II.* Fascinated by the unique sound, Simon immersed himself in South African music, and the next year he traveled to Johannesburg to work with some of the musicians there. The result of Simon's visit to South Africa was *Graceland,* 1987's Grammy–winner for Record of the Year.

The songs on the album range from the country sound of "Graceland" to the distinctly African flavor of "Homeless," which Simon cowrote with Joseph Shabalala and performed with the group Ladysmith Black Mambazo. In addition to Simon's South African collaborators, American performers such as Linda Ronstadt and Los Lobos contributed their talents to the album. The diverse musical styles on *Graceland* lend it an infectiously optimistic tone, in contrast to much of Simon's previous work.

On his next album, *The Rhythm of the Saints* (1990), Simon continued to explore new musical territory, drawing from Brazilian tradition. Lyrically, he once again avoided excessive introspection in favor of social observation. In "Can't Run But," he describes the 1986 Chernobyl nuclear disaster: "A cooling system/ Burns out in the Ukraine/ Trees and umbrellas/ Protect us from the new rain." Once again, caution is balanced with optimism, however, as "Born at the Right Time" celebrates the promise of a better world for a new generation: "Born at the instant/ The church bells chime/ And the whole world whispering/ Born at the right time."

Broadway Bound. In May, 1992, Simon married Edie Brickell of the New Bohemians; in December the couple had a son, Adrian, who in 1995 became a brother to his new sister, Lulu. Meanwhile, Simon fulfilled his ambition to write a musical. *The Capeman,* which premiered at the Marquis Theater in January, 1998, is the true story of Salvador Agron, a Puerto Rican immigrant convicted of murder in 1959 and sentenced to death at the age of sixteen. "It felt like a very New York story with a great musical environment," Simon explained. "It raised the possibility of examining changing musical styles as the story unfolded and moved back and forth between Puerto Rico and New York." Simon collaborated on the lyrics with poet Derek Walcott, and singer Rubén Blades portrayed the older Salvador Agron. Simon has not been content to write music solely for other musicians to perform, however; *Songs from the Capeman,* released in 1997, features Simon's own renditions of eleven songs from the musical.

—Ed McKnight

SELECT DISCOGRAPHY

■ ALBUMS

The Paul Simon Song Book, 1965
Paul Simon, 1972
There Goes Rhymin' Simon, 1973

Live Rhymin', 1974
Still Crazy After All These Years, 1975
Greatest Hits, Etc., 1977
One Trick Pony, 1980
Hearts and Bones, 1983
Graceland, 1986
Negotiations and Love Songs 1971-1986, 1988 (compilation)
The Rhythm of the Saints, 1990
Songs from the Capeman, 1997

SELECT AWARDS

Grammy Awards for Album of the Year for *Still Crazy After All These Years* (with Phil Ramone) and Best Pop Vocal Performance, Male, for "Still Crazy After All These Years," 1975

Grammy Award for Album of the Year for *Graceland*, 1986

SEE ALSO: Blades, Rubén; Los Lobos; Ronstadt, Linda; Simon and Garfunkel.

Simon and Garfunkel

ORIGINAL MEMBERS: Paul Simon (b. 1941), Art Garfunkel (b. 1941)

FIRST ALBUM RELEASE: *Wednesday Morning, 3 A.M.*, 1964

MUSICAL STYLES: Folk, pop

Simon and Garfunkel were one of the most successful vocal duos in history, and the lyrical blending of their voices became one of the most recognizable sounds of the 1960's. Together they gave the world such classics as "The Sound of Silence" and "Bridge over Troubled Water." However, the pair did not use their soothing voices to distract listeners from contemporary issues. Instead, their lyrics focused on the afflictions of modern society, such as alienation and class division. Their breakup signaled the end of the decade as much as that of the Beatles did, but when the duo reunited for a single evening in 1981, half a million fans attended their concert in New York City's Central Park.

Tom and Jerry. Paul Simon and Art Garfunkel were born less than one month apart and grew up blocks from each other in the Forest Hills neighborhood of Queens, New York. Simon's parents were Hungarian Jews, and Garfunkel's grandfather was a Romanian immigrant. The two boys met during a sixth-grade production of Lewis Carroll's *Alice in Wonderland*, and by the time they were thirteen they were singing together at school assemblies and parties.

In addition to performing the popular songs of the day, the two created their own music as well, experimenting with double tracking on the two tape recorders that belonged to Garfunkel's parents. They would regularly visit Manhattan's famed Brill Building to try to sell their songs to the music publishers that occupied its floors. In order to disguise their ethnicity, the two boys took the stage name of Tom and Jerry. Simon even borrowed his current girlfriend's last name and copyrighted his songs under the name Jerry Landis.

In 1957 their hard work paid off with the Top-100 hit "Hey, Schoolgirl," which sold 100,000 copies and peaked at number 54 on the charts. That brought with it an appearance on Dick Clark's *American Bandstand*, following Jerry Lee Lewis and his new hit, "Great Balls of Fire."

"The Sound of Silence." "Hey, Schoolgirl" was followed by three unsuccessful releases, and Simon and Garfunkel went on to pursue their educations and individual musical careers. Then, in 1964, Simon was offered an audition by CBS, to which he insisted that Garfunkel be invited. As a result of that audition, the pair were given the opportunity to record an album under their own names. *Wednesday Morning, 3 A.M.* (1964) included some traditional folk songs, covers of "The Sun Is Burning" and "The Times They Are a-Changin'," and one classical piece that Garfunkel had discovered in his university library. The five original songs written by Simon included the quietly poetic "Bleecker Street" as well as the song that won them the audition to begin with, "He Was My Brother." In it Simon grieves for a friend and classmate killed while participating in the Civil Rights movement of the 1950's and 1960's.

The album sold a disappointing three thousand copies the first year, and the two again parted ways, Garfunkel to Columbia University for a mas-

For the Record

Although "Mrs. Robinson" won a Grammy Award for Record of the Year, and *The Graduate* earned Mike Nichols an Academy Award for Best Director, Simon and Garfunkel failed to win the Academy Award for Best Song. Instead, that year's winner was "Talk to the Animals" from *Dr. Dolittle.*

ter's degree, and Simon to Europe. In September of 1965, however, Simon picked up a copy of *Billboard* in Denmark to discover that one of the songs from the album had broken into the Top 100. "The Sound of Silence" was a hit in the United States. The musicians decided to take immediate advantage of their newfound success and released two albums within the next year, prudently naming the first after their current hit. *Sounds of Silence* (1966) included not only a new version of the title song, but such hits as "Homeward Bound" and "I Am a Rock," powerful anthems of loneliness and isolation. In addition, the album featured a pair of beautiful meditations on the fleeting quality of time, "Leaves That Are Green" and "April Come She Will."

Their next album, *Parsley, Sage, Rosemary and Thyme* (1966), reveals Simon and Garfunkel at the height of their remarkable ability to blend voice and melody into a unified whole. "Scarborough Fair/Canticle" takes two traditional tunes from disparate sources and combines them so skillfully that they seem as one. "The Dangling Conversation" is a song about a couple's inability to communicate, inspired by the work of poet T. S. Eliot. "Cloudy" and "Flowers Never Bend with the Rainfall" feature unparalleled harmonies as well as lyrical intensity. The latter returns to the theme of transience with the chorus: "So I continue to continue to pretend/ My life will never end/ And flowers never bend with the rainfall." The final song on the album, "7 O'Clock News/Silent Night," juxtaposes the Christmas carol with a news broadcast detailing the horrors of the modern world. The effect is both stunning and chilling.

"Mrs. Robinson." The next project that Simon and Garfunkel worked on was the sound track to the 1967 film *The Graduate,* an effort for which they received their first pair of Grammys. Although "Mrs. Robinson" was the only song written specifically for the film, director Mike Nichols found that several of their earlier songs, including "Scarborough Fair/Canticle," "The Sound of Silence," and "April Come She Will," blended seamlessly into the fabric of the film. "Mrs. Robinson" won Grammies for Record of the Year and Best Pop Performance by a Duo.

In 1968 Simon and Garfunkel released their fourth album, *Bookends,* featuring both the Grammy Award-winning "Mrs. Robinson" and "America," a song that became an anthem for a generation in search of its true homeland. "Old Friends," a somber variation on the Beatles'

Simon and Garfunkel (National Archives)

"When I'm Sixty-Four," imagines the vocalists "years from today sharing a park bench quietly." The duo also displayed a rarely seen capacity for levity in "At the Zoo," a song that later became a children's book, and "Punky's Dilemma," which contained the memorable line "I prefer boysenberry more than any ordinary jam/ I'm a Citizens for Boysenberry Jam fan."

Troubled Waters. The close of the 1960's saw Simon and Garfunkel's artistic ambitions straining against the limitations placed upon them by corporate America and their own partnership. On November 30, 1969, Simon and Garfunkel appeared in their own television special, *Songs of America*, but they were compelled to eliminate much of what the sponsor, AT&T, regarded as political commentary, including film footage of civil rights leader Martin Luther King, Jr. *Bridge over Troubled Water*, released in 1970, achieved more in the way of commercial success and critical acclaim than any of their previous work, but the singers themselves were unable to agree on a twelfth song for the album. Simon wanted to conclude it with a protest song entitled "Cuba Si, Nixon No," while Garfunkel preferred a Bach chorale. The album, released with only eleven songs, won the Grammy Award for Album of the Year, while the title track was named Record of the Year. However, the success of *Bridge over Troubled Water* proved to be the climax of their career together.

Old Friends. Simon and Garfunkel followed different paths through the next decade. Simon married Peggy Harper, his former manager's former wife, in 1970, while Garfunkel married a graphic designer named Linda Grossman in 1972, the year that Simon's son, Harper, was born. Both marriages ended in divorce, and when Garfunkel's girlfriend, Laurie Bird, committed suicide in 1979, he was devastated.

Both singers released a number of solo albums, and although Simon met with greater musical success, Garfunkel extended his artistic interests in pursuit of an acting career. In 1974 the two recorded "My Little Town," a song that Simon wrote especially for his former partner and which appeared on albums by both singers. The bleak view of small-town life that the song depicts is summarized by the lines: "And after it rains there's a rainbow/ But all of the colors are black/ It's not that the colors aren't there/ It's just imagination they lack."

On September 19, 1981, Simon and Garfunkel appeared together once again, at a reunion concert in Central Park. Half a million devoted fans attended the free concert, which was recorded for a live album released the following year. Creative differences scuttled subsequent plans for the two to record an album of new material together, but on that September night the lasting impact of Simon and Garfunkel's contribution to music was felt again. *—Ed McKnight*

SELECT DISCOGRAPHY

■ SINGLES

"The Sound of Silence," 1965
"Homeward Bound," 1966
"I Am a Rock," 1966
"A Hazy Shade of Winter," 1966
"At the Zoo," 1967
"Scarborough Fair/Canticle," 1968
"Mrs. Robinson," 1968
"Bridge over Troubled Water," 1970
"My Little Town," 1975

■ ALBUMS

Wednesday Morning, 3 A.M., 1964
Sounds of Silence, 1966
Parsley, Sage, Rosemary and Thyme, 1966
The Graduate, 1968 (sound track)
Bookends, 1968
Bridge over Troubled Water, 1970
The Concert in Central Park, 1982

SELECT AWARDS

Grammy Awards for Record of the Year (with Roy Halee) and Best Contemporary Pop Performance, Vocal, Duo, or Group, for "Mrs. Robinson," 1968

Grammy Awards for Record of the Year for "Bridge over Troubled Water" and Album of the Year for *Bridge over Troubled Water*, 1970 (with Roy Halee)

Rock and Roll Hall of Fame, inducted 1990

SEE ALSO: Simon, Paul.

Frank Sinatra

BORN: Hoboken, New Jersey; December 12, 1915
DIED: Los Angeles, California; May 14, 1998
FIRST SINGLE RELEASE: "From the Bottom of My Heart," 1939
MUSICAL STYLES: Pop, jazz, swing

Frank Sinatra was the son of Martin Sinatra and Dolly Garavente Sinatra, Italian immigrants. To avoid anti-Italian prejudice, Martin Sinatra boxed under the name of Marty O'Brien before becoming a firefighter. Dolly Sinatra owned a bar in 1917 when, two years before national prohibition of alcohol sales, President Woodrow Wilson imposed prohibition upon Hoboken to protect troops leaving for World War I battlefields abroad (the underworld connections established during this time were to be used against Sinatra throughout his professional career). Dolly Sinatra also became a politically powerful Democratic committeewoman.

Frank Sinatra was an adored only child and his family was economically secure. Hoboken, however, provided a tough environment, and prejudice was part of his childhood; he became a lifelong fighter for racial and religious equality. His volatile temper, his insistence on giving and receiving loyalty, and his determination to mingle with people of his choice, whether criminals or U.S. presidents, were also part of this heritage.

The Early Years. Frank Sinatra shared his mother's ambition. He was impatient with formal education, dropped out of high school, and loathed the manual labor available to the uneducated. By 1932, Sinatra had decided to sing for a living; his parents bought him a portable sound system, and he sang at nightclubs, roadhouses, parties, weddings, school dances, and Democratic Party meetings, less interested in pay than in experience. A performance by his hero Bing Crosby determined his style. Crosby (1903-1977) was among the first generation to benefit from sophisticated microphones and amplification techniques developed in the 1920's, which enabled a relaxed, low-key, almost conversational style to be projected to large audiences in halls, on radio, and in films. Crosby's style was labeled "crooning."

Sinatra's first break came in 1935, when he auditioned for a popular radio talent show, *Major Bowes Original Amateur Hour*, broadcast from New York. A Hoboken trio called the Three Flashes also auditioned. Major Edward E. Bowes suggested they perform with Sinatra as the Hoboken Four. The radio audience was enthusiastic. Bowes signed the group for a three-month road tour during which Sinatra learned how to use the microphone as if it were a musical instrument for the intimate projection of his voice.

Returning to New Jersey, Sinatra sang in roadhouses, preferring those broadcasting their entertainment on local radio. At the Englewood, New Jersey, Rustic Cabin, for twenty-five dollars per week, his distinctive style attracted the attention of bandleader and trumpeter Harry James. Sinatra signed with James and cut his first record with the James band, but, in need of money and wider exposure, he moved to the popular Tommy Dorsey band in 1940. He had new responsibilities; in 1939, he had married Nancy Barbato. His first daughter, Nancy, was born in June, 1940; a son, Frank Sinatra, Jr., was born in 1944, and Christina (Tina) in 1948.

The Swoonatra Years. During the big-band era of the 1930's and early 1940's, singers often delivered lyrics in an almost wooden fashion. Crosby and Sinatra changed that, adapting the intimate delivery of jazz to the big-band sound. Of the ten songs Sinatra recorded with James, eight were arranged by Andy Gibson, who also wrote for jazz greats Duke Ellington, Count Basie, and Cab Calloway. In his early years with James and Dorsey, Sinatra learned to dramatize lyrics. He developed an intensity that allowed him to give nuanced readings of even the most banal lyrics and to sound as if he were communicating individually with each member of the audience. Through physical training, especially underwater swimming, he learned the breath control that allowed him to deliver long, uninterrupted lines without pauses for breath.

Although the first few girls who fainted or "swooned" at a Sinatra performance may have been paid by a press agent, the phenomenon spread without paid assistance. By 1942, when Sinatra left Dorsey to go on his own, performances, radio shows, records (made mostly with arranger Axel Stordahl), and guest appearances in films (*Las Vegas Nights*, 1941; *Ship Ahoy*, 1942) had brought him wealth and fame. He became known simply as "The Voice." In January, 1942, *Billboard* named him Top Band Vocalist. On December 30, 1942, he opened as an added attraction at the Paramount Theatre in New York; the main attractions were a Bing Crosby film, *Star-Spangled Rhythm*, and the Benny Goodman band. To Goodman's amazement, some five thousand teenagers stomped, screamed, and fainted at Sinatra's appearance. Sinatra became the show, not the added feature.

Frank Sinatra (Arkent Archive)

The "Columbus Day riot" of October 11, 1944, marked the pinnacle of Sinatra's early success. On that day, he opened a three-week engagement at New York's Paramount Theatre. Young people began lining up for tickets at 4:30 A.M. By 8:30 A.M., the theater was filled for the first show (at noon), while ten thousand people were lined outside and another twenty thousand milled around in Times Square, creating a massive traffic jam. When the audience in the theater refused to leave, enraged fans broke windows and destroyed the ticket booth. The mob was not brought under control until late that night.

Sinatra's success took many other forms. In 1943, Sinatra became a regular on the popular radio show *Lucky Strike Hit Parade*, which featured the most popular songs of the week, and he performed on other radio shows, in clubs, and at war bond fund-raisers. He began a series of increasingly well-made and popular musical films. In early films such as *Reveille with Beverly* (1943), he was only one of several musical performers, but he was featured in *Higher and Higher* (1943), *Step Lively* (1944), *Anchors Aweigh* (1945, with Gene Kelly), *It Happened in Brooklyn* (1947, with Jimmy Durante), *Take Me out to the Ball Game* (1949, with Kelly and swimming star Esther Williams), and, most important, *On the Town* (1949, with Kelly). He briefly appeared in MGM studio's lavish tribute to songwriter Jerome Kern, *Till the Clouds Roll By* (1946). In addition, in 1943, despite complaints by music critics who wanted a clear separation between classical and popular music, Sinatra performed with the Cleveland Philharmonic, the Philadelphia Philharmonic, and in concert at the Hollywood Bowl.

In 1945, Sinatra, playing himself, starred in a short feature, *The House I Live In*, singing the title song and arguing against racial and religious intolerance. Profits were donated to charities; the Academy of Motion Picture Arts and Sciences awarded the film a special Academy Award. That year, Sinatra also began a lecture tour at schools around the country, talking about intolerance and juvenile delinquency. He appeared in Gary, Indiana, for example, in an attempt to defuse a strike by white students protesting the admission of African Americans.

Years of Failure. By the late 1940's, however, personal and professional problems were increasing. While Sinatra had never given as much attention to films as to concerts and recording dates, he was miscast in his first dramatic role in *The Miracle of the Bells* (1948) and in *The Kissing Bandit* (1948). Following a 1950 wisecrack about MGM head Louis B. Mayer that was reported to Mayer, Sinatra was fired from the studio. Films made for RKO and Universal Studios failed. Record sales also fell, in part because of changing tastes in music. His appearance on *Hit Parade* required him to sing the most popular songs of the week; these songs, including such hits as "Feudin', Fussin' and a Fightin'" and the "Too Fat Polka," were increasingly inappropriate to his voice and style. As his record sales fell, Columbia Records producer Mitch Miller encouraged him to produce novelty records, such as "Mama Will Bark," generally considered Sinatra's worst record. By 1952, Sinatra had been dropped by Columbia Records, MGM, his agents, and CBS radio.

Personal problems, in part, caused this decline. After well-publicized Hollywood romances with top stars, Sinatra began pursuit of film star Ava Gardner in 1949. Some fans were offended by this headline-making courtship, as well as by his divorce from the Roman Catholic mother of his children. Gardner and Sinatra were married in 1951. Their tumultuous marriage continued to make headlines until they were divorced in 1957.

In addition to these personal problems, this was the period of the House Committee on Un-American Activities (HUAC) investigation of entertainers. Sinatra's 1945 film *The House I Live In* had been written by Albert Maltz, a victim of the McCarthy-era blacklist; the title song was written by lyricist Lewis Allen, writer of "Strange Fruit," a powerful song about lynching made famous by Billie Holiday. Even before Joseph McCarthy's HUAC hearings, this film, together with Sinatra's outspoken support of President Franklin D. Roosevelt's administration and of racial and religious equality, led to Sinatra's being called a Communist by conservative journalists and broadcasters. In 1949, McCarthy accused Sinatra of following or appeasing the Communist Party. No charge was substantiated. Neither were charges of associating with gangsters, although Sinatra was frequently investigated. These headlines helped damage the singer's career during the conservative late 1940's and early 1950's. Sinatra's notoriously poor relationship with journalists began during this period. He found it difficult even to get nightclub work.

A Fresh Start. At this low point, through the influence of friends and Ava Gardner, he signed with Capitol Records, and he began filming his first serious dramatic role, as Angelo Maggio in *From Here to Eternity*, both in April, 1953. He won an Academay Award for Best Supporting Actor. He sustained his reputation as a dramatic actor with his portrait of a killer in *Suddenly* (1954) and as a drug addict in *The Man with the Golden Arm* (1955). In his music career, the development of long-playing records allowed him to record concept albums such as *Songs for Young Lovers*, *Swing Easy!* (both 1954), *In the Wee Small Hours* (1955), and *Only the Lonely* (1958). *Swing Easy!* was named

For the Record

When Frank Sinatra opened at New York's Paramount Theatre on October 11, 1944, more than four hundred police reservists, twenty radio cars, two emergency trucks, four lieutenants, six sergeants, two captains, two assistant chief inspectors, two inspectors, seventy patrolmen, fifty traffic officers, twelve mounted police, twenty policewomen, and two hundred detectives were needed to control the crowd.

Billboard's Album of the Year, and Sinatra was named Top Male Vocalist by *Billboard*, *Down Beat*, and *Metronome* magazines. His voice became deeper and less pure but more dramatic, and he worked primarily with arranger Nelson Riddle. Many of the albums featured upbeat swing music, reviving the big-band sound. His musical films of the 1950's included *Young at Heart* (1955), *The Tender Trap* (1955), *Guys and Dolls* (1955), *High Society* (1956, with Grace Kelly and Bing Crosby), and *Pal Joey* (1957). Sinatra's recording of "Young at Heart," the title song from the film, brought him to the top of the charts in 1955.

In the late 1950's and early 1960's, working with Billy May, he began to experiment with new rhythms, from bossa nova to soft rock. His Las Vegas appearances with his hard-living friends—the group, sometimes called the Rat Pack or Clan, included Joey Bishop, Sammy Davis, Jr., Dean Martin, and Peter Lawford—were spontaneous, rowdy, anti-authoritarian, and extremely popular. The pure baritone of his early years was gone, but life experience gave his music a greater depth and intensity.

The 1960's was a period of extremes. In 1960, Sinatra left Capitol to form his own record company, Reprise, producing a series of successful albums, notably *Ring-a-Ding Ding!* (1961); a tribute to Tommy Dorsey, *I Remember Tommy* (1961); *The Concert Sinatra* (1963) and *It Might as Well Be Swing* (1964), the latter with Count Basie and arrangements by Quincy Jones; *Sinatra: A Man and His Music (1960-1965)*; and *September of My Years* (1965). As far as singles go, Sinatra had minor successes in the early 1960's but suddenly had a triumphant year in 1966, when he had a number 1 hit with "Strangers in the Night" and had three other Top-40 hits that became Sinatra signature pieces and standards, "It Was a Very Good Year," "Summer Wind," and "That's Life." The ending of "Strangers in the Night" provided the famous "doo-be-doo-be-doo" phrase that became associated with Sinatra. In 1967 a lightweight duet with daughter Nancy, "Somethin' Stupid," went to number 1 as well. In 1969 came "My Way," another signature piece.

His personal life in the 1960's contained both highs and lows. In 1962, he embarked on an ambitious humanitarian gesture, a World Tour for Children. Sinatra paid expenses; profits went to children's organizations. Upon his return, however, new scandals concerning criminal associates broke in the press. A supporter of President John F. Kennedy, Sinatra was horrified by Kennedy's assassination in 1963. Two weeks later, Frank Sinatra, Jr., was kidnapped; the kidnappers falsely claimed that Sinatra had hired them as a publicity stunt. The press periodically revived the rumors for decades. In 1966, Sinatra married actress Mia Farrow, but the marriage lasted only thirteen months.

Retirement and Back. Sinatra announced his retirement in 1971; two years later he was back, beginning a rigorous series of performances and tours that eventually included "The Main Event" (1974), "The Concert for the Americas" (1982), "The Ultimate Event" (with Sammy Davis, Jr., and Liza Minnelli, 1988), and the "Diamond Jubilee World Tour" (1991). He married Barbara Marx in 1976, and the couple stayed together to the end of his life. A year later, Sinatra's mother, Dolly, probably the most profound influence in his life, was killed in an airplane crash on the way to meet Sinatra in Las Vegas.

In 1980 Sinatra released his version of a motion-picture theme that had originally come out three years before. The song was "New York, New York" and by the end of his life the song had become a standard and was as strongly associated with Sinatra as any he had done previously in his long career. In 1980, he appeared for the first time in Brazil; 175,000 people gathered to hear him at the Maracaña Stadium, setting a new world record for concert attendance. President Ronald Reagan presented him with the Medal of Freedom in 1985.

As he aged, Sinatra needed TelePrompTers to assist him with lyrics, and his voice sometimes failed him, but he remained a remarkable and popular entertainer. Sinatra released new recordings into the 1990's. His attempts to record popular music in *Duets* (1993) and *Duets II* (1994) met with commercial, although not critical, success. Sinatra also intensified his benefit concerts. The money he raised went to a broad range of charities. These included the Martin Sinatra Medical Education Center, named after his father, who had died in 1969, the Frank Sinatra International Youth Center for Arab and Jewish Children in Israel, and the Barbara Sinatra Children's Center (for abused children).

Sinatra's public appearances had become infrequent by the mid-1990's. He appeared on February 25, 1995, at the Frank Sinatra Desert Classic golf tournament. Congress awarded him a Congressional Gold Medal in 1997. By 1997, Sinatra's health was failing, and there were frequent hospital visits and recurrent rumors that he might be nearing death. He suffered a heart attack in early 1997, and was not seen in public again. He died of heart failure in May, 1998. —*Betty Richardson*

SELECT DISCOGRAPHY

■ SINGLES

"Learnin' the Blues," 1955
"Love and Marriage," 1955
"Hey! Jealous Lover," 1956
"All the Way," 1957
"Witchcraft," 1958
"Softly, as I Leave You," 1964
"It Was a Very Good Year," 1966
"Strangers in the Night," 1966
"That's Life," 1966
"Somethin' Stupid," 1967 (with Nancy Sinatra)
"My Way," 1969
"Theme from *New York, New York*," 1980

■ ALBUMS

Songs for Young Lovers, 1954
Swing Easy, 1954
In the Wee Small Hours, 1955
Songs for Swingin' Lovers! 1956
Close to You, 1957
A Swingin' Affair, 1957
Come Fly with Me, 1957
Only the Lonely, 1958
Nice 'n' Easy, 1960
Ring-a-Ding Ding! 1961
I Remember Tommy, 1961
All Alone, 1962
Sinatra & Strings, 1962
The Concert Sinatra, 1963
It Might as Well Be Swing, 1964 (with Count Basie)
September of My Years, 1965
Sinatra: A Man and His Music (1960-1965), 1965 (two-record album)
Francis Albert Sinatra & Antonio Carlos Jobim, 1967
A Man Alone, 1969
Watertown, 1970
Ol' Blue Eyes Is Back, 1973
The Capitol Years, 1990 (three-CD boxed set)
The Reprise Collection, 1990 (four-CD boxed set)
Sinatra, 1992 (two-CD sound track)
Frank Sinatra: The Columbia Years 1943-1952, the Complete Recordings, 1993 (twelve-CD boxed set)
Duets, 1993
Duets II, 1994
The Song Is You, 1994 (five-CD boxed set)
Portrait of Sinatra: Columbia Classics, 1997 (two-CD boxed set)

SELECT AWARDS

Grammy Awards for Album of the Year and Best Vocal Performance, Male, for *Come Dance with Me*, 1959
Grammy Awards for Album of the Year for *September of My Years* and Best Vocal Performance, Male, for "It Was a Very Good Year," and Lifetime Achievement, 1965
Emmy Award for Outstanding Musical Program for *Frank Sinatra: A Man and His Music*, 1965
Peabody Award for Distinguished Achievement in Video Programming for *Frank Sinatra: A Man and His Music*, 1965
Grammy Awards for Record of the Year and Best Vocal Performance, Male, for "Strangers in the Night" and Album of the Year for *Sinatra: A Man and His Music (1960-1965)*, 1966
Songwriters of America Entertainer of the Century Award, 1973
Variety Clubs International Humanitarian Award, 1980
Kennedy Center Honor for Lifetime Achievement Award, 1983
Boy Scouts of America Distinguished American Award, 1984
American Cinema Awards Distinguished Lifetime Achievement Award, 1992
Grammy Legend Award, 1994

SEE ALSO: Bennett, Tony; Davis, Sammy, Jr.

Ricky Skaggs

BORN: Cordell, Kentucky; July 18, 1954
FIRST ALBUM RELEASE: *Sweet Temptation*, 1979
MUSICAL STYLES: Bluegrass, progressive country

A musical prodigy, Ricky Skaggs received his first mandolin from his father, Hobart, at age five, and although his father lacked the time to teach him to play, Skaggs became sufficiently self-taught that year to perform "Ruby Are You Mad at Your Man" on stage with Bill Monroe before a very receptive audience. He delighted an audience once again when, at the age of seven, he performed on Lester Flatt and Earl Scruggs's television program. As an adolescent, Ricky became equally proficient on the mandolin, guitar, and fiddle, and thus played with his parents in the Skaggs Family band. Although traditional bluegrass was the musical heritage of the rural Kentuckian, the youthful Skaggs became influenced by the honky-tonk of George Jones and Ray Price and enjoyed the music of such rock groups as the Beatles and the Rolling Stones. In his adolescence he played briefly in rock-and-roll bands, but he never abandoned his traditional musical roots.

Early Bands. In his mid-teens Skaggs met Keith Whitley, another teenage fiddler, and the two formed a band that included Keith's brother, Dwight, on banjo. Based upon the success they experienced playing at local radio stations, the band was invited to open a show for Ralph Stanley, and the patriarch of bluegrass was so impressed by Skaggs and Whitley's rendering of Stanley Brothers songs that he hired them to be members of his band, the Clinch Mountain Boys. Skaggs was fifteen years of age at the time. In addition to gaining professional experience as a member of the Clinch Mountain Boys, Skaggs appeared on Stanley's record *Cry from the Cross.* In 1972 Skaggs also played on Whitley's solo album, *2nd Generation Bluegrass.*

After three years with Ralph Stanley and the Clinch Mountain Boys, Skaggs grew weary of the demanding road schedule and left the band to relocate in the Washington, D.C., area. For a short time he left music and worked in a boiler room for the Virginia Electric Power Company, but he returned to his first love in 1973 when invited to play fiddle for the Country Gentlemen. In 1974, he left the Gentlemen to accept a position with the new progressive bluegrass band J. D. Crowe and the New South (which included Tony Rice and Jerry Douglas).

Skaggs returned to the studio in 1975, assisting Keith Whitley with his second album, *That's It,* and in 1976 he formed his own band, Boone Creek. Although the band specialized in bluegrass, Skaggs integrated elements of honky-tonk and country swing, reflecting his own musical past, which gave the band a distinct, "newgrass" sound. Country star Emmylou Harris was one of those captivated by the new Boone Creek sound, and she became persistent in her efforts to retain the musical services of Ricky Skaggs. In 1977, after repeated offers, Skaggs joined Harris's Hot Band, replacing Rodney Crowell. Between 1977 and 1980, Skaggs had a major influence on Harris's career as he directed her more toward traditional country music, as is best reflected in her classic album *Roses in the Snow* (1980).

While with Harris, Skaggs participated in several recording projects with other artists. In 1978 he recorded his final project with Boone Creek, *One Way Track,* and participated in two duet projects with Tony Rice: *Take Me Home Tonight in a Song* (1978) and *Skaggs & Rice* (1980). The most significant event of this period however, was his first solo project, for Sugar Hill Records, *Sweet Temptation* (1979), which was a major bluegrass hit and helped to launch his Nashville career.

Major Contribution. In 1980 Skaggs moved to Nashville, Tennessee, and, based upon the strength of his first solo album, signed a contract with Epic Records. At the time, country music was experiencing a creative and financial slump, a problem Skaggs was soon to remedy. Few of his peers could match his instrumental prowess (on mandolin, fiddle, guitar, and banjo) and vocal talents, and along with his extensive experience in traditional music, he clearly stood alone. Skaggs can be credited as a major force in shaping the new traditionalist sound that sparked a renewed interest in country music and opened doors for performers such as George Strait and Randy Travis. New traditionalism was a back-to-basics movement that saw the integration of classic bluegrass, traditional country, and honky-tonk with contemporary production techniques that resulted in a commercially viable product. With his bluegrass tenor voice and enormous talent, Skaggs proved that traditional country music could compete with pop music. His first Epic release, *Waitin' for the Sun to Shine* (1981), produced two number 1 songs on the country charts and received rave reviews in both country and rock-and-roll publications. Skaggs had become a star. No less an authority than Chet Atkins suggested that Skaggs single-handedly saved country music.

Stardom and Afterward. Skaggs charged onto the country music scene in 1982 with five number 1 country hits: "Crying My Heart Out over You," "I Don't Care," "Heartbroke," "I Wouldn't Change You If I Could," and "Highway 40 Blues." Late in 1982 he was made the youngest member of the Grand Ole Opry. Among the dozens of awards earned by Skaggs are a total of eight Country Music Association (CMA) trophies, four Grammy Awards, and the coveted CMA Entertainer of the Year Award, which he received in 1985. By 1997 he had hit the country charts with eighteen Top-10 songs and twelve number 1 hits. After becoming a country star, Skaggs continued to pay homage to his bluegrass roots, making number 1 country hits of Lester Flatt and Earl Scruggs's "Crying My Heart Out over You," and Bill Monroe's "Uncle Penn."

In the early 1990's, new traditionalist country music became a bit slicker and demonstrated an overt rock influence that began to erode Skaggs's popularity. In 1992 Columbia Records dropped him from their label due to a decline in his record sales, but he remained in high demand for festivals and concerts. In 1994 he began a syndicated radio program, *The Simple Life*, and in 1995 he returned to recording with his first album on Atlantic Records, *Solid Ground*. In 1997 he released *Bluegrass Rules*! on Rounder Records, a label under which he recorded fifteen years earlier.

In 1996, Skaggs became the creator and host of *Monday Night Concerts* on the Nashville Network, where each week he assembles, at the historic Ryman Auditorium in Nashville, Tennessee, top artists from country, rock, bluegrass, and roots music. Guests on the show have included Alison Krauss and Union Station, George Jones, Elvis Costello, Lyle Lovett, Béla Fleck, Bruce Hornsby, Clint Black, Michael McDonald, and Wynonna Judd. Although his music has waned in popularity, Ricky Skaggs is perceived as a country music icon worldwide.

—*Wayne M. Bledsoe*

Ricky Skaggs (Paul Natkin)

SELECT DISCOGRAPHY

■ ALBUMS

Sweet Temptation, 1979
Skaggs & Rice, 1980
Waitin' for the Sun to Shine, 1981
Highways & Heartaches, 1982
Family and Friends, 1982
Don't Cheat in Our Hometown, 1983
Country Boy, 1984
Favorite Country Songs, 1985
Live in London, 1985
Love's Gonna Get Ya! 1986
Comin' Home to Stay, 1988
Kentucky Thunder, 1989
Radio Special, 1990
My Father's Son, 1991
Solid Ground, 1995
Country Pride, 1995
Crying My Heart Out, 1996
Life Is a Journey, 1997
Bluegrass Rules! 1997
That's It, 1997

SELECT AWARDS

Country Music Association Male Vocalist of the Year and Horizon Awards, 1982

Country Music Association Instrumental Group of the Year Award, 1983, 1984, 1985 (with the Ricky Skaggs Band)

Grammy Award for Best Country Instrumental Performance for "Wheel Hoss," 1984

Grammy Award for Best Country Instrumental Performance (Orchestra, Group, or Soloist) for "Raisin' the Dickens," 1986

Country Music Association Vocal Duo of the Year Award, 1987 (with Sharon White)

Country Music Association Vocal Event of the Year Award for *Mark O'Connor and the New Nashville Cats*, 1991 (with Mark O'Connor, Vince Gill, and Steve Wariner)

Grammy Award for Best Country Vocal Collaboration for "Restless," 1991 (with Vince Gill and Steve Wariner)

SEE ALSO: Gill, Vince; Harris, Emmylou; Monroe, Bill, and the Blue Grass Boys; Strait, George; Travis, Randy.

Sly and the Family Stone

ORIGINAL MEMBERS: Sly Stone (b. Sylvester Stewart, 1944), Freddie Stone (b. Freddie Stewart, 1946), Larry Graham, Jr. (b. 1946), Cynthia Robinson (b. 1946), Greg Errico (b. 1946), Rosie Stone (b. 1945), Jerry Martini (b. 1943)

FIRST ALBUM RELEASE: *A Whole New Thing*, 1967

MUSICAL STYLES: Soul, funk, rhythm and blues

Beginning in the late 1960's, Sly and the Family Stone embarked on a new musical path that combined elements of rock, soul, and pop along with a distinct influence from James Brown. From the group's beginning, they succeeded in drawing a wide range of listeners. The band was begun as an ensemble that would reflect the inclusiveness of the hippie movement in the San Francisco Bay area, composed of black and white, male and female members. Their music was extremely conscious of the racial strife of the late 1960's, and many of the band's songs sought to convey messages of racial harmony and social equality. Formed in 1967, Sly and the Family Stone were one of the very first bands associated with the funk style and have gained the reputation of being one of the most influential groups on the later funk bands of the 1970's.

Formation. Born in Dallas, Texas, in 1944, Sly Stone moved to the San Francisco Bay area with his family shortly thereafter. His first musical experiences were gained singing gospel music in church. In his youth, he also learned to play many instruments, including trumpet and guitar. As a rising musician on the San Francisco scene, he was involved in the production of albums for several local bands on the Autumn Records label, which included the Beau Brummels, Bobby Freeman, the Mojo Men, and Grace Slick's first band, the Great Society. At the same time, Stone worked as a disc jockey for radio stations KSOL and KDIA, both of which played soul music. He also gained valuable musical education at Vallejo Junior College, where he studied trumpet, music theory, and composition.

In 1966, Sly and his brother, singer and guitarist Freddie Stone (Stewart), along with trumpeter

Sly Stone (Archive Photos)

Cynthia Robinson, joined efforts to form the group Stoners. This group existed for only about one year. After the failure of this band, the three members, along with other new musicians, reformed as Sly and the Family Stone. Their first album, *A Whole New Thing* (1967) saw little commercial success. The band's second release, *Dance to the Music* (1968), fared slightly better due in part to the rise of the title track to number 8 on the U.S. pop charts. This song, which combined the multirhythmic textures of James Brown, the distorted guitar associated with Jimi Hendrix, and the stress of all four beats similar to Motown music, helped define the group's sound.

At Their Height. In 1968, Sly and the Family Stone released their third album, *Life*, which saw disappointing sales. This was turned around, however, when the group released the single "Everyday People"/"Sing a Simple Song" which went to number 1 on the U.S. pop charts and propelled their popularity to a much wider audience. The group's biggest success, however, came with the release of their 1969 album, *Stand!* This album contains some of their boldest political statements, along with a more refined style of dance music first seen with "Dance to the Music." It was with these dance hits that the group established the essential elements of funk music that were taken up by the bands of the 1970's such as Kool and the Gang, Parliament and Funkadelic, the Ohio Players, and the Isley Brothers.

Among the songs on *Stand!* that took a bold stance on racial and political issues were the title track, "Don't Call Me Nigger, Whitey," "Sex Machine," and "Somebody's Watching You." The record company feared that the inclusion of these songs would create controversy and hurt record sales. Due to the way in which the statements were presented, however, sales of the album *Stand!* remained remarkably high. For instance, in the song "Don't Call Me Nigger, Whitey" the second line of the song states the opposite, "Don't call me whitey, nigger," showing the band's concern not only for racism against blacks, but also for a true equality between both races. It was because of the band's image as a multiracial group that the song was presented in this way and thus made its statement applicable to both black and white audiences.

Dance tracks from *Stand!* such as "I Want to Take You Higher" (number 38, pop; number 24, rhythm and blues), "Hot Fun in the Summertime" (number 2, pop; number 3, rhythm and blues), and "Thank You Falettinme Be Mice Elf Agin" (number 1, pop and rhythm and blues) helped

For the Record

Sly and the Family Stone's *Stand!* was the first album recorded by predominantly black musicians to sell millions of copies.

establish the band as one of the premier groups of the late 1960's. Their appearance at the Woodstock festival in 1969, where they performed "Dance to the Music" and "I Want to Take You Higher," took Sly Stone to the point of superstardom.

Contributions to Funk. From 1967 to 1970, Sly and the Family Stone produced songs important to the development of funk. Of these, "Dance to the Music," "I Want to Take You Higher," "Sing a Simple Song," and especially "Thank You Falettinme Be Mice Elf Agin" are the most important. The use of distorted guitars, wa-wa pedal, Hammond organ, and a prominent horn section were all influential to the instrumentation of later funk bands.

Most important in musical style, however, was the bass playing of Larry Graham, Jr. Graham single-handedly transformed soul and funk bass playing by innovating a highly rhythmic style which basically hovered around one or two notes. This style made the bass into more of a rhythmic instrument, adding to the many layers of rhythm already created by the drums, guitar, organ, and horns. Graham's innovative playing is best heard on "Dance to the Music" and "I Want to Take You Higher." It was this style of playing that would not only affect the entire funk movement of the 1970's but also the realms of disco and soul music of that era.

The most important contribution made by the band as a whole was their single "Thank You Falettinme Be Mice Elf Agin." This song stands apart from other Sly and the Family Stone dance-oriented tracks as one that laid the groundwork for later funk music. The characteristics that seem to foreshadow the work of later funk bands include a repetitive bass riff played in a "slap" style, a prominent guitar with wa-wa pedal, and the use of an extended song form (verse-chorus form where the chorus is repeated extensively toward the end of the song). This song proved to be so influential to later funk that even the unorthodox spelling of the title was often copied by such bands as Parliament and Funkadelic.

Fading Out. In 1970, a compilation of *Greatest Hits* marked the band's prominence in the last three years of the 1960's. The next year saw the release of the band's last successful album, *There's a Riot Goin' On.* Carried by the success of the single "Family Affair" (number 1, pop and rhythm and blues), the album itself reached number 1 on the charts in 1971. This album was darker in tone, and the troubles that the band was facing at the time began to reveal themselves.

The difficulties of stardom were visible as early as 1970, when the reputation for late and missed concerts became a stigma for the band. It was widely known that drugs had become a problem, and there were also signs of internal strife. In 1972, Larry Graham Jr., and drummer Greg Errico left the group and were replaced by Rusty Allen and Andy Newmark. It was at this point that the decline of Sly and the Family Stone became apparent.

Their last album releases, *Fresh* (1973), *Small Talk* (1974), and *Heard Ya Missed Me, Well I'm Back* (1976), were met with little public acclaim and gradually brought the band to its end. Sly Stone's career continued, most often unsuccessfully, in the 1980's and 1990's. His most notable appearances have been collaborating with Parliament on their 1981 album, *The Electric Spanking of War Babies* and touring with George Clinton and his P-Funk All-Stars. —*Andrew Cook*

SELECT DISCOGRAPHY

■ ALBUMS

A Whole New Thing, 1967
Dance to the Music, 1968
Life, 1968
Stand! 1969
Greatest Hits, 1970
There's a Riot Goin' On, 1971
Fresh, 1973
Small Talk, 1974
Heard Ya Missed Me, Well I'm Back, 1976

SELECT AWARDS
Rock and Roll Hall of Fame, inducted 1993

SEE ALSO: Brown, James; Clinton, George / Parliament / Funkadelic; Kool and the Gang; Ohio Players, The.

Smashing Pumpkins

ORIGINAL MEMBERS: Billy Corgan (b. 1967), James Iha (b. 1968), D'Arcy Wretzky (b. 1968), Jimmy Chamberlin (b. 1964)
OTHER MEMBERS: Dennis Flemion
FIRST ALBUM RELEASE: *Gish,* 1991
MUSICAL STYLE: Alternative

Many of Smashing Pumpkin's young fans think of this Chicago band as an alternative rock group in the spirit of Nirvana, and indeed, Smashing Pumpkins mastermind Billy Corgan has at least two traits in common with the late Kurt Cobain: He grew up idolizing Cheap Trick and writes music that reflects the anger and confusion of a troubled childhood. Unlike the grunge bands that call Seattle home, however, Smashing Pumpkins always made music that reflected a taste for 1960's and 1970's "arena rock" and heavy metal along the lines of Led Zeppelin and Black Sabbath. They have also shown that they are not afraid to push their sound and approach into new musical realms that defy any single label or category.

From Basketball to Pumpkins. Corgan, the group's lead vocalist and songwriter, grew up in Glendale Heights, Illinois, a suburb of Chicago. A self-described "stupid, non-groovy" fan of bad heavy metal and basketball, the six-foot-three-inch youth turned his energies from sports to the guitar and formed a band called the Marked. In August, 1988, that band became Smashing Pumpkins, with guitarist James Iha, bassist D'Arcy Wretzky, and drummer Jimmy Chamberlin.

Corgan, who described his new band as somewhere between "neo-glam and hypnotic drone grunge," seemed proud that his influences were out of style. One of the band's earliest cover songs was a sneering version of Blue Öyster Cult's "Godzilla." However, Corgan's group boasted a distinctive sound from its earliest shows, described by one reviewer as "a mix of metal roar and confessional whisper, bombast and beauty—and a demeanor to match: dour, serious, self-possessed."

"I've never had a stable life," Corgan told *Chicago Tribune* rock critic Greg Kot during the band's formative years. "I lived in five different places before I was 5. I saw divorces, messy break-ups, boyfriends, girlfriends, drugs. I don't trust stability. I understand chaos. I muck things up because it forces you to react. I don't understand what it is to have everyone like you and think you're great." Still, Corgan set his sights on a guitar-driven hard-rock sound and would not be denied. Long before the band signed to a major label, Corgan said, "Success to me would be to be able to put out the exact type of records I want to put out and play the shows I want to play and have people accept that."

From Early Gigs to Gish. The band was treated with hostility by Chicago's tight-knit and cliquish alternative music community, and the mainstream bar bands did not know what to make of Smashing Pumpkins either. However, the band attracted the attention of Joe Shanahan, manager of Chicago's Cabaret Metro, a mainstay of the city's alternative music scene. By their fourth show, Smashing Pumpkins were warming up for Jane's Addiction. A few months later, they were opening for punk legends the Buzzcocks at yet another sold-out local show. At the end of 1990, they released a single, "Tristessa"/"La Dolly Vita" for Seattle's Sub Pop Records, which discovered Nirvana. Before the single came out, major record labels were already courting the band with offers in the six-figure range.

For the Record

Billy Corgan has said that the name Smashing Pumpkins "means absolutely nothing. It's the most ambiguous name I could think of."

Corgan chose a label that many observers considered to be a long shot: He signed with Caroline Records, an independent label based in New York City. Corgan explained that he felt Caroline Records would allow the band to grow and continue to create excitement on its own terms. Smashing Pumpkins released their first album for Caroline Records in May, 1991. *Gish,* which took its title from the actress Lillian Gish, was filled with swirling textures and combined elements of funk, psychedelic rock, hard rock, and, occasionally, folk music. It went over big with music critics and listeners alike, selling 300,000 copies, an astonishing number for an independently released album.

Fame and Misfortune. At the New Music Seminar in New York in the summer of 1991, Smashing Pumpkins packed the historic CBGB-OMFUG rock club. The show fueled more interest from big record companies, and, in the fall of 1991, Smashing Pumpkins signed with Virgin Records. They also landed an opening spot on a Red Hot Chili Peppers tour, an ideal opportunity to reach new fans.

Their first album for Virgin Records, *Siamese Dream,* came out in the summer of 1993 amid band turmoil. Corgan, frustrated with the performance of his bandmates, played many of the instruments himself. Meanwhile, the lyrics of songs such as "Disarm" and "Today" reflected more anger and aggression as Corgan, singing in an agitated whine, dredged up painful childhood memories. The booklet that came with the album played on this theme, with its family-album snapshots, pictures of suburbia, and lyrics scrawled in ransom-note fashion. The album sold more than three million copies and led to a headline spot on the 1994 Lollapalooza tour.

Smashing Pumpkins in 1995: from left, James Iha, Billy Corgan, Jimmy Chamberlin, D'arcy Wretzky (AP/Wide World Photos)

In October, 1995, Smashing Pumpkins released *Mellon Collie and the Infinite Sadness.* The twenty-eight-song double compact disc further established the band's ability to effectively embrace musical extremes. It was impossible to assign any one style to the album, as it alternated between the dreamy string arrangements of "Tonight, Tonight" and the overdriven guitars of "Bullet with Butterfly Wings."

Just as the band should have been enjoying its greatest success, tragedy hit. On July 12, 1996, Jonathan Melvoin, a touring keyboardist with Smashing Pumpkins, was found dead in his Manhattan hotel room of a heroin overdose. Police alleged that Chamberlin was with Melvoin when the keyboardist died. Chamberlin was immediately fired and the band hired drummer Matt Walker of the industrial rock band Filter to take over his touring duties. Dennis Flemion of the Milwaukee pop band the Frogs eventually replaced Melvoin. Chamberlin, who pleaded guilty to disorderly conduct, entered a drug rehabilitation program.

The album *Adore* was released in June, 1998. The band ultimately resorted to using a drum machine. Smashing Pumpkins took their menacing sound back a notch, creating a record that the *Chicago Tribune*'s Kot says "seduces with its loveliness, then reveals its depth with repeated listens."

—*Louis R. Carlozo*

SELECT DISCOGRAPHY

■ ALBUMS

Gish, 1991
Siamese Dream, 1993
Pisces Iscariot, 1994 (previously released material)
Mellon Collie and the Infinite Sadness, 1995
Adore, 1998

SELECT AWARDS

Grammy Award for Best Hard Rock Performance for "Bullet with Butterfly Wings," 1996
Grammy Award for Best Hard Rock Performance for "The End Is the Beginning Is the End," 1997

SEE ALSO: Black Sabbath / Ozzy Osbourne; Cheap Trick; Led Zeppelin; Nirvana; Pearl Jam.

Patti Smith

BORN: Chicago, Illinois; December 31, 1946
FIRST ALBUM RELEASE: *Horses*, 1975
MUSICAL STYLES: Alternative, punk rock

Originally a poet and rock journalist, Patti Smith helped pave the way for musical alternatives to the "glam rock" and stadium rock which reigned in the mid-1970's. Though she has enjoyed little commercial success, her influence is universally acknowledged by critics, and her music inspired a generation of alternative artists, including Michael Stipe of R.E.M., PJ Harvey, Courtney Love of Hole, and Sonic Youth.

Influences. Smith grew up in the working-class melting pot of Pitman, New Jersey. While working in a factory after high school and briefly attending community college, she began reading the poetry of American writer William Burroughs and the nineteenth century French symbolist Arthur Rimbaud, becoming a poet herself. She admired cultural figures as diverse as Irish poet William Butler Yeats, Italian artist Amedeo Modigliani, Swedish American actor Greta Garbo, and Spanish poet Federico García Lorca. She was also deeply enthralled with contemporary rock and roll. Through the music of Bob Dylan she came to appreciate the musical possibilities of communicating her cultural sensibility. Collectively these diverse cultural influences inspired an avant-garde consciousness which led her to New York's Greenwich Village in the late 1960's.

Combining her new poetic horizons with a love of Jimi Hendrix, the Doors' Jim Morrison, and the Rolling Stones, Smith became a vital part of alternative culture in New York. By 1972 she was regularly reading her poetry at venues such as St. Mark's Church and the Mercer Art Center and had already published two volumes of poetry. She wrote for rock publications such as *Rolling Stone*, *Crawdaddy*, and *Creem*. Smith collaborated with playwright Sam Shepard on a book of plays, *Mad Dog Blues*, and together they performed in an Off-Broadway production of their own *Cowboy Mouth*. She also wrote lyrics for Blue Öyster Cult and Todd Rundgren.

Poetry and Music. In 1973 Smith invited guitarist Lenny Kaye and pianist Richard Sohl to provide a musical backdrop to her readings. This artistic marriage enabled Smith to combine her interests in rock music and poetry and gave her a new avenue for experimentation. In 1974 she released what many consider to be the first punk record, the single "Hey Joe"/"Piss Factory" for Robert Mapplethorpe's Mer label. As Smith gravitated toward full-fledged rock music, she added guitarist Ivan Kral and drummer Jay Dee Daugherty to her ensemble, and together the Patti Smith Group landed a major record deal with Arista in 1975. For seven weeks they played the CBGB club, which had been home to early

For the Record

When pop-culture maven Andy Warhol met Patti Smith, he found her a bit too grungy for his own taste. Afterward he said, "She wouldn't be bad-looking if she would wash up and glue herself together a little bit."

alternative acts such as Television. Journalists and fans flocked to the club, putting the Patti Smith Group on the musical map.

The group's first album, *Horses* (number 47), released in 1975, was produced by John Cale of the Velvet Underground. It was an artistic sensation, combining traditional rock with avant-garde abandon, and managed to crack the Top 50. The follow-up, *Radio Ethiopia* (1976), was less popular, representing the peak of the Patti Smith Group's improvised rock. After sustaining serious neck injuries following a fall from a stage, Smith took a year and a half off. She returned with her two most commercially successful albums, *Easter* (1978, number 20) and *Wave* (1979, number 18). Smith enjoyed her only Top-40 single when "Because the Night," a revision of fellow New Jersey rocker Bruce Springsteen's song, went to number 13 on the pop charts.

By the late 1970's, Smith's music had lost most of its edge. She dropped out of the music scene after her marriage to former MC5 guitarist Fred "Sonic" Smith, and from 1979 to 1988 rarely made appearances, instead focusing on raising her family. In 1988 she returned to produce *Dream of Life* (number 65), and in 1996 she released *Gone Again*. Many fans admired her artistic development, but the albums were commercially unsuccessful. In 1993 she made a rare appearance at Central Park's Summerstage, reading poetry and singing a capella. Her performance was in honor of two friends who had recently died, band member Richard Sohl and photographer Robert Mapplethorpe.

Legacy. Because of the mixed poetic, cultural, and musical messages inherent in Smith's performances, many fans and critics argue that her best work was found in her live shows. Given the sincerity of her message and its establishment-smashing attitude, traditional recordings did not do justice to her vision. According to critic Richie Unterberger, the bootleg recording of her Roxy concert of January, 1976, entitled *Teenage Perversity and Ships in the Night*, "may be her best album, and one of the best '70's punk/new wave albums of all."

—*John Powell*

Patti Smith in 1996 (AP/Wide World Photos)

SELECT DISCOGRAPHY

■ ALBUMS

Horses, 1975
Radio Ethiopia, 1976
Easter, 1978
Wave, 1979
Dream of Life, 1988
Gone Again, 1996
Peace and Noise, 1997

SEE ALSO: Hendrix, Jimi; Springsteen, Bruce; Velvet Underground.

The Smithereens

ORIGINAL MEMBERS: Jim Babjak (b. 1957), Dennis Diken (b. 1957), Pat DiNizio (b. 1955), Mike Mesaros (b. 1957)

FIRST ALBUM RELEASE: *Girls About Town*, 1980 (EP)

MUSICAL STYLE: Pop

If the British band Squeeze represented the cute, quirky, and perky extreme of 1980's power pop, then New Jersey's Smithereens stood at the other end, with their beatnik-black romantic broodings and bruising backbeat. If Squeeze gave listeners a playful hug, the Smithereens blew them to bits with their blend of crunchy guitars and relentless rhythm.

Band Wanted. Jim Babjak, Mike Mesaros, and Dennis Diken began playing music together in high school. Pat DiNizio, who started playing guitar at age seven, was influenced by Brian Wilson, Ray Davies, the Beatles, and his idol, Buddy Holly. Along with his pop-oriented influences, DiNizio also listened to heavier-sounding bands such as the Who, Led Zeppelin, Steppenwolf, Black Sabbath, and Uriah Heep.

DiNizio formed the Smithereens in March, 1980, after Diken answered his advertisement for a drummer in a music paper. The drummer immediately called on Babjak and Mesaros, and later that year the group released its first EP, *Girls About Town*. The Smithereens soon began building a following in the New York and northern New Jersey area. In 1983, the Smithereens released a follow-up EP, *Beauty and Sadness*, which showcased the band's hook-laden, guitar-driven pop. DiNizio's writing obsessed about broken-hearted relationships, and his songs, combined with his cool baritone singing, gave the pop group a dark edge from its earliest days. The foursome was especially popular at Rutgers University, where Babjak ran a local record store, and the college radio station played their music in heavy rotation. When DiNizio and company failed to attract the attention of major record labels, they briefly considered calling it quits. The members wondered whether they were too old to get signed.

In 1985, DiNizio sent a tape to the newly formed independent record label Enigma Records. The tape reached Scott Vanderbilt, who had become a Smithereens fan during his days as a college disc jockey. Vanderbilt signed the band and, in 1987, they released their first full-length album, *Especially for You*. The album featured a guest appearance by singer Suzanne Vega, who had formerly been DiNizio's boss at a nonmusical day job. (Although it is rumored that Vega fired him, the two remained on good terms.) The hit single off the album, "Blood and Roses," spawned an MTV video and was featured in the film *Dangerously Close* (1987).

Turning up to *11*. As the Smithereens began touring further outside their Carteret, New Jersey, home base, they expanded their fan base. The 1988 album *Green Thoughts* proved that they could avoid the dreaded "sophomore slump," and the band's contract switched over to Capitol Records (the parent label of Enigma) with the 1989 release *11*. The album took its name from the 1960 movie *Ocean's Eleven*, which featured Frank Sinatra and members of the "Rat Pack."

Unlike most rock albums, *11* took only about one month to record and mix. Producer Ed Stasium replaced Don Dixon, who had produced the first two Smithereens albums. The result was an even harder beat-heavy sound with dashes of cello and harpsichord and the group's first Top-40 single, "A Girl Like You." The song was originally written for the film *Say Anything* (1989), but when the film's producer asked DiNizio to change the lyrics, DiNizio refused. The sound track used Peter Gabriel's "In Your Eyes" instead.

Soon after *11* became a gold record, the Smithereens' popularity crested. Their 1991 album *Blow*

For the Record

The Smithereens are among a tiny minority of bands that have taken their names from Bugs Bunny cartoons. Their name comes from Yosemite Sam's constant threat to blow Bugs to "smithereens."

Up spawned the minor hit "Too Much Passion." Soon after, the band left Capitol Records for RCA Records and released *A Date with the Smithereens* in 1994. Though the album featured Lou Reed and reunited the band with Dixon, it fell far short of the band's commercial success with *11*, and the Smithereens left RCA Records as well. At the end of 1997, DiNizio released the solo album *Songs and Sounds* to favorable reviews. *—Louis R. Carlozo*

SELECT DISCOGRAPHY

■ ALBUMS

Girls About Town, 1980 (EP)
Especially for You, 1987
Green Thoughts, 1988
11, 1989
Blow Up, 1991
A Date with the Smithereens, 1994

SEE ALSO: Reed, Lou; Vega, Suzanne.

The Smiths / Morrissey

Smiths

ORIGINAL MEMBERS: Morrissey (b. 1959), Johnny Marr (b. John Maher, 1963), Mike Joyce (b. 1963), Andy Rourke (b. 1963)

FIRST ALBUM RELEASE: *The Smiths*, 1984

Morrissey

BORN: Manchester, England; May 22, 1959

FIRST ALBUM RELEASE: *Viva Hate*, 1988

MUSICAL STYLES: Alternative, rock and roll, pop

The story of the Smiths's formation is somewhat mystical and fateful. In 1982 in the grim, industrial city of Manchester, England, the British charts were dominated by vapid, lifeless dance-pop, most of which would soon disappear. Budding guitarist Johnny Marr heard rumors about a strange local poet named Steven Morrissey. Marr, it is said, simply knocked on Morrissey's door one day and asked if he would be interested in writing songs. Both recall the meeting in mystical terms; Morrissey once summed it up by saying, "It was an event I'd always been looking forward to and unconsciously waiting for since my childhood." One of the most influential bands of the 1980's was thus born.

Completion. It took several months of careful searching by Morrissey and Marr to find bassist Andy Rourke and drummer Mike Joyce. Once the lineup was firm, the group would remain in high gear until their breakup in 1987. In 1982 and 1983, the Smiths's popularity skyrocketed in England. Incessant touring and the release of three singles were certainly a catalyst, but it was the enigmatic presence of Morrissey—who preferred that no one use his first name—which caused the greatest stir, both among insatiable fans and harsh critics. Morrissey was the antithesis of the early 1980's pop star. He wore glasses and sang in a warbly falsetto; he had flowers teeming from his back pockets; he sang about love and the world without the calculated detachment of his peers. He was loved and hated for it.

The Smiths was released in 1984 to acclaim and controversy (controversy would forever plague Morrissey's career). The first track, "Reel Around the Fountain," was mistakenly interpreted as an ode to child molestation. The beautiful, empathetic "Suffer Little Children," a song based on true child-murders in England, was seen as crass. Those who understood, however, realized that Morrissey was one of the most poignant lyricists to emerge in ages, and that Marr's guitar work and songwriting were unlike anything that had been heard before. *Hatful of Hollow* (1984), a compilation of radio session tracks and B-sides, was released soon after the debut and included what would become the Smiths' best-known song, "How Soon Is Now?"

Meat is Murder. As if Morrissey's interviews—which included wishes of death for royalty, Margaret Thatcher, and certain journalists, declarations of complete celibacy, and a hint of homoeroticism—did not provide enough ammunition for his detractors, he decided to name the Smiths' 1985 album after its highly political title track, "Meat Is Murder." The song was a call to arms for one of Morrissey's favorite causes, vegetarianism. It was, in fact, the weakest track on an otherwise caustic and funny album. The record housed some classic Smiths lines, such as "I smoke, be-

The Smiths (Sire/Jo Novark)

album tracks in no particular order, while *Singles* (1995) collected easily available album tracks in chronological order.

After leaving the Smiths, Johnny Marr never reached the musical heights he had with his first group. He acted as a guitarist for hire, working with Billy Bragg, Pet Shop Boys, Bryan Ferry, the The and countless others. In 1991, Marr began a collaboration with Bernard Sumner, singer for Manchester's other favorite sons, New Order. The duo was called Electronic, and they released two relatively unremarkable synth-pop records, *Electronic* (1991) and *Raise the Pressure* (1995).

cause I'm hoping for an early death/ And I need to cling to something."

The Smiths' potential was to be fully realized in 1986 with their classic album *The Queen Is Dead.* In spite of its antiroyalty title, the album was almost universally praised as an instant classic. From the epic opening title track to Morrissey's tongue-in-cheek "Some Girls Are Bigger than Others," *The Queen Is Dead* achieved near-perfection. Marr had finally written and, more importantly, produced the record the Smiths had always wanted to make. December of that year, however, would see the Smiths play their last show.

One more proper studio album, 1987's underrated *Strangeways, Here We Come,* would be released before the public announcement of the Smiths's demise. Officially, Johnny Marr left the group to pursue other musical avenues, but intense infighting seemed to be the real cause. A testament to the Smiths's lasting popularity is the sheer number of compilations that were released after their breakup. *Louder Than Bombs* (released in 1987) is a collection of singles and B-sides that stands easily aside any of the proper albums. In 1988 the live album *Rank* was released. *Best I* and *Best II* (both 1992) simply collected easily available

Solo. Morrissey began a solo career in earnest. His first single, "Suedehead," was released early in 1988 and was as strong a song as any he had written with the Smiths. An album, *Viva Hate,* followed. Cowritten with well-known producer Stephen Street and performed by Street and Durutti Column guitarist Vini Reilly, *Viva Hate* was a forceful departure from the Smiths. Morrissey's lyrics remained strong and controversial, and his pop-sounding hits ("Suedehead," "Everyday Is Like Sunday") were balanced with more introspective, quieter numbers ("Little Man, What Now?," "Late Night, Maudlin Street"). It would be three years before Morrissey would release another solo album, but in the interim, he released enough singles to justify a collection, 1990's *Bona Drag.* Notoriously difficult to work with, Morrissey collaborated with many different players through his early years, including all of the former Smiths (with the exception of Marr). The most fruitful work was done with Stephen Street.

Morrissey's second solo album, 1991's *Kill Uncle,* was hailed by the press as Morrissey's death knell. Written largely with former Fairground Attraction guitarist Mark Nevin and produced by pop legends Clive Langer and Alan Winstanley, *Kill Uncle*'s biggest fault was that it tried too hard to be commercial—and failed. While there are touching moments, the album was the first that Morrissey had been involved with that was less than solid.

For his "Kill Uncle" tour, Morrissey found both a band and a pair of new collaborators in Boz Boorer and Alain Whyte. Whyte and Morrissey cowrote 1992's *Your Arsenal*, which was produced by David Bowie collaborator and producer Mick Ronson. The album was Morrissey's foray into a more physical rock sound, and while it contained some gems, such as "We'll Let You Know" and the Bowie-tinged "I Know It's Gonna Happen Someday," it was certainly the weakest overall record he had released.

That pattern continued, to the chagrin of many Morrissey fans. Unlike the Smiths' catalog, which was consistently good, Morrissey's next three solo records—1994's *Vauxhall and I*, 1995's *Southpaw Grammar*, and 1997's *Maladjusted*—were largely unsuccessful, the odd classic Morrissey track surrounded by lifeless material. *—Josh Modell*

SELECT DISCOGRAPHY

the Smiths

■ ALBUMS

The Smiths, 1984
Hatful of Hollow, 1984
Meat Is Murder, 1985
The Queen Is Dead, 1986
Louder Than Bombs, 1987 (compilation)
Strangeways, Here We Come, 1987
Rank, 1988
Best I, 1992
Best II, 1992
Singles, 1995

Morrissey

■ ALBUMS

Viva Hate, 1988
Bona Drag, 1990
Kill Uncle, 1991
Your Arsenal, 1992
Vauxhall and I, 1994
World of Morrissey, 1995 (singles collection)
Southpaw Grammar, 1995
Maladjusted, 1997

SEE ALSO: Bowie, David.

Snoop Doggy Dogg

(Calvin Broadus)

BORN: Long Beach, California; October 20, 1972
FIRST ALBUM RELEASE: *Doggystyle*, 1993
MUSICAL STYLES: Rap, hip-hop

Affectionately nicknamed Snoop by his parents because as a baby he was thought to resemble Snoopy of the *Peanuts* comic strip, Calvin Broadus was raised by his mother in Long Beach, California. He spent his free time rapping with his friend Warren Griffin, later famous as the rapper Warren G.

Snoop was a good student and athlete in high school, with several college basketball programs out to recruit him. However, he joined the Long Beach Insane Crips gang and frequently ran into trouble with the law. Soon after his high school graduation, he was arrested for possession of cocaine and spent most of the next three years in jail. Meanwhile, Warren G played some of Snoop's homemade tapes for his stepbrother, N.W.A.'s

Snoop Doggy Dogg (Ken Settle)

Dr. Dre, cofounder of Death Row Records. Dre was impressed with Snoop's style and the two began collaborating.

First Hits. In 1992, Dre invited Snoop to rap the title song for the film *Deep Cover*, starting a buzz about the new artist. That grew into full-fledged mania when Dre released his own debut album, *The Chronic*, late in 1992, prominently featuring Snoop's drawled, laconic rhyming. The singles "Nuthin' but a 'G' Thang" and "Dre Day" became Top-10 pop crossover hits in 1993, setting the stage for Snoop Doggy Dogg's much anticipated debut album, *Doggystyle*.

Arrested Again. While recording the album with Dre in August, 1993, Snoop was arrested in connection with the drive-by shooting death of Phillip Woldermarian. The arrest certainly fortified his urban image and gave the violence implied in his lyrics an uncanny ring of truth. According to the charges, the rapper's bodyguard, McKinley Lee, shot Woldermarian from the vehicle Snoop was driving. The rapper claimed it was self-defense, alleging that the victim was stalking him. Following a performance at the MTV Video Music Awards in September, 1993, Snoop turned himself over to authorities.

Debut Album. *Doggystyle* finally came out on the Death Row label in November, 1993. The album, boosted as much by Snoop's talent as the controversy surrounding his arrest and colorful lyrics, became the first debut album to enter the charts at number 1. The album's Top-10 singles "What's My Name?" and "Gin & Juice" kept *Doggystyle* at the top of the charts during early 1994. Snoop Doggy Dogg blurred the lines between reality and myth and quickly became the most famous star in rap.

In the long run, though he was cleared of the murder charges in February, 1996, the arrest stalled his career. He spent more time in court than in the studio throughout 1994 and 1995. *Tha Doggfather*, his second album, was not released until November of 1996. It debuted at number 1, but lacking any breakout singles, it sold only two million copies, half as many as its predecessor. Snoop was still a star, but without the influence he had enjoyed just two years before.

The album's timing may have also tightened the leash on *Tha Doggfather*. By this time, the pop- and hip-hop-buying public had wearied of "gangsta" rap (the more violent side of rap) and especially the too real news stories about its stars. Tupac Shakur, a friend and labelmate of Snoop Doggy Dogg, had been murdered just three months before the release of the album. Dr. Dre had left Death Row Records to his partner Suge Knight, who in early 1997 was indicted on racketeering charges and given a nine-year jail term for parole violations. The murder of another peer, the Notorious B.I.G., in March, 1997, led to Snoop's decision to cancel a planned 1997 tour.

Career Renewal. By June the same year, Snoop was back in the game. He signed up to tour with rock's Lollapalooza summer festival tour, accepted his first film role, married his longtime girlfriend, Shantay Taylor, and became a father. He collaborated with Tony Toni Toné's Raphael Saddiq and with Rage Against the Machine for the extended-play single *Doggumentary* and also recorded a track on the sound track of the hugely successful 1997 film *Men in Black*. Also planned were separate collaborations with Beck and Marilyn Manson, as well as a third album release in 1998, *Da Game Is to Be Sold, Not to Be Told* on the No Limit label. —*Tim Bradley*

SELECT DISCOGRAPHY

■ ALBUMS

Doggystyle, 1993
Tha Doggfather, 1996
Da Game Is to Be Sold, Not to Be Told, 1998

SELECT AWARDS

Rolling Stone, named Best Rap Artist, 1994
MTV Video Music Award for Best Rap Video for "Doggy Dogg World," 1994

SEE ALSO: Dr. Dre; N.W.A.; Rage Against the Machine.

Sonic Youth

ORIGINAL MEMBERS: Kim Gordon (b. 1953), Thurston Moore (b. 1958), Lee Ranaldo (b. 1956), Richard Edson

BEST-KNOWN LINEUP: Kim Gordon, Thurston Moore, Lee Ranaldo, Steve Shelley (b. 1962)
OTHER MEMBERS: Bob Bert, Jim Sclavunos
FIRST RELEASE: *Sonic Youth*, 1982 (extended-play single)
MUSICAL STYLES: Punk rock, alternative

Formed in New York City in 1981, Sonic Youth combined the noise experimention of "no wave" and the intensity of punk rock to create a unique style of music that seemed nearly inaccessible to most listeners. However, tireless touring and networking with underground musicians across the United States not only helped them develop a dedicated following but also helped them become extremely influential in the alternative music scene.

No Wave. The underground music scene in New York City in 1979 was in a state of transition. The explosive energy of punk rock had expended itself and given way to the dissonance of "no wave," a short-lived but highly influential period of experimentation by performance artists and untrained musicians who were more interested in exploring their potential for making noise than in writing conventional songs. Hundreds of bands with names such as Teenage Jesus and the Jerks, Tone Death, the Static, and the Contortions formed and played at the small clubs of New York's Lower East Side.

Guitarists Thurston Moore and Lee Ranaldo both moved to Manhattan, New York, in the late 1970's (Moore from Bethel, Connecticut, and Ranaldo from Long Island, New York) to be part of the punk scene, but they were too late. Instead, they played in various no-wave bands before they met while playing in one of avant-garde composer Glenn Branca's dissonant "guitar army" ensembles, which often featured six or more guitarists playing cacophonous but highly structured noise. Branca's experiments with feedback and alternate guitar tunings would become hallmarks of Sonic Youth's guitar sound.

In 1981, Moore helped organize the Noise Festival at the White Columns performance space in Manhattan. It was here that Sonic Youth made their live debut with Moore on guitar and vocals, visual artist Kim Gordon (whom Moore had met at a no-wave show and whom he would later marry) on bass and vocals, Ann DeMarinis on keyboards, and Richard Edson on drums. DeMarinis and Edson quit the band almost immediately after the first show, while Gordon convinced Ranaldo, who had performed with Branca at the Noise Festival, to join. The trio began rehearsing the songs that would appear on their debut album. During early live performances, the band compensated for the lack of a drummer by hitting their guitars with steel pipes and drum sticks, while Ranaldo found a way to rig a power drill to a guitar effects pedal for added noise. Vocal duties were divided between Moore and Gordon, both of whom eschewed actual singing in favor of a monotonous drone that worked perfectly with the sounds they created with their instruments. In December, 1981, Edson returned to play drums during the recording of *Sonic Youth*, which became the first extended-play single to be released on Branca's Neutral Records label.

Diversification and Experimentation. In the following months, Moore became interested in the rise of hardcore punk, a louder, faster offspring of punk rock that emphasized a do-it-yourself ethos to ensure complete autonomy from major record labels. This aesthetic was particularly apparent on Sonic Youth's first full-length

For the Record

After playing under names such as Male Bonding, Red Milk, and the Arcadians, Thurston Moore renamed the group Sonic Young when it performed at an art gallery during a 1981 festival. The name combined the names of two bands he admired: Sonic's Rendezvous Band and a reggae band called Big Youth.

§

"We always hated being called an art band. I never took art in high school."

—*Thurston Moore*

Sonic Youth: Lee Ranaldo, Thurston Moore, Kim Gordon, Steve Shelley (Geffen/Christian Lantry)

album, *Confusion Is Sex* (1983). Whereas *Sonic Youth* boasted clean, professional production, *Confusion Is Sex* was recorded in a rudimentary basement studio under chaotic circumstances. The result was an unremarkable album of heavily layered and muddy-sounding songs.

In subsequent rehearsals, the band allowed more diverse influences to enter their music. The alternate guitar tunings that Moore and Ranaldo learned from Branca became increasingly apparent, but so too did a pop music influence. The album *Bad Moon Rising* (1985) demonstrated Sonic Youth's willingness to look to the 1960's for both musical and lyrical inspiration: "Death Valley 69," a fairly straightforward song centered on a classic rock guitar riff, was a frenzied if somewhat ironic "tribute" to mass murderer Charles Manson. The following year, having already lost three drummers, the band settled on Steve Shelley and signed to SST Records, a large independent label in Los Angeles that had released seminal alternative albums by Black Flag, Hüsker Dü, and the Minutemen. The resulting albums, *EVOL* (1986) and *Sister* (1987), continued Sonic Youth's move toward more conventional song structures and revealed the band members' obsessions with such topics as death, insanity, and dysfunction in the world.

Sonic Youth's breakthrough came with their 1988 double album *Daydream Nation*, which gained wide airplay on college radio stations and topped the lists of several music industry journals that track airplay and record sales. The first pressing sold 100,000 copies, a figure that, although astoundingly high for an independent release, does not come near to gauging the album's influence on countless alternative bands, most notably those in the fledgling Seattle, Washington, grunge scene.

Major Label. The album was also instrumental in Sonic Youth's attainment of a recording contract with Geffen Records. Wary of the way that major-label deals had compromised the music of other alternative pioneers, Sonic Youth demanded, and received, a contract that allowed them complete creative control over their output. *Goo* (1990), the band's major-label debut, gave them more media attention than they had ever received. The album had an uneven quality to it: Although the song structure tended to be more conventional than previous efforts, the larger studio allowed the band members to coax new sounds out of their instruments, thus expanding the opportunity for experimentation. Shortly after the album's release, Neil Young invited them to open for him on his "Ragged Glory" tour, which became Sonic Youth's first real confrontation with the mainstream. Although Sonic Youth may have won a few converts during the three-month tour, the band usually found themselves confronted and booed by an audience that was described by Gordon as primarily "redneck" and "conservative." More successful was Sonic Youth's own tour in support of *Goo*, during which they invited the unknown Seattle band Nirvana to open their West Coast shows. The sales of *Goo* had already set off a frenzy of major-label signing among independent bands. The members of Sonic Youth successfully urged Geffen Record Co. to sign Nirvana, who would go on to sell millions of albums.

Sonic Youth's next ablum, *Dirty* (1992), approached the mainstream sound as it had been envisioned by the wave of grunge bands emerging from the Seattle underground. Although the album sold well, it was a creative low point in that Sonic Youth seemed to be attempting to imitate the bands they themselves had inspired. However, *Dirty* still contained many surprising aspects that set the group apart from the now-predictable Seattle scene, including a muddy version of an early 1980's hardcore punk song and several tracks in which Gordon's previously monotonous vocals gave way to an angry, intimidating growl.

Return to Experimentation. With *Experimental Jet Set, Trash and No Star* (1994), Sonic Youth took a turn toward a sound that was both more subdued and more adventurous than their previous major-label releases. Despite this apparent attempt to turn their backs to the mainstream, the release became their best-selling album to that point, reaching number 34 on the U.S. album charts. In response to this success, the group released *Washing Machine* the following year, an even less accessible album that marked an overt return to guitar noise experimentation. Rather than duplicating their sound of the early to mid-1980's, however, the band maintained their more recent dedication to song structure, creating, at times, a complex, ambient layering of guitar noise. The follow-up album, *A Thousand Leaves* (1998), continued these experiments but seemed to gain inspiration from a surprising source: 1970's pop ballads. This is not to say that Sonic Youth became sentimental in their middle age. Many songs evoked their earlier obsession with death, but in a more melancholy form, most notably "Hits of Sunshine," dedicated to Beat poet Allen Ginsberg, who had died the previous year.

From the start of their careers, the members of Sonic Youth involved themselves in numerous side projects and played in other bands, including the Dim Stars (Moore and Shelley), Free Kitten (Gordon), From Here → Infinity (Ranaldo), and Ciccone Youth (a pseudonym for Sonic Youth under which the band recorded sarcastic tributes to Madonna and other pop icons). Sonic Youth also played on several tracks on writer William S. Burroughs's spoken-word album *Dead City Radio* (1990), while Gordon coproduced Hole's *Pretty on the Inside* (1991) with Don Fleming. —*Douglas Long*

SELECT DISCOGRAPHY

■ SINGLES

Sonic Youth, 1982 (extended-play single)
Kill Yr. Idols, 1983 (extended-play single)
Death Valley 69, 1985 (extended-play single)

■ ALBUMS

Confusion Is Sex, 1983
Sonic Death, 1984
Bad Moon Rising, 1985
EVOL, 1986
Sister, 1987
Daydream Nation, 1988
Goo, 1990
Dirty, 1992
Experimental Jet Set, Trash and No Star, 1994
Made in USA, 1995
Screaming Fields of Sonic Love, 1995 (compilation)
Washing Machine, 1995
A Thousand Leaves, 1998

SEE ALSO: Hole; Nirvana; Young, Neil.